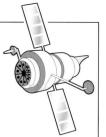
SOUTH AMERICA

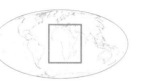

AFRICA

EUROPE

ASIA

AUSTRALASIA & OCEANIA

POLAR REGIONS

☐ KEY TO MAP SYMBOLS ON FRONT ENDPAPER
☐ FLAGS ON BACK ENDPAPER

AMAZING EARTH

Earth is unique among the nine planets that circle the Sun. It is the only one that can support life, because it has enough oxygen in its atmosphere and plentiful water. In fact, seen from space, the Earth looks almost entirely blue. This is because about 70% of its surface is under water, submerged beneath four huge oceans: the Pacific, Atlantic, Indian and Arctic oceans. Land makes up about 30% of the Earth's surface. It is divided into seven landmasses of varying shapes and sizes called continents. These are, from largest to smallest: Asia, Africa, North America, South America, Antarctica, Europe and Australia.

THE SHAPE OF THE EARTH

Photographs taken from space by astronauts in the 1960s, and more recently from orbiting satellites, have proven beyond doubt what humans had already worked out long ago – that the Earth is shaped like a ball. But it is not perfectly round. The force of the Earth's rotation makes the world bulge very slightly at the Equator and go a little flat at the North and South poles. So the Earth is actually a flattened sphere, or a 'geoid'.

WET EARTH

Tropical rainforests grow in areas close to the Equator, where it is wet and warm all year round. Although they cover just 7% of the Earth's land, these thick, damp forests form the richest ecosystems on the planet. More plant and animal species are found here than anywhere else on Earth.

DRY EARTH

Deserts are among the most inhospitable places on the planet. Some deserts are scorching hot, others are freezing cold, but they have one thing in common – they are all dry. Very few plant and animal species can survive in these harsh conditions. The world's coldest and driest continent, Antarctica (*left*), is a cold desert.

WATERY WORLD

The Earth's oceans and seas cover more than 367 million sq km – that is twice the surface of Mars and nine times the surface of the moon.

Beneath the ocean waves lies the biggest and most unexplored landscape on Earth. Here are coral reefs, enormous, open plains, deep canyons and the longest mountain range on Earth – the Mid-Atlantic Ridge – which stretches almost from pole to pole.

☐ HEIGHTS AND DEPTHS

The Pacific Ocean contains the deepest places on the Earth's surface – the ocean trenches. The very deepest is Challenger Deep in the Mariana Trench which plunges 11,034 m into the Earth's crust. If Mount Everest, the highest point on land at 8,850 m, was dropped into the trench, its peak wouldn't even reach the surface of the Pacific.

☐ WATER

Over 97% of the Earth's water is salt water. The total amount of salt in the world's oceans and seas would cover the whole of Europe to a depth of five km. Less than 3% of the Earth's water is fresh. Of this, 2.24% is frozen in ice sheets and about 0.6% is stored underground as groundwater. The remainder is in lakes and rivers.

☐ COASTS

The total length of the Earth's coastlines is more than 500,000 km – that is the equivalent of 12 times around the globe. A high percentage of the world's people live in coastal zones: of the ten most populated cities on Earth, seven are situated on estuaries or the coast.

☐ BIODIVERSITY

Today, almost 6,800,000,000 humans, approximately 1.2 million animal species and 300,000 known plant species depend on the air, water and land of planet Earth.

☐ VANISHING FORESTS

10,000 years ago, thick forests covered about half of the Earth's land surface. Today, 33% of those forests no longer exist, and more than half of what remains has been dramatically altered. During the 20th century, more than 50% of the Earth's rainforests were felled.

STUDENT
ATLAS

WORLD

DK

LONDON NEW YORK MELBOURNE MUNICH AND DELHI

DK

LONDON, NEW YORK, MELBOURNE, MUNICH AND DELHI

FOR THE SIXTH EDITION

Managing Cartographer David Roberts   Senior Cartographic Editor Simon Mumford
Jacket Designer Mark Cavanagh   Production Controller Rebecca Short   Production Editor Joanna Byrne
Publisher Jonathan Metcalf   Art Director Philip Ormerod   Associate Publisher Liz Wheeler

DORLING KINDERSLEY CARTOGRAPHY
CARTOGRAPHERS

MANAGING EDITOR
Lisa Thomas

MANAGING ART EDITOR
Philip Lord

PROJECT EDITORS
Debra Clapson, Wim Jenkins, Jill Hamilton (US)

PROJECT DESIGNERS
Rhonda Fisher, Karen Gregory

EDITORIAL CONTRIBUTORS
Thomas Heath, Kevin McRae, Constance Novis,
Iris Rossoff (US), Siobhan Ryan

DESIGNERS
Carol Ann Davis, David Douglas,
Nicola Liddiard

MANAGING CARTOGRAPHER
David Roberts

SENIOR CARTOGRAPHIC EDITOR
Roger Bullen

Pamela Alford, James Anderson, Chris Atkinson, Dale Buckton, Tony Chambers, Jan Clark,
Martin Darlison, Damien Demaj, Paul Eames, Sally Gable, Jeremy Hepworth, Michael Martin,
Ed Merritt, Simon Mumford, John Plumer, Gail Townsley, Julie Turner,
Sarah Vaughan, Jane Voss, Peter Winfield

DATABASE MANAGER
Simon Lewis

DIGITAL MAPS CREATED IN DK CARTOPIA BY
Phil Rowles, Rob Stokes

PLACENAMES DATABASE TEAM
Natalie Clarkson, Julia Lynch,

EDITORIAL DIRECTION
Andrew Heritage

PICTURE RESEARCH
Louise Thomas

EDUCATIONAL CONSULTANTS
Dr. David Lambert, Institute of Education, University of London, David R Wright, BA MA

TEACHER REVIEWERS
US: Ramani DeAlwis; UK: Kevin Ball, Pat Barber, Stewart Marson

First published in Great Britain in 1998 by
Dorling Kindersley Limited,
80 Strand, London WC2R ORL
Penguin Group (UK)

2 4 6 8 10 9 7 5 3 1

001 – 175652 – Feb/2011

Second Edition 2002, Reprinted 2003, Third Edition 2004,
Fourth Edition 2006, Fifth Edition 2008, Sixth Edition 2011

Copyright © 1998, 1999, 2002, 2003, 2004, 2006, 2008, 2011 Dorling Kindersley Limited, London.

ACKNOWLEDGMENTS
The publishers are grateful for permission to reproduce the following photographs:

t=top, b=bottom, a=above, l=left, r=right, c=centre

Axiom: Jiri Rezac 64br; J Spaull 92br. **Bridgeman Art Library**: Hereford Cathedral, Trustees of the Hereford Mappa Mundi 8tr. **J Allan Cash**: 120cr. **Bruce Coleman Ltd**: C Ott 28cr (below); Dr E Pott 4bc; H Reinhard 19cr; J Murray 130bl; Peter Terry 19crr. **Colourific**: Black Star/R Rogers 113br; Frank Herrmann 119bc. **Comstock**: 17tc. **Corbis**: Bob Daemmrich 30bl. **James Davis Travel Photography**: 44tr, 119tr. **Robert Harding Picture Library**: 6tr (below); 21c, 21cr, 22br, 92cr (above); 28bl, 30cr, 30br, 31bl, 38tr, 118bl; A Tovy 120br; Adam Woollitt 62br; C Bowman 112tr; Charcrit Boonson 90cr (below); David Lomax 20tr; Franz Joseph Land 19tr; G Boutin 120cl (below); G Renner 17c, 118cr(above); Gavin Hellier 31tr; Geoff Renner 39cr (above); H P Merten 23tl; Jane Sweeney 23bl; Louise Murray 93tr; Peter Scholey 91tr; Robert Francis 23cr; Schuster/Keine 62cr (above); Simon Westcott 90br. **Hutchison Library**: A Zvoznikov 19cl; J Nowell 93bl; R Ian Lloyd 10cl. **Image Bank**: Carlos Navajas 17bl; M Isy-Schwart 17bc; P Grumann 64cr (below); Steve Proehl 30cr (below); Terje Rakke 17br. **Images Colour Library**: 19c, 62cr (below), 118br. **Impact**: Jeremy Nicholl 121cl (below); Mark Henley 20bl; Paul O'Driscoll 63cr; Robin Lubbock 118br. **Frank Lane Picture Agency**: D Smith 19bc; W Wisniewski 17cr. **Magnum**: Chris Steele Perking 120tr (below); Jean Gaumy 65cl. **N.A.S.A**: 9tc. **N.H.P.A**: M Wendler 4cl; 110bl. **Oxford Scientific Films**: Konrad Wothe 19tc; L Gould 4tr; Nobert Rosing 28cl. **Panos Pictures**: Alain le Garsheur 92cr; Alain le Garsmeur 31cl (below); Alberto Arzoz 63tr; Bruce Paton 121bl; Jeremy Hartley 120bl; Maria Luiza M Cavalho 112cl (below); Paul Smith 111cr; Rhodri Jones 113bl; Ron Gilling 119cr; Trygve Bolstad 22bl. **Edward Parker**: 17cr (above). **Pictor International**: 4tc, 10bc, 18tr, 20br, 36bc, 38br. **Planet Earth Pictures**: J Waters 113bc. **South American Pictures**: Robert Francis 29br; Tony Morrison 110cr, 111cl. **Spectrum Colour Library**: 29br. **Frank Spooner Pictures**: Gamma/E Baitel 91cl. **Still Pictures**: J Frebet 113cl; R Seitre 90cr (above). **Tony Stone Images**: 17tr, 112cl; A Sacks 28cr; Alan Levenson 92cr; Charles Thatcher 39tr; D Austen 131cr; D Hanson 17cl; Donald Johnson 62bc; Earth Imaging 6tr (above); G Johnson 90bl; H Strand 113tr; Hans Schlapfer 38bc; J Jangoux 19bcr; J Warden 110bc; John Garrett 121br; L Resnick 121tr; Larry Ulrich 37br; P Chesley 130tr; Paul Chesley 36br; Randy Wells 19br; Robert Frerck 65tr; Tom Walker 36bl; Tony Craddock 65cr. **Telegraph Colour Library**: 29tr. **Travel Ink**: Colin Marshall 22bc. **Trip**: A Kuznetsov 92bc; H Rogers 90cr; M Barlow 112bl; N Ray 10tr; Robert Belbin 92bl; V Kolpakov 93cr (above); V Sidoropolev 64cr; W Jacobs 130c. **World Pictures**: 131tr. **ZEFA Picture Library**: 19bcl, 19cll, 63bc; Damm 119cl; Heilman 110cr (below); K Siewert 110cl; Kitchen 19bll; Sunak 91cr; Surpress 111tr. **JACKET IMAGES**: Front: **Corbis**: Richard Berenholtz br; Bob Krist tc, bl; JamesRandklev tr, bl; Keren Su tl. **Science Photo Library/NOAA**. Back: **Corbis**: Robert Y. Ono bc; James Randklevbl; Paul A. Souders br; Royalty Free Images: Cobis tc. Corbis tr. Spine: **Corbis**: Robert Y. Ono.

CONTENTS

DIFFERENT WORLD VIEWS

Because the Earth is round, we can only see half of it at any one time. This half is called a hemisphere, which means 'half a sphere'. There are always two hemispheres – the half that you see and the other half that you don't see. Two hemispheres placed together will always make a complete sphere.

PLANET WATER, PLANET LAND

The Earth can also be divided into land and water hemispheres. The land hemisphere shows most of the land on the Earth's surface. The water hemisphere is dominated by the vast Pacific Ocean – from this view, the Earth appears to be almost entirely covered by water.

Equator 0°

NORTH AND SOUTH

The Equator is an imaginary line drawn around the middle of the Earth, where its circumference is greatest. If we cut along the Equator, the Earth separates into two hemispheres: the northern and southern hemispheres. Most of the Earth's land is the northern hemisphere. Europe and North America are the only continents which lie entirely in the northern hemisphere. Australia and Antarctica are the only continents that lie wholly in the southern hemisphere.

The southern hemisphere contains three of the Earth's four great oceans: the Pacific, Indian and Atlantic oceans.

EAST AND WEST

The Earth can also be divided along two other imaginary lines – the Prime Meridian (0°) and 180° – which run opposite each other between the North and South poles. This creates eastern and western hemispheres. The continents in the eastern hemisphere are traditionally called the Old World while those in the western hemisphere – the Americas – were named the New World by the Europeans who explored them in the 15th century.

Prime Meridian (0°)
North Pole
180°

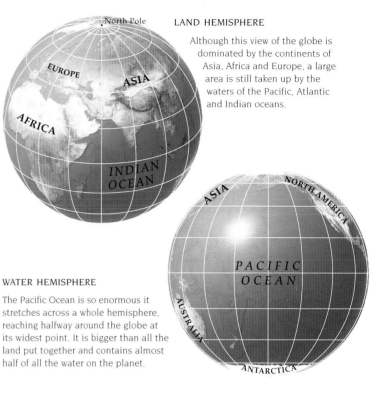

LAND HEMISPHERE

Although this view of the globe is dominated by the continents of Asia, Africa and Europe, a large area is still taken up by the waters of the Pacific, Atlantic and Indian oceans.

WATER HEMISPHERE

The Pacific Ocean is so enormous it stretches across a whole hemisphere, reaching halfway around the globe at its widest point. It is bigger than all the land put together and contains almost half of all the water on the planet.

THE SEASONS

As the Earth orbits the Sun, it is also spinning around an imaginary line called its axis, which joins the North and South poles. The Earth's axis is not quite at right angles to the Sun, but tilts over at an angle of 23.5°. As a result, each place gradually moves closer to the Sun and then further away from it again. Summer in the northern hemisphere is when the north is closest to the Sun. In winter, the northern hemisphere tilts away from the Sun, receiving far less heat and light. In the southern hemisphere the seasons are reversed, with summer in December and winter in June.

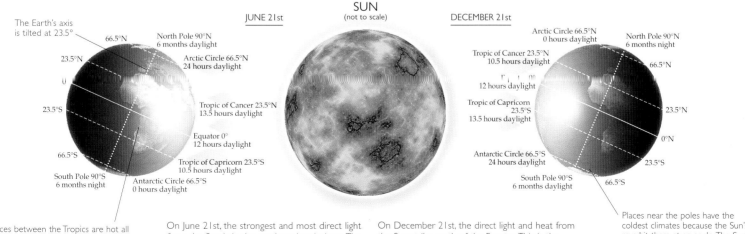

JUNE 21st

SUN (not to scale)

DECEMBER 21st

The Earth's axis is tilted at 23.5°
66.5°N
North Pole 90°N 6 months daylight
23.5°N
Arctic Circle 66.5°N 24 hours daylight
0
23.5°S
Tropic of Cancer 23.5°N 13.5 hours daylight
Equator 0° 12 hours daylight
66.5°S
Tropic of Capricorn 23.5°S 10.5 hours daylight
South Pole 90°S 6 months night
Antarctic Circle 66.5°S 0 hours daylight

Arctic Circle 66.5°N 0 hours daylight
North Pole 90°N 6 months night
Tropic of Cancer 23.5°N 10.5 hours daylight
66.5°N
12 hours daylight
Tropic of Capricorn 23.5°S 13.5 hours daylight
23.5°N
0°N
Antarctic Circle 66.5°S 24 hours daylight
23.5°S
South Pole 90°S 6 months daylight
66.5°S

Places between the Tropics are hot all year round. This is because the Sun's rays strike the Equator almost vertically, heating the land more intensely.

On June 21st, the strongest and most direct light from the Sun is in the northern hemisphere. The Arctic Circle has 24 hours of daylight, and the northern hemisphere has its longest day.

On December 21st, the direct light and heat from the Sun strike south of the Equator. This is the longest day in the southern hemisphere. The northern hemisphere has its shortest day and longest night.

Places near the poles have the coldest climates because the Sun's rays hit them at an angle. The Sun's warmth is therefore spread out over a much wider area.

MAPPING THE WORLD

The main purpose of a map is to show, or locate, where things are. The only truly accurate map of the whole world is a globe – a round model of the Earth. But a globe is impractical to carry around, so map-makers (cartographers) produce flat paper maps instead. Changing the globe into a flat map is not simple. Imagine cutting a globe in half and trying to flatten the two hemispheres. They would be stretched in some places, and squashed in others. In fact, it is impossible to make a map of the round Earth on flat paper without some distortion of area, distance or direction.

MODELS OF THE WORLD

Satellite images can show the whole world as it appears from space. However, this image shows only one half of the world, and is distorted at the edges.

A globe (right) is the only way to illustrate the shape of the Earth accurately. A globe also shows the correct positions of the continents and oceans and how large they are in relation to one another.

LATITUDE

We can find out exactly how far north or south, east or west any place is on Earth by drawing two sets of imaginary lines around the world to make a grid. The horizontal lines on the globe below are called lines of latitude. They run from east to west. The most important is the Equator, which is given the value 0°. All other lines of latitude run parallel to the Equator. and are numbered in degrees either north or south of the Equator.

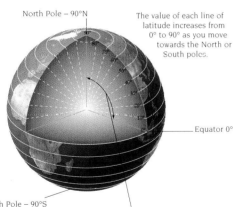

North Pole – 90°N

The value of each line of latitude increases from 0° to 90° as you move towards the North or South poles.

Equator 0°

South Pole – 90°S

Lines of latitude are measured from the centre of the Earth. An angle is then measured from here in relation to the Equator.

One degree of latitude is approximately 113 km.

Lines of latitude divide the world into 'slices' of equal thickness on either side of the Equator.

LONGITUDE

The vertical lines on the globe below run from north to south between the poles. They are called lines of longitude. The most important passes through Greenwich, London and is numbered 0°. It is called the Prime Meridian. All other lines of longitude are numbered in degrees either east or west of the Prime Meridian. The line directly opposite the Prime Meridian is numbered 180°.

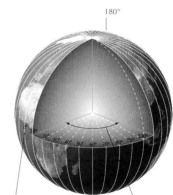

180°

Prime Meridian – 0°

Lines of longitude are also measured from the centre of the Earth. This time, the angle is taken in relation to the Prime Meridian.

Lines of longitude divide the world into segments, like those of an orange – wide near the Equator, but narrow at the poles.

WHERE ON EARTH?

When lines of latitude and longitude are combined on a globe, or as here, on a flat map, they form a grid. Using this grid, we can locate any place on land, or at sea, by referring to the point where its line of latitude intersects with its line of longitude. Even when a place is not located exactly where the lines cross, you can still find its approximate position.

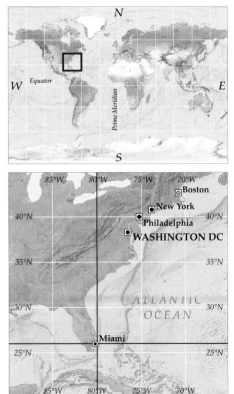

The map above is of the eastern USA. It is too small to show all the lines of latitude and longitude, so they are given at intervals of 5°. Miami is located at about 26° north of the Equator and 80° west of the Prime Meridian. We write its location like this: 26°N 80°W.

MAKING A FLAT MAP FROM A GLOBE

Cartographers use a technique called projection to show the Earth's curved surface on a flat map. Many different map projections have been designed. The distortion of one feature – either area, distance, or direction – can be minimized, while other features become more distorted. Cartographers must choose which of these things it is most important to show correctly for each map that they make. Three major families of projections can be used to solve these questions.

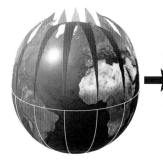

To make a globe, the Earth is divided into segments or 'gores' along lines of longitude.

1 CYLINDRICAL PROJECTIONS

These projections are 'cylindrical' because the surface of the globe is transferred onto a surrounding cylinder. This cylinder is then cut from top to bottom and 'rolled out' to give a flat map. These maps are very useful for showing the whole world.

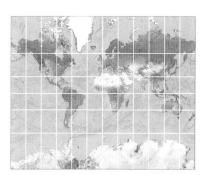

The cylinder touches the globe at the Equator. Here, the scale on the map will be exactly the same as it is on the globe. At the northern and southern edges of the cylinder, which are furthest away from the surface of the globe, the map is most distorted. The Mercator projection (*above*), created in the 16th century, is a good example of a cylindrical projection.

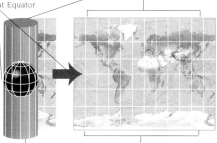

Scale accurate at Equator — Greatest distortion

Greatest distortion

2 AZIMUTHAL PROJECTIONS

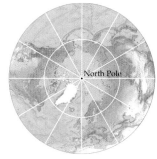

North Pole

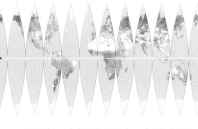

Azimuthal projections put the surface of the globe onto a flat circle. 'Azimuthal' means that the direction or 'azimuth' of any line coming from the centre point of that circle is correct. Azimuthal maps are useful for viewing hemispheres, continents and the polar regions. Mapping any area larger than a hemisphere gives great distortion at the outer edges of the map.

Accurate scale at central point

Greatest distortion

The circle only touches the globe's surface at one central point. The scale is only accurate at this point and becomes less and less accurate the further away the circle is from the globe. This kind of projection is good for maps centering on a major city or on one of the poles.

3 CONIC PROJECTIONS

Conic projections are best used for smaller areas of the world, such as country maps. The surface of the globe is projected onto a cone which rests on top of it. After cutting from the point to the bottom of the cone, a flat map in the shape of a fan is left behind.

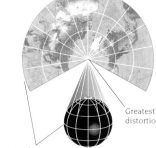

The conic projection touches the globe's surface at one latitude. This is where the scale of the map will be most accurate. The parts of the cone furthest from the globe will be the most distorted and are usually omitted from the map itself.

Greatest distortion

Most accurate scale

PROJECTIONS USED IN THIS ATLAS

The projections which are appropriate for showing maps at a world, continental or country scale are quite different. The projections for this atlas have been carefully chosen. They are ones that show areas as familiar shapes and ensure that they are distorted as little as possible.

1 World Maps

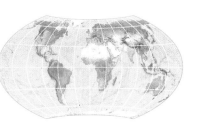

The **Wagner VII** projection is used for our world maps as it shows all the countries at their correct sizes relative to one another.

2 Continents

The **Lambert Azimuthal Equal Area** is used for continental maps. The shape distortion is relatively small and countries retain their correct sizes relative to one another.

3 Countries

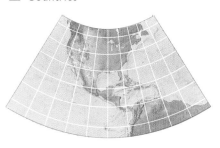

The **Lambert Conformal Conic** shows countries with as little distortion as possible. The angles from any point on the map are the same as they would be on the surface of the globe.

HOW MAPS ARE MADE

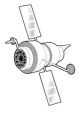

New technologies have revolutionized map making. Computers and information from satellites have replaced drawing boards and drafting pens, and the process of creating new maps is now far easier. But map making is still a skilled and often time-consuming process. Information about the World must be gathered, sorted and checked. The cartographer must make decisions about the function of the map and what information to select in order to make it as clear as possible.

THE MAPPA MUNDI

Maps have been made for thousands of years. The 13th century Mappa Mundi, meaning 'known world' shows the Mediterranean Sea and the Don and Nile rivers. Asia is at the top, with Europe on the left, and Africa to the right. The oceans are shown as a ring surrounding the land. The map reflects a number of biblical stories.

HISTORICAL MAP MAKING

This detailed hand-drawn map of the southern coast of Spain was made in about 1750. The mountains are illustrated as small hills and the labels have been hand lettered.

For centuries, maps were drawn by hand. Very early maps were no more than a pictorial representation of what the surface of the ground looked like. Where there were hills, pictures were drawn to represent them. Later maps were drawn using information gathered by survey teams. They would carefully mark out and calculate the height of the land, the positions of towns and other geographical features. As knowledge and techniques improved, maps became more accurate.

NEW TECHNIQUES

Computers make it easier to change map information and styles quickly. This map of the southern coast of Spain, made in 1997 has been made using digital terrain modelling (see below) and traditional cartography.

Today, cartographers have access to far more data about the Earth than in the past. Satellites collect and process information about its surface. Further elements may then be added in the traditional way. Computers are now widely used to combine these different sorts of map information. More recently, the use of Global Positioning Systems (GPS) linked to satellites, and the increased availability of Internet based mapping, has revolutionised the way that maps are created and used.

MODERN MAP MAKING

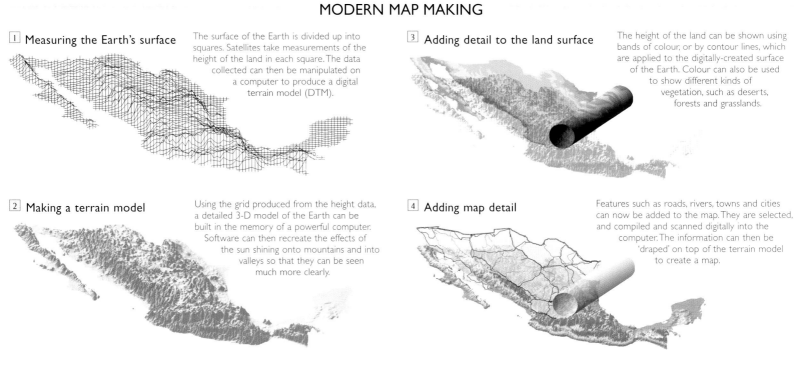

1 **Measuring the Earth's surface**
The surface of the Earth is divided up into squares. Satellites take measurements of the height of the land in each square. The data collected can then be manipulated on a computer to produce a digital terrain model (DTM).

2 **Making a terrain model**
Using the grid produced from the height data, a detailed 3-D model of the Earth can be built in the memory of a powerful computer. Software can then recreate the effects of the sun shining onto mountains and into valleys so that they can be seen much more clearly.

3 **Adding detail to the land surface**
The height of the land can be shown using bands of colour, or by contour lines, which are applied to the digitally-created surface of the Earth. Colour can also be used to show different kinds of vegetation, such as deserts, forests and grasslands.

4 **Adding map detail**
Features such as roads, rivers, towns and cities can now be added to the map. They are selected, and compiled and scanned digitally into the computer. The information can then be 'draped' on top of the terrain model to create a map.

SHOWING INFORMATION ON A MAP

A map is a selective diagram of a place. It is the cartographer's job to decide what kind of information to show on a map. They can choose to highlight certain kinds of features – such as roads, rivers and land height. They can also show other features such as sea depth, place names, and borders which would be impossible to see either on the ground or from a photograph. The information that can be shown in a map is influenced by a number of factors, most notably by its scale.

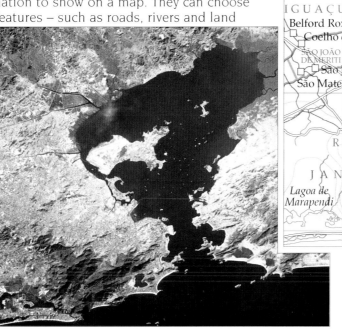

This is a satellite photograph of the harbour area of Rio de Janeiro in Brazil. Although you can see the bay and where most of the housing is, it is impossible to see roads or get any sense of the position of places relative to one another.

This is a map of the same area as you can see in the photograph. Much of the detail has been greatly simplified. Towns are named and marked; contours indicate the height of the land; and roads, railways and borders between districts have been added.

SCALE

To make a map of an area it needs to be greatly reduced in size. This is known as drawing to scale. The scale of the map shows us by how much the area has been reduced. The smaller the scale, the greater the area of land that can be shown on the map. There will be far less detail and the map will not be as accurate. The maps below show the different kinds of information that can be shown on maps of varying scales.

WAYS TO SHOW SCALE

When using a map to work out what areas or distances are in reality, we need to refer to the scale of that particular map. Map scales can be shown in several ways.

1 Representative fraction

One unit on the map would be equal to 1,000,000 units on the ground.

1:1,000,000

2 Linear scale

The line is marked off in units which represent the real distances of the map, given in both miles and kilometres.

SCALE BAR
0 km   10   20
0 miles   10   20

3 Statement of scale

It means that 1-mm on the map represents 1-km on the ground.

1 mm represents 1 km

LONDON 1:21,000,000

This small-scale map shows the position of London in relation to Europe. Very little detail can be seen at this scale – only the names of countries and the largest towns.

LONDON 1:5,500,000

At a scale of 1 to 5,500,000 you can see the major road network in the southeast of the UK. Many towns are named and you can see the difference in size and status.

LONDON 1:900,000

This map is at a much larger scale. You can see the major roads that lead out from London and the names of many suburbs, places of interest and airports.

LONDON 1:12,500

This is a street map of central London. The streets are named, as are places of interest, train and underground stations. The scale is large enough to show plenty of detail.

READING MAPS

Maps use a unique visual language to convey a great deal of detailed information in a relatively simple form. Different features are marked out using special symbols and styles of print. These symbols are explained in the key to the map and you should always read a map alongside its key or legend. This page explains how to look for different features on the map and how to unravel the different layers of information that you can find on it.

PHYSICAL FEATURES

All the regional and country maps in this atlas are based on a model of the Earth's surface. The computer-generated relief gives an accurate picture of the surface of the land. Colours are used to show the relative heights of the land; green is for low-lying land, and yellows, browns and greys are for higher land. Water features like streams, rivers and lakes are also shown.

1 WATER FEATURES

On this map extract, the blue lines show a number of rivers, including the Salween and the Irrawaddy. The Irrawaddy forms a huge delta, splitting into many streams as it reaches the sea.

2 RELIEF

These mountains are in the north of Southeast Asia. The underlying relief on the map and the coloured bands help you to see the height of the land.

HUMAN FEATURES

Maps also reveal a great deal about the human geography of an area. As well as showing where towns and roads are, different symbols can tell you more about the size of towns and the importance of a road. Borders between countries or regions can only be seen on a map.

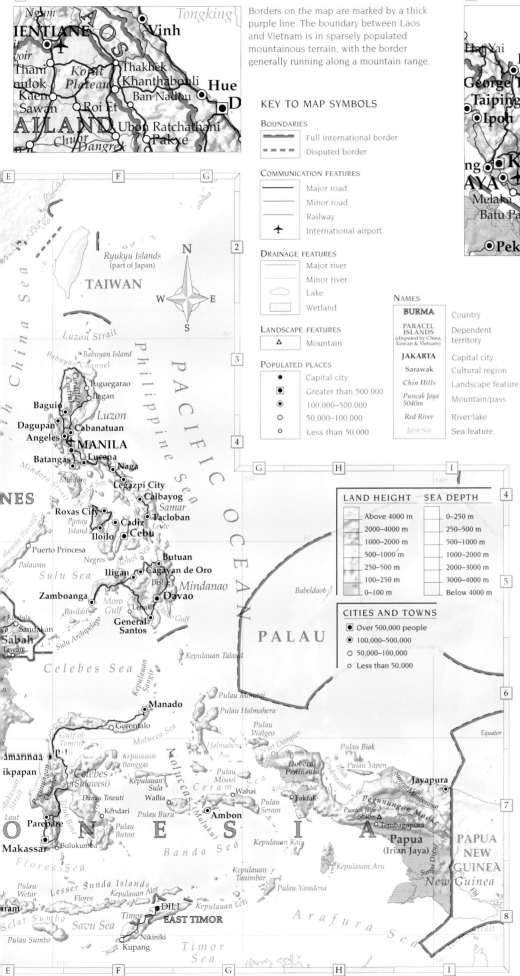

3 BORDERS

Borders on the map are marked by a thick purple line. The boundary between Laos and Vietnam is in sparsely populated mountainous terrain, with the border generally running along a mountain range.

KEY TO MAP SYMBOLS

BOUNDARIES

————	Full international border
– – – –	Disputed border

COMMUNICATION FEATURES

————	Major road
————	Minor road
————	Railway
✈	International airport

DRAINAGE FEATURES

	Major river
	Minor river
	Lake
	Wetland

LANDSCAPE FEATURES

△	Mountain

POPULATED PLACES

●	Capital city
▣	Greater than 500,000
◉	100,000–500,000
○	50,000–100,000
○	Less than 50,000

NAMES

BURMA	Country
PARACEL ISLANDS (disputed by China, Taiwan & Vietnam)	Dependent territory
JAKARTA	Capital city
Sarawak	Cultural region
Chin Hills	Landscape feature
Puncak Jaya 5040m	Mountain/pass
Red River	River/lake
Java Sea	Sea feature

LAND HEIGHT

Above 4000 m
2000–4000 m
1000–2000 m
500–1000 m
250–500 m
100–250 m
0–100 m

SEA DEPTH

0–250 m
250–500 m
500–1000 m
1000–2000 m
2000–3000 m
3000–4000 m
Below 4000 m

CITIES AND TOWNS

▣	Over 500,000 people
◉	100,000–500,000
○	50,000–100,000
○	Less than 50,000

4 SETTLEMENTS

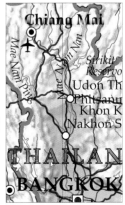

The symbol for a settlement can tell you its position, population and political status. Most towns are shown by a circle or a square. These represent the size of their population. Where a town is coloured red, this shows that it is a capital city such as Kuala Lumpur in Malaysia.

FINDING PLACES

Alphanumeric grid references

All the maps in this book are indexed using their alphanumeric grid reference – for example, G4. To find a place you must first look up its page number and then its grid reference. Read the letters and numbers off the bottom and side of the grid. Using rulers held at right angles to one another you will find the point where the lines meet. The place will be located within this square.

Latitude and longitude references

The lines of latitude and longitude are known as graticules. They are shown on the map as thin blue lines with the value of their latitude or longitude given as a blue number at the edge of the map.

5 ROADS AND RAILWAYS

a The major road and railway links between Hue and Nha Trang hug the Vietnamese coast. A string of coastal towns is often connected by road and rail in this manner.

Chiang Mai, in northern **b** Thailand, is linked to the capital Bangkok to the south by railway and road. At Chiang Mai, the mountains are too high for the railway to continue, and only roads go north into Burma.

USING THE ATLAS

This Atlas has been designed to develop map-reading skills and to introduce readers to a wide range of different maps. It also provides a wealth of detailed geographic information about the world today. The Atlas is divided into four sections: **Learning Map Skills**; The World About Us, covering global geographic patterns; the World Atlas, dealing with the world's regions, and an **Index**.

THE WORLD ABOUT US

These pages contain a series of world maps which show important themes, such as physical features, climate, life zones, population and the world economy, at a global scale. They give a worldwide picture of concepts which are explored in more detail later in the book.

Text introduces themes and concepts in each spread.

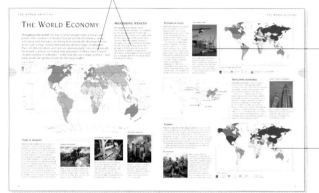

Photographs illustrate examples of places or topics shown on the main map.

World maps show geographic patterns at a global scale.

LEARNING MAP SKILLS

Maps show the Earth – which is three-dimensional – in just two dimensions. This section shows how maps are made; how different kinds of information are shown on maps; how to choose what to put on a map and the best way to show it. It also explains how to read the maps in this Atlas.

Introduction to projections: different projections and how they work.

Choosing the best projections: the map projections used in this book.

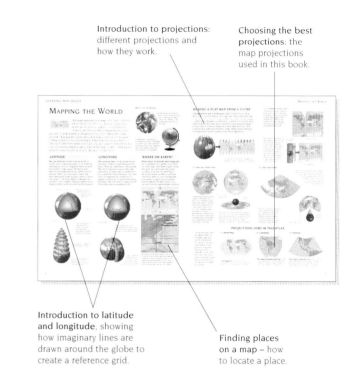

Introduction to latitude and longitude, showing how imaginary lines are drawn around the globe to create a reference grid.

Finding places on a map – how to locate a place.

CONTINENTAL MAPS

A cross-section through the continent shows the relative height of certain features.

A detailed physical map of the continent shows major natural geographic features, including mountains, lakes and rivers.

Photographs and locator maps illustrate the main geographic regions and show you where they are.

The industry map shows the main industrial towns and cities and the main industries in each continent. It also shows the wealth of each country relative to the rest of the world.

The political map of the continent shows country boundaries and country names.

CONTINENTAL PAGES

These pages show the physical shape of each continent and the impact that humans have made on the natural landscape – building towns and roads and creating borders between countries. They show where natural features such as mountain ranges and rivers have created physical boundaries, and where humans have created their own political boundaries between states.

CONTINENTAL GEOGRAPHY PAGES

Humans have colonized and changed all the continents except Antarctica. These pages show the factors which have affected this process: climate, the availability of resources such as coal, oil and minerals, and varying patterns of land use. Mineral resources are directly linked to many industries, and most agriculture is governed both by the quality of the land and the climate.

The climate map shows the main types of climates across the continent and where the hottest and coldest, wettest and driest places are.

The mineral resources map shows where the most important reserves of minerals, including coal and precious metals, are found.

The land use map shows different types of land and the main kinds of farming that take place in each area.

REGIONAL MAPS

The main part of the Atlas contains detailed maps of countries and regions. Each of these is accompanied by a series of small thematic maps, models and charts, which give information about the climate, where people live, how they use the land, the different kinds of industry, and important environmental issues.

TERRAIN MODEL

A computer-generated landscape model shows what the land really looks like. There are no roads or towns to mask the physical geography of the country or region. Mountain ranges, plains and river basins can be easily seen.

COLOURED THUMB TAGS

Each section has its own colour code.

- Learning Map Skills
- The World About Us
- North America
- South America
- Africa
- Europe
- Asia
- Australasia and Oceania
- Antarctica and the Arctic

CLIMATE MAPS

These maps show the temperature and rainfall patterns in January and July. Coloured bands indicate temperatures: blue for low temperatures, orange for high ones. Rainfall is represented by black lines with a number giving the average amount of rain. These are called isohyets.

Isohyets show the rainfall patterns in millimetres per year. The areas between the lines are either over or under the figures shown on the isohyets.

Here the rainfall is between 50 and 100 mm per year.

LOCATOR GLOBE

This shows the location of the country or region both within its continent, and in relation to the rest of the world.

MAP GRID

Each main map has a grid. Using the grid will help you to find a place on the map. Grid references are expressed as letters (running from left to right across the frame), and numbers (running from the top to the bottom of the frame), for example, A-4, G-6. Everything on the map is referenced in the **Index** at the back of the book.

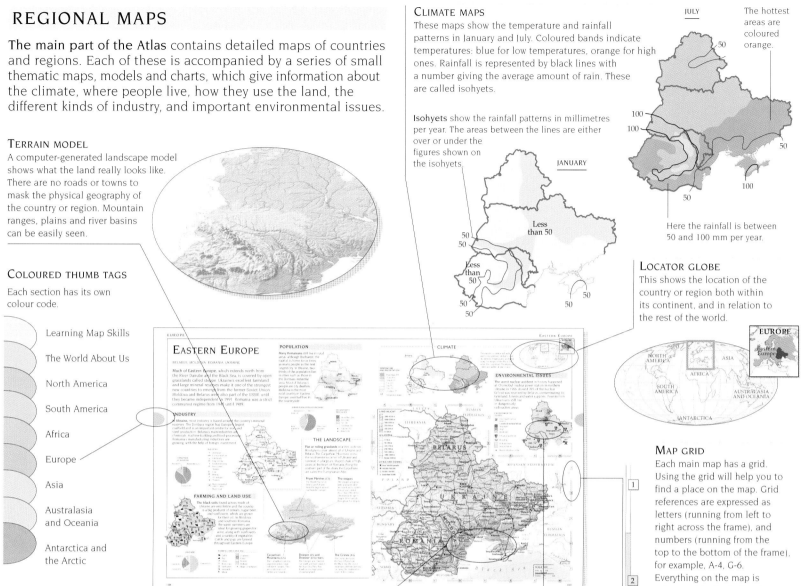

REGIONAL MAPS

The main map on each regional page shows the main topographical features of the area: the height of the land, the major roads, the rivers and lakes. It also shows the main cities and towns in the region – represented by different symbols.

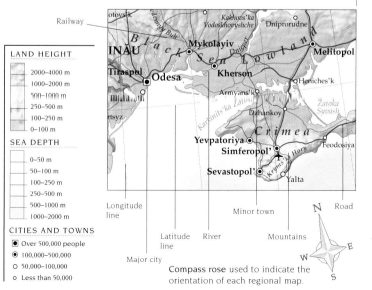

LAND HEIGHT
- 2000–4000 m
- 1000–2000 m
- 500–1000 m
- 250–500 m
- 100–250 m
- 0–100 m

SEA DEPTH
- 0–50 m
- 50–100 m
- 100–250 m
- 250–500 m
- 500–1000 m
- 1000–2000 m

CITIES AND TOWNS
- Over 500,000 people
- 100,000–500,000
- 50,000–100,000
- Less than 50,000

Railway · Longitude line · Latitude line · River · Minor town · Mountains · Road · Major city

Compass rose used to indicate the orientation of each regional map.

THEMATIC MAPS

These small maps show various aspects of the geography of the country or region. The environment maps cover topics such as the effects of pollution. Industry, land use and population maps locate the major industries, types of agriculture and the distribution of population.

Diagrams are used to show the geographic information on the map statistically.

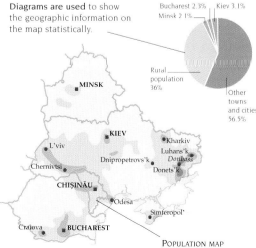

Bucharest 2.3% · Kiev 3.1% · Minsk 2.1% · Rural population 36% · Other towns and cities 56.5%

POPULATION MAP

INDUSTRY MAP

LAND USE MAP

ENVIRONMENT MAP

THE PHYSICAL WORLD

This map shows the main physical features of the world: the mountain ranges, the great rivers and lakes, deserts, grassland plains, seas and oceans. No human settlements are named on this map – only the physical or landscape features.

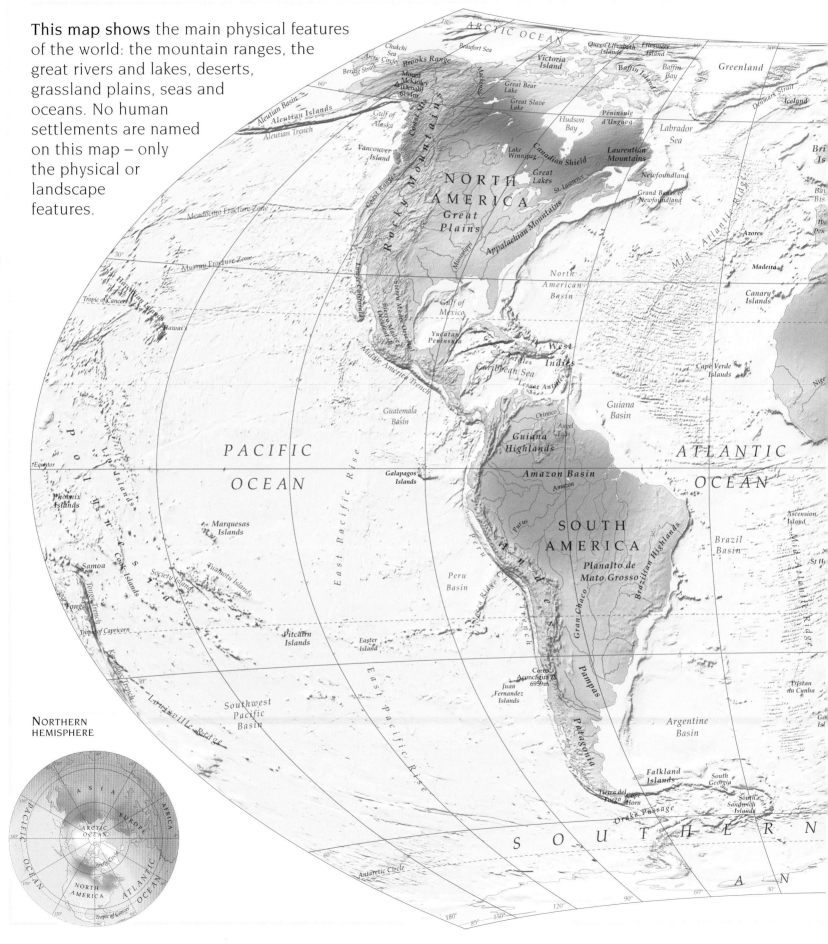

NORTHERN
HEMISPHERE

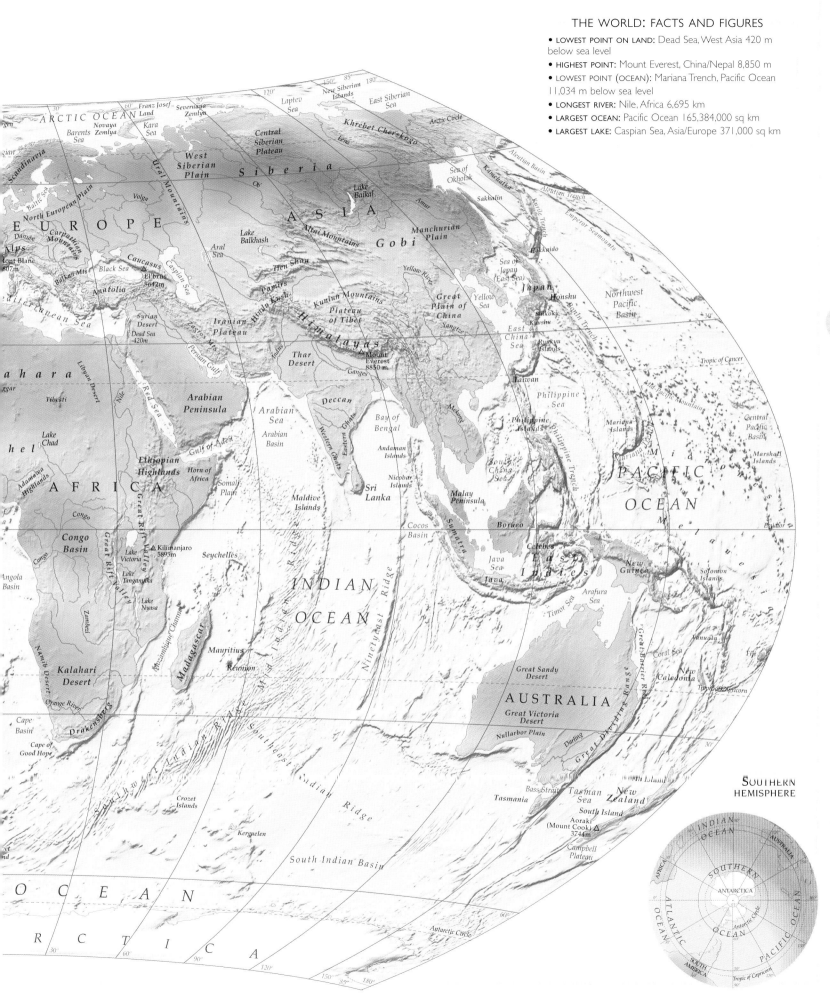

THE WORLD: FACTS AND FIGURES

- **LOWEST POINT ON LAND:** Dead Sea, West Asia 420 m below sea level
- **HIGHEST POINT:** Mount Everest, China/Nepal 8,850 m
- **LOWEST POINT (OCEAN):** Mariana Trench, Pacific Ocean 11,034 m below sea level
- **LONGEST RIVER:** Nile, Africa 6,695 km
- **LARGEST OCEAN:** Pacific Ocean 165,384,000 sq km
- **LARGEST LAKE:** Caspian Sea, Asia/Europe 371,000 sq km

SOUTHERN
HEMISPHERE

THE EARTH'S STRUCTURE

The shape and position of the Earth's oceans and continents make a familiar pattern. This is just the latest in a series of forms which the Earth has taken in the hundreds of millions of years since its creation. Massive forces inside the Earth cause the continents and oceans to move apart and together again, forming larger landmasses and then breaking them apart – a process known as plate tectonics. The movement is very slow – but over millions of years, the changes can be enormous.

DYNAMIC EARTH

The heart of the Earth is a solid core of iron surrounded by several layers of very hot – sometimes liquid – rock. The crust is relatively thin and is made up of a series of 'plates' which fit closely together. Movement of the molten rock deep within the mantle of the Earth causes the plates to move, creating changes in the surface features of the Earth.

THE EARTH'S PLATES

Continental plate

Oceanic plate

Plate boundary or margin

Continental and oceanic plates are tectonic plates – made from crustal rock

INSIDE THE EARTH

Rocky crust

Inner core – made of iron

Outer core – liquid iron and nickel

Mantle – mad from solid an molten roc

TECTONIC PLATES, VOLCANOES AND EARTHQUAKES

▲ Volcanic zone

Earthquake zone on land

⇨ Direction of plate movement

ᵛᵛᵛᵛ Rift valley

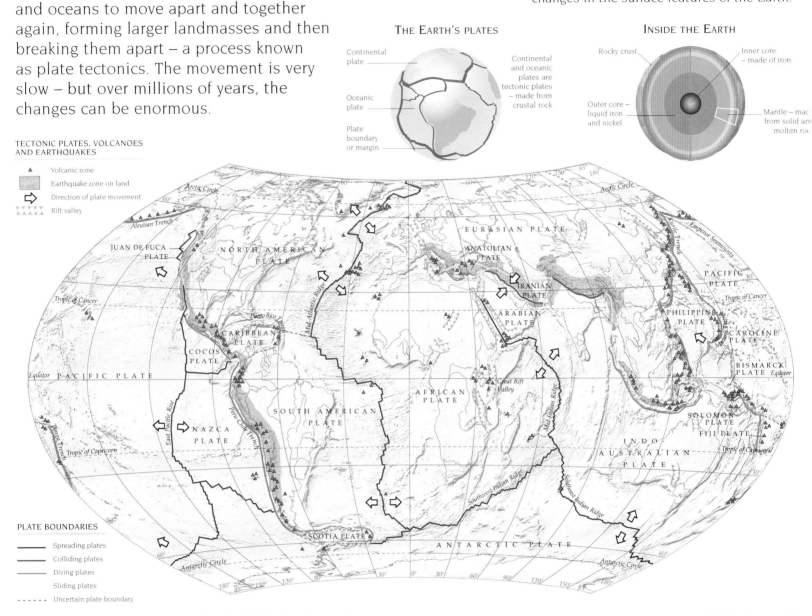

PLATE BOUNDARIES

—— Spreading plates

—— Colliding plates

—— Diving plates

—— Sliding plates

- - - - - Uncertain plate boundary

PLATE BOUNDARIES

The point where two plates meet is known as a plate boundary. As the Earth's plates move together or apart or slide alongside one another, the great forces which result cause great changes in the landscape. Mountains can be created, earthquakes occur and there may be frequent volcanic eruptions.

SPREADING PLATES

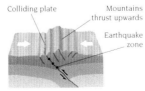

Earthquake zone   Ocean floor

Magma pushed upwards   Solid mantle

As plates move apart, magma rises through the outer mantle. When it cools, it forms new crust. The Mid-Atlantic Ridge is caused by spreading plates.

COLLIDING PLATES

Colliding plate   Mountains thrust upwards

Earthquake zone

When two plates bearing landmasses collide with one another, the land is crumpled upwards into high mountain peaks such as the Alps, and the Himalayas.

DIVING PLATES

Earthquake zone   Mountains

Ocean plate   Continental plate

When an ocean-bearing plate collides with a continental plate it is forced downwards under the other plate and into the mantle. Volcanoes occur along these boundaries.

SLIDING PLATES

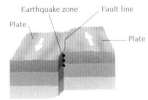

Earthquake zone   Fault line

Plate   Plate

As two plates slide past each other, great friction is set up along the fault line which lies between them. This can lead to powerful earthquakes.

SHAPING THE LANDSCAPE

The Earth's surface is made from solid rock or water. The land is constantly re-shaped by external forces. Water flowing as rivers or in the oceans erodes and deposits material to create valleys and lakes and to shape coastlines. When water is built up and compressed into solid sheets of ice, it can erode more deeply, creating deeper, wider valleys. Wind also has a powerful effect; stripping away vegetation and transporting rock particles vast distances.

RIVERS

Most rivers have their sources in mountain areas. They flow fast through the mountains, eroding deep V-shaped valleys. As they reach flatter areas they begin to meander in great loops, both eroding and then depositing rock particles as they slow down.

GLACIERS

In cold areas, close to the poles or on mountain tops, snow is built up into rivers of ice called glaciers. They move slowly, eroding deep U-shaped valleys. When the glacier melts, ridges of eroded rock called moraines are left at the sides and end of the glacier.

SEA ACTION

The oceans change the landscape in two major ways. They batter cliffs, causing rock to break away and the land to retreat, and they carry eroded material along the coast, to make beaches and sand bars.

WIND

Wind can erode and break down rock into smaller boulders and stones and eventually into sand. Desert sand dunes are shaped by the force of the wind and vary from ripples to hills 200 m high.

LANDSLIDES

Heavy rain can loosen soil and rock beneath the surface of slopes. As this moves, the top layers slip forward, to form heaps of rubble at the base of the slope.

THE WORLD'S OCEANS

Just over two-thirds of the Earth's surface is covered by water and more than 97% of this water is contained in the oceans. Movements within the Earth shape the ocean floor in the same way as they do the land surface, creating mountain ranges, trenches and plateaus, and changing the shape and size of the oceans. The difference between an ocean and a sea is simply its size; oceans are much bigger.

POLAR OCEANS

The Southern and Arctic Oceans contain large icebergs, that have broken away from the ice shelf.

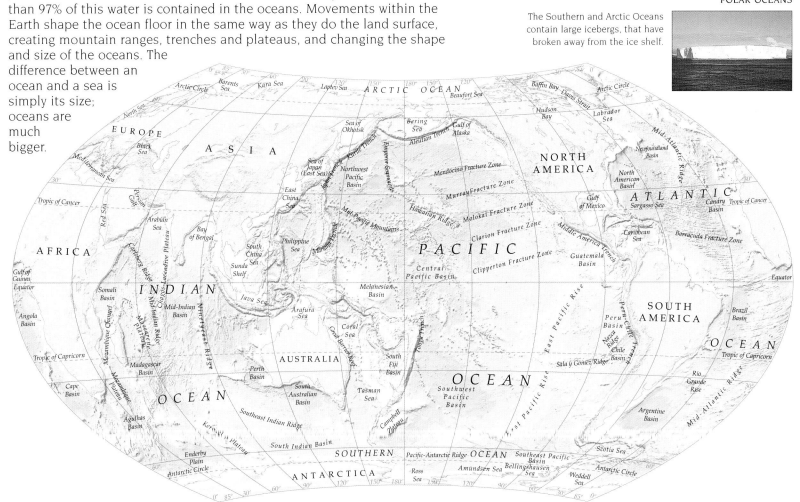

INDIAN OCEAN

The Indian Ocean covers about 20% of the world's surface. Ocean swells, starting deep in the Southern Ocean, often cause flooding in Sri Lanka and the Maldives.

PACIFIC OCEAN

The Pacific is the largest and deepest ocean in the world. It is surrounded an arc of volcanoes, including Japan, Indonesia and the Andes, known as the 'Ring of Fire'.

ATLANTIC OCEAN

The Atlantic Ocean was formed about 180 million years ago. The land which now forms Europe and Africa pulled apart from the Americas to create an ocean 3,000 km wide.

CLIMATE AND LIFE ZONES

This map shows the different climates found around the world. Climates are particular combinations of temperature and humidity. Climates are affected by latitude, the height of the land, winds and ocean currents. Climates can change, but not overnight. Weather is local and consists of short-term events such as thunderstorms, hurricanes and blizzards.

HURRICANES

Hurricanes are violent cyclonic windstorms, driven by heat energy gathered from tropical seas. The Caribbean islands and the east coast of the USA are particularly prone to hurricanes.

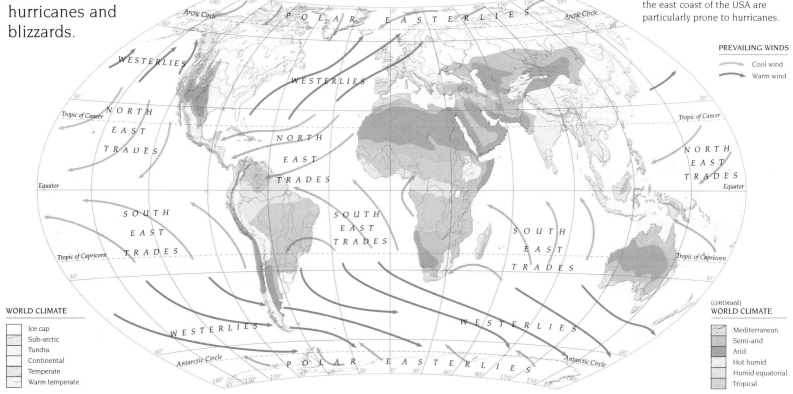

PREVAILING WINDS

Cool wind
Warm wind

WORLD CLIMATE

Ice cap
Sub-arctic
Tundra
Continental
Temperate
Warm temperate

(continued)
WORLD CLIMATE

Mediterranean
Semi-arid
Arid
Hot humid
Humid equatorial
Tropical

CLIMATE CHANGE

The Earth's climate is a constantly changing system resulting from a complex interaction of different geographical factors. Throughout history there have been several periods when the Earth's climate has been either hotter or colder than today. However, many scientists think that human activity is causing problems to this system by increasing levels of 'greenhouse gases' in the atmosphere. These gases, including carbon dioxide (CO_2), allow heat from the Sun to enter the atmosphere and then trap some of this heat like a greenhouse. Most scientists believe that unless action is taken to reduce greenhouse gases, temperatures will rise in a process known as global warming.

MAP KEY

Predicted change in average surface air temperature between 1960–1990 and 2070–2100

4 to 5°C
3 to 4°C
2 to 3°C
1 to 2°C
0 to 1°C

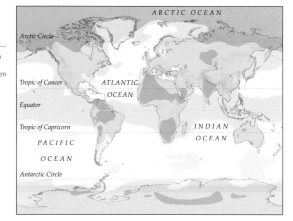

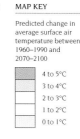

OCEAN CURRENTS

Ocean currents help to distribute heat around the Earth and have a great influence on climate. Convection currents circulate massive amounts of warm and cold water around the oceans. Warm water is moved away from the tropics to higher latitudes and cold water is moved toward the tropics.

OCEAN CURRENTS AND SURFACE TEMPERATURES

Cold currents
Warm currents
El Niño

20 to 30°C
10 to 20°C
0 to 10°C
Sea-water −2° to 0°C
Sea-ice (average) below −2°C

LIFE ZONES

The map below shows the Earth divided into different biomes – also called biogeographical regions. The combination of climate, the type of landscape, and the plants and animals that live there, are used to classify a region. Similar biomes are found in very different places around the world.

POLAR REGIONS
The North and South poles are permanently covered by ice. Only a few plants and animals can live here.

TUNDRA
Tundra is flat, cold and dry with few trees. Plants such as mosses and lichens grow close to the ground.

DESERTS
Very little rain falls in desert areas, whether they are hot deserts such as the Sahara or cold deserts like the Gobi.

NEEDLELEAF FORESTS
Tall coniferous trees such as pine and spruce, with spines or needles instead of leaves, grow in the far north of Scandinavia, Canada and the Russian Federation.

BROADLEAF FORESTS
Broadleaf or deciduous forests once covered temperate regions over most of the northern hemisphere. They contain trees of many varieties – all of which shed their leaves every year.

TEMPERATE RAINFORESTS
Evergreen, broadleaved trees need a warmer, wetter climate than deciduous trees. They are known as temperate rainforests.

MEDITERRANEAN
Close to the shores of the Mediterranean Sea, the vegetation consists mainly of herbs, shrubs and drought-resistant trees.

BIOME TYPES

- Mountains
- Polar regions
- Tundra
- Tropical rainforests
- Dry woodlands
- Savannah
- Temperate grasslands

(continued)
BIOME TYPES

- Mediterranean
- Needleleaf forests
- Temperate rainforests
- Broadleafs forests
- Cold deserts
- Hot deserts
- Wetlands

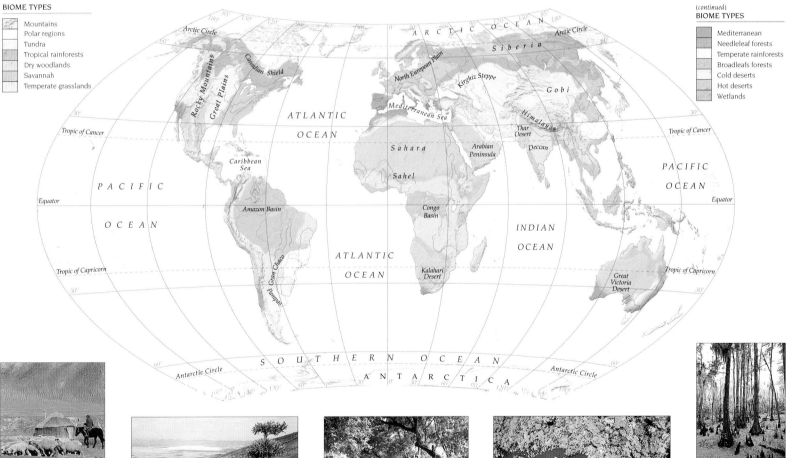

TEMPERATE GRASSLANDS
Grasslands cover the central areas of the continents. They are known in the middle latitudes as prairies, steppe and pampas.

SAVANNAH
The savannah consists of woodland, interspersed with grassland. These regions lie between the tropical rainforest and hot desert regions.

DRY WOODLANDS
Dry woodlands are found at the edge of grasslands. They contain small trees and shrubs adapted to dry conditions.

TROPICAL RAINFORESTS
Around the Equator, where temperatures are high and there is plenty of rain, tropical rainforests can flourish. Trees grow continuously and are tall with huge, broad leaves.

WETLANDS
Low-lying swamps and marshes are known as wetlands. They are often home to a rich variety of animal, plant and bird species.

WORLD POPULATION

There are now nearly 6.5 billion people on Earth. The population has increased nearly four times since 1900. Before that date, the number of people increased slowly as people were born and died at similar rates. With improved living conditions, better medical care and more efficient food production, more people survived to adulthood and the population began to grow much faster. If growth continues at the present rate, the world's population is likely to reach 7.5 billion by the year 2020.

Favelas – or shanty towns – have grown up around many South American cities because of overcrowding.

POPULATION STRUCTURES

Measuring the numbers of old and young people gives the age structure of a country or continent. If there are large numbers of young people and a high birth rate, the population is said to be youthful – as is the case in many African, Asian and South American countries. If the birth-rate is low but many people survive into old age, the population distribution is said to be ageing – this is true of much of Europe, Japan, Canada and the USA. Extreme events like wars can distort the population, leading to a loss of population in certain age groups.

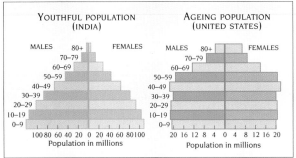

POPULATION DENSITY

The main map (*centre*) and the map below both show population density – the number of people who live in a given area. The map below shows the average population density per country. You can see that European countries and parts of Asia are very densely populated. The large map shows where people actually live. While the average population density in Brazil and Egypt is quite low, the coasts of Brazil and the areas close to the River Nile in Egypt are very densely populated.

DENSE POPULATION

Huge crowds near the Haora Bridge in Kolkata (Calcutta), India – one of the world's most densely populated cities.

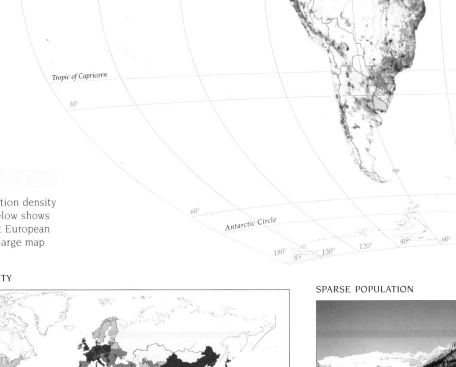

POPULATION DENSITY

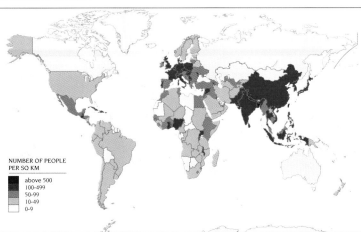

NUMBER OF PEOPLE PER SQ KM

- above 500
- 100-499
- 50-99
- 10-49
- 0-9

SPARSE POPULATION

The cold north of Canada has one of the lowest population densities in the world. Some people live in extreme isolation, separated from others by lakes and forests.

URBAN GROWTH

The 20th century saw a huge increase in the number of people living in cities. This has led to more large cities and the development of some 'super cities' such as Mexico City and Tokyo, each with more than 20 million people. In 1900, only about 10% of the population lived in cities. Now it is closer to 50% and soon the figure may be nearer two in three people. Some continents are far more 'urbanized' than others: in South America nearly 80% of people live in cities, whereas in Africa the figure is only about 30%.

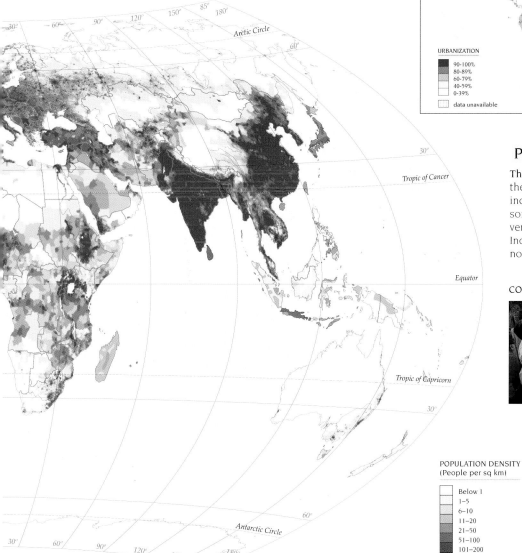

POPULATION DENSITY
(People per sq km)

- Below 1
- 1–5
- 6–10
- 11–20
- 21–50
- 51–100
- 101–200
- Above 200

LEVELS OF URBANIZATION

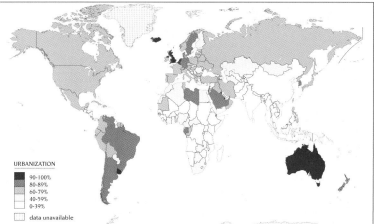

URBANIZATION

- 90-100%
- 80-89%
- 60-79%
- 40-59%
- 0-39%
- data unavailable

POPULATION GROWTH

The rate of population growth varies dramatically between the continents. Europe has a large population but it is increasing slowly. Africa is still sparsely populated, but in some countries such as Kenya, the population is growing very rapidly, increasing pressure on the land. China and India have the world's largest populations. Both countries now have laws to try and curb the birth rate.

CONTROLLING GROWTH

In 1980, fewer than 25% of women in less developed countries used birth control. Education programmes and more widely available contraceptives are thought to have doubled this figure. But many families still have no access to contraception.

AN AGEING POPULATION

In some countries, a low birth-rate, and an increasingly long-lived elderly population has greatly increased the ratio of old people to younger people, putting a strain on health and social services. For example, in Japan, most people can now expect to live to at least 80 years of age.

BIRTH RATE

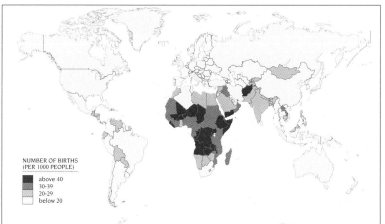

NUMBER OF BIRTHS
(PER 1000 PEOPLE)

- above 40
- 30-39
- 20-29
- below 20

LIFE EXPECTANCY

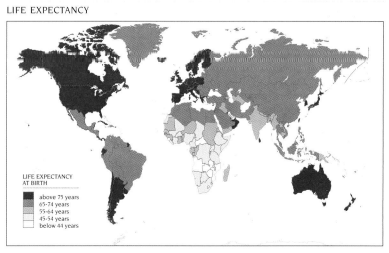

LIFE EXPECTANCY
AT BIRTH

- above 75 years
- 65-74 years
- 55-64 years
- 45-54 years
- below 44 years

THE WORLD ECONOMY

Throughout the world, the way in which people make a living varies greatly. The countries of Western Europe and North America, along with Japan and Australia, are the most economically developed in the world, with a long- established and very diverse range of industries. They sell their products and services internationally. Less economically developed countries in Central Asia and much of Africa, have a much smaller number of industries – some may rely on a single product – and many goods are produced only for the local market.

MEASURING WEALTH

The wealth of a country can be measured in several ways: for example, by the average annual income per person; by the volume of its trade; and by the total value of the goods and services that the country produces annually – its Gross Domestic Product or GDP. The map below shows the average GDP per person for each of the world's countries, expressed in US$. Most of the highest levels of GDP are in Europe and the US; most of the lowest are in Africa.

WORLD ECONOMIES

Average GNP per capita (in US$)

- Above 20,000
- 5,000–20,000
- 1,000–5,000
- Below 1,000
- Data unavailable

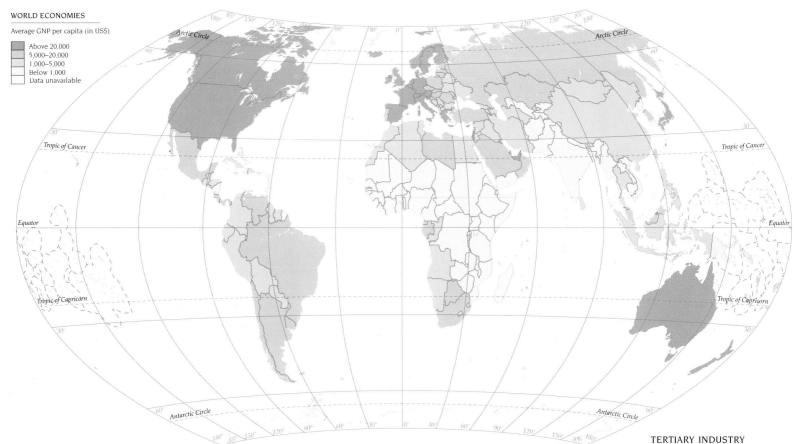

TYPES OF INDUSTRY

Industries are usually defined in one of three ways. Primary industries such as farming or mining involve the production of raw materials such as food or minerals. Secondary industries make or manufacture finished products out of raw materials: clothing and car manufacture are examples of secondary industries. People who work in tertiary industries provide different kinds of services. Banking, insurance and tourism are all examples of tertiary industries. Some economically advanced nations such as Germany or USA now have quaternary industries such as biotechnology which are knowledge-creation industries, devoted to the research and development of new products.

PRIMARY INDUSTRY

Tobacco leaves are picked and laid out for drying in Cuba, one of the world's great producers of cigars. Many countries rely on one or two high-value 'cash crops' like tobacco to earn foreign currency.

SECONDARY INDUSTRY

This skilled Thai weaver is producing an intricately patterned silk fabric on a hand loom. Fabric manufacture is an important industry throughout South and Southeast Asia. In India and Pakistan, vast quantities of cotton are produced in highly mechanized factories, but many fabrics are still hand woven.

TERTIARY INDUSTRY

The City of London is one of the world's great finance centres. Branches of many banks and insurance companies, including the world famous Lloyds of London, are clustered into the City's 'square mile'.

PATTERNS OF TRADE

Almost all countries trade goods with one another in order to obtain products they cannot produce themselves, and to make money from goods they have produced. Some countries – for example those in the Caribbean – rely mainly on a single export, usually a foodstuff or mineral, and can suffer a loss of income when world prices drop. Other countries, such as Germany and Japan, export a vast range of both raw materials and manufactured goods throughout the world. A number of huge companies, known as multinational corporations or MNCs, are responsible for more than 70% of world trade, with divisions all over the world. They include firms like BP, Coca Cola and Microsoft.

CONTAINER SHIPS

Many products are transported around the world on container ships. Containers are of a standard size so that they can be efficiently transported to their destinations. Some ships are specially designed to carry perishable goods such as fruit and vegetables.

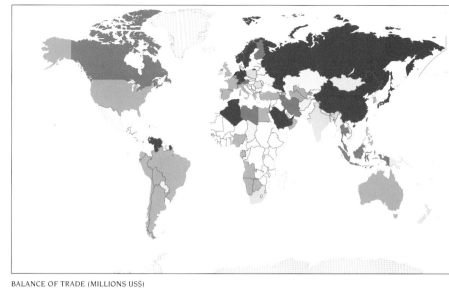

BALANCE OF TRADE (MILLIONS US$)

Surplus		Deficit		
■ Over 30,000	■ 1,000–9,999	□ 0–999	■ 10,000–29,999	□ Data unavailable
■ 10,000–29,999	□ 0–999	□ 1,000–9,999	■ Over 30,000	

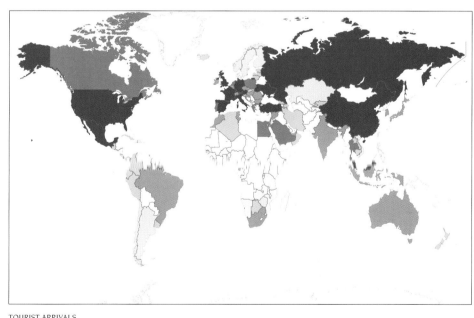

IRELAND
LUXEMBOURG
CYPRUS
CHINA
SOUTH KOREA
INDIA
TAIWAN
THAILAND
MALAYSIA
SINGAPORE
BOTSWANA
MAURITIUS

DEVELOPING ECONOMIES

Although world trade is still dominated by the more economically developed countries, since the 1970s, less economically developed countries have increased their share of world trade from less than 10% to nearly 30%. Countries such as China, India, Malaysia and South Korea, aided by investment from their governments or from wealthier countries, have become able to manufacture and export a wide variety of goods. Products include cars, electronic goods, clothing and footwear. Multinational companies can take advantage of cheaper labour costs to manufacture goods in these countries. Moves are being made to limit the exploitation of workers who are paid low wages for producing luxury goods.

ASIAN 'TIGER' ECONOMIES

The economies of Malaysia, Taiwan and South Korea, boomed in the late 1980s, attracting investment for buildings such as the Petronas Towers.

TOURISM

Tourism is now the world's largest industry. More than 700 million people travel both abroad and in their own countries as tourists each year. People in more developed countries have more money and leisure time to travel. Tourism can bring large amounts of cash into the local economy, but local people do not always benefit. They may have to take low-paid jobs and experience great intrusions into their lives. Tourist development and pollution may damage the environment – sometimes destroying the very attractions that led to the development of tourism in the first place.

ECOTOURISM

These tourists are being introduced to a giant tortoise, one of the many unique animals found in the Galapagos Islands. A number of places with special animals and ecosystems have introduced schemes to teach visitors about them. This not only educates more people about the need to safeguard these environments, but brings in money to help protect them.

TOURIST ARRIVALS

■ Over 20 million	■ 5–10 million	□ 1–2.5 million	□ Under 700,000
■ 10–20 million	□ 2.5–5 million	□ 700,000–1 million	□ Data unavailable

BORDERS AND BOUNDARIES

There are more countries in the world today than ever before – over 190 – whereas in 1950, there were only 82. Since then, many former European colonies and Soviet states have become independent. The establishment of borders for each of these countries has often been the subject of disagreement.

Military borders
At the end of wars, new borders are often drawn up between the countries – frequently along ceasefire lines. They may remain there for many years. At the end of the Korean War in 1953, North and South Korea were divided close to the 38° line of latitude. This border has remained heavily fortified.

Enclaves
If part of a country's territory has become separated from the rest of the country, and is surrounded by foreign territory, it is called an enclave. Kaliningrad is part of the Russian Federation, but is cut off from it by Lithuania and Belarus.

River borders
Over one-sixth of the world's national borders are formed by rivers. Long stretches of the Danube form natural borders in southeastern Europe.

Long borders
The border between the USA and Canada is the second longest continuous border in the world. It cuts through the centre of the Great Lakes. To the west of the Great Lakes, the border runs along the 49° line of latitude.

Mountain borders
Mountain ranges such as the Pyrenees, Alps and Himalayas form natural borders between many countries. In the Andes, border disputes between Chile and Argentina centred on finding the highest point in the mountain range which divided them.

Straight line borders
The borders of many countries in Africa and other former colonial territories are straight lines. This was the simplest solution for colonial administrators, who often knew little of the country's geography or population.

Lake boundaries
Countries which lie next to lakes usually fix their borders in the middle of the lake. Complicated agreements between colonial powers led to the awkward division of Lake Nyasa in Africa.

Territorial disputes
There are still many disputed territories and borders. One of the most serious territorial disputes is between India and Pakistan over Jammu and Kashmir, which has led to three wars since 1947.

THE ATLAS
OF THE
WORLD

THE NATIONS OF THE WORLD

The world is divided into 195 independent countries, and about 60 overseas territories or dependencies. The largest country is the Russian Federation covering 17,075,200 sq km; the smallest is Vatican City in Rome, with an area of 0.44 sq km.

ARCTIC OCEAN

Arctic Circle Alaska (part of USA)

Bering Sea

Aleutian Is (part of USA)

Great Bear Lake

Great Slave Lake

Hudson Bay

Baffin Bay

Greenland (to Denmark)

Jan M (to N

ICELAND

Faeroe Islands (to Denmark)

C A N A D A

Lake Winnipeg

Lake Superior

Lake Michigan Lake Huron Lake Ontario Lake Erie

UNITED STATES OF AMERICA

St Pierre & Miquelon (to France)

UN KIN

IRELAND

Isle of Man (to UK)

Channe Islands (to UK)

P A C I F I C   O C E A N

Midway Islands (to USA)

Tropic of Cancer

Hawaii (part of USA)

Johnston Atoll (to USA)

Guadalupe (part of Mexico)

Revillagigedo Islands (part of Mexico)

MEXICO

Gulf of Mexico

BAHAMAS

Turks & Caicos Is (to UK)

Bermuda (to UK)

A T L A N T I C   O C E A N

Azores (part of Portugal) PORTUGAL

Gibraltar (to UK)
Ceuta (part of Spain)
Melilla (part of Spain)

Madeira (part of Portugal)

Canary Islands (part of Spain)

MORO

CUBA

Cayman Is (to UK)

JAMAICA

BELIZE

Navassa I (to USA)

Puerto Rico (to USA)

Virgin Is (to USA)

HAITI DOM. REP.

ST KITTS & NEVIS

British Virgin Is (to UK)
Anguilla (to UK)
ANTIGUA & BARBUDA
Guadeloupe (to France)
DOMINICA
Martinique (to France)
ST LUCIA
ST VINCENT & THE GRENADINES
BARBADOS
GRENADA

Montserrat (to UK)

WESTERN SAHARA (disputed)

MAURITANIA

CAPE VERDE

SENEGAL MA

GAMBIA

GUINEA-BISSAU BU.

GUINEA

SIERRA LEONE IVO COA

LIBERIA

GUATEMALA
HONDURAS
EL SALVADOR
NICARAGUA

Caribbean Sea

Netherlands Antilles
Aruba (to Neth.)

TRINIDAD & TOBAGO

COSTA RICA

Clipperton Island (to French Polynesia)

PANAMA

VENEZUELA

COLOMBIA

GUYANA
SURINAM
French Guiana (to France)

Kingman Reef (to USA)

Palmyra Atoll (to USA)

Baker & Howland Is (to USA)

Jarvis I (to USA)

Equator

Galapagos Is (part of Ecuador)

ECUADOR

P E R U

B R A Z I L

Fernando de Noronha (part of Brazil)

Ascension (to St Helena)

K I R I B A T I

Tokelau (to NZ)

SAMOA

Wallis & Futuna (to France)

American Samoa (to USA)

Cook Islands (to NZ)

French Polynesia (to France)

TONGA

Niue (to NZ)

P A C I F I C   O C E A N

Lake Titicaca

BOLIVIA

A T L A N T I C   O C E A N

Trindade (part of Brazil)

St He (to

Tropic of Capricorn

Pitcairn Islands (to UK)

Kermadec Islands (part of NZ)

Easter Island (part of Chile)

Sala y Gomez (part of Chile)

San Felix Island (part of Chile) San Ambrosio Island (part of Chile)

C H I L E

PARAGUAY

A R G E N T I N A

URUGUAY

Juan Fernandez Islands (part of Chile)

Chatham Islands (part of NZ)

Falkland Islands (to UK)

South Georgia & South Sandwich Islands (to UK)

Tristan da Cunha (to St Helena)

Gough Islan (part of Tristan da

S O U T H E E

South Shetland Islands South Orkney Islands

Peter I Island (to Norway)

Antarctic Circle

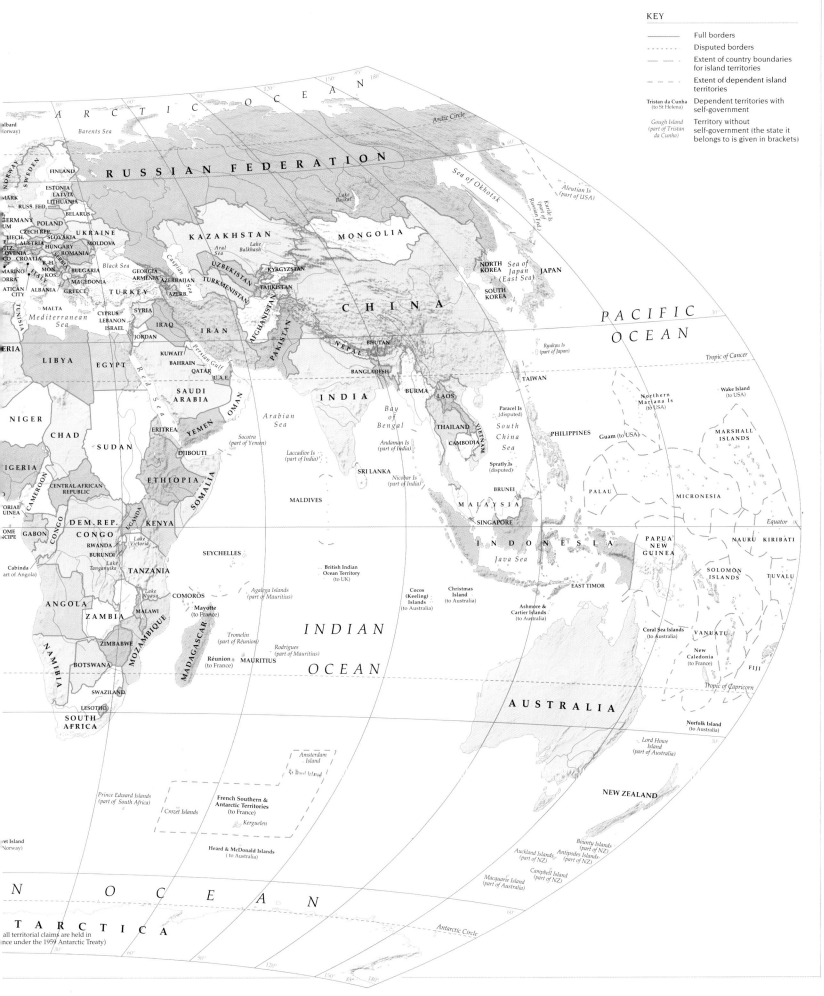

CONTINENTAL NORTH AMERICA

North America is the world's third largest continent, stretching from icy Greenland to the tropical Caribbean. The first people came from Asia more than 20,000 years ago. Their descendants spread across the continent, ate fish, meat, and wild and cultivated plants, and developed a wide variety of cultures and languages. About 500 years ago, immigrants from Europe, Africa, and Asia began to arrive in North America, bringing their own languages and cultures.

CROSS-SECTION THROUGH NORTH AMERICA

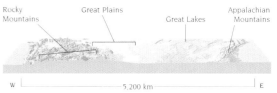

In the west, the land rises from the Pacific Ocean to the coastal ranges and the Rocky Mountains. Further east, the continent flattens into the Great Plains and the Great Lakes – gouged out by glaciers at the end of the last Ice Age. The Appalachian Mountains are older than the Rockies, and very worn down.

PHYSICAL NORTH AMERICA

The high peaks of the Rocky Mountains of Canada and the USA tower above the lower ranges of the western coasts. These ranges stretch from the icy north of Alaska, south to Mexico and Central America. The heart of the continent is flatter, and much of it is drained by the mighty Mississippi-Missouri river system.

1 THE FAR NORTH

Much of Canada's far north is covered by ice and snow. Only in summer, when the ice thaws, can hardy lichens grow. Great pine forests are found further south.

2 THE MOUNTAINOUS WEST

A huge mountain chain runs down the western side of the continent. These mountains are young, and are still being formed.

ELEVATION

- 6000 m
- 5000 m
- 4000 m
- 3000 m
- 2000 m
- 1000 m
- 500 m
- 250 m
- 100 m
- sea level
- below sea level

▶◀ cross-section

SCALE 1:52,000,000

0 km   500   1000

0 miles 250   500   750   1000

3 THE GREAT PLAINS

The fertile soils of much of the Great Plains – at the heart of the continent – allow cereal crops like wheat and corn to be grown.

THE DESERT REGIONS 4

The Sonoran Desert, in southwestern USA, is typical of North America's extensive desert regions.

5 THE TROPICAL SOUTH

The Yucatan Peninsula, in Mexico, is full of caves and sinkholes because the humid tropical climate accelerates erosion.

POLITICAL NORTH AMERICA

The USA, Canada and Mexico are all federal countries. This means that political power is shared between the national government and the state or provincial governments. Canada and the USA are democracies with a long history of freedom and equal rights. Governments in the countries south of the USA have been less stable, often ruled by dictators or harsh regimes. Many people have suffered for their political beliefs. During the 1960's and 1970's many of the Caribbean islands gained independence from their European colonial rulers.

THE SPACE RACE

The USA pioneered some of the great achievements of 20th century technology, including mass production of the motor car and the development of space craft.

POPULATION

The most densely populated parts of North America are the east and west coasts of the USA, central Mexico, the countries of Central America and the Caribbean islands. The far north of Canada, covered by ice, lakes and forests, has a very small and scattered population.

Largest city
NEW YORK
21.7 million people

POPULATION DENSITY
(People per sq km)

Below 9
10–49
50–99
100–249
250–499
Above 500

STANDARDS OF LIVING

The USA and Canada are two of the world's wealthiest countries, although pockets of poverty remain. In Central America and the Caribbean, people are less well off. Many in Mexico City live in overcrowded and inadequate housing.

STANDARD OF LIVING
(UN Human Development Index)

low   high

GREAT DISTANCES

Most people in the USA and Canada rely on automobiles to transport them from place to place. Since the 1930s, great highway systems have been built to link all parts of the continent.

STATE ABBREVIATIONS

AL   Alabama
IN   Indiana
MS   Mississippi
PA   Pennsylvania
VT   Vermont
WV   West Virginia

POPULATION

◉ Above 500,000
◎ 100,000 to 500,000
● 50,000 to 100,000
• Below 50,000

SCALE 1:47,500,000

0 km   500   1000

0 miles 250   500   750   1000

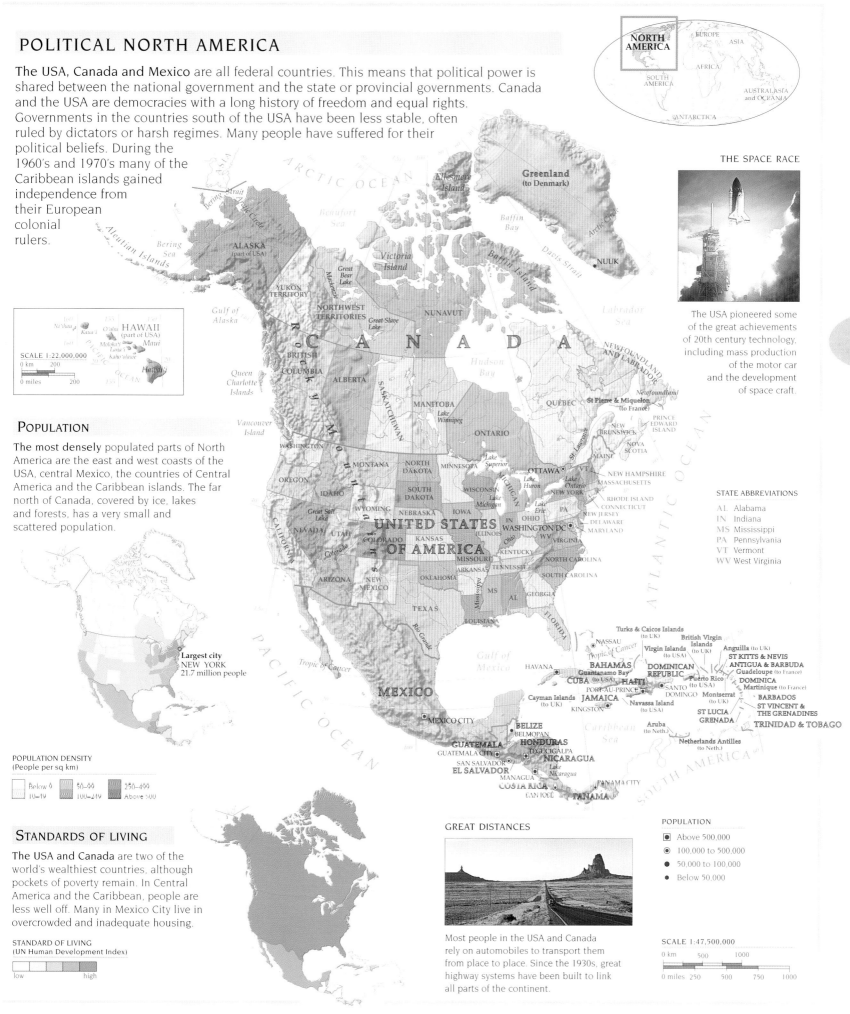

NORTH AMERICAN GEOGRAPHY

Canada and the USA are among the world's wealthiest countries. They have rich natural resources, good farmland and thriving, varied industries. The range of different industries in Mexico is growing, but other Central American countries and the Caribbean islands rely on one or two important cash crops and tourism for most of their incomes. They have a lower standard of living than Canada and the USA.

MINERAL RESOURCES

North America still has large amounts of mineral resources. Canada has important nickel reserves, Mexico is renowned for its silver, and bauxite – used to make aluminum – is found in Jamaica. Oil and gas are plentiful, particularly in the arctic northwest by the Beaufort Sea, and further south by the Gulf of Mexico.

INDUSTRY

The USA and Canada have an extremely wide range of industries, from mining and the processing of farm produce, to heavy and light manufacturing and service industries like banking. A variety of goods are produced, including aeroplanes, cars and computers. Oil exports and machine assembly are Mexico's main industries. In Central America and the Caribbean nations, most industry is based on agricultural produce.

MINERAL RESOURCES

- Bauxite
- Copper
- Iron
- Nickel
- Phosphates
- Silver
- Uranium
- Oil/gas field
- Coal field

TIMBER PROCESSING

Huge tracts of forest are found toward the north of the continent; nearly 30% of Canada is covered by forest. Timber is processed to make paper in cities such as Portland and Vancouver.

HI-TECH INDUSTRY

The Santa Clara Valley, just south of San Francisco is also known as Silicon Valley, because of the number of firms producing computer hardware and software and micro-electronics which have set up in the area.

INDUSTRY

- ✈ Aerospace
- ♦ Brewing
- ➤ Car/vehicle manufacture
- ⚗ Chemicals
- ⛏ Coal
- ⚔ Defence
- ⚙ Engineering
- ✹ Film industry
- 🅂 Finance
- ⬚ Food processing
- 🖥 Hi-tech industry
- ⬛ Iron & steel
- ♦ Oil & gas
- ✎ Pharmaceuticals
- ▥ Printing & publishing
- ✪ Research & development
- ⚓ Shipbuilding
- ☂ Textiles
- ♣ Timber processing

GNI per capita (US$)

- Below 1,999
- 2,000–4,999
- 5,000–9,999
- 10,000–19,999
- 20,000–24,999
- Above 25,000
- • Industrial centre

FOOD PROCESSING

Jamaica has been famous for its rum since the 16th century. Syrup is extracted from sugar cane which is then fermented to make rum.

MANUFACTURING

Mexico has many car part assembly plants. Labour costs in Mexico are low, making it cheap to assemble car parts here.

CLIMATE

Much of northern Canada lies within the Arctic Circle and is permanently covered by ice or the sparse vegetation known as tundra. Southern Canada and much of central USA have a continental climate, with hot summers and cold winters. The southern parts of the USA, Central America and the Caribbean have a hot, humid tropical climate. The Caribbean and the eastern and central states of the USA often experience hurricane-force winds, waterspouts and tornadoes.

EXTREME WEATHER EVENTS

Symbols indicate climatic extremes

Coldest place
NORTHICE (Greenland)
Temperature -66°C

Wettest place
HENDERSON LAKE (BC, Canada)
Annual rainfall 6650mm

Hottest place
DEATH VALLEY (CA, USA)
Temperature 57°C

Driest place
BATAQUES (Mexico)
Annual rainfall 30mm

CLIMATE

- Ice cap
- Tundra
- Sub-arctic
- Cool continental
- Warm temperate
- Mediterranean
- Semi-arid
- Arid
- Humid equatorial
- Tropical
- Hot Humid

NORTH AMERICA'S HOTTEST PLACE

Death Valley in California is the hottest and driest place in the USA. Strong, dry winds sweep through the valley, constantly reshaping the sand and salt deposits which cover its floor.

LAND USE AND AGRICULTURE

On the Great Plains and Prairies of the USA and Canada, vast quantities of cereal crops, including corn and wheat, grow in the fertile soils. Cattle are also raised on great ranches throughout these regions and on the foothills of the Rocky Mountains. In California, vegetables and fruits are grown with the aid of irrigation. Bananas, coffee and sugar cane are grown for export in Central America and the Caribbean, while sorghum and maize are grown as subsistence crops.

BANANA PLANTATION

Banana plantations are common in the Caribbean and Central America. The fruit is grown for local consumption and for export to the USA and Europe, where they are valued for their flavour and nutritional qualities.

FISHING

The Grand Banks off the eastern coast of Canada were once home to almost limitless fish stocks. Overfishing has reduced the number of fish to very low levels. Quotas limiting the numbers of fish caught are helping numbers to rise.

LAND USE AND AGRICULTURE

- Cattle
- Poultry
- Pigs
- Reindeer
- Sheep
- Bananas
- Cereals
- Citrus fruits
- Coffee
- Corn (maize)
- Cotton
- Fishing
- Fruit
- Peanuts
- Rice
- Shellfish
- Soya beans
- Sugarcane
- Timber
- Tobacco
- Vineyards

- Cropland
- Desert
- Forest
- Ice cap
- Mountain region
- Pasture
- Tundra
- Wetland
- Major conurbation

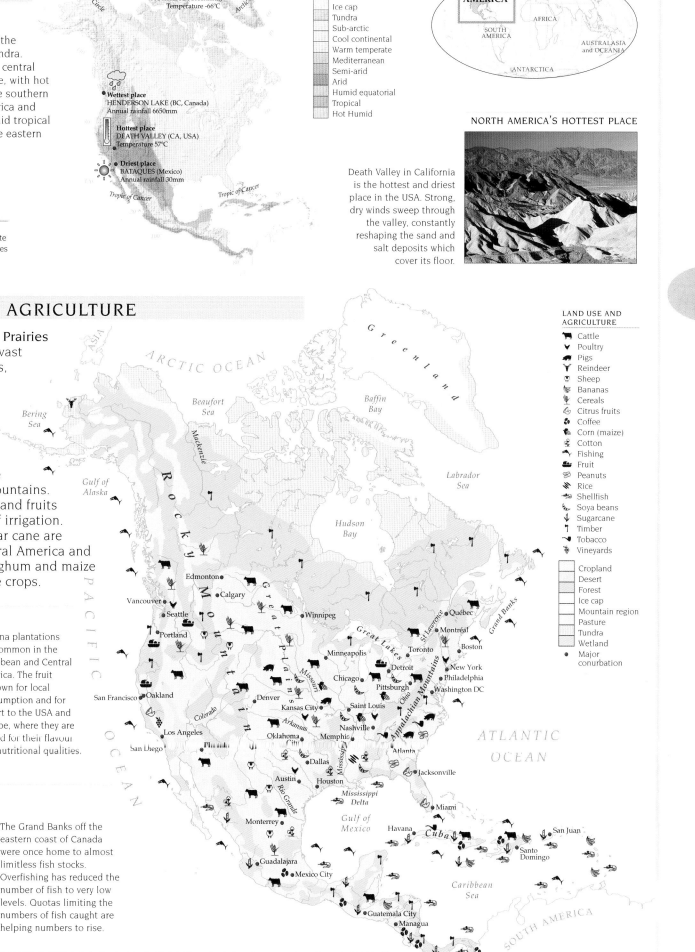

WESTERN CANADA

ALBERTA, BRITISH COLUMBIA, MANITOBA, NORTHWEST
TERRITORIES, NUNAVUT, SASKATCHEWAN, YUKON TERRITORY

The first inhabitants of Canada's western provinces
were Native Americans. By the late 1800s, the Canadian
Pacific Railroad was completed and European settlers
moved west, turning most of the prairie into huge grain
farms. North of the prairies lie the vast, empty territories
that have significant Native American populations.
In 1999, part of the Northwest Territories, known as
Nunavut, became a self-governing Inuit homeland.

INDUSTRY

The major industries in the prairie provinces
are related to agriculture, such as
meat-processing in Manitoba. Alberta
has huge reserves of fossil fuels,
and the other provinces are rich in
minerals, including zinc, nickel, silver
and uranium. British Columbia's
economy depends on manufacturing,
especially automobiles, chemicals
and machinery, along with paper
and timber industries.

STRUCTURE OF
INDUSTRY

Primary 6%
Services 64%
Manufacturing 30%

INDUSTRY
- 🚗 Car manufacturing
- 🧪 Chemicals
- ⚙ Engineering
- 🍴 Food processing
- △ Metal refining
- ◊ Oil and gas
- ⛏ Mining
- 🪵 Timber processing
- ⓘ Tourism
- ▣ Major industrial centre / area
- — Major road

Resolute
Kitimat
Edmonton
Vancouver
Calgary
Regina
Winnipeg
Flin Flon

ENVIRONMENTAL ISSUES

For hundreds of years sailors have searched in vain for
a route from Europe to Asia via the Northwest Passage,
through the north of this region. In recent summers the sea
ice has retreated further north, and in 2007 the route was
completely navigable.
Many of the extensive forests in
British Columbia are used for
commercial lumbering. The
province produces more than
half of Canada's timber.

ENVIRONMENTAL
ISSUES
- 🏭 Lumbering activity
- ▢ Permafrost zone
- • Major industrial centre
- ---- Northwest Passage - direct route

Vancouver
Winnipeg

FARMING AND LAND USE

More than 20% of the world's wheat is
grown in Canada's prairie provinces:
Manitoba, Alberta and
Saskatchewan. Beef cattle graze
on the ranches of Alberta and
British Columbia. Fruits,
especially apples, flourish
in the sheltered southern
valleys of British Columbia,
and Pacific salmon and
herring are caught off
the west coast.

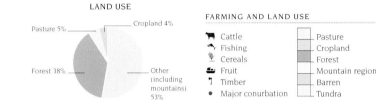

Vancouver
Calgary
Edmonton
Winnipeg

LAND USE

Pasture 5%
Cropland 4%
Forest 38%
Other (including mountains) 53%

FARMING AND LAND USE
- 🐄 Cattle
- 🐟 Fishing
- 🌾 Cereals
- 🦞 Fruit
- 🌲 Timber
- • Major conurbation
- ▢ Pasture
- ▨ Cropland
- ▨ Forest
- ▨ Mountain region
- ▢ Barren
- ▢ Tundra

THE LANDSCAPE

The prairie provinces are mostly flat. Occasionally,
the level plains are broken up by river valleys such
as that of the Qu'Appelle in Saskatchewan. In the
west, the jagged peaks and steep passes of the Rocky
Mountains and the Coast Mountains are covered
in snow for months on end. West of the Rockies,
the land descends sharply towards the coast of
British Columbia. The far north is covered by dense
forests and many glacial lakes.

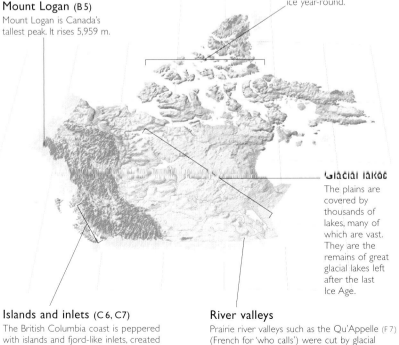

The Arctic
Most of Canada's northern
islands are within the Arctic
Circle. They are covered by
ice year-round.

Mount Logan (B 5)
Mount Logan is Canada's
tallest peak. It rises 5,959 m.

Glacial lakes
The plains are
covered by
thousands of
lakes, many of
which are vast.
They are the
remains of great
glacial lakes left
after the last
Ice Age.

Islands and inlets (C 6, C7)
The British Columbia coast is peppered
with islands and fjord-like inlets, created
by the force of the Pacific Ocean.

River valleys
Prairie river valleys such as the Qu'Appelle (F 7)
(French for 'who calls') were cut by glacial
meltwater thousands of years ago.

NORTH AMERICA
Western Canada

POPULATION

Most of the people in western Canada live near the Canada/USA border, taking advantage of the warmer climate and convenient transport routes. In the cold, forested north, the population is sparse, with only a few people per 100 sq km – many of them Native Americans such as the Inuit.

Edmonton
Vancouver
Calgary
Saskatoon
Regina
Winnipeg

URBAN/RURAL POPULATION DIVISION

Vancouver 22.7%
Other towns and cities 38%
Calgary 10.8%
Edmonton 10.5%
Rural population 18%

INHABITANTS PER SQ KM

More than 10
1–10
Less than 1
• Major city

CLIMATE

Parts of northern Canada are frozen all year round. The prairie provinces have warm summers and cold winters. Coastal British Columbia is mild and wet.

January

July

TEMPERATURE AND PRECIPITATION

More than 20°C | 0 to -5°C
15 to 20°C | -5 to -10°C
10 to 15°C | -10 to -15°C
5 to 10°C | Less than -15°C
0 to 5°C
100 Precipitation (mm)

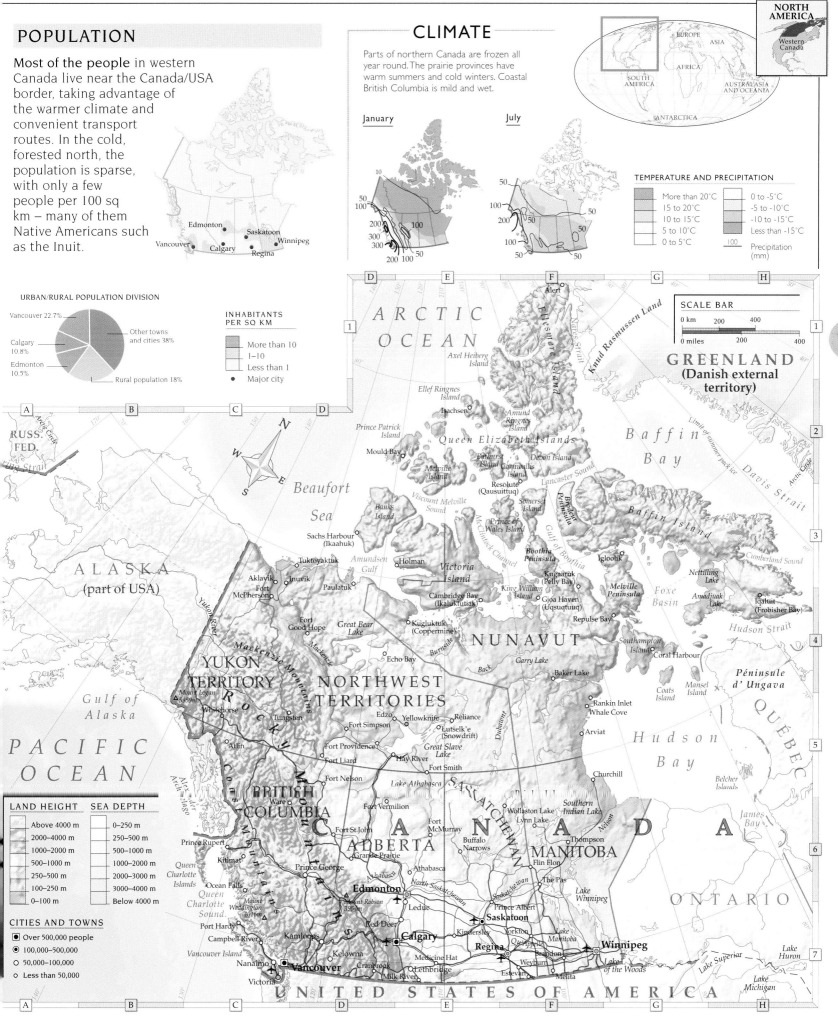

SCALE BAR

0 km 200 400
0 miles 200 400

LAND HEIGHT / SEA DEPTH

LAND HEIGHT
Above 4000 m
2000–4000 m
1000–2000 m
500–1000 m
250–500 m
100–250 m
0–100 m

SEA DEPTH
0–250 m
250–500 m
500–1000 m
1000–2000 m
2000–3000 m
3000–4000 m
Below 4000 m

CITIES AND TOWNS

◉ Over 500,000 people
● 100,000–500,000
◦ 50,000–100,000
○ Less than 50,000

ARCTIC OCEAN

GREENLAND (Danish external territory)

Alert
Ellesmere Island
Knud Rasmussen Land
Axel Heiberg Island
Baffin Bay
Ellef Ringnes Island
Isachsen
Prince Patrick Island
Amund Ringnes Island
Queen Elizabeth Islands
Mould Bay
Bathurst Island
Cornwallis Island
Devon Island
Melville Island
Resolute (Qausuittuq)
Lancaster Sound
Davis Strait
Viscount Melville Sound
Somerset Island
Boothia Peninsula
Brodeur Peninsula
Baffin Island
Banks Island
Prince of Wales Island
Gulf of Boothia
Igloolik
Cumberland Sound
Sachs Harbour (Ikaahuk)
Amundsen Gulf
Holman
Victoria Island
Nettilling Lake
Tuktoyaktuk
Melville Peninsula
Foxe Basin
Amadjuak Lake
Iqaluit (Frobisher Bay)
Aklavik
Inuvik
King William Island
Kugaaruk (Pelly Bay)
Fort McPherson
Paulatuk
Cambridge Bay (Ikaluktutiak)
Gjoa Haven (Uqsuqtuuq)
Repulse Bay
Hudson Strait
Fort Good Hope
Great Bear Lake
Kugluktuk (Coppermine)
NUNAVUT
Southampton Island
Coral Harbour
Echo Bay
Burnside
Garry Lake
Baker Lake
Coats Island
Mansel Island
Péninsule d'Ungava
YUKON TERRITORY
Mackenzie Mountains
Mackenzie
Back
Dubawnt
QUÉBEC
Mount Logan 5959m
NORTHWEST TERRITORIES
Rankin Inlet
Whale Cove
ALASKA (part of USA)
Yukon River
Whitehorse
Tungsten
Edzo
Yellowknife
Reliance
Arviat
Hudson Bay
Fort Simpson
Lutselk'e (Snowdrift)
Atlin
Fort Providence
Great Slave Lake
Fort Liard
Hay River
Fort Smith
Churchill
PACIFIC OCEAN
Gulf of Alaska
Rocky Mountains
Fort Nelson
Lake Athabasca
Belcher Islands
Coast Mountains
BRITISH COLUMBIA
Fort Vermilion
SASKATCHEWAN
Ware
Alexander Archipelago
Fort St.John
Fort McMurray
Wollaston Lake
Southern Indian Lake
James Bay
Prince Rupert
CANADA
ALBERTA
Grande Prairie
Buffalo Narrows
Lynn Lake
Flin Flon
Thompson
MANITOBA
Nelson
ONTARIO
Kitimat
Athabasca
North Saskatchewan
Queen Charlotte Islands
Prince George
The Pas
Ocean Falls
Athabasca
Saskatchewan
Lake Winnipeg
Queen Charlotte Sound
Mount Waddington 4016m
Edmonton
Leduc
Mount Robson 3954m
Prince Albert
Saskatoon
Lake Winnipeg
Port Hardy
Red Deer
Yorkton
Lake Manitoba
Campbell River
Kamloops
Calgary
Kindersley
Qu'Appelle
Winnipeg
Lake Superior
Lake Huron
Vancouver Island
Kelowna
Medicine Hat
Regina
Brandon
Melita
Nanaimo
Vancouver
Cranbrook
Lethbridge
Weyburn
Estevan
Lake of the Woods
Lake Michigan
Victoria
Milk River

UNITED STATES OF AMERICA

RUSS. FED.
Bering Strait
Arctic Circle
Beaufort Sea

33

EASTERN CANADA

NEW BRUNSWICK, NEWFOUNDLAND AND LABRADOR, NOVA SCOTIA, ONTARIO, PRINCE EDWARD ISLAND, QUÉBEC

The first European settlements grew up in the Atlantic provinces, and along the St. Lawrence River, where Québec City and Montréal were founded. People gradually migrated further west along the St. Lawrence River and the Great Lakes, establishing other cities including Toronto. Although the majority of Canadians speak English, people in Québec speak mainly French, and both English and French are official languages in Canada.

INDUSTRY

In the Atlantic provinces the traditional fishing industry has declined, causing unemployment. However, Newfoundland has a thriving food processing industry. Ontario and Québec have a wide range of industries, including the generation of hydro-electricity, mining, and chemicals, car manufacturing and fruit canning in the great cities. Large amounts of wood pulp and paper are also produced.

STRUCTURE OF INDUSTRY

Primary 7%
Services 64%
Manufacturing 29%

INDUSTRY

Car manufacture	Timber processing
Chemicals	Hi-tech industry
Fish processing	Tourism
Food processing	
Hydro-electric power	Major industrial centre / area
Metal refining	Major road
Mining	

Labrador City

Thunder Bay · Timmins · Chicoutimi · St. John's
Sudbury · Québec · Sydney
Sault Ste. Marie · Ottawa · Montréal · Saint John · Halifax
Toronto · Yarmouth

FARMING AND LAND USE

The best farmland lies on the flat, fertile plains close to the St. Lawrence River and on the strip of land between Lake Erie and Lake Ontario. It is used to grow fruits such as grapes, cherries and peaches, and to raise cattle. Nova Scotia has fruit farms, and the rich red soils of Prince Edward Island produce a big potato crop. The vast forests that grow across the north are a major source of timber.

Thunder Bay · St. John's · Ottawa · Québec · Montréal · Halifax · Toronto

LAND USE

Pasture 2%   Cropland 2%

Other (including mountains) 32%

Forest 64%

FARMING AND LAND USE

Cattle	Pasture
Fishing	Cropland
Fruit	Forest
Potatoes	Tundra
Timber	Major conurbation

ENVIRONMENTAL ISSUES

Acid rain caused by emissions from factories in the USA and along the St. Lawrence River destroys forests and kills marine life. Massive hydro-electric power projects in James Bay on Hudson Bay have flooded huge areas of land, affecting the environment and the local Cree people. Overfishing in the Atlantic has led to limits being set on the number of fish that can be caught.

ENVIRONMENTAL ISSUES

James Bay

Depleted fish stocks	
Major dam	
Urban air pollution	
Affected by acid rain	
Severe sea/lake pollution	
Major industrial centre	

Sudbury · Montréal · Hamilton · Toronto

THE LANDSCAPE

A huge, ancient mass of rock called the Canadian Shield lies beneath much of eastern Canada. It is covered by low hills, rocky outcrops, thousands of lakes, and huge areas of forest. Much of the Canadian Shield is permanently frozen. The St. Lawrence River flows out of Lake Ontario and into the Atlantic Ocean. It is surrounded by rolling hills and flat areas of very fertile farmland.

Scoured by ice
About 20,000 years ago, Labrador and northern Québec were completely covered by ice. The glaciers scraped hollows in the rock beneath. When the ice melted, lakes were left in the hollows that remained.

Lake Superior (B 5)
Lake Superior is the largest freshwater lake in the world. It covers an area of 83,270 sq km and lies between Canada and the USA.

St. Lawrence River (E 5)
The St. Lawrence River is 1,197 km long. Parts of it have become silted up, causing it to be braided into many different channels. Between December and mid-April the river freezes over.

Highlands
The highlands of New Brunswick, Nova Scotia and Newfoundland are the most northerly part of the Appalachian mountain chain.

The Bay of Fundy (F 5)
This bay has the world's highest tides. It is shaped like a funnel, and as the Atlantic flows into it, the ever narrowing shores cause the water level to rise 6–15 m at every high tide.

POPULATION

Colonists from both France and Britain settled in Canada from the early 1600s onward. Ontario and the Atlantic provinces are mainly English speaking. Québec is the centre of French settlement; 80% of the people there have French as a first language. Most people in eastern Canada now live in large towns and cities close to the St. Lawrence River.

URBAN/RURAL POPULATION DIVISION

- Toronto 19.7%
- Montréal 14.5%
- Ottawa 3.7%
- Other towns and cities 46.1%
- Rural population 16%

INHABITANTS PER SQ KM

- More than 50
- 10–50
- 1–10
- Less than 1
- ■ Capital city
- ● Major city

CLIMATE

Winters are very cold, but warm winds from the Gulf of Mexico can bring hot summers to southern Ontario and the areas bordering the St. Lawrence River.

TEMPERATURE AND PRECIPITATION

- More than 20°C
- 15 to 20°C
- 10 to 15°C
- 5 to 10°C
- 0 to 5°C
- 0 to -5°C
- -5 to -15°C
- -15 to -25°C
- Less than -25°C

100 — Precipitation (mm)

January

July

NORTH AMERICA
Eastern Canada

CITIES AND TOWNS

- ◉ Over 500,000 people
- ● 100,000–500,000
- ○ 50,000–100,000
- ○ Less than 50,000

LAND HEIGHT

- 500–1000 m
- 250–500 m
- 100–250 m
- 0–100 m

SEA DEPTH

- 0–250 m
- 250–500 m
- 500–1000 m
- 1,000–2000 m
- 2,000–3000 m
- 3,000–4000 m
- Below 4000 m

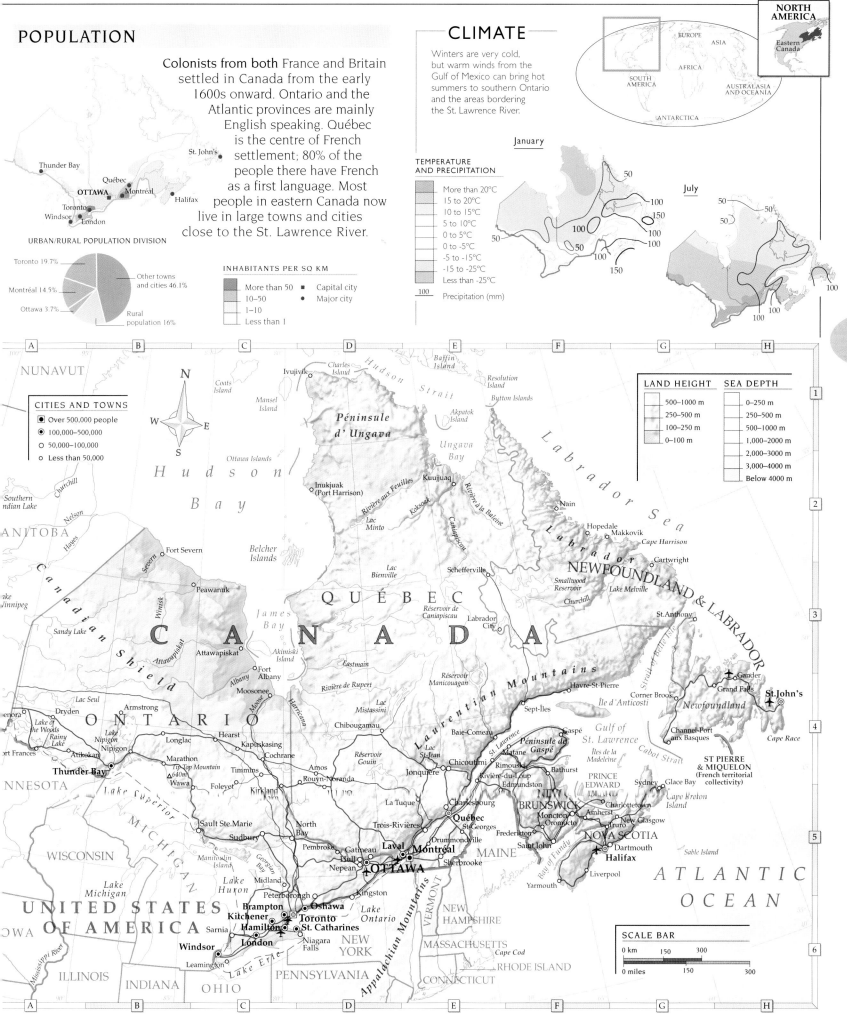

SCALE BAR

0 km 150 300

0 miles 150 300

USA: THE NORTHEASTERN STATES

CONNECTICUT, DELAWARE, MAINE, MASSACHUSETTS, NEW-HAMPSHIRE, NEW JERSEY, NEW YORK, PENNSYLVANIA, RHODE ISLAND, VERMONT

The dynamic 200-year boom of the northeastern states has been the result of a combination of factors. Between 1855 and 1924, over 20 million people poured into the region from all over the world, hoping to build a new life. Natural resources, including coal and iron, fuelled new industries and fertile farmland provided food for the region's growing population. The 'gateway' cities of the Atlantic seaboard, New York and Boston, enabled manufacturers to export their goods worldwide.

INDUSTRY

Boston, New York and Philadelphia are international centres of industry and commerce. Electronics and communications are growing throughout the Northeast alongside traditional industries such as fishing and wood products. Tourism is vital for the northeastern states, particularly along the Atlantic coast.

STRUCTURE OF INDUSTRY

Manufacturing 16.5%
Primary 0.5%
Services 83%

INDUSTRY
- ⚗ Chemicals
- ⚙ Engineering
- 🥫 Food processing
- ⚒ Iron and steel
- ⚕ Pharmaceuticals
- 👕 Textiles
- 🪵 Timber processing
- ⚓ Defence
- $ Finance
- 💻 High-tech
- ⚗ Research and development
- 🏛 Tourism
- ▪ Major industrial centre / area
- — Major road

FARMING AND LAND USE

The varied landscape of the northeastern states supports a great range of farming. Livestock, including cattle, horses, poultry and pigs, are raised throughout the region. The main crops are fruits and vegetables. Fishing is important, especially off the Atlantic coast of Maine.

FARMING AND LAND USE
- 🐂 Cattle
- 🐖 Pigs
- 🦃 Poultry
- 🐟 Fishing
- 🌾 Cereals
- 🍒 Cranberries
- 🍓 Fruit
- 🍁 Maple syrup
- ⌐ Timber
- ▨ Cropland
- ▨ Forest
- □ Pasture
- ● Major conurbation

LAND USE

Pasture 6%
Cropland 14%
Other 16%
Forest 64%

THE LANDSCAPE

The Appalachian and Adirondack Mountains form a barrier between the marshy lowlands of the Atlantic coast and the lowlands further west. The interior consists of rolling hills, fertile valleys and thousands of lakes created by the movement of glaciers.

Appalachians (E3)
The Appalachian Mountains, which run through most of this region, are the eroded remnants of peaks that were once much higher.

Rocky coastline (G3)
The coast of Maine is made up of rocky bays, islands, and inlets. If the shoreline were stretched out, it would be 4,000 km long.

Adirondacks (E3)
The Adirondacks are a broad, wide mountain range, formed when older rocks were forced into a 'dome' shape by movements in the Earth's crust many millions of years ago.

Long Island Sound (F5)
Long Island Sound is a river valley that was drowned by rising sea levels.

Finger Lakes (D3)
The long, narrow Finger Lakes lie in upper New York state. They were cut by glaciers.

Delaware Bay (D6)
Deep bays such as Delaware Bay are often surrounded by salt marshes and barrier beaches that create ideal breeding conditions for a wide variety of birds and animals.

ENVIRONMENTAL ISSUES

The high level of industry and the large population puts great pressure on the environment. Air pollution from vehicles and industry led to poor air quality in many cities and caused acid rain. The problem is worse close to the Great Lakes, where severe lake pollution has occurred.

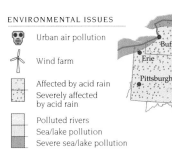

ENVIRONMENTAL ISSUES
- 😷 Urban air pollution
- 🌀 Wind farm
- ▦ Affected by acid rain
- ▨ Severely affected by acid rain
- □ Polluted rivers
- ▨ Sea/lake pollution
- ▨ Severe sea/lake pollution
- ● Major industrial centre

POPULATION

The areas along the eastern seaboard were settled by some of the earliest European colonists. The Northeast is now one of the most densely populated parts of the USA. A few of the largest cities in the USA, such as New York and Philadelphia, are in this region, but in the six states known as New England many towns and cities have populations of less than 30,000 inhabitants.

CLIMATE

Although the climate is mild during spring and autumn, summers can be hot and extremely humid, while winters are often very cold with heavy snowfall.

NORTH AMERICA

USA: The Northeastern States

January

July

INHABITANTS PER SQ KM

- More than 200
- 100–200
- 50–100
- 25–50
- Less than 25
- ● Major city

URBAN/RURAL POPULATION DIVISION

- New York 14.6%
- Philadelphia 2.7%
- Boston 1.1%
- Rural population 17%
- Other towns and cities 64.6%

TEMPERATURE AND PRECIPITATION

- More than 20°C
- 15 to 20°C
- 0 to 5°C
- -5 to 0°C
- -10 to -5°C
- Less than -10°C
- 100 Precipitation (mm)

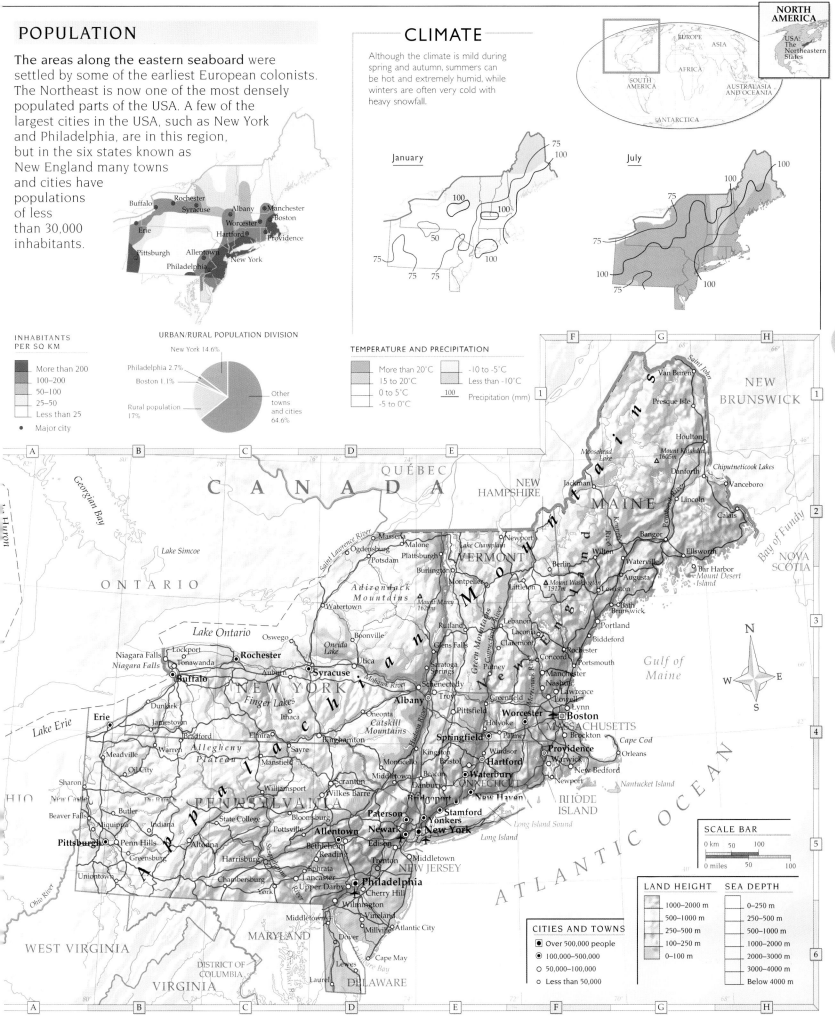

SCALE BAR
0 km 50 100
0 miles 50 100

CITIES AND TOWNS
- ■ Over 500,000 people
- ◉ 100,000–500,000
- ○ 50,000–100,000
- ○ Less than 50,000

LAND HEIGHT
- 1000–2000 m
- 500–1000 m
- 250–500 m
- 100–250 m
- 0–100 m

SEA DEPTH
- 0–250 m
- 250–500 m
- 500–1000 m
- 1000–2000 m
- 2000–3000 m
- 3000–4000 m
- Below 4000 m

USA: THE SOUTHERN STATES

ALABAMA, ARKANSAS, DISTRICT OF COLUMBIA, FLORIDA, GEORGIA, KENTUCKY, LOUISIANA, MARYLAND, MISSISSIPPI, NORTH CAROLINA, SOUTH CAROLINA, TENNESSEE, VIRGINIA, WEST VIRGINIA

The southern states suffered great devastation and poverty as a result of the Civil War (1861–65). Recovery has come with the discovery and exploitation of resources and the development of major commercial and industrial centres. Yet these states retain the vibrant mix of cultures that reflect their French, Spanish, English and African heritage.

INDUSTRY

Tourism is a major industry in the 'sunbelt' states, especially Florida, and many people move to the area when they retire to enjoy the climate. Oil and gas are extracted along the coast of the Gulf of Mexico, and there are many related chemical industries. Textiles are still produced in North and South Carolina, but aerospace and other high-tech industries have been established as well.

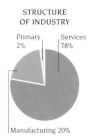

STRUCTURE OF INDUSTRY

Primary 2%
Services 78%
Manufacturing 20%

INDUSTRY

- ✈ Aerospace
- ⚗ Chemicals
- ⚙ Engineering
- 🏭 Food processing
- Iron and steel
- 👕 Textiles
- ⚒ Coal
- ⛏ Oil and gas
- 💻 High-tech
- ⊕ Research and development
- 🛍 Tourism
- ⊡ Major industrial centre / area
- — Major road

POPULATION

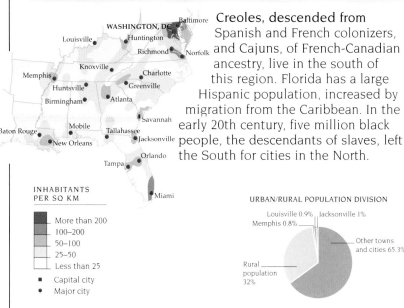

Creoles, descended from Spanish and French colonizers, and Cajuns, of French-Canadian ancestry, live in the south of this region. Florida has a large Hispanic population, increased by migration from the Caribbean. In the early 20th century, five million black people, the descendants of slaves, left the South for cities in the North.

INHABITANTS PER SQ KM

- More than 200
- 100–200
- 50–100
- 25–50
- Less than 25
- ■ Capital city
- ● Major city

URBAN/RURAL POPULATION DIVISION

Louisville 0.9%   Jacksonville 1%
Memphis 0.8%
Other towns and cities 65.3%
Rural population 32%

FARMING AND LAND USE

Cotton is still the South's main crop, but many old cotton fields are now pastures where all types of livestock are raised. Florida is famous for citrus fruits, while Georgia is renowned for peanuts. Sugarcane, soya beans, tobacco, corn, fruits and rice are grown in other areas.

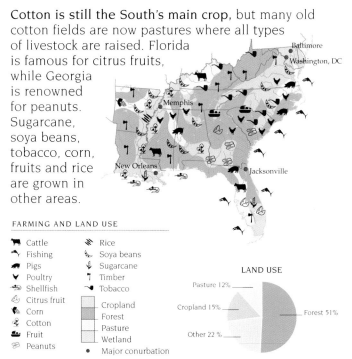

FARMING AND LAND USE

- 🐄 Cattle
- 🎣 Fishing
- 🐖 Pigs
- 🐓 Poultry
- 🦐 Shellfish
- 🍊 Citrus fruit
- 🌽 Corn
- ⚓ Cotton
- 🍐 Fruit
- 🥜 Peanuts
- ≋ Rice
- Soya beans
- ↓ Sugarcane
- ⼂ Timber
- ⼂ Tobacco
- Cropland
- Forest
- Pasture
- Wetland
- ● Major conurbation

LAND USE

Pasture 12%
Cropland 15%
Other 22%
Forest 51%

THE LANDSCAPE

The South is a land of contrasts – the uplands of the Appalachians, the foothills of the Piedmont, and low-lying coastal regions are all featured. The interior lowlands are drained by the Mississippi. Florida is dotted with thousands of lakes and is home to the Everglades, a giant sawgrass swamp.

Mississippi River (C 4)
A major transport artery, the Mississippi was an essential route in opening up the interior region. With its main tributary, the Missouri, it is nearly 6,115 km long, making it the world's fourth-longest river.

Kentucky Bluegrass (E 2)
The gently rolling bluegrass landscape of northern Kentucky is ideal country for raising horses and livestock.

Barrier beaches (I 3)
Sandy barrier beaches and islands line the eastern and southern coasts, along with sheltered lagoons and salt marshes.

The Everglades (G 8)
The Everglades cover 13,000 sq km and support abundant wild animals and plants, many unique to the area.

Thermal springs (B 4)
Hot Springs National Park in Arkansas has 47 thermal springs and is a popular tourist and health resort. Visitors relax here in the hot water that trickles from the hillsides.

Tennessee River (D 4)
The Tennessee River is 1,000 km long. Dams along the river generate hydro-electricity to provide most of the region's energy needs.

Limestone caves (E 4)
Cathedral Caverns in Alabama is a collection of enormous limestone caves. The main entrance is more than 300 m high and 45 m wide.

ENVIRONMENTAL ISSUES

Factories in the Great Lakes region have contributed to the large blanket of acid rain across the northern part. Towards the south, hurricanes sweep in from the Atlantic Ocean and Gulf of Mexico during the hurricane season, which lasts from May to October each year.

ENVIRONMENTAL ISSUES

- Path of recent, devastating hurricane
- Affected by acid rain
- Polluted river
- Sea pollution
- • Major city

NORTH AMERICA

USA: The Southern States

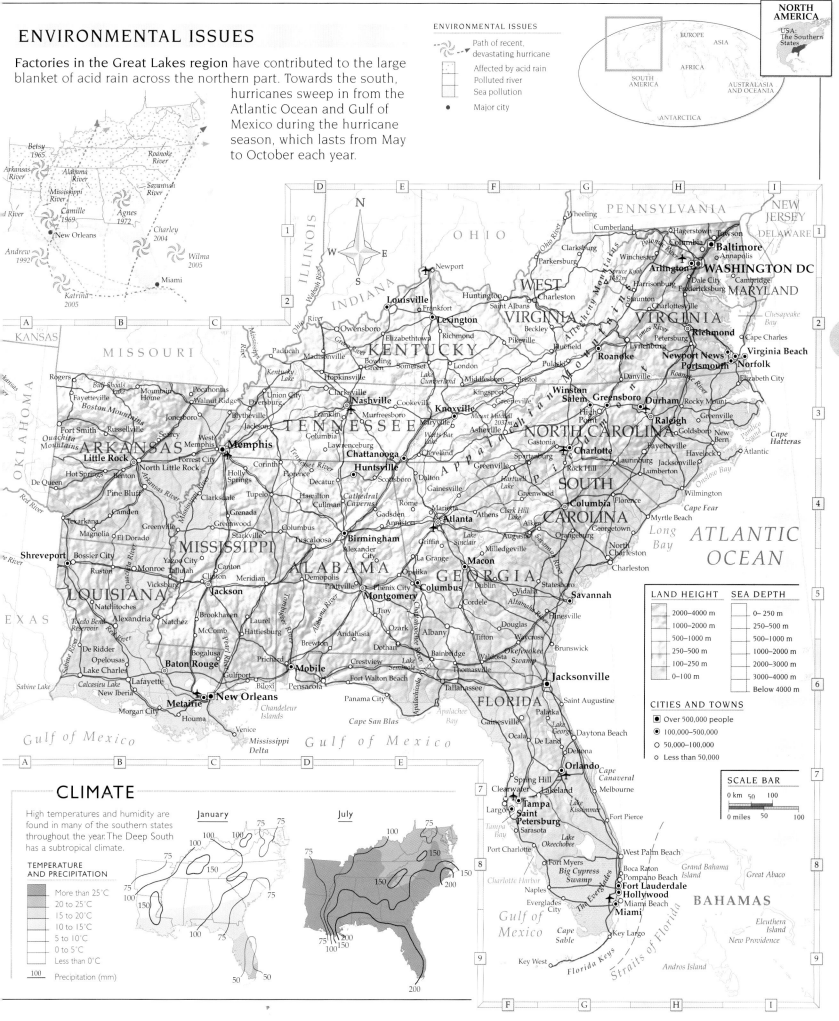

CLIMATE

High temperatures and humidity are found in many of the southern states throughout the year. The Deep South has a subtropical climate.

TEMPERATURE AND PRECIPITATION

- More than 25°C
- 20 to 25°C
- 15 to 20°C
- 10 to 15°C
- 5 to 10°C
- 0 to 5°C
- Less than 0°C

100 Precipitation (mm)

January
July

LAND HEIGHT
- 2000–4000 m
- 1000–2000 m
- 500–1000 m
- 250–500 m
- 100–250 m
- 0–100 m

SEA DEPTH
- 0–250 m
- 250–500 m
- 500–1000 m
- 1000–2000 m
- 2000–3000 m
- 3000–4000 m
- Below 4000 m

CITIES AND TOWNS
- Over 500,000 people
- 100,000–500,000
- 50,000–100,000
- Less than 50,000

SCALE BAR
0 km 50 100
0 miles 50 100

USA: THE GREAT LAKES STATES

ILLINOIS, INDIANA, MICHIGAN, OHIO, WISCONSIN

Good transport links, excellent farmland and a wealth of natural resources drew settlers from Europe and the south and east of the USA to the Great Lakes states during the late 19th century. By the 1930s, they had become one of the world's most prosperous industrial and agricultural regions. In recent years, the decline in traditional heavy industries has hit some cities hard, leading to unemployment and a rising crime rate.

POPULATION

The Great Lakes states are one of the most densely populated parts of the USA. Many of the largest cities in this region – Chicago, Detroit and Milwaukee – grew up on the banks of the lakes and are connected to each other and the rest of the USA by an impressive road and rail network.

INHABITANTS PER SQ KM

- More than 200
- 100–200
- 50–100
- 25–50
- Less than 25
- • Major city

URBAN/RURAL POPULATION DIVISION

Detroit 2% Chicago 6.3%
Indianapolis 1.7%
Other towns and cities 66%
Rural population 24%

CLIMATE

Plentiful rainfall waters the agricultural lands. In winter, strong winds sweep across the lakes, and water close to the shore may freeze.

January

July

TEMPERATURE AND PRECIPITATION

- More than 25°C
- 20 to 25°C
- 15 to 20°C
- 0 to 5°C
- -5 to 0°C
- -10 to -5°C
- Less than -10°C
- 100 Precipitation (mm)

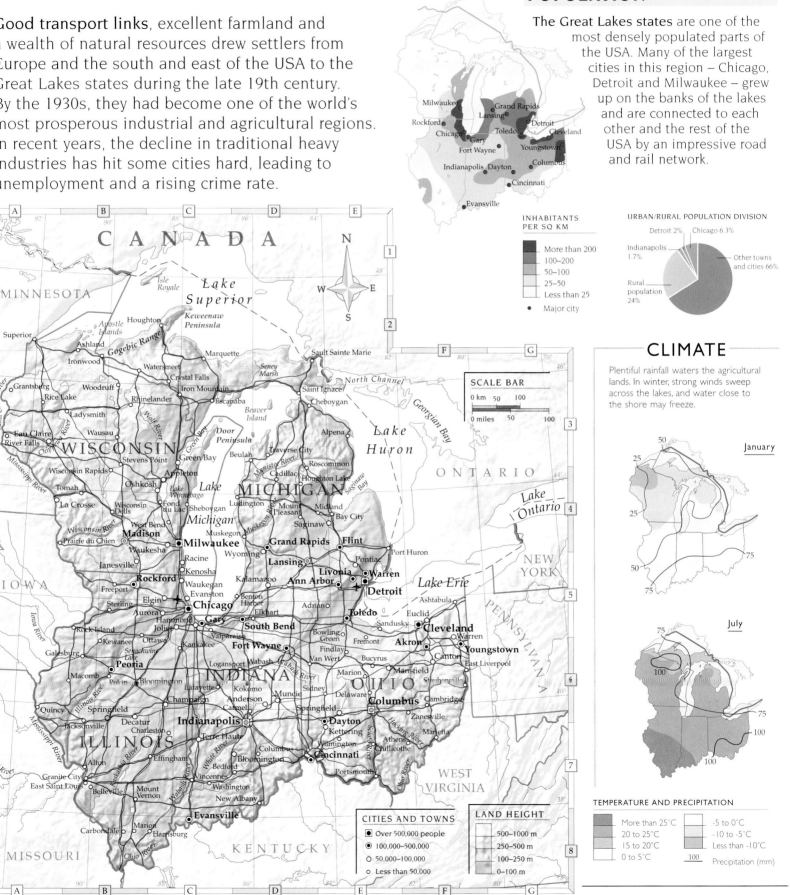

SCALE BAR

0 km 50 100

0 miles 50 100

CITIES AND TOWNS

- ● Over 500,000 people
- ◉ 100,000–500,000
- ○ 50,000–100,000
- ○ Less than 50,000

LAND HEIGHT

- 500–1000 m
- 250–500 m
- 100–250 m
- 0–100 m

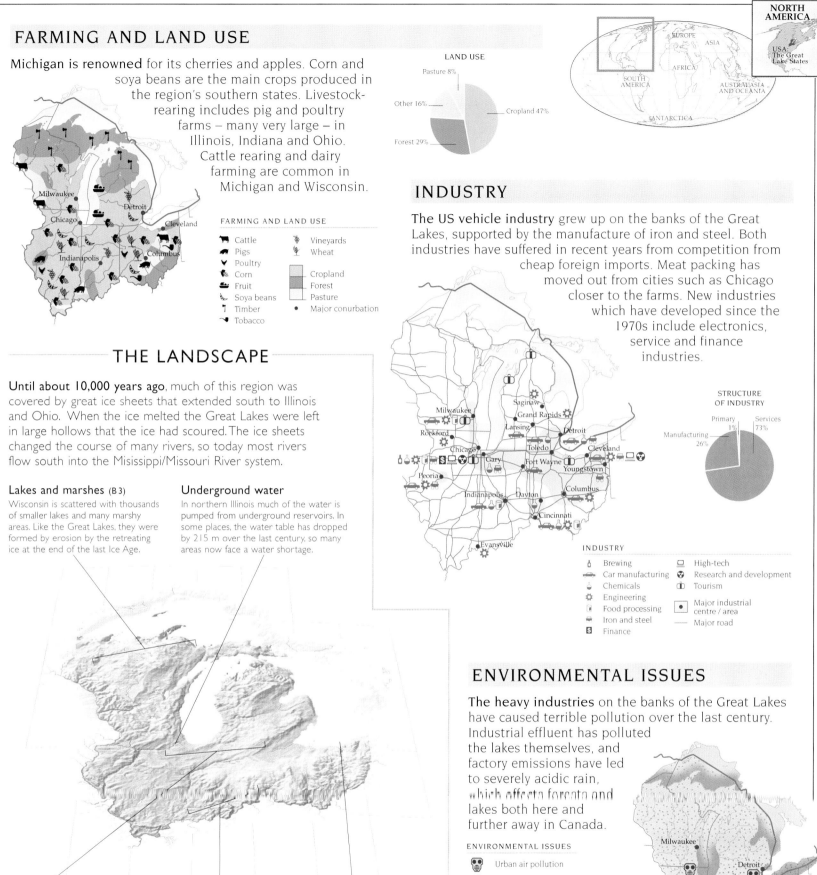

FARMING AND LAND USE

Michigan is renowned for its cherries and apples. Corn and soya beans are the main crops produced in the region's southern states. Livestock-rearing includes pig and poultry farms – many very large – in Illinois, Indiana and Ohio. Cattle rearing and dairy farming are common in Michigan and Wisconsin.

LAND USE

Pasture 8%
Other 16%
Cropland 47%
Forest 29%

FARMING AND LAND USE

- 🐄 Cattle
- 🐖 Pigs
- Ⓥ Poultry
- 🌽 Corn
- 🍓 Fruit
- Soya beans
- Timber
- Tobacco
- 🍇 Vineyards
- Wheat
- Cropland
- Forest
- Pasture
- • Major conurbation

Milwaukee, Detroit, Chicago, Cleveland, Indianapolis, Columbus

THE LANDSCAPE

Until about 10,000 years ago, much of this region was covered by great ice sheets that extended south to Illinois and Ohio. When the ice melted the Great Lakes were left in large hollows that the ice had scoured. The ice sheets changed the course of many rivers, so today most rivers flow south into the Mississippi/Missouri River system.

Lakes and marshes (B3)

Wisconsin is scattered with thousands of smaller lakes and many marshy areas. Like the Great Lakes, they were formed by erosion by the retreating ice at the end of the last Ice Age.

Underground water

In northern Illinois much of the water is pumped from underground reservoirs. In some places, the water table has dropped by 215 m over the last century, so many areas now face a water shortage.

Moraines

When the last ice age ended, the retreating ice sheets left long ridges and piles of rock to the south of Lake Michigan. Some of these ridges, known as moraines, can be up to 90 m high.

Limestone region

Limestone in the hills of southern Indiana has been dissolved by acid rainwater. This has produced features such as sinkholes and underground caves.

Lake Erie (F5)

Lake Erie is the shallowest of the Great Lakes. Its average depth is about 19 m. Storms that sweep across from Canada have eroded its shores and caused the silting of its harbours.

INDUSTRY

The US vehicle industry grew up on the banks of the Great Lakes, supported by the manufacture of iron and steel. Both industries have suffered in recent years from competition from cheap foreign imports. Meat packing has moved out from cities such as Chicago closer to the farms. New industries which have developed since the 1970s include electronics, service and finance industries.

Milwaukee, Saginaw, Grand Rapids, Lansing, Rockford, Detroit, Chicago, Toledo, Cleveland, Gary, Fort Wayne, Youngstown, Peoria, Indianapolis, Dayton, Columbus, Cincinnati, Evansville

STRUCTURE OF INDUSTRY

Primary 1%
Services 73%
Manufacturing 26%

INDUSTRY

- 🍶 Brewing
- 🚗 Car manufacturing
- Chemicals
- ⚙ Engineering
- Food processing
- Iron and steel
- Ⓢ Finance
- 💻 High-tech
- ☢ Research and development
- ⓘ Tourism
- ⊡ Major industrial centre / area
- — Major road

ENVIRONMENTAL ISSUES

The heavy industries on the banks of the Great Lakes have caused terrible pollution over the last century. Industrial effluent has polluted the lakes themselves, and factory emissions have led to severely acidic rain, which affects forests and lakes both here and further away in Canada.

ENVIRONMENTAL ISSUES

- 😷 Urban air pollution
- Wind farm
- Affected by acid rain
- Severely affected by acid rain
- Polluted rivers
- Lake pollution
- Severe lake pollution
- • Major industrial centre

Milwaukee, Detroit, Chicago, Gary, Cleveland, Mississippi River, Ohio River

USA: THE CENTRAL STATES

IOWA, KANSAS, MINNESOTA, MISSOURI, NEBRASKA,
NORTH DAKOTA, OKLAHOMA, SOUTH DAKOTA

The prairie states of the central USA became
one of America's richest agricultural regions in
the mid-19th century. Despite the 'Dustbowl'
crisis of the 1930s, which led many farmers to
leave their ruined lands, agriculture is still crucial
to the economy, and one third of the people still
live in rural areas rather than large cities.

FARMING AND LAND USE

Wheat and corn grow on the fertile plains.
Kansas is the leading grower of wheat in
the entire USA, while Iowa is one of the
leaders in corn and livestock. Irrigation
projects to combat drought are crucial
in large areas. Livestock – including
cattle in vast herds; pigs, particularly
in Iowa, the Dakotas and Nebraska;
sheep; and turkeys – are raised
throughout these states.

LAND USE

Other 37%

Cropland 43%

Forest 11%

Pasture 9%

FARMING AND LAND USE

Cattle	Cropland
Pigs	Forest
Poultry	Pasture
Sheep	● Major conurbation
Corn	
Soya beans	
Wheat	

INDUSTRY

Industries related to agriculture, such as food processing and
the production of farm machinery, are traditional in these states
but high-tech industries – such as aeronautical engineering – are
increasing and large aerospace plants
are found in Wichita and Saint Louis. Oil
and gas are extracted in great quantities
toward the south of the region, especially
in Oklahoma and Kansas.

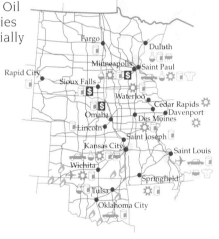

INDUSTRY

✈ Aerospace
🚗 Car manufacturing
Chemicals
⚙ Engineering
Food processing
Iron and steel
Textiles
◊ Oil and gas
S Finance

▪ Major industrial
centre / area
— Major road

STRUCTURE OF INDUSTRY

Primary 4%
Services 76%
Manufacturing 20%

THE LANDSCAPE

Most of the eastern edge of this region is marked
by the Mississippi River, while the Missouri bisects
it, running from northwest to southeast. The Great
Plains cover most of this area, gradually rising
towards the Rocky Mountains at the far western
edge of the Central States.

The Badlands (A 4)
The Badlands cover an
area of about 5,200 sq km
in South Dakota. Heavily
eroded by wind and water,
almost nothing grows there.

Minnesota
Minnesota is filled with lakes,
hills strewn with boulders,
and mineral-rich deposits that
have been left behind by the
scouring movement of glaciers.

Chimney Rock (A-5)
Chimney Rock
stands 150 m
above the plains.
It is a remnant of
an ancient land
surface that was
eroded by the
North Platte River.

ENVIRONMENTAL ISSUES

Intensive agriculture requires large quantities of
water to grow crops. Over-intensive use of the land
has destroyed the balance of soil and water in the
past, leading to fertile farmland being turned into
useless areas of 'Dustbowl'. These states have a
great underground store
of water known as the
Ogallala Aquifer, but over-
extraction for irrigation is
reducing the amount of
available water.

ENVIRONMENTAL ISSUES

☠ Urban air pollution

Wind farm

Affected by acid rain
Aquifer
Polluted river
Risk of desertification
● Major industrial centre

Great Plains (D 7)
Little more than a century ago the great flat plains
that cover most of these states were home to wild
grasses and massive herds of buffalo. In areas where
lack of water has made farming impossible, large tracts
of land are being allowed to return to grassland.

Great Salt Plains (D 7)
These arid salt plains cover about
120 sq km of northern Oklahoma.
An ancient salt lake once occupied
the area. When the salt evaporated,
only the salt flats were left.

NORTH AMERICA

USA: The Central States

POPULATION

The inhabitants are largely the descendants of Europeans who came to the region in the late 1800s. The entire region is primarily rural, with enormous tracts of land devoted to growing crops. North Dakota has no city with a population greater than 100,000.

URBAN/RURAL POPULATION DIVISION

Kansas City 1.9%   Oklahoma City 2.3%
Omaha 1.8%
Other towns and cities 60%
Rural population 34%

INHABITANTS PER SQ KM

More than 50
25–50
Less than 25
● Major city

CLIMATE

The Central States have a continental climate, with hot, dry summers and long, cold winters. Unreliable rainfall can be a problem for farmers on the Great Plains.

January

July

TEMPERATURE AND PRECIPITATION

More than 25°C
20 to 25°C
15 to 20°C
10 to 15°C
5 to 10°C
0 to 5°C
-5 to 0°C
-10 to -5°C
-15 to -10°C
Less than 15°C
Precipitation (mm)

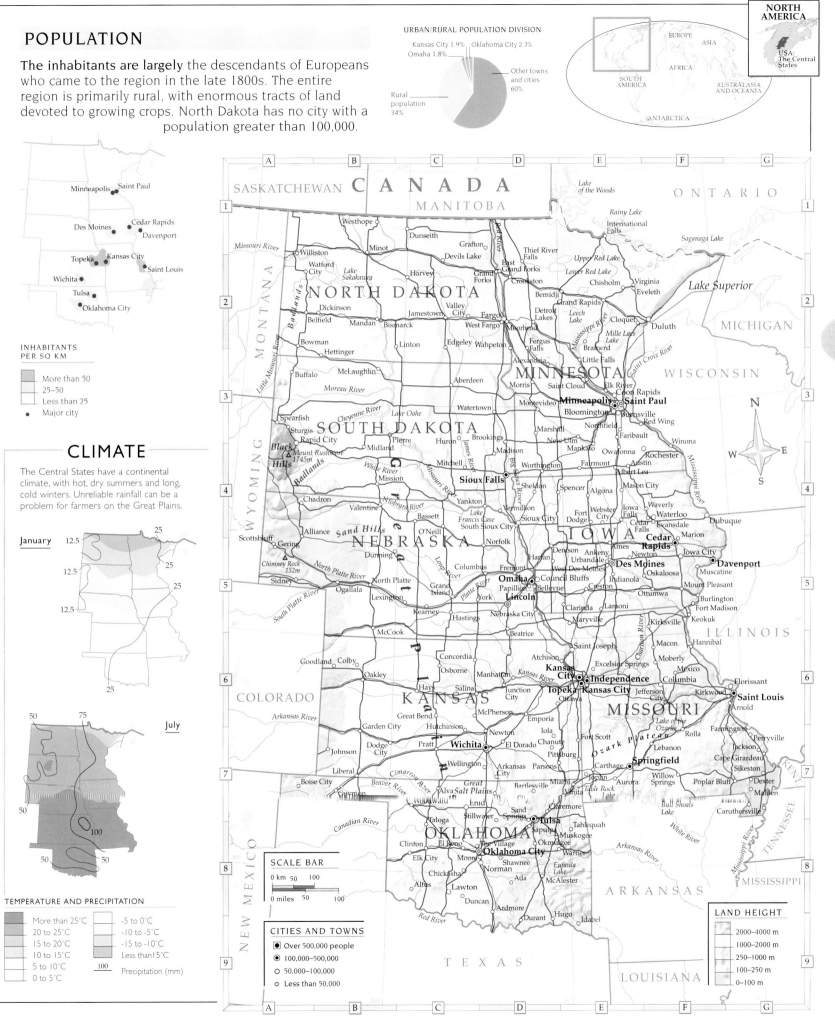

SCALE BAR

0 km 50 100
0 miles 50 100

CITIES AND TOWNS
■ Over 500,000 people
◉ 100,000–500,000
◯ 50,000–100,000
○ Less than 50,000

LAND HEIGHT
2000–4000 m
1000–2000 m
250–1000 m
100–250 m
0–100 m

USA: THE SOUTHWESTERN STATES

ARIZONA, NEW MEXICO, TEXAS

Large parts of the southwestern states were purchased from Mexico in 1848. This land of expansive plateaus, spectacular canyons, prairies and deserts is home to several distinct peoples, whose customs and traditions are still practised. The Navaho and Hopi own one-third of the land in Arizona, and the ruins of thousand-year-old cliff dwellings built by the Anasazi people are still preserved there today.

ENVIRONMENTAL ISSUES

Desertification is a serious problem in the southwestern states. Lack of water combined with intensive farming has allowed soils to erode. Drought is held at bay by irrigation, but falling water table levels are a cause for concern. New Mexico was the site for many early nuclear weapons tests, and some places remain contaminated.

ENVIRONMENTAL ISSUES

- Urban air pollution
- Former nuclear test site
- Path of recent, devastating hurricane
- Wind farm

- Desert area
- Risk of desertification
- Polluted river
- Major industrial centre

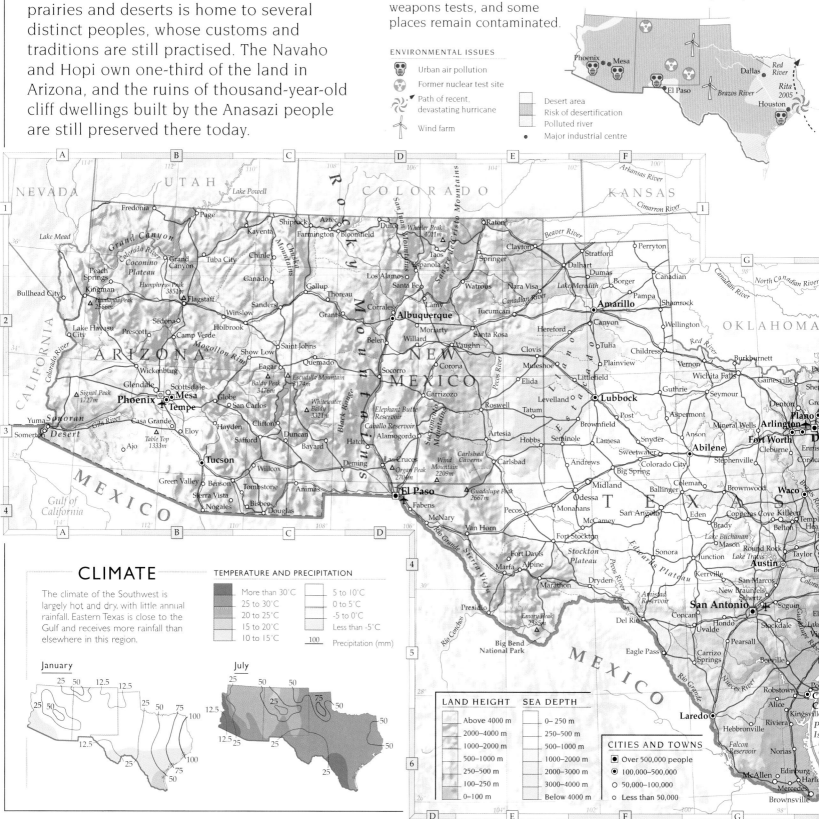

CLIMATE

The climate of the Southwest is largely hot and dry, with little annual rainfall. Eastern Texas is close to the Gulf and receives more rainfall than elsewhere in this region.

TEMPERATURE AND PRECIPITATION

Temperature	
More than 30°C	5 to 10°C
25 to 30°C	0 to 5°C
20 to 25°C	-5 to 0°C
15 to 20°C	Less than -5°C
10 to 15°C	

100 — Precipitation (mm)

January

July

LAND HEIGHT

- Above 4000 m
- 2000–4000 m
- 1000–2000 m
- 500–1000 m
- 250–500 m
- 100–250 m
- 0–100 m

SEA DEPTH

- 0–250 m
- 250–500 m
- 500–1000 m
- 1000–2000 m
- 2000–3000 m
- 3000–4000 m
- Below 4000 m

CITIES AND TOWNS

- Over 500,000 people
- 100,000–500,000
- 50,000–100,000
- Less than 50,000

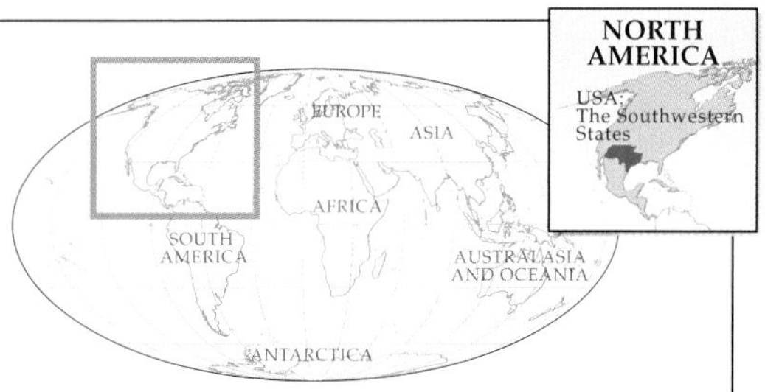
NORTH AMERICA
USA: The Southwestern States
EUROPE
ASIA
AFRICA
SOUTH AMERICA
AUSTRALASIA AND OCEANIA
ANTARCTICA

THE LANDSCAPE

The arid, mountainous Colorado Plateau covers nearly half of Arizona, dipping towards the south to form desert basins. Parts of northern New Mexico are forested, but the south consists primarily of semi-arid plains. Eastern Texas is bordered by the waters of the Gulf of Mexico, and the farmland of this area is well watered. Western Texas is covered by the Llano Estacado and, in the south, much of the land is arid.

Big Bend (E5)
Big Bend National Park gets its name from the 90° bend that the Rio Grande makes there.

Invading sea
The crust of southeastern Texas is warping, causing the land to subside and allowing the sea to invade. Hurricanes make the situation worse.

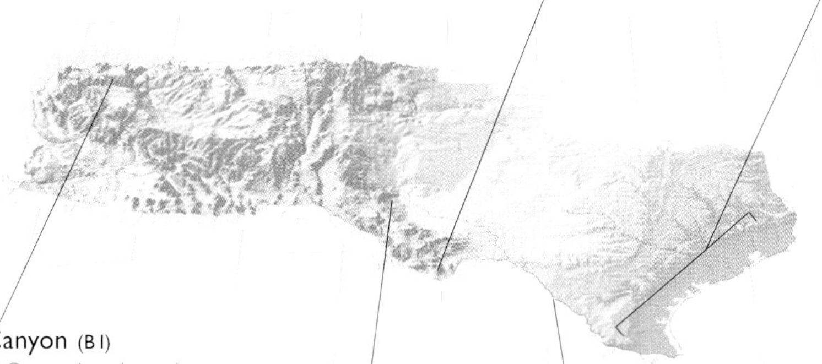

Grand Canyon (B1)
The Grand Canyon is a dramatic gorge cut in the rock by the Colorado River. It is about 350 km long, 675 km wide, and up to 1.6 km deep.

Carlsbad Caverns (B3)
Carlsbad Caverns are a series of underground caves, consisting of a three-level chain of limestone chambers studded with towering stalactites and stalagmites. They are millions of years old.

Rio Grande (G5)
The Rio Grande, or 'Great River' forms all of the border between Texas and Mexico. It flows from its source high up in the Rocky Mountains, to the Gulf of Mexico.

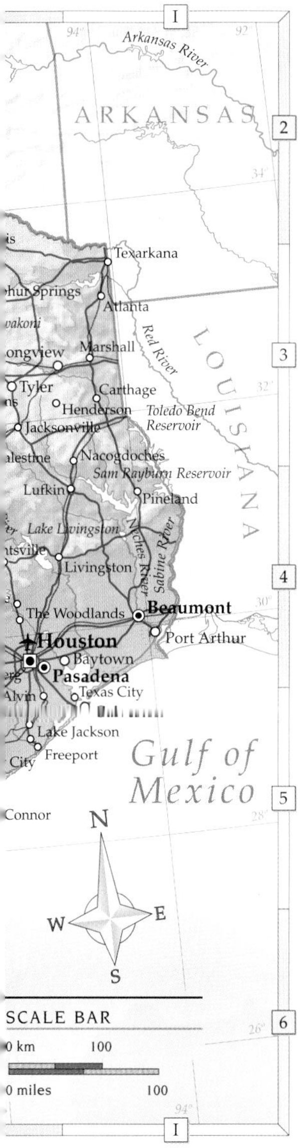
I
2
3
4
5
6
Arkansas River
ARKANSAS
LOUISIANA
Texarkana
Atlanta
Red River
Marshall
Tyler
Carthage
Henderson
Toledo Bend Reservoir
Jacksonville
Nacogdoches
Sam Rayburn Reservoir
Lufkin
Pineland
Lake Livingston
Livingston
Sabine River
The Woodlands
Beaumont
Port Arthur
Houston
Baytown
Pasadena
Texas City
Lake Jackson
Freeport
Gulf of Mexico
N
E
S
W
SCALE BAR
0 km 100
0 miles 100

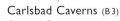

INDUSTRY

Mining and related industries are one of the most important sources of income in the Southwest. Great deposits of oil lie under about 65% of Texas; copper and coal are mined in Arizona and New Mexico. Defence-related industries, including NASA have encouraged the development of many high-tech companies in Texas – and high-tech is also growing in larger cities such as Santa Fe and Phoenix.

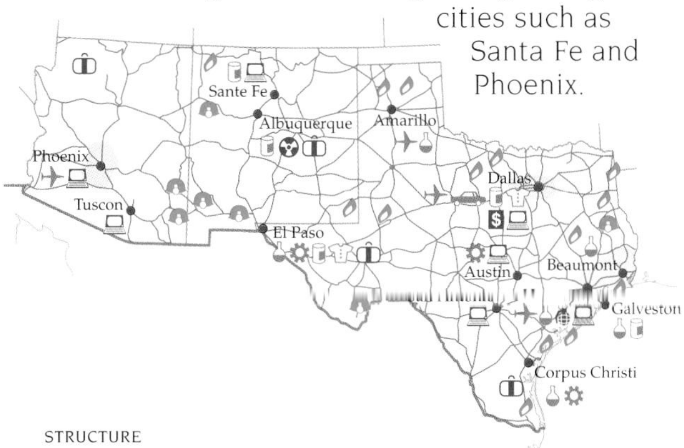
Sante Fe
Albuquerque
Amarillo
Phoenix
Tuscon
Dallas
El Paso
Austin
Beaumont
Galveston
Corpus Christi

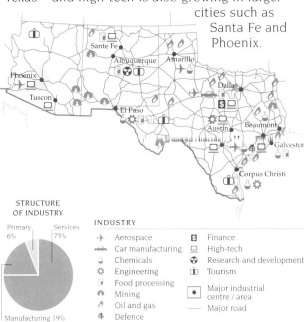

STRUCTURE OF INDUSTRY

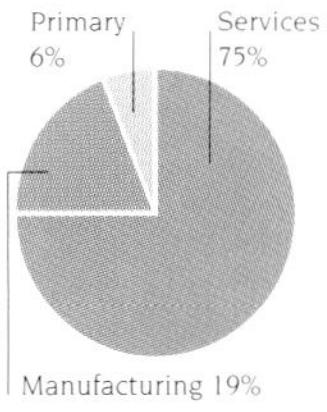
Primary 6%
Services 75%
Manufacturing 19%

INDUSTRY

- Aerospace
- Car manufacturing
- Chemicals
- Engineering
- Food processing
- Mining
- Oil and gas
- Defence
- Finance
- High-tech
- Research and development
- Tourism
- Major industrial centre / area
- Major road

FARMING AND LAND USE

Many cattle and sheep ranches have been set up on the open plateaus. Fruit and vegetables, grown in hothouses and cotton, hay and wheat are among the major crops. Beef cattle and broiler chickens are raised on huge farms while sheep graze the drier parts of Texas. Extensive irrigation has made farming possible in even the most arid areas.

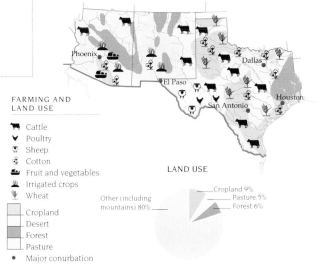

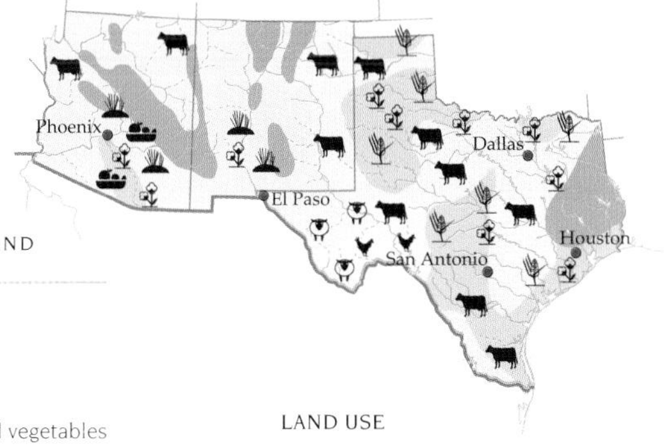
Phoenix
Dallas
El Paso
Houston
San Antonio

FARMING AND LAND USE

- Cattle
- Poultry
- Sheep
- Cotton
- Fruit and vegetables
- Irrigated crops
- Wheat
- Cropland
- Desert
- Forest
- Pasture
- Major conurbation

LAND USE

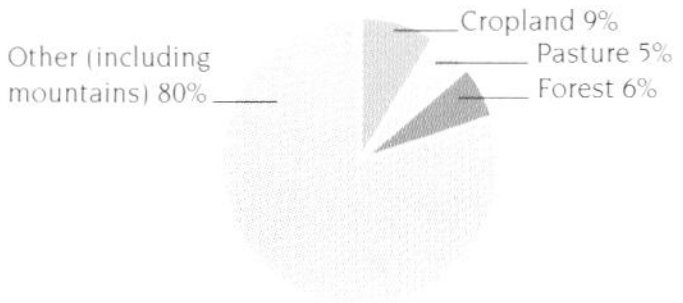
Cropland 9%
Pasture 5%
Forest 6%
Other (including mountains) 80%

POPULATION

The descendants of Mexican and Spanish settlers and numerous groups of Native Americans live in the southwestern states. The great cities of Texas grew up on income from cattle-ranching and the oil industry. Much of Arizona and New Mexico is sparsely populated, but today people are moving to these states to escape the cold winters elsewhere.

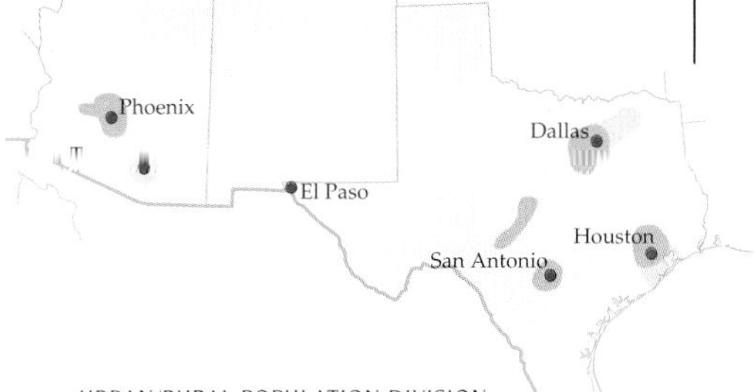
Phoenix
Dallas
El Paso
Houston
San Antonio

INHABITANTS PER SQ KM

- More than 50
- 25–50
- Less than 25
- Major city

URBAN/RURAL POPULATION DIVISION

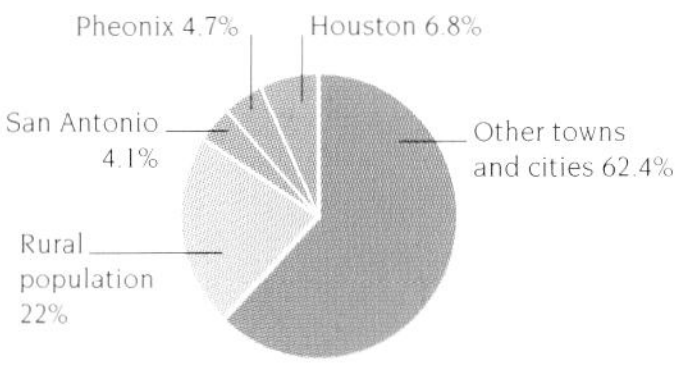
Pheonix 4.7%
Houston 6.8%
San Antonio 4.1%
Other towns and cities 62.4%
Rural population 22%

USA: THE MOUNTAIN STATES

COLORADO, IDAHO, MONTANA, NEVADA, UTAH, WYOMING

These states are home to some of the nation's most fantastic landscapes: endless treeless plains, craggy peaks, incredible desert landforms, and the salt flats of Utah. Although this was one of the last regions of the USA to be settled, great mineral reserves have been exploited here in recent years, and new industries have grown up in some of the larger cities. Utah is the headquarters of the Mormon religion.

INDUSTRY

Rich mineral reserves, including coal, oil and gas, are mined throughout the region and forests are a source of good-quality timber. In the larger cities of Colorado and Utah, growing industries include high-tech computer firms. Many tourists are drawn to this region to ski in the resorts of Colorado and to explore the wilderness.

STRUCTURE OF INDUSTRY

Manufacturing 16%
Primary 4%
Services 80%

INDUSTRY

- Chemicals
- Food processing
- Textiles
- Coal
- Mining
- Oil and gas
- Timber processing
- Gambling
- High-tech
- Research and development
- Tourism

- Major industrial centre / area
- Major road

FARMING AND LAND USE

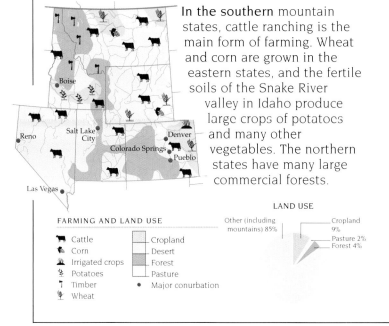

In the southern mountain states, cattle ranching is the main form of farming. Wheat and corn are grown in the eastern states, and the fertile soils of the Snake River valley in Idaho produce large crops of potatoes and many other vegetables. The northern states have many large commercial forests.

FARMING AND LAND USE

- Cattle
- Corn
- Irrigated crops
- Potatoes
- Timber
- Wheat

- Cropland
- Desert
- Forest
- Pasture
- Major conurbation

LAND USE

Other (including mountains) 85%
Cropland 9%
Pasture 2%
Forest 4%

POPULATION

Colorado, with the growing city of Denver, is the most populous of the mountain states. In other states, people have settled close to sources of water such as Great Salt Lake in Utah. Many towns have less than 10,000 people and are far apart.

INHABITANTS PER SQ KM

- More than 50
- 25–50
- Less than 25
- Major city

URBAN/RURAL POPULATION DIVISION

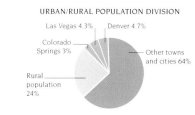

Las Vegas 4.3%
Denver 4.7%
Colorado Springs 3%
Other towns and cities 64%
Rural population 24%

THE LANDSCAPE

The great Rocky Mountains and many smaller mountain ranges cover almost all of this region. Only eastern Montana is not mountainous. Here western parts of the Great Plains rise to meet the mountains. Parts of the southern mountain states are very arid with spectacular scenery, including block-like *mesas*, formed by erosion.

Continental Divide
From this watershed, crossing the Lewis Range, rivers flow in different directions across North America. Some flow east to Hudson Bay, some south to the Gulf of Mexico and others west to the Pacific Ocean.

Yellowstone National Park (D 3)
Yellowstone was set up in 1872 as the first national park in the USA. Water from hot springs has deposited minerals as it cools, forming white rock terraces close to the springs.

Snake River (C 4)

Great Plains (E 2)

North Platte River (F 4)

Artificial lake (C 7)
Lake Mead – more than 285 km long, is one of the largest artificial lakes in the world. It was formed in 1936, when the Hoover Dam was built across the Colorado River.

Great Salt Lake (C 5)

Mountainous state
Colorado has more than 1,500 peaks more than 3000 m high – this is six times the number of high mountains found in the Swiss Alps.

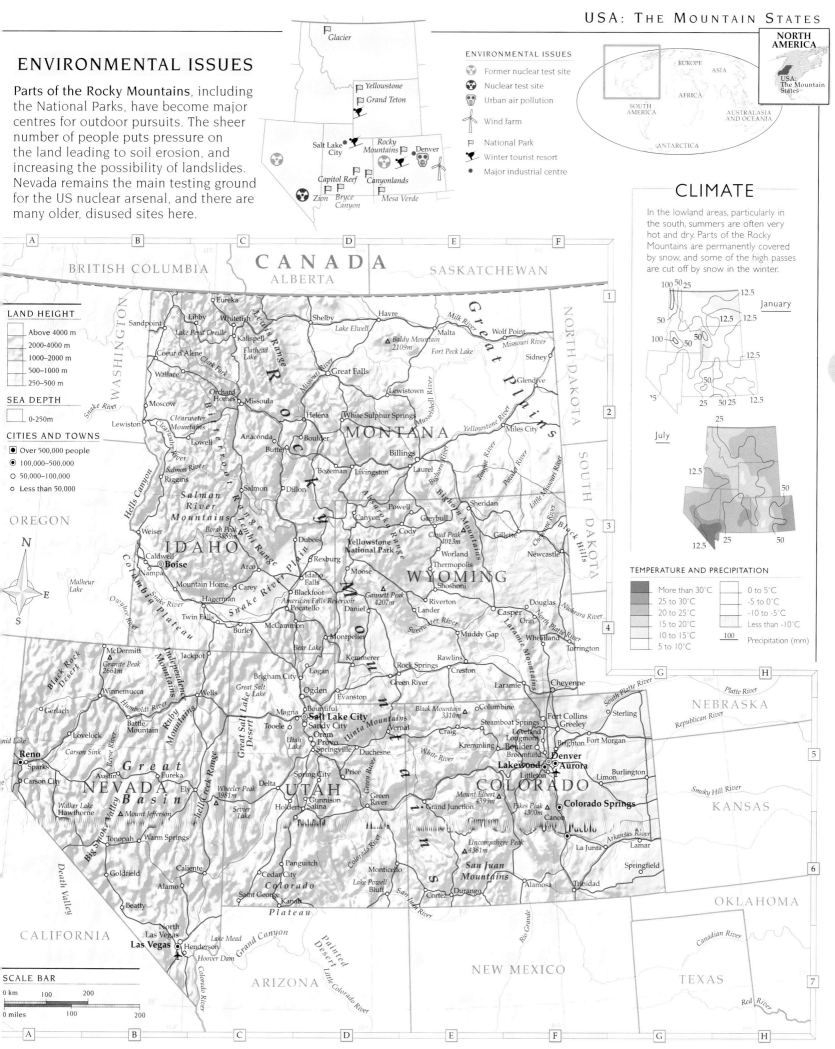

ENVIRONMENTAL ISSUES

Parts of the Rocky Mountains, including the National Parks, have become major centres for outdoor pursuits. The sheer number of people puts pressure on the land leading to soil erosion, and increasing the possibility of landslides. Nevada remains the main testing ground for the US nuclear arsenal, and there are many older, disused sites here.

ENVIRONMENTAL ISSUES

- Former nuclear test site
- Nuclear test site
- Urban air pollution
- Wind farm
- National Park
- Winter tourist resort
- Major industrial centre

CLIMATE

In the lowland areas, particularly in the south, summers are often very hot and dry. Parts of the Rocky Mountains are permanently covered by snow, and some of the high passes are cut off by snow in the winter.

January

July

TEMPERATURE AND PRECIPITATION

More than 30°C	0 to 5°C
25 to 30°C	-5 to 0°C
20 to 25°C	-10 to -5°C
15 to 20°C	Less than -10°C
10 to 15°C	
5 to 10°C	100 Precipitation (mm)

NORTH AMERICA

LAND HEIGHT
- Above 4000 m
- 2000–4000 m
- 1000–2000 m
- 500–1000 m
- 250–500 m

SEA DEPTH
- 0–250m

CITIES AND TOWNS
- Over 500,000 people
- 100,000–500,000
- 50,000–100,000
- Less than 50,000

SCALE BAR
0 km 100 200
0 miles 100 200

USA: THE PACIFIC STATES

CALIFORNIA, OREGON, WASHINGTON

The earliest European visitors to the West Coast were fur-trappers and miners, but the Gold Rush of 1849 brought in the first major wave of settlers. Drawn by tales of the beautiful scenery, pleasant climate, and fertile valleys, more people arrived on the newly built railways. People from all over the world are still moving into this region, seeking jobs in the dynamic economy and the famous laid-back lifestyle.

INDUSTRY

The Pacific States are the centre of the high-tech computer industry with Silicon Valley between San Francisco and San Jose, and electronics industries growing in Portland and Seattle. Other major industries include research and development for the defence industry, film making in Los Angeles, food processing and lumbering. Tourism is well developed throughout the Pacific States.

STRUCTURE OF INDUSTRY

Primary 2%
Services 81%
Manufacturing 17%

INDUSTRY

✈ Aerospace	☀ Film industry
⚗ Chemicals	▭ High-tech
⚙ Engineering	◉ Research and development
⬛ Food processing	⬚ Tourism
⬛ Iron and steel	▪ Major industrial centre / area
⬙ Shipbuilding	— Major road
👕 Textiles	
⚘ Timber processing	

FARMING AND LAND USE

California's Central Valley and the river valleys of Washington and Oregon provide ideal conditions for a wide range of fruit and vegetables, including citrus fruit and grapes. Poultry farming is widespread in the northwest and there are many large cattle ranches. Millions of hectares of commercial forest are located in this region.

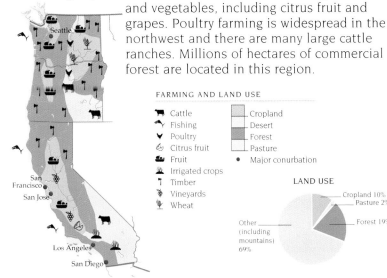

FARMING AND LAND USE

🐂 Cattle	▢ Cropland
🐟 Fishing	▢ Desert
V Poultry	▢ Forest
🍋 Citrus fruit	▢ Pasture
🦐 Fruit	• Major conurbation
🌾 Irrigated crops	
🌲 Timber	
🌿 Vineyards	
🌾 Wheat	

LAND USE

Cropland 10%
Pasture 2%
Forest 19%
Other (including mountains) 69%

ENVIRONMENTAL ISSUES

Some of the great national parks of the USA, including Yosemite and Sequoia, are found here. The immense numbers of visitors put great pressure on the landscape. Water is in short supply in large parts of California, and desertification, caused by over-intense farming methods, is a problem. Wind farms have been set up on the hills above the San Joaquin valley to provide alternative energy.

ENVIRONMENTAL ISSUES

⚑ National park	▢ Desert area
😷 Urban air pollution	▢ Risk of desertification
	▢ Severe risk of desertification
⊹ Wind farm	▢ Polluted rivers
	• Major industrial centre
⚒ Risk of wild fire	

THE LANDSCAPE

The Coast and Cascade ranges run north–south through Oregon and Washington while further south, the high Sierra Nevada run along California's eastern fringes. Two broad valleys, the Sacramento and San Joaquin, are known as the Central Valley, and form a trough beneath the Sierra Nevada. The south is extremely dry – Death Valley is the hottest place in the entire USA.

Northern rain forest (B 2)

The ocean-facing side of the Olympic Mountains receives 3,600 mm of rain every year, supporting the only true temperate rainforest in the Northern Hemisphere.

Hells Canyon (D 3)

Hells Canyon is North America's deepest gorge. Running through part of Oregon, it was created as the Snake River cut down through the land.

Volcanic eruption (B 2)

Mount St. Helens erupted in 1980, killing 57 people and destroying a vast area.

San Andreas Fault

The San Andreas Fault runs for 1,050 km underneath California. When both sides of the fault move at different rates, tremors and earthquakes result.

Hottest place (D 7)

In 1913, Death Valley set the record for the highest temperature ever recorded in the US, at 56.6°C.

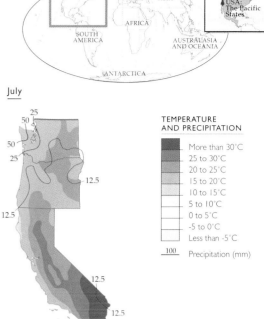

NORTH AMERICA

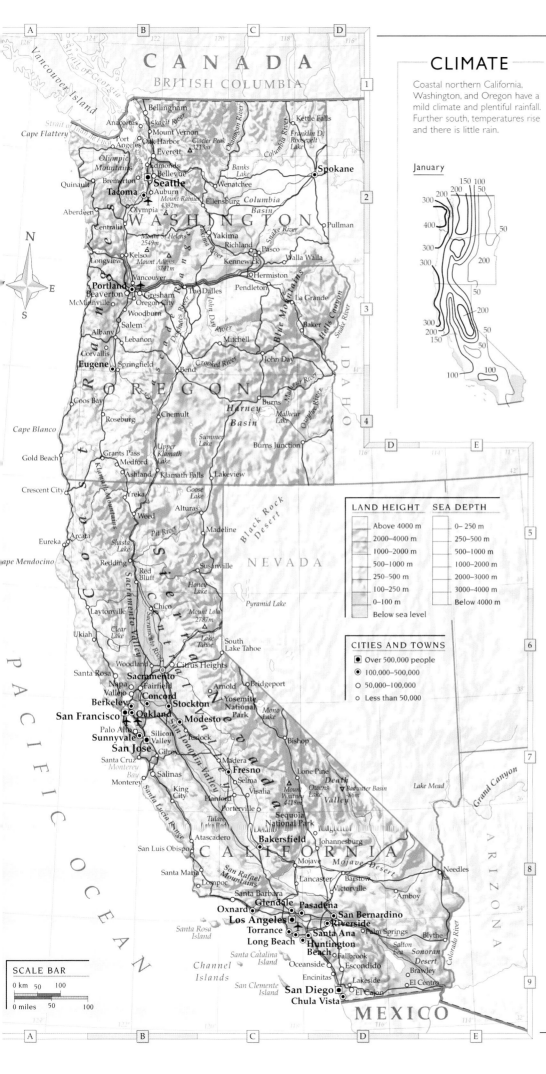

CLIMATE

Coastal northern California, Washington, and Oregon have a mild climate and plentiful rainfall. Further south, temperatures rise and there is little rain.

January

July

TEMPERATURE AND PRECIPITATION

More than 30°C
25 to 30°C
20 to 25°C
15 to 20°C
10 to 15°C
5 to 10°C
0 to 5°C
-5 to 0°C
Less than -5°C

—100— Precipitation (mm)

POPULATION

California has the most diverse population in the entire USA and is one of the most populated states. Oregon and Washington are far less densely populated, but increasing numbers of people are moving into the Northwest and to cities such as Seattle. Los Angeles is one of the world's most sprawling urban centres.

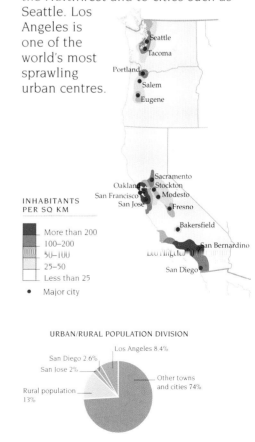

INHABITANTS PER SQ KM

More than 200
100–200
50–100
25–50
Less than 25

• Major city

Seattle
Tacoma
Portland
Salem
Eugene

Sacramento
Stockton
Modesto
Oakland
San Francisco
San Jose
Fresno
Bakersfield
Los Angeles
San Bernardino
San Diego

URBAN/RURAL POPULATION DIVISION

Los Angeles 8.4%
San Diego 2.6%
San Jose 2%
Other towns and cities 74%
Rural population 13%

Map labels

CANADA
BRITISH COLUMBIA

Vancouver Island
Strait of Georgia
Cape Flattery
Strait of Juan de Fuca

Bellingham
Anacortes
Skagit River
Mount Vernon
Kettle Falls
Port Angeles
Oak Harbor
Glacier Peak 3213m
Columbia River
Franklin D. Roosevelt Lake
Everett
Edmonds
Olympic Mountains
Bellevue
Bremerton
Seattle
Spokane
Quinault
Banks Lake
Wenatchee
Tacoma
Auburn
Ellensburg
Columbia Basin
Aberdeen
Olympia
WASHINGTON
Mount Rainier 4392m
Centralia
Yakima
Pullman
Mount St Helens 2549m
Richland
Snake River
Longview
Kelso
Pasco
Kennewick
Walla Walla
Mount Adams 3741m
Vancouver
Hermiston
Portland
Beaverton
The Dalles
Pendleton
Gresham
McMinnville
Oregon City
John Day River
La Grande
Woodburn
Salem
Blue Mountains
Albany
Lebanon
Baker
Corvallis
Mitchell
Hells Canyon
Snake River
Eugene
Springfield
Crooked River
John Day
OREGON
Bend
Coos Bay
Harney Basin
Burns
Roseburg
Chemult
Malheur Lake
Malheur River
Owyhee River
Cape Blanco
Summer Lake
Grants Pass
Upper Klamath Lake
Burns Junction
Gold Beach
Medford
Ashland
Klamath Falls
Lakeview
Crescent City
Yreka
Goose Lake
Alturas
Weed
Eureka
Arcata
Shasta Lake
Redding
Black Rock Desert
NEVADA
Cape Mendocino
Red Bluff
Honey Lake
Laytonville
Susanville
Ukiah
Chico
Mount Lola 2787m
Clear Lake
Pyramid Lake
Pit River
Madeline
Coast Ranges
Sierra Nevada
Sacramento Valley
Woodland
Lake Tahoe
Santa Rosa
Citrus Heights
South Lake Tahoe
Sacramento
Napa
Fairfield
Arnold
Bridgeport
Vallejo
Concord
Stockton
Berkeley
Oakland
Yosemite National Park
San Francisco
Modesto
Mono Lake
Palo Alto
Silicon Valley
Sunnyvale
Turlock
San Jose
Gilroy
Madera
Bishop
Santa Cruz
Monterey Bay
Salinas
Fresno
Lone Pine
Monterey
Selma
Death Valley
Lake Mead
King City
Visalia
Owens Lake
Badwater Basin -86m
Hanford
Porterville
Mount Whitney 4418m
Grand Canyon
Tulare Lake
Sequoia National Park
Santa Lucia Range
Atascadero
Bakersfield
Johannesburg
San Luis Obispo
CALIFORNIA
ARIZONA
Santa Maria
Mojave
Mojave Desert
Needles
San Rafael Mountains
Lancaster
Barstow
Santa Barbara
Victorville
Amboy
Oxnard
Glendale
Pasadena
San Bernardino
Los Angeles
Riverside
Torrance
Santa Ana
Palm Springs
Long Beach
Huntington Beach
Blythe
Santa Rosa Island
Salton Sea
Sonoran Desert
Colorado River
Channel Islands
Oceanside
Fallbrook
Brawley
Santa Catalina Island
Escondido
Encinitas
Lakeside
El Centro
San Clemente Island
San Diego
El Cajon
Chula Vista
MEXICO
PACIFIC OCEAN
IDAHO

N
E
S

LAND HEIGHT
Above 4000 m
2000–4000 m
1000–2000 m
500–1000 m
250–500 m
100–250 m
0–100 m
Below sea level

SEA DEPTH
0–250 m
250–500 m
500–1000 m
1000–2000 m
2000–3000 m
3000–4000 m
Below 4000 m

CITIES AND TOWNS
■ Over 500,000 people
◉ 100,000–500,000
○ 50,000–100,000
∘ Less than 50,000

SCALE BAR
0 km 50 100
0 miles 50 100

ALASKA

A **magnificent land** of mountains, forests and snowfields, with rich oil and mineral reserves, Alaska was purchased from Russia for $1 million in 1867. Almost 650,000 people live here, many drawn by the oil industry. Some of Alaska's native peoples like the Aleuts and Inupiaq still live by hunting and fishing.

ENVIRONMENTAL ISSUES

Much of northern Alaska is covered by permafrost (permanently frozen ground). The Trans-Alaska Pipeline, which brings oil from Prudhoe Bay to Valdez, was built above ground to stop the permafrost melting. A number of major oil spills have threatened Alaska's unique envrionment.

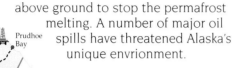

Trans-Alaska
Pipeline
Prudhoe Bay
Valdez
Exxon Valdez 1993

ENVIRONMENTAL ISSUES

- 🛢 Major oil spill
- - - Oil pipeline
- 🗼 Oil wells
- ▢ Permafrost zone
- ● Major town

INDUSTRY

Prudhoe Bay
Anchorage
Valdez
Juneau

The Alaskan economy is dominated by the oil business. The oilfields of Alaska are of a similar size to those in the Persian Gulf. Minerals including gold are mined in the mountains, and paper products are exported to countries on the Pacific Rim.

INDUSTRY

- Chemicals
- Mining
- Oil and gas
- Timber processing
- ■ Major industrial centre
- — Major road

FARMING AND LAND USE

Anchorage

Salmon are caught in great numbers in the waters of the north Pacific. Much of the state – more than 9 million hectares – is covered by forest which is commercially lumbered. Most food must be imported, although fruit is grown in hothouses near the larger cities.

FARMING AND LAND USE

- 🎣 Fishing
- 🦀 Fruit
- 🌲 Timber
- ▢ Barren
- ▢ Forest
- ▢ Mountains
- ▢ Tundra
- ● Major conurbation

Near Islands
Attu Island
A B C D E F
RUSS. FED.
Arctic Circle
Bering Bering Strait
Wevok Point Lay Barrow
Kivalina
Beaufort Sea
Sea
1
Gambell
Saint Lawrence Island
Wales
Deering
Colville River
Prudhoe Bay
Umiat
Kaktovik
Rat Islands
Norton Sound
Brooks Range
Alakanuk
Amchitka Island
Aleutian Islands
Nunivak Island
Grayling
Yukon River
Kokrines
Fort Yukon
2
Andreanof Islands
Atka
Pribilof Islands
Kwigillingok
A L A S K A
(part of USA)
Fairbanks
Yukon River
Arctic Circle
Platinum
Kuskokwim Mts
Alaska Range
McKinley Park
Mount McKinley
(Denali) 6194m
Susitna
Anchorage
Umnak Island
Dutch Harbor
Bristol Bay
Iliamna Lake
Hope
Gulkana
C A N A D A
Unalaska Island
Unimak Island
Belkofski
Alaska Peninsula
Valdez
Chitina
Cordova
3
Shumagin Islands
Kodiak
Katalla
Kodiak Island
Gulf of Alaska
Yakutat
PACIFIC OCEAN
Haines
Gustavus
Juneau
Kake
Alexander Archipelago
4
Port Alexander
Ketchikan

LAND HEIGHT
- Above 4000 m
- 2000–4000 m
- 1000–2000 m
- 500–1000 m
- 250–500 m
- 100–250 m
- 0–100 m

SEA DEPTH
- 0–250 m
- 250–500 m
- 500–1000 m
- 1000–2000 m
- 2000–3000 m
- 3000–4000 m
- Below 4000 m

CITIES AND TOWNS
- ◉ 100,000–500,000
- ◎ 50,000–100,000
- ○ Less than 50,000

SCALE BAR
0 km 200 400
0 miles 200 400

CLIMATE

Parts of northern Alaska are frozen year-round and can be cut off entirely in the winter. Summers are milder – especially in the Aleutians.

January
10
10
50
100
200
50
200

July
50
50
100
100
200
200
100

TEMPERATURE AND PRECIPITATION
- More than 15°C
- 10 to 15°C
- 5 to 10°C
- 0 to 5°C
- -5 to 0°C
- -10 to -5°C
- -15 to -10°C
- Less than -15°C
- 100 Precipitation (mm)

HAWAII

Hawaii is the 50th US state. It lies far from the mainland in the middle of the Pacific Ocean. The island chain was formed by volcanoes, only one of which, Mauna Loa, remains active today. The islands' indigenous peoples are Polynesians, but continued immigration means that they now make up only 9% of the population.

INDUSTRY AND LAND USE

Tourism is the most important industry in Hawaii, accounting for one in every three jobs. The naval base at Pearl Harbor also provides jobs for numerous people. The many large plantations grow sugarcane, bananas and tropical fruit for export.

FARMING AND LAND USE

- 🐂 Cattle
- 🎣 Fishing
- 🍓 Fruit
- ↧ Sugarcane
- Cropland
- Forest
- Mountain region
- Pasture

INDUSTRY

- Tourism
- Major town

ENVIRONMENTAL ISSUES

Climatic occurrences, combined with the growth of tourism, have an adverse effect on the indigenous flora and fauna. Eruptions from Mauna Loa are an accepted risk for the population.

ENVIRONMENTAL ISSUES

- Tourist resort
- ⛰ Volcanic eruption
- Major town

Mauna Loa – 1984
Kilauea – 1983

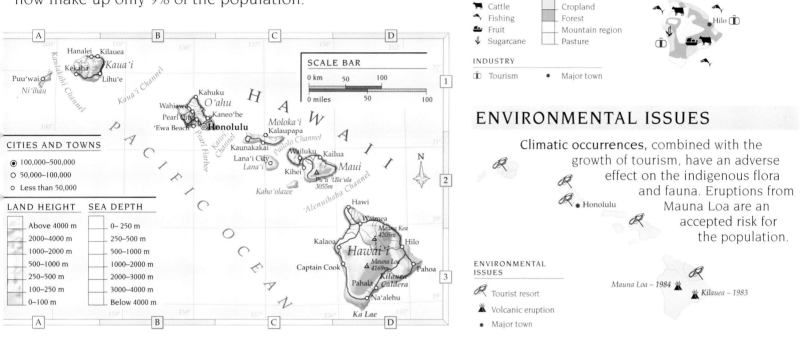

CITIES AND TOWNS
- ◉ 100,000–500,000
- ○ 50,000–100,000
- ○ Less than 50,000

LAND HEIGHT
- Above 4000 m
- 2000–4000 m
- 1000–2000 m
- 500–1000 m
- 250–500 m
- 100–250 m
- 0–100 m

SEA DEPTH
- 0– 250 m
- 250–500 m
- 500–1000 m
- 1000–2000 m
- 2000–3000 m
- 3000–4000 m
- Below 4000 m

SCALE BAR
- 0 km ... 50 ... 100
- 0 miles ... 50 ... 100

UNITED STATES OVERSEAS TERRITORIES

America's overseas territories have traditionally been seen as strategically or economically important. In most cases, the local population has been given a say in deciding whether it wants to govern itself. A US commonwealth territory has a greater level of independence than a US unincorporated or external territory. The US has 13 overseas territories; the four largest are shown here.

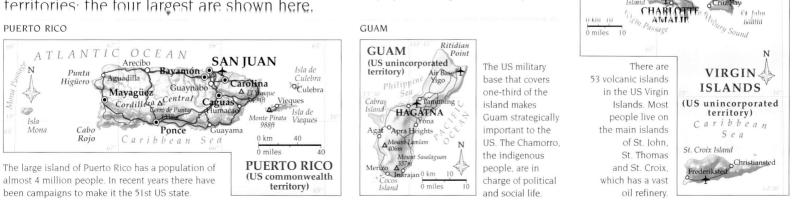

AMERICAN SAMOA

AMERICAN SAMOA
(US unincorporated territory)
PAGO PAGO

American Samoa consists of five volcanic islands and two coral atolls in the south Pacific. The people are among the last true Polynesians.

US VIRGIN ISLANDS

There are 53 volcanic islands in the US Virgin Islands. Most people live on the main islands of St. John, St. Thomas and St. Croix, which has a vast oil refinery.

VIRGIN ISLANDS
(US unincorporated territory)

PUERTO RICO

The large island of Puerto Rico has a population of almost 4 million people. In recent years there have been campaigns to make it the 51st US state.

PUERTO RICO
(US commonwealth territory)

GUAM

GUAM
(US unincorporated territory)

The US military base that covers one-third of the island makes Guam strategically important to the US. The Chamorro, the indigenous people, are in charge of political and social life.

MEXICO

Mexico is a large country with a rich mixture of traditions and cultures. The ancient civilization of the Aztecs which flourished here was crushed by Spanish invaders in the 16th century. Spain ruled Mexico until its independence in 1836 and today, the country has the world's largest Spanish-speaking population. Mexico is mostly dry and mountainous, and farm land is limited, so the country has to import most of the basic foods it needs to feed its people.

FARMING AND LAND USE

Most of the land suitable for farming is planted with corn – a big part of the Mexican diet. Along the Gulf coast coffee, sugarcane and cotton are grown on plantations for export. Parts of the dry north are irrigated to grow cotton, but most of the land is taken up by large cattle ranches. Fishing, especially for shellfish such as lobster and shrimp is important in coastal areas.

FARMING AND LAND USE

- Cattle
- Fishing
- Sheep
- Bananas
- Coffee
- Corn (maize)
- Cotton
- Fruit
- Grapes
- Shellfish
- Sugarcane
- Timber

- Cropland
- Desert
- Forest
- Pasture
- Wetland
- Major conurbation

LAND USE

- Cropland 14%
- Other 15%
- Forest 29%
- Pasture 42%

THE LANDSCAPE

Much of Mexico is made up of a high plateau. The climate there is very dry and varies between true desert in the north, and semi-desert further south. The plateau is separated from the coastal plains by two long, rugged mountain chains: the Eastern Sierra Madre and the Western Sierra Madre. Towards the south, the mountain ranges join, meeting in the region of high volcanic peaks that surround Mexico City.

Lower California (B 3)
This long and very dry peninsula, separates the Gulf of California from the Pacific Ocean. The Gulf was formed after the last Ice Age, when the sea rose to flood a major rift valley.

The Rio Grande (D 2)
This river flows from Colorado in the USA and forms much of Mexico's northern border. It crosses a vast arid area on its way to the Gulf of Mexico.

Earthquakes and volcanoes
Volcanic activity is common in Mexico. Popocatépetl (F 5) and Volcán El Chichónal (G 5) have erupted recently, and Mexico City was hit by a devastating earthquake in 1985

Western Sierra Madre (C 3).

Eastern Sierra Madre (D 5).

Yucatan Peninsula (H 4)
The Yucatan Peninsula is a low, wide tableland, formed by layers of limestone. Limestone absorbs water, so there are few rivers on the peninsula, and the tropical rainforests found there are fed mainly by streams and underground water.

POPULATION

Most of the north is sparsely populated due to the hot, dry climate and lack of cultivable farm land. As people have migrated from the countryside in search of work, the cities have grown dramatically; almost 75% of Mexicans now live in urban areas. Mexico City is home to almost a fifth of the population and is one of the world's largest cities.

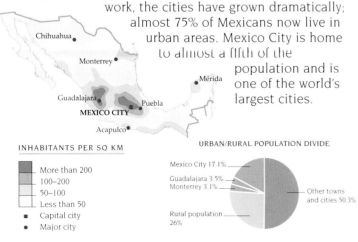

INHABITANTS PER SQ KM

- More than 200
- 100–200
- 50–100
- Less than 50
- ■ Capital city
- ● Major city

URBAN/RURAL POPULATION DIVIDE

- Mexico City 17.1%
- Guadalajara 3.5%
- Monterrey 3.1%
- Other towns and cities 50.3%
- Rural population 26%

ENVIRONMENTAL ISSUES

Fast, unplanned growth has led to poor sanitation and water supplies in Mexico City, while the wall of mountains which surround the city traps pollution from cars and factories, giving it some of the world's worst air pollution. Much of Mexico's tropical rainforest has been felled, leading to increased soil erosion. Land clearance further north is also causing desertification.

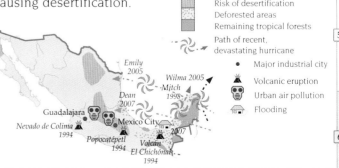

ENVIRONMENTAL ISSUES

- Risk of desertification
- Deforested areas
- Remaining tropical forests
- Path of recent, devastating hurricane
- ● Major industrial city
- Volcanic eruption
- Urban air pollution
- Flooding

NORTH AMERICA

INDUSTRY

Oil and gas on the Gulf coast are the biggest source of income. Mexico is also rich in other minerals; it is the world's top silver producer. Manufacturing is centred around Mexico City and along the US border, where mainly foreign owned factories assemble products for export. Tourism is also very important to Mexico.

STRUCTURE OF INDUSTRY

Primary 4%
Services 70%
Manufacturing 26%

INDUSTRY

- 🚗 Car manufacture
- 📱 Electronics
- ⚙ Engineering
- 🏭 Food processing
- 🏗 Iron & steel
- 🛢 Oil refining
- 👕 Textiles
- ⛏ Mining
- 🛢 Oil and gas
- 🏛 Tourism
- ● Major industrial centre / area
- — Major road

CLIMATE

Northern Mexico and the peninsula of Lower California are dry, hot and largely desert. Towards the south, rainfall increases, especially in July. Moist, warm conditions allow rainforests to grow.

January

July

TEMPERATURE AND PRECIPITATION

- More than 30°C
- 25 to 30°C
- 20 to 25°C
- 15 to 20°C
- 10 to 15°C
- 5 to 10°C
- Less than 5°C

100 Precipitation (mm)

LAND HEIGHT
- Above 4000 m
- 2000–4000 m
- 1000–2000 m
- 500–1000 m
- 250–500 m
- 100–250 m
- 0–100 m

SEA DEPTH
- 0–250 m
- 250–500 m
- 500–1000 m
- 1000–2000 m
- 2000–3000 m
- 3000–4000 m
- Below 4000 m

CITIES AND TOWNS
- ■ Over 500,000 people
- ◉ 100,000–500,000
- ○ 50,000–100,000
- ○ Less than 50,000

SCALE BAR

km 200

miles 200

CENTRAL AMERICA

BELIZE, COSTA RICA, EL SALVADOR, GUATEMALA, HONDURAS, NICARAGUA, PANAMA

Central America lies on a narrow bridge of land which links North and South America. All the countries here, except Belize, were once governed by Spain. Today, most of their people are *mestizos* – a mix of the original Maya Indian inhabitants and Spanish settlers. The hot, steamy climate is ideal for growing tropical crops, such as coffee and bananas, which are exported worldwide.

FARMING AND LAND USE

About half of all the agricultural products grown here are exported. The Pacific coast has fertile, well-watered land suitable for growing cotton and sugarcane. In the central highlands are big coffee plantations, and ranches where beef cattle are raised. Bananas grow well along the humid Caribbean coastal plain, and shrimp and lobster are caught offshore.

FARMING AND LAND USE

- 🐃 Cattle
- 🦐 Shellfish
- 🍌 Bananas
- ☕ Coffee
- 🌽 Corn (maize)
- 🌿 Cotton
- 🌾 Sugarcane
- ⚑ Timber
- Cropland
- Forest
- Pasture
- • Major conurbation

LAND USE

Pasture 27%
Forest 35%
Cropland 15%
Other 23%

ENVIRONMENTAL ISSUES

Central America's rainforests are rapidly being cut down for timber and to make way for farmland and land for building. Over half of Guatemala's forests have been felled, mostly in the last 30 years. The situation is also bleak in Honduras, Costa Rica and Nicaragua. Central America has a line of volcanoes running through the region which are still active.

Mitch 1998
Felix 2007
Volcán Tacaná 1986
Volcán de Fuego 1974
Volcán de Izalco 1958
Volcán San Cristobal 2000
Volcán Cerro Negro 1995
Volcán Masaya 2001
Volcán Concepcion 1986
Volcán Arenal 1998, 2000
Volcán Rincon de la Vieja 1998

ENVIRONMENTAL ISSUES

- 🌋 Volcanic eruption
- Deforested areas
- Remaining forests
- Path of recent, devastating hurricane

POPULATION

Central America's people live mainly in the valleys of the central highlands or along the Pacific coastal plains. Despite the threat of volcanic eruptions and earthquakes, towns and cities developed in these areas because of the fertile volcanic soils found there. Around half the population still live in rural areas, mostly in small villages or remote settlements, but the cities have expanded rapidly and overcrowding has become a serious problem.

BELMOPAN
GUATEMALA CITY
TEGUCIGALPA
SAN SALVADOR
MANAGUA
SAN JOSÉ
PANAMA CITY

INHABITANTS PER SQ KM

- More than 50
- 25–50
- Less than 25
- ■ Capital city

URBAN/RURAL POPULATION DIVIDE

- Managua 2.2%
- Tegucigalpa 2%
- Guatemala City 2.4%
- Other towns and cities 43.4%
- Rural population 50%

THE LANDSCAPE

The Sierra Madre in the north and the Cordillera Central to the south form a mountainous ridge that stretches down most of Central America. Along the Pacific coast north of Panama is a belt of more than 40 active volcanoes. The mountains are broken by valleys and basins with large, fertile areas of rich, volcanic soil.

Sierra Madre (A 3)

Coral reef (C 2)
Off the coast of Belize is a 290 km long coral reef – the second longest in the world. Its waters contain spectacular marine life. In places, the reef has become built up into dozens of small sandy islands called cayes.

The Mosquito Coast (E 4)
The Mosquito Coast is a remote area of tropical rainforests, lagoons, and rivers lined with mangroves. Most of it is uninhabited by humans, but there is a huge variety of animal species, including monkeys and alligators.

Lake Nicaragua (E 5)
This large freshwater lake contains about 400 islands, some of which are active volancoes like Volcán Concepcion. The lake is also home to the world's only freshwater sharks.

Cordillera Central (G 6)

The Panama Canal (H 6)
The Panama Canal links the Atlantic and Pacific oceans along a distance of 82 km. Half of its route passes through Lake Gatún, a freshwater lake which acts as a reservoir for the canal, providing water to operate the locks.

MEXICO
Yucatan
BELMOPAN
Carm
Río Usumacinta
Barillas
Jacaltenango
GUA
Chajul
Nebaj
Huehuetenango
Volcán Tacaná 4093m
Santa Cruz del Quiché
San Marcos
Quezaltenan
GUATEMALA CITY
Champerico
San Jos

NORTH AMERICA

CLIMATE

Temperatures are high all year round, although in January the Caribbean side of Central America is is cooler and wetter than the Pacific side. Summers are generally much wetter, especially in the Sierra Madre in Guatemala and on the Pacific coasts of Costa Rica and Panama.

TEMPERATURE AND PRECIPITATION

More than 25°C
20 to 25°C
Less than 20°C
100 ――― Precipitation (mm)

January

July

INDUSTRY

Coffee, fish, and timber processing, fruit exporting and textile-weaving are typical of the small-scale industries found in Central America. Most industries are based in the capital cities and larger towns. In Panama, many people work at the Panama Canal, which is one of the world's busiest shipping routes. The country is also a major financial centre, with many banking and insurance companies.

INDUSTRY

- Chemicals
- Coffee processing
- Fish processing
- Food processing
- Textiles
- Banana exporting
- Timber processing
- S Finance
- ● Major industrial centre / area
- ―― Major road

STRUCTURE OF INDUSTRY

Primary 18%
Services 60%
Manufacturing 22%

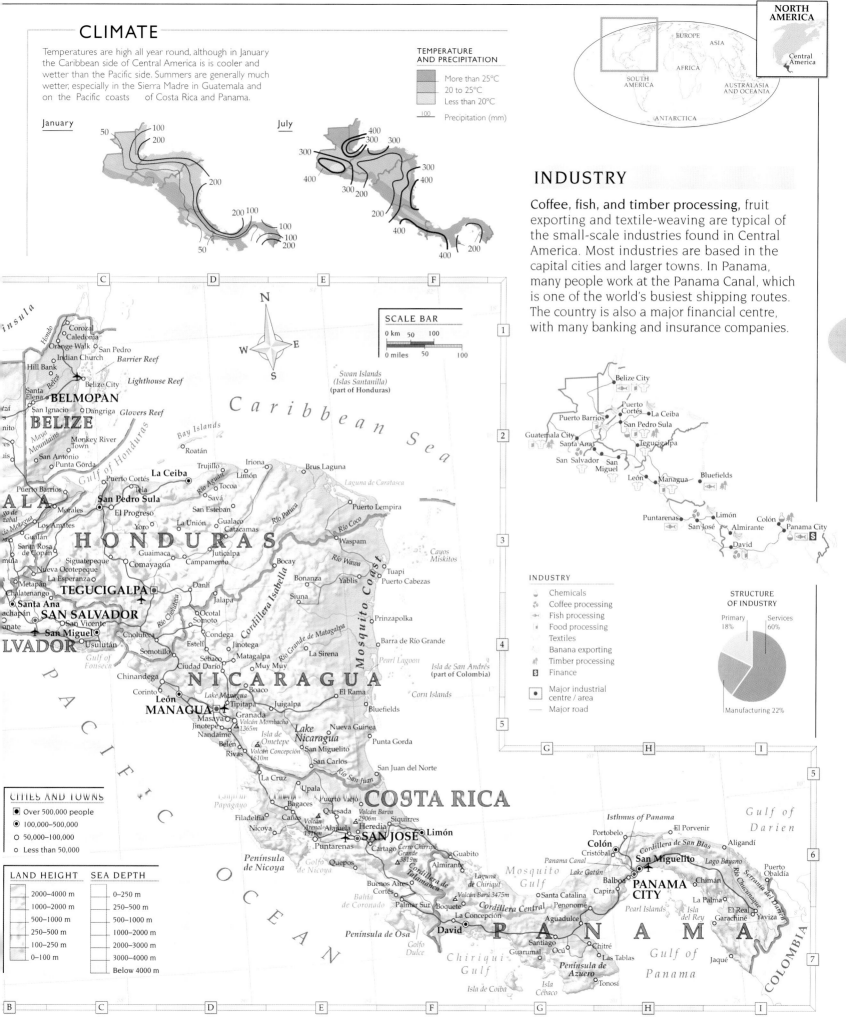

CITIES AND TOWNS
- ● Over 500,000 people
- ◉ 100,000–500,000
- ○ 50,000–100,000
- ○ Less than 50,000

LAND HEIGHT / **SEA DEPTH**

LAND HEIGHT	SEA DEPTH
2000–4000 m	0–250 m
1000–2000 m	250–500 m
500–1000 m	500–1000 m
250–500 m	1000–2000 m
100–250 m	2000–3000 m
0–100 m	3000–4000 m
	Below 4000 m

THE CARIBBEAN

The Caribbean Sea is enclosed by an arc of many hundreds of islands, islets and offshore reefs which reach from Florida in the USA round to Venezuela in South America. From 1492, Spain, France, Britain and the Netherlands claimed the islands as colonies. Most of the islands' original inhabitants were wiped out by disease and a wide mixture of peoples – of African, Asian and European descent – now make up the population. The islands are prone to earthquakes, hurricanes and volcanic eruptions.

THE LANDSCAPE

The Bahamas
The Bahamas are low-lying, islands formed from limestone rock. Their coastlines are fringed by coral reefs, lagoons and mangrove swamps. Some of the bigger islands are covered by forests.

The islands are formed from two main mountain chains: the Greater Antilles, which are part of a chain running from west to east, and the Lesser Antilles, which run from north to south. The mountains are now almost submerged under the Atlantic Ocean and Caribbean Sea. Only the higher peaks reach above sea level to form islands.

Hispaniola (F 4)
Two countries, Haiti and the Dominican Republic occupy the island of Hispaniola. The land is mostly mountainous, broken by fertile valleys.

Cuba (C 3)
Cuba is the largest island in the Antilles. Its landscape is made up of wide, fertile plains with rugged hills and mountains in the southeast.

The Lesser Antilles
Most of these small volcanic islands have mountainous interiors. Barbados and Antigua & Barbuda are flatter, with some higher volcanic areas. Montserrat was evacuated in 1997, following volcanic eruptions on the island.

FARMING AND LAND USE

Agriculture is an important source of income, with over half of all produce exported. Many islands have fertile, well-watered land and large areas are set aside for commercial crops such as sugarcane, tobacco and coffee. Some islands rely heavily on a single crop; in Dominica, bananas provide over half the country's income. Cuba is one of the world's biggest sugar producers.

FARMING AND LAND USE

- Cattle
- Fishing
- Pigs
- Poultry
- Shellfish
- Bananas
- Coffee
- Sugarcane
- Tobacco

- Cropland
- Forest
- Pasture
- • Major conurbation

ENVIRONMENTAL ISSUES

The islands of the Caribbean are often under threat from hurricane storm systems which sweep in from the Atlantic Ocean between May and October. The winds can reach speeds of up to 300 km per hour, devastating everything that lies in their path and causing severe flooding. The storms themselves are enormous; a hurricane can extend outwards for 650 km from its calm centre, which is known as the 'eye'.

TOURISM

Tourism is thriving in the Caribbean, often bringing more income to the region than other, traditional industries. Long sandy beaches, clear, warm waters and the climate are the main attractions. In Cuba and the Dominican Republic, tourism is expanding at some of the fastest rates in North America. As hotel complexes and new roads and airports are developed, the environment is often damaged. Local people who work in the industry often receive little of the extra cash brought in by the tourists.

TOURISM

Major tourist destinations

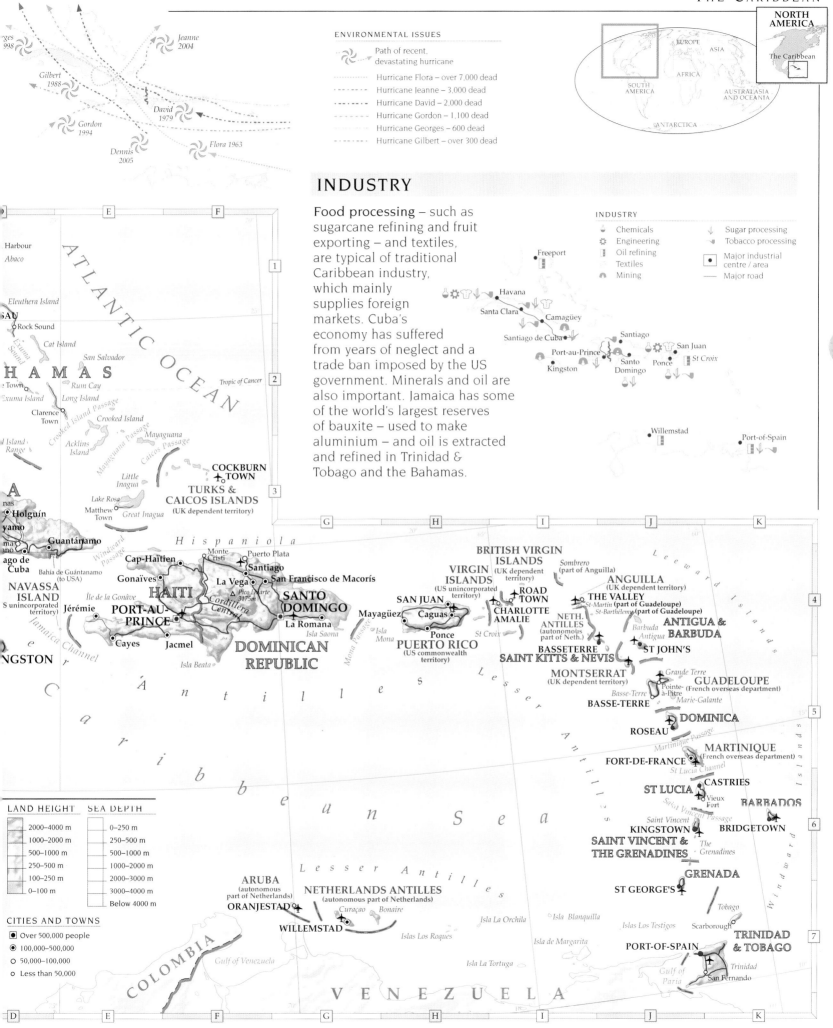

NORTH
AMERICA

The Caribbean

ENVIRONMENTAL ISSUES

Path of recent, devastating hurricane

Hurricane Flora – over 7,000 dead

Hurricane Jeanne – 3,000 dead

Hurricane David – 2,000 dead

Hurricane Gordon – 1,100 dead

Hurricane Georges – 600 dead

Hurricane Gilbert – over 300 dead

Jeanne 2004

Gilbert 1988

David 1979

Gordon 1994

Dennis 2005

Flora 1963

INDUSTRY

Food processing – such as sugarcane refining and fruit exporting – and textiles, are typical of traditional Caribbean industry, which mainly supplies foreign markets. Cuba's economy has suffered from years of neglect and a trade ban imposed by the US government. Minerals and oil are also important. Jamaica has some of the world's largest reserves of bauxite – used to make aluminium – and oil is extracted and refined in Trinidad & Tobago and the Bahamas.

INDUSTRY

- Chemicals
- Engineering
- Oil refining
- Textiles
- Mining
- Sugar processing
- Tobacco processing
- Major industrial centre / area
- Major road

Freeport

Havana
Santa Clara
Camagüey
Santiago de Cuba
Santiago
San Juan
St Croix
Port-au-Prince
Kingston
Santo Domingo
Ponce

Willemstad
Port-of-Spain

LAND HEIGHT

- 2000–4000 m
- 1000–2000 m
- 500–1000 m
- 250–500 m
- 100–250 m
- 0–100 m

SEA DEPTH

- 0–250 m
- 250–500 m
- 500–1000 m
- 1000–2000 m
- 2000–3000 m
- 3000–4000 m
- Below 4000 m

CITIES AND TOWNS

- Over 500,000 people
- 100,000–500,000
- 50,000–100,000
- Less than 50,000

Harbour
Abaco

ATLANTIC OCEAN

Eleuthera Island
Rock Sound
Cat Island
San Salvador

Tropic of Cancer

BAHAMAS

Town
Rum Cay
Exuma Island
Long Island
Clarence Town
Crooked Island
Acklins Island
Mayaguana
Caicos Passage

Island Range

Little Inagua
Lake Rosa
Matthew Town
Great Inagua

COCKBURN TOWN
TURKS & CAICOS ISLANDS
(UK dependent territory)

Holguín
yamo
ma
ago de Cuba
Guantánamo

NAVASSA ISLAND
S unincorporated territory

Hispaniola

Cap-Haïtien
Monte Cristi
Puerto Plata
Santiago
San Francisco de Macorís
Gonaïves
La Vega
HAITI
Pico Duarte
3175m
Cordillera Central
SANTO DOMINGO
Bahía de Guántanamo
(to USA)
Île de la Gonâve
Jérémie
PORT-AU-PRINCE
La Romana
Cayes
Jacmel
DOMINICAN REPUBLIC
Isla Saona

Windward Passage

Jamaica Channel

NGSTON

Isla Beata

Isla Mona
Mayagüez
Caguas
Isla Mona
Ponce
St Croix
PUERTO RICO
(US commonwealth territory)

SAN JUAN

VIRGIN ISLANDS
(US unincorporated territory)

BRITISH VIRGIN ISLANDS
(UK dependent territory)

ROAD TOWN

CHARLOTTE AMALIE

Sombrero
(part of Anguilla)

ANGUILLA
(UK dependent territory)
THE VALLEY
St-Martin (part of Guadeloupe)
St-Barthélemy (part of Guadeloupe)

NETH. ANTILLES
(autonomous part of Neth.)

Barbuda
Antigua
ANTIGUA & BARBUDA
ST JOHN'S

BASSETERRE
SAINT KITTS & NEVIS

MONTSERRAT
(UK dependent territory)

Leeward Islands

Grande Terre
Pointe-à-Pitre
GUADELOUPE
(French overseas department)
Basse-Terre
Marie-Galante
BASSE-TERRE

DOMINICA
ROSEAU

Martinique Passage

MARTINIQUE
(French overseas department)
FORT-DE-FRANCE
St Lucia Channel

ST LUCIA
CASTRIES
Vieux Fort
Saint Vincent Passage

BARBADOS
KINGSTOWN
BRIDGETOWN
SAINT VINCENT & THE GRENADINES
The Grenadines

GRENADA
ST GEORGE'S

Lesser Antilles

Windward Islands

Antilles

Caribbean Sea

ARUBA
(autonomous part of Netherlands)
ORANJESTAD

NETHERLANDS ANTILLES
(autonomous part of Netherlands)
Curaçao
Bonaire
WILLEMSTAD

Isla La Orchila
Isla Blanquilla
Islas Los Testigos

Islas Los Roques
Isla de Margarita

COLOMBIA

Gulf of Venezuela

VENEZUELA

Isla La Tortuga

Tobago
Scarborough

TRINIDAD & TOBAGO
PORT-OF-SPAIN

Gulf of Paria
Trinidad
San Fernando

CONTINENTAL SOUTH AMERICA

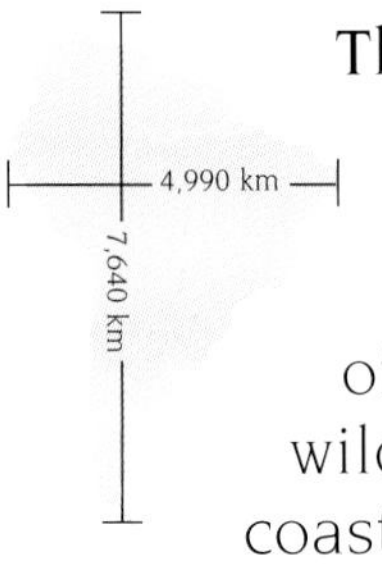

The towering peaks of the Andes stand high above the western side of South America. They act as a barrier to the sparsely inhabited interior of the continent which includes the dense rainforest of the Amazon Basin – one of the Earth's last great wildernesses. Most people live on South America's coastal fringes. Brazil is both the largest country, and the most populous. Over half the continent's land area and half its people are found there.

— 4,990 km —
7,640 km

CROSS-SECTION ACROSS SOUTH AMERICA

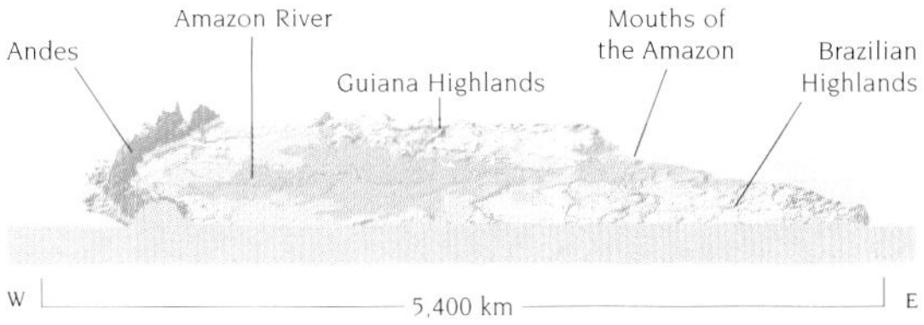

Andes Amazon River Mouths of the Amazon Brazilian Highlands Guiana Highlands

W — 5,400 km — E

The high peaks of the Andes rise up from a narrow strip of land bordering the Pacific Ocean. East of the Andes, the land flattens into a broad, shallow basin into which the Amazon River flows. To the north are the older Guiana Highlands where rock has been eroded to form flat-topped 'table' mountains.

PHYSICAL SOUTH AMERICA

Ancient masses of rocks, like the Guiana and Brazilian highlands, which are known as shields, form the core of South America. The Andes are the solid backbone of the continent. They are relatively young, formed by collisions between different plates of the Earth's crust. The major rivers; the Paraná and the mighty Amazon flow in deep depressions to the east of the mountains.

ELEVATION

6000 m
5000 m
4000 m
3000 m
2000 m
1000 m
500 m
250 m
100 m
sea level
below sea level
cross-section

SCALE 1:40,000,000

0 km 400 800
0 miles 400 800

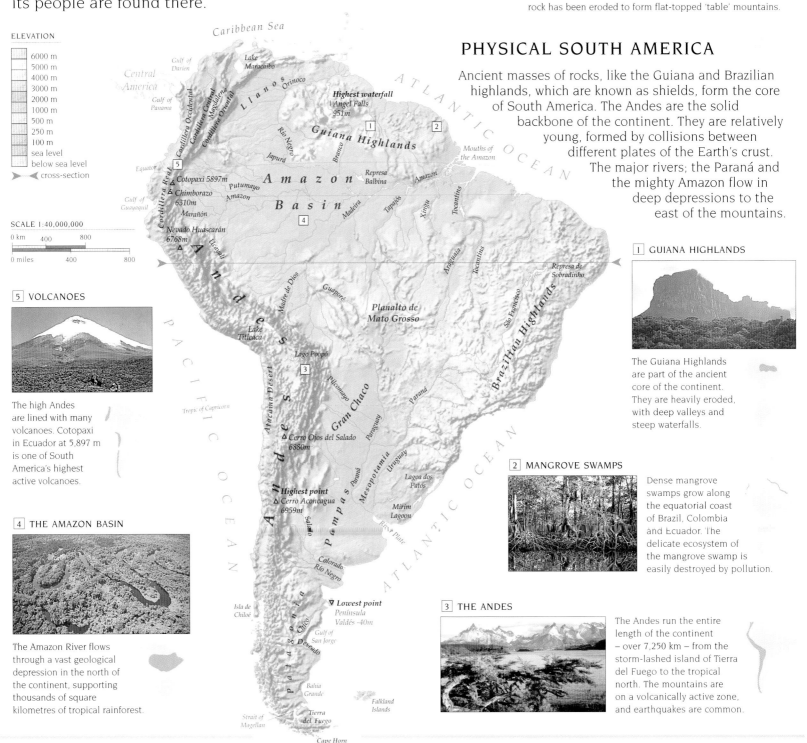

5 VOLCANOES

The high Andes are lined with many volcanoes. Cotopaxi in Ecuador at 5,897 m is one of South America's highest active volcanoes.

4 THE AMAZON BASIN

The Amazon River flows through a vast geological depression in the north of the continent, supporting thousands of square kilometres of tropical rainforest.

1 GUIANA HIGHLANDS

The Guiana Highlands are part of the ancient core of the continent. They are heavily eroded, with deep valleys and steep waterfalls.

2 MANGROVE SWAMPS

Dense mangrove swamps grow along the equatorial coast of Brazil, Colombia and Ecuador. The delicate ecosystem of the mangrove swamp is easily destroyed by pollution.

3 THE ANDES

The Andes run the entire length of the continent – over 7,250 km – from the storm-lashed island of Tierra del Fuego to the tropical north. The mountains are on a volcanically active zone, and earthquakes are common.

Map labels: Caribbean Sea, Gulf of Darien, Central America, Gulf of Panama, Lake Maracaibo, Llanos, Orinoco, Highest waterfall Angel Falls 951m, Guiana Highlands, Río Negro, Branco, Japurá, Mouths of the Amazon, ATLANTIC OCEAN, Cordillera Occidental, Cordillera Central, Cordillera Oriental, Magdalena, Equator, Cordillera Real, Cotopaxi 5897m, Chimborazo 6310m, Putumayo, Amazon, Represa Balbina, Amazon, Marañón, Amazon Basin, Madeira, Tapajós, Xingu, Tocantins, Nevado Huascarán 6768m, Gulf of Guayaquil, Ucayali, Andes, Madre de Dios, Guaporé, Planalto de Mato Grosso, São Francisco, Represa de Sobradinho, Brazilian Highlands, Lake Titicaca, Lago Poopó, Pilcomayo, Paraná, Atacama Desert, Tropic of Capricorn, Cerro Ojos del Salado 6880m, Gran Chaco, Paraguay, Paraná, Uruguay, Mesopotamia, Lagoa dos Patos, PACIFIC OCEAN, Highest point Cerro Aconcagua 6959m, Pampas, Salado, Mirim Lagoon, Río Plate, ATLANTIC OCEAN, Colorado, Río Negro, Isla de Chiloé, Lowest point Península Valdés -40m, Patagonia, Chaco, Gulf of San Jorge, Deseado, Bahía Grande, Falkland Islands, Strait of Magellan, Tierra del Fuego, Cape Horn

POLITICAL SOUTH AMERICA

In the 17th century, explorers from Spain and Portugal claimed most of South America for their rulers in Europe. Their influences are still strong today: Brazilians speak Portuguese, while much of the rest of the continent is Spanish-speaking. The small nations of the north, Surinam and Guyana, were Dutch and British colonies and French Guiana is a French overseas department. The mix of peoples is mainly European, native American and African. Some native peoples still live in the dense Amazon rainforest.

BORDER DISPUTES

Many of South America's borders have been, or remain, disputed. Bolivia is landlocked as a result of a dispute with Chile in 1883, when it lost its lands bordering the Pacific Ocean.

TRANSPORT LINKS

The Pan American Highway is a vital transport link, running from the far south of the continent, northwards along the Pacific coast. Its route takes it through sparsely populated areas like the Atacama Desert.

POPULATION

Many South American countries have a similar pattern of population distribution. The largest numbers of people are found near the coasts. Migration to the coastal cities has led to rocketing population figures, and growing social problems. São Paulo is now one of the world's largest cities; its outskirts are fringed with sprawling, shantytown suburbs – known as *favelas*.

URBAN GROWTH

Urban growth has transformed São Paulo into a major population and industrial centre. Its rapid growth has created many problems, like traffic congestion, overcrowding, and inadequate sewerage.

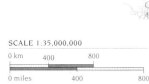

SCALE 1:35,000,000

POPULATION

Capital cities
- ▣ Above 500,000
- ◉ 100,000 to 500,000
- ● 50,000 to 100,000
- • Below 50,000

Other cities
- ▫ Above 500,000
- ○ 50,000 to 100,000

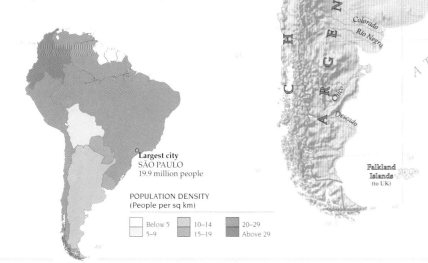

Largest city
SÃO PAULO
19.9 million people

POPULATION DENSITY
(People per sq km)
- Below 5
- 5–9
- 10–14
- 15–19
- 20–29
- Above 29

STANDARDS OF LIVING

There are many inequalities in living standards across South America. Argentina's economy has suffered during the regional recession but living standards are still above those of Guyana and Bolivia, which have weak economies, and are heavily reliant upon trade in raw materials. The booming black market drug trade increases crime and corruption.

STANDARD OF LIVING
(UN Human Development Index)
low   high   no data

SOUTH AMERICAN GEOGRAPHY

Agriculture is still the most common form of employment in South America. Cattle and cash crops of coffee, cocoa and, in some places, coca for cocaine, provide the main sources of income. Brazil has the greatest range of industries, followed by Argentina, Venezuela and Chile. The large coastal cities such as Rio de Janeiro, Lima and Buenos Aires are where most of the jobs are found. This encourages people to migrate from the country to the city, in search of employment.

INDUSTRY

Brazil is the continent's leading industrial producer and São Paulo the major industrial city. Manufactured products include iron and steel, automobiles, chemicals, textiles, and meat and leather products from the continent's vast cattle herds. In the mountains of Bolivia and Colombia, coca plants are grown to make cocaine, which has created a black market for this illegal drug.

OIL AND GAS

Under the waters of Lake Maracaibo, Venezuela, lie some of South America's biggest oil reserves. Oil exploitation has brought great wealth to Venezuela. The money has helped the country to build new roads and develop other industries.

INDUSTRIAL CENTRE

São Paulo, Brazil, is the largest city in South America and a leading industrial centre. A wide range of goods is manufactured here, including automobiles, chemicals, textiles and electronic products. São Paulo is also a leading financial centre. Hundreds of people flock to the city daily in search of work.

TRADE AND EXPORTS

The Chilean port of Valparaíso ships many different products out of South America. Trade is growing with Japan and other countries around the Pacific Ocean.

CLIMATE

South America's mineral resources are highly localized. Few countries have both fossil fuels and metallic ores. The richest oilfields are in the north, especially in Venezuela. Coal, however, is scarce. When the Andes formed, heat helped create the many metallic minerals which are mined today.

MINERAL RESOURCES

- Bauxite
- Copper
- Iron
- Lead
- Silver
- Tin
- Oil/Gas field
- Coal field

COPPER MINES

Metallic mineral reserves are abundant in the Andes. Chuquicamata, northern Chile, is one of the world's largest copper mines.

ECONOMIC ACTIVITY

- Aerospace
- Brewing
- Car/vehicle manufacture
- Chemicals
- Coal
- Electronics
- Engineering
- Finance
- Fish processing
- Food processing
- Hi-tech industry
- Iron & steel
- Metal refining
- Narcotics
- Oil and gas
- Pharmaceuticals
- Printing & publishing
- Shipbuilding
- Textiles
- Timber processing
- Tobacco processing

GNI per capita (US$)

- Below 1,000
- 1,000-1,999
- 2,000-2,999
- 3,000-3,999
- 4,000-4,999
- Above 5,000
- Industrial centre

CLIMATE

South America has four main climatic regions; tropical, arid, temperate, and the cold climate of the far south. The Amazon Basin, covered by massive rain forests, and the Guiana Highlands have a humid, tropical climate which allows vegetation to flourish. West of the Andes the climate tends to be very dry. Moist air flowing west from the Atlantic Ocean is prevented from reaching the shores of the Pacific Ocean by the Andes and rain falls before it can pass over the mountains. This creates arid deserts like the Atacama.

EXTREME WEATHER EVENTS

Symbols indicate climatic extremes

Wettest place
QUIBDO (Colombia)
Annual rainfall 899cm

Driest place
ARICA (Chile)
Annual rainfall 0.08cm

Hottest place
RIVADAVIA (Argentina)
Temperature 49°C

Coldest place
SARMIENTO (Argentina)
Temperature -33°C

CLIMATE

- Subarctic
- Cool continental
- Warm temperate
- Semi-arid
- Arid
- Temperate
- Tropical
- Humid equatorial

PATAGONIAN ICEFIELDS

Towards the south of the continent, the climate becomes very cold. Large expanses of ice, forming glaciers are found in southern Patagonia and on islands such as Tierra del Fuego at the tip of South America.

LAND USE AND AGRICULTURE

Many plants now found throughout the world originated in South America, like the tomato, potato and cassava. Today, coffee, cocoa, rubber, soya beans, corn (maize), and sugarcane are widely cultivated, and grapes are grown in sheltered valleys in the Andes. Much of the Amazon Basin is covered by dense rainforest and is unsuitable for cultivation, although some farmers practise 'slash and burn' techniques to make land for crops and cattle farming, which destroy ancient forest.

LAND USE AND AGRICULTURE

- Cattle
- Pigs
- Sheep
- Bananas
- Corn (Maize)
- Citrus fruits
- Coca
- Cocoa
- Cotton
- Coffee
- Fishing
- Oil palms
- Peanuts
- Rubber
- Shellfish
- Soya beans
- Sugarcane
- Vineyards
- Wheat

- Barren land
- Cropland
- Desert
- Forest
- Mountain region
- Pasture
- Wetland
- • Major conurbation

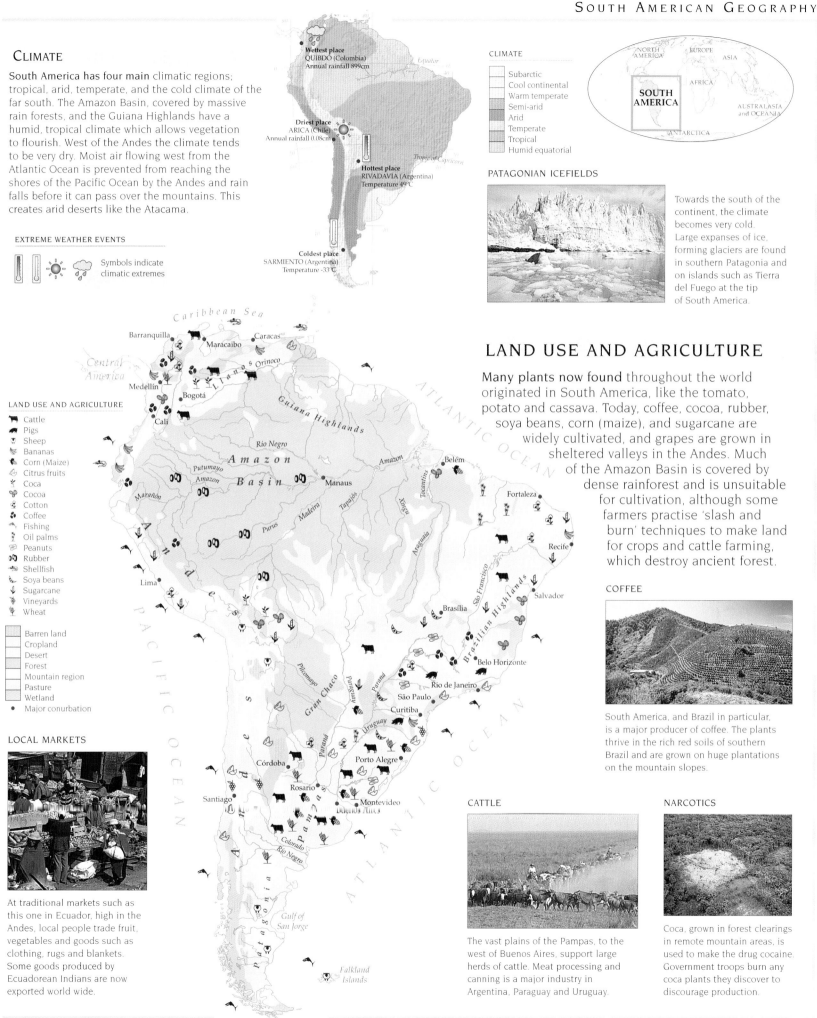

COFFEE

South America, and Brazil in particular, is a major producer of coffee. The plants thrive in the rich red soils of southern Brazil and are grown on huge plantations on the mountain slopes.

LOCAL MARKETS

At traditional markets such as this one in Ecuador, high in the Andes, local people trade fruit, vegetables and goods such as clothing, rugs and blankets. Some goods produced by Ecuadorean Indians are now exported world wide.

CATTLE

The vast plains of the Pampas, to the west of Buenos Aires, support large herds of cattle. Meat processing and canning is a major industry in Argentina, Paraguay and Uruguay.

NARCOTICS

Coca, grown in forest clearings in remote mountain areas, is used to make the drug cocaine. Government troops burn any coca plants they discover to discourage production.

NORTHERN SOUTH AMERICA

BRAZIL, COLOMBIA, ECUADOR, GUYANA, PERU, SURINAM, VENEZUELA

High mountains, steamy rain forests and hot, grassy plains cover much of northern South America. From the 16th century, after the conquest of the Incas, the western countries were ruled by Spain, while Brazil was governed by Portugal, Guyana by Britain, and Surinam by the Dutch. The more recent history of some of these countries has included periods of civil war and military rule. Most are still troubled by widespread poverty.

FARMING AND LAND USE

The variety of climates means a wide range of crops including sugarcane, cocoa and bananas can be grown for export. Coffee is the most important cash crop; Brazil is the world's leading coffee grower. Cattle are farmed on the plains of Colombia, Venezuela and southern Brazil. Much of the good farmland is owned by a few rich landowners, and many peasant farmers do not have enough land to make a living.

FARMING AND LAND USE

🐂 Cattle	⚓ Sugarcane		
🐟 Fishing	🎋 Timber		
🐐 Goats			
🐑 Sheep	Cropland		
🍌 Bananas	Forest		
🍫 Cocoa	Mountain region		
Cotton	Pasture		
☕ Coffee	Wetland		
Rubber	● Major conurbation		

LAND USE

Cropland 6%
Other (including mountains) 15%
Pasture 23%
Forest 56%

INDUSTRY

Important oil reserves are found in Venezuela and parts of the Amazon Basin; Venezuela is one of the world's top oil producers. Brazil's cities have a wide range of industries including chemicals, clothes and shoes, and textiles. Metallic minerals, particularly iron ore, are mined throughout the area and specially-built industrial centres like Ciudad Guayana have been developed to refine them.

STRUCTURE OF INDUSTRY

Primary 11%
Services 50%
Manufacturing 39%

INDUSTRY

✈ Aerospace	♠ Oil	
⚗ Chemicals	🎋 Timber processing	
Food processing	⚓ Tourism	
Iron & steel		
△ Metal refining	▣ Major industrial centre / area	
Textiles		
⛏ Mining	— Major road	

THE LANDSCAPE

The Andes run down the western side of South America. There are many volcanoes among their peaks, and earthquakes are common. The tropical rainforests surrounding the River Amazon take up most of western Brazil. Huge, dry, flat grasslands called *llanos* cover central Venezuela and part of eastern Colombia.

Angel Falls (D 2)
Venezuela's Angel Falls is the world's highest waterfall. Twenty times as high as Niagara Falls, it drops 979 m from a spectacular plateau deep in the Guiana Highlands.

River Amazon (D 4)
The Amazon is the longest river in South America, and the second longest in the world. It flows over 6,516 km from the Peruvian Andes to the coast of Brazil. One-fifth of the world's fresh water is carried by the river.

POPULATION

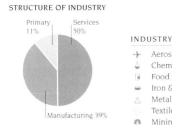

Most of the population lives in urban areas. Many cities are extremely overcrowded, with poor housing. São Paulo in Brazil is one of the world's fastest-growing cities. The rainforests of the interior and high Andes are sparsely populated. The few native American peoples live in remote areas.

INHABITANTS PER SQ KM

More than 200   ■ Capital city
100–200   ● Major city
50–100
10–50
Less than 10

URBAN/RURAL POPULATION DIVIDE

Rio de Janeiro 4%
São Paulo 6.4%
Bogotá 2.6%
Rural population 21%
Other towns and cities 66%

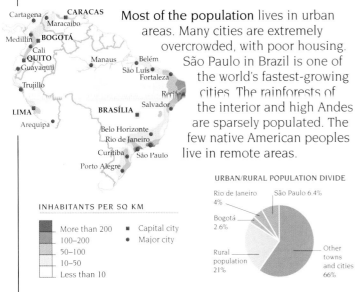

Andes (B 5)
The snow-capped Andes are the longest mountain range on Earth. They stretch 7,250 km down the whole length of South America.

Lake Titicaca (C 6)
South America's largest lake is the highest navigable lake in the world at 3,810 m above sea level. It lies across the border between Peru and Bolivia.

Pantanal (E 6)
This is the largest area of wetlands in the world. It spreads across 130,000 sq km of Brazil. Many hundreds of plant and animal species are found here.

Amazon rainforest (D 4)
The enormous rainforest surrounding the River Amazon and its tributaries covers 6,500,000 sq km, an area almost as big as Australia. It is estimated that at least half of all known living species are found in the forest.

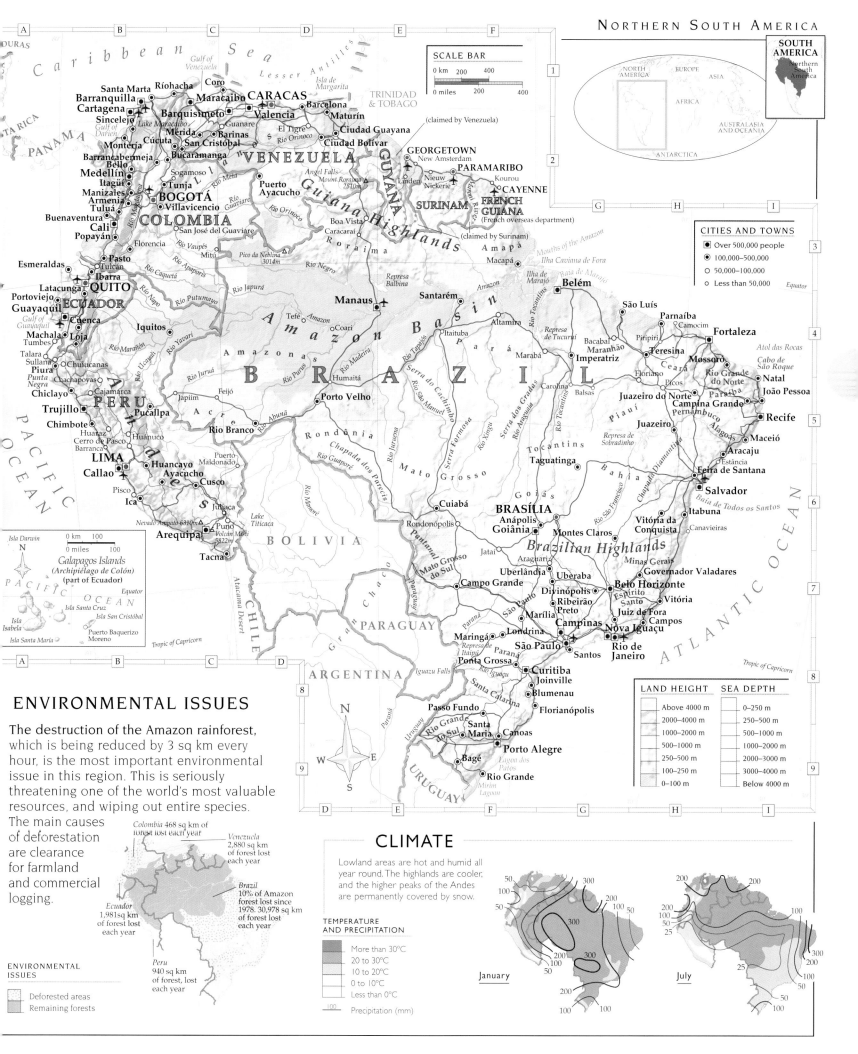

SOUTH AMERICA
Northern South America

SCALE BAR

0 km 200 400

0 miles 200 400

CITIES AND TOWNS
- ■ Over 500,000 people
- ◉ 100,000–500,000
- ○ 50,000–100,000
- ○ Less than 50,000

ENVIRONMENTAL ISSUES

The destruction of the Amazon rainforest, which is being reduced by 3 sq km every hour, is the most important environmental issue in this region. This is seriously threatening one of the world's most valuable resources, and wiping out entire species. The main causes of deforestation are clearance for farmland and commercial logging.

Colombia 468 sq km of forest lost each year

Venezuela 2,880 sq km of forest lost each year

Brazil 10% of Amazon forest lost since 1978. 30,978 sq km of forest lost each year

Ecuador 1,981 sq km of forest lost each year

Peru 940 sq km of forest, lost each year

ENVIRONMENTAL ISSUES
- Deforested areas
- Remaining forests

LAND HEIGHT	SEA DEPTH
Above 4000 m	0–250 m
2000–4000 m	250–500 m
1000–2000 m	500–1000 m
500–1000 m	1000–2000 m
250–500 m	2000–3000 m
100–250 m	3000–4000 m
0–100 m	Below 4000 m

CLIMATE

Lowland areas are hot and humid all year round. The highlands are cooler, and the higher peaks of the Andes are permanently covered by snow.

TEMPERATURE AND PRECIPITATION
- More than 30°C
- 20 to 30°C
- 10 to 20°C
- 0 to 10°C
- Less than 0°C
- Precipitation (mm)

January

July

SOUTHERN SOUTH AMERICA

ARGENTINA, BOLIVIA, CHILE, PARAGUAY, URUGUAY

The southern half of South America forms a long, narrow cone, with landscapes ranging from barren desert in the west, to frozen glaciers in the far south. The whole area was governed by Spain until the early 19th century, and Spanish is still the main language spoken, although the few remaining native American groups use their own languages. Most people now live in vast cities such as Buenos Aires and Santiago.

POPULATION

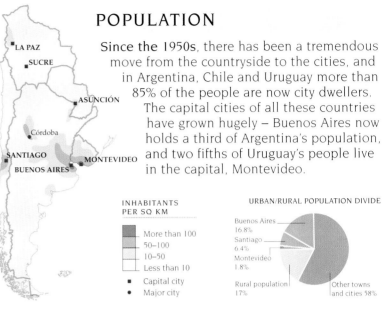

Since the 1950s, there has been a tremendous move from the countryside to the cities, and in Argentina, Chile and Uruguay more than 85% of the people are now city dwellers. The capital cities of all these countries have grown hugely – Buenos Aires now holds a third of Argentina's population, and two fifths of Uruguay's people live in the capital, Montevideo.

INHABITANTS PER SQ KM
- More than 100
- 50–100
- 10–50
- Less than 10
- ■ Capital city
- ● Major city

URBAN/RURAL POPULATION DIVIDE
- Buenos Aires 16.8%
- Santiago 6.4%
- Montevideo 1.8%
- Rural population 17%
- Other towns and cities 58%

INDUSTRY

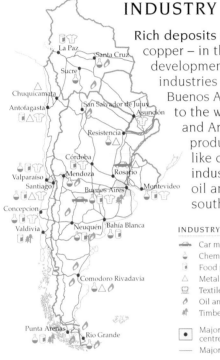

Rich deposits of minerals – especially copper – in the Andes have led to the development of large metal refining industries in Chile. The capital cities, Buenos Aires and Santiago, are home to the widest range of industries and Argentina is an important producer of processed foods like canned beef. There are fewer industries in the south, although oil and gas are extracted in southern Argentina and Chile.

INDUSTRY
- Car manufacture
- Chemicals
- Food processing
- Metal refining
- Textiles
- Oil and gas
- Timber processing
- Major industrial centre / area
- Major road

STRUCTURE OF INDUSTRY
- Primary 10%
- Services 55%
- Manufacturing 35%

THE LANDSCAPE

Southern South America's landscape varies from tropical forest and dry desert in the north, to sub-Antarctic conditions in the south. The towering Andes divide Chile from Argentina. East of the Andes lie forests and rolling grasslands. To the west is a thin coastal strip. The wet, windswept, freezing southern tip of the continent has volcanoes alongside glaciers and fjords.

Gran Chaco (C3)
This huge stretch of forest and grassland runs from Bolivia, through Paraguay and into Argentina. The south and east provide grazing for cattle.

The Paraná River (C4)
South America's second longest river is the Paraná. It stretches 4,000 km from the Brazilian Highlands, finally flowing into the River Plate near Buenos Aires in Argentina.

Iguazu Falls (D4)
The Iguazu River drops 80 m over the Iguazu Falls. When the river is at its fullest, the water flowing over the falls could fill six Olympic swimming pools every second.

Atacama Desert (A3)
The Atacama Desert in northern Chile is the driest place on Earth. In some parts, rain has not fallen for hundreds of years.

The Pampas (B5)
The grassy plains in central Argentina – known as the Pampas – cover 650,000 sq km. The western part is semi-desert, but the east gets plenty of rain.

Chile
The far south of Chile has a dramatic landscape of fjords, lakes, jagged mountain peaks and spectacular glaciers.

Patagonia (B8)
The high, windswept plateau of Patagonia covers 770,000 sq km of southern Argentina. The south is dry and freezing cold, with very little vegetation.

ENVIRONMENTAL ISSUES

Many of southern South America's rivers are polluted, particularly close to Buenos Aires. The Itaipú Dam on the Paraná River is the world's largest hydro-electric power project. Deforestation is a persistent problem in Bolivia, Paraguay and northern Argentina with 6,000 sq km cut down every year. Air quality in Buenos Aires and Santiago is poor, especially in Santiago which is surrounded by mountains, making it difficult for pollution to escape.

ENVIRONMENTAL ISSUES
- Major dam
- Urban air pollution
- Deforested areas
- Polluted river
- Major industrial centre

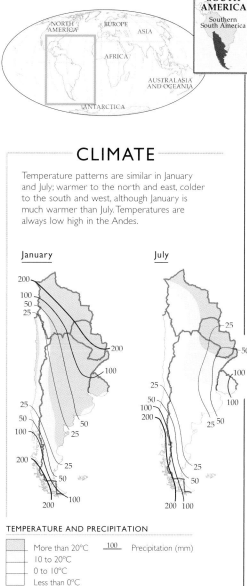

SOUTH AMERICA
Southern
South America

LAND HEIGHT

- Above 4000 m
- 2000–4000 m
- 1000–2000 m
- 500–1000 m
- 250–500 m
- 100–250 m
- 0–100 m

SEA DEPTH

- 0–250 m
- 250–500 m
- 500–1000 m
- 1000–2000 m
- 2000–3000 m
- 3000–4000 m
- Below 4000 m

CITIES AND TOWNS

- ■ Over 500,000 people
- ◉ 100,000–500,000
- ◎ 50,000–100,000
- ○ Less than 50,000

BOLIVIA'S TWO CAPITALS

LA PAZ – legislative and administrative capital

SUCRE – legal capital

CLIMATE

Temperature patterns are similar in January and July; warmer to the north and east, colder to the south and west, although January is much warmer than July. Temperatures are always low high in the Andes.

January

July

TEMPERATURE AND PRECIPITATION

- More than 20°C
- 10 to 20°C
- 0 to 10°C
- Less than 0°C

100 — Precipitation (mm)

SCALE BAR

0 km — 200 — 400

0 miles — 200 — 400

FALKLAND ISLANDS
(UK dependent territory)

N W E S

FARMING AND LAND USE

The enormous grasslands to the east of the Andes provide good grazing for cattle and sheep, and Argentina is one of the world's leading suppliers of meat, milk and hides. The country is also an important grower of wheat and fruit. Chile is the world's top producer of fishmeal, and grows grapes for its successful wine industry, and for eating. The illegal growing of coca, used to make the drug cocaine, is a major source of income in Bolivia.

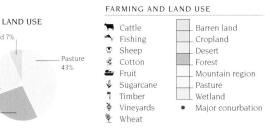

LAND USE

- Cropland 7%
- Pasture 43%
- Other (including mountains) 23%
- Forest 27%

FARMING AND LAND USE

- 🐄 Cattle
- 🎣 Fishing
- 🐑 Sheep
- Cotton
- Fruit
- Sugarcane
- Timber
- Vineyards
- Wheat
- Barren land
- Cropland
- Desert
- Forest
- Mountain region
- Pasture
- Wetland
- ● Major conurbation

CONTINENTAL AFRICA

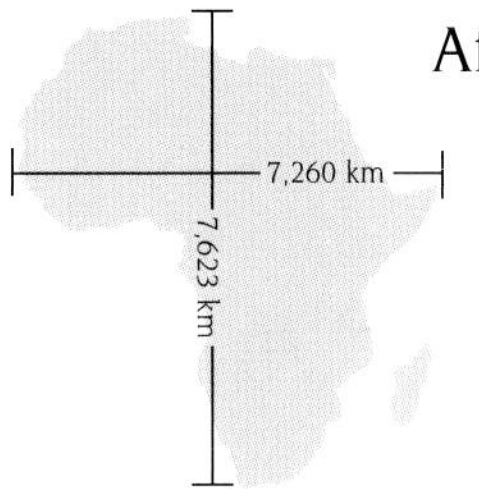

Africa is the second largest continent in the world. Its dramatic landscapes include arid deserts, humid rainforests, and the valleys of the east African rift – the place where humans first evolved. Today, there are 53 separate countries in Africa, and its people speak a rich variety of languages. The world's highest temperatures have been recorded in Africa's deserts.

7,260 km

7,623 km

CROSS-SECTION THROUGH AFRICA

Niger Delta · Congo Basin · Great Rift Valley · Ethiopian Highlands · Lake Victoria · Horn of Africa

W ⊢ 5,200 km ⊣ E

In the west, the Niger River flows into the Atlantic Ocean through the swampy Niger Delta. Further east is the immense Congo Basin, where the Congo River winds its way through thick rainforests. In the east is the Great Rift Valley, and the Ethiopian Highlands. The Horn of Africa is Africa's most easterly point.

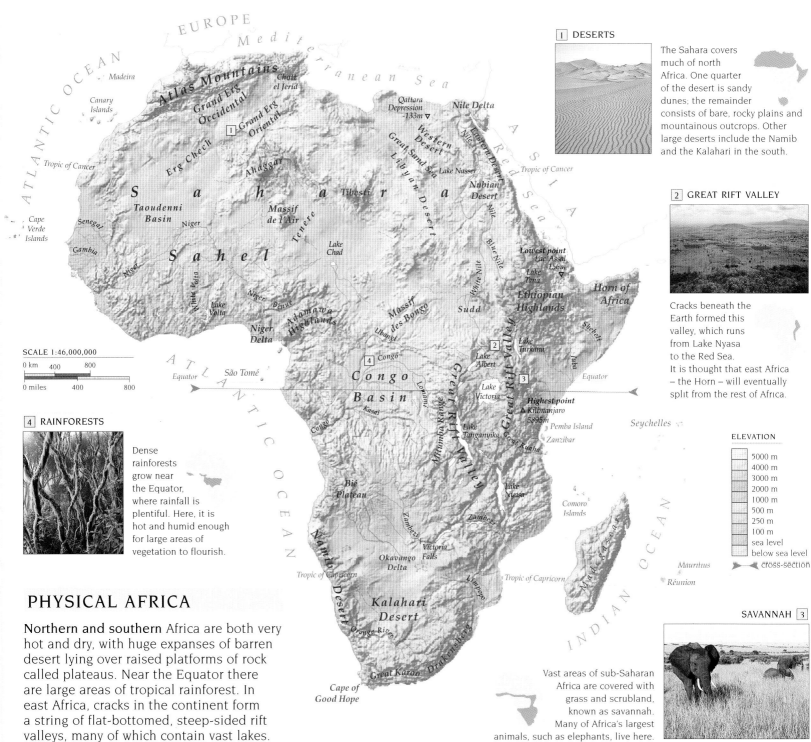

1 DESERTS

The Sahara covers much of north Africa. One quarter of the desert is sandy dunes; the remainder consists of bare, rocky plains and mountainous outcrops. Other large deserts include the Namib and the Kalahari in the south.

2 GREAT RIFT VALLEY

Cracks beneath the Earth formed this valley, which runs from Lake Nyasa to the Red Sea. It is thought that east Africa – the Horn – will eventually split from the rest of Africa.

4 RAINFORESTS

Dense rainforests grow near the Equator, where rainfall is plentiful. Here, it is hot and humid enough for large areas of vegetation to flourish.

ELEVATION

5000 m
4000 m
3000 m
2000 m
1000 m
500 m
250 m
100 m
sea level
below sea level
cross-section

SAVANNAH 3

Vast areas of sub-Saharan Africa are covered with grass and scrubland, known as savannah. Many of Africa's largest animals, such as elephants, live here.

PHYSICAL AFRICA

Northern and southern Africa are both very hot and dry, with huge expanses of barren desert lying over raised platforms of rock called plateaus. Near the Equator there are large areas of tropical rainforest. In east Africa, cracks in the continent form a string of flat-bottomed, steep-sided rift valleys, many of which contain vast lakes.

SCALE 1:46,000,000

0 km   400   800
0 miles   400   800

Map labels: EUROPE, Mediterranean Sea, ATLANTIC OCEAN, Madeira, Canary Islands, Atlas Mountains, Chott el Jerid, Grand Erg Occidental, Grand Erg Oriental, Qattara Depression -133m, Nile Delta, Western Desert, Great Sand Sea, Lake Nasser, Eastern Desert, Red Sea, Tropic of Cancer, Erg Chech, Ahaggar, Tibesti, Libyan Desert, Nile, Nubian Desert, ASIA, Sahara, Taoudenni Basin, Massif de l'Air, Ténéré, Senegal, Niger, Cape Verde Islands, Gambia, Sahel, Lake Chad, Blue Nile, Lowest point Lac Assal -156m, Lake Tana, Ethiopian Highlands, Horn of Africa, White Nile, Shebeli, White Volta, Lake Volta, Niger, Benue, Adamawa Highlands, Massif des Bongo, Sudd, Juba, Niger Delta, Ubangi, Lake Turkana, São Tomé, Equator, ATLANTIC OCEAN, Congo, Lake Albert, Lake Victoria, Highest point Kilimanjaro 5895m, Pemba Island, Seychelles, Equator, Congo Basin, Kasai, Lomami, Lomani, Mitumba Range, Great Rift Valley, Lake Tanganyika, Great Ruaha, Zanzibar, Bié Plateau, Lake Nyasa, Comoro Islands, Zambezi, Namib Desert, Okavango Delta, Victoria Falls, Zambezi, Madagascar, INDIAN OCEAN, Mauritius, Réunion, Tropic of Capricorn, Kalahari Desert, Orange River, Limpopo, Tropic of Capricorn, Great Karoo, Drakensberg, Cape of Good Hope

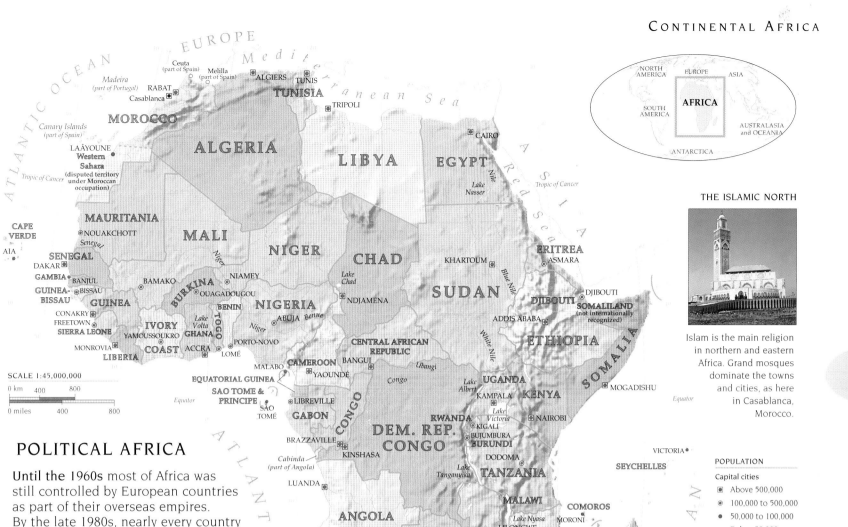

THE ISLAMIC NORTH

Islam is the main religion in northern and eastern Africa. Grand mosques dominate the towns and cities, as here in Casablanca, Morocco.

POLITICAL AFRICA

Until the 1960s most of Africa was still controlled by European countries as part of their overseas empires. By the late 1980s, nearly every country had gained its independence. Many problems must still be solved in order to improve quality of life, and several countries have experienced severe droughts and civil wars. Fifteen countries are land-locked, which means that they do not have access to the sea. This restricts their trade and communications.

CITY LIFE

Most Africans still live in rural areas, although there are large cities, like Cairo in Egypt. Cairo is the continent's largest city and 15.3 million people live here.

POPULATION

Capital cities
- ◉ Above 500,000
- ◉ 100,000 to 500,000
- ● 50,000 to 100,000
- • Below 50,000

Other cities
- ○ 50,000 to 100,000

INDEPENDENCE

This grand cathedral at Yamoussoukro, Ivory Coast, has been built since independence, when the city became the country's new capital. Building a new capital symbolized the break from Ivory Coast's colonial past.

POPULATION

Despite its great size, Africa's population is relatively low, especially in the desert areas. The highest populations are found where water and fertile land are available. African birth rates are high which means that populations are increasing rapidly.

POPULATION DENSITY
(People per sq km)

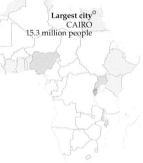

Largest city
CAIRO
15.3 million people

Below 49	100–149	200–299
50–99	150–199	Above 300

CONFLICT AND WARFARE

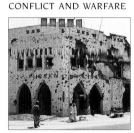

Many African nations contain several ethnic groups, who often have little in common. Inter-ethnic conflict has led to bitter civil war; these buildings in Ndjamena, Chad's capital, still bear the scars.

STANDARDS OF LIVING

The majority of Africa's people have a very simple way of life, although access to western consumer goods is growing. In many countries standards of health and literacy are improving slowly through education programmes.

STANDARD OF LIVING
(UN Human Development Index)

low ▢▢▢▢▢ high

AFRICAN GEOGRAPHY

Africa's massive reserves of minerals, including oil, gold, copper and diamonds, are amongst the largest in the world. Mining is a very important industry for many countries, and has provided money for growth and development. Africa's wide range of environments means that many different types of crops can be grown. Rubber, bananas and oil palms are grown for export in the tropics, and east Africa is especially famous for its tea and coffee.

INDUSTRY

Most African industries are based on processing raw materials such as food crops or mineral ores. Some African countries depend on one product or crop for most of their income, but in many larger cities different industries are developing. Northern Africa, Nigeria, and South Africa have the widest range of industries.

MINERAL RESOURCES

The southern countries, in particular South Africa, have large reserves of diamonds, gold, uranium and copper. The large copper deposits in Dem. Rep. Congo and Zambia are known as the 'copper belt'. Oil and gas are extracted in Algeria, Angola, Egypt, Libya, and Nigeria.

MINING

One of the world's largest uranium mines is at Rössing, Namibia. Uranium is used to fuel nuclear power stations. and is also mined in Niger and South Africa,

MINERAL RESOURCES

- Bauxite
- Copper
- Diamonds
- Iron
- Phosphates
- Gold
- Uranium
- Oil/gas field
- Coal field

OIL AND GAS

In the desert wastes of Algeria, a drilling rig searches for new sources of oil in the rich north African oilfields. There are several large oil fields in the Niger delta, and north Africa.

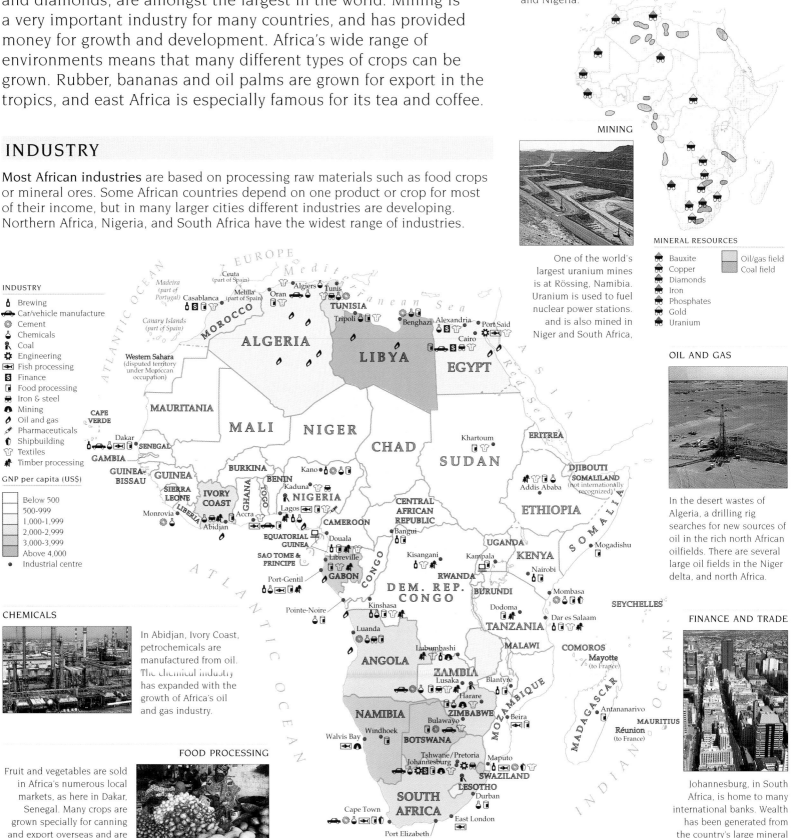

INDUSTRY

- Brewing
- Car/vehicle manufacture
- Cement
- Chemicals
- Coal
- Engineering
- Fish processing
- Finance
- Food processing
- Iron & steel
- Mining
- Oil and gas
- Pharmaceuticals
- Shipbuilding
- Textiles
- Timber processing

GNP per capita (US$)

- Below 500
- 500-999
- 1,000-1,999
- 2,000-2,999
- 3,000-3,999
- Above 4,000
- Industrial centre

CHEMICALS

In Abidjan, Ivory Coast, petrochemicals are manufactured from oil. The chemical industry has expanded with the growth of Africa's oil and gas industry.

FOOD PROCESSING

Fruit and vegetables are sold in Africa's numerous local markets, as here in Dakar, Senegal. Many crops are grown specially for canning and export overseas and are known as 'cash crops.'

FINANCE AND TRADE

Johannesburg, in South Africa, is home to many international banks. Wealth has been generated from the country's large mineral resources, such as diamonds.

CLIMATE

Africa is the world's hottest continent: temperatures of more than 50°C have been recorded in the Sahara. The northern coast has a hot, dry climate with little rainfall. Further inland, the Sahara is extremely arid, with strong, dry winds. South of the Sahara is the Sahel, where cutting down trees for fuel has turned farmland into desert. Close to the Equator there is more rainfall, and huge rainforests can grow in western and central Africa. In the south, the climate is much drier, and drought is a problem.

EXTREME WEATHER EVENTS

Symbols indicate climatic extremes

Coldest place
IFRANE (Morocco)
Temperature -24°C

Tropic of Cancer

Hottest place
AL 'AZĪZĪYAH (Libya)
Temperature 58°C

Driest place
WADI HALFA (Sudan)
Annual rainfall <2.5mm

Equator

Wettest place
CAPE DEBUNDSHA (Cameroon)
Annual rainfall 10290mm

Tropic of Capricorn

CLIMATE

- Warm temperate
- Mediterranean
- Semi-arid
- Arid
- Humid equatorial
- Tropical

AFRICA

THE ENCROACHING DESERT

Africa has three main desert areas: the Sahara in the north and the Namib and Kalahari deserts in the south. They are a mixture of sandy dunes and bare, rocky plateaus. At the desert's edges, low rainfall and land clearance is causing the deserts to expand into areas that were once grassland.

LAND USE AND AGRICULTURE

The quality of land and the amount of rainfall has a great impact on the type of farming. In the mountain regions of countries such as Rwanda, Uganda, and Kenya, tea and coffee are grown. In the north, there is not enough water to produce staple crops such as wheat for all the population, but 'cash crops' such as citrus fruits, dates and olives are grown for export. Sub-tropical west Africa grows peanuts, cocoa and coffee. In the southern part of the continent, South Africa grows many different crops: citrus fruits are grown for export, as well as grapes, which are used to make wine.

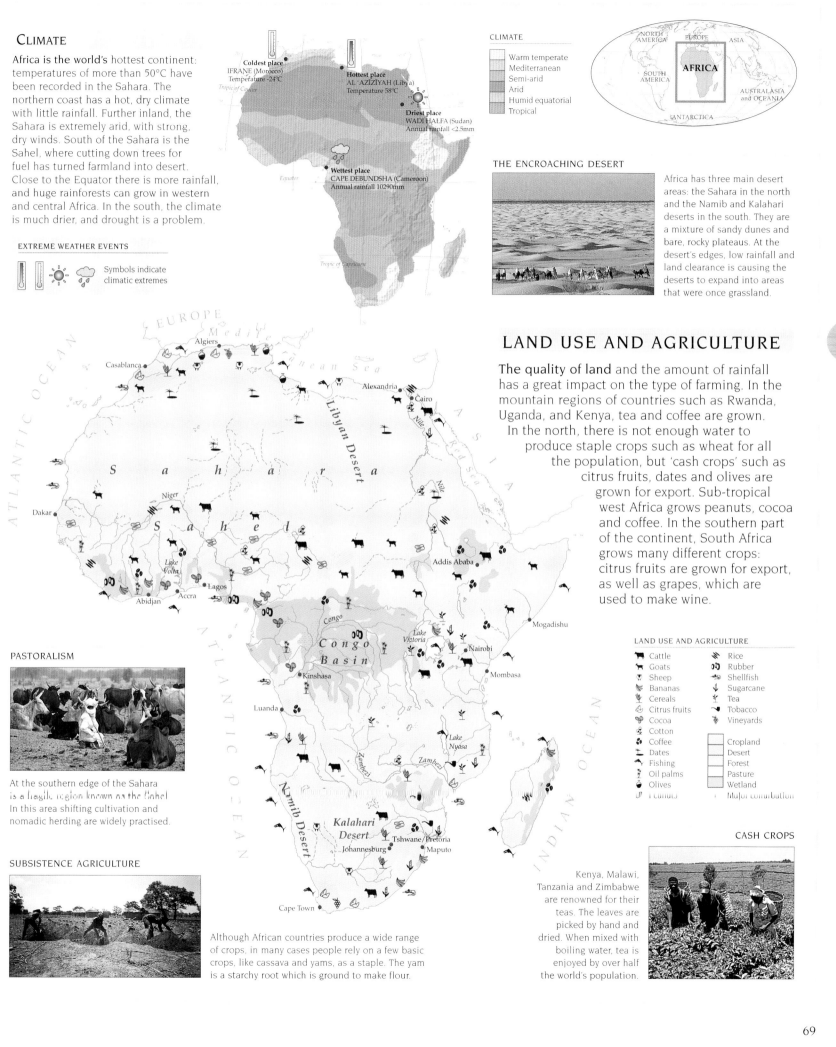

PASTORALISM

At the southern edge of the Sahara is a fragile region known as the Sahel. In this area shifting cultivation and nomadic herding are widely practised.

SUBSISTENCE AGRICULTURE

Although African countries produce a wide range of crops, in many cases people rely on a few basic crops, like cassava and yams, as a staple. The yam is a starchy root which is ground to make flour.

LAND USE AND AGRICULTURE

- Cattle
- Goats
- Sheep
- Bananas
- Cereals
- Citrus fruits
- Cocoa
- Cotton
- Coffee
- Dates
- Fishing
- Oil palms
- Olives
- Peanuts
- Rice
- Rubber
- Shellfish
- Sugarcane
- Tea
- Tobacco
- Vineyards

- Cropland
- Desert
- Forest
- Pasture
- Wetland
- Major conurbation

CASH CROPS

Kenya, Malawi, Tanzania and Zimbabwe are renowned for their teas. The leaves are picked by hand and dried. When mixed with boiling water, tea is enjoyed by over half the world's population.

NORTH AFRICA

ALGERIA, EGYPT, LIBYA, MOROCCO, TUNISIA.

Sandwiched between the Mediterranean and the Sahara, North Africa has a history dating back to the dawn of civilization. 6,000 years ago, settlements were established along the banks of the River Nile, and since that time, waves of settlers, including Romans, Arabs and Turks have brought a mix of different cultures to the area. In the 19th century, Spain, France and Britain claimed colonies in the region, but today North Africa is independent, although Western Sahara is occupied by Morocco.

FARMING AND LAND USE

Most farming in North Africa is restricted to the fertile Mediterranean coastal strip, and the banks of the Nile where it relies heavily on irrigation. In spite of these seemingly inhospitable conditions, the region is a major producer of dates, which grow in desert oases, and of cork, made from the bark of the cork oak tree. A wide variety of other crops is also grown, including grapes, olives and cotton.

FARMING AND LAND USE

- Fishing
- Goats
- Sheep
- Citrus Fruits
- Cork
- Cotton
- Dates
- Olives
- Vineyards

- Cropland
- Desert
- Forest
- Pasture
- Major conurbation

CLIMATE

Most of north Africa is desert, and the climate is harsh. Rainfall is scarce, and drought is common. Temperatures are freezing at night, scorching by day and have been known to climb to over 50°C.

January

July

whole area has below 25mm rainfall

LAND USE

Forest 1%

Pasture 13%

Cropland 5%

Other (including desert) 81%

TEMPERATURE AND PRECIPITATION

- More than 35°C
- 30 to 35°C
- 25 to 30°C
- 20 to 25°C
- 15 to 20°C
- 10 to 15°C
- 5 to 10°C
- Less than 5°C

100 — Precipitation (mm)

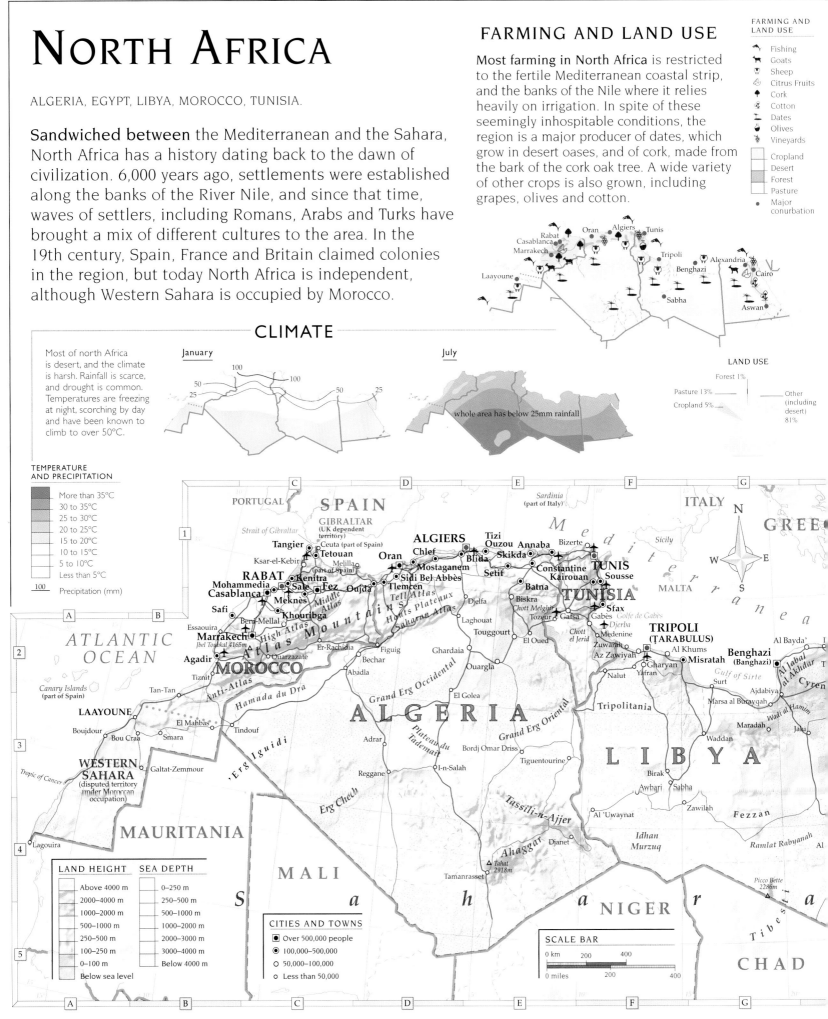

LAND HEIGHT
- Above 4000 m
- 2000–4000 m
- 1000–2000 m
- 500–1000 m
- 250–500 m
- 100–250 m
- 0–100 m
- Below sea level

SEA DEPTH
- 0–250 m
- 250–500 m
- 500–1000 m
- 1000–2000 m
- 2000–3000 m
- 3000–4000 m
- Below 4000 m

CITIES AND TOWNS
- ■ Over 500,000 people
- ◉ 100,000–500,000
- ○ 50,000–100,000
- ○ Less than 50,000

SCALE BAR

0 km   200   400

0 miles   200   400

POPULATION

The majority of the population, and all of the big towns and cities, are found on the coastal plains, or along the banks of the Nile – about 99% of Egyptians live along the river. Egypt's capital, Cairo, is Africa's largest city, with over 15 million people. Western Sahara, and the southern portions of Egypt, Algeria and Libya are sparsely populated by Tuareg nomads who roam the Sahara.

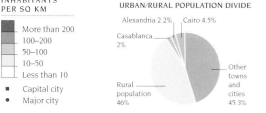

INHABITANTS PER SQ KM

- More than 200
- 100–200
- 50–100
- 10–50
- Less than 10
- ■ Capital city
- ● Major city

URBAN/RURAL POPULATION DIVIDE

Alexandria 2.2%
Cairo 4.5%
Casablanca 2%
Rural population 46%
Other towns and cities 45.3%

THE LANDSCAPE

The parched rocks and endless sandy expanses of the Sahara occupy much of North Africa. The only major river here is the Nile, with a delta that extends into the Mediterranean Sea. The old, eroded Atlas Mountains are the highest mountain range.

Sand dunes
Winds blowing across the Sahara cause the sand to build up into dunes which can reach heights of up to 430 m.

Nile Delta (I2)
As the River Nile nears the Mediterranean, it separates into many small streams, which flow over a fertile triangle of land. Mud and rock carried by the river and deposited in the delta have formed new land.

Red Sea (J3)
The Red Sea may get its name from red algae that live on the sea floor and occasionally make the water appear red during algae blooms.

Atlas Mountains (C2)
The Atlas Mountains are made up of a number of different ranges – the Anti-Atlas, High Atlas, Middle Atlas, Tell Atlas and Saharan Atlas. They stretch some 2,250 km from the north of Tunisia to the Atlantic coast of Morocco.

Qattara Depression (I3)
In the northwest of Egypt is a huge desert depression 320 km long and 120 km wide. Its floor, part of which is 134 m below sea level, is covered with sand, brackish ponds and salt marshes.

The River Nile (I3)
The world's longest river flows 6,695 km to the Mediterranean Sea. The system of rivers and lakes that flow into the Nile drain some 2,850,000 sq km – about 10% of the entire African continent.

INDUSTRY

Oil and natural gas have brought wealth to the area, particularly to Libya, which has enough oil reserves to last into the middle of this century. Textile manufacture is widespread – North Africa is famous for its exotic cloths and rugs. Several large chemical refineries and steel plants have been established along the coast, especially in the major industrial cities like Alexandria and Cairo in Egypt.

STRUCTURE OF INDUSTRY

Primary 16%
Services 44%
Manufacturing 40%

INDUSTRY

- Chemicals
- Food processing
- Iron and steel
- Textiles
- Oil and gas
- Tourism
- ● Major industrial centre / area
- — Major road

ENVIRONMENTAL ISSUES

Droughts, overgrazing and the stripping of vegetation for fuelwood and animal fodder have caused the Sahara to expand northwards. This has reduced the already limited amount of land available for farming. The risk of desertification is acute in many coastal areas. North Africa is very dry, and there are severe droughts periodically. Many of the larger cities like Alexandria and Cairo have very poor air quality.

ENVIRONMENTAL ISSUES

- Drought
- Urban air pollution
- Existing desert
- Risk of desertification
- Severe risk of desertification
- Non-affected area
- ● Major industrial centre

WEST AFRICA

BENIN, BURKINA, CAMEROON, CENTRAL AFRICAN REPUBLIC, CHAD, EQUATORIAL GUINEA, GAMBIA, GHANA, GUINEA, GUINEA-BISSAU, IVORY COAST, LIBERIA, MALI, MAURITANIA, NIGER, NIGERIA, SAO TOME & PRINCIPE, SENEGAL, SIERRA LEONE, TOGO

West Africa's varied climate and agricultural and mineral wealth have provided the foundation for some of Africa's greatest civilizations, like those of the Malinke and Asante people. The area remains ethnically and culturally diverse today, as well as densely populated; Nigeria is by far the most populous country in Africa. Since independence from European colonial powers in the 1960s, political instability has been a feature of many countries here.

INDUSTRY

Agricultural products still form the basis of most economies in West Africa. Food processing is widespread – oil palms and peanuts are processed for their valuable vegetable oils. Oil and gas are found off the coast of Ivory Coast and around the Niger delta, where a large chemical industry has developed.

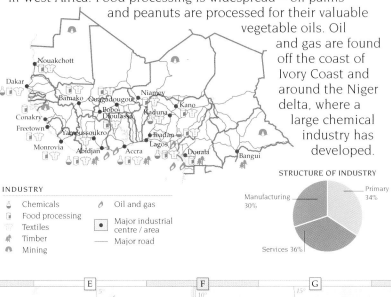

INDUSTRY

Chemicals	Oil and gas
Food processing	Major industrial centre / area
Textiles	Major road
Timber	
Mining	

STRUCTURE OF INDUSTRY

Manufacturing 30%
Primary 34%
Services 36%

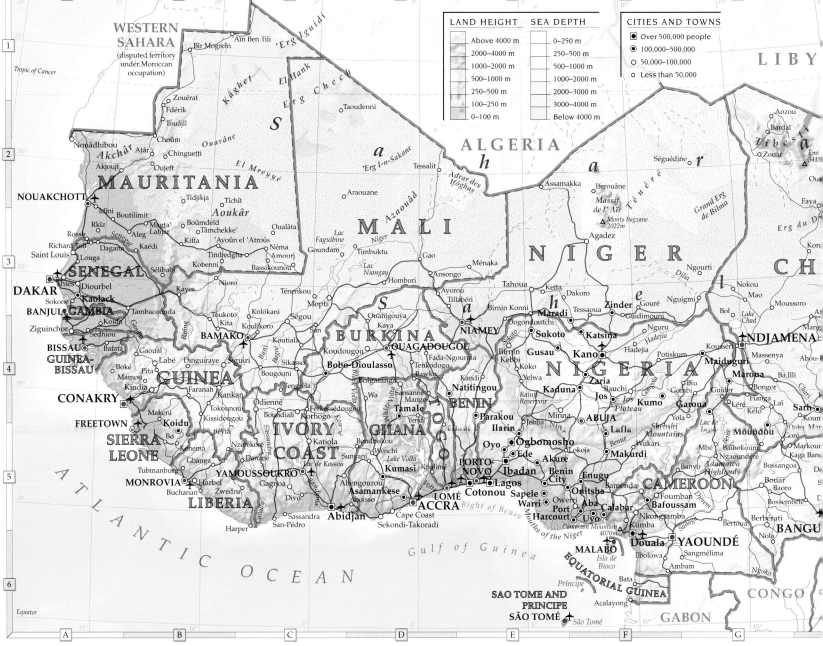

FARMING AND LAND USE

Well-watered land along the coast allows a wide variety of crops to be grown, including cocoa and oil palms, both of which provide important cash crops. In the drier north, goats and sheep are grazed, and subsistence crops such as yams, millet and cassava are grown.

FARMING AND LAND USE

- 🐐 Goats
- 🐑 Sheep
- 🦐 Shellfish
- 🌿 Cassava
- 🌰 Cocoa
- 🌼 Cotton
- 🌾 Millet
- 🌴 Oil palms
- 🥜 Peanuts
- Cropland
- Desert
- Forest
- Pasture
- Wetland
- ● Major conurbation

Dakar, Conakry, Monrovia, Abidjan, Accra, Cotonou, Ibadan, Lagos, Yaoundé, Bangui, Ndjamena

LAND USE

Cropland 10%
Pasture 26%
Forest 16%
Other (including desert) 48%

CLIMATE

The climate differs immensely from the hot desert north, through to the tropical rainforest south. July is the wet season, and rainfall is heavy in the south, while the desert areas remain dry throughout the year.

January | July

TEMPERATURE AND PRECIPITATION

- More than 35°C
- 30 to 35°C
- 25 to 30°C
- 20 to 25°C
- Less than 20°C
- 100 — Precipitation (mm)

ENVIRONMENTAL ISSUES

Persistent droughts are the main concerns in the north of the region. The problem is made worse by a shortage of wood needed for fuel, which leads to the cutting down of any available trees for fuelwood. In the tropical south, the timber industry is destroying much of the ancient forest. In 2007 huge floods affected almost all of the region.

1968–1977, 1983–1985, 2003, 2005–2006, 2007, 1973–1974
1968–1977, 1982–1985, 1991, 1993, 1997, 2001, 2005–2006, 2007
1971–1974, 1983–1985, 1967–1974, 1983–1985, 1971–1974, 1983–1984

ENVIRONMENTAL ISSUES

- Drought
- Severe fuelwood shortage
- Flooding
- Existing desert
- Risk of desertification
- Severe risk of desertification
- Deforested area

POPULATION

Most of the population lives in the southern coastal regions. In the drier north, settlement becomes more sporadic, and nomadic tribespeople are best suited to live in the desert north. Nigeria is the most populated country in Africa and Lagos is one of the continent's larger cities, although West Africa's population remains mainly rural.

INHABITANTS PER SQ KM

- More than 200
- 100–200
- 50–100
- 10–50
- Less than 10
- ■ Capital city
- ● Major city

NOUAKCHOTT, DAKAR, BANJUL, BISSAU, CONAKRY, FREETOWN, MONROVIA, BAMAKO, OUAGADOUGOU, NIAMEY, ABUJA, PORTO-NOVO, ACCRA, Abidjan, Lagos, YAOUNDÉ, Port Harcourt, Kano, Kaduna, NDJAMENA, BANGUI

URBAN/RURAL POPULATION DIVIDE

Abidjan 1.1% Lagos 1.9%
Kano 0.8%
Other towns and cities 36.2%
Rural population 60%

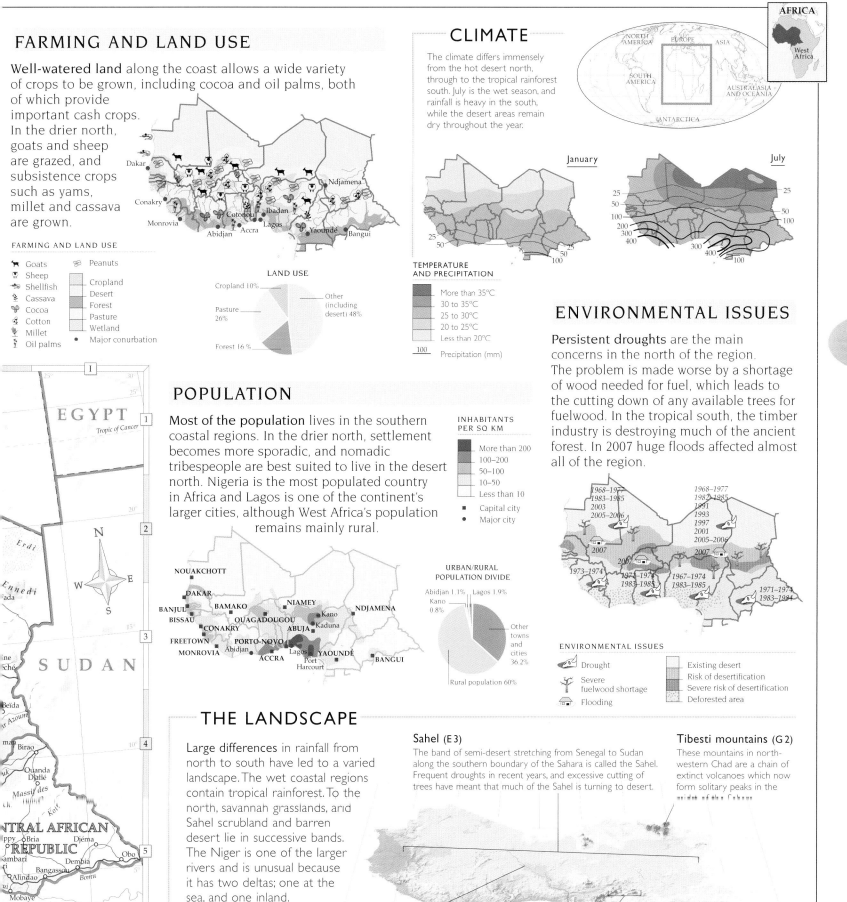

THE LANDSCAPE

Large differences in rainfall from north to south have led to a varied landscape. The wet coastal regions contain tropical rainforest. To the north, savannah grasslands, arid Sahel scrubland and barren desert lie in successive bands. The Niger is one of the larger rivers and is unusual because it has two deltas; one at the sea, and one inland.

Sahel (E 3)

The band of semi-desert stretching from Senegal to Sudan along the southern boundary of the Sahara is called the Sahel. Frequent droughts in recent years, and excessive cutting of trees have meant that much of the Sahel is turning to desert.

Tibesti mountains (G 2)

These mountains in north-western Chad are a chain of extinct volcanoes which now form solitary peaks in the
midst of the Sahara.

River Niger (D 3)

The River Niger is West Africa's longest river. When it reaches the sea, it flows through a vast delta of mud flats and mangrove swamps. Great oil deposits have been found here.

Adamawa Highlands (G 5)

This mountainous spine separates West Africa from the vast Congo Basin to the southeast.

EGYPT
Tropic of Cancer
SUDAN
NTRAL AFRICAN REPUBLIC
EM. REP. CONGO
Equator

N, E, S, W

SCALE BAR
km 200 400
miles 200 400

Erdi, Ennedi, Beïda, Azoum, Birao, Ouanda Djallé, Massif des, Kou, ppy, Bria, Djéma, Obo, Dembia, Bangassou, Bomu, Alindao, Mobaye

EAST AFRICA

BURUNDI, DJIBOUTI, ERITREA, ETHIOPIA, KENYA, RWANDA, SOMALIA, SUDAN, TANZANIA, UGANDA

Much of East Africa is covered by long grass, scrub and scattered trees, called savannah. This land is grazed by both domestic animals and a great variety of wild animals including lions, giraffes and elephants. The east of the region is known as the Horn of Africa, because it is shaped like an animal horn. Along with Sudan, the countries there have recently been devastated by civil wars, and periods of drought and famine. In contrast, Kenya in the south is more stable but still has to battle with corruption.

FARMING AND LAND USE

Much of the north and east is too dry for farming, but in Sudan, cotton is grown on land irrigated by the River Nile. The Lake Victoria basin and rich volcanic soils of the highlands in Kenya, Uganda and Tanzania support staple food crops, and those grown for export, such as tea and coffee. Kenya also grows high-quality vegetables, like mangetout, and exports them by air to supermarkets abroad. Sheep, goats and cattle are herded on the savannah.

LAND USE

Cropland 9%
Pasture 40%
Other 26%
Forest 25%

FARMING AND LAND USE

- Cattle
- Fishing
- Goats
- Sheep
- Bananas
- Coffee
- Cotton
- Dates
- Market gardening
- Sugarcane
- Sisal
- Tea

Cropland
Desert
Forest
Pasture
Wetland
- Major conurbation

INDUSTRY

East Africa has few mineral resources, and industry is mainly based on processing raw materials. Coffee, tea, sugarcane and sisal, are harvested and processed before being exported. Textile production is widespread, but is only on a small scale. Tourism is increasingly important in Kenya and Tanzania; each year, many thousands of people visit the wildlife reserves there.

INDUSTRY

- Cement manufacturing
- Chemicals
- Food processing
- Textiles
- Tourism
- Major industrial centre / area
- Major road

STRUCTURE OF INDUSTRY

Primary 38%
Services 44%
Manufacturing 18%

THE LANDSCAPE

The south of East Africa is savannah grassland, broken by the rugged mountains – some of them active volcanoes – and large fresh and saltwater lakes that make up part of the Great Rift Valley. The River Nile has its source here, flowing through lakes Victoria, Kyoga and Albert as it takes much-needed water to the arid desert areas in the north.

Great Rift Valley (D 6) (D 4)
The Great Rift Valley is like a deep scar running 7,000 km from north to south through East Africa. It has been formed by the movements of two of the Earth's plates over millions of years. If these movements continue, East Africa may eventually become an island, separated by the ocean from the rest of the continent.

Sudd (B 4)
The north of Sudan is rocky desert, but in the south, the waters of the White Nile run into a swampy area called the Sudd where much of its water disperses and evaporates.

River Juba (E 5)
This river rises in the highlands of Ethiopia and flows some 1,200 km southwards to the Indian Ocean. It, and the River Shebeli, which joins it about 30 km from the coast, are the only permanent rivers in Somalia.

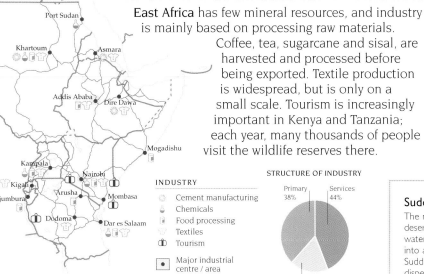

Lake Victoria (C 5)
Lake Victoria is Africa's largest lake and the second largest freshwater lake in the world. It lies on the Equator, between Kenya, Tanzania and Uganda, and covers 68,880 sq km. Its only outlet is the River Nile in the north.

Kilimanjaro (D 6)
This old volcano, made up of alternating layers of lava and ash, is Africa's highest mountain, rising to 5,895 m. Although it lies only three degrees from the Equator, its peak is permanently covered with snow.

ENVIRONMENTAL ISSUES

Rapid population growth has created a need for increasing amounts of land for farming. This, as well as the need for fuelwood, has led to tree cover being stripped, allowing the soil to be washed or blown away. Over the past 30 years, eastern Africa has been stricken by many catastrophic droughts which have made desertification worse, and brought much human suffering.

1973
1980
1984–1985
1990
1997
2000
2003–2004

1973–1975
1980
1984–1985
1989
1991–1994
1999–2000
2003
2005–2006
2007–2009

1973–1975
1980
1985
1989
1992
1999
2004
2005–2006
2007–2009

2007

2007

1986
2001
2005

2007

1972–1974

1973–1975
1980
1985
1987
1989
1999–2000
2004-2005
2007–2009

1973–1974
1991–1992
1996–1997
1999
2000
2004
2007–2009

ENVIRONMENTAL ISSUES

- Drought
- Severe fuelwood shortage
- Flooding
- Existing desert
- Risk of desertification
- Severe risk of desertification

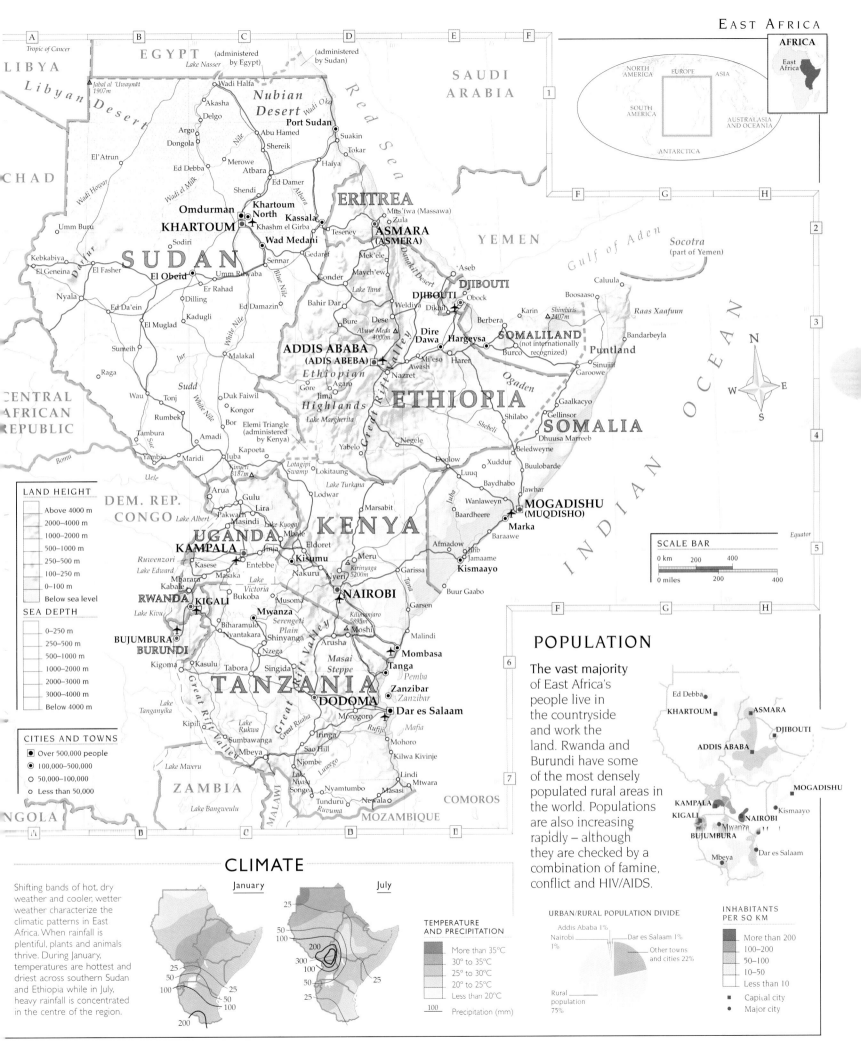

LAND HEIGHT

	Above 4000 m
	2000–4000 m
	1000–2000 m
	500–1000 m
	250–500 m
	100–250 m
	0–100 m
	Below sea level

SEA DEPTH

	0–250 m
	250–500 m
	500–1000 m
	1000–2000 m
	2000–3000 m
	3000–4000 m
	Below 4000 m

CITIES AND TOWNS

- ◼ Over 500,000 people
- ◉ 100,000–500,000
- ○ 50,000–100,000
- ○ Less than 50,000

SCALE BAR

0 km   200   400

0 miles   200   400

POPULATION

The vast majority of East Africa's people live in the countryside and work the land. Rwanda and Burundi have some of the most densely populated rural areas in the world. Populations are also increasing rapidly – although they are checked by a combination of famine, conflict and HIV/AIDS.

INHABITANTS PER SQ KM

	More than 200
	100–200
	50–100
	10–50
	Less than 10
◼	Capital city
●	Major city

CLIMATE

Shifting bands of hot, dry weather and cooler, wetter weather characterize the climatic patterns in East Africa. When rainfall is plentiful, plants and animals thrive. During January, temperatures are hottest and driest across southern Sudan and Ethiopia while in July, heavy rainfall is concentrated in the centre of the region.

January

July

TEMPERATURE AND PRECIPITATION

	More than 35°C
	30° to 35°C
	25° to 30°C
	20° to 25°C
	Less than 20°C

100   Precipitation (mm)

URBAN/RURAL POPULATION DIVIDE

Addis Ababa 1%
Nairobi 1%
Dar es Salaam 1%
Other towns and cities 22%
Rural population 75%

75

SOUTHERN AFRICA

ANGOLA, BOTSWANA, COMOROS, CONGO, DEM. REP. CONGO, GABON, LESOTHO, MADAGASCAR, MALAWI, MOZAMBIQUE, NAMIBIA, SOUTH AFRICA, SWAZILAND, ZAMBIA, ZIMBABWE

Southern Africa contains the richest deposits of valuable minerals on the continent. South Africa is the wealthiest and most industrialized country in the region. Most of the surrounding countries rely on it for trade and work. Racial segregation under apartheid operated from 1948 until 1994, when South Africa held its first multiracial elections.

FARMING AND LAND USE

Most of southern Africa's farmers grow just enough food to feed their families, though much of the farmland is in the hands of a few wealthy landowners. In the tropical north, oil palms and rubber are grown on large commercial plantations. Fruits are cultivated in the south, and tea and coffee are important in the east. Cattle farming is widespread across the dry grasslands.

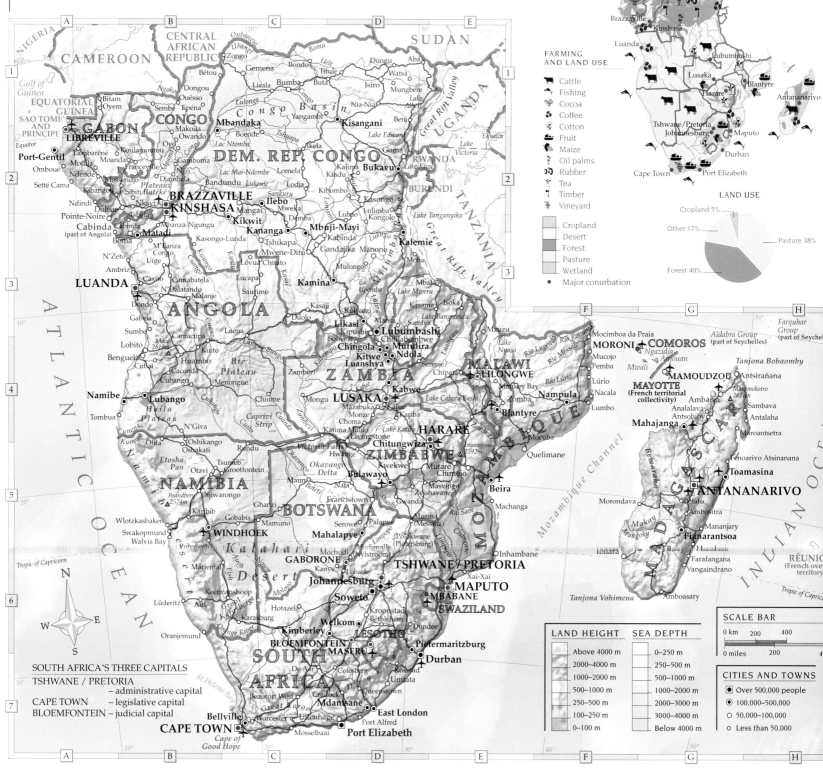

FARMING
AND LAND USE

- 🐂 Cattle
- 🐟 Fishing
- 🌰 Cocoa
- ☕ Coffee
- 🌱 Cotton
- 🍓 Fruit
- 🌾 Maize
- 🌴 Oil palms
- 🍃 Rubber
- 🌿 Tea
- 🌲 Timber
- 🍇 Vineyard

LAND USE

- Cropland
- Desert
- Forest
- Pasture
- Wetland
- ● Major conurbation

Cropland 5%
Other 17%
Pasture 38%
Forest 40%

SOUTH AFRICA'S THREE CAPITALS

TSHWANE / PRETORIA
– administrative capital
CAPE TOWN – legislative capital
BLOEMFONTEIN – judicial capital

LAND HEIGHT | SEA DEPTH

LAND HEIGHT	SEA DEPTH
Above 4000 m	0–250 m
2000–4000 m	250–500 m
1000–2000 m	500–1000 m
500–1000 m	1000–2000 m
250–500 m	2000–3000 m
100–250 m	3000–4000 m
0–100 m	Below 4000 m

SCALE BAR

0 km   200   400

0 miles   200   400

CITIES AND TOWNS

- ▣ Over 500,000 people
- ◉ 100,000–500,000
- ○ 50,000–100,000
- • Less than 50,000

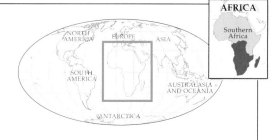

CLIMATE

During January, temperatures are highest in the Kalahari Desert and rainfall is plentiful in the centre of southern Africa. July is cooler and drier with rainfall concentrated in north Dem. Rep. Congo. The Atlantic coast of Namibia receives little rain all year round.

January

July

TEMPERATURE AND PRECIPITATION

- More than 35°C
- 30 to 35°C
- 25 to 30°C
- 20 to 25°C
- 15 to 20°C
- Less than 15°C
- 100 Precipitation (mm)

ENVIRONMENTAL ISSUES

The immense rain forests of the Congo Basin in the north remain relatively untouched, but deforestation is beginning to occur at their edges, with more forest due to be cleared in the future. Large parts of Madagascar have also been deforested. Further south, occasional drought and the clearing of bushlands for fuelwood can cause soil loss.

Congo Basin

1991–1992 1995 2005
1971–1974 1979–1985 1991–1992 2002, 2005, 2008
1985 1989
1982–1984 1992 1997–1998, 2001 2007–2008
2000 2007
1983–1985 1992–1993 2002–2003
1983 1985 2001 2004 2007

ENVIRONMENTAL ISSUES

- Drought
- Severe fuelwood shortage
- Flooding
- Existing desert
- Risk of desertification
- Severe risk of desertification
- Deforested area
- Remaining tropical forest

THE LANDSCAPE

Southern Africa stretches from just north of the equator down to the southern tip of the continent. It is an area with an extremely varied climate and geography. In the north are the tropical rain forests of the Congo Basin, while arid desert covers much of the southwest. The eastern regions are mostly grasslands, with lush vegetation found on the tropical coast of Mozambique.

Congo Basin (C 1)
The Congo River is Africa's second longest river, flowing in an arc through the dense tropical forests of the Congo Basin before emptying into the Atlantic Ocean.

Namib Desert (B 5)
The Namib is one of the world's driest deserts. The only water it receives is from mists that roll in from the sea. Where the desert meets the coast is known as the Skeleton Coast because of sailors who were shipwrecked and died there.

Okavango Delta (C 5)
The Okavango River terminates in the Kalahari Desert, forming a vast, swampy inland delta.

Victoria Falls (D 5)
On its way to the Indian Ocean, the Zambezi River plunges over a 128 m cliff into a narrow chasm. The resultant spray rises up to 490 m, and the thunder of the water can be heard up to 40 km away.

Madagascar (G 5)
The world's fourth largest island lies in isolation 250 km off the east coast of southern Africa. It became separated from the African continent 135 million years ago, and its plant and animal life are unique. The rich biodiversity of the rain forests is being threatened by lumbering for wood and timber.

Drakensberg (D 4)
The Drakensberg are a chain of mountains that lie at the edge of a broad plateau that has tilted because of the movement of the Earth's plates. Rivers have carved through the high mountains, creating dramatic gorges and waterfalls.

INDUSTRY

Southern Africa has extraordinary mineral resources. Angola has large deposits of oil, and diamonds are found in Angola, Botswana, Namibia, and South Africa. Copper is mined in the region known as the 'copper belt', that runs from Dem. Rep. Congo into Zambia. South Africa is the world's largest gold producer. Manufacturing, such as fruit canning and steel production, is most developed in South Africa.

INDUSTRY
- Car manufacture
- Chemicals
- Engineering
- Food processing
- Iron & steel
- Metal refining
- Textiles
- Oil and gas
- Mining
- Timber processing
- Tourism
- Major industrial centre / area
- Major road

STRUCTURE OF INDUSTRY
Primary 10%
Services 59%
Manufacturing 31%

POPULATION

The population is still mostly rural with two thirds of southern Africa's residents living in the countryside. Dense tropical rain forest in the north and arid desert in the southwest have kept habitation to a bare minimum. Malawi is the most densely populated country in the region.

INHABITANTS PER SQ KM
- More than 100
- 50–100
- 10–50
- Less than 10
- Capital city
- Major city

Luanda 1.4% Kinshasa 2.4%
Cape Town 1.2%
Other towns and cities 34%
Rural population 61%

CONTINENTAL EUROPE

Europe is the world's second smallest continent, occupying the western tip of the vast Eurasian landmass. To the north and west are old highlands, with the high peaks of the Alps in the south. Most people live on the densely populated North European Plain, which runs from southern England, through northern France, across Germany into Russia.

CROSS-SECTION THROUGH EUROPE

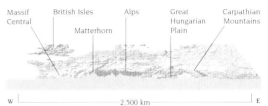

Massif Central · British Isles · Matterhorn · Alps · Great Hungarian Plain · Carpathian Mountains

W · 2,500 km · E

In the west, the land rises up from the Atlantic coast towards the Massif Central in France, and the high peaks of the Alps. Between the Alps and the Carpathian Mountains is the Great Hungarian Plain, where the River Danube flows on its way to the Black Sea.

PHYSICAL EUROPE

The ancient mountains of northwest Europe were scoured and smoothed by glaciers in the last Ice Age. The Alps are newer and more jagged – pushed up when Africa collided with Europe. In between is the North European Plain, where thick layers of fertile soils allow many different crops to be grown.

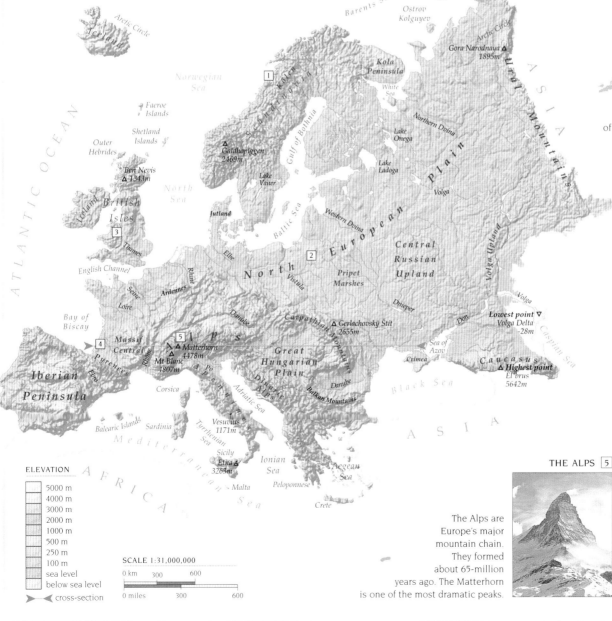

Novaya Zemlya
Barents Sea
Ostrov Kolguyev
Arctic Circle
Iceland
Norwegian Sea
Kola Peninsula
White Sea
Gora Narodnaya △ 1895m
Faeroe Islands
Shetland Islands
Outer Hebrides
Scandinavia
Kjølen
Gulf of Bothnia
Lake Onega
Northern Dvina
Ural Mountains
ASIA
Galdhøpiggen 2469m
Lake Vänern
Lake Ladoga
Ben Nevis △ 1343m
North Sea
Jutland
Baltic Sea
Volga
British Isles
Thames
Elbe
Vistula
North European Plain
Pripet Marshes
Central Russian Upland
Volga Upland
English Channel
Rhine
Dnieper
Seine
Ardennes
Loire
Danube
Carpathian Mountains
Gerlachovský Štít 2655m
Don
Volga
Lowest point ▽ Volga Delta -28m
Bay of Biscay
Massif Central
Alps
Matterhorn 4478m
Rhône
Mt Blanc 4807m
Pyrenees
Ebro
Po
Apennines
Great Hungarian Plain
Dinaric Alps
Danube
Sea of Azov
Crimea
Caucasus
△ Highest point Elbrus 5642m
Caspian Sea
Iberian Peninsula
Corsica
Adriatic Sea
Balkan Mountains
Black Sea
ASIA
Balearic Islands
Sardinia
Tyrrhenian Sea
Vesuvius 1171m
Sicily
Etna △ 3263m
Ionian Sea
Aegean Sea
Mediterranean Sea
Malta
Peloponnese
Crete
AFRICA
ATLANTIC OCEAN

ELEVATION

	5000 m
	4000 m
	3000 m
	2000 m
	1000 m
	500 m
	250 m
	100 m
	sea level
	below sea level

✕ cross-section

SCALE 1:31,000,000

0 km · 300 · 600

0 miles · 300 · 600

1 THE FROZEN NORTH

Europe's northern coastline stretches deep into the Arctic Circle. Here in Norway, icebergs drift into the deep, wide-bottomed fjords.

THE NORTH EUROPEAN PLAIN 2

The North European Plain has low, rolling hills and plains. Much of the area is cultivated and used for growing crops like wheat and sugar beet.

3 ANCIENT HIGHLANDS

Some of the world's oldest rocks are found in northwest Europe. Erosion by glaciers in the last Ice Age created smoothed hills such as the mountains of Wales.

4 THE ATLANTIC COAST

On Europe's Atlantic coast, the force of waves and winds has created striking landforms like this huge sand dune in southwest France.

THE ALPS 5

The Alps are Europe's major mountain chain. They formed about 65-million years ago. The Matterhorn is one of the most dramatic peaks.

POLITICAL EUROPE

Europe's population increased rapidly during the 18th and 19th centuries, following the Industrial Revolution. In the 20th century, Europe suffered a series of wars which redrew the political map. From 1989–1991, communist governments in eastern Europe and the former Soviet Union collapsed, as political reform swept through the countries behind the 'Iron Curtain'. In 2007 the European Union admitted two new states in a further expansion.

EUROPEAN UNION

- six original members, 1957
- nine further members, 1973 – 1995
- ten further members, 2004
- two new members, 2007

REGIONAL IDENTITY

Throughout Europe, there is a growing call to recognize regional cultural identity. The Basque region, straddling southwest France and Spain, is one example.

RURAL LIFE

Away from Europe's bustling cities, traditional rural lifestyles survive. Here in Ireland, a winter shelter is being made for cattle.

POPULATION

Capital cities
- ◉ Above 500,000
- ◎ 100,000 to 500,000
- ● 50,000 to 100,000

SCALE 1:27,500,000

0 km   300   600

0 miles   300   600

POPULATION

More than 725 million people live in Europe, and its population is highly urbanized. In Belgium and the Netherlands, almost 90% of people live in cities. In the south and east, more people still live in rural areas. The northern countries have the smallest populations, because much of the land is too cold to be habitable.

POPULATION DENSITY
(People per sq km)
- Below 49
- 50–99
- 100–149
- 150–199
- 200–299
- Above 300

Largest city
MOSCOW
10.1 million people

SPREADING CITIES

Amsterdam, in the Netherlands, is part of a conurbation, a large built-up area where several towns or cities have merged together to form a single urban area.

STANDARDS OF LIVING

Living standards are generally much lower in eastern Europe than in the wealthier west. Homelessness and unemployment are still problems, even in the most prosperous countries.

STANDARD OF LIVING
(UN Human Development Index)

low   high

EUROPEAN GEOGRAPHY

Europe is blessed with a temperate climate, ample mineral reserves, and good transport links. During the 18th and 19th centuries the continent was transformed, as new methods of production made industry and farming more efficient and productive. Today, in many countries, 'heavy' industries have been replaced by hi-tech and service industries. Agriculture is still important and many crops thrive on Europe's fertile plains.

INDUSTRY

Western Europe has some of the world's wealthiest countries. In countries such as France, Germany and the UK, traditional industries like iron and steel-making are now being replaced by light industries such as electronics, and services like finance and insurance. In Eastern Europe, industry was subsidized by the communist governments for years. Many factories are old fashioned and need investment to improve their equipment and production methods.

MINERAL RESOURCES

Europe has few sizeable reserves of metallic minerals; most were used up by industry during the 19th century. Oil, gas and coal are found in large quantities – gas in the North Sea and oil in the Volga basin. Coal, though abundant, is being steadily depleted.

MINERAL RESOURCES

- Bauxite
- Chromium
- Copper
- Iron
- Manganese
- Nickel
- Uranium
- Oil/gas field
- Coal field

OIL AND GAS

Oil and gas reserves are plentiful in the Russian Federation. South of Rostov-on-Don, oil is pumped from the ground and piped to nearby refineries.

CAR MANUFACTURE

Germany is one of the world's largest and oldest manufacturer of cars. Companies like BMW, Mercedes-Benz and Volkswagen export cars across the world.

FINANCE

London, Frankfurt and Paris are among the most important financial centres in the world. Many banks and financial institutions have their headquarters here. At the London Stock Exchange, people buy and sell stocks and shares.

ECONOMIC ACTIVITY

- Aerospace
- Car/vehicle manufacture
- Chemicals
- Coal
- Defence
- Electronics
- Engineering
- Finance
- Food processing
- Hi-tech industry
- Iron & steel
- Oil and gas
- Printing & publishing
- Textiles
- Timber processing

GNI per capita (US$)

- Below 1,999
- 2,000–4,999
- 5,000–9,999
- 10,000–19,999
- 20,000–24,999
- Above 25,000
- Industrial centre

CLIMATE

Europe's climate is temperate with few climatic extremes. In the far north, Europe extends into the Arctic Circle and the climate is so cold that in the winter, the Baltic Sea freezes over. Towards the Atlantic coast in the west, the climate becomes wetter and warmer because of a warm ocean current, known as the Gulf Stream. Countries such as Italy and Spain which border the Mediterranean Sea, have long, hot summers and low rainfall, which can sometimes lead to problems such as drought.

EXTREME WEATHER EVENTS

Symbols indicate climatic extremes

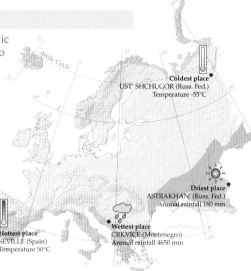

Coldest place
UST' SHCHUGOR (Russ. Fed.)
Temperature -55°C

Driest place
ASTRAKHAN (Russ. Fed.)
Annual rainfall 160 mm

Hottest place
SEVILLE (Spain)
Temperature 50°C

Wettest place
CRKVICE (Montenegro)
Annual rainfall 4650 mm

CLIMATE
- Tundra
- Subarctic
- Cool continental
- Temperate/humid
- Mediterranean
- Semi-arid

THE MEDITERRANEAN CLIMATE

The mild, warm climate around the Mediterranean Sea allows olives, citrus fruits and grapes to thrive. Long, sunny days also help the fruits ripen. Grapes are harvested and crushed to make many different wines.

LAND USE AND AGRICULTURE

Europe's agricultural heart is the North European Plain, where fertile soils and ample rainfall mean that a variety of crops can be grown. Wheat is the main grain crop, and a wide range of fruit and vegetables are also grown. Dairy and beef cattle are raised for their milk and meat throughout Europe. In the south, the Mediterranean climate allows citrus fruits and olives to grow. Forests cover much of northern Scandinavia, while in the hills of the British Isles, sheep farming is common.

FISHING

The north Atlantic Ocean provides a rich marine harvest for fishermen. Today the cod, haddock and mackerel stocks have to be protected from over-fishing.

CROPLANDS

Many different crops are grown on the North European Plain. Sunflowers, wheat, and sugar beet – used to make sugar – are amongst the main crops grown there.

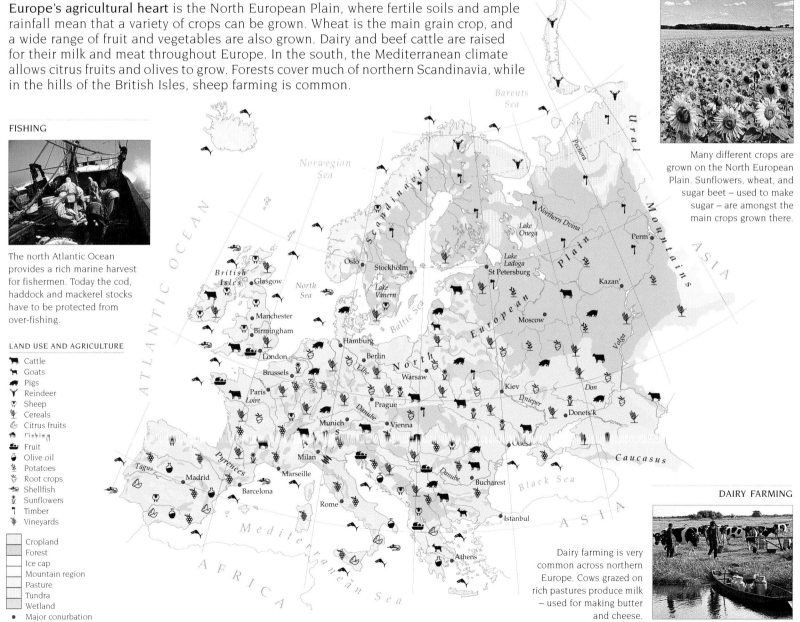

LAND USE AND AGRICULTURE
- Cattle
- Goats
- Pigs
- Reindeer
- Sheep
- Cereals
- Citrus fruits
- Fishing
- Fruit
- Olive oil
- Potatoes
- Root crops
- Shellfish
- Sunflowers
- Timber
- Vineyards

- Cropland
- Forest
- Ice cap
- Mountain region
- Pasture
- Tundra
- Wetland
- Major conurbation

DAIRY FARMING

Dairy farming is very common across northern Europe. Cows grazed on rich pastures produce milk – used for making butter and cheese.

NORTHERN EUROPE

DENMARK, ESTONIA, FINLAND, ICELAND, LATVIA, LITHUANIA, NORWAY, SWEDEN

Denmark, Sweden and Norway are together known as Scandinavia. These countries, along with the North Atlantic island of Iceland, have similar languages and cultures. Finland has a very different language and a separate identity from its Scandinavian neighbours. Estonia, Latvia and Lithuania, known as the Baltic states, were part of the Soviet Union until 1989, when each became an independent country.

INDUSTRY

In Scandinavia, many natural resources are used in industry: timber for paper and furniture; iron ore for steel and cars; and fish and natural gas from the seas. Hydro-electric power is generated by water flowing down steep mountain slopes. The Baltic states still rely on Russia to supply their raw materials and energy.

INDUSTRY

- 🚗 Car manufacture
- 🝙 Chemicals
- ⚙ Engineering
- 🐟 Fish processing
- ⌁ Hydro-electric power
- ⚓ Shipbuilding
- 🌲 Timber processing
- ⓘ Tourism

- ▪ Major industrial centre / area
- — Major road

STRUCTURE OF INDUSTRY

Primary 4%
Services 65%
Manufacturing 31%

POPULATION

The population is distributed mainly along the warmer and flatter southern and coastal areas. Population totals and densities are low for all of the countries, and Iceland has the lowest population density in Europe, with just three people per sq km. Many Scandinavians have holiday homes on the islands, along the lake shores, or in coastal areas.

INHABITANTS PER SQ KM

- More than 200
- 100–200
- 50–100
- Less than 50
- ▪ Capital city
- ● Major city

URBAN/RURAL POPULATION DIVIDE

- Copenhagen 3.4%
- Stockholm 3.8%
- Helsinki 3.3%
- Other towns and cities 66.5%
- Rural population 23%

FARMING AND LAND USE

Southern Denmark and Sweden are the most productive areas, with pig farming, dairy-farming and crops such as wheat, barley and potatoes. Sheep farming is important in southern Norway and Iceland. In the Baltic states, cereals, potatoes and sugar beet are the main crops and cattle graze on damp pasture.

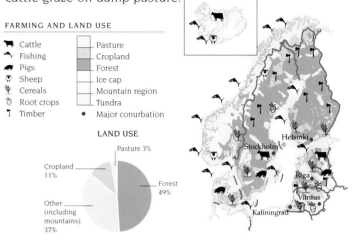

FARMING AND LAND USE

- 🐄 Cattle
- 🐟 Fishing
- 🐖 Pigs
- 🐑 Sheep
- 🌾 Cereals
- 🥔 Root crops
- 🌲 Timber

- Pasture
- Cropland
- Forest
- Ice cap
- Mountain region
- Tundra
- ● Major conurbation

LAND USE

- Pasture 3%
- Cropland 11%
- Forest 49%
- Other (including mountains) 37%

THE LANDSCAPE

The north and west of Scandinavia is extremely rugged and mountainous, with landscapes eroded by ice. In the south of Scandinavia the land is flatter, with fertile soils deposited by glaciers. Much of Finland, Norway and Sweden is covered by dense forests. The Baltic states are much lower, with rounded hills and many lakes and marshes.

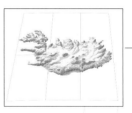

The land of ice and fire. Iceland is one of the world's most active volcanic areas. There are about 200 volcanoes on the island, along with bubbling hot springs, mud-holes, and geysers which spurt boiling water and steam high into the air.

Fjords
Norway has many fjords: deep, wide valleys carved by glaciers, drowned by seawater when the ice melted at the end of the last Ice Age.

Baltic Sea (D 7)
Ships from Finland, Sweden and the Baltic states use the Baltic Sea as their route to the north Atlantic Ocean. In winter, much of the sea is frozen.

Glacial lakes
Finland and Sweden have many thousands of lakes. During the last Ice Age, glaciers scoured hollows which filled with water when the ice melted.

Courland Spit (D 7)
This wide sandspit runs f[...] 100 km along the Baltic [...] of Lithuania and the Russ[...] enclave of Kaliningrad. It encloses a huge lagoon[...]

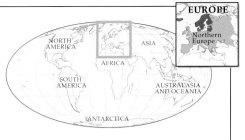

EUROPE
Northern Europe

ENVIRONMENTAL ISSUES

Northern Europe has been badly affected by industrial pollution from other parts of Europe. Polluted air moves north, and mixes with the rain to create acid rain. This poisons forests and lakes, destroying the plants and animals living in them. Renewable energy plays a major role in this region, hydro-electric, geothermal and wind power are all exploited.

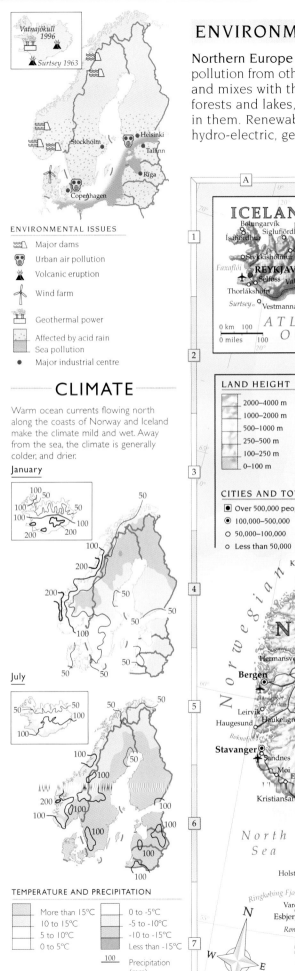

Vatnajökull 1996
▲ Surtsey 1963

Stockholm
Helsinki
Tallinn
Riga
Copenhagen

ENVIRONMENTAL ISSUES

- Major dams
- Urban air pollution
- Volcanic eruption
- Wind farm
- Geothermal power
- Affected by acid rain
  Sea pollution
- Major industrial centre

CLIMATE

Warm ocean currents flowing north along the coasts of Norway and Iceland make the climate mild and wet. Away from the sea, the climate is generally colder, and drier.

January

100 50 50
100 50
100 200
100
200
100 50
200 50 50

July

50 50 50
100
100
200 100
100 50
100 100
200 100 100
100 100

TEMPERATURE AND PRECIPITATION

More than 15°C	0 to -5°C
10 to 15°C	-5 to -10°C
5 to 10°C	-10 to -15°C
0 to 5°C	Less than -15°C

100 Precipitation (mm)

ICELAND

Norwegian Sea
Arctic Circle

Bolungarvík
Ísafjördhur
Raufarhöfn
Siglufjördhur
Húsavík
Stykkishólmur
Akureyri
REYKJAVÍK
Seydhisfjördhur
Neskaupstadhur
Selfoss
Djúpivogur
Faxaflói
Thorlákshöfn
Hvannadalshnúkur 2119m
Surtsey
Vestmannaeyjar

ATLANTIC OCEAN

0 km 100
0 miles 100

SCALE BAR

0 km 100 200
0 miles 100 200

LAND HEIGHT

- 2000–4000 m
- 1000–2000 m
- 500–1000 m
- 250–500 m
- 100–250 m
- 0–100 m

SEA DEPTH

- 0–50 m
- 50–100 m
- 100–250 m
- 250–500 m
- 500–1000 m
- 1000–2000 m
- Below 2000 m

CITIES AND TOWNS

- Over 500,000 people
- 100,000–500,000
- 50,000–100,000
- Less than 50,000

NORWAY
SWEDEN
FINLAND
DENMARK
ESTONIA
LATVIA
LITHUANIA
GERMANY
POLAND
RUSSIAN FEDERATION
BELARUS

North Cape (Nordkapp)
Barents Sea
Magerøya
Søroya
Kirkenes
Lakselv
Tana Bru
Talvik
Alta
Karasjok
Karigasniemi
Inari
Kaamanen
Ivalo
Saariselkä
Tromsø
Finnmarksvidda
Kebnekaise 2117m
Kiruna
Muonio
Sattanen
Sodankylä
Kolari
Rovaniemi
Kemijärvi
Bodø
Fauske
Malmberget
Gällivare
Jokkmokk
Kuusamo
Mo i Rana
Boden
Haparanda
Tornio
Kemi
Pudasjärvi
Arvidsjaur
Luleå
Piteå
Oulu
Skellefteå
Kajaani
Sotkamo
Kuhmo
Namsos
Vilhelmina
Dorotea
Hoting
Umeå
Kokkola (Karleby)
Nurmes
Steinkjer
Verdalsøra
Levanger
Strömsund
Holmsund
Jakobstad (Pietarsaari)
Iisalmi
Pielinen
Siilinjärvi
Joensuu
Trondheim
Heimdal
Stjørdalshalsen
Östersund
Örnsköldsvik
Vaasa (Vasa)
Kuopio
Kristiansund
Molde
Andalsnes
Ålesund
Storlien
Røros
Dombås
Remunden
Kramfors
Timrå
Härnösand
Sundsvall
Kankaanpää
Lapua
Seinäjoki
Keuruu
Närpes (Närpiö)
Jyväskylä
Varkaus
Saimaa
Glittertind 2472m
Ringebu
Lillehammer
Hudiksvall
Pori
Nokia
Tampere
Lappeenranta
Imatra
Lake Ladoga
Hermansverk
Jotunheimen
Gol
Gjøvik
Hamar
Mora
Rättvik
Leksand
Rauma
Hämeenlinna
Riihimäki
Hyvinkää
Kouvola
Bergen
Gol
Hønefoss
Malung
Falun
Sandviken
Tierp
Turku (Åbo)
Salo
Porvoo
Kotka
Leirvik
Eidfjord
Hardangervidda
Sandvika
Drammen
Lillestrøm
OSLO
Ski
Filipstad
Sala
Uppsala
Hanko (Hangö)
Kunda
Narva
Haugesund
Haukeligrend
Kongsberg
Horten
Moss
Grums
Karlstad
Nora
Västerås
Norrtälje
Täby
HELSINKI
Espoo
TALLINN
Kohtla-Järve
Stavanger
Sandnes
Sarpsborg
Halden
Säffle
Örebro
Södertälje
STOCKHOLM
Hiiumaa
Lake Peipus
ESTONIA
RUSS. FED.
Moi
Evje
Fredrikstad
Strömstad
Åmål
Vänern
Askersund
Nyköping
Saaremaa
Pärnu
Tartu
Räpina
Arendal
Uddevalla
Mariefred
Vättern
Linköping
Gotland
Gulf of Riga
Mõisaküla
Võru
Kristiansand
Trollhättan
Borås
Jönköping
Visby
Ventspils
Valka
Gothenburg (Göteborg)
Mölndal
Kungsbacka
Varberg
Oskarshamn
Kolka
Saulkrasti
LATVIA
Viļaka
Ludza
Hjørring
Aalborg
Läsø
Borgholm
Liepāja
RIGA
Jūrmala
Skrīveri
Hobro
Randers
Halmstad
Ljungby
Växjö
Kalmar
Öland
Jelgava
Western Dvina
Dagda
Holstebro
Viborg
Laholm
Karlskrona
Pakruojis
Rokiškis
Jutland
Kattegat
Helsingborg
Kristianstad
Salantai
Dotnuva
Panevėžys
Daugavpils
DENMARK
COPENHAGEN (KØBENHAVN)
Lund
Malmö
Hanöbukten
Klaipėda
Šiauliai
LITHUANIA
Zarasai
Esbjerg
Kolding
Slagelse
Zealand
Šilutė
Ukmergė
Giedraičiai
Odense
Fyn
Møn
Falster
Rønne
Bornholm
Nida
Courland Lagoon
Neman
Kaunas
Jonava
VILNIUS
Salčininkai
Zelenogradsk
Kaliningrad
Gulf of Danzig
Mamonovo
KALININGRAD (part of Russian Federation)
Alytus
Veisiejai

Norwegian Sea
North Sea
Skagerrak
Baltic Sea
Gulf of Bothnia
Gulf of Finland
Åland Islands
Åland Sea

THE LOW COUNTRIES

BELGIUM, LUXEMBOURG, NETHERLANDS

Belgium, Luxembourg and the Netherlands are called the Low Countries because most of their land is flat and low-lying. Much of the Netherlands lies below sea level, and over hundreds of years the Dutch have built dykes and dams to prevent flooding, and have pumped water off large areas of land to reclaim them from the sea. The Low Countries are Europe's most densely populated countries, but most of their people have a high living standard.

ENVIRONMENTAL ISSUES

Huge land reclamation projects in the Netherlands, such as the IJsselmeer project, have created some new land for agricultural use, and also for houses, roads and open spaces. However, because of this work, sea-level rise is a major threat to large parts of the Netherlands.

ENVIRONMENTAL ISSUES

- Urban air pollution
- Built-up areas
- Reclaimed land
- Polluted river
- • Major industrial centre

CLIMATE

The Low Countries share a similar climate, with mild winters and warm summers. Only in the upland Ardennes region does rainfall increase and temperatures decrease.

January

July

Less than 50

Less than 50

100

100

TEMPERATURE AND PRECIPITATION

- More than 15°C
- 10 to 15°C
- 5 to 10°C
- 0 to 5°C
- Less than 0°C

100 Precipitation (mm)

NETHERLANDS' TWO CAPITALS
AMSTERDAM - capital
THE HAGUE - seat of governme

West Frisian Islands (Waddeneilanden)

Schiermonnikoog
Ameland
Terschelling
Vlieland
Waddenzee
Texel

Eemshaven
Delfzijl
Appingedam
Loppersum
Bedum
Zuidhorn
Groningen
Hoogezand-Sappe
Winschoten
Veendam
Vlagtwedde
Stadskanaal

Ferwerd
Dokkum
Winsum
Menaldum
Leeuwarden
Leek
Haren
Harlingen
Drachten
Roden
Zuidlaren
Assen

Den Helder
Sneek
Joure
Heerenveen
Wolvega
Beilen
Borger
Odoorn
Emmen

NETHERLANDS

Schagen
Opmeer
Heerhugowaard
Emmeloord
Steenwijk
Hoogeveen Klazienaveen
Coevorden

Heiloo
Bergen
IJsselmeer
Meppel
Dedemsvaart
Hardenberg

Heemskerk
Castricum
Purmerend
Broek-in-Waterland
Lelystad
Zwolle
Ommen
Velsen-Noord
Almere
Wezep
Hattem
Den Ham
Tubbergen
Zaanstad
Zeewolde
Oldebroek
Heerde
Wierden
Almelo
Oldenzaal
Haarlem
Weesp
Nunspeet
Raalte
Borne
AMSTERDAM
Hillegom
Amstelveen
Blaricum
Nijkerk
Vaassen
Deventer
Hengelo
Noordwijk aan Zee
Aalsmeer
Hilversum
Ermelo
Gorssel
Goor
Enschede
Sassenheim
Uithoorn
Baarn
Apeldoorn
Voorst
Lochem
Haaksbergen
Lisse
Mijdrecht
Amersfoort
Lunteren
Zutphen
Needle
Eibergen
Leiden
Alphen aan den Rijn
De Bilt
Ede
Brummen
Winterswijk
THE HAGUE ('S-GRAVENHAGE)
Zeist
Veenendaal
Oosterbeek
Dieren
Lichtenvoorde
Zoetermeer
Nieuwegein
Arnhem
Aalten
's-Gravenzande
Delft
Vianen
Wijk bij Duurstede
Elst
Duiven
Ulft
Gouda
Capelle aan den IJssel
Geldermalsen
Bemmel
Zevenaar
Waal
Rotterdam
Spijkenisse
Barendrecht
Gorinchem
Oss
Wijchen
Nijmegen
Goeree
Hellevoetsluis
Woudrichem
Werkendam
Rosmalen
Grave
Cuijk
Groesbeek
Overflakkee
Raamsdonksveer
Vlijmen
's-Hertogenbosch
Gennep
Rhine (Rhein)
Schouwen
Middelharnis
Made
Oosterhout
Sint-Michielsgestel
Boxmeer
Zierikzee
Zevenbergen
Breda
Schijndel
Nieuw-Bergen
Noord-Beveland
Tholen
Roosendaal
Zundert
Tilburg
Oirschot
Helmond
Horst
Middelburg
Goes
Kapelle
Baarle-Hertog
Deurne
Venlo
Vlissingen
Zuid-Beveland
Essen
Baarle-Nassau
Eindhoven
Someren
Tegelen
Western Scheldt
Kalmthout
Veldhoven
Eersel
Nederweert
Reuver
Zeebrugge
Knokke-Heist
Oostburg
Terneuzen
Brecht
Turnhout
Bergeyk
Valkenswaard
Weert
Beesel
Blankenberge
Axel
Hulst
Schoten
Lommel
Peer
Bree
Posterholt
Ostend (Oostende)
Assenede
Beveren
Wilrijk
Nijlen
Duffel
Tessenderlo
Beringen
Maaseik
Echt
Middelkerke
Bruges (Brugge)
Eeklo
Zelzate
Antwerp (Antwerpen)
Geel
Balen
Kinrooi
Susteren
Koksijde
Aalter
Sint-Niklaas
Mol
Genk
Geleen
Sittard
Veurne
Torhout
Oostakker
Willebroek
Mechelen
Haacht
Herselt
Zonhoven
Heerlen
Flanders
Ghent (Gent)
Laarne
Zele
Vilvoorde
Herk-de-Stad
Hasselt
Kerkrade
Izegem
Deinze
Melle
Aalst
Leuven
Diepenbeek
Bilzen
Simpelveld
Poperinge
Roeselare
Gavere
Wemmel
Tienen
Tongeren
Maastricht
Ieper
BRUSSELS (BRUSSEL/BRUXELLES)
Schaerbeek
Landen
Riemst
Vaals
Kortrijk
Zwevegem
Sint-Pieters-Leeuw
Tervuren
Waremme
Herstal
Mouscron
Halle
Overijse
Wavre
Eupen
BELGIUM
Enghien
Ottignies
Louvain-la-Neuve
Seraing
Liège
Verviers
Tournai
Ath
Braine-le-Comte
Gembloux
Éghezée
Amay
Huy
Hautes Fagnes
Péruwelz
Leuze-en-Hainaut
Andenne
Botrange 694m
Mons
Binche
La Louvière
Namur
Ciney
Malmédy
Jemappes
Anderlues
Charleroi
Châtelet
Gerpinnes
Dinant
Fagne
Walcourt
Thuin
Couvin
Rochefort
Weiswampach
Marche-en-Famenne
Ourthe
Ardennes
Bastogne
Houffalize
Recogne
Sûre
GERMANY
Neufchâteau
Diekirch
Ettelbrück
Mosel
FRANCE
Étalle
Arlon
Grevenmacher
LUXEMBOURG
Virton
Aubange
LUXEMBOURG
Esch-sur-Alzette
Differdange
Dudelange

LAND HEIGHT

- 500–1000 m
- 250–500 m
- 100–250 m
- 0–100 m
- Below sea level

SEA DEPTH

- 0–100 m

CITIES AND TOWNS

- ■ Over 500,000 people
- ● 100,000–500,000
- ○ 50,000–100,000
- ○ Less than 50,000

SCALE BAR

0 km   25   50

0 miles   25   50

Amsterdam
IJssel
Lek
Rhine
Rotterdam
Bergse Maas
Antwerp
Brussels
Meuse

EUROPE
Low Countries

POPULATION

More than **27 million people** live in the Low Countries and nine out of every ten people live in a town or city. The largest urban area – known as the *Randstad Holland* – is in the Netherlands. It runs in an unbroken line from Rotterdam in the south, to Amsterdam in the west. Even most rural areas in the Low Countries are densely populated.

INHABITANTS
PER SQ KM

More than 200
100–200
50–100
0–50

■ Capital city
● Major city

URBAN/RURAL
POPULATION DIVIDE

Amsterdam 2.8%　Brussels 3.9%
Rotterdam 2.3%
Rural
population
8%

Other towns
and cities 83%

FARMING AND LAND USE

The Low Countries' fertile soils and flat plains provide excellent conditions for farming. The main crops grown are barley, potatoes, and flax for making linen. In the Netherlands, much farmland is used for dairy-farming. The country is also famous for growing flowers, which are exported around the world. Flowers and vegetables are grown either in open fields or in enormous greenhouses, which allow production all year round.

LAND USE

Forest
16%

Other
(including
urban)
29%

Pasture
26%　Cropland
29%

FARMING AND LAND USE

🐄 Cattle
🐖 Pigs
🌾 Cereals
✳ Flax
🌷 Flowers
🐂 Market gardening
🌱 Sugar beet

　Pasture
　Cropland
　Forest
　Wetland
● Major
conurbation

THE LANDSCAPE

The Low Countries are largely flat and low-lying. The ancient hills of the Ardennes, in the far southeast, are the only higher region. They rise to heights of more than 500 m. Two major rivers – the Meuse and the Rhine – flow across the Low Countries to their mouths in the North Sea. At the coast, the River Rhine deposits large quantities of sediment to form a delta.

Polders

In the Netherlands, land has been reclaimed from the sea since the Middle Ages by building dykes and drainage ditches. These areas of land are called polders. They are very fertile.

The River Rhine (E4)

The River Rhine erodes and carries large amounts of sediment along its course. When it reaches the Netherlands it divides into three rivers. As they approach the North Sea, the rivers slow down, depositing the sediment to form a delta.

Low-lying Netherlands

Over two-thirds of the Netherlands lies at or below sea level. This makes flooding a constant threat in coastal areas.

Flanders (B6)

The plains of Flanders in western Belgium have fertile soils which were deposited by glaciers during the last Ice Age. They provide excellent land for growing crops.

Heathlands

The heathlands on the Dutch-Belgian border have thin, sandy soils. The only plants which grow well here are heathers and gorse.

The Ardennes (D8)

The hills of the Ardennes were formed over 300 million years ago. They have many deep valleys, which have been eroded by rivers like the Meuse.

INDUSTRY

The Low Countries are an important centre for the hi-tech and electronics industries. Good transport links to the rest of Europe allow them to sell their products in other countries. The built-up area stretching from Amsterdam in the Netherlands to Antwerp in Belgium has the greatest number of factories. Luxembourg is also an important banking centre; many international banks have their headquarters in its capital city.

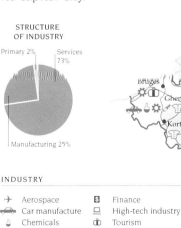

STRUCTURE
OF INDUSTRY

Primary 2%　Services
73%

Manufacturing 25%

INDUSTRY

✈ Aerospace
🚗 Car manufacture
⚗ Chemicals
⚙ Engineering
💊 Pharmaceuticals
👕 Textiles

Ⓢ Finance
🖥 High-tech industry
🏛 Tourism
● Major industrial
centre / area
— Major road

THE BRITISH ISLES

IRELAND, UNITED KINGDOM

The British Isles lie off the northwest coast of mainland Europe. They are made up of two large islands and over 5,000 smaller ones. Politically, the region is divided into two countries: the United Kingdom – England, Wales, Scotland and Northern Ireland – and Ireland. Geographically, the British Isles are divided between highlands to the north and west, and lowlands to the south and east.

THE LANDSCAPE

Low rolling hills, high moorlands, and small fields with high hedges are all typical of the British Isles. Ireland is known as the Emerald Isle, because heavy rainfall gives it a lush, green appearance. Scotland and Wales are mountainous; the rocks forming the mountains there are some of the oldest in the world.

Indented coastlines
The west coast of the British Isles faces the Atlantic Ocean, and over 3,000 km of open sea to the North American continent. Storms and high waves constantly batter the hard, rocky coastline, giving it a jagged outline.

Ben Nevis (C 4)
This mountain is the highest point in the British Isles. It is 1,343 m above sea level.

The Lake District (D 5)
The Lake District National Park has England's highest peak, Scafell Pike, at 978 m (E4), its deepest lake, Wast Water (80 m), and its largest lake, Windermere (16 km long).

The Pennines (D 6)
The Pennines are a chain of high hills, topped by moorland. They run for over 400 km, and are known as the 'backbone of England'.

The Burren (A 6)
The Burren is a large area of limestone rock in the west of Ireland. Its flat surfaces are known as limestone 'pavements'. There are also many caves and sinkholes in the area.

The Fens (E 6)
This is the flattest area in England. Much of the land here has been reclaimed from the sea.

Rias
Rias are river valleys that have been drowned by rising sea levels. The southern coast of southwest England has many good examples.

FARMING AND LAND USE

The English lowlands and the wide, flat stretches of land in East Anglia are the agricultural heartland of the United Kingdom. The country is no longer self-sufficient in food, but wheat, potatoes and other vegetables, and fruits, are widely grown. In Ireland, and in central and southern England, dairy and beef cattle feed off grassy pastures. In the hilly and mountainous areas, sheep farming is more usual.

FARMING AND LAND USE

- 🐂 Cattle
- 🎣 Fishing
- 🐑 Sheep
- 🌾 Cereals
- 🐖 Market gardening
- 🌱 Root crops
- ☐ Pasture
- ☐ Cropland
- ☐ Forest
- ☐ Mountain region
- ● Major conurbation

LAND USE

Cropland 24%
Pasture 50%
Other (including urban) 17%
Forest 9%

INDUSTRY

The United Kingdom's traditional industries, such as coal mining, iron and steel-making, and textiles, have declined in recent years. Today, newer industries make cars, chemicals, electronic and hi-tech goods. Service industries, especially banking and insurance, have grown in importance. The country's most valuable natural resource is its large North Sea oil and gas fields.

INDUSTRY

- ✈ Aerospace
- 🚗 Car manufacture
- 🧪 Chemicals
- ⚙ Engineering
- 👕 Textiles
- 💲 Finance
- 💻 Hi-tech industry
- ⓘ Tourism
- ▪ Major industrial centre / area
- — Major road

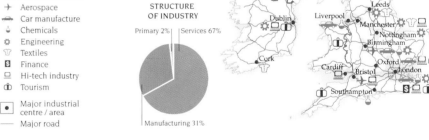

STRUCTURE OF INDUSTRY

Primary 2% | Services 67%
Manufacturing 31%

POPULATION

The United Kingdom is densely populated, with most of the people living in urban areas. The southeast is the most crowded part of the country. The Scottish Highlands are less populated today than they were 200 years ago. Ireland is still mainly rural, with many Irish people making their living from farming.

URBAN/RURAL POPULATION DIVIDE

Birmingham 1.6%
London 11.4%
Glasgow 1%
Rural population 12%
Other towns and cities 74%

INHABITANTS PER SQ KM

- ☐ More than 200
- ☐ 100–200
- ☐ 50–100
- ☐ Less than 50
- ▪ Capital city
- ● Major city

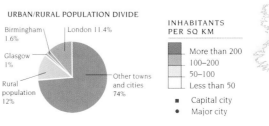

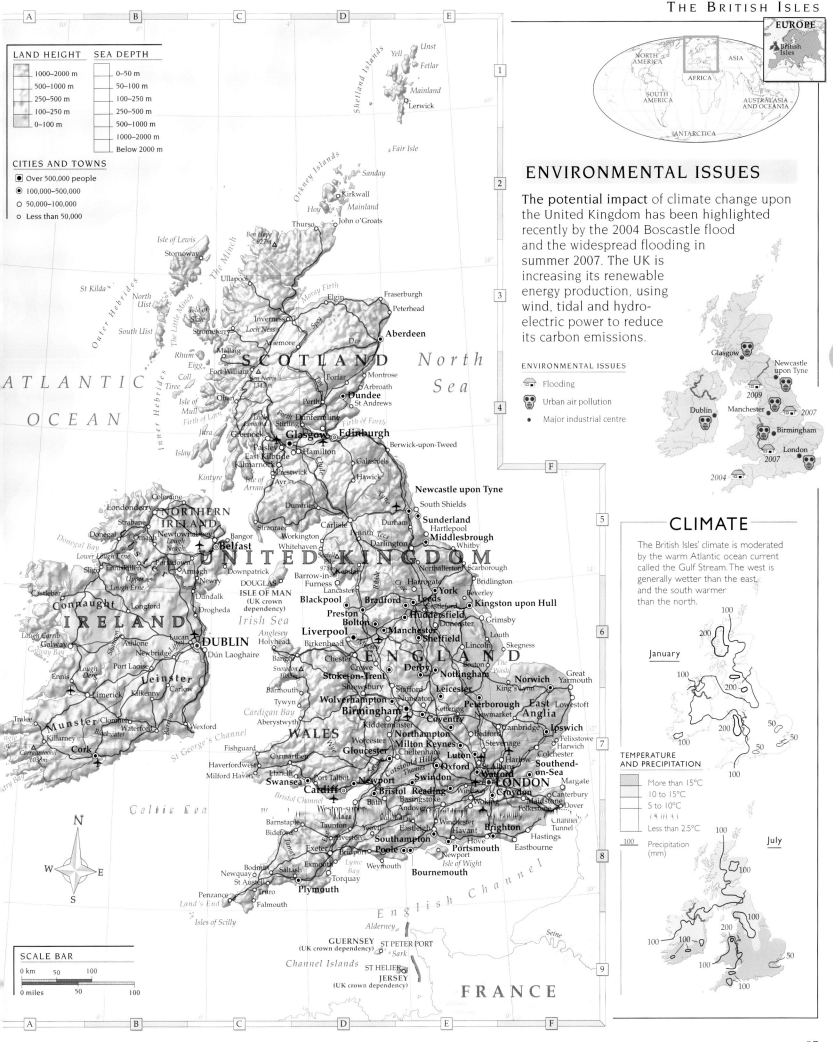

EUROPE
British Isles

ENVIRONMENTAL ISSUES

The potential impact of climate change upon the United Kingdom has been highlighted recently by the 2004 Boscastle flood and the widespread flooding in summer 2007. The UK is increasing its renewable energy production, using wind, tidal and hydro-electric power to reduce its carbon emissions.

ENVIRONMENTAL ISSUES

- Flooding
- Urban air pollution
- Major industrial centre

CLIMATE

The British Isles' climate is moderated by the warm Atlantic ocean current called the Gulf Stream. The west is generally wetter than the east, and the south warmer than the north.

TEMPERATURE AND PRECIPITATION

- More than 15°C
- 10 to 15°C
- 5 to 10°C
- 2.5 to 5°C
- Less than 2.5°C

100 Precipitation (mm)

January

July

LAND HEIGHT
- 1000–2000 m
- 500–1000 m
- 250–500 m
- 100–250 m
- 0–100 m

SEA DEPTH
- 0–50 m
- 50–100 m
- 100–250 m
- 250–500 m
- 500–1000 m
- 1000–2000 m
- Below 2000 m

CITIES AND TOWNS
- Over 500,000 people
- 100,000–500,000
- 50,000–100,000
- Less than 50,000

SCALE BAR
0 km   50   100
0 miles   50   100

IRELAND

IRELAND, NORTHERN IRELAND

Ireland faces the north Atlantic Ocean and is one of the remotest parts of the European Union. Since 1921 the island has been divided into two separate states: Northern Ireland, which is part of the United Kingdom, and Ireland, which has its own government in Dublin. The eastern side of the island has more people and industry. In the west, traditional ways of life based on farming remain strong and the native Irish language is still spoken by some people.

INDUSTRY

Ireland has few mineral resources, around 15% of its electricity is produced by burning peat. In the last 20 years the European Union has given money to help the Irish economy and many new factories have been set up, mainly in the area around Dublin. Hi-tech industries expanded rapidly, as a result of low set-up costs and tax benefits.

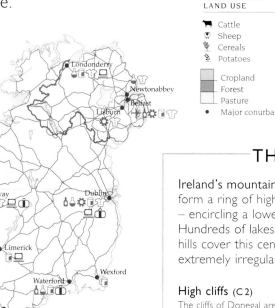

INDUSTRY

✈ Aerospace	⬜ Hi-tech industry
🍷 Brewing	ⓣ Tourism
🍶 Chemicals	
⚙ Engineering	▣ Major industrial centre / area
🥫 Food processing	— Major road
👕 Textiles	

POPULATION

The population of Ireland has actually fallen over the last century as a result of mass emigration, mainly to North America. The rate of people leaving the country to live abroad is still high, although one of Europe's highest birth rates and economic immigration are finally causing the population to rise again, with one person in every three being less than 20-years old.

INHABITANTS PER SQ KM

	More than 250	■	Capital city
	100–250	●	Major city
	50–100		
	Less than 50		

FARMING AND LAND USE

Potatoes were once the traditional staple food of the Irish; potatoes and cereals flourish in the drier east. The climate is too wet for many types of crop, particularly in the west, where the soils are thin and the land is mostly used for sheep grazing. In bog areas a type of soil called peat is cut from the ground and dried to be burned as fuel.

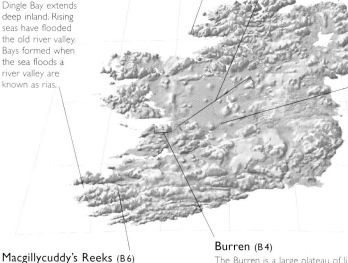

FARMING AND LAND USE

🐄 Cattle	
🐑 Sheep	
🌾 Cereals	
☘ Potatoes	
	Cropland
	Forest
	Pasture
●	Major conurbation

THE LANDSCAPE

Ireland's mountains are nearly all close to the sea. They form a ring of high ground – broken in only a few places – encircling a lower lying plain which fills the central areas. Hundreds of lakes, large areas of bogland and low, grassy hills cover this central plain. The west coast follows an extremely irregular line, with many long bays and headlands.

High cliffs (C 2)
The cliffs of Donegal are some of the highest in Europe. Slieve League has been half cut away by sea erosion, so that the cliff rises vertically, all the way up from the shore to its 670 m summit.

Lakes made by glaciers
The central plain is covered with lakes of many different sizes. Most of these lakes were formed by huge blocks of ice which remained lying around as the last Ice Age came to an end, slowly melting over hundreds of years to leave sunken pits in the land surface.

Flooded river valleys (A 6)
Dingle Bay extends deep inland. Rising seas have flooded the old river valley. Bays formed when the sea floods a river valley are known as rias.

Shannon (C 4)
The Shannon is Ireland's longest river and also its main source of hydro-electric power. The main power station lies to the north of Limerick.

Macgillycuddy's Reeks (B 6)
This is the highest mountain range in Ireland. The jagged peaks and steep-sided valleys were cut from the highly resistant rocks by glacial erosion, during the last Ice Age.

Burren (B 4)
The Burren is a large plateau of limestone rock. Limestone is permeable, which means that water sinks below the surface and flows underground. The bare rock is visible at the surface in many places, where it is called a limestone pavement.

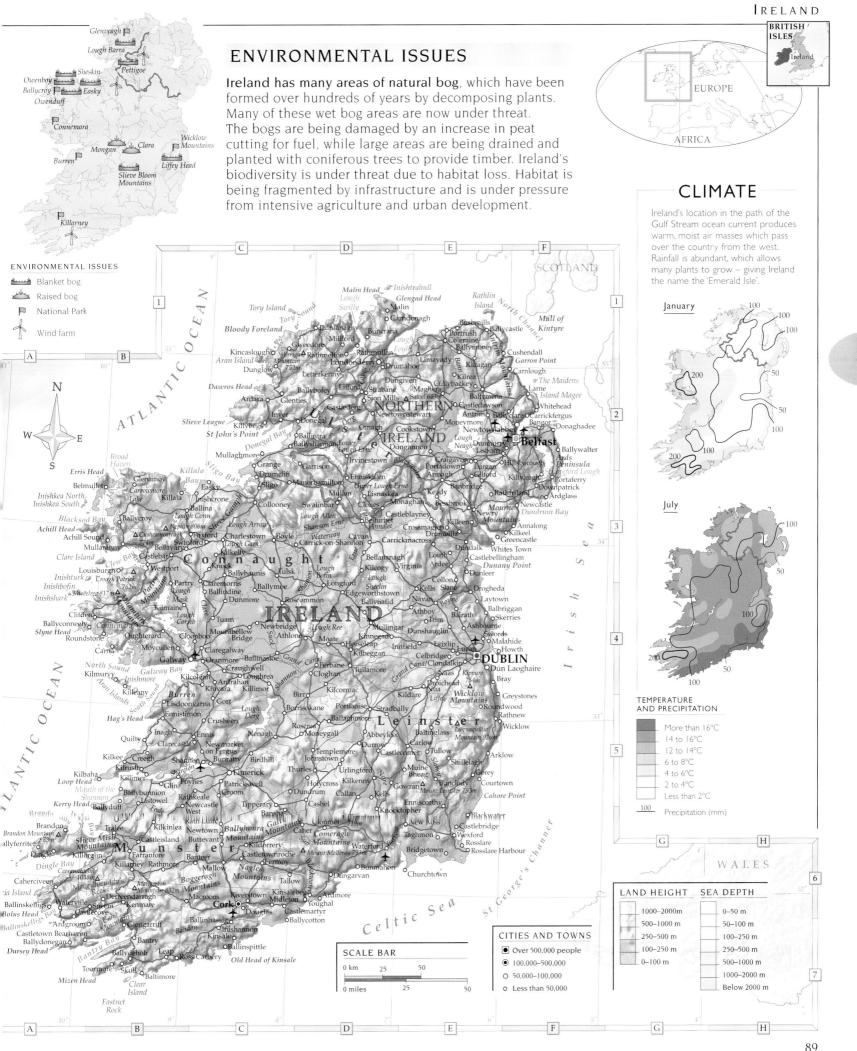

BRITISH ISLES

ENVIRONMENTAL ISSUES

Ireland has many areas of natural bog, which have been formed over hundreds of years by decomposing plants. Many of these wet bog areas are now under threat. The bogs are being damaged by an increase in peat cutting for fuel, while large areas are being drained and planted with coniferous trees to provide timber. Ireland's biodiversity is under threat due to habitat loss. Habitat is being fragmented by infrastructure and is under pressure from intensive agriculture and urban development.

CLIMATE

Ireland's location in the path of the Gulf Stream ocean current produces warm, moist air masses which pass over the country from the west. Rainfall is abundant, which allows many plants to grow – giving Ireland the name the 'Emerald Isle'.

January

July

TEMPERATURE AND PRECIPITATION

- More than 16°C
- 14 to 16°C
- 12 to 14°C
- 6 to 8°C
- 4 to 6°C
- 2 to 4°C
- Less than 2°C

100 — Precipitation (mm)

ENVIRONMENTAL ISSUES

- Blanket bog
- Raised bog
- National Park
- Wind farm

SCALE BAR

0 km   25   50

0 miles   25   50

CITIES AND TOWNS

- Over 500,000 people
- 100,000–500,000
- 50,000–100,000
- Less than 50,000

LAND HEIGHT

- 1000–2000m
- 500–1000 m
- 250–500 m
- 100–250 m
- 0–100 m

SEA DEPTH

- 0–50 m
- 50–100 m
- 100–250 m
- 250–500 m
- 500–1000 m
- 1000–2000 m
- Below 2000 m

SCOTLAND

Scotland occupies the northern third of Britain and has three main regions: the northern highlands and islands, the Southern Uplands and, between these two mountain areas, the central lowlands, where around three quarters of the population live and work. Scotland was once an independent country and, after nearly 300 years of union with England, has regained its own parliament, with certain autonomous powers. Scotland's economy has been boosted over the last 30 years by the North Sea oil industry.

INDUSTRY

A century ago, the area around the River Clyde was one of the great industrial regions of the world. The old heavy industries have since declined and been replaced by hi-tech and electronics industries, earning the area the name of 'Silicon Glen'. North Sea oil has brought many jobs and attracted new, oil-based industries such as chemicals and plastics production to the east coast.

INDUSTRY

✈ Aerospace	⬦ Oil and gas
⬦ Brewing	⬚ Hi-tech industry
⚖ Chemicals	⬚ Printing and publishing
✿ Engineering	⬚ Tourism
Fish processing	
Food processing	⬚ Major industrial centre / area
Textiles	— Major road

ENVIRONMENTAL ISSUES

During a storm in January 1993, the Braer oil tanker struck the cliffs of southern Shetland. The ship broke up, shedding its entire load of crude oil into the sea. Although the oil was washed away within weeks, it did have some long-term effects upon the shellfish industry. Due to its favourable landscape, Scotland has seen a significant rise in the number of wind farms built in recent years.

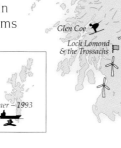

Aviemore
Cairngorms
Glen Coe
Loch Lomond & the Trossachs
Braer – 1993

ENVIRONMENTAL ISSUES

🛢	Major oil spill
⛷	Skiing resort
🌬	Wind farm
⚑	National Park

FARMING AND LAND USE

The eastern side of Scotland has a drier climate than the west and is suitable for growing cereal crops and vegetables. Most of the mountain areas are too wet and barren for arable farming and are put to a variety of uses, which include sheep and deer farming, game-keeping, forestry, tourism and recreation. Scottish fishermen currently land about two-thirds of all the fish caught by the UK.

FARMING AND LAND USE

🐂	Cattle
🦌	Deer
🐟	Fishing
🐑	Sheep
🌾	Cereals
🌱	Root crops
🌲	Timber
▨	Cropland
	Forest
	Mountains
	Pasture
•	Major conurbation

Aberdeen
Dundee
Glasgow
Edinburgh

THE LANDSCAPE

Much of Scotland is rugged and mountainous. During the last Ice Age, around 18,000 years ago, glaciers and great sheets of ice attacked Scotland's hard, ancient rocks, leaving behind a landscape of high moorlands and steep-sided mountains separated by deep valleys, often filled by lakes known as lochs.

Glen Mor (D 3)
Glen Mor is a deep valley which runs right across Scotland. It marks a major line of rock fracture, known as a fault. Much of the fault line is filled by Loch Ness (D 3) and Loch Linnhe (C 4).

Grampians (D 4)
The Grampians are Britain's largest and highest mountain region. They include the spectacular Cairngorm range (E 3) and, to the west, Ben Nevis (D 4), the highest point in the British Isles, at 1,343 m.

Hebrides (A 2), (B 6)
The Inner and Outer Hebrides comprise several large islands and hundreds of small ones. Many of these were formed following the last Ice Age, as the sea level rose, cutting off parts of the mountainous landscape from the mainland.

Firth of Forth (F 5)
The Firth of Forth is one of several great sea inlets, known as firths, along the Scottish coast. They include the Firths of Clyde (D 6), Tay (F 5) and Moray (E 3).

Lochs (D 5)
The many sea lochs (fjords) of the west coast were formed as the sea level rose after the last Ice Age, flooding the deep valleys that had been cut by glaciers. The sea lochs cause the coast to follow a highly irregular line.

Rannoch Moor (D 5)
Rannoch Moor is the largest wild moorland in Scotland. A great ice sheet covered the area during the last Ice Age, leaving behind a vast expanse of bleak, bare ground, pitted with small depressions.

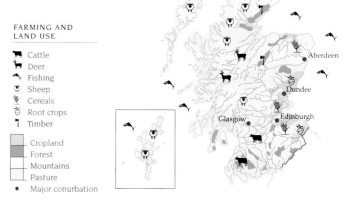

Wick
Stornoway
Banff
Inverness
Peterhead
Aberdeen
Fort William
Perth
Dundee
Glasgow
Dunfermline
Greenock
Edinburgh
Paisley
Kilmarnock
East Kilbride
Ayr
Prestwick
Dumfries
Lerwick

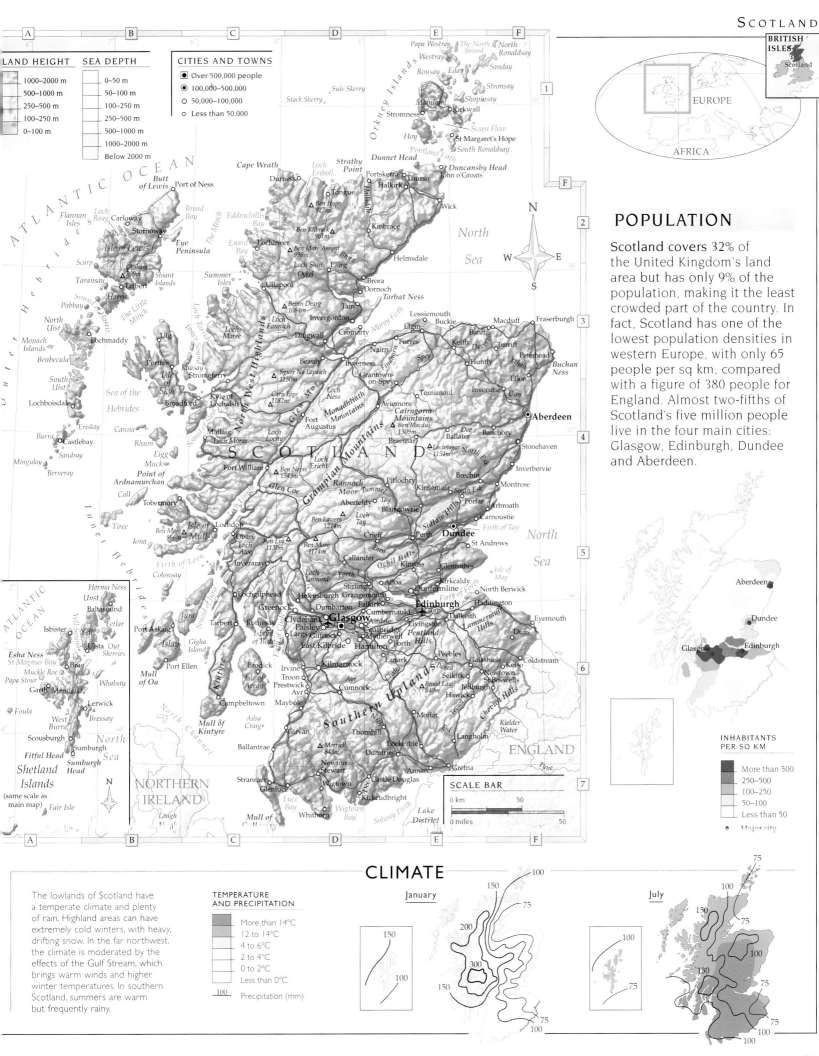

LAND HEIGHT
- 1000–2000 m
- 500–1000 m
- 250–500 m
- 100–250 m
- 0–100 m

SEA DEPTH
- 0–50 m
- 50–100 m
- 100–250 m
- 250–500 m
- 500–1000 m
- 1000–2000 m
- Below 2000 m

CITIES AND TOWNS
- ◼ Over 500,000 people
- ◉ 100,000–500,000
- ◎ 50,000–100,000
- ○ Less than 50,000

BRITISH ISLES

EUROPE

AFRICA

Scotland

POPULATION

Scotland covers 32% of the United Kingdom's land area but has only 9% of the population, making it the least crowded part of the country. In fact, Scotland has one of the lowest population densities in western Europe, with only 65 people per sq km, compared with a figure of 380 people for England. Almost two-fifths of Scotland's five million people live in the four main cities: Glasgow, Edinburgh, Dundee and Aberdeen.

INHABITANTS PER SQ KM
- More than 500
- 250–500
- 100–250
- 50–100
- Less than 50
- ● Major city

SCALE BAR
0 km 50
0 miles 50

CLIMATE

The lowlands of Scotland have a temperate climate and plenty of rain. Highland areas can have extremely cold winters, with heavy, drifting snow. In the far northwest, the climate is moderated by the effects of the Gulf Stream, which brings warm winds and higher winter temperatures. In southern Scotland, summers are warm but frequently rainy.

TEMPERATURE AND PRECIPITATION
- More than 14°C
- 12 to 14°C
- 4 to 6°C
- 2 to 4°C
- 0 to 2°C
- Less than 0°C

100 Precipitation (mm)

January

July

NORTHERN ENGLAND & WALES

The Industrial Revolution of the 18th and 19th centuries began in northern England, exploiting rich local resources to begin a new era of mass production. Today, these industries have declined, but despite a number of difficult years, northern England is becoming more prosperous again. Similarly, south Wales was once a major coal-mining and heavy industrial area but this has largely been replaced by new service industries. The magnificent scenery throughout this region attracts many tourists and outdoor enthusiasts.

INDUSTRY

Traditional industries such as iron and steel, coal-mining and textiles have been in decline for many years. More recently, the type of industries have changed to light engineering and hi-tech industries, producing microchips and computers, together with service industries such as insurance and retailing, printing and publishing. Tourism is important; large numbers of people visit the area's stunning national parks each year.

INDUSTRY

✈	Aerospace	☇	Pharmaceuticals
♦	Brewing	⚓	Shipbuilding
🚗	Car manufacture	👕	Textiles
◎	Ceramics	🛢	Oil refining
⚗	Chemicals	💻	Hi-tech industry
✿	Engineering	📠	Printing and publishing
🐟	Fish processing	⌂	Tourism
🍴	Food processing		
⚒	Iron & steel	▪	Major industrial centre / area
△	Metal refining	—	Major road

ENVIRONMENTAL ISSUES

Some of the UK's most dramatic scenery is found in this area, and national parks have long been established to protect the environment. These parks have proved so popular that in some places tourists are in danger of destroying the environment. Coal-fired power stations in the region power the large cities, but recently there has been an increase in renewable energy production.

Milford Haven – 1996

Severn Barrage (proposed)

ENVIRONMENTAL ISSUES

- ⌂ Coal-fired power station
- ⌂ Barrage scheme
- ≈ Hydro-electric scheme
- ⚑ National park
- 🌀 Wind farm
- ⛴ Major oil spill
- • Major industrial city

FARMING AND LAND USE

The eastern lowlands have an ideal climate for arable crops, while oats and potatoes grow in the north and west. The southwest is used mainly for grazing cattle and sheep, which also graze rough in the upland areas of the Pennines and Wales. Forestry is increasingly important in mountain areas.

FARMING AND LAND USE

- 🐂 Cattle
- 🐑 Sheep
- 🌾 Cereals
- 🥬 Market gardening
- 🍓 Root crops
- ▢ Cropland
- ▨ Forest
- ▢ Pasture
- • Major conurbation

THE LANDSCAPE

The Pennines form the backbone of northern England. Likewise, the Cambrian Mountains, including the spectacular landscape of Snowdonia, run the length of central Wales. To the east, the Aire and Ouse rivers have cut a broad flood plain between the Pennines and the North York Moors, while in the far northwest, Cumbria's Lake District has many long, deep lakes, which were formed during the last Ice Age.

Limestone pavements
Bare 'pavements' of weathered limestone are also known as karst scenery. They have a block-like appearance, with deep cracks between the blocks that have been dissolved by rainwater.

Spurn Head (F4)
Spurn Head is a long sand bar (called a spit) at the mouth of the Humber estuary. It was formed by waves which deposited sand across the mouth of the bay. Constant erosion has often made Spurn Head almost inaccessible from the mainland.

Lake District (C3)
The Lake District covers a small area of the Cumbrian Mountains. The 15 lakes here form a radial pattern, spreading out from a central zone of volcanic rock.

The Pennines (D3)

North York Moors (E3)

Snowdonia (B5)
These spectacular mountains include Snowdon, the highest point in England and Wales, at 1,085 m. The spectacular sheer sides and jagged ridges were carved by glaciers during the last Ice Age.

Cambrian Mountains (B6)
The Cambrian range runs the whole length of the country and contains some of the oldest rocks in Britain. The rock is rich in minerals. Slate was also once mined in great quantities in northern and central areas.

POPULATION

The cities of Liverpool, Manchester, Leeds and Bradford have spread out to form great conurbations. In the West Midlands, large populations grew up in and around the industrial cities of Coventry and Birmingham. The northeastern coast from Middlesbrough to Newcastle upon Tyne is also densely populated. The area around Newport, Cardiff and Swansea is home to more than 60% of the population of Wales. Upland regions are sparsely populated.

INHABITANTS PER SQ KM

- More than 500
- 250–500
- 100–250
- 50–100
- Less than 50
- • Major city

CLIMATE

Northern England tends to be cooler and wetter than the south, especially in the summer months. High rainfall totals are recorded in the upland areas of the west. The east, in the 'rainshadow' of the Pennines, is drier.

January

July

TEMPERATURE AND PRECIPITATION

- More than 16°C
- 14 to 16°C
- 12 to 14°C
- 4 to 6°C
- 2 to 4°C
- Less than 2°C
- 100 Precipitation (mm)

LAND HEIGHT

- 500–1000 m
- 250–500 m
- 100–250 m
- 0–100 m

SEA DEPTH

- 0–10 m
- 10–25 m
- 25–50 m
- 50–100 m
- 100–250 m
- 250–500 m
- Below 500 m

CITIES AND TOWNS

- ■ Over 500,000 people
- ◉ 100,000–500,000
- ○ 50,000–100,000
- ○ Less than 50,000

SCALE BAR

0 km   25   50

0 miles   25   50

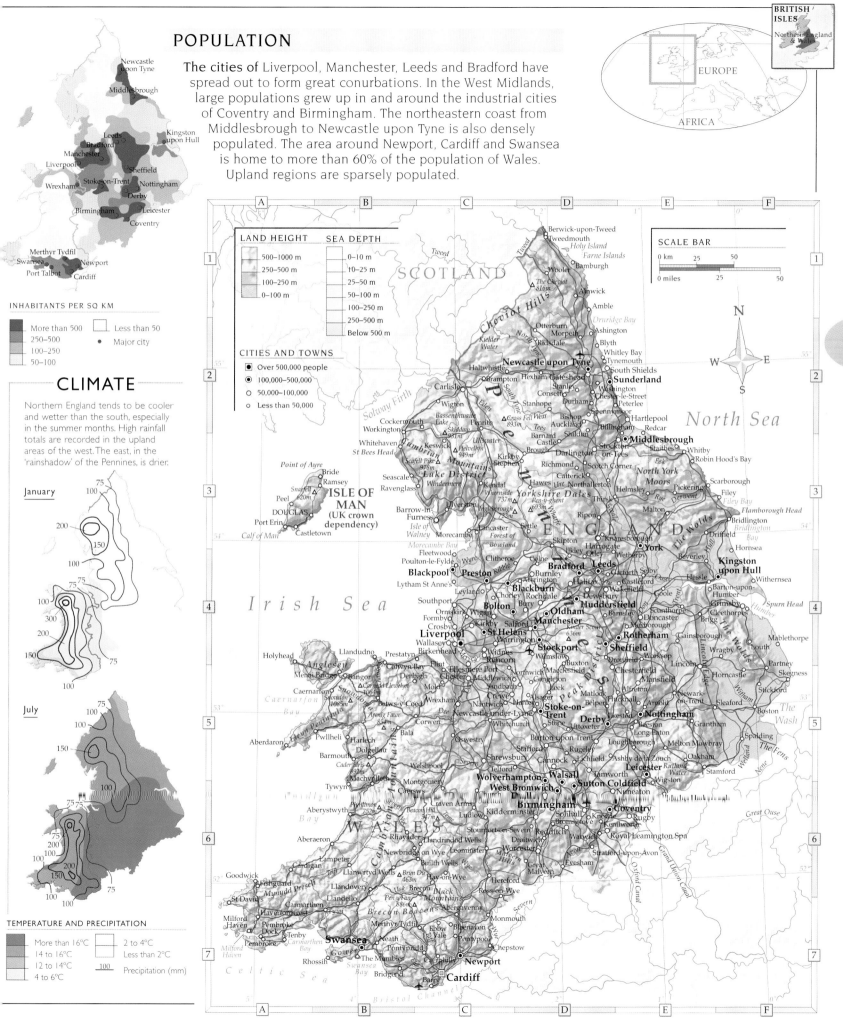

93

SOUTHERN ENGLAND

The southern counties of England, and particularly Greater London, are the most densely populated part of the British Isles. There are more industries and more jobs here than anywhere else in the UK. In contrast, the counties of the far west and east are much less heavily populated and more rural, although towns in the eastern counties have been growing rapidly since the 1980s. Following the completion of the Channel Tunnel, the UK has had a direct rail link to Europe.

INDUSTRY

London is one of the world's top financial centres and is also a leading centre for other service industries including insurance, the media and publishing. Many car manufacturers are based in southern England, though the numbers of people employed have greatly decreased. Several cities, including Cambridge and Swindon, are centres for hi-tech industry. Thousands of tourists visit the historic and cultural centres in southern England every year.

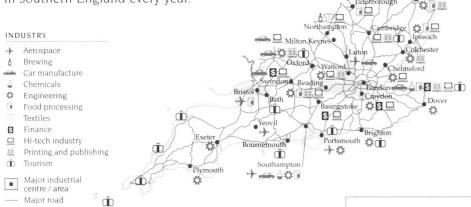

INDUSTRY

- ✈ Aerospace
- 🍺 Brewing
- 🚗 Car manufacture
- 🧪 Chemicals
- ⚙ Engineering
- 🍽 Food processing
- 👕 Textiles
- S Finance
- 💻 Hi-tech industry
- 📖 Printing and publishing
- 🏛 Tourism
- ● Major industrial centre / area
- —— Major road

ENVIRONMENTAL ISSUES

The large and growing population of southern England has increased pressure for the development of 'green belt' land, designed to protect the countryside surrounding large cities. Alternatives include infilling in urban areas, 'brownfield' redevelopment and building on flood plains. The proposed expansion of Heathrow airport has been cancelled.

ENVIRONMENTAL ISSUES

- 'Green belt' areas
- National Park
- Wind farm
- ● Major town/city

FARMING AND LAND USE

Fertile soils and reliable rainfall mean that a wide range of crops can be grown in southern England. Large arable farms growing wheat and barley are found in the flat eastern counties, and a great variety of soft and orchard fruits and vegetables are grown in market gardens in the far southeast. Beef and dairy cattle and large flocks of sheep are grazed throughout the south.

FARMING AND LAND USE

- 🐂 Cattle
- 🐟 Fishing
- 🐑 Sheep
- 🌾 Cereals
- 🥬 Market gardening

- Cropland
- Forest
- Pasture
- ● Major conurbation

THE LANDSCAPE

The landscape of southern England is very varied. Cornwall in the far west has craggy hills, and a jagged coastline shaped by the Atlantic Ocean. The Cotswolds and the North and South Downs are gentle hills, while towards the east, the land becomes flatter. Near the east coast, low-lying areas are occasionally prone to flooding.

Chalk hills The rounded hills of the Chilterns (F 3) are made from chalk. Because chalk is a porous rock, water quickly seeps through it, so few rivers can be seen in chalk areas.

The Broads (H 2) The Broads in Norfolk are a series of wide waterways flowing across flat meadows. The channels were cut by peat cutters and are not 'natural'. They then flooded, forming shallow inland lakes.

Steep cliffs The coasts of north Devon and Cornwall are battered by great waves from the Atlantic Ocean. The force of the waves weakens the rock at the foot of the cliffs, causing them to be 'undercut'. The top layer of rock breaks off and the cliffs recede.

Dartmoor (B 5) Dartmoor is the visible part of a great dome of granite rock. It was formed when molten rock seeped into and cooled in the Earth's crust. Because granite is so hard it erodes very slowly, so outcrops of rock known as tors can be seen all over Dartmoor.

River Thames (F 3) The Thames has its source close to the Cotswolds, and meanders through Oxford and London before reaching the North Sea in a wide estuary.

BRITISH ISLES
Southern England

CLIMATE

Southern England has a warm, temperate climate. The eastern counties are more windy and exposed, and low rainfall means that drought has become a major problem in the far southeast.

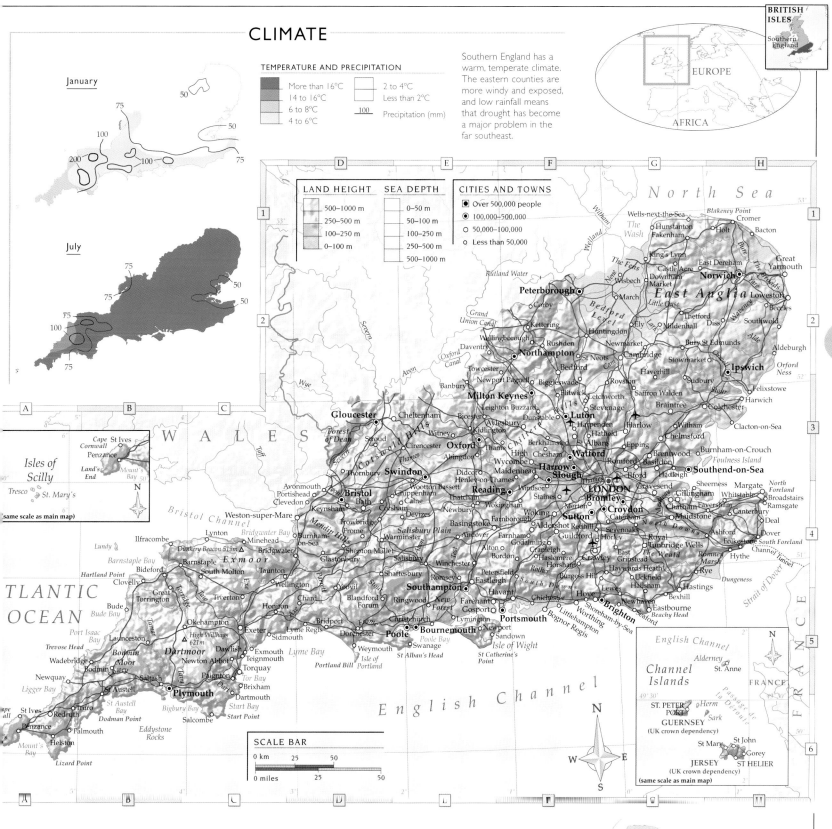

POPULATION

Greater London and the southeastern counties are the most heavily populated areas of England. More than seven million people live in Greater London, a conurbation which extends almost to the boundary of the M25 motorway. Other large population centres are found along the south coast and close to motorways – Brighton, Southampton, Portsmouth, Oxford, Swindon and Reading are among the biggest. Many people live a long distance from their workplaces and commute into cities by car and train.

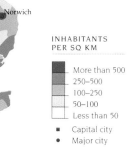

INHABITANTS PER SQ KM
More than 500
250–500
100–250
50–100
Less than 50
■ Capital city
● Major city

FRANCE

ANDORRA, FRANCE, MONACO

France has helped to shape the history and culture of Europe for centuries. Today, as a founder-member of the European Union, France is a keen supporter of the eventual political and economic integration of Europe's different countries. France is Western Europe's leading farming nation, and one of the world's top industrial powers. Its cultural attractions and scenery draw tourists from around the world.

FARMING AND LAND USE

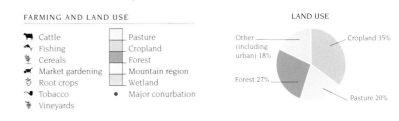

France is able to produce a variety of crops because of its rich soils and mild climate. Wheat is grown in many parts of the north, along with potatoes and other vegetables. Fields of maize and sunflowers and fruit orchards, are found in the south, while grapes for the famous wine industry are grown across the country. Beef and dairy cattle are grazed on low-lying pasture.

FARMING AND LAND USE

- 🐂 Cattle
- 🎣 Fishing
- 🌾 Cereals
- 🐄 Market gardening
- 🌱 Root crops
- 🚬 Tobacco
- 🍇 Vineyards

- Pasture
- Cropland
- Forest
- Mountain region
- Wetland
- ● Major conurbation

LAND USE

Other (including urban) 18%
Cropland 35%
Forest 27%
Pasture 20%

THE LANDSCAPE

The north and west of France is made up of mainly flat, grassy plains or low hills. Wooded mountains line the country's borders in the south and east, and much of central France is taken up by the Massif Central, an enormous plateau, cut by deep river valleys and scattered with extinct volcanoes. Three major rivers, the Loire, Seine and Garonne drain the lowland basins.

Paris Basin

The Paris Basin is a saucer-shaped hollow made up of layers of hard and soft rock, covered with very fertile soils. It runs across about 100,000 sq km of northern France.

Alps (E 5)

The western end of the European Alpine mountain chain stretches into southeast France. The French Alps can be crossed by several passes, which give access to Italy and Switzerland.

Normandy

The coast of Normandy is lined with high chalk cliffs.

Pyrenees (C 7)

These mountains form a natural barrier between France and Spain. Several of their peaks reach heights of over 3,000 m. The Pyrenees are difficult to cross, due to their height, and because they have few low passes.

Massif Central (D 5)

This vast granite plateau was formed over 200 million years ago. Volcanic activity here only stopped within the last 10,000 years and the region's rounded hills are the worn down remains of volcanic mountains.

Mont Blanc (E 5)

This mountain in the French Alps is the tallest in Western Europe. It is 4,807 m high.

Camargue (D 7)

The Camargue is an area of marshes, pastures, sand dunes and salt flats at the mouth of the River Rhône. Rare animal and plant species are found there.

INDUSTRY

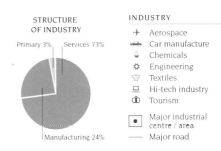

France is one of the world's top manufacturing nations, with a variety of both traditional and hi-tech industries. Cars, machinery and electronic products are exported worldwide, along with luxury goods such as perfumes, fashions and fine wines. Extensive use of nuclear power has allowed France to become the world's largest net exporter of electricity.

STRUCTURE OF INDUSTRY

Primary 3%
Services 73%
Manufacturing 24%

INDUSTRY

- ✈ Aerospace
- 🚗 Car manufacture
- 🧪 Chemicals
- ⚙ Engineering
- 👕 Textiles
- 💻 Hi-tech industry
- 🍺 Tourism
- ▣ Major industrial centre / area
- — Major road

POPULATION

In the past 50 years, most people have moved from the countryside into urban areas. Paris and its suburbs, the industrial cities, and the Côte d'Azur in the southeast are the most economically developed parts of France and now have the biggest populations.

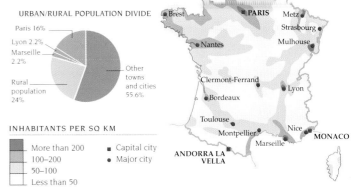

URBAN/RURAL POPULATION DIVIDE

Paris 16%
Lyon 2.2%
Marseille 2.2%
Rural population 24%
Other towns and cities 55.6%

INHABITANTS PER SQ KM

- More than 200
- 100–200
- 50–100
- Less than 50
- ■ Capital city
- ● Major city

ENVIRONMENTAL ISSUES

Many of France's coastal areas have been polluted by industry and tourism. A summer heatwave in 2003 severeley affected France, with temperatures of up to 40°C contributing to the deaths of an estimated 15,000 people. France's reliance on nuclear energy – over 75% of its electricity is generated by nuclear power – means that it suffers less from the pollution caused by burning fossil fuels than many other countries in Europe.

ENVIRONMENTAL
ISSUES

⌐ Nuclear power station
▨ Sea pollution
☐ Polluted rivers
● Major industrial centre

CLIMATE

In winter, the coldest areas of France are the mountains of the Massif Central, and the Alps. Summers are hottest on the Mediterranean coast.

TEMPERATURE
AND PRECIPITATION

More than 20°C
15 to 20°C
10 to 15°C
5 to 10°C
0 to 5°C
0 to -5°C
Less than -5°C

100 Precipitation (mm)

January

July

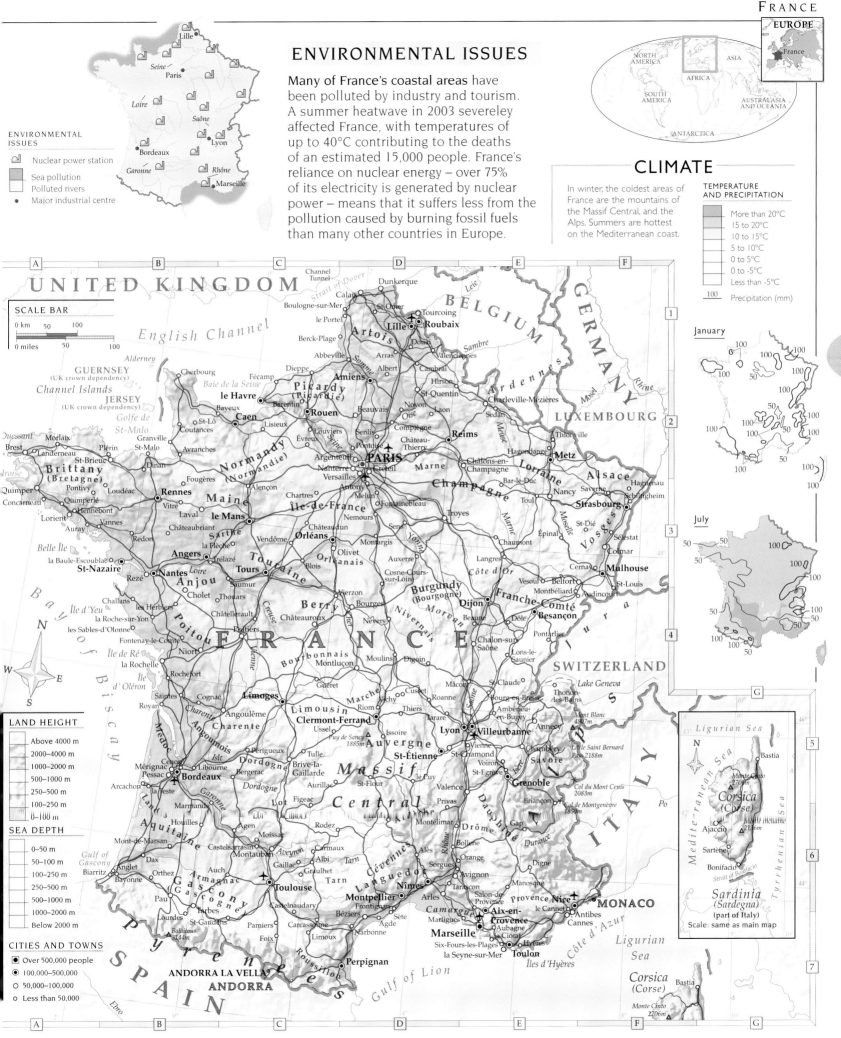

SCALE BAR
0 km   50   100
0 miles   50   100

LAND HEIGHT
Above 4000 m
2000–4000 m
1000–2000 m
500–1000 m
250–500 m
100–250 m
0–100 m

SEA DEPTH
0–50 m
50–100 m
100–250 m
250–500 m
500–1000 m
1000–2000 m
Below 2000 m

CITIES AND TOWNS
● Over 500,000 people
◉ 100,000–500,000
◉ 50,000–100,000
○ Less than 50,000

SPAIN AND PORTUGAL

PORTUGAL, SPAIN

Spain and Portugal occupy the Iberian Peninsula, which is cut off from the rest of Europe by the Pyrenees. Over the centuries, Iberia has been invaded and settled by many different peoples. The Moors, who arrived from North Africa in the 8th century, ruled much of Spain for almost 800 years and their influence can still be seen in Spanish culture. Portugal has modernized it's economy since joining the European Union, and both countries have changed their currencies to the euro.

INDUSTRY

Madrid, Barcelona and the northern ports are Spain's industrial centres. Here, iron ore from Spanish mines is used to make steel, and factories produce cars, machinery and chemicals. Portugal exports textiles, clothing and footwear, along with fish such as sardines and tuna, caught off the Atlantic coast. In both countries, tourism is very important to the economy.

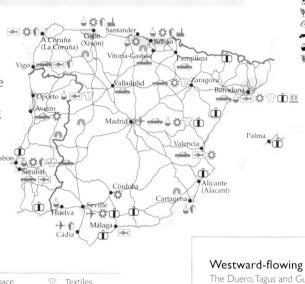

STRUCTURE OF INDUSTRY

Primary 4%
Services 67%
Manufacturing 29%

INDUSTRY

✈ Aerospace	⬦ Textiles
🚗 Car manufacture	⚒ Mining
⚗ Chemicals	🛆 Tourism
⚙ Engineering	▥ Publishing
⌕ Fish processing	
⚓ Shipbuilding	⬛ Major industrial centre / area
⚒ Steel	— Major road

POPULATION

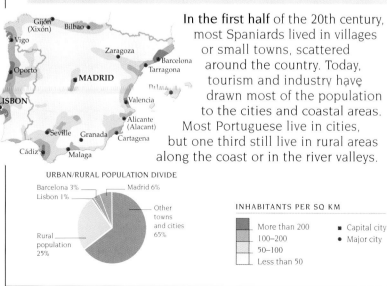

In the first half of the 20th century, most Spaniards lived in villages or small towns, scattered around the country. Today, tourism and industry have drawn most of the population to the cities and coastal areas. Most Portuguese live in cities, but one third still live in rural areas along the coast or in the river valleys.

URBAN/RURAL POPULATION DIVIDE

Barcelona 3%
Madrid 6%
Lisbon 1%
Other towns and cities 65%
Rural population 25%

INHABITANTS PER SQ KM

	More than 200	■ Capital city
	100–200	● Major city
	50–100	
	Less than 50	

FARMING AND LAND USE

Cereals, especially wheat and barley, are Iberia's chief crops. In the dry south of Spain, the land is irrigated to grow citrus fruits, especially oranges, and vegetables. In both countries, olive trees and vineyards occupy large areas of land; olive oil and wine are important exports. Cork oak trees from Iberia's forests supply 80% of the world's cork.

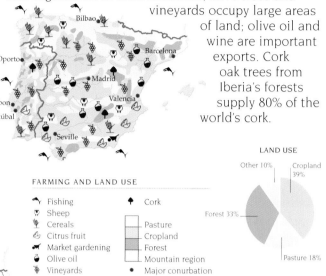

FARMING AND LAND USE

⌁ Fishing	⬥ Cork
🐑 Sheep	
🌾 Cereals	☐ Pasture
🍊 Citrus fruit	▨ Cropland
🐐 Market gardening	▦ Forest
🫒 Olive oil	▧ Mountain region
🍇 Vineyards	● Major conurbation

LAND USE

Other 10%
Cropland 39%
Forest 33%
Pasture 18%

THE LANDSCAPE

Most of inland Spain is taken up by the Meseta, a dry, almost treeless plateau surrounded by steep mountain ranges. The only lowlands, apart from narrow strips along the Mediterranean coast, are the valleys of the Ebro, Tagus, Guadiana and Guadalquivir rivers. Portugal's coast is lined by wide plains. Inland, the River Tagus divides the country in two. To the north the land is hilly and wooded; to the south it is low-lying and drier.

Westward-flowing rivers
The Duero, Tagus and Guadalquivir rivers flow across the Meseta on their courses to the Atlantic Ocean.

River Ebro (E 2)
The River Ebro carries vital irrigation water to Spain's northeastern plains before flowing into the Mediterranean Sea.

Cordillera Cantábrica (C 1)
These rugged, forested mountains rise on Spain's Atlantic coast. They form the northern edge of the Meseta.

The Pyrenees (F 2)
These high mountains form a natural boundary with France.

River Duero (D 2)

River Tagus (B 4)

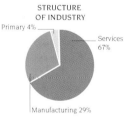

The Meseta
Much of this vast plateau of ancient rock is covered with dry, dusty high plains. It has thin soils and is mainly used to graze sheep and goats.

Sierra Morena (C 5)
The southern end of the Meseta is marked by this low range of mountains.

Guadalquivir Basin (C 5)
The River Guadalquivir has deposited layers of rich soil called alluvium on its flood plain, making this one of Spain's most fertile regions.

Mulhacén (D 5)
Mulhacén, in the snow-capped Sierra Nevada range in southern Spain, is 3,481 m high. It is Iberia's tallest mountain.

ENVIRONMENTAL ISSUES

Soil erosion – where the top layer of soil has been worn away by wind and rain – has affected much of the Iberian Peninsula. This is caused by farming, combined with drought and deforestation. In Spain, a national tree-planting scheme has been started to combat this problem. Industrial and tourist development along the Mediterranean coast of Spain, and in the Balearic Islands, has damaged natural habitats on both land and sea.

ENVIRONMENTAL ISSUES

- Major oil spill
- Overbuilding
- Soil degradation
- Severe soil degradation
- Polluted rivers
- Sea pollution

CLIMATE

Northern Spain is wetter and cooler than the south. On the central plateau, summers are very hot and dry, and winters often freezing. The north of Portugal is cooled by winds blowing off the Atlantic Ocean. The south is warmer, with dry, mild winters.

EUROPE

TEMPERATURE AND PRECIPITATION

- More than 25°C
- 20 to 25°C
- 15 to 20°C
- 10 to 15°C
- 5 to 10°C
- 0 to 5°C
- 0 to -5°C
- -5 to -10°C
- Less than -10°C

100 Precipitation (mm)

January

July

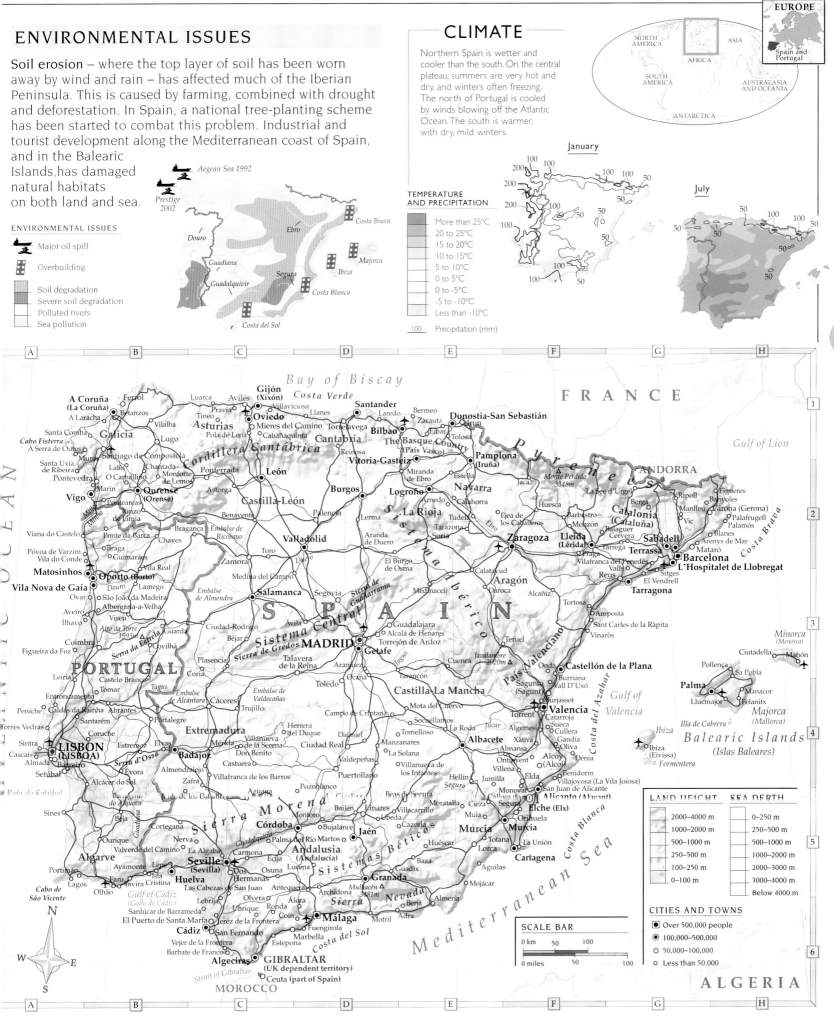

LAND HEIGHT / SEA DEPTH

LAND HEIGHT	SEA DEPTH
2000–4000 m	0–250 m
1000–2000 m	250–500 m
500–1000 m	500–1000 m
250–500 m	1000–2000 m
100–250 m	2000–3000 m
0–100 m	3000–4000 m
	Below 4000 m

CITIES AND TOWNS
- Over 500,000 people
- 100,000–500,000
- 50,000–100,000
- Less than 50,000

SCALE BAR
0 km   50   100
0 miles   50   100

GERMANY AND THE ALPINE STATES

AUSTRIA, GERMANY, LIECHTENSTEIN, SLOVENIA, SWITZERLAND

Germany lies at the heart of Europe and is the biggest industrial power in the continent. In 1945, Germany was divided into two separate countries, East and West Germany, which were reunited in 1990. To the south, the snow-capped peaks of the Alps, Europe's highest mountains, tower over the Alpine states – Switzerland, Austria, Liechtenstein and the former Yugoslavian state of Slovenia.

INDUSTRY

Germany is a leading manufacturer of cars, chemicals, machinery and transport equipment. Switzerland and Liechtenstein, with few raw materials, make high-value products such as watches and pharmaceuticals, and provide services such as banking. The Alpine states are a popular tourist location all year round.

INDUSTRY

- Aerospace
- Car manufacture
- Chemicals
- Engineering
- Iron & steel
- Shipbuilding
- Pharmaceuticals
- Finance
- Hi-tech industry
- Tourism
- Major industrial centre / area
- Major road

STRUCTURE OF INDUSTRY

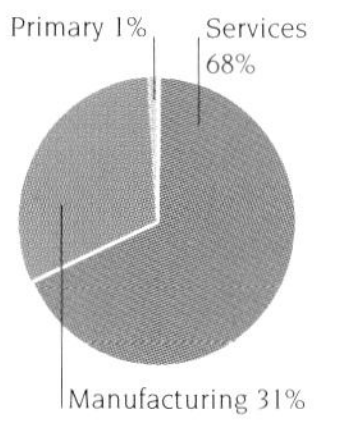

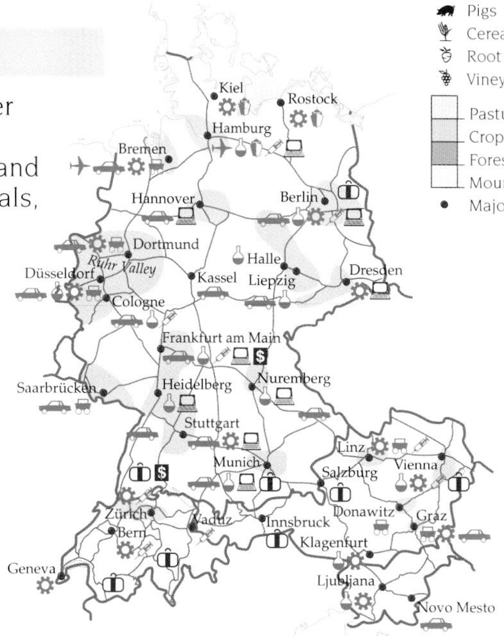

POPULATION

Western and central Germany are the most densely populated areas in this region – particularly in and around the Rhine and Ruhr valleys, where there are many industries. In the south, the steep slopes of the Alps and permanent snow cover on the higher peaks means that most large towns and cities are in scattered lowland areas.

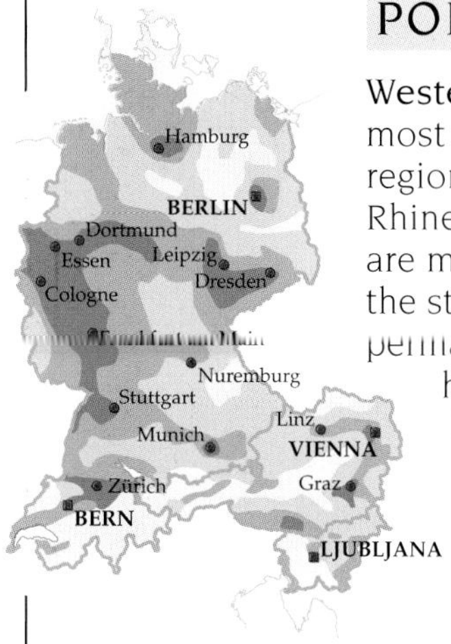

INHABITANTS PER SQ KM

- More than 200
- 100–200
- 50–100
- Less than 50
- Capital city
- Major city

URBAN/RURAL POPULATION DIVIDE

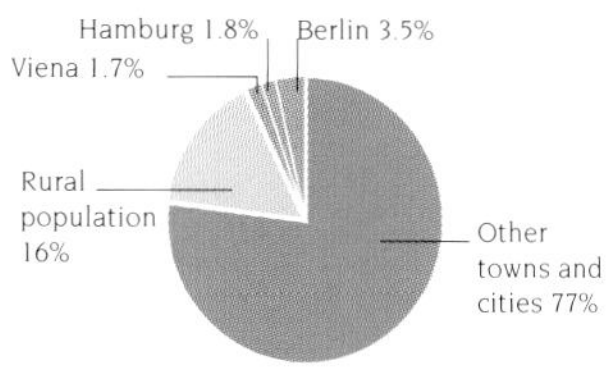

FARMING AND LAND USE

Germany produces three-quarters of its own food. Crop farming is widespread, with cereals and root crops grown in flat, fertile areas. Cattle and pig farming supplies meat and dairy products. Across the Alps, the mountains limit farming, although vines are grown on the warmer, south-facing slopes. The rich pastures of the lower slopes are used to graze beef and dairy cattle.

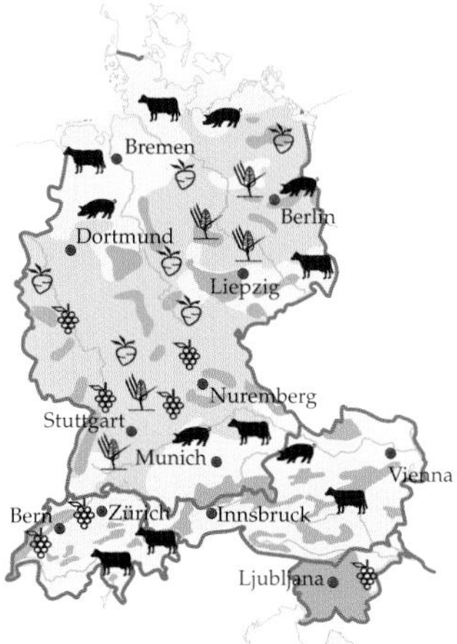

FARMING AND LAND USE

- Cattle
- Pigs
- Cereals
- Root crops
- Vineyards
- Pasture
- Cropland
- Forest
- Mountain region
- Major conurbation

LAND USE

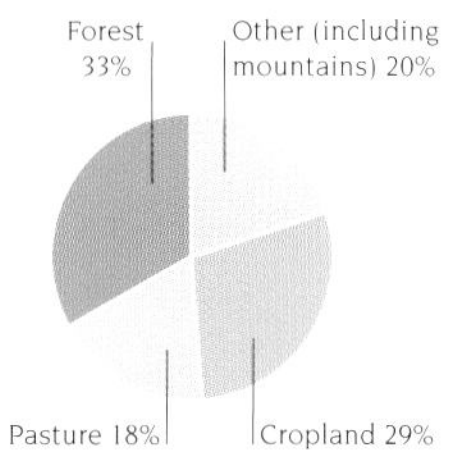

THE LANDSCAPE

To the north, flat plains and heathlands surround the North Sea coast. Further south are Germany's central uplands, which are lower and older than the jagged peaks of the Alps, which began to form about 65 million years ago. From its source in the Black Forest, the River Danube flows eastward across Germany and Austria on its course to the Black Sea. The other major river, the Rhine, flows northward.

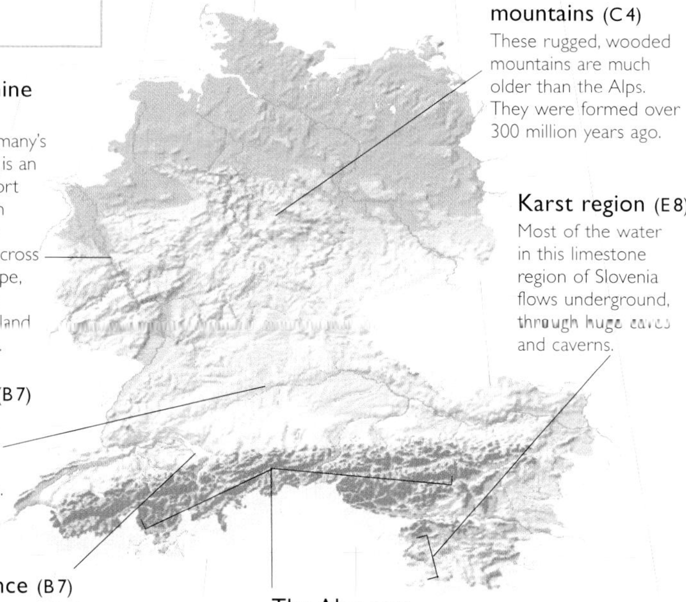

The River Rhine (B5)
The Rhine is Germany's main waterway. It is an important transport route to and from northern ports. It twists and turns across 1,320 km of Europe, from its source in southeast Switzerland to the North Sea.

The Danube (B7)
The Danube is Europe's second longest river, flowing 2,840 km.

Lake Constance (B7)
Lake Constance covers 540 sq km and is Germany's largest lake, although its waters are shared by Austria and Switzerland.

The Harz mountains (C4)
These rugged, wooded mountains are much older than the Alps. They were formed over 300 million years ago.

Karst region (E8)
Most of the water in this limestone region of Slovenia flows underground, through huge caves and caverns.

The Alps (C8)
The Alps were formed when the African Plate collided with the Eurasian Plate, pushing up and crushing huge amounts of rock, to form mountains.

EUROPE
Germany and the Alpine States

SCALE BAR

km 50 100
miles 50 100

CITIES AND TOWNS
■ Over 500,000 people
● 100,000–500,000
○ 50,000–100,000
○ Less than 50,000

ENVIRONMENTAL ISSUES

The large number of industries in Germany, especially in the east of the country, has led to high levels of pollution in cities, and in rivers like the Rhine. Acid rain from car fumes and industrial pollution has poisoned many of Germany's forests. The popularity of the Alps as a year-round tourist destination puts great demands on the environment. The development of new resorts has destroyed the natural habitats of many plants and animals.

ENVIRONMENTAL ISSUES
Urban air pollution
Flooding
Winter tourist resort
Affected by acid rain
Polluted rivers
● Major industrial centre

CLIMATE

Winter temperatures decrease eastwards, and the high Alpine region is coldest. Rainfall is higher in the summer. Climate variations in the Alps are common, due to turbulent air flows.

January

July

TEMPERATURE AND PRECIPITATION
More than 20°C   0 to -5°C
15 to 20°C   -5 to -10°C
10 to 15°C   Less than -10°C
5 to 10°C
0 to 5°C   100 Precipitation (mm)

LAND HEIGHT
Above 4000 m
2000–4000 m
1000–2000 m
500–1000 m
250–500 m
100–250 m
0–100 m

SEA DEPTH
0–10 m
10–25 m
25–50 m
50–100 m

ITALY

ITALY, SAN MARINO, VATICAN CITY

Italy has played an important role in Europe since the Romans based their mighty empire here over 2,000 years ago. The famous boot shape divides into two very different halves. Northern Italy has a varied range of industries and agriculture. Beautiful cities like Venice, Florence, and Rome draw tourists from all over the world. Southern Italy is poorer and less developed than the north, with a hotter, drier climate and less productive land.

THE LANDSCAPE

Italy is a peninsula jutting south from mainland Europe into the Mediterranean Sea. In northern and central Italy the land is mainly mountainous. Most of the flat land is in the Po Valley and along the eastern coast. Italy lies within an earthquake zone, which makes the land unstable, and there are also a number of active volcanoes.

Italian lakes
Great lakes like Garda (B3) and Como (B2) fill several south-facing valleys once occupied by glaciers.

The Dolomites (D 2)
These high mountains are part of the same range as the Alps. They were formed 65 million years ago.

Po Valley (C 2)
The basin of the River Po has the best soils in Italy. Rich alluvium is washed from the mountains by the river to form a wide plain.

The Apennines (C 4)
This mountain range forms the 'backbone' of Italy, dividing the rocky west coast from the flatter sandy east coast.

Earthquakes
The southern Apennines, as well as coastal areas of southwestern Italy, often experience earthquakes and mudslides.

Tyrrhenian Sea (C 6)
This sea, which divides the Italian mainland from Sardinia, is gradually filling with sediment from the rivers which flow into it.

Sardinia
The island of Sardinia is made from very old rocks which were thrust up to form mountains.

Sicily
Sicily is the largest island in the Mediterranean. It has a famous active volcano called Mount Etna, and often experiences earthquakes

Gulf of Taranto (F 7)
During earthquakes, great blocks of land have broken away and sunk into the sea, forming the Gulf's square shape.

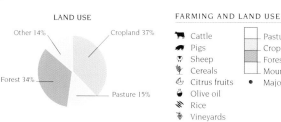

FARMING AND LAND USE

The Po Valley is a broad, flat plain in the north of Italy. It contains the most fertile land in the country, and wheat and rice are the main cereal crops grown here. Grapes for wine are grown everywhere in Italy. In much of the south, the land must be irrigated to support crops. Where there is enough water, citrus fruits, olives, and many kinds of tomatoes are grown.

LAND USE
- Other 14%
- Cropland 37%
- Forest 34%
- Pasture 15%

FARMING AND LAND USE
- Cattle
- Pigs
- Sheep
- Cereals
- Citrus fruits
- Olive oil
- Rice
- Vineyards
- Pasture
- Cropland
- Forest
- Mountain region
- • Major conurbation

INDUSTRY

Italian industry is located mainly in the north. Design is extremely important to Italians and they are proud of the elegant designs of their furniture, clothes and shoes. Though many firms are small, they are very efficient. Italy has few mineral resources so it needs to import raw materials to make cars, engines and other hi-tech products.

INDUSTRY
- Car manufacture
- Chemicals
- Iron & steel
- Textiles
- Finance
- Hi-tech industry
- Tourism
- ▪ Major industrial centre / area
- — Major road

STRUCTURE OF INDUSTRY
- Primary 3%
- Services 66%
- Manufacturing 31%

POPULATION

Most of Italy's population lives in the north, mainly in and around the Po Valley, which is home to over 25 million people. Most people here have a high standard of living. Southern Italy is much more rural; towns are smaller and life is often much harder.

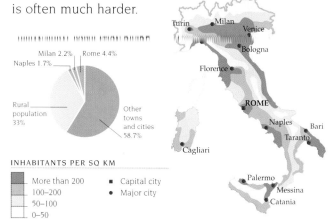

INTERNATIONAL POPULATION BLAH
- Milan 2.2%
- Rome 4.4%
- Naples 1.7%
- Rural population 33%
- Other towns and cities 58.7%

INHABITANTS PER SQ KM
- More than 200
- 100–200
- 50–100
- 0–50
- ▪ Capital city
- • Major city

ITALY

ENVIRONMENTAL ISSUES

Sewage and chemical by-products from industry have polluted the Mediterranean and Adriatic seas. Southern Italy is subject to natural dangers like volcanoes, earthquakes and mudslides. Mount Etna is one of the most active volcanoes in the world.

ENVIRONMENTAL ISSUES
- ◉ Catastrophic earthquakes
- Urban air pollution
- Acid rain
- Sea pollution
- Severe sea pollution
- • Major industrial centre

CLIMATE

The Alpine north has cold winters, often with snow. Further south, temperatures are higher. Sicily has Italy's highest temperatures, due to warm African winds.

January

July

TEMPERATURE AND PRECIPITATION
- More than 25°C
- 20 to 25°C
- 15 to 20°C
- 10 to 15°C
- 5 to 10°C
- 0 to 5°C
- 0 to -5°C
- -5 to -10°C
- Less than -10°C
- 100 Precipitation (mm)

SCALE BAR
0 km 40 80
0 miles 40 80

CITIES AND TOWNS
- ■ Over 500,000 people
- ◉ 100,000–500,000
- ○ 50,000–100,000
- ○ Less than 50,000

LAND HEIGHT
- Above 4000 m
- 2000–4000 m
- 1000–2000 m
- 500–1000 m
- 250–500 m
- 100–250 m
- 0–100 m

SEA DEPTH
- 0–50 m
- 50–100 m
- 100–250 m
- 250–500 m
- 500–1000 m
- 1000–2000 m
- Below 2000 m

CENTRAL EUROPE

CZECH REPUBLIC, HUNGARY, POLAND, SLOVAKIA

Central Europe has been invaded many times throughout history. The countries have changed shape frequently as their borders have shifted backwards and forwards. From the end of the Second World War until 1989, they were ruled by communist governments, which were supported by the Soviet Union. In 1993, the state of Czechoslovakia voted to split into two separate nations, called the Czech Republic and Slovakia.

INDUSTRY

Brown coal, or lignite, is central Europe's main fuel, and one of Poland's major exports. A variety of minerals are mined in the mountains of the Czech Republic and Slovakia. Hungary has a wide range of industries producing vehicles, metals, and chemicals, as well as textiles and electrical goods. The Czech Republic is famous for its breweries and glass-making.

STRUCTURE
OF INDUSTRY

Primary 3%
Services 65%
Manufacturing 32%

INDUSTRY

- ⚗ Brewing
- 🚗 Car manufacture
- ⚗ Chemicals
- ⚙ Engineering
- Food processing
- Iron & steel
- ⚒ Coal mining
- ■ Major industrial centre / area
- — Major road

ENVIRONMENTAL ISSUES

The growth of heavy industries that took place under communist rule has caused terrible environmental pollution in some places. Hungary's oil and Poland's brown coal have a high sulphur content. Burning these fuels to produce electricity causes air pollution, and the sulphur dioxide produced combines with moisture in the air, leading to acid rain.

ENVIRONMENTAL
ISSUES

- Severe industrial pollution
- Flooding
- Urban air pollution
- Affected by acid rain
  Polluted rivers
- Major industrial centre

FARMING AND LAND USE

Central Europe's main crops are cereals such as maize, wheat and rye, along with sugar beet and potatoes. In Hungary, sweet peppers grow, helped by the warm summers and mild winters. They are used to make paprika. Grapes are also grown, to make wine. Large areas of the plains of Hungary and Poland are used for rearing pigs and cattle. Trees for timber grow in the mountains of Slovakia and the Czech Republic.

FARMING AND LAND USE

- 🐄 Cattle
- 🐖 Pigs
- 🌾 Cereals
- Root crops
- Potatoes
- Timber
- Vineyards

- ☐ Pasture
- ☐ Cropland
- ☐ Forest
- • Major conurbation

LAND USE

Other 11%
Cropland 47%
Forest 29%
Pasture 13%

THE LANDSCAPE

The high Carpathian Mountains sweep across northern Slovakia. The lower Sudeten Mountains lie on the border of the Czech Republic and Poland. Together, these mountains form a barrier which divides the Great Hungarian Plain and the River Danube basin in the south from Poland and the vast rolling lowlands of the North European Plain.

Pomerania (C 2)
This is a sandy coastal area with lakes formed by glaciers. It stretches west from the River Vistula to just beyond the German border.

River Vistula (F 4)
Poland's largest river is the Vistula. It flows northwards, passing through the capital, Warsaw, on its way to the Baltic Sea.

North European Plain

Hot springs
The Sudeten mountains (C5) are famous for their hot mineral springs. These occur where water heated deep within the Earth's crust finds its way to the surface along fractures in the rock.

River Danube (D 7)
The River Danube forms the border between Slovakia and Hungary for over 162 km. It then turns south to flow across the Great Hungarian Plain.

Great Hungarian Plain (E 8)
This huge plain covers almost half of Hungary's land area. It is a mixture of farmland and steppe.

Tatra Mountains (E 6)
The Tatra Mountains are a small range at the northern end of the Carpathian Mountains. They include Gerlachovsky Stít, which is Central Europe's highest point at 2,655 m.

POPULATION

Most people in central Europe live in low-lying areas, for example, along the River Vistula in Poland, and in the lowlands of the Czech Republic. In mountainous Slovakia, many people still live in rural towns and villages. The industrial areas and capital cities have the highest population densities.

URBAN/RURAL POPULATION DIVIDE

Warsaw 2.6% Budapest 2.7%
Prague 1.7%
Other towns and cities 59%
Rural population 34%

EUROPE

INHABITANTS PER SQ KM

More than 200
100–200
50–100
Less than 50

■ Capital city
● Major city

CLIMATE

The Carpathian Mountains are both the coldest and the wettest part of central Europe. Temperatures plunge below zero across the whole region during winter. In summer, eastern Hungary is the hottest place.

January

July

TEMPERATURE AND PRECIPITATION

More than 20°C
15 to 20°C
10 to 15°C
5 to 10°C
0 to 5°C
0 to -5°C
Less than -5°C

—100— Precipitation (mm)

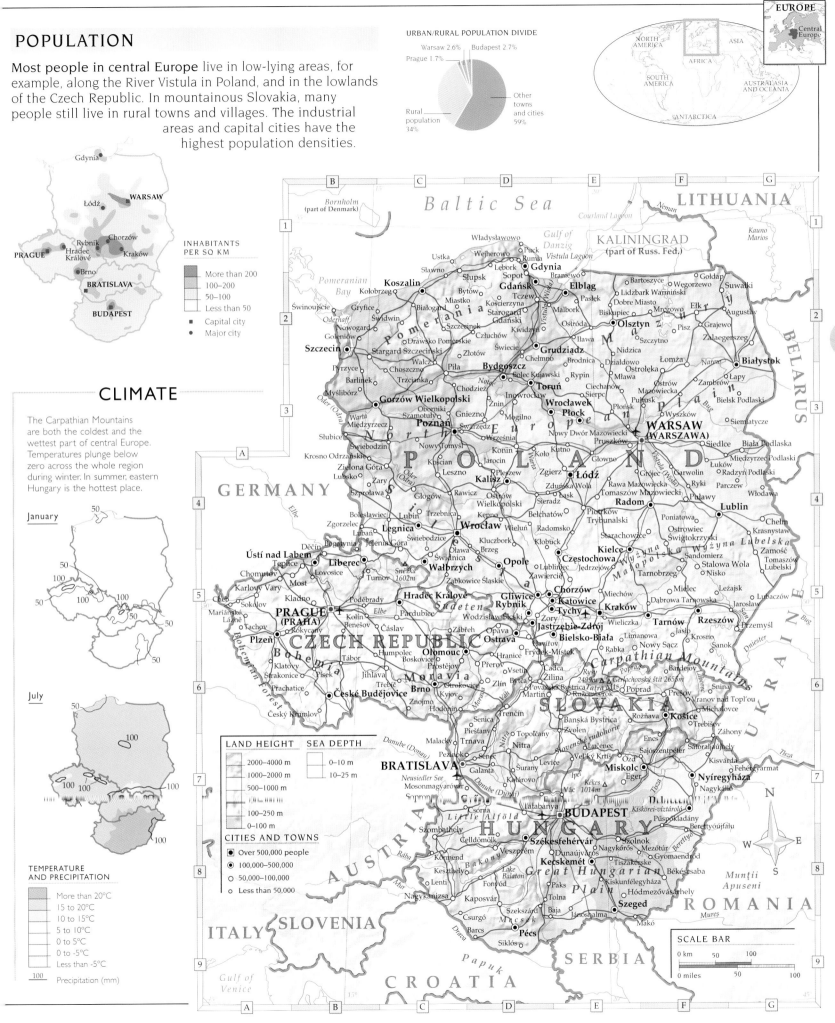

LAND HEIGHT
2000–4000 m
1000–2000 m
500–1000 m
250–500 m
100–250 m
0–100 m

SEA DEPTH
0–10 m
10–25 m

CITIES AND TOWNS
■ Over 500,000 people
● 100,000–500,000
◉ 50,000–100,000
○ Less than 50,000

SCALE BAR
0 km   50   100
0 miles   50   100

SOUTHEAST EUROPE

ALBANIA, BOSNIA AND HERZEGOVINA, BULGARIA, CROATIA, GREECE, KOSOVO, MACEDONIA, MONTENEGRO, SERBIA

Southeast Europe extends inland from the coasts of the Aegean, Adriatic and Black seas. Ancient Greece was the birthplace of European civilization. Albania and Bulgaria were ruled by communists for over 50 years, until the early 1990s. The rest of the region was part of a communist union of states called Yugoslavia. The collapse of this union in 1991 led to a civil war, after which seven separate countries emerged.

THE LANDSCAPE

Southeast Europe is largely mountainous, with ranges running from northwest to southeast. The Dinaric Alps run parallel to the Dalmatian coast, and the Pindus Mountains continue this line into Greece. In the Aegean Sea, the drowned peaks of an old mountain chain form thousands of islands.

Earthquakes
Bulgaria, Greece, and Macedonia lie in earthquake zones. Major earthquakes have hit the Ionian Islands in 1953, and Macedonia in 1963.

Great Hungarian Plain (D1)
The Vojvodina region of Serbia is the southern part of the Great Hungarian Plain. The plain is flat and fertile soils allow grain crops like corn and wheat to be grown.

Dinaric Alps (C2)

Balkan Mountains (F3)
The mountains form a spur running east to west through Bulgaria and separate the two main rivers, the Danube and the Maritsa.

Dalmatian coast (B2)
The Dalmatian coast has many long, narrow islands near the shore. These were formed as the Adriatic Sea flooded the river valleys which ran parallel to the coast.

Greek Islands

The Peloponnese (E6)
The Peloponnese is a mountainous peninsula linked to the Greek mainland only by a narrow strip of land, only 6 km wide, called the Isthmus of Corinth.

Greek Islands
There are two groups of Greek Islands, the Ionian Islands to the west of mainland Greece, and the more numerous islands to the east in the Aegean Sea.

FARMING AND LAND USE

Cereals like wheat, and fruits, vegetables and grapes are grown in the fertile north of the region. The band of mountains across southeast Europe is used mainly for grazing sheep and goats. Further south, and in coastal areas, the warm Mediterranean climate is ideal for growing grapes, olives and tobacco.

FARMING AND LAND USE

- Fishing
- Goats
- Pigs
- Sheep
- Fruit
- Olive oil
- Tobacco
- Vineyards
- Wheat
- Cropland
- Forest
- Mountains
- Pasture
- Major conurbation

LAND USE

- Pasture 27%
- Forest 34%
- Cropland 30%
- Other 9%

STRUCTURE OF INDUSTRY

- Primary 10%
- Services 64%
- Manufacturing 26%

INDUSTRY

Mainland Greece and the many islands in the Aegean Sea are centres of a thriving tourist trade, while tourism on the Black Sea coast continues to grow. The Dalmatian coast's growing tourist industry is recovering after the civil war in former Yugoslavia disrupted it, and other industries. Heavy industries like chemicals, engineering and shipbuilding remain an important source of income in Bulgaria.

INDUSTRY

- Car manufacture
- Chemicals
- Engineering
- Food processing
- Metal refining
- Shipbuilding
- Textiles
- Mining
- Tourism
- Major industrial centre / area
- Major road

POPULATION

Greece's population is two thirds urban; over 35% live in the capital, Athens and in Salonica. In Bulgaria, most people live in cities. About half of Albania's and Macedonia's people are still rural. Since the civil war, the different ethnic groups in Bosnia and Herzegovina, Montenegro, Serbia and Croatia have lived apart from one another.

URBAN/RURAL POPULATION DIVIDE

- Belgrade 3.5%
- Athens 8%
- Sofia 2.5%
- Other towns and cities 42%
- Rural population 44%

INHABITANTS PER SQ KM

- More than 200
- 100–200
- 50–100
- Less than 50
- Capital city
- Major city

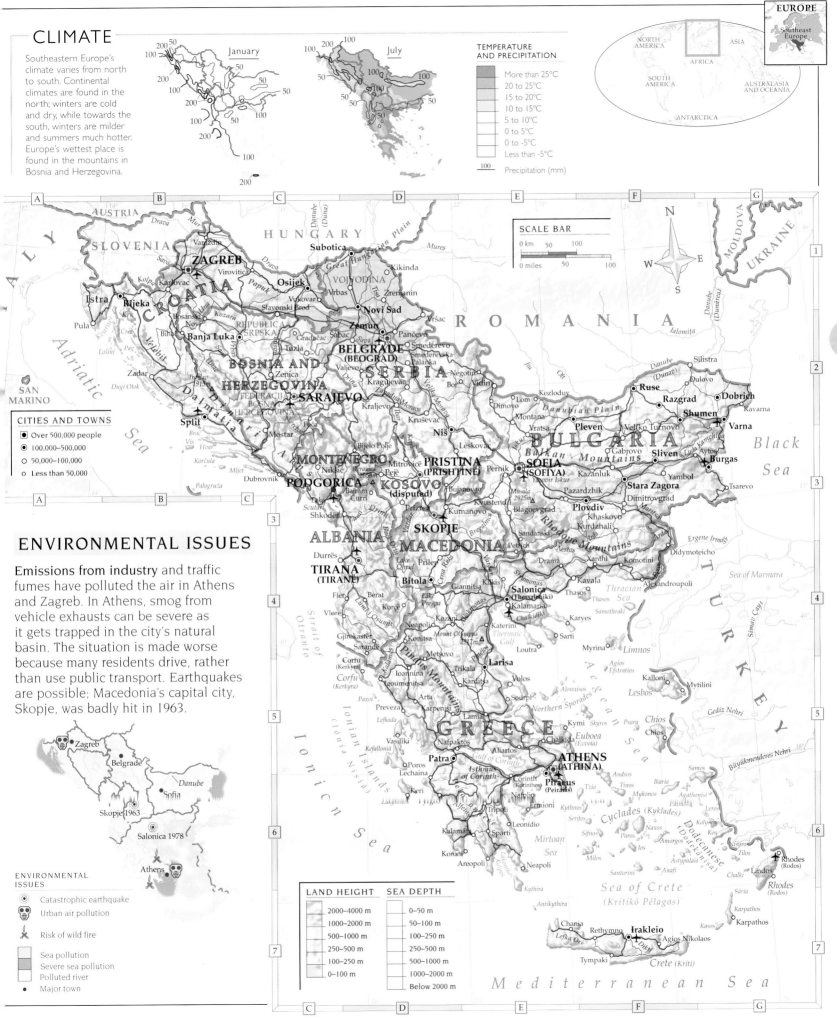

CLIMATE

Southeastern Europe's climate varies from north to south. Continental climates are found in the north; winters are cold and dry, while towards the south, winters are milder and summers much hotter. Europe's wettest place is found in the mountains in Bosnia and Herzegovina.

January

July

TEMPERATURE AND PRECIPITATION

- More than 25°C
- 20 to 25°C
- 15 to 20°C
- 10 to 15°C
- 5 to 10°C
- 0 to 5°C
- 0 to -5°C
- Less than -5°C

100 ──── Precipitation (mm)

EUROPE

Southeast Europe

NORTH AMERICA
SOUTH AMERICA
ASIA
AFRICA
AUSTRALASIA AND OCEANIA
ANTARCTICA

SCALE BAR

0 km 50 100
0 miles 50 100

CITIES AND TOWNS

- ■ Over 500,000 people
- ◉ 100,000–500,000
- ○ 50,000–100,000
- ∘ Less than 50,000

ENVIRONMENTAL ISSUES

Emissions from industry and traffic fumes have polluted the air in Athens and Zagreb. In Athens, smog from vehicle exhausts can be severe as it gets trapped in the city's natural basin. The situation is made worse because many residents drive, rather than use public transport. Earthquakes are possible; Macedonia's capital city, Skopje, was badly hit in 1963.

Zagreb
Belgrade
Danube
Sofia
Skopje 1963
Salonica 1978
Athens

ENVIRONMENTAL ISSUES

- ◉ Catastrophic earthquake
- ☠ Urban air pollution
- ✗ Risk of wild fire
- Sea pollution
- Severe sea pollution
- Polluted river
- • Major town

LAND HEIGHT

- 2000–4000 m
- 1000–2000 m
- 500–1000 m
- 250–500 m
- 100–250 m
- 0–100 m

SEA DEPTH

- 0–50 m
- 50–100 m
- 100–250 m
- 250–500 m
- 500–1000 m
- 1000–2000 m
- Below 2000 m

EASTERN EUROPE

BELARUS, MOLDOVA, ROMANIA, UKRAINE

Much of Eastern Europe, which extends north from the River Danube and the Black Sea, is covered by open grasslands called steppe. Ukraine's excellent farmland and large mineral reserves make it one of the strongest new countries to emerge from the former Soviet Union. Moldova and Belarus were also part of the USSR, until they became independent in 1991. Romania was a strict communist regime from 1945 until 1989.

INDUSTRY

In Ukraine, most industry is based around the country's mineral reserves. The Donbass region has Europe's largest coalfield and is an important centre for iron and steel production. Belarus's main industries are chemicals, machine building and food-processing. Romania's manufacturing industries are growing, with the help of foreign investment.

STRUCTURE
OF INDUSTRY

Primary 15%   Manufacturing 42%

Services 43%

INDUSTRY

✈ Aerospace
🚗 Car manufacture
🝙 Chemicals
⚙ Engineering
🗄 Food processing
⚒ Iron & steel
👕 Textiles
⚒ Coal
⛏ Mining
⛽ Oil and gas
🏛 Tourism

▪ Major industrial centre / area
Major road

POPULATION

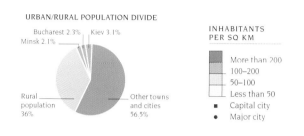

Many Romanians still live in rural areas, although Bucharest, the capital, is home to six times as many people as the next largest city. In Ukraine, two-thirds of the population live in cities such as those in the Donbass industrial area. Most of Belarus's people are city dwellers. Moldova is the most rural country in Eastern Europe; over half live in the countryside.

URBAN/RURAL POPULATION DIVIDE

Bucharest 2.3%   Kiev 3.1%
Minsk 2.1%

Rural population 36%

Other towns and cities 56.5%

INHABITANTS
PER SQ KM

More than 200
100–200
50–100
Less than 50
▪ Capital city
● Major city

THE LANDSCAPE

Flat or rolling grasslands, marshes and river flood plains cover almost all of Ukraine and Belarus. The Carpathian Mountains cross the southwestern corner of Ukraine and continue in a large arc-shaped chain of high peaks at the heart of Romania. Along the southern part of this chain, the Carpathians are called the Transylvanian Alps.

Pripet Marshes (C 3)
The Pripet Marshes in Belarus and Ukraine form the largest area of marshland in Europe.

The steppes
The steppes are great, wide grasslands which are found across eastern Europe and central Asia. Over 70% of the Ukrainian landscape is steppe. Little rain falls throughout the steppes.

FARMING AND LAND USE

The black soils found across much of Ukraine are very fertile and the country is a big producer of cereals, sugar beet, and sunflowers, which are grown for their oil. In Moldova and southern Romania, the warm summers are ideal for growing grapes for wine, along with sunflowers and a variety of vegetables. Cattle and pigs are farmed throughout Eastern Europe.

LAND USE

Other 11%

Forest 24%

Pasture 15%

Cropland 50%

FARMING AND LAND USE

🐂 Cattle
🐖 Pigs
🐑 Sheep
🥕 Root crops
🌻 Sunflowers
🍇 Vineyards
🌾 Wheat

Cropland
Forest
Pasture
Wetland
● Major conurbation

Carpathian Mountains (C 5)
The Carpathians are the largest mountain range in Eastern Europe. They are a rich source of timber and minerals.

Dnieper (E 5) **and Dniester** (D 5) **rivers**
The Dnieper and Dniester run south and east towards the Black Sea. They flow slowly across huge areas of low-lying land.

The Crimea (F 6)
This peninsula divides the Sea of Azov from the Black Sea. The steep mountains of Kryms'ki Hory run along the southeastern coast of the Crimea.

EUROPE
Eastern
Europe

CLIMATE

January

July

The climate is continental, with warm, dry summers and very cold, dry winters. Temperatures are higher along the fringes of the Black Sea, while the Carpathian Mountains are colder and wetter all year round.

Less than 50

50

50

Less than 50

50

50

50

100

100

100

50

50

100

TEMPERATURE AND PRECIPITATION

More than 20°C
15 to 20°C
10 to 15°C
5 to 10°C
0 to 5°C
0 to -5°C
Less than -5°C

100 — Precipitation (mm)

ENVIRONMENTAL ISSUES

The worst nuclear accident in history happened at Chornobyl' nuclear power station in northern Ukraine in 1986. Around 70% of the nuclear fallout was received by Belarus, contaminating its farmland, forests and water supplies. Four million Ukrainians still live in dangerously radioactive areas.

ENVIRONMENTAL ISSUES

Destroyed nuclear reactor
Levels of nuclear fallout
Very high
High
Moderate
Urban air pollution
Flooding
Polluted river
Sea pollution
● Major industrial centre

Minsk
Chornobyl'
Kiev
Kharkiv
Dnipropetrovs'k
Donets'k
Arad
Târgu Mures
2005
Bucharest
Volganeft-139
2007

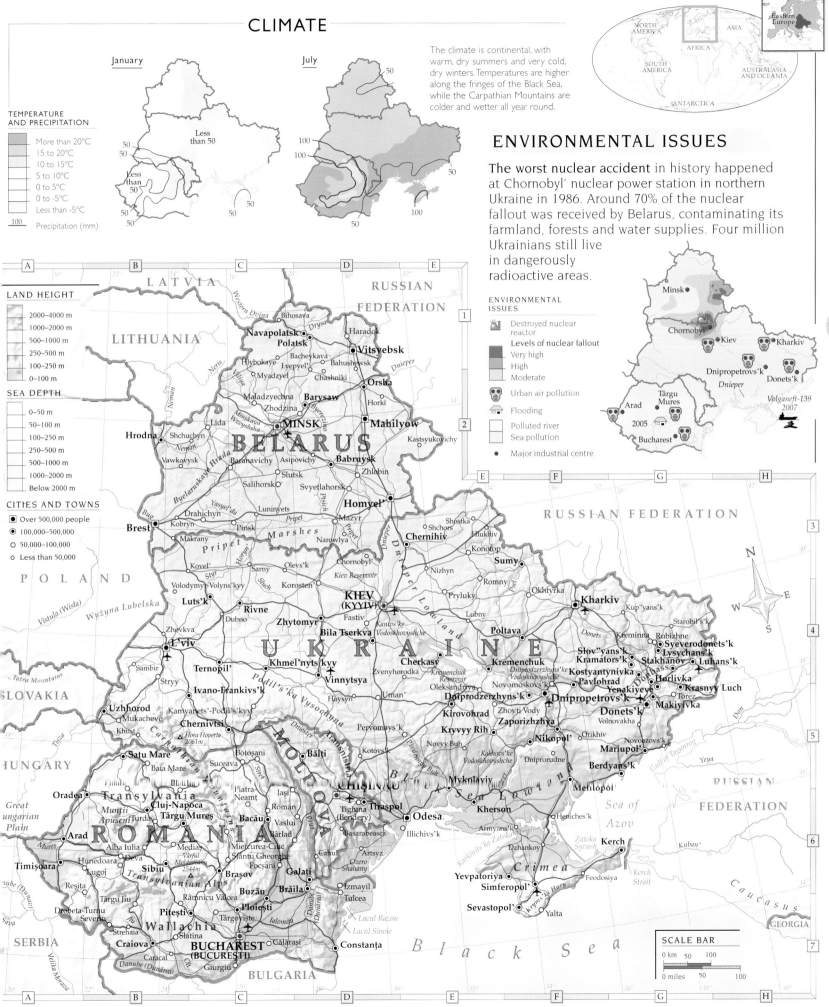

LAND HEIGHT
2000–4000 m
1000–2000 m
500–1000 m
250–500 m
100–250 m
0–100 m

SEA DEPTH
0–50 m
50–100 m
100–250 m
250–500 m
500–1000 m
1000–2000 m
Below 2000 m

CITIES AND TOWNS
■ Over 500,000 people
● 100,000–500,000
◉ 50,000–100,000
○ Less than 50,000

LATVIA

RUSSIAN FEDERATION

LITHUANIA

Western Dvina

Drysa

Bihosava

Navapolatsk
Polatsk

Haradok

Vitsyebsk

Neris

Hlybokaye
Bacheykava
Bahushewsk

Lyepyel'
Myadzyel
Chashniki

Orsha

Dnieper

Maladzyechna

Barysaw

Zhodzina

Horki

Vilija

Lida

Minskaya Wzvyshsha

MINSK

Mahilyow

Neman

Hrodna
Shchuchyn

Vawkavysk
Baranavichy
Asipovichy

Babruysk

Kastsyukovichy

Byelaruskaya Hrada

Slutsk
Zhlobin

Yasyel'da
Salihorsk

Svyetlahorsk

Bug

Drahichyn
Luninyets

Homyel'

POLAND

Brest
Kobryn
Pinsk

Pripet

Mazyr

Shchors

Chernihiv

Hlukhiv

Marshes
Narowlya

Chornobyl'

Konotop

Sumy

Wyżyna Lubelska

Makrany

Horyn

Sarny

Olevs'k

Korosten'

Kiev Reservoir

Nizhyn

Romny

Okhtyrka

Vistula (Wisła)

Kovel'

Styr

Sluch

Luts'k

Volodymyr-Volyns'kyy

Dubno

Rivne

KIEV (KYYIV)

Fastiv

Pryluky

Lubny

Kharkiv

Kup"yans'k

Starobil's'k

Zhytomyr

Bila Tserkva

Kaniv's'ke Vodoskhovyshche

UKRAINE

Poltava

Donets

Kreminna

Rubizhne

L'viv

Zhovkva

Khmel'nyts'kyy

Cherkasy

Kremenchuk

Slov"yans'k

Kramators'k

Syeverodonets'k

Lysychans'k

Stakhanov

Luhans'k

Ternopil'

Kremenchuk Reservoir

Dniprodzerzhyns'ke Vodoskhovyshche

Kostyantynivka

Horlivka

SLOVAKIA

Sambir

Vinnytsya

Zvenyhorodka

Oleksandriya

Novomoskovs'k

Pavlohrad

Yenakiyeve

Krasnyy Luch

Stryy

Ivano-Frankivs'k

Podil's'ka Vysochyna

H,ysyn

Uman'

Dniprodzerzhyns'k

Dnipropetrovs'k

Torez

Makiyivka

Uzhhorod

Mukacheve

Kamyanets'-Podil's'kyy

Kirovohrad

Zhovti Vody

Donets'k

Tatra Mountains

Khust

Chernivtsi

Pervomays'k

Novvy Buh

Kryvyy Rih

Zaporizhzhya

Volnovakha

Dniester

Podbennaya Bug

Nikopol'

Orikhiv

Novoazovs'k

HUNGARY

Tisza

△ Hora Hoverla 2061m

Satu Mare

Botosani

MOLDOVA

Bălți

Kotovsk

Kakhovs'ke Vodoskhovyshche

Dniprorudne

Mariupol'

Berdyans'k

Gulf of Taganrog

Yeya

RUSSIAN FEDERATION

Carpathian Mountains

Baia Mare

Suceava

Siret

Prut

Háysyn

Southern Buh

Novyy Buh

Mykolayiv

Melitopol'

Sea of Azov

Oradea

Transylvania

Piatra Neamţ

Iaşi

Roman

CHIŞINĂU

Tighina (Bendery)

Tiraspol

Kherson

Heniches'k

Cluj-Napoca

Muntii Apuseni

Turda

Târgu Mures

Bacău

Vaslui

Bârlad

Odesa

Armyans'k

Zatoka Sivash

Kerch

Arad

Alba Iulia

Mediaş

Varful Moldoveanu 2544m

Miercurea-Ciuc
Sfântu Gheorghe

Focşani

Cahul

Basarabeasca

Illichivs'k

Dzhankoy

Crimea

Karkinits'ka Zatoka

Zatoka Syvash

Kerch Strait

Timişoara

Mureş

Hunedoara

Deva

ROMANIA

Brașov

Galați

Izmayil

Ozero Shahany

Artsyz

Yevpatoriya

Simferopol'

Feodosiya

Caucasus

Lugoj

Reşiţa

Sibiu

Transylvanian Alps

Buzău

Brăila

Tulcea

Sevastopol'

Kryms'ki Hory

Yalta

GEORGIA

Great Hungarian Plain

Târgu Jiu

Râmnicu Vâlcea

Ploieşti

Ialomiţa

Lacul Razim

Drobeta-Turnu Severin

Piteşti

Târgovişte

Danube (Dunărea)

Lacul Sinoie

Strehaia

Wallachia

Slatina

Călăraşi

Constanţa

Black Sea

SERBIA

Veliki Morava

Caracal

Craiova

Jiu

BUCHAREST (BUCUREŞTI)

Giurgiu

BULGARIA

Sava

Danube (Dunărea)

SCALE BAR
0 km 50 100
0 miles 50 100

N
W   E
S

EUROPEAN RUSSIA

RUSSIAN FEDERATION

European Russia is separated from the Asiatic part of the Russian Federation by the Ural Mountains. It is home to two-thirds of the country's population. Russia was the largest and most powerful republic of the communist Soviet Union, which collapsed in 1991. Though new businesses were set up when communism ended, many old state industries closed down, causing unemployment and further hardship for many people.

POPULATION

Three-quarters of European Russia's people live in towns and cities, most in a broad band stretching south from Saint Petersburg to Moscow, and eastwards to the Urals. The capital, Moscow, and Saint Petersburg are very crowded cities. Living conditions there are cramped, with two families often sharing one flat. The southeast is also heavily populated. Over 12 million people live in the cities and towns which line the banks of the River Volga.

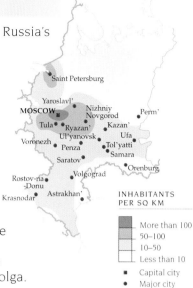

INHABITANTS PER SQ KM

- More than 100
- 50–100
- 10–50
- Less than 10
- ■ Capital city
- ● Major city

INDUSTRY

European Russia is rich in natural resources. Minerals are mined on the Kola Peninsula, and in the Urals, while dense forests are felled and processed in many of the larger northern cities. The Volga basin is one of Europe's largest sources of oil and gas. Moscow, and the cities near the Volga are centres of skilled labour for a wide range of manufacturing industries like cars, chemicals and heavy engineering and steel production.

INDUSTRY

- ⇌ Car manufacture
- ♨ Chemicals
- ✿ Engineering
- ⊜ Iron & steel
- ▭ Textiles
- ⌂ Mining
- ⬗ Oil & gas
- ♠ Timber processing
- ◉ Major industrial centre/area
- — Major road

THE LANDSCAPE

European Russia lies on the North European Plain, a huge, rolling lowland with wide river basins. The northern half of the plain, which was once covered by glaciers, has many lakes and swamps. The River Volga drains much of the plain as it flows south to the Caspian Sea. The Caucasus and Ural mountains form natural boundaries in the south and east.

Northern European Russia (C 3)
Northern European Russia reaches into the Arctic Circle. It is a region of pine and birch forests, marshes and tundra. There are also tens of thousands of lakes, including the biggest in Europe, Ladoga, which covers about 17,700 sq km.

Ural Mountains (E 5)
The Ural Mountains run from north to south, stretching almost 4,020 km.

Lake Ladoga (B 4)

Valdai Hills (A 5)
The Valdai Hills are a high, swampy region of the North European Plain. Two of Europe's biggest rivers, the Volga and the Western Dvina, have their sources here.

Caucasus (A 9)
This massive barrier of mountains stretches from the Black Sea to the Caspian Sea. It includes El'brus, the highest peak in Europe, at 5,642 m.

Caspian Sea (C 9)

River Volga (C 7)
The River Volga flows for 3,688 km, making it Europe's longest river and Russia's most important inland waterway. It is used for transport and to generate hydro-electric power.

The North European Plain (C 4)
The North European Plain sweeps west from the Ural Mountains, all the way to the River Rhine in Germany. In European Russia it includes a number of hill ranges, such as the Volga Uplands and the Central Russian Upland.

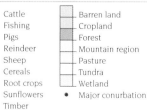

FARMING AND LAND USE

Russia's best farmland lies within this region. Big crops of wheat, barley and oats, potatoes and sunflowers are produced in the fertile black soil which forms a thick band across the country to the south of Moscow. The far north is cold and frozen, with bare mountains and tundra making cultivation impossible. Further south there are extensive forests, and rough pastures used for herding and hunting.

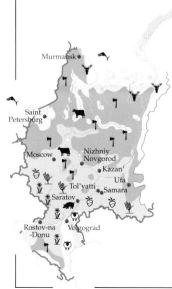

FARMING AND LAND USE

- ⊼ Cattle
- ⚲ Fishing
- ⍦ Pigs
- ⍟ Reindeer
- ⍦ Sheep
- ⍦ Cereals
- ⍦ Root crops
- ⍦ Sunflowers
- ⍦ Timber
- ▭ Barren land
- ▭ Cropland
- ▭ Forest
- ▭ Mountain region
- ▭ Pasture
- ▭ Tundra
- ▭ Wetland
- ● Major conurbation

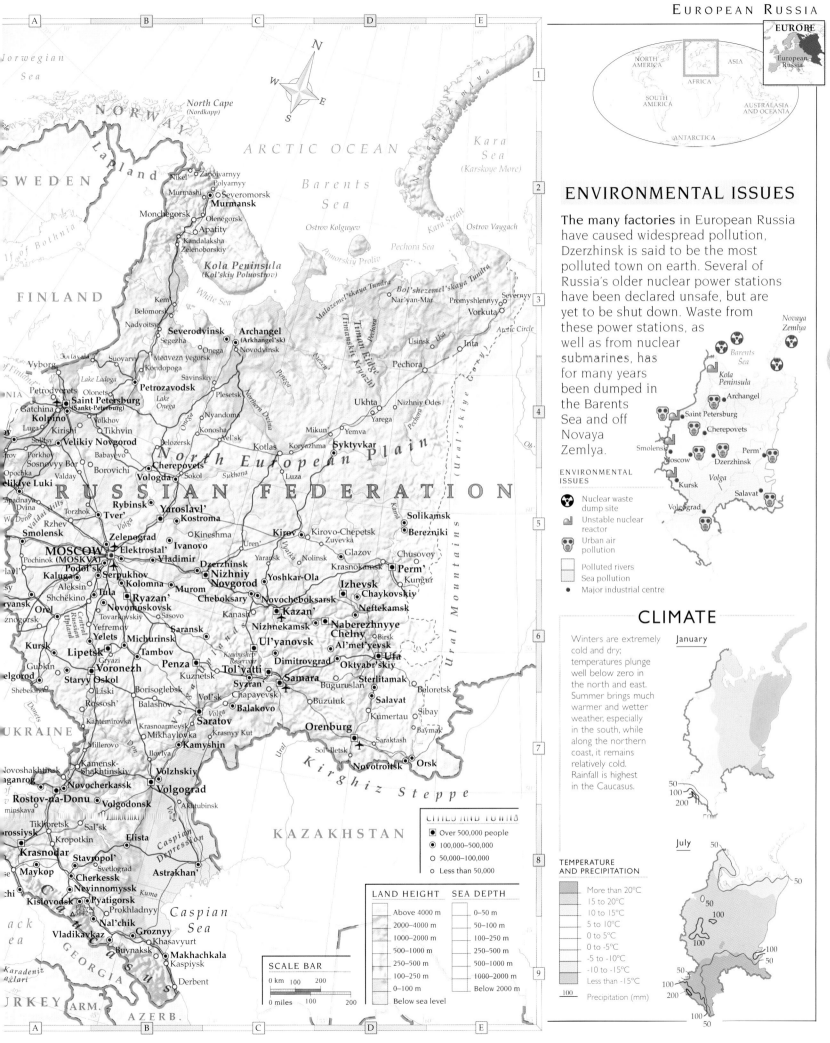

ENVIRONMENTAL ISSUES

The many factories in European Russia have caused widespread pollution, Dzerzhinsk is said to be the most polluted town on earth. Several of Russia's older nuclear power stations have been declared unsafe, but are yet to be shut down. Waste from these power stations, as well as from nuclear submarines, has for many years been dumped in the Barents Sea and off Novaya Zemlya.

ENVIRONMENTAL ISSUES

- Nuclear waste dump site
- Unstable nuclear reactor
- Urban air pollution
- Polluted rivers
- Sea pollution
- Major industrial centre

CLIMATE

Winters are extremely cold and dry; temperatures plunge well below zero in the north and east. Summer brings much warmer and wetter weather, especially in the south, while along the northern coast, it remains relatively cold. Rainfall is highest in the Caucasus.

January

July

TEMPERATURE AND PRECIPITATION

- More than 20°C
- 15 to 20°C
- 10 to 15°C
- 5 to 10°C
- 0 to 5°C
- 0 to -5°C
- -5 to -10°C
- -10 to -15°C
- Less than -15°C

Precipitation (mm)

CITIES AND TOWNS
- ■ Over 500,000 people
- ◉ 100,000–500,000
- ○ 50,000–100,000
- ○ Less than 50,000

LAND HEIGHT	SEA DEPTH
Above 4000 m	0–50 m
2000–4000 m	50–100 m
1000–2000 m	100–250 m
500–1000 m	250–500 m
250–500 m	500–1000 m
100–250 m	1000–2000 m
0–100 m	Below 2000 m
Below sea level	

SCALE BAR
0 km 100 200
0 miles 100 200

THE MEDITERRANEAN

The Mediterranean Sea separates Europe from Africa. It stretches more than 4,000 km from east to west and is almost completely enclosed by land. Many great civilizations, including the Greek and Roman empires grew up around the Mediterranean. It has been a crossroads of international trade routes for many centuries. More than 100 million people live in the 28 countries which border the sea and their numbers are increased by the large crowds of tourists who regularly visit the area.

ENVIRONMENTAL ISSUES

Sea pollution is widespread in the Mediterranean, especially near the large coastal resorts where raw sewage and industrial effluent is pumped out to sea and often ends up on the beaches. Oil refining and oil spills have also furthered pollution.

ENVIRONMENTAL ISSUES

🌢 Oil spill

☐ Mild sea pollution
☐ Severe sea pollution

SCALE BAR

0 km   100   200
0 miles   100   200

LAND HEIGHT

Above 4000 m
2000–4000 m
1000–2000 m
500–1000 m
250–500 m
100–250 m
0–100 m
Below sea level

SEA DEPTH

0–250 m
250–500 m
500–1000 m
1000–2000 m
2000–3000 m
3000–4000 m
Below 4000 m

CITIES AND TOWNS

■ Over 500,000 people
● 100,000–500,000
◉ 50,000–100,000
○ Less than 50,000

MALTA

Victoria · Nadur
Gozo · Mġarr · Comino
Mellieħa
Mosta · St Julian's
Ħamrun · Sliema
Rabat · Paola · VALLETTA
Birżebbuġa
0 km   10
0 miles   10

CYPRUS

Mediterranean Sea
Yenierenköy (Agialoúsa)
Lapta · Girne (Kerýneia)
Güzelyurt (Mórfou)
Değirmenlik (Kythréa)
TURKISH REPUBLIC OF NORTHERN CYPRUS (recognized only by Turkey)
Famagusta Bay
Pólis · NICOSIA · Famagusta (Ammóchostos) (Onzimágusa)
Troódos · Larnaca (Lárdaka)
Páfos · Dhekelia Sovereign Base Area (to UK)
Akrotiri Sovereign Base Area (to UK)
Limassol (Lemesós)
0 km   25
0 miles   25

THE LANDSCAPE

The Mediterranean Sea would be an enormous lake if it were not for the Strait of Gibraltar, a narrow opening only 13 km wide, which joins it to the Atlantic Ocean. The Mediterranean lies over the boundary of two continental plates. Where they meet, earthquakes and volcanoes are common.

Strait of Gibraltar

Sandy beaches
The Mediterranean coasts are bordered by several thousand miles of sandy beaches.

Shallow shelves
The area of sea off the coast of Tunisia and also the Adriatic sea, are shallower than the rest of the Mediterranean.

Greek islands
Greece has thousands of islands which lie both in the Mediterranean and in the smaller Aegean Sea. Some of them are the remains of old volcanoes which have left black sand on the beaches.

Suez Canal
The Suez Canal links the Mediterranean to the Gulf of Suez and the Red Sea. Before it was built, ships had to sail around the whole of Africa to reach Asia.

Atlas Mountains
The rugged Atlas Mountains run through most of Morocco and Algeria. They form a barrier between the Mediterranean coast and the Sahara which lies south of them.

TOURISM

The **tourist industry in and around the Mediterranean** is one of the most highly developed in the world. More than half the world's income from tourism is generated here. Resorts have grown up along the northwest coast of Africa, and in Egypt, in southern Spain, France, Italy, Greece and Turkey. Tourism brings huge economic benefits, but the ever-increasing number of visitors has also damaged the environment.

TOURISM

- Major tourist destinations/resorts
- Tourist centre

INDUSTRY

The **Mediterranean has a large fishing industry,** although most of the fishing is small-scale. Tuna and sardines are caught throughout the region and mussels are farmed off the coast of Italy. Fish canning and packing takes place at most of the larger ports. Small oil and gas reserves are extracted off the coast of North Africa and near Greece, Spain and Italy.

INDUSTRY

- Fishing ports
- Oil and gas
- Major city

CONTINENTAL ASIA

Asia is the world's largest continent, and has the greatest range of physical extremes. Some of the highest, lowest, and coldest places on Earth are found in Asia: Mount Everest in the Himalayas is the highest, the Dead Sea in the west is the lowest, and the frozen wastes of northern Siberia are among the coldest. More people live in Asia than on any other continent – 1.3 billion of them in China, and 1.2 billion in India.

6,500 km

9,700 km

CROSS-SECTION THROUGH ASIA

Persian Gulf   Iranian   Plateau of Tibet   Yellow River
Arabian   Plateau   Mouth of
Peninsula   Himalayas   the Ganges   Taiwan

W   7,800 km   E

The Arabian Peninsula and the mountainous Iranian Plateau are divided by the Persian Gulf, fed by the Tigris and Euphrates rivers. Further east, the land begins to rise, the mountains spreading north to the Plateau of Tibet, and south to the Himalayas. The plains to the south of the Himalayas are drained by the Indus and Ganges, and to the east of the Plateau of Tibet by the Yellow River.

PHYSICAL ASIA

Northern Asia is made up of old mountains and ancient, stable plateaus. The jagged Himalayan mountains dominate the central part of the continent, along with the Plateau of Tibet, which stretches north into China. In Southeast Asia, there are many islands. Volcanoes and earthquakes are common, and some of the islands are volcanically-formed.

TUNDRA AND PERMAFROST 1

In the far north of Asia, the land is permanently frozen – this is known as permafrost. During the summer, the surface thaws and lakes appear.

2 GREAT RIVERS

Asia is watered by many great rivers. India's Ganges has its source high in the Himalayas. The huge delta is a maze of inlets and marshes.

TROPICAL RAINFORESTS 3

Tropical forests blanket the landscape across much of Southeast Asia, especially in Burma, Thailand and the islands of Borneo, Celebes, Java and Sumatra.

4 DESERTS

The Takla Makan is one of several deserts in central Asia. Moist air is prevented from reaching them by the mountain chains to the south.

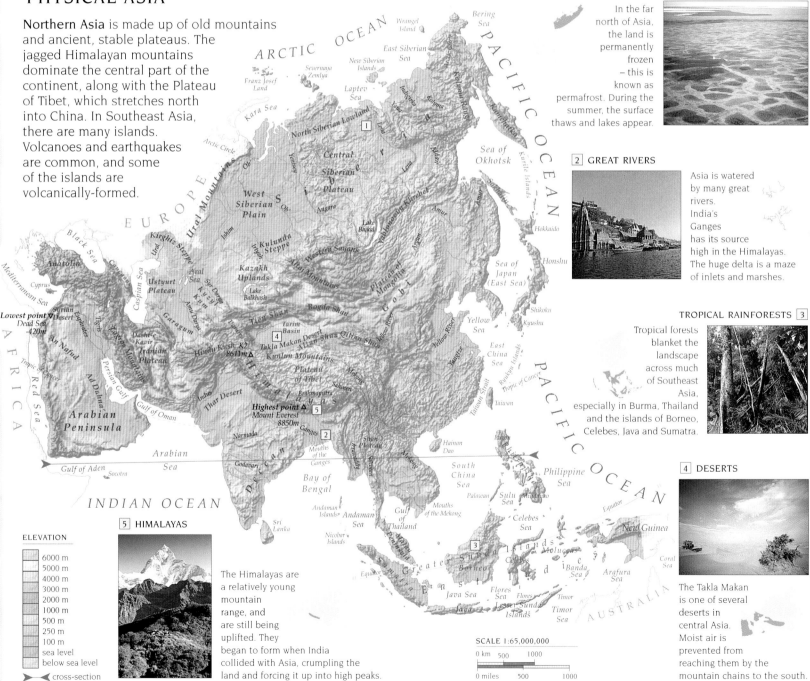

5 HIMALAYAS

The Himalayas are a relatively young mountain range, and are still being uplifted. They began to form when India collided with Asia, crumpling the land and forcing it up into high peaks.

ELEVATION

6000 m
5000 m
4000 m
3000 m
2000 m
1000 m
500 m
250 m
100 m
sea level
below sea level

cross-section

SCALE 1:65,000,000

0 km   500   1000

0 miles   500   1000

POLITICAL ASIA

Asia is a continent of many contrasts: in its lands, its peoples and its traditions. The break up of the Soviet Union, which once stretched south from Russia to Iran, produced the new central Asian republics of Kazakhstan, Kyrgyzstan, Tajikistan, Turkmenistan and Uzbekistan. The countries in southwest Asia are mainly Muslim, and include monarchies, republics and theocracies. India is the world's largest democracy, while China is a communist power regaining its economic influence in the world.

POPULATION

Capital cities
● 50,000 to 100,000
⊡ Above 500,000
● Below 50,000
◉ 100,000 to 500,000

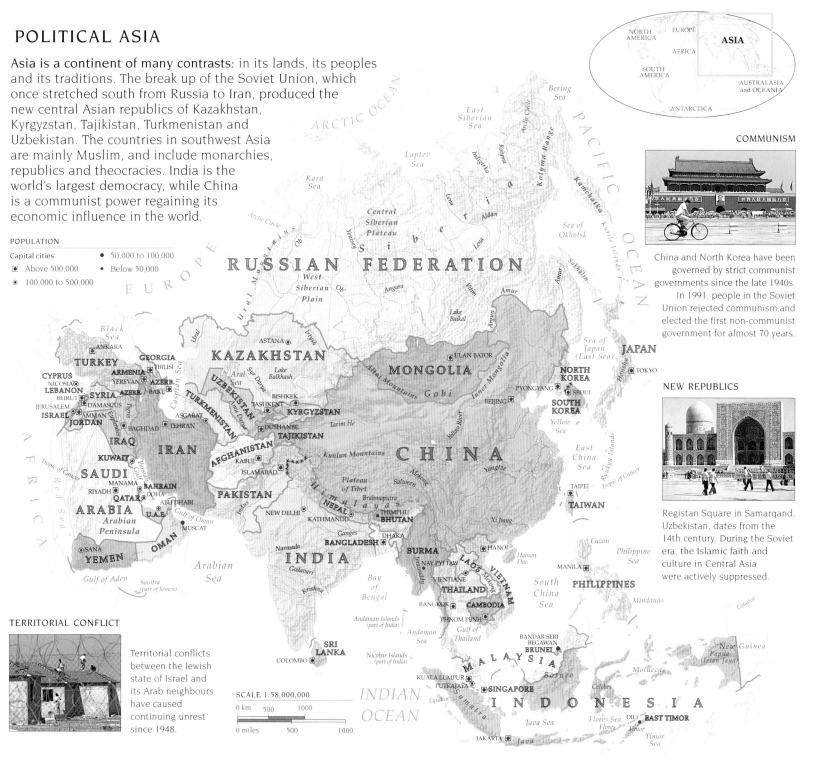

COMMUNISM

China and North Korea have been governed by strict communist governments since the late 1940s. In 1991, people in the Soviet Union rejected communism, and elected the first non-communist government for almost 70 years.

NEW REPUBLICS

Registan Square in Samarqand, Uzbekistan, dates from the 14th century. During the Soviet era, the Islamic faith and culture in Central Asia were actively suppressed.

TERRITORIAL CONFLICT

Territorial conflicts between the Jewish state of Israel and its Arab neighbours have caused continuing unrest since 1948.

SCALE 1:58,000,000

0 km   500   1000

0 miles   500   1000

POPULATION

The deserts and high mountains of Asia are almost uninhabited and much of the Russian Federation is very sparsely populated. Singapore is one of the world's most densely populated places. Japan and India also have very high densities. Over 20% of the world's people live in China, but India is fast catching up.

POPULATION DENSITY
(People per sq km)

Below 9
10–49
50–99
100–249
250–3,999
Above 4,000

Largest city
TOKYO
34 million
people

STANDARDS OF LIVING

Asian living standards differ greatly; the industrial wealth of Japan, and the oil wealth of the Gulf states, contrast sharply with some of the world's poorest countries. Elsewhere, factors such as civil war, recurring droughts or flooding and a scarcity of suitable farmland keep standards of living low.

STANDARD OF LIVING
(UN Human Development Index)

low   high   no data

115

ASIAN GEOGRAPHY

Asia's forbidding mountain ranges, barren deserts, and fertile plains have affected the way in which people settled the continent. Intensive agriculture is found in the more fertile areas, and the largest concentrations of people grew up near fertile land and close to great rivers. Asia's mineral wealth has brought people to the more inhospitable parts of the continent: the deserts of southwest Asia for oil, and frozen Siberia for oil, gas and minerals.

MINERAL RESOURCES

Over half of the world's oil and gas reserves are in Asia, most importantly around the Persian Gulf and in western Siberia. Coal in Siberia and China has provided power for steel industries. Metallic minerals are also abundant: tin in Southeast Asia, and platinum and nickel in Siberia.

MINERAL RESOURCES

- Chromium
- Tin
- Nickel
- Iron
- Platinum
- Gold
- Lead
- Oil/gas field
- Coal field

INDUSTRY

Many people in Asia still rely on agriculture as a source of income, and some countries have very few industries. Heavy industry dominates eastern China and Russia, but Japan is the most industrially productive country. In recent years, booming 'tiger' economies have developed in countries such as Taiwan, that border the Pacific Ocean.

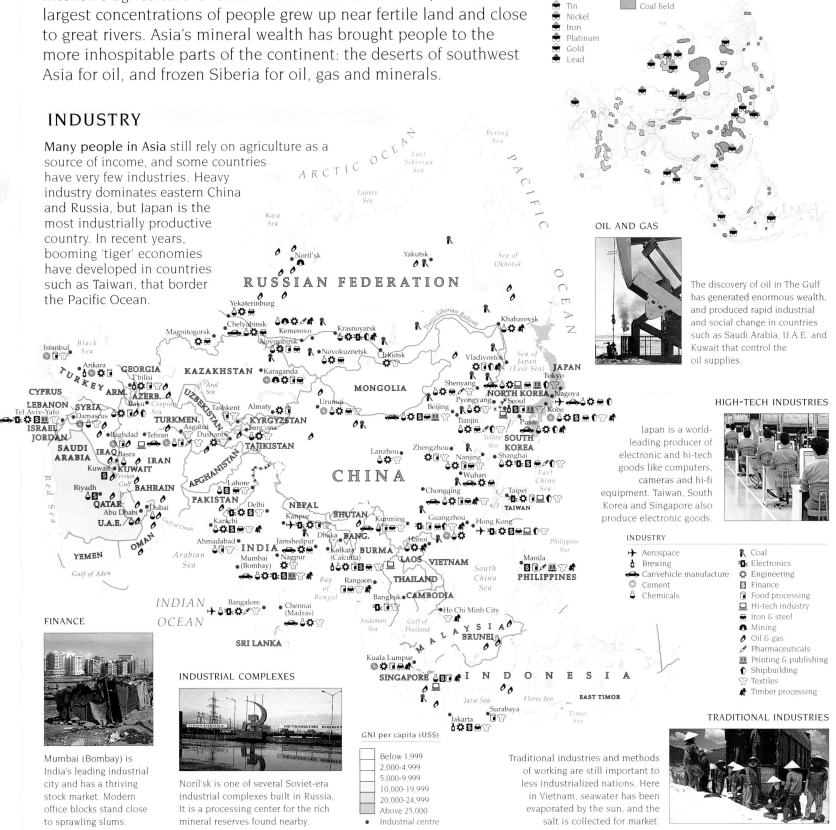

OIL AND GAS

The discovery of oil in The Gulf has generated enormous wealth, and produced rapid industrial and social change in countries such as Saudi Arabia, U.A.E. and Kuwait that control the oil supplies.

HIGH-TECH INDUSTRIES

Japan is a world-leading producer of electronic and hi-tech goods like computers, cameras and hi-fi equipment. Taiwan, South Korea and Singapore also produce electronic goods.

INDUSTRY

- ✈ Aerospace
- Brewing
- Car/vehicle manufacture
- Cement
- Chemicals
- Coal
- Electronics
- Engineering
- Finance
- Food processing
- Hi-tech industry
- Iron & steel
- Mining
- Oil & gas
- Pharmaceuticals
- Printing & publishing
- Shipbuilding
- Textiles
- Timber processing

FINANCE

Mumbai (Bombay) is India's leading industrial city and has a thriving stock market. Modern office blocks stand close to sprawling slums.

INDUSTRIAL COMPLEXES

Noril'sk is one of several Soviet-era industrial complexes built in Russia, It is a processing center for the rich mineral reserves found nearby.

GNI per capita (US$)

- Below 1,999
- 2,000-4,999
- 5,000-9,999
- 10,000-19,999
- 20,000-24,999
- Above 25,000
- Industrial centre

Traditional industries and methods of working are still important to less industrialized nations. Here in Vietnam, seawater has been evaporated by the sun, and the salt is collected for market.

TRADITIONAL INDUSTRIES

CLIMATE

Most of Asia has a continental climate, apart from coastal areas. Without the moderating effects of the ocean, temperatures can soar during the day and plummet at night, while rainfall is generally low – producing several large deserts. Temperatures as low as –68°C have been recorded in the frozen wastes of Siberia, while the islands in southeast Asia have tropical climates. Southern and eastern Asia are also affected by a seasonal wind called the monsoon. This originates in the Indian Ocean and brings heavy rainfall and high winds, often devastating small coastal and low-lying villages and towns.

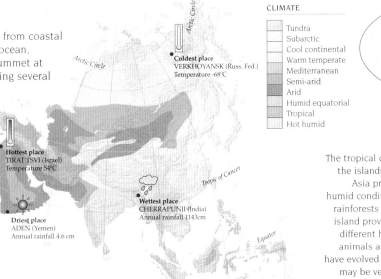

Coldest place
VERKHOYANSK (Russ. Fed.)
Temperature -68°C

Hottest place
TIRAT TSVI (Israel)
Temperature 54°C

Driest place
ADEN (Yemen)
Annual rainfall 4.6 cm

Wettest place
CHERRAPUNJI (India)
Annual rainfall 1143cm

EXTREME WEATHER EVENTS

Symbols indicate climatic extremes

CLIMATE

	Tundra
	Subarctic
	Cool continental
	Warm temperate
	Mediterranean
	Semi-arid
	Arid
	Humid equatorial
	Tropical
	Hot humid

ASIA

NORTH AMERICA EUROPE
AFRICA
SOUTH AMERICA
ANTARCTICA
AUSTRALASIA and OCEANIA

RAINFORESTS

The tropical climate across the islands of southeast Asia produces warm, humid conditions in which rainforests flourish. Each island provides a slightly different habitat, so the animals and plants that have evolved on one island may be very different to those on the next.

LAND USE AND AGRICULTURE

Large expanses of Asia are uncultivated because the soil is too poor, or the climate is too cold or dry for crops to grow. The Plateau of Tibet, much of Siberia and the Arabian Peninsula have limited agriculture. Some of the most fertile land is found in eastern China and India, where rice is a staple. Elsewhere, cash crops are grown for profit, such as dates in southwest Asia; rubber in Southeast Asia; tea in India, China and Sri Lanka; and coconuts throughout the island archipelago of Southeast Asia.

RICE

China is the world's largest producer of rice, which is grown in muddy fields called paddy fields. Water buffaloes are used to plough the ground before planting.

COTTON

Uzbekistan is the world's fifth largest producer of cotton. Water has been diverted from nearby rivers to water the crops, which has led to the drying up of the Aral Sea.

LAND USE AND AGRICULTURE

- Cattle
- Goats
- Pigs
- Sheep
- Cereals
- Coconuts
- Corn (maize)
- Cotton
- Dates
- Fishing
- Fruit
- Jute
- Peanuts
- Rice
- Root crops
- Rubber
- Shellfish
- Sugarcane
- Soya beans
- Tea
- Timber

	Mountains
	Cropland
	Desert
	Forest
	Pasture
	Wetland
●	Major conurbation

DATES

Dates have been cultivated on the Arabian Peninsula since ancient times. They are an important cash crop, grown for export in dry sandy areas where few other crops can grow.

Map labels: Arctic Circle, Tropic of Cancer, Equator, ARCTIC OCEAN, PACIFIC OCEAN, INDIAN OCEAN, EUROPE, AFRICA, Siberia, Ural Mountains, Ob', Yenisey, Lena, Amur, Sea of Okhotsk, Altai Mountains, Tien Shan, Gobi, Plateau of Tibet, Himalayas, Iranian Plateau, Arabian Peninsula, Caucasus, Black Sea, Caspian Sea, Aral Sea, Red Sea, Gulf of Aden, Arabian Sea, South China Sea, Sumatra, Borneo, Java, New Guinea, Syr Darya, Amu Darya, Indus, Ganges, Brahmaputra, Mekong, Salween, Irrawaddy, Yangtze, Yellow River, Tigris, Euphrates

City labels: Yekaterinburg, Chelyabinsk, Omsk, Novosibirsk, Karaganda, Istanbul, Ankara, T'bilisi, Baku, Damascus, Baghdad, Tehran, Riyadh, Tashkent, Almaty, Urumqi, Harbin, Changchun, Sapporo, Tokyo, Kobe, Kitakyushu, Pusan, Seoul, Beijing, Tianjin, Taiyuan, Zhengzhou, Lanzhou, Xi'an, Wuhan, Nanjing, Shanghai, Chengdu, Chongqing, Nanchang, Taipei, Guangzhou, Hong Kong, Kunming, Hanoi, Lahore, Delhi, Jaipur, Karachi, Kanpur, Lucknow, Ahmadabad, Kolkata (Calcutta), Dhaka, Chittagong, Mumbai (Bombay), Bangalore, Chennai (Madras), Rangoon, Bangkok, Ho Chi Minh City, Manila, Kuala Lumpur, Singapore, Jakarta, Surabaya

RUSSIA AND KAZAKHSTAN

Russia lies partly in Europe, but mostly in Asia. The land to the east of the Ural Mountains is called Siberia. This immense stretch of grasslands, thick, evergreen forest and tundra is crossed by giant rivers. Vast areas of Siberia are almost untouched by human activity, yet in the industrial regions set up under communism (1922–1991), air, water and soil are heavily polluted with harmful substances. Along with the former Soviet state of Kazakhstan, Siberia is rich in a huge variety of minerals.

INDUSTRY

The discovery of gold in the 19th century opened Siberia up to economic and industrial development. Later, vast reserves of oil, coal and gas were found, especially in the west, which is now the main centre for oil extraction. Gold and diamonds are mined in the east. In Kazakhstan, mining and other industries are growing, with the help of foreign investors.

STRUCTURE OF INDUSTRY

Primary 5%
Services 60%
Manufacturing 35%

INDUSTRY

- Car manufacture
- Chemicals
- Engineering
- Iron & steel
- Textiles
- Diamonds
- Mining
- Oil and gas
- Timber manufacturing
- Major industrial centre / area
- Major road

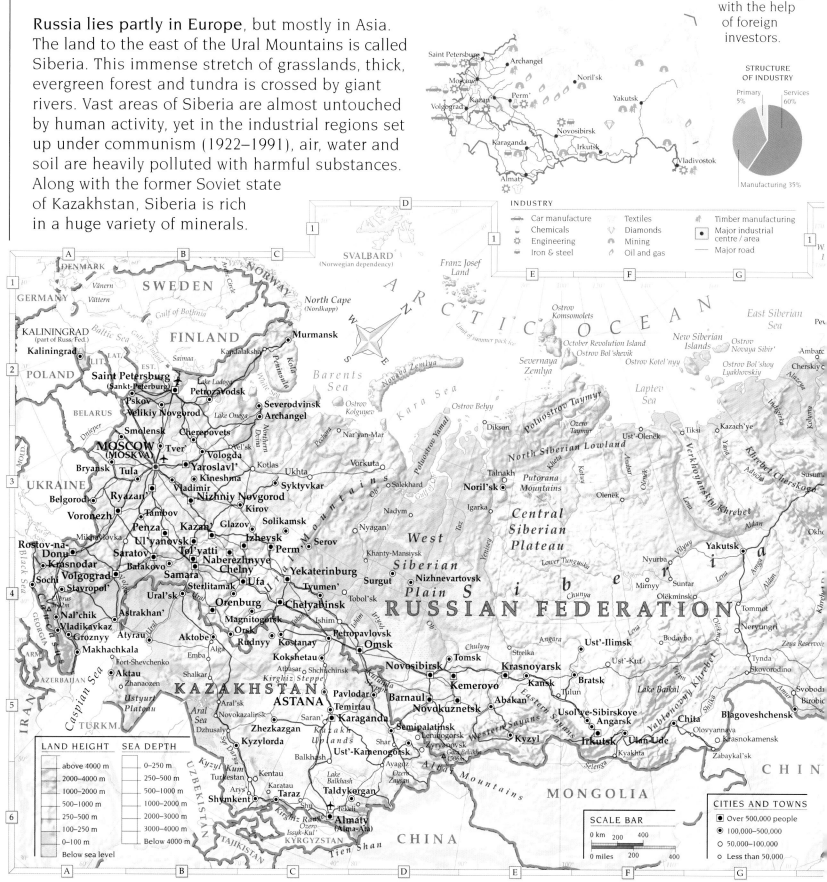

LAND HEIGHT
- above 4000 m
- 2000–4000 m
- 1000–2000 m
- 500–1000 m
- 250–500 m
- 100–250 m
- 0–100 m
- Below sea level

SEA DEPTH
- 0–250 m
- 250–500 m
- 500–1000 m
- 1000–2000 m
- 2000–3000 m
- 3000–4000 m
- Below 4000 m

SCALE BAR
0 km   200   400
0 miles   200   400

CITIES AND TOWNS
- Over 500,000 people
- 100,000–500,000
- 50,000–100,000
- Less than 50,000

THE LANDSCAPE

East of the Ural Mountains lies the West Siberian Plain – the world's biggest area of flat ground. The plain gradually rises to the Central Siberian Plateau, and then again to highlands in the southeast. Great coniferous forests called *taiga* stretch across most of this land. The far north of Siberia extends into the Arctic Circle. There, the landscape is made up of frozen plains called tundra. Much of Kazakhstan is covered by huge rolling grasslands, or steppe; in the south are arid sandy deserts.

Tundra and *taiga*

Stubby birch trees, dwarf bushes, moss and lichen huddle close to the ground in the frozen tundra wastes of northern Russia. They lie between the permanent ice and snow of the Arctic, and the thick *taiga* forests which cover an area greater than the Amazon rainforest.

The Caspian Sea (A 5)

The Caspian Sea covers 371,000 sq km and is the world's largest expanse of inland water. It is fed by the Volga and Ural rivers, which flow in from the plains of the north.

West Siberian Plain (D 4)

This vast, flat expanse is covered with a network of marshes and streams. The Ob' river, which winds its way north across the plains, is frozen for up to half the year.

Lake Baikal (F 5)

Lake Baikal is the deepest lake in the world, and the largest freshwater one – it is more than 1.6 km deep, and covers 32,500 sq km. It is fed by 336 rivers and contains around 20% of all the fresh water in the world.

CLIMATE

Russia and Kazakhstan have strongly continental climates, and their distance away from seas and oceans means that temperatures fluctuate wildly, both daily and seasonally. Temperatures in eastern Siberia have been known to reach -68°C.

TEMPERATURE AND PRECIPITATION

- More than 30°C
- 25 to 30°C
- 20 to 25°C
- 15 to 20°C
- 10 to 15°C
- 5 to 10°C
- 0 to 5°C
- 0 to -5°C
- -5 to -10°C
- -10 to -15°C
- Less than -15°C

—— 100 —— Precipitation (mm)

January

July

FARMING AND LAND USE

Siberia's harsh climate has restricted farming to the south, where there are a few areas warm enough to grow cereal crops, such as wheat and oats, and to raise cattle on the small pockets of pasture. The rest of the region is used for hunting, herding reindeer, and forestry – the *taiga* forests contain the world's biggest timber reserves. In Kazakhstan, big herds of cattle, goats and sheep are raised for wool and meat, and wheat is cultivated in the fertile north.

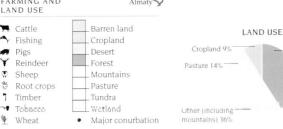

FARMING AND LAND USE

- 🐂 Cattle
- 🐟 Fishing
- 🐗 Pigs
- 🦌 Reindeer
- 🐑 Sheep
- 🌱 Root crops
- 🌾 Timber
- 🍃 Tobacco
- 🌾 Wheat

- Barren land
- Cropland
- Desert
- Forest
- Mountains
- Pasture
- Tundra
- Wetland

● Major conurbation

LAND USE

- Cropland 9%
- Pasture 14%
- Forest 41%
- Other (including mountains) 36%

POPULATION

Siberia has some of the world's largest areas of uninhabited land – the bitingly cold climate and harsh living conditions have kept the population small. The industrial cities in the west hold the most people. Despite its huge size, Kazakhstan has only 16 million people; just over half live in urban areas.

INHABITANTS PER SQ KM

- More than 100
- 50–100
- 10–50
- Less than 10

■ Capital city
● Major city

URBAN/RURAL POPULATION DIVIDE

- Saint Petersburg 2.6%
- Novosibirsk 1%
- Moscow 6.4%
- Rural population 24%
- Other towns and cities 66%

ENVIRONMENTAL ISSUES

Decades of industrial development during the communist regime brought new industries to undeveloped parts of the region, like Siberia. This industrial development has now led to environmental degradation on a massive scale and river, air and land pollution in Russia is among the worst in the world.

ENVIRONMENTAL ISSUES

- 😷 Urban air pollution
- Polluted rivers
- Sea pollution
- ● Major industrial centre

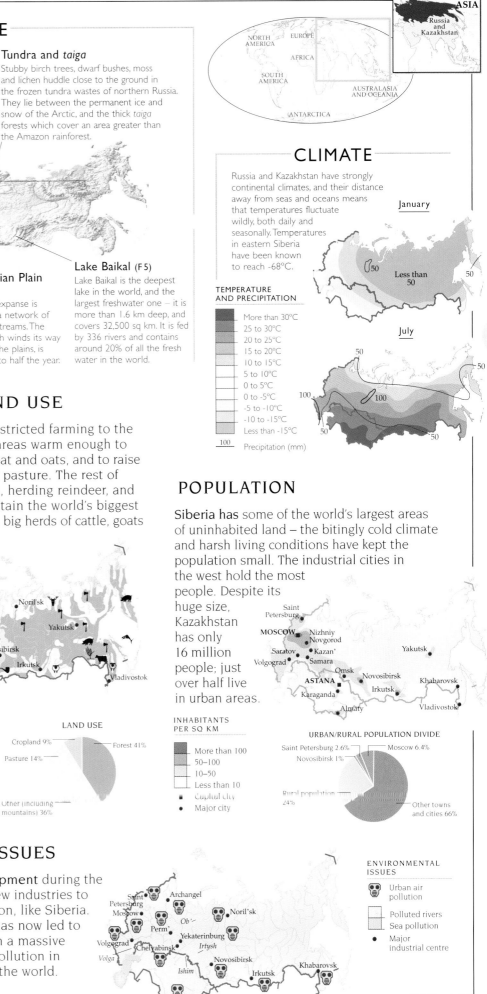

TURKEY AND THE CAUCASUS

ARMENIA, AZERBAIJAN, GEORGIA, TURKEY

Turkey and the Caucasus lie partly in Europe, partly in Asia. Turkey has a long Islamic tradition, and although the country is now a secular (non-religious) one, most Turks are Muslims. Turkey is becoming more industrialized, although one third of its workforce is still employed in agriculture. The countries of the Caucasus were under Russian rule for 70 years, until 1991. They are home to more than 50 different ethnic groups.

INDUSTRY

Turkey has a wide range of industries, including tourism and growing trade links with Europe. Azerbaijan has large oil reserves and is able to export oil. The other states use imported fuel and hydro-electric power generated by their rushing rivers. Georgia produces industrial machinery and chemicals. Armenia's economy is recovering from the conflict with Azerbaijan.

FARMING AND LAND USE

With its warm climate and good soils, Turkey is able to produce all of its own food. Cattle and goats are kept on the central plateau. Along the Mediterranean coast, farmers grow olives, figs, grapes and peaches. Hazelnuts are cultivated along the shores of the Black Sea. Across the Caucasus, the limited fertile land is used to grow wine grapes, tobacco and cotton.

FARMING AND LAND USE

- 🐄 Livestock
- 🐟 Fishing
- 🌿 Cotton
- 🍓 Fruit
- Hazelnuts
- Root crops
- Tobacco
- 🍇 Vineyards
- ▢ Pasture
- ▢ Cropland
- ▢ Forest
- ● Major conurbation

LAND USE

- Cropland 34%
- Pasture 20%
- Forest 15%
- Other 31%

INDUSTRY

- 🚗 Car manufacture
- Cement manufacturing
- Chemicals
- ✿ Engineering
- Food processing
- 👕 Textiles
- ✈ Oil field
- Tourism
- Major industrial centre / area
- —— Major road

STRUCTURE OF INDUSTRY

- Primary 12%
- Services 57%
- Manufacturing 31%

THE LANDSCAPE

A huge semi-arid plateau called Anatolia runs across the centre of Turkey. It is rimmed by several mountain ranges along the Black Sea coast, and the steep Taurus Mountains in the south. A narrow strip of lowland separates the Caucasus and the Lesser Caucasus mountains in the northeast.

Anatolia
Anatolia has large areas of soft limestone rock. Over a long period of time, layers of rock have been worn away by water to produce strange landscapes with caves, and tall, isolated rock pinnacles.

Caucasus Mountains (H 1)

Lesser Caucasus (H 2)

Earthquakes
In 1988, 25,000 people were killed in an earthquake in the west of Armenia.

Between two continents
The city of Istanbul (B2) in Turkey is divided in two by a narrow channel of water called the Bosporus. One part of the city is in Europe, the other in Asia. The two parts are linked by bridges.

Taurus Mountains (D 5)
The Taurus Mountains were formed around 60 to 65 million years ago. Weathering has formed caves and deep gorges.

Lake Van (H 4)
Lake Van is one of the shallow salt lakes found in Anatolia. Salt lakes develop in hot, dry areas where large quantities of water evaporate, leaving behind salty deposits.

POPULATION

Over 75% of Turks live in large towns or cities, mostly in the western half of the country. The eastern and southeastern parts of Anatolia are home to the Kurdish people. The Caucasian republics became more industrialized under Russian rule, and today, two thirds of their people live in urban places.

ENVIRONMENTAL ISSUES

Turkey has built many large dams to use water from rivers – especially the Euphrates – to irrigate its farmland. Syria and Iraq, which lie downstream, have opposed the dams, because they will have less water flowing into their countries. The safety of old-style nuclear plants such as Metsamor in Armenia has caused concern.

ASIA

Turkey & the Caucasus

NORTH AMERICA
EUROPE
AFRICA
SOUTH AMERICA
AUSTRALASIA AND OCEANIA
ANTARCTICA

CLIMATE

Winters are coldest in the Caucasus Mountains and in Anatolia, while the shores of the Mediterranean and Black seas remain mild. Summers are hottest around the edge of the Mediterranean and near Turkey's border with Syria and Iraq.

January

July

TEMPERATURE AND PRECIPITATION

- More than 30°C
- 25 to 30°C
- 20 to 25°C
- 15 to 20°C
- 10 to 15°C
- 5 to 10°C
- 0 to 5°C
- 0 to -5°C
- -5 to -10°C
- Less than -10°C

100 Precipitation (mm)

URBAN/RURAL POPULATION DIVIDE

Istanbul 10%
Ankara 3.7%
Izmir 2.5%
Other towns and cities 55.8%
Rural population 28%

INHABITANTS PER SQ KM

- More than 200
- 100–200
- 50–100
- Less than 50
- ■ Capital city
- ● Major city

ENVIRONMENTAL ISSUES

- ◎ Earthquake zone
- 🌊 Major dam
- ⌂ Unstable nuclear power station
- Urban air pollution
- Sea pollution
- ● Major industrial centre

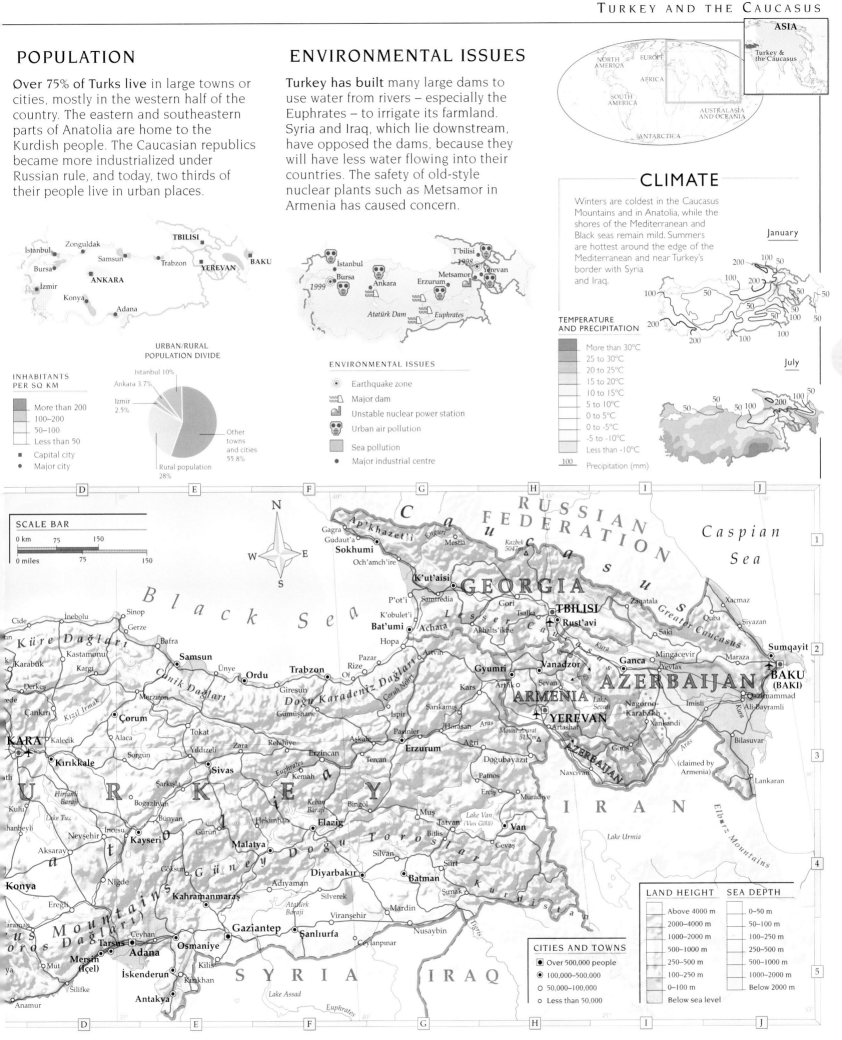

SCALE BAR
0 km 75 150
0 miles 75 150

CITIES AND TOWNS
- ■ Over 500,000 people
- ● 100,000–500,000
- ○ 50,000–100,000
- ○ Less than 50,000

LAND HEIGHT
- Above 4000 m
- 2000–4000 m
- 1000–2000 m
- 500–1000 m
- 250–500 m
- 100–250 m
- 0–100 m
- Below sea level

SEA DEPTH
- 0–50 m
- 50–100 m
- 100–250 m
- 250–500 m
- 500–1000 m
- 1000–2000 m
- Below 2000 m

SOUTHWEST ASIA

BAHRAIN, IRAN, IRAQ, ISRAEL, JORDAN, KUWAIT, LEBANON, OMAN, QATAR, SAUDI ARABIA, SYRIA, UNITED ARAB EMIRATES, YEMEN

Most of southwest Asia is barren desert, yet the world's first cities developed here, over 5,000 years ago. It was also the birthplace of three major religions: Islam, Judaism and Christianity. In recent years, the discovery of oil has brought great wealth to much of the region, but it has been torn by internal conflicts and wars between neighbouring countries. Most people here are Muslims, although Israel is the world's only Jewish state.

INDUSTRY

Oil has made the previously poor Arab states very wealthy. Oil and natural gas continue to be the main source of income for many of the countries here, although other industries are being developed to support their economies when these resources run out. Iran is famous for its carpets, which are woven from wool or silk.

INDUSTRY

- ⚙ Cement manufacturing
- 🍴 Food processing
- ⚒ Iron and steel
- 🛢 Oil refining
- 👕 Textiles
- ⬗ Oil and gas
- 🆂 Finance

- ▣ Major industrial centre / area
- — Major road

STRUCTURE OF INDUSTRY

Primary 10%
Services 49%
Manufacturing 41%

FARMING AND LAND USE

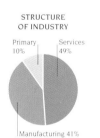

The best farmland is found along the Mediterranean coast, and in the fertile valleys of the Tigris, Euphrates and Jordan rivers. Wheat is the main cereal crop, and cotton, dates, citrus and orchard fruits are grown for export. Elsewhere, modern irrigation techniques have created patches of fertile land in the desert. Dates, wheat and coffee are cultivated in the oases and along the Persian Gulf coast.

LAND USE

Forest 2%
Pasture 45%
Cropland 6%
Other (including desert) 47%

FARMING AND LAND USE

- 🐐 Goats
- 🐟 Fishing
- 🐑 Sheep
- 🍊 Citrus fruits
- ☕ Coffee
- 🌿 Cotton
- 🌴 Dates
- 🍇 Fruit
- 🌿 Tobacco
- 🌾 Wheat

- ▢ Cropland
- ▨ Desert
- ▣ Forest
- ▤ Pasture
- ▦ Wetland
- ● Major conurbation

ENVIRONMENTAL ISSUES

Water shortages are common because of the hot, dry climate and the lack of rivers. Desalination plants convert sea water into fresh water, and are found along the Red Sea and Gulf coasts. Lack of water also makes the risk of desertification greater. Iran has had many catastrophic earthquakes; in 2003 an earthquake in Bam killed 26,000 people.

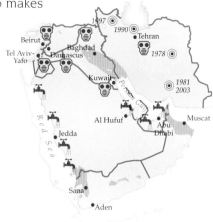

ENVIRONMENTAL ISSUES

- 🚰 Area with many desalination plants
- ◉ Catastrophic earthquake
- 😷 Urban air pollution

- ▢ Existing desert
- ▨ Risk of desertification
- ▨ Sea pollution
- • Major industrial centre

THE LANDSCAPE

Great desert plateaus, both sandy and rocky, cover much of southwest Asia. On the enormous Arabian Peninsula, which covers an area almost the size of India, narrow, sandy plains along the Red Sea and south coast rise to dry mountains. In the centre is a vast, high plateau that slopes gently down to the flat shores of the Persian Gulf. The mountainous areas of Iran experience frequent earthquakes.

Wadis

Valleys or riverbeds, called *wadis*, are found in the Saudi Arabian desert. Usually they are dry, but after heavy rains, they are briefly filled by fast flowing rivers.

Syrian Desert (B 2)

The Syrian Desert extends from the Jordan valley in the west, to the fertile plains of the Tigris and Euphrates rivers in the east. It is mainly a rocky desert, as the sand has been swept away by winds and occasional heavy rainstorms.

Oases

Oases are areas within a desert where water is available for plants, and human use. They are usually formed when a fault, or split, in the rock allows water to come to the surface. Oases can be no bigger than a few palm trees, or cover several hundred sq km.

Dead Sea (A 2)

This large lake on the border between Israel and Jordan is the lowest point on the Earth's surface – its shores lie 420 m below sea level. It is also the world's saltiest body of water, and can support no life forms.

Ar Rub' al Khali (D 5)

The Ar Rub' al Khali desert, also known as the 'Empty Quarter', is the largest uninterrupted stretch of sand on Earth. It covers some 650,000 sq km and is one of the world's driest and most hostile deserts.

Iranian Plateau (E 3)

Central Iran is taken up by a vast, semi-arid plateau, which rises steeply from the coastal lowlands bordering the Persian Gulf. It is ringed by the high Zagros and Elburz mountains.

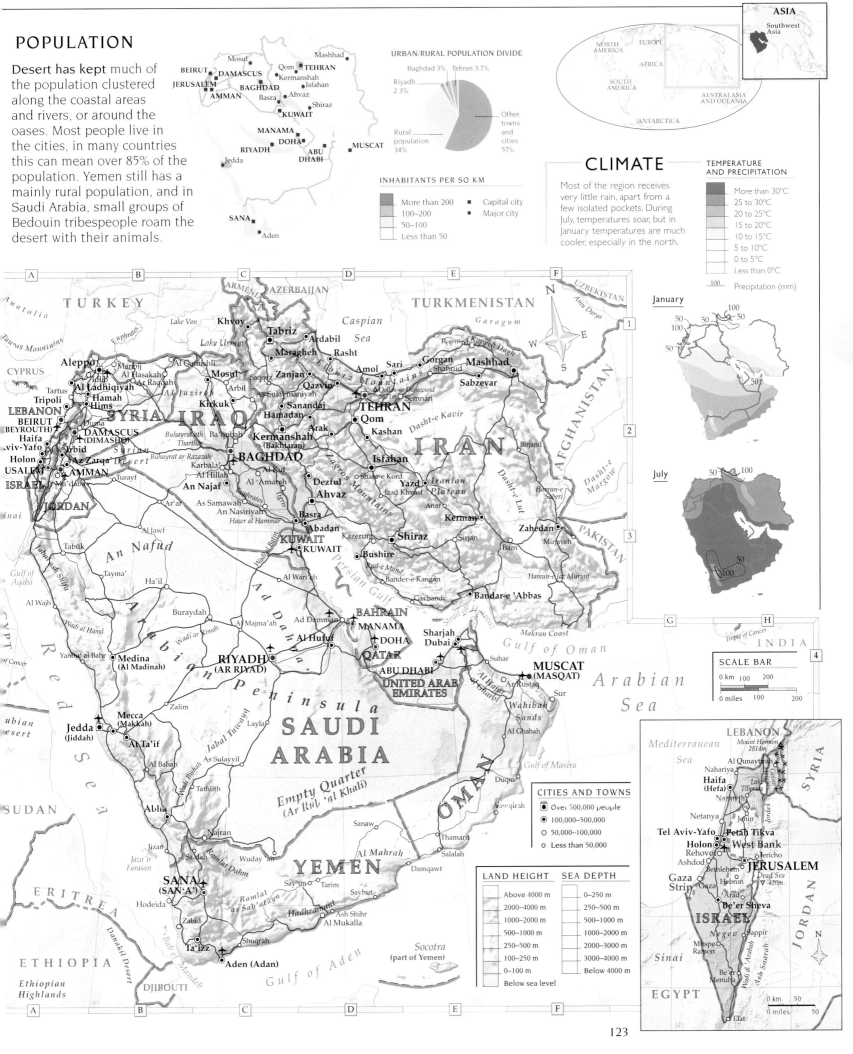

POPULATION

Desert has kept much of the population clustered along the coastal areas and rivers, or around the oases. Most people live in the cities, in many countries this can mean over 85% of the population. Yemen still has a mainly rural population, and in Saudi Arabia, small groups of Bedouin tribespeople roam the desert with their animals.

URBAN/RURAL POPULATION DIVIDE

Baghdad 3% Tehran 3.7%
Riyadh 2.3%
Other towns and cities 57%
Rural population 34%

INHABITANTS PER SQ KM

More than 200
100–200
50–100
Less than 50

■ Capital city
● Major city

CLIMATE

Most of the region receives very little rain, apart from a few isolated pockets. During July, temperatures soar, but in January temperatures are much cooler, especially in the north.

TEMPERATURE AND PRECIPITATION

More than 30°C
25 to 30°C
20 to 25°C
15 to 20°C
10 to 15°C
5 to 10°C
0 to 5°C
Less than 0°C

100 Precipitation (mm)

January

July

CITIES AND TOWNS
■ Over 500,000 people
◉ 100,000–500,000
◎ 50,000–100,000
○ Less than 50,000

SCALE BAR
0 km 100 200
0 miles 100 200

LAND HEIGHT	SEA DEPTH
Above 4000 m	0–250 m
2000–4000 m	250–500 m
1000–2000 m	500–1000 m
500–1000 m	1000–2000 m
250–500 m	2000–3000 m
100–250 m	3000–4000 m
0–100 m	Below 4000 m
Below sea level	

123

CENTRAL ASIA

AFGHANISTAN, KYRGYZSTAN, TAJIKISTAN, TURKMENISTAN, UZBEKISTAN

Central Asia is a land of hot, dry deserts and high, rugged mountains. It lies on the ancient Silk Road, an important trade route between China and Europe for over 400 years, until the 15th century. All of the countries here, apart from Afghanistan, were part of the Soviet Union from the 1920s, until 1991, when they gained independence. Since then, their people have re-established their local languages and Islamic faith, all of which were restricted under Russian rule.

INDUSTRY

Fossil fuels, especially coal, natural gas and oil, are extracted and processed throughout Central Asia. Agriculture supplies the raw materials for many industries, including food and textile processing, and the manufacture of leather goods and clothing. The region is famous for its colourful traditional carpets, hand-woven from the wool of the Karakul sheep. The Fergana Valley, southeast of Tashkent, is the main industrial area.

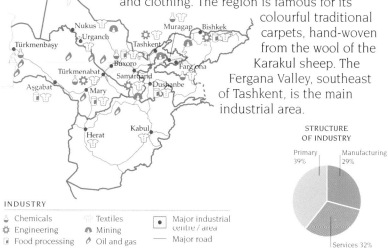

Nukus, Urganch, Türkmenbaşy, Türkmenabat, Muragap, Tashkent, Bishkek, Buxoro, Samarqand, Farg'ona, Dushanbe, Aşgabat, Mary, Herat, Kabul

INDUSTRY

- ⚗ Chemicals
- ✿ Engineering
- ▤ Food processing
- ⊤ Textiles
- ◠ Mining
- ◊ Oil and gas
- • Major industrial centre / area
- — Major road

STRUCTURE OF INDUSTRY

- Primary 39%
- Manufacturing 29%
- Services 32%

POPULATION

The peoples of Central Asia are mostly rural farmers, living in the river valleys and in oases. There are few large cities. A few still lead a traditional nomadic lifestyle, moving from place to place with their animals, in search of new pastures. Large areas of Afghanistan, the western deserts and the mountain regions in the east, are virtually uninhabited.

BISHKEK, TASHKENT, Samarqand, Farg'ona, AŞGABAT, DUSHANBE, KABUL

INHABITANTS PER SQ KM

- More than 100
- 50–100
- 10–50
- Less than 10
- ■ Capital city
- • Major city

URBAN/RURAL POPULATION DIVIDE

- Tashkent 3.2%
- Kabul 4%
- Bishkek 1.1%
- Other towns and cities 22.7%
- Rural population 69%

FARMING AND LAND USE

Farming is concentrated around the fertile river valleys in the east, like the Fergana Valley. A variety of cereals, and fruits, including peaches, melons and apricots, are grown. In drier areas, animal breeding is important, with goats, sheep and cattle supplying wool, meat and hides. Big crops of cotton, which is a major export, are produced on land irrigated by the Amu Darya river.

Bishkek, Tashkent, Samarqand, Aşgabat, Dushanbe, Fergana Valley, Herat, Kabul

FARMING AND LAND USE

- 🐄 Cattle
- 🐐 Goats
- 🐑 Sheep
- ✿ Cotton
- 🍇 Fruit
- ⚘ Opium poppies
- 🌱 Tobacco
- 🌾 Wheat
- Cropland
- Desert
- Mountains
- Pasture
- Wetland
- • Major conurbation

LAND USE

- Forest 5%
- Cropland 9%
- Pasture 51%
- Other (including mountains and deserts) 35%

THE LANDSCAPE

Two of the world's great deserts, the Garagum and the Kyzyl Kum, cover much of the western portion of Central Asia. In the east, a belt of high mountain ranges – the Hindu Kush, the Tien Shan and the Pamirs – tower above the land. Few rivers cross the deserts, apart from the Amu Darya, which flows from the Pamirs to the shrinking Aral Sea.

The Aral Sea (D 1)

The Aral Sea was once the fourth largest lake in the world, but it has shrunk by 75% since 1960. Diversion of its water for irrigation has made the lake shallower, so its waters evaporate faster.

Garagum (D 3)

The sandy desert of the Garagum occupies over 70% of Turkmenistan. Its surface consists of wind-sculpted dunes and depressions. Human settlement is limited to the desert's fringes.

Tien Shan (H 2)

Fergana Valley (G 3)

Stresses and strains in the Earth created the Fergana Valley, a deep depression encircled by high mountains. The valley's fertile soils are irrigated by water from the Syr Darya river, and underground sources.

Amu Darya river (E 3)

Hindu Kush (G 4)

Pamirs (G 4)

The Pamirs lie mainly in Tajikistan. Their highest point, at 7,495 m, is Qullai Ismoili Somoni, previously known as Communism Peak because it was the highest peak in the former Soviet Union.

RUSSIAN FEDERATION, AZERBAIJAN, Elbu

ENVIRONMENTAL ISSUES

The Aral Sea is rapidly drying up, as the rivers feeding it are being diverted to irrigate fields of cotton. Central Asia is a very dry area, and desertification is a constant threat, especially in Afghanistan. Severe urban and industrial air pollution is a legacy from the communist era, when heavy industries were established in the countries here.

ENVIRONMENTAL ISSUES

- Urban air pollution
- Existing desert
- Risk of desertification
- Severe risk of desertification
- Polluted river
- Sea pollution
- Major industrial centre

CLIMATE

Central Asia's climate is strongly inflenced by its position deep within Asia, far from the moderating effects of the oceans. Winters are cold, summers are very hot everywhere. Rainfall is virtually non-existent all year round.

ASIA — Central Asia

January
Less than 50mm precipitation

July
Less than 50mm precipitation

TEMPERATURE AND PRECIPITATION

- More than 30°C
- 25 to 30°C
- 5 to 10°C
- 0 to 5°C
- Less than 0°C

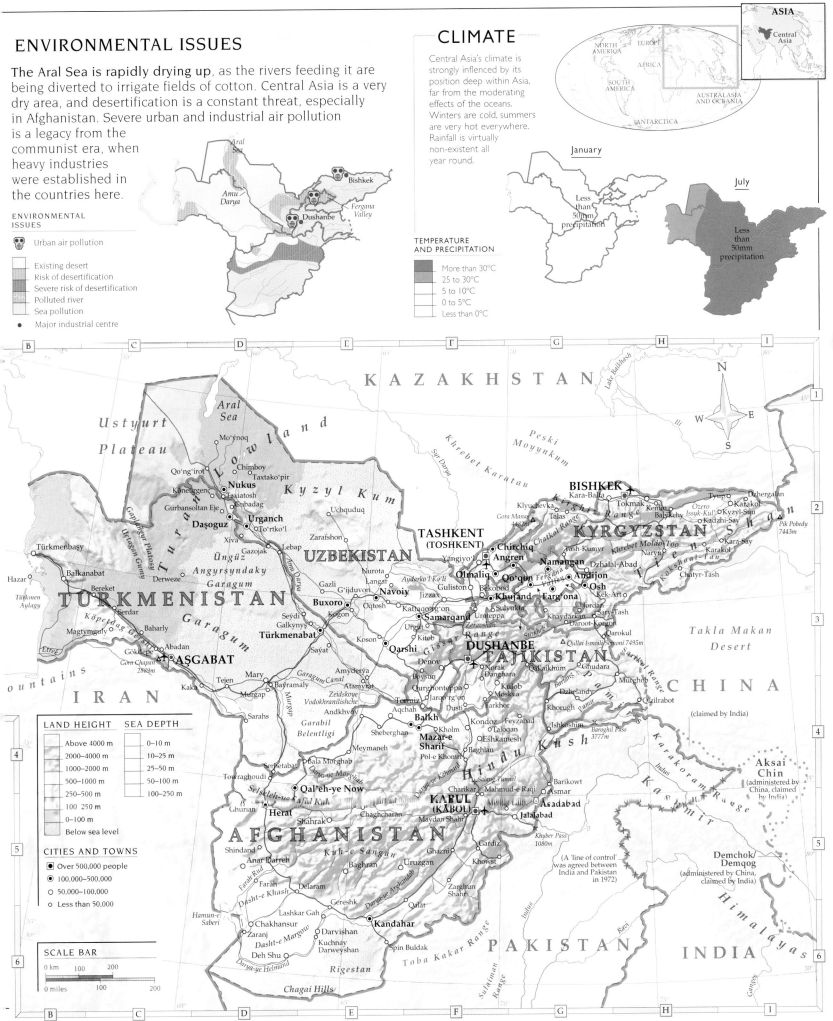

LAND HEIGHT
- Above 4000 m
- 2000–4000 m
- 1000–2000 m
- 500–1000 m
- 250–500 m
- 100–250 m
- 0–100 m
- Below sea level

SEA DEPTH
- 0–10 m
- 10–25 m
- 25–50 m
- 50–100 m
- 100–250 m

CITIES AND TOWNS
- Over 500,000 people
- 100,000–500,000
- 50,000–100,000
- Less than 50,000

SCALE BAR
0 km | 100 | 200
0 miles | 100 | 200

South Asia

BANGLADESH, BHUTAN, INDIA, NEPAL, PAKISTAN, SRI LANKA

South Asia is a land of many contrasts. Its landscape ranges from the mighty peaks of the Himalayas in the north, through vast plains and arid desert, to tropical forests and palm-fringed beaches in the south. More than one-fifth of the world's people live here, and a long history of foreign invasions has left a mosaic of hugely different cultures, religions and traditions, and thousands of languages and dialects.

Farming and Land Use

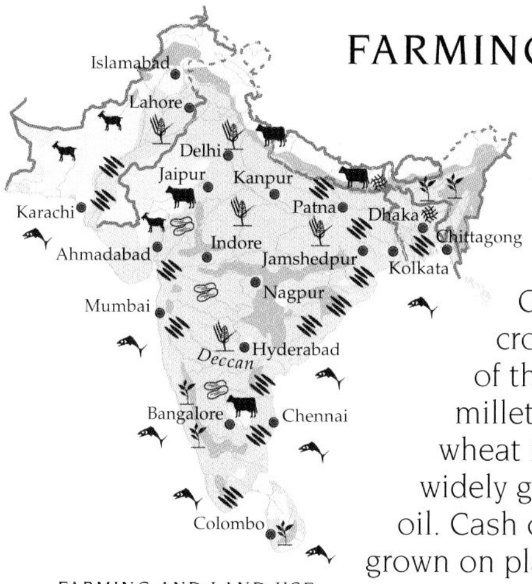

Over 60% of the population is involved in agriculture, but most farms are small, and produce only enough food to feed one family. Grains are the staple food crops – rice in the wetter parts of the east and west, corn and millet on the Deccan plateau, and wheat in the north. Groundnuts are widely grown as a source of cooking oil. Cash crops include tea, which is grown on plantations, and jute.

FARMING AND LAND USE

- Cattle
- Fishing
- Goats
- Cereals
- Groundnuts
- Jute
- Rice
- Tea
- Cropland
- Desert
- Forest
- Pasture
- Wetland
- Major conurbation

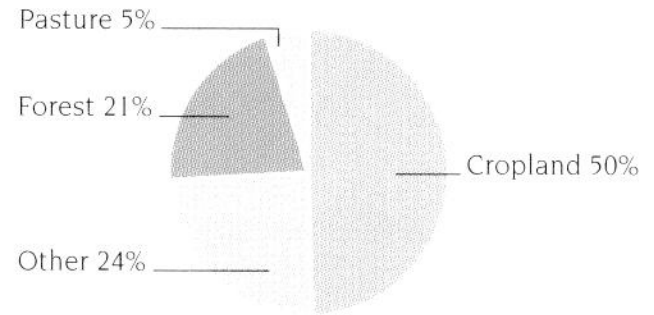

Industry

Industry has expanded in India in recent years, and in the cities a variety of goods are produced and processed, including cars, aeroplanes, chemicals, food and drink. Service industries such as tourism and banking are also growing. Elsewhere, small-scale cottage industries serve the needs of local people, but many products, mainly silk and cotton textiles, clothing, leather and jewellery, are also exported.

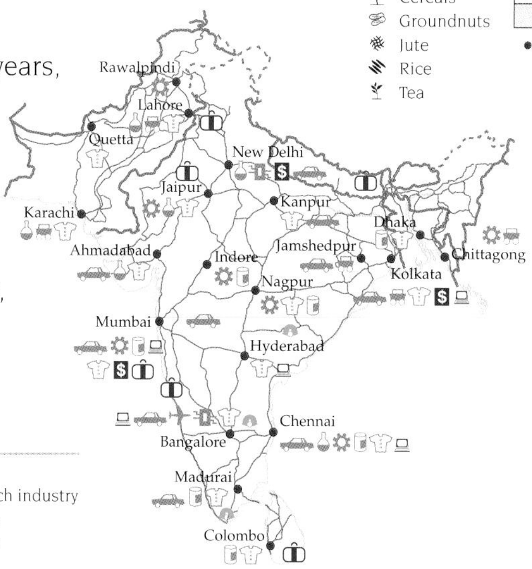

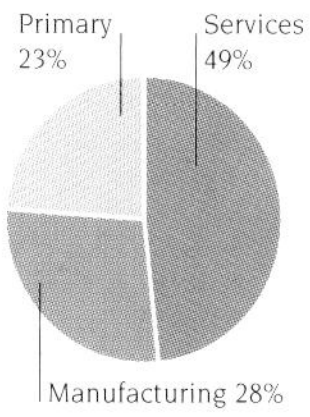

INDUSTRY

- Aerospace
- Car manufacture
- Chemicals
- Electronics
- Engineering
- Food processing
- Iron and steel
- Textiles
- Mining
- High-tech industry
- Finance
- Tourism
- Major industrial centre / area
- Major road

The Landscape

A massive, towering wall of snow-capped mountains stretches in an arc across the north, isolating South Asia from the rest of the continent. The huge floodplains and deltas of the Indus, Ganges and Brahmaputra rivers separate the mountains from the rest of the peninsula: a great rolling plateau, bordered on either side by coastal hills called the Eastern and Western Ghats.

Himalayas (E 2)
The Himalayas are the highest mountain system in the world. They were formed about 40 million years ago when two of the Earth's plates collided, thrusting up huge masses of land.

Mount Everest (F 3)
The northern ranges of the Himalayas average 7,000 m in height. They include the highest point on Earth, Mount Everest on the Nepal–China border, which soars to 8,850 m.

Thar Desert (C 3)
The border between India and Pakistan runs through the arid, sandy Thar Desert.

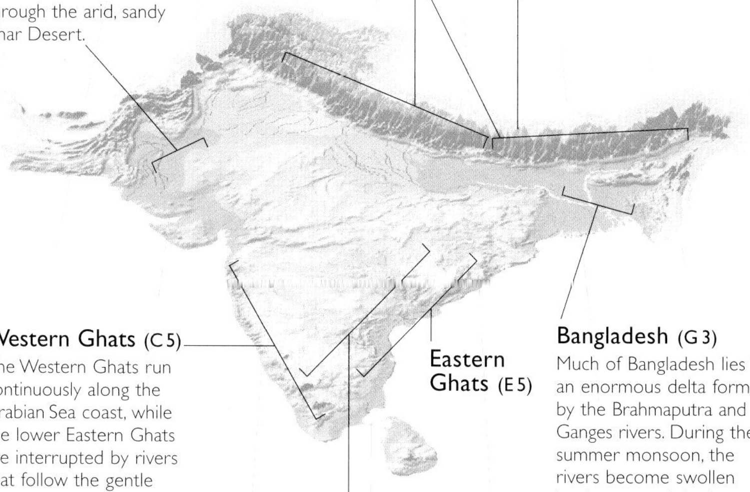

Western Ghats (C 5)
The Western Ghats run continuously along the Arabian Sea coast, while the lower Eastern Ghats are interrupted by rivers that follow the gentle slope of the Deccan plateau and flow across broad lowlands into the Bay of Bengal. This is one of the wettest regions in the world.

Eastern Ghats (E 5)

Deccan plateau (D 5)
This giant plateau makes up most of central and southern India. Its volcanic rock has been deeply cut by rivers such as the Krishna, creating stepped valleys called *traps*.

Bangladesh (G 3)
Much of Bangladesh lies in an enormous delta formed by the Brahmaputra and Ganges rivers. During the summer monsoon, the rivers become swollen by the torrential rains – and meltwater from the Himalayas – and the delta floods. Over the years, millions of people have drowned or been made homeless by heavy flooding.

Population

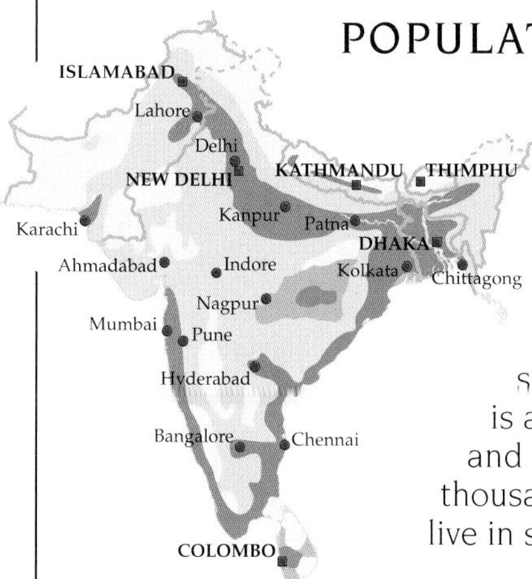

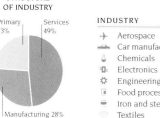

Most of South Asia's people live in villages scattered across the fertile river floodplains, in mountain valleys or along the coasts, but increasing numbers are migrating to the cities in search of work. Overcrowding is a serious problem in both rural and urban areas; in many cities, thousands of people are forced to live in slums, or on the streets.

INHABITANTS PER SQ KM

- More than 200
- 100–200
- 50–100
- Less than 50
- Capital city
- Major city

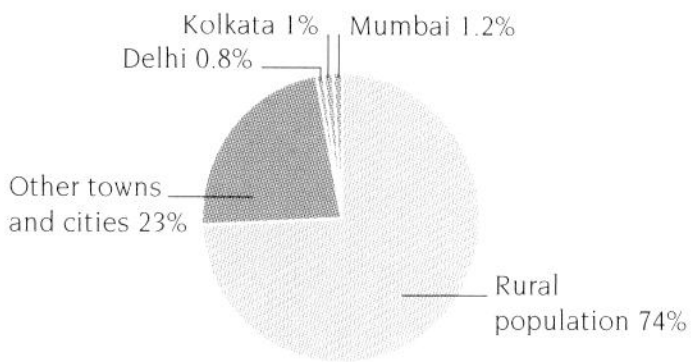

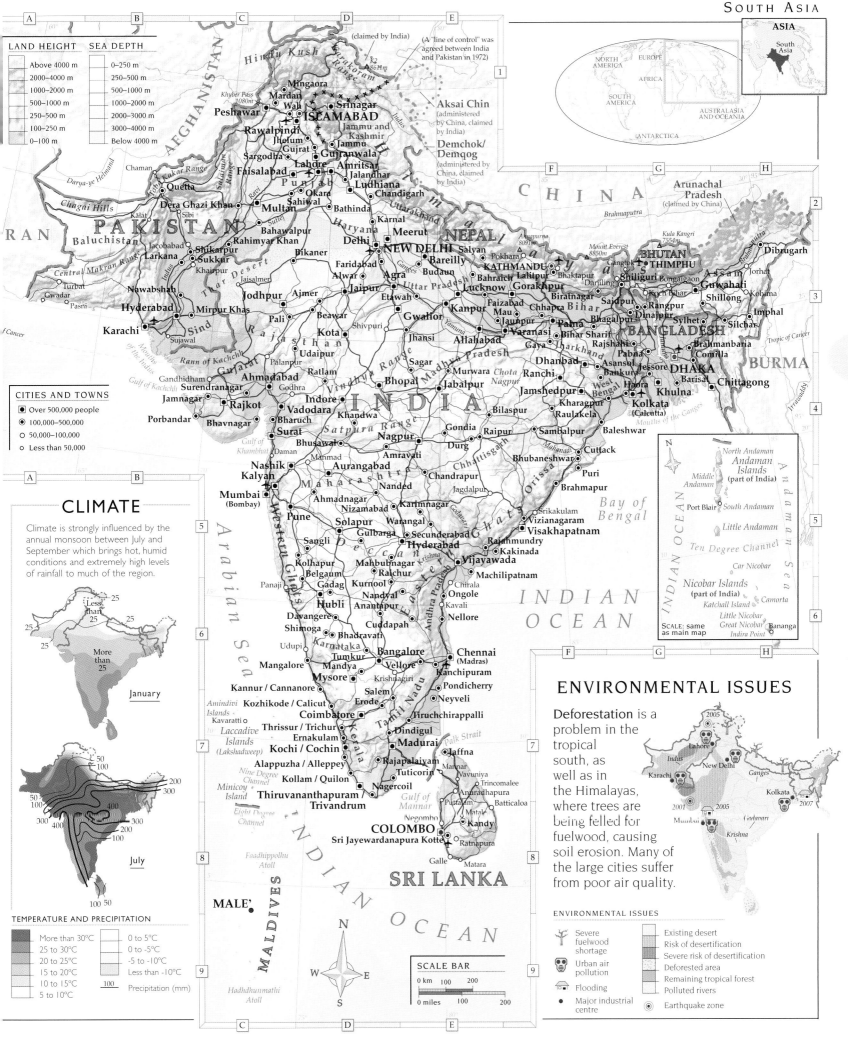

CLIMATE

Climate is strongly influenced by the annual monsoon between July and September which brings hot, humid conditions and extremely high levels of rainfall to much of the region.

ENVIRONMENTAL ISSUES

Deforestation is a problem in the tropical south, as well as in the Himalayas, where trees are being felled for fuelwood, causing soil erosion. Many of the large cities suffer from poor air quality.

EAST ASIA

CHINA, MONGOLIA, TAIWAN

China is the world's fourth largest country and its most populous – over 1.3 billion people live there. Under its communist government, which came to power in 1949, China has become a major industrial nation, but most of its people still live and work on the land, as they have for thousands of years. Taiwan also has a booming economy and exports its products around the world. Mongolia is a vast, remote country with a small population, many of whom are nomads.

INDUSTRY

Chemicals, iron and steel, engineering and textiles are the main industries in China's east coast cities, and in industrial centres like Shenyang. Shanghai, Hong Kong and Beijing are also important financial centres. In the interior, large deposits of coal support the heavy industries in major cities such as Chengdu and Wuhan. Taiwan specializes in textiles and shoe manufacture, along with electronic goods. Mongolia's economy is mainly agricultural.

INDUSTRY

- ✈ Aerospace
- 🚗 Car manufacture
- 🧪 Chemicals
- ⚡ Electronics
- 💻 Electronic goods
- ⚙ Engineering
- 🥫 Food processing
- 🏭 Iron & steel
- ⚓ Shipbuilding
- 👕 Textiles
- ⛏ Coal
- ⛏ Mining
- $ Finance
- ● Major industrial centre / area
- — Major road

STRUCTURE OF INDUSTRY

Services 37%
Manufacturing 50%
Primary 13%

POPULATION

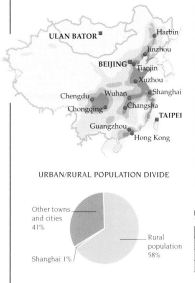

ULAN BATOR
Harbin
Jinzhou
BEIJING
Tianjin
Xuzhou
Chengdu
Wuhan
Shanghai
Chongqing
Changsha
TAIPEI
Guangzhou
Hong Kong

Most of China's people live in the eastern part of the country, where the climate, landscape and soils are most favourable. Urban areas there house over 250 million people, but almost 60% of the population lives in villages and farm the land. Taiwan's lowlands are very densely populated. In Mongolia, one third of the people live in the countryside.

URBAN/RURAL POPULATION DIVIDE

Other towns and cities 41%
Rural population 58%
Shanghai 1%

INHABITANTS PER SQ KM
- More than 200
- 100–200
- 50–100
- Less than 50
- ■ Capital city
- ● Major city

FARMING AND LAND USE

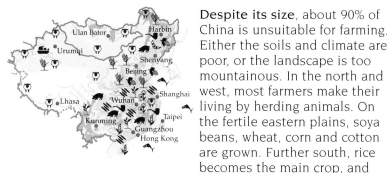

Ulan Bator
Harbin
Urumqi
Shenyang
Beijing
Lhasa
Wuhan
Shanghai
Kunming
Taipei
Guangzhou
Hong Kong

Despite its size, about 90% of China is unsuitable for farming. Either the soils and climate are poor, or the landscape is too mountainous. In the north and west, most farmers make their living by herding animals. On the fertile eastern plains, soya beans, wheat, corn and cotton are grown. Further south, rice becomes the main crop, and pigs are raised in large numbers.

FARMING AND LAND USE

- 🎣 Fishing
- 🐖 Pigs
- 🐑 Sheep
- 🌽 Corn (maize)
- Cotton
- 🍎 Fruit
- 🌾 Rice
- Soya beans
- Sugarcane
- 🍃 Tea
- Tobacco
- 🌾 Wheat
- Cropland
- Desert
- Forest
- Mountain region
- Pasture
- ● Major conurbation

LAND USE

Cropland 14%
Pasture 49%
Other (including mountains) 21%
Forest 16%

THE LANDSCAPE

China's landscape divides into three areas. The vast Plateau of Tibet in the southwest is the highest and largest plateau on Earth. It contains both dry deserts and pockets of pasture surrounded by high mountains. Northwest China has dry highlands. The great plains of eastern China were formed from soils deposited by rivers like the Yellow River over thousands of years. Most of Mongolia is dry, grassland steppe and cold, arid desert.

Tien Shan mountains (B 2)

The Tien Shan, or 'Heavenly Mountains' reach heights of 7,443 m. They surround fields of permanent ice and spectacular glaciers.

Gobi (E 2) and Takla Makan (B 3) deserts

The arid landscapes of the Gobi and Takla Makan deserts are made up of bare rock surfaces and huge areas of shifting sand dunes. They are hot in summer, but unlike most other deserts, are extremely cold in winter.

Takla Makan Desert

A handmade landscape

'The Roof of the World'

The cold, remote Plateau of Tibet (C 4) averages 4,000 m in height. Many of China's great rivers have their sources here. The world's highest human settlement, a town called Wenquan, is found in the east of the plateau. It lies 5,099 m above sea level.

The Yellow River (E 3)

The Yellow River (Huang He) is the world's muddiest river, carrying hundreds of lorry loads of sediment to the sea every minute. The river has burst its banks many times throughout history, causing enormous damage and claiming millions of human lives.

A handmade landscape

In the farming areas of eastern and southern China, terraces have been carved into the hillsides to make them flat enough to grow rice and other crops. This method of farming has been used for over 7,000 years.

ENVIRONMENTAL ISSUES

China is now the world's largest emitter of greenhouse gases. Its rapid economic growth has had a huge impact upon the environment. The Yangtze and Yellow Rivers are badly polluted. Urbanization is increasing, with over 100 cities in China having populations above 1 million.

The Three Gorges Dam is the largest hydro-electric project in the world.

CLIMATE

Two air masses control climate; one cold and dry from Siberia, and one moist and warm from the Pacific. Winters are long and cold away from the coast – especially on the Plateau of Tibet.

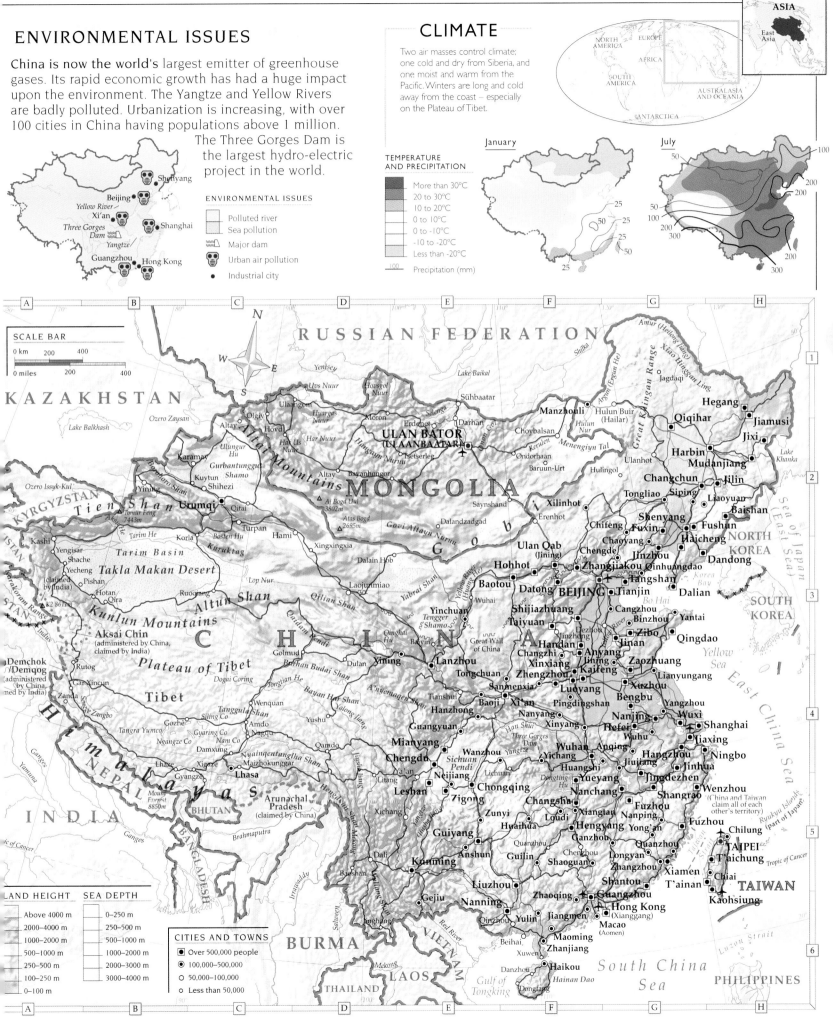

SOUTHEAST ASIA

BRUNEI, BURMA, CAMBODIA, EAST TIMOR, INDONESIA, LAOS,
MALAYSIA, PHILIPPINES, SINGAPORE, THAILAND, VIETNAM

Southeast Asia is made up of a mainland area and many thousands of tropical islands. The region has great natural wealth – from precious stones to oil – and has recently experienced fast industrial growth. Some countries here, especially Singapore and Malaysia, have become prosperous, but Laos and Cambodia remain poor, and are still recovering from years of terrible warfare.

ENVIRONMENTAL ISSUES

In Burma, Malaysia and Indonesia, ancient rainforests are being cut down faster than they can grow back. On 26th of December, 2004 a tsunami devastated the west of the region, it is estimated that over 225,000 people died around the Indian Ocean.

ENVIRONMENTAL ISSUES
- Urban air pollution
- Deforested area
- Remaining tropical forest
- Major industrial centre

POPULATION

On the mainland, the population is concentrated in the river valleys, plateaus or plains. Upland areas are inhabited by small groups of hill peoples. Most people still live in rural areas, but the cities are growing fast. In Indonesia and the Philippines, the population is unevenly distributed. Some islands, such as Java, are densely settled; others are barely occupied.

INHABITANTS PER SQ KM
- More than 200
- 100–200
- 50–100
- Less than 50
- ■ Capital city
- ● Major city

URBAN/RURAL POPULATION DIVIDE
- Bangkok 1.2%
- Jakarta 1.5%
- Manilla 1.8%
- Rural population 37%
- Other towns and cities 58.5%

INDUSTRY

Industries based on the processing of raw materials, like metallic minerals, timber, oil and gas and agricultural produce, are important here, but manufacturing has grown dramatically in recent years. Many foreign firms, attracted by low labour costs, have invested in the region. Malaysia and Singapore are major producers of electronic goods like disk drives for computers.

STRUCTURE OF INDUSTRY
- Primary 19%
- Services 45%
- Manufacturing 36%

INDUSTRY
- Chemicals
- Engineering
- Food processing
- Textiles
- Mining
- Oil and gas
- Timber
- $ Finance
- Hi-tech
- Tourism
- Major industrial centre / area
- Major road

THE LANDSCAPE

On the mainland, a belt of mountain ranges, cloaked in thick forest, runs north–south. The mountains are cut through by the wide valleys of five great rivers. On their route to the sea, these rivers have deposited sediment, forming immense, fertile flood plains and deltas. To the southeast of the mainland lies a huge arc of over 20,000 mountainous, volcanic islands.

Borneo (D 7)
Borneo is the world's third-largest island, with a total area of 757,050 sq km. Lying on the Equator and in the path of two monsoons, the island is hot, and one of the wettest places on Earth. The landscape contains thickly-forested central highlands and swampy lowlands.

Asian Tsunami (A6)
On December 26th, 2004 the second largest earthquake ever recorded occured under the sea off the west coast of Sumatra. This triggered a huge Tsunami wave, up to 30 m high in places, that devastated coastal communities causing the deaths of over 225,000 people in eleven countries.

Philippines (E4)
The Philippines' 7,000 islands are mountainous and volcanic with narrow coastal plains.

Papua (Irian Jaya) (I7)
Papua is a province of Indonesia. Its dense rainforests are some of the last unexplored areas on Earth and are inhabited by many rare plant and animal species.

Volcanoes
Indonesia is the most active volcanic region in the world; Java alone has over 50 active volcanoes out of the country's total of more than 220.

Indonesia (C7)
Indonesia is an archipelago of 13,677 islands, scattered over almost 5,000 km. The islands lie on the boundary between two of the Earth's tectonic plates and frequently experience earthquakes.

FARMING AND LAND USE

The staple crop here is rice, which grows in low-lying flooded fields called paddies, or on terraces cut into the hillsides. Sugarcane, coconuts, bananas and pineapples are widely grown as cash crops, and Malaysia produces 25% of the world's rubber. Freshwater and marine fish are caught in large quantities; fish is one of the main foods in this region.

FARMING AND LAND USE

- Cattle
- Fishing
- Pigs
- Shellfish
- Coconuts
- Fruit
- Rice
- Rubber
- Sugarcane
- Timber
- Cropland
- Forest
- Pasture
- Wetland
- Major conurbation

LAND USE

- Pasture 4%
- Cropland 21%
- Forest 51%
- Other 24%

ASIA
Southeast Asia

CLIMATE

Southeast Asia's climate is strongly affected by the monsoon, which brings warm, humid air and high rainfall to mainland Southeast Asia during July, and to maritime southeast Asia during January.

January

July

TEMPERATURE AND PRECIPITATION

- More than 30°C
- 20 to 30°C
- 10 to 20°C
- Less than 10°C
- 100 Precipitation (mm)

LAND HEIGHT
- Above 4000 m
- 2000–4000 m
- 1000–2000 m
- 500–1000 m
- 250–500 m
- 100–250 m
- 0–100 m

SEA DEPTH
- 0–250 m
- 250–500 m
- 500–1000 m
- 1000–2000 m
- 2000–3000 m
- 3000–4000 m
- Below 4000 m

CITIES AND TOWNS
- Over 500,000 people
- 100,000–500,000
- 50,000–100,000
- Less than 50,000

MALAYSIA'S TWO CAPITALS
KUALA LUMPUR - capital
PUTRAJAYA - administrative capital

131

JAPAN AND KOREA

JAPAN, NORTH KOREA, SOUTH KOREA

Japan is a curved chain of over 4,000 islands in the Pacific Ocean. To the west, Korea juts out from northern China. Japan has few natural resources but it has become one of the world's most successful industrial nations due to investment in new technology and a highly efficient workforce. North Korea is a communist state with limited contact with the outside world, while South Korea is a democracy with major international trade links.

THE LANDSCAPE

Most of Japan is covered by forested mountains and hills, among which are many short, fast-flowing rivers and small lakes. Only about a quarter of the land is suitable for building and farming and new land has been created by cutting back hillsides and reclaiming land from the sea. North and South Korea are mostly mountainous, with some coastal plains.

Hokkaido, Honshu, Shikoku and Kyushu
Japan's four main islands were formed when two giant plates making up the Earth's crust collided, making their edges buckle upwards.

T'aebaek-sanmaek (C 5)
This wooded mountain range forms the 'backbone' of the Korean peninsula. It runs from north to south close to the east coast.

Tsunamis
Huge sea waves called tsunamis frequently threaten the east coast of Japan. They are set off by submarine earthquakes. The waves increase in size as they near the shore, and can flood coastal areas and sink ships.

Earthquakes
In Japan, earthquakes are part of everyday life. The islands lie on a fault line, and earthquake tremors occur, on average, 5,000 times a year. Most of these are mild, and may go unnoticed, but there is a constant threat of disaster.

Volcanoes
Japan's mountain ranges are studded with volcanoes, 60 of which are still active. Mount Fuji is a 3,776 m snow-capped volcano and the highest mountain in Japan. It last erupted in 1707.

FARMING AND LAND USE

Modern farming methods allow Japan to grow much of its own food, despite a shortage of farmland. Rice is the main crop grown throughout the region. Japan has a large fishing fleet; the Japanese eat more fish than any other nation. In North Korea, farming is controlled by the government.

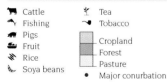

FARMING AND LAND USE

🐂 Cattle	🍃 Tea	
🐟 Fishing	🍂 Tobacco	
🐖 Pigs		Cropland
🍐 Fruit		Forest
🌾 Rice		Pasture
🫘 Soya beans	● Major conurbation	

LAND USE

Pasture 1%
Cropland 16%
Other (including mountains) 18%
Forest 65%

POPULATION

Most of Japan's 128 million people live in crowded cities on the coasts of the four main islands. The Kanto Plain around Tokyo is Japan's biggest area of flat land, and the most populous part of the country. In South Korea, a quarter of the population lives in the capital, Seoul. Most North Koreans live on the coastal plains.

URBAN/RURAL POPULATION DIVIDE

Tokyo-Yokohama 5.9%
Seoul 5.2%
Kobe-Osaka 2.1%
Rural population 22%
Other towns and cities 64.8%

INHABITANTS PER SQ KM

■ More than 200	■ Capital city	
100–200	● Major city	
50–100		
Less than 50		

INDUSTRY

Japan is a world leader in hi-tech electronic goods like computers, televisions and cameras, as well as cars. South Korea also has a thriving economy. It produces ships, cars, hi-tech goods, shoes and clothes for worldwide export. Both countries have to import most of their raw materials and energy. North Korea has little trade with other countries, but it is rich in minerals such as coal and silver.

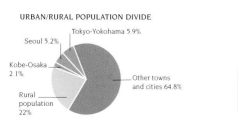

STRUCTURE OF INDUSTRY

Primary 2%
Services 70%
Manufacturing 28%

INDUSTRY

🚗 Car manufacture	⛏ Mining	
⚗ Chemicals	S Finance	
⚙ Engineering	💻 Hi-tech	
Food processing	Research & Development	
Iron & steel		
Shipbuilding	▣ Major industrial centre / area	
👕 Textiles	— Major road	

ENVIRONMENTAL ISSUES

Industrial pollution from Korea and China has produced acid rain, and pollution in Japanese cities has led to people wearing masks to filter the air. Russia regularly dumps nuclear waste into the Sea of Japan. In 1995, an earthquake caused great destruction to the city of Kobe.

ENVIRONMENTAL ISSUES

- Catastrophic earthquake
- Nuclear waste dump site
- Urban air pollution
- Affected by acid rain
- Site of nuclear accident
- Major industrial area

CLIMATE

Korea has hot summers and dry, very cold winters, especially in the north, where snow is common. In Japan, winters are less cold than on the Asian mainland; summers are hot, wet and humid.

January

July

TEMPERATURE AND PRECIPITATION

- More than 20°C
- 15 to 20°C
- 10 to 15°C
- 5 to 10°C
- 0 to 5°C
- 0 to -5°C
- Less than -5°C
- 100 Precipitation (mm)

ASIA
Japan and Korea

NORTH AMERICA · EUROPE · ASIA · AFRICA · SOUTH AMERICA · AUSTRALASIA AND OCEANIA · ANTARCTICA

SCALE BAR

km 100 200
miles 100 200

JAPAN

Hokkaido

Wakkanai, Rebun-to, Rishiri-to, Monbetsu, Abashiri, Nayoro, Shibetsu, Kitami, Nemuro, Asahikawa, Takikawa, Asahi-dake 2290m, Obihiro, Kushiro, Akkeshi, Otaru, Ebetsu, Sapporo, Chitose, Horoshiri-dake 2052m, Iwanai, Tomakomai, Noboribetsu, Muroran, Okushiri-to, Hakodate

Sea of Okhotsk

Kurile Islands (administered by Russian Federation, claimed by Japan)

Tsugaru-kaikyo

Honshu

Aomori, Goshogawara, Hachinohe, Hirosaki, Kuji, Odate, Iwate, Miyako, Noshiro, Gojome, Morioka, Akita, Yokote, Kesennuma, Honjo, Shizugawa, Sakata, Shinjo, Funakawa, Tsuruoka, Ishinomaki, Yamagata, Sendai, Fukushima, Soma, Haramachi, Niigata, Sado, Koriyama, Nagaoka, Inawashiro-ko, Iwaki, Sukagawa, Joetsu, Hitachi, Itoigawa, Shinano, Utsunomiya, Mito, Takaoka, Nagano, Oyama, Kanazawa, Toyama, Kawagoe, Matsumoto, Kasumiga-ura, Choshi, Komatsu, TOKYO, Chiba, Fukui, Kofu, Kawasaki, Nakatsugawa, Mount Fuji 3776m, Yokohama, Tsuruga, Gifu, Shizuoka, Izu-hanto, Ogaki, Toyota, O-shima, Nagoya, Okazaki, Nii-jima, Tottori, Biwa-ko, Hamamatsu, Kozu-shima, Matsue, Yonago, Kyoto, Otsu, Tsu, Miyako-jima, Mikura-jima, Himeji, Kobe, Ise, Okayama, Osaka, Wakayama, Kurashiki, Takamatsu, Gobo, Shingu, Hiroshima, Iwakuni, Niihama, Tokushima, Tanabe, Yamaguchi, Horu, Matsuyama, Shikoku, Shimonoseki, Ube, Kochi, Kitakyushu, Oita, Fukuoka, Kurume, Saga, Omuta, Kumamoto, Nobeoka, Sasebo, Nagasaki, Yatsushiro, Miyazaki, Kyushu, Sendai, Miyakonojo, Kagoshima

Sea of Japan / East Sea

Liancourt Rocks (under South Korean control)

Oki-shoto, Dogo, Dozen

PACIFIC OCEAN

NORTH KOREA

Hoeryong, Najin, Paektu-san 2750m, Ch'ongjin, Hyesan, Huch'ang, Kilchu, Kanggye, Kimch'aek, Ch'osan, Pukch'ong, Huich'on, Sinp'o, Namsan-ni, Hamhung, Sinuiju, Anju, Chongju, Yonghung, Namp'o, Sunch'on, Wonsan, Changyon, Sariwon, PYONGYANG, Sokch'o, Haeju, Kaesong, Ch'unch'on, Kangnung

(North and South Korea have been divided by a ceasefire agreement since 1953)

SOUTH KOREA

Ongjin, SEOUL (SOUL), Wonju, Tonghae, Inch'on, Suwon, Ch'onan, Ch'ungju, Andong, P'ohang, Taejon, Taegu, Ulsan, Kunsan, Namwon, Masan, Pusan, Kwangju, Sunch'on, Mokp'o, Chindo

Yellow Sea, East Korea Bay, Korea Strait, Tsushima, Kyushu, Ryukyu Islands (part of Japan), Okinawa, Naze, Amami-oshima, Cheju Strait, Cheju-do, East China Sea, Philippine Sea

LAND HEIGHT
- 2000–4000 m
- 1000–2000 m
- 500–1000 m
- 250–500 m
- 100–250 m
- 0–100 m

SEA DEPTH
- 0–250 m
- 250–500 m
- 500–1000 m
- 1000–2000 m
- 2000–3000 m
- 3000–4000 m
- Below 4000 m

CITIES AND TOWNS
- Over 500,000 people
- 100,000–500,000
- 50,000–100,000
- Less than 50,000

AUSTRALASIA & OCEANIA

Australasia and Oceania encompasses the ancient land mass of Australia, the islands of New Zealand, and the scattering of thousands of small islands that stretch out into the Pacific Ocean. Indigenous peoples of the South Pacific, such as the Aborigines, Maoris, Polynesians, Micronesians and Melanesians, inhabit the region. In Australia and New Zealand, they live alongside people of European origin who settled in the 18th century, and more recent arrivals from East and Southeast Asia.

7,300 km

9,800 km

PACIFIC ISLANDS

Micronesia is one of the Pacific's island nations, consisting of a group of volcanic islands, low-lying coral reefs and lagoons. Many of the smaller Pacific islands are only a few metres above sea level.

LAND USE AND AGRICULTURE

Much of the centre of Australia is a dry, barren desert and unsuitable for agriculture. At its fringes, sheep farming is practised, and Australia and New Zealand alike are massive producers of wool and lamb. The Pacific islands export many exotic fruits and crops – especially oil palms and coconut palms. Oil from the palms is processed and sold, as well as the fruits themselves. Small-scale fishing is common, but larger scale operations are run by foreign fishing fleets, especially the Japanese, who fish tuna from the deeper waters of the Pacific.

SHEEP FARMING

New Zealand and Australia are the world's biggest producers of wool. In New Zealand, sheep outnumber people by 12 to 1.

POPULATION

Capital cities
- ◼ Above 500,000
- ◉ 100,000 to 500,000
- ● 50,000 to 100,000
- ● Below 50,000

State capitals
- ◼ Above 500,000
- ◉ 100,000 to 500,000
- ○ 50,000 to 100,000

BORDERS

	full international border
	indication of maritime country extent
	indication of maritime dependent territory extent
	state border

SCALE 1:37,250,000

0 km 300 600

0 miles 300 600

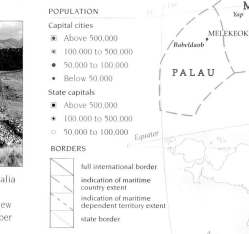

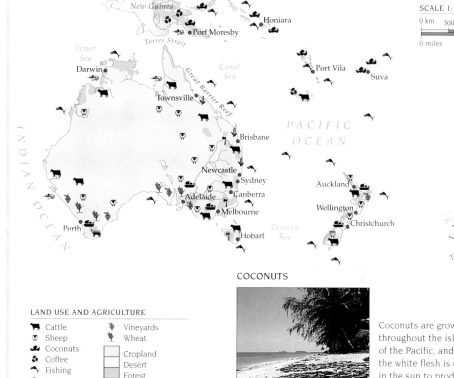

LAND USE AND AGRICULTURE

- 🐂 Cattle
- 🐑 Sheep
- 🥥 Coconuts
- ☕ Coffee
- 🐟 Fishing
- 🍎 Fruit
- 🦐 Shellfish
- 🌾 Sugarcane
- 🌲 Timber
- 🍇 Vineyards
- 🌾 Wheat

	Cropland
	Desert
	Forest
	Mountain region
	Pasture
●	Major conurbation

COCONUTS

Coconuts are grown throughout the islands of the Pacific, and the white flesh is dried in the sun to produce copra. Copra is a valuable export crop for many islands.

MINERAL RESOURCES

Mineral resources are not widespread, but where they are found, it is in great abundance. Most of the small Pacific islands have no mineral resources, but Australia has enormous reserves of bauxite and iron ore, and also sizeable reserves of gold and zinc. Copper is found in Papua New Guinea, and New Caledonia has large nickel reserves. There are ample supplies of fossil fuels and although coal is plentiful in eastern Australia, oil and gas are found only in isolated pockets around Australia's coast.

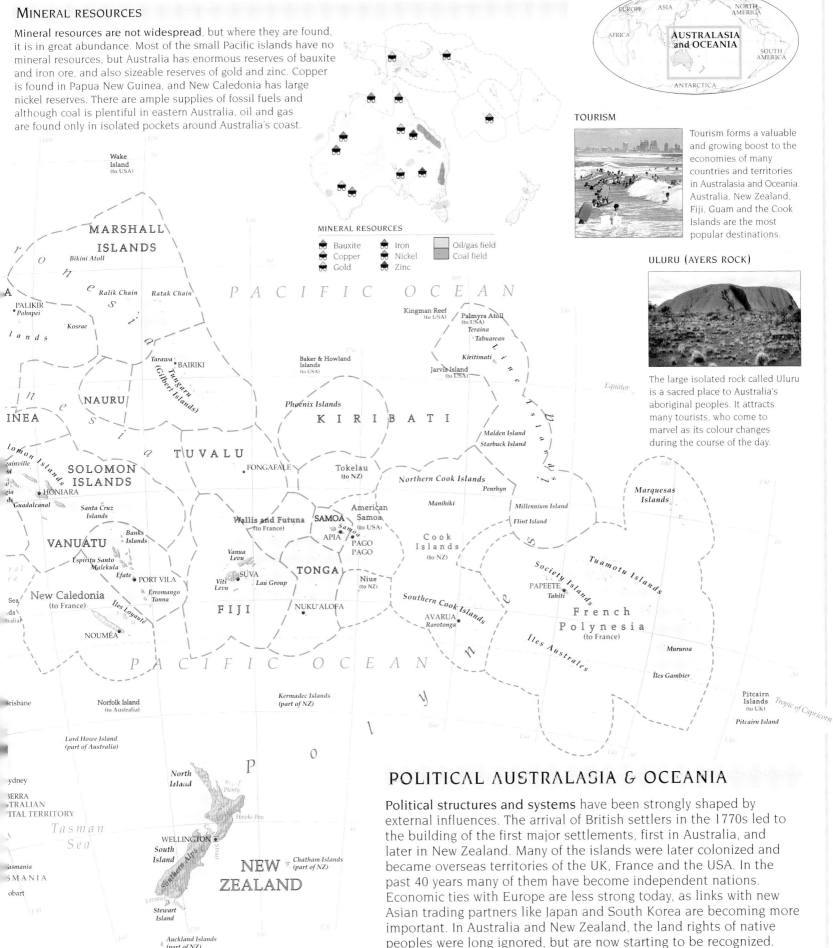

MINERAL RESOURCES

Bauxite	Iron		Oil/gas field
Copper	Nickel		Coal field
Gold	Zinc		

AUSTRALASIA and OCEANIA

EUROPE ASIA NORTH AMERICA
AFRICA
SOUTH AMERICA
ANTARCTICA

TOURISM

Tourism forms a valuable and growing boost to the economies of many countries and territories in Australasia and Oceania. Australia, New Zealand, Fiji, Guam and the Cook Islands are the most popular destinations.

ULURU (AYERS ROCK)

The large isolated rock called Uluru is a sacred place to Australia's aboriginal peoples. It attracts many tourists, who come to marvel as its colour changes during the course of the day.

PACIFIC OCEAN

MARSHALL ISLANDS
Bikini Atoll
Ralik Chain Ratak Chain
PALIKIR
Pohnpei
Kosrae
Tarawa BAIRIKI
Tungaru
(Gilbert Islands)
NAURU
NEA
INEA

Wake Island (to USA)

Kingman Reef (to USA)
Palmyra Atoll (to USA)
Teraina
Tabuaeran
Kiritimati
Jarvis Island (to USA)

Baker & Howland Islands (to USA)

Phoenix Islands

K I R I B A T I

Malden Island
Starbuck Island

Equator

Line Islands

TUVALU
FONGAFALE
Tokelau (to NZ)

Northern Cook Islands
Penrhyn
Manihiki
Millennium Island
Flint Island

Marquesas Islands

olomon Islands
SOLOMON ISLANDS
HONIARA
Guadalcanal
Santa Cruz Islands
Banks Islands
VANUATU
Espiritu Santo
Malekula
Efate PORT VILA
Erromango
Tanna
New Caledonia (to France)
Îles Loyauté
NOUMÉA

Wallis and Futuna (to France)
SAMOA
Samoa
APIA
PAGO PAGO
(to USA)
American Samoa

Vanua Levu
SUVA
Viti Levu Lau Group
TONGA
FIJI
NUKU'ALOFA

Niue (to NZ)

Cook Islands (to NZ)

Southern Cook Islands
AVARUA
Rarotonga

Society Islands
PAPEETE
Tahiti

Tuamotu Islands

French Polynesia (to France)
Îles Australes

Mururoa
Îles Gambier

PACIFIC OCEAN

Brisbane
Norfolk Island (to Australia)
Kermadec Islands (part of NZ)
Pitcairn Islands (to UK)
Pitcairn Island
Tropic of Capricorn

Lord Howe Island (part of Australia)

ydney
BERRA
TRALIAN
ITAL TERRITORY

Tasman Sea

North Island
Bay of Plenty
Hawke Bay

WELLINGTON
South Island Southern Alps
asmania
SMANIA
obart

NEW ZEALAND

Chatham Islands (part of NZ)

Stewart Island
Auckland Islands (part of NZ)

POLITICAL AUSTRALASIA & OCEANIA

Political structures and systems have been strongly shaped by external influences. The arrival of British settlers in the 1770s led to the building of the first major settlements, first in Australia, and later in New Zealand. Many of the islands were later colonized and became overseas territories of the UK, France and the USA. In the past 40 years many of them have become independent nations. Economic ties with Europe are less strong today, as links with new Asian trading partners like Japan and South Korea are becoming more important. In Australia and New Zealand, the land rights of native peoples were long ignored, but are now starting to be recognized.

AUSTRALIA

Australia is the world's sixth-largest country, and also the smallest, flattest continent, with the lowest rainfall. Most Australians are of European, mainly British, origin. However, since 1945 almost six million settlers from more than 170 countries have made Australia their home. The Aboriginal peoples, now only a tiny minority, were the first inhabitants. Recently, there have been several moves to restore their ancient lands.

INDUSTRY

Australia has one of the world's biggest mining industries. Bauxite, coal, copper, gold and iron ore are mined and exported, especially to Japan. In the cities, service industries, particularly tourism, are growing fast; Australia's sunshine and dramatic scenery are attracting an increasing number of overseas visitors.

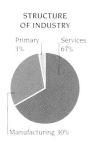

STRUCTURE
OF INDUSTRY

Primary 3%
Services 67%
Manufacturing 30%

INDUSTRY
- Brewing
- Car manufacture
- Chemicals
- Electronics
- Engineering
- Food processing
- Coal
- Mining
- Oil and gas
- Tourism
- Major industrial centre / area
- Major road

POPULATION

Despite its vast size, Australia is sparsely populated. The desert 'outback', which covers most of the interior, is too dry and barren to support many people. About 85% of the population live in the cities and towns on the east and southeast coasts, and around Perth in the west.

INHABITANTS
PER SQ KM
- More than 50
- 10–50
- 1–10
- Less than 1
- Capital city
- Major city

URBAN/RURAL POPULATION DIVIDE

Sydney 17.8%
Melbourne 16%
Brisbane 7.7%
Other towns and cities 43.5%
Rural population 15%

FARMING AND LAND USE

Away from the coasts, much of the land is too dry for agriculture. Fields of sugarcane grow close to the east coast, and grapes for the thriving wine industry are cultivated in the south and west, along with wheat. Vast numbers of cattle and sheep are raised for their meat and wool – both of which are major exports. They are grazed in the desert, on huge farms called 'stations', and in more fertile areas.

FARMING AND LAND USE
- Cattle
- Sheep
- Wheat
- Sugarcane
- Timber
- Vineyards
- Cropland
- Desert
- Forest
- Pasture
- Major conurbation

LAND USE

Cropland 6%
Other (including desert) 21%
Forest 19%
Pasture 54%

THE LANDSCAPE

Most of Australia is dry, flat and barren; all of the wetter, fertile land is found along its coastline. Huge sun-baked deserts, fringed by semi-arid plains of scrub and grassland cover most of the west and centre of the country. In the east, the land rises to the highlands of the Great Dividing Range, which run the whole length of the east coast. The tropical north coast has rainforests and mangrove swamps.

Blue Mountains (G 6)
The Blue Mountains lie towards the southern end of the Great Dividing Range. They get their name from the blue haze of oil droplets given off by the eucalyptus trees covering their slopes.

Great Barrier Reef (G 2)
This spectacular coral reef, which stretches for over 2,000 km off the coast of Queensland, is the largest living structure on Earth. The reef has built up over millions of years and its waters are home to thousands of different species of coral and marine animals.

Uluru (Ayers Rock) (D 4)
Uluru is an enormous block of red sandstone, standing almost in the middle of Australia. It is the world's biggest free-standing rock – 9.4 km around the base, and 867 m high. It is the summit of a sandstone hill that is buried beneath the sands of the desert.

Simpson Desert (E 4)
The Simpson Desert covers around 130,000 sq km. It contains long, parallel lines of sand dunes and is scattered with large salt pans and salt lakes, which were created when old rivers evaporated. They are now fed by the seasonal rains.

Murray River (F 5)
Together with its tributaries, the Murray River is Australia's main river system. It winds slowly westwards for more than 2,500 km from the Great Dividing Range to the Indian Ocean. It is fed by snow from mountains in the far southeast.

Great Dividing Range (H 5)
These highlands separate the desert regions from the fertile eastern plains. Rivers and streams have eroded them, creating deep valleys and gorges.

ENVIRONMENTAL ISSUES

Australia's dry climate and low rainfall make it susceptible to desertification. Between 2001 and 2007, southeast Australia experienced one of its worst droughts on record. The Murray-Darling basin, one of Australia's most productive agricultural regions, was very badly affected. During the dry season, vegetation becomes tinder-dry, and bush fires are common, burning huge tracts of land.

2001–2007

CLIMATE

Much of Australia's climate is continental, and temperatures soar during the day and fall rapidly at night. The climate is also arid and very little rain falls, apart from in the summer months when the north is affected by tropical storms.

January

July

TEMPERATURE AND PRECIPITATION

- More than 35°C
- 30 to 35°C
- 25 to 30°C
- 20 to 25°C
- 15 to 20°C
- 10 to 15°C
- 5 to 10°C
- Less than 5°C

100 — Precipitation (mm)

ENVIRONMENTAL ISSUES

- Area at risk from bushfires
- Drought
- Existing desert
- Risk of desertification
- Severe risk of desertification

LAND HEIGHT
- 2000–4000 m
- 1000–2000 m
- 500–1000 m
- 250–500 m
- 100–250 m
- 0–100 m
- Below sea level

SEA DEPTH
- 0–250 m
- 250–500 m
- 500–1000 m
- 1000–2000 m
- 2000–3000 m
- 3000–4000 m
- Below 4000 m

CITIES AND TOWNS
- Over 500,000 people
- 100,000–500,000
- 50,000–100,000
- Less than 50,000

SCALE BAR
0 km 100 200
0 miles 100 200

NEW ZEALAND

New Zealand is one of the most remote populated places in the world. The first people to settle on the islands were the Maori, a Polynesian people. When European settlers arrived during the 19th century, the Maori became a minority, and now only make up about 8% of the population. With a small population and rich natural resources, New Zealand's people have high living standards. The country's magnificent rugged scenery is popular with tourists.

INDUSTRY

Hi-tech industries such as electronics and computing are growing in the major cities of Auckland and Wellington, although agricultural products such as meat, wool and milk are still among New Zealand's major exports, and large pine forests supply wood for paper pulp and timber. The exciting scenery and varied climate draw tourists from all over the world, especially for walking and adventure holidays.

STRUCTURE
OF INDUSTRY

Primary 5%
Services 68%
Manufacturing 27%

INDUSTRY

- Chemicals
- Electronics
- Engineering
- Fish processing
- Food processing
- Iron and steel
- Textiles
- Timber
- Tourism

- Major industrial centre / area
- Major road

POPULATION

Most of the population is descended from European settlers, although immigrants from Asia and from the Pacific islands are increasing. About one-third of New Zealand's 4 million people live in Auckland on North Island, which also has the largest Polynesian population of any city in the Pacific. Elsewhere, the population is clustered along the coasts, where the land is lower.

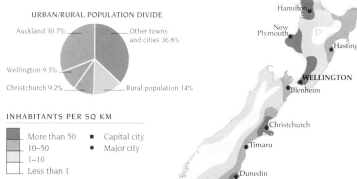

URBAN/RURAL POPULATION DIVIDE

Auckland 30.7%
Other towns and cities 36.8%
Wellington 9.3%
Christchurch 9.2%
Rural population 14%

INHABITANTS PER SQ KM

- More than 50
- 10–50
- 1–10
- Less than 1

- Capital city
- Major city

ENVIRONMENTAL ISSUES

New Zealand is one of the world's least polluted countries – largely due to its low population and lack of heavy industries, although air quality is occasionally poor in Auckland and Christchurch. Environment-friendly geothermal energy is tapped to make electricity in the volcanic region of North Island. Recently, logging companies have begun to exploit the rich forest reserves, although this has been widely opposed.

ENVIRONMENTAL ISSUES

- Geothermal power generation
- Logging activity
- Urban air pollution
- Major industrial centre

THE LANDSCAPE

Two large, mountainous islands form New Zealand's main land areas. A large crack or fault – the Alpine Fault, in the west of South Island – is the boundary between two plates in the Earth's crust. Land either side of the fault tends to move, causing earthquakes. Volcanoes, many of them still active, are also found, on both islands. South Island has many high peaks, several more than 3,000 m high.

Geysers and boiling mud

Geysers occur when hot volcanic rocks come into contact with underground water. The water boils and turns to steam forcing the water above it to burst through the Earth's surface into the air. There are many geysers and boiling mud pools in the areas around Rotorua and Taupo.

Northland (C1)

This is a tropical region in the far northwest. Many of the inlets are fringed by mangrove swamps.

Mount Taranaki (C4)

The dormant volcano of Mount Taranaki lies on New Zealand's North Island. It rises to a height of 2,518 m.

Probable location of Alpine Fault

Lake Taupo (D3)

New Zealand's largest lake, Lake Taupo, covers 606 sq km of North Island. It lies in the crater of an extinct volcano.

Southern Alps

New Zealand's Southern Alps stretch more than 483 km down the backbone of South Island. They were formed by the collision of the Indo-Australian and Pacific plates. Heavy snowfalls here, brought by westerly winds, feed the Fox Glacier which moves at a speed of 0.5–4.5 m a day.

FARMING AND LAND USE

Large areas of rich, sweet grasslands have made New Zealand one of the world's top areas for rearing sheep. There are around 12 sheep for every person, grazing alongside about ten million cattle. Fruits, including apples, strawberries, oranges, peaches, and the famous kiwi fruit, are cultivated, particularly on South Island, and are exported throughout the world. Fish caught off the Pacific coast are another important source of income.

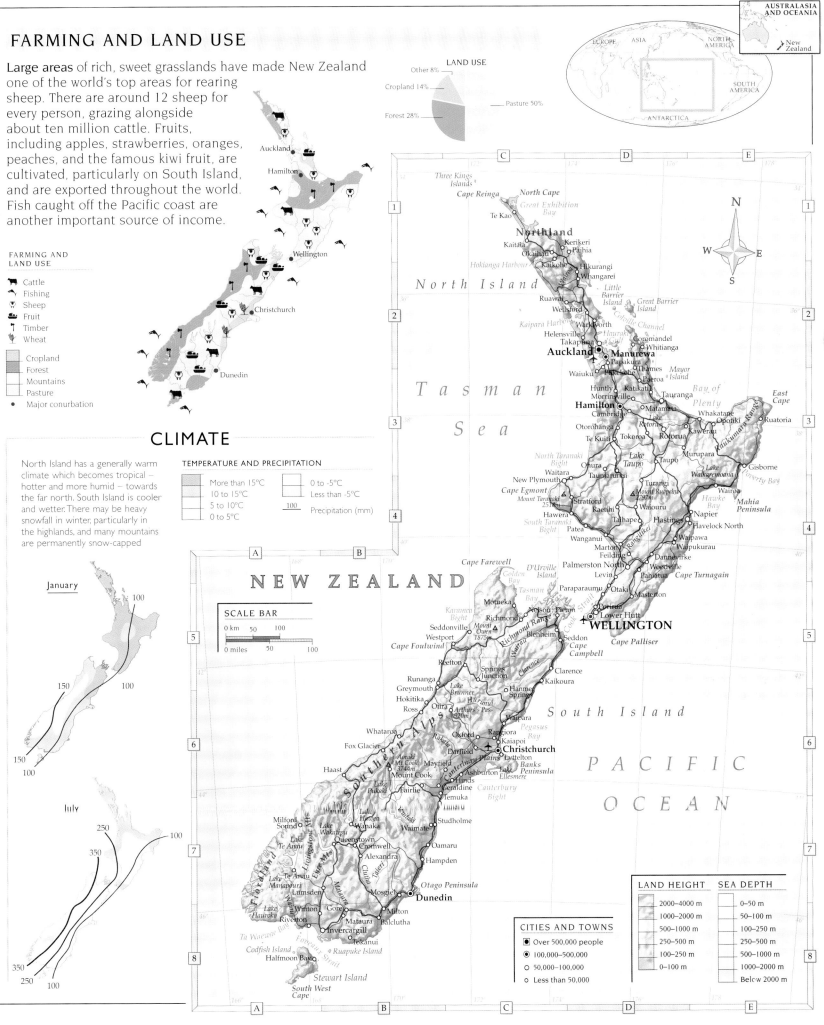

AUSTRALASIA AND OCEANIA

LAND USE

Other 8%
Cropland 14%
Forest 28%
Pasture 50%

FARMING AND LAND USE

- Cattle
- Fishing
- Sheep
- Fruit
- Timber
- Wheat

- Cropland
- Forest
- Mountains
- Pasture
- • Major conurbation

CLIMATE

North Island has a generally warm climate which becomes tropical – hotter and more humid – towards the far north. South Island is cooler and wetter. There may be heavy snowfall in winter, particularly in the highlands, and many mountains are permanently snow-capped

TEMPERATURE AND PRECIPITATION

- More than 15°C
- 10 to 15°C
- 5 to 10°C
- 0 to 5°C
- 0 to -5°C
- Less than -5°C
- 100 Precipitation (mm)

January
100
150
100
150
100

July
250
350
100
350
250
100

NEW ZEALAND

SCALE BAR

0 km 50 100
0 miles 50 100

LAND HEIGHT
- 2000–4000 m
- 1000–2000 m
- 500–1000 m
- 250–500 m
- 100–250 m
- 0–100 m

SEA DEPTH
- 0–50 m
- 50–100 m
- 100–250 m
- 250–500 m
- 500–1000 m
- 1000–2000 m
- Below 2000 m

CITIES AND TOWNS
- Over 500,000 people
- 100,000–500,000
- 50,000–100,000
- Less than 50,000

SOUTHWEST PACIFIC

The many thousands of islands in the Pacific Ocean are scattered across an enormous area. The original inhabitants, the Polynesians, Melanesians and Micronesians, settled the islands following the last Ice Age. In the 1700s Europeans arrived. They colonized all of the Pacific islands, introducing their culture, languages and religion. Today, many, though not all, of the islands have become independent. Their economies are simple, based largely on fishing and agriculture. Many are increasingly relying on their beautiful scenery and tropical climates to attract tourists and give a valuable boost to their economies.

LANDSCAPE

Most of the Pacific islands are extremely small, the largest land mass is the half of the island of New Guinea occupied by Papua New Guinea. The edges of the Indo-Australian and Pacific plates meet on the western edge of the area, leading to much volcanic and earthquake activity. Many of the islands are coral atolls, originally formed by volcanic activity, and some are no more than a few metres above sea level.

New Guinea (A 2)
A mountainous spine runs through the centre of the island, separating the northern coast from the dense forests and mangroves found in the south.

Pacific Ocean
The Pacific Ocean is the Earth's oldest and deepest ocean. Its name means peaceful, though it is far from being so; the highest wave ever recorded on open ocean – 34 m – occurred during a hurricane in the Pacific.

Kavachi
Kavachi is a submarine volcano lying off the coast of New Georgia, in the Solomon Islands. It still erupts every few years.

Ring of Fire
The 'Ring of Fire' is the term used to describe the string of volcanoes which surround the entire Pacific Ocean and erupt frequently because of intense stress and movement from within the Earth. The ring crosses the south Pacific, running between Vanuatu and New Caledonia, along the edge of the Solomon Islands, and between New Britain and New Guinea.

Sea trenches
Deep trenches mark the sea floor boundary where the Indo-Australian plate 'dives' under the Pacific plate.

Coral atolls
Volcanic activity in the Pacific has led to the creation of many islands. These islands become fringed with a ring of coral. When the islands subside beneath the sea once again, only the circle of coral is left, forming an atoll.

INDUSTRY

Today, the main industry for many of the Pacific islands is tourism. Food processing and small-scale textile industries are also common on many islands.

INDUSTRY

- 🍶 Brewing
- Food processing
- Textiles
- Timber processing
- ⛰ Mining
- Tourism

- ▪ Major industrial centre
- — Major road

FARMING AND LAND USE

Most farming that takes place on the Pacific islands is at a subsistence level, and many people keep pigs and chickens. A few crops are grown for export, especially oil palms, and coconuts, which are dried in the sun to produce copra. Many islanders make their living from the rich fishing grounds of the Pacific. The thick forests of Papua New Guinea are increasingly cut down for timber.

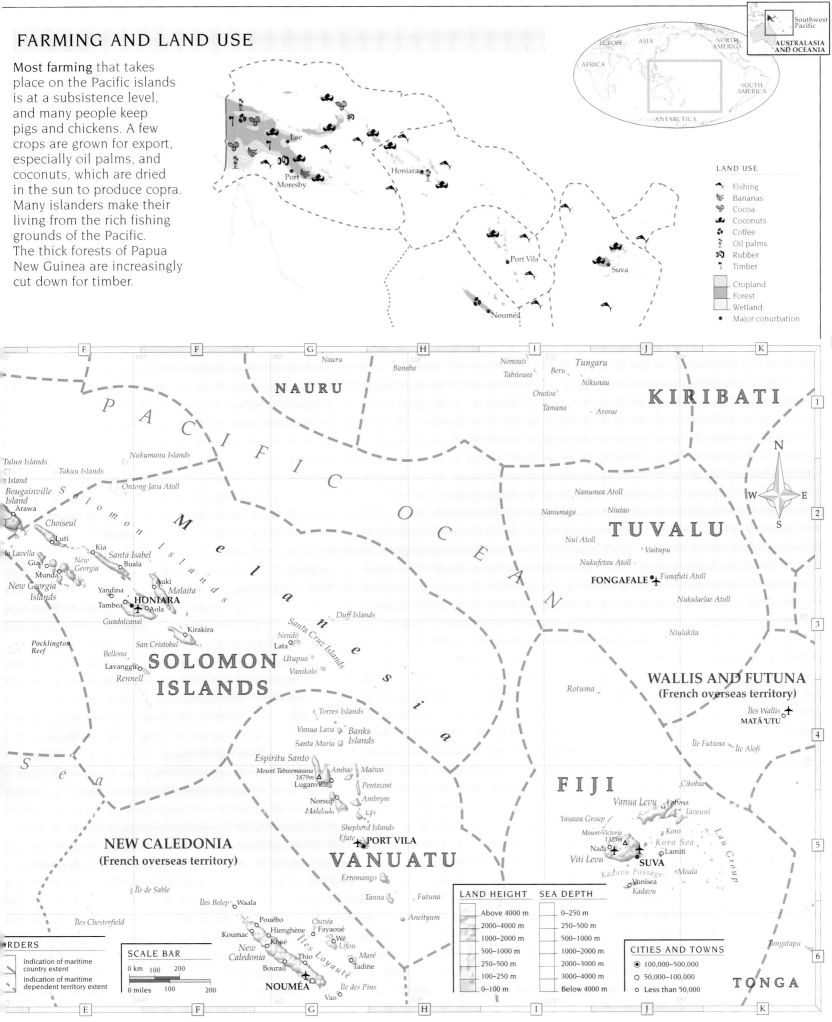

EUROPE ASIA NORTH AMERICA
AFRICA
SOUTH AMERICA
ANTARCTICA

Southwest Pacific
AUSTRALASIA AND OCEANIA

Lae
Honiara
Port Moresby
Port Vila
Suva
Nouméa

LAND USE

- Fishing
- Bananas
- Cocoa
- Coconuts
- Coffee
- Oil palms
- Rubber
- Timber

Cropland
Forest
Wetland
● Major conurbation

Main map

NAURU

Nauru
Banaba
Nonouti Tungaru
Tabiteuea Beru
Onotoa Nikunau
Tamana Arorae

KIRIBATI

P A C I F I C   O C E A N

Tulun Islands
Takuu Islands
Nukumanu Islands

Bougainville Island
Arawa
Choiseul
Luti
Kia Santa Isabel
Gizo New Buala
Munda Georgia
New Georgia Islands
Yandina Auki
Tambea Malaita
HONIARA
Aola
Guadalcanal
San Cristobal
Kirakira
Pocklington Reef
Bellona
Lavanggu
Rennell

SOLOMON ISLANDS

Nanumea Atoll
Nanumaga Niutao
TUVALU
Nui Atoll Vaitupu
Nukufetau Atoll
FONGAFALE ✈ Funafuti Atoll
Nukulaelae Atoll
Niulakita

M e l a n e s i a

Duff Islands
Nendö Santa Cruz Islands
Lata
Utupua
Vanikolo

Torres Islands
Vanua Lava Banks Islands
Santa Maria

Espiritu Santo
Mount Tabwemasana 1879m Ambae Maéwo
Luganville Pentecost
Norsup Ambrym
Malakula Lopi
Shepherd Islands
Efate **PORT VILA**
VANUATU
Erromango
Tanna Futuna
Aneityum

Rotuma

WALLIS AND FUTUNA
(French overseas territory)

Îles Wallis ✈
MATĂ'UTU
Île Futuna Île Alofi

FIJI
Cikobia
Vanua Levu Labasa
Yasawa Group Taveuni
Mount Victoria 1323m Koro
Nadi Koro Sea
Viti Levu **SUVA** Lamiti
Kadavu Passage Moala
Vunisea
Kadavu

Lau Group

NEW CALEDONIA
(French overseas territory)

S e a

Île de Sable
Îles Belep Waala
Îles Chesterfield
Pouébo
Koumac Hienghène Ouvéa
Koné Fayaoué
Wé
New Lifou
Caledonia Maré
Thio Tadine
Bourail
NOUMÉA Île des Pins
Vao

Tongatapu

TONGA

N
W E
S

BORDERS

— indication of maritime country extent
— indication of maritime dependent territory extent

SCALE BAR

0 km 100 200
0 miles 100 200

LAND HEIGHT

- Above 4000 m
- 2000–4000 m
- 1000–2000 m
- 500–1000 m
- 250–500 m
- 100–250 m
- 0–100 m

SEA DEPTH

- 0–250 m
- 250–500 m
- 500–1000 m
- 1000–2000 m
- 2000–3000 m
- 3000–4000 m
- Below 4000 m

CITIES AND TOWNS

- ◉ 100,000–500,000
- ◎ 50,000–100,000
- ○ Less than 50,000

ANTARCTICA

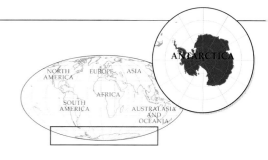

The continent of Antarctica has no permanent human population and very few animals can survive on the frozen land, although the surrounding seas teem with fish and mammals. Even in the summer the temperature is rarely above freezing and the sea-ice only partly melts; in winter, temperatures plummet to –80°C. The only people who live in Antarctica are teams of scientists who study the wildlife and monitor the ice for changes in the Earth's atmosphere.

THE LANDSCAPE

Frozen seas
During the cold winter months, the seas surrounding Antarctica freeze, almost doubling the size of the continent.

Antarctica is the world's most southerly continent. It is also the world's coldest continent and its highest, mainly due to the great ice sheet – up to 2 km thick in parts – which lies over the mountains of the Antarctic Peninsula and the plateau of East Antarctica.

Lambert Glacier (E 4)
The Lambert Glacier is the world's largest series of glaciers. It is 80 km wide at the coast and reaches more than 300 km inland.

Transantarctic Mountains (C 5)
The Transantarctic Mountains run across the continent, splitting it into East and West Antarctica.

Ice sheet
A massive sheet of ice, about 4,800 m thick at its deepest point, covers almost the entire area of Antarctica. It contains most of the fresh water on Earth. The weight of the ice pushes the land down below sea level.

The Ross Ice Shelf (C 5)
The Ross Sea is part of the Southern Ocean. This deep bay is covered by a thick sheet of ice which floats on the ocean.

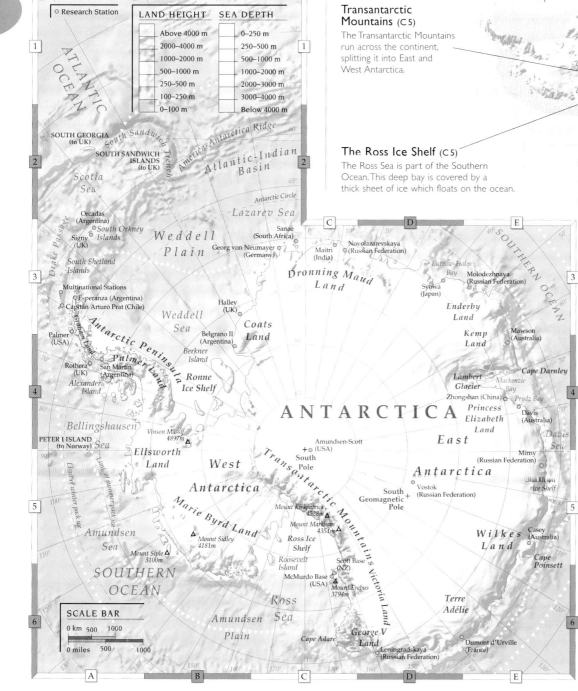

○ Research Station

LAND HEIGHT	SEA DEPTH
Above 4000 m	0–250 m
2000–4000 m	250–500 m
1000–2000 m	500–1000 m
500–1000 m	1000–2000 m
250–500 m	2000–3000 m
100–250 m	3000–4000 m
0–100 m	Below 4000 m

SCALE BAR
0 km 500 1000
0 miles 500 1000

RESOURCES

The mountains of Antarctica have rich mineral reserves. Gold, iron and coal are found, and there is natural gas in the surrounding seas. The unique and abundant marine wildlife is Antarctica's greatest resource. Colonies of penguins breed on the ice sheet, and whales, seals and many bird and fish species thrive in the icy waters.

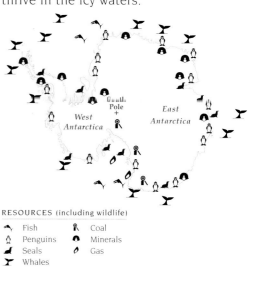

West Antarctica
East Antarctica

RESOURCES (including wildlife)
- Fish
- Penguins
- Seals
- Whales
- Coal
- Minerals
- Gas

THE ARCTIC

The ice-covered Arctic Ocean is encircled by the most northerly parts of Europe, North America and Asia. Very few people live in the often freezing conditions. Those who do, including the Sami of northern Scandinavia, the Siberian Yugyt and Nenet people and the Canadian Inuit, were nomads who lived by hunting and herding. Some live like this today, but many have now settled in small towns.

THE LANDSCAPE

The Arctic Ocean is the smallest ocean in the world, covering a total area of 15,100,000 sq km. The ocean is divided into two large basins, divided by three great underwater mountain ranges including the Lomonosov Ridge which is more than 3,000 m high on average.

Lomonosov Ridge (C 4)

Arctic islands (A 4)

In the far north of Canada, there are many thousands of islands including Baffin Island and Victoria Island. Many of them are almost entirely surrounded by pack-ice.

Pack-ice

Much of the Arctic Ocean is permanently covered by pack-ice. When the ice breaks up, it forms enormous floating ice-masses called icebergs.

Greenland (A 3)

Greenland is the world's largest island. It is covered by a huge ice sheet, more than 1,683,400 sq km across. The weight of the ice has pushed most of the land below sea level.

Sastrugi

Snow, blown by strong winds can scratch deep patterns in the snow. These patterns are known as sastrugi and line up with the direction of the wind.

RESOURCES

Coal, oil and gas are found beneath the Arctic Ocean and in Canada, Alaska and Russia. Fears about damage to the environment and the cost of extracting these resources have restricted the quantities removed. Overfishing has reduced fish stocks to very low levels. Quotas have been put in place to allow them to revive.

RESOURCES

- ⌐ Fish
- ⚑ Coal
- ⬠ Minerals
- ◊ Oil and gas
- ● Major town/city

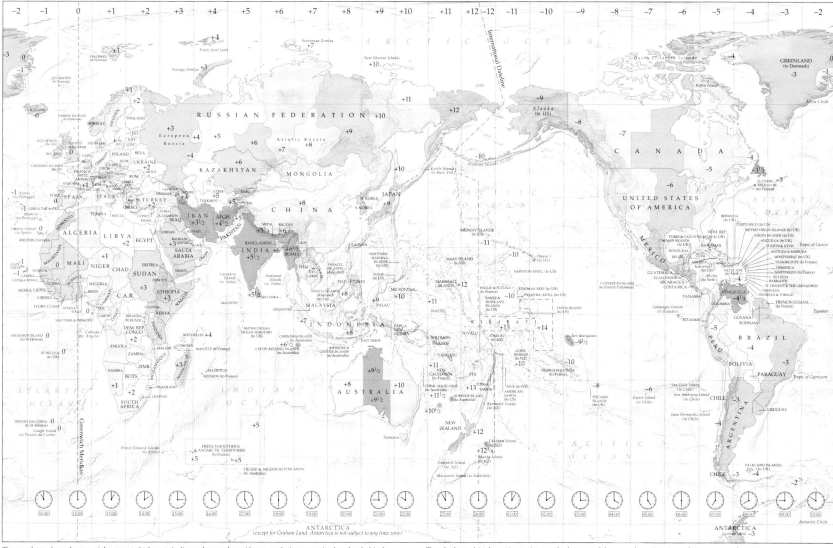

The numbers along the top of the map (+2/-2 etc.), indicate the number of hours each time zone is ahead or behind UTC (Coordinated Universal Time)

The clocks and 24-hour times given at the bottom of the map show time in each time zone when it is 12.00 hours noon UTC

TIME ZONES

The Earth is a rotating sphere, and because of this the Sun only shines on half of its surface at any one time. This means that it is morning, evening and night time in different parts of the world (*see diagram below*). Because of these differences, each country or part of a country uses a local time. A region of Earth's surface which uses a single local time is called a time zone. There are 24 one-hour time zones around the world, arranged roughly in vertical longitudinal bands.

DAY AND NIGHT AROUND THE WORLD

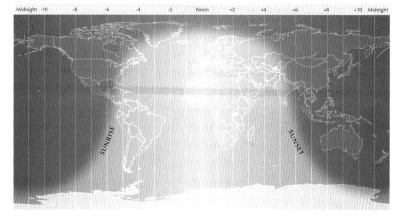

STANDARD TIME

Standard time is the official local time in a particular country or part of a country. Although time zones are arranged roughly in longitudinal bands, in many places the borders of a zone do not fall exactly along a line of longitude, as can be seen on the map, but are determined by geographical factors or by borders between countries.

Most countries have just one time zone, but some large countries (such as the USA, Canada and Russia) are split between several time zones, so standard time varies across those countries. For example, mainland USA crosses four time zones and so has four standard times, called the Eastern, Central, Mountain and Pacific standard times. China is unusual in that just one standard time is used for the whole country, even though it extends across 60° of longitude from west to east.

COORDINATED UNIVERSAL TIME (UTC)

Coordinated Universal Time (UTC) is an international reference used to set the local time in each time zone. For example, Australian Western Standard Time (the local time in Western Australia) is set 8 hours ahead of UTC (it is UTC+8), so if it were 12.00 noon UTC in London, UK, it would be 8.00pm in Perth, Western Australia. UTC has replaced Greenwich Mean Time (GMT) because UTC is based on an atomic clock, which is more accurate and convenient than GMT. Greenwich Mean Time was determined by the Sun's position in the sky relative to the 0° line of longitude, also known as the Greenwich Meridian, which runs through Greenwich, UK.

THE INTERNATIONAL DATELINE

The International Dateline is an imaginary line from pole to pole that roughly corresponds to the 180° line of longitude. It is an arbitrary marker between calendar days. The dateline is needed because of the use of local times around the world rather than a single universal time. When moving from west to east across the dateline, travellers have to set their watches back one day. Those travelling in the opposite direction, from east to west, must add a day.

DAYLIGHT SAVING TIME

Daylight saving is a summertime adjustment to the local time in a country or region, designed to increase the hours of daylight that occur during people's normal waking hours. To follow the system, clocks are advanced by an hour on a pre-decided date in spring and reverted back in autumn. About half of the world's nations use daylight saving.

LARGEST COUNTRIES

Russian Federation	6,592,735 sq miles (17,075,200 sq km)
Canada	3,885,171 sq miles (9,984,670 sq km)
USA	3,717,792 sq miles (9,629,091 sq km)
China	3,705,386 sq miles (9,596,960 sq km)
Brazil	3,286,470 sq miles (8,511,965 sq km)
Australia	2,967,893 sq miles (7,686,850 sq km)
India	1,269,339 sq miles (3,287,590 sq km)
Argentina	1,068,296 sq miles (2,766,890 sq km)
Kazakhstan	1,049,150 sq miles (2,717,300 sq km)
Sudan	967,493 sq miles (2,505,810 sq km)

SMALLEST COUNTRIES

Vatican City	0.17 sq miles (0.44 sq km)
Monaco	0.75 sq miles (1.95 sq km)
Nauru	8.1 sq miles (21 sq km)
Tuvalu	10 sq miles (26 sq km)
San Marino	24 sq miles (61 sq km)
Liechtenstein	62 sq miles (160 sq km)
Marshall Islands	70 sq miles (181 sq km)
St. Kitts & Nevis	101 sq miles (261 sq km)
Maldives	116 sq miles (300 sq km)
Malta	122 sq miles (316 sq km)

MOST POPULOUS COUNTRIES

China	1,345,751,000
India	1,198,003,300
USA	314,658,800
Indonesia	229,964,700
Brazil	193,733,800
Pakistan	180,808,100
Bangladesh	162,220,800
Nigeria	154,728,892
Russian Federation	140,873,600
Japan	127,156,200

LEAST POPULOUS COUNTRIES

Vatican City	800
Nauru	9800
Tuvalu	11,100
Palau	20,400
San Marino	31,400
Monaco	32,000
Liechtenstein	35,000
St. Kitts & Nevis	46,100
Marshall Islands	54,100
Dominica	70,400

MOST DENSELY POPULATED COUNTRIES

Monaco	42,667 people per sq mile (16,410 per sq km)
Singapore	20,072 people per sq mile (7765 per sq km)
Vatican City	4706 people per sq mile (1818 per sq km)
Malta	3296 people per sq mile (1277 per sq km)
Bangladesh	3138 people per sq mile (1211 per sq km)
Bahrain	2899 people per sq mile (1121 per sq km)
Maldives	2667 people per sq mile (1031 per sq km)
Taiwan	1844 people per sq mile (712 per sq km)
Mauritius	1794 people per sq mile (693 per sq km)
Barbados	1542 people per sq mile (595 per sq km)

MOST SPARSELY POPULATED COUNTRIES

Mongolia	4 people per sq mile (2 per sq km)
Namibia	7 people per sq mile (3 per sq km)
Australia	7 people per sq mile (3 per sq km)
Mauritania	8 people per sq mile (3 per sq km)
Surinam	8 people per sq mile (3 per sq km)
Iceland	8 people per sq mile (3 per sq km)
Botswana	9 people per sq mile (3 per sq km)
Canada	9 people per sq mile (4 per sq km)
Libya	9 people per sq mile (4 per sq km)
Guyana	10 people per sq mile (4 per sq km)

RICHEST COUNTRIES (GNI PER CAPITA, IN US$)

Liechtenstein	99,160
Qatar	93,204
Norway	87,068
Luxembourg	84,892
Switzerland	65,334
Denmark	59,129
UAE	54,067
San Marino	53,910
Sweden	50,943
Netherlands	50,150

POOREST COUNTRIES (GNI PER CAPITA, IN US$)

Burundi	135
Congo, Dem. Rep	153
Liberia	167
Zimbabwe	237
Guinea-Bissau	245
Ethiopia	282
Malawi	288
Somalia	288
Eritrea	299
Sierra Leone	321

MOST WIDELY SPOKEN LANGUAGES

1. Chinese (Mandarin)	6. Arabic
2. English	7. Bengali
3. Hindi, Hindustani, Urdu	8. Portuguese
4. Spanish	9. Malay-Indonesian
5. Russian	10. French

LARGEST DESERTS

Sahara	3,450,000 sq miles (9,065,000 sq km)
Gobi	500,000 sq miles (1,295,000 sq km)
Empty Quarter (Ar Rub al Khali)	289,600 sq miles (750,000 sq km)
Great Victorian	249,800 sq miles (647,000 sq km)
Sonoran	120,000 sq miles (311,000 sq km)
Kalahari	120,000 sq miles (310,800 sq km)
Garagum	115,800 sq miles (300,000 sq km)
Takla Makan	100,400 sq miles (260,000 sq km)
Namib	52,100 sq miles (135,000 sq km)
Thar	33,670 sq miles (130,000 sq km)

NB – Most of Antarctica is a polar desert, with only 2 inches (50 mm) of precipitation annually

LARGEST ISLANDS

Greenland	849,400 sq miles (2,200,000 sq km)
New Guinea	312,000 sq miles (808,000 sq km)
Borneo	292,222 sq miles (757,050 sq km)
Madagascar	229,300 sq miles (594,000 sq km)
Sumatra	202,300 sq miles (524,000 sq km)
Baffin Island	183,800 sq miles (476,000 sq km)
Honshu	88,800 sq miles (230,000 sq km)
Britain	88,700 sq miles (229,800 sq km)
Victoria Island	81,900 sq miles (212,000 sq km)
Ellesmere Island	75,700 sq miles (196,000 sq km)

HIGHEST MOUNTAINS (HEIGHT ABOVE SEA LEVEL)

Everest	29,035 ft (8850 m)
K2	28,253 ft (8611 m)
Kanchenjunga I	28,210 ft (8598 m)
Makalu I	27,767 ft (8463 m)
Cho Oyu	26,907 ft (8201 m)
Dhaulagiri I	26,796 ft (8167 m)
Manaslu I	26,783 ft (8163 m)
Nanga Parbat I	26,661 ft (8126 m)
Annapurna I	26,547 ft (8091 m)
Gasherbrum I	26,471 ft (8068 m)

DEEPEST OCEAN FEATURES

Challenger Deep, Mariana Trench (Pacific)	36,201 ft (11,034 m)
Vityaz III Depth, Tonga Trench (Pacific)	35,704 ft (10,882 m)
Vityaz Depth, Kurile-Kamchatka Trench (Pacific)	34,588 ft (10,542 m)
Cape Johnson Deep, Philippine Trench (Pacific)	34,441 ft (10,497 m)
Kermadec Trench (Pacific)	32,964 ft (10,047 m)
Ramapo Deep, Japan Trench (Pacific)	32,758 ft (9984 m)
Milwaukee Deep, Puerto Rico Trench (Atlantic)	30,185 ft (9200 m)
Argo Deep, Torres Trench (Pacific)	30,070 ft (9165 m)
Meteor Depth, South Sandwich Trench (Atlantic)	30,000 ft (9144 m)
Planet Deep, New Britain Trench (Pacific)	29,988 ft (9140 m)

LARGEST BODIES OF INLAND WATER (AREA & DEPTH)

Caspian Sea	143,243 sq miles (371,000 sq km) ...... 3215 ft (980 m)
Lake Superior	32,151 sq miles (83,270 sq km) ...... 1289 ft (393 m)
Lake Victoria	26,560 sq miles (68,880 sq km) ...... 328 ft (100 m)
Lake Huron	23,436 sq miles (60,700 sq km) ...... 751 ft (229 m)
Lake Michigan	22,402 sq miles (58,020 sq km) ...... 922 ft (281 m)
Lake Tanganyika	12,703 sq miles (32,900 sq km) ...... 4700 ft (1435 m)
Great Bear Lake	12,274 sq miles (31,790 sq km) ...... 1047 ft (319 m)
Lake Baikal	11,776 sq miles (30,500 sq km) ...... 5712 ft (1741 m)
Great Slave Lake	10,981 sq miles (28,440 sq km) ...... 459 ft (140 m)
Lake Erie	9915 sq miles (25,680 sq km) ...... 197 ft (60 m)

LONGEST RIVERS

Nile (NE Africa)	4160 miles (6695 km)
Amazon (South America)	4049 miles (6516 km)
Yangtze (China)	3915 miles (6299 km)
Mississippi/Missouri (US)	3710 miles (5969 km)
Ob'-Irtysh (Russ. Fed.)	3461 miles (5570 km)
Yellow River (China)	3395 miles (5464 km)
Congo (Central Africa)	2900 miles (4667 km)
Mekong (Southeast Asia)	2749 miles (4425 km)
Lena (Russian Federation)	2734 miles (4400 km)
Mackenzie (Canada)	2640 miles (4250 km)
Yenisey (Russian Federation)	2541 miles (4090 km)

GREATEST WATERFALLS (MEAN FLOW OF WATER)

Boyoma (Congo)	600,400 cu. ft/sec (17,000 cu.m/sec)
Khône (Laos/Cambodia)	410,000 cu. ft/sec (11,600 cu.m/sec)
Niagara (USA/Canada)	195,000 cu. ft/sec (5500 cu.m/sec)
Grande (Uruguay)	160,000 cu. ft/sec (4500 cu.m/sec)
Paulo Afonso (Brazil)	100,000 cu. ft/sec (2800 cu.m/sec)
Urubupunga (Brazil)	97,000 cu. ft/sec (2750 cu.m/sec)
Iguaçu (Argentina/Brazil)	62,000 cu. ft/sec (1700 cu.m/sec)
Maribondo (Brazil)	53,000 cu. ft/sec (1500 cu.m/sec)
Victoria (Zimbabwe)	39,000 cu. ft/sec (1100 cu.m/sec)
Kabalega (Uganda)	42,000 cu. ft/sec (1200 cu.m/sec)
Churchill (Canada)	35,000 cu. ft/sec (1000 cu.m/sec)
Cauvery (India)	33,000 cu. ft/sec (900 cu.m/sec)

HIGHEST WATERFALLS

Angel (Venezuela)	3212 ft (979 m)
Tugela (South Africa)	3110 ft (948 m)
Utigard (Norway)	2625 ft (800 m)
Mongefossen (Norway)	2539 ft (774 m)
Mtarazi (Zimbabwe)	2500 ft (762 m)
Yosemite (USA)	2425 ft (739 m)
Ostre Mardola Foss (Norway)	2156 ft (657 m)
Tyssestrengane (Norway)	2119 ft (646 m)
*Cuquenan (Venezuela)	2001 ft (610 m)
Sutherland (New Zealand)	1903 ft (580 m)
*Kjellfossen (Norway)	1841 ft (561 m)

* indicates that the total height is a single leap

			GENERAL FACTS		
Country	Capital city	Land area (sq km)	Main languages spoken	Unit of currency	Population (2009)

NORTH AMERICA

Country	Capital city	Land area (sq km)	Main languages spoken	Unit of currency	Population (2009)
Antigua & Barbuda	St John's	442	English, English patois	East Caribbean dollar	82 8
Bahamas	Nassau	13 940	English, English Creole, French Creole	Bahamian dollar	341 7
Barbados	Bridgetown	430	Bajan (Barbadian English), English	Barbados dollar	255 9
Belize	Belmopan	22 966	English Creole, Spanish, English, Mayan, Garifuna (Carib)	Belizean dollar	306 8
Canada	Ottawa	9 984 670	English, French, Chinese, Italian, German, Ukrainian, Portuguese, Inuktitut, Cree	Canadian dollar	33 573 5
Costa Rica	San José	51 100	Spanish, English Creole, Bribri, Cabecar	Costa Rican colón	4 578 9
Cuba	Havana	110 860	Spanish	Cuban peso	11 204 2
Dominica	Roseau	754	French Creole, English	East Caribbean dollar	70 4
Dominican Republic	Santo Domingo	48 380	Spanish, French Creole	Dominican Republic peso	10 090 1
El Salvador	San Salvador	21 040	Spanish	Salvadorean colón, US $	6 163 1
Grenada	St George's	340	English, English Creole	East Caribbean dollar	103 9
Guatemala	Guatemala City	108 890	Quiché, Mam, Cakchiquel, Kekchí, Spanish	Quetzal	14 026 9
Haiti	Port-au-Prince	27 750	French Creole, French	Gourde	10 032 6
Honduras	Tegucigalpa	112 090	Spanish, Garífuna (Carib), English Creole	Lempira	7 466 0
Jamaica	Kingston	10 990	English Creole, English	Jamaican dollar	2 718 8
Mexico	Mexico City	1 972 550	Spanish, Nahuatl, Mayan, Zapotec, Mixtec, Otomi, Totonac, Tzotzil, Tzeltal	Mexican peso	109 610 0
Nicaragua	Managua	129 494	Spanish, English Creole, Miskito	Córdoba oro	5 742 8
Panama	Panama City	78 200	English Creole, Spanish, Amerindian languages, Chibchan languages	Balboa, US dollar	3 453 9
St Kitts & Nevis	Basseterre	261	English, English Creole	East Caribbean dollar	46 1
St Lucia	Castries	620	English, French Creole	East Caribbean dollar	172 2
St Vincent & the Grenadines	Kingstown	389	English, English Creole	East Caribbean dollar	109 2
Trinidad & Tobago	Port-of-Spain	5 128	English Creole, English, Hindi, French, Spanish	Trinidad and Tobago dollar	1 338 6
United States	Washington D.C.	9 626 091	English, Spanish, Chinese, French, German, Tagalog, Vietnamese, Italian, Korean, Russian, Polish	US dollar	314 658 8

SOUTH AMERICA

Country	Capital city	Land area (sq km)	Main languages spoken	Unit of currency	Population (2009)
Argentina	Buenos Aires	2 766 890	Spanish, Italian, Amerindian languages	Argentine peso	40 276 4
Bolivia	La Paz/Sucre	1 098 580	Aymara, Quechua, Spanish	Boliviano	9 862 9
Brazil	Brasília	8 511 965	Portuguese, German, Italian, Spanish, Polish, Japanese, Amerindian languages	Real	193 733 8
Chile	Santiago	756 950	Spanish, Amerindian languages	Chilean peso	16 970 3
Colombia	Bogotá	1 138 910	Spanish, Wayuu, Páez, other Amerindian languages	Colombian peso	45 659 7
Ecuador	Quito	283 560	Spanish, Quechua, other Amerindian languages	US dollar	13 625 1
Guyana	Georgetown	214 970	English Creole, Hindi, Tamil, Amerindian languages, English	Guyanese dollar	762 5
Paraguay	Asunción	406 750	Guaraní, Spanish, German	Guaraní	6 348 9
Peru	Lima	1 285 200	Spanish, Quechua, Aymara	Nuevo sol	29 164 8
Surinam	Paramaribo	163 270	Sranan (creole), Dutch, Javanese, Sarnami Hindi, Saramaccan, Chinese, Carib	Surinamese dollar	519 7
Uruguay	Montevideo	176 220	Spanish	Uruguayan peso	3 360 9
Venezuela	Caracas	912 050	Spanish, Amerindian languages	Bolívar fuerte	28 583 4

AFRICA

Country	Capital city	Land area (sq km)	Main languages spoken	Unit of currency	Population (2009)
Algeria	Algiers	2 381 740	Arabic, Tamazight (Kabyle, Shawia, Tamashek), French	Algerian dinar	34 895 5
Angola	Luanda	1 246 700	Portuguese, Umbundu, Kimbundu, Kikongo	Readjusted kwanza	18 497 6
Benin	Porto-Novo	112 620	Fon, Bariba, Yoruba, Adja, Houeda, Somba, French	CFA franc	8 935 0
Botswana	Gaborone	600 370	Setswana, English, Shona, San, Khoikhoi, isiNdebele	Pula	1 949 8
Burkina	Ouagadougou	274 200	Mossi, Fulani, French, Tuareg, Dyula, Songhai	CFA franc	15 756 9
Burundi	Bujumbura	27 830	Kirundi, French, Kiswahili	Burundian franc	8 303 3
Cameroon	Yaoundé	475 400	Bamileke, Fang, Fulani, French, English	CFA franc	19 521 6
Cape Verde	Praia	4 033	Portuguese Creole, Portuguese	Escudo	505 6
Central African Republic	Bangui	622 984	Sango, Banda, Gbaya, French	CFA franc	4 422 4
Chad	N'Djamena	1 284 000	French, Sara, Arabic, Maba	CFA franc	11 206 1
Comoros	Moroni	2 170	Arabic, Comoran, French	Comoros franc	676 0
Congo, Democratic Republic	Kinshasa	2 345 410	Kiswahili, Tshiluba, Kikongo, Lingala, French	Congolese franc	66 020 4

POPULATION					HEALTH AND EDUCATION					ECONOMIC DEVELOPMENT			TECHNOLOGICAL DEVELOPMENT		
Population density per sq km (2009)	Birth rate per 1000 population (2005–2010)	Death rate per 1000 population (2005–2010)	Life expectancy at birth (years; 2007)		Medical doctors per 10 000 people (1997–2007)	Infant mortality (deaths per 1000 live births; 2007)	Adult literacy rate (percentage of adults over 15; 2000–2007)		Average calorie intake per person (2005)	GNI per person (US$; 2008)	Annual electricity consumption per person (kWh; 2007)	Annual military expenditure as percentage of GDP (2005–2008)	Mobile telephones per 1000 population (2008)	Internet users per 1000 population (2008)	ICT Dev. Index (IDI), compiled by the ITU (2009)
			Male	Female			Male	Female							
188	17	6	74	75	1.80	9	98.4	99.0	2 267	13 617	1468	0.6	1 577	750	-
34	17	6	71	77	10.65	12	95.0	96.7	2 665	21 688	6223	0.7	1 060	315	-
595	11	8	72	78	11.97	11	99.0	99.0	2 920	13 829	3346	0.8	1 591	737	-
13	25	4	64	72	12.50	22	-	-	2 800	3 819	676	1.0	532	113	-
4	11	7	78	83	19.10	5	99.0	99.0	3 551	41 729	16 293	1.4	664	754	19
90	17	4	77	81	13.00	10	95.7	96.2	2 808	6 064	1 792	0.4	418	323	66
101	10	7	76	81	58.90	5	99.0	99.0	3 286	5 512	1 233	4.2	30	129	95
94	16	8	72	76	5.14	12	-	-	3 072	4 767	1 091	0.0	1 497	412	-
209	23	6	70	74	18.40	31	88.8	89.5	2 306	4 392	1 396	0.6	725	216	90
297	20	7	68	75	12.20	21	84.9	79.7	2 509	3 482	659	0.5	1 133	106	99
306	19	6	67	70	8.00	15	-	-	2 320	5 709	1 734	-	580	232	-
129	33	6	65	72	8.98	29	79.0	68.0	2 285	2 679	539	0.5	1 092	143	103
364	28	9	59	64	2.60	57	60.1	64.0	1 829	661	31	0.4	324	101	136
67	28	5	68	74	5.66	20	83.7	83.5	2 593	1 799	626	0.7	849	131	102
251	20	7	69	74	8.34	26	80.5	91.1	2 814	4 871	2 350	0.5	1 006	569	53
57	19	5	73	78	15.00	18	94.4	91.4	3 243	9 981	1 833	0.4	694	217	75
48	25	5	70	76	3.72	28	78.1	77.9	2 362	1 079	451	0.6	548	33	111
45	21	5	74	79	15.28	18	94.0	92.8	2 399	6 178	1 567	1.0	1 152	275	61
128	18	8	69	76	11.22	16	-	-	2 426	10 961	3 075	-	1 567	313	-
282	18	7	72	78	49.00	12	-	-	2 755	5 530	1 770	-	995	587	-
321	18	8	66	75	7.71	15	-	-	2 743	5 141	1 050	-	1 192	605	-
261	15	8	66	73	7.72	31	99.0	98.3	2 767	16 538	5 411	0.3	1 129	170	56
34	14	8	76	81	26.25	6	99.0	99.0	3 855	47 577	12 912	4.3	868	740	17
15	17	8	71	19	30.10	14	97.6	97.7	3 043	7 201	2 512	0.8	1 166	281	47
9	27	8	64	68	12.15	48	96.0	86.0	2 160	1 457	491	1.5	498	108	98
23	16	6	70	76	11.66	20	89.8	90.2	3 118	7 351	2 107	1.5	785	375	60
23	15	5	75	81	10.90	8	96.6	96.5	2 999	9 396	3 451	3.5	881	325	48
44	21	6	72	79	13.50	17	92.4	92.8	2 688	4 658	821	3.7	919	385	70
49	21	5	70	76	14.60	20	87.3	81.7	2 365	3 643	727	2.9	856	288	82
4	18	8	57	63	4.25	45	99.0	99.0	2 836	1 416	867	1.8	368	269	-
16	25	6	71	77	10.96	24	95.7	93.5	2 620	2 180	834	0.8	955	143	96
23	21	5	75	77	11.80	17	94.9	84.6	2 547	3 987	938	1.3	727	247	74
3	19	8	66	73	4.58	27	92.7	88.1	2 725	4 990	3 116	0.6	808	97	-
19	15	9	72	79	36.42	12	97.4	98.2	2 941	8 259	2 040	1.2	1 047	400	49
32	21	5	72	78	19.51	17	95 4	94.9	2 433	9 226	2 997	1.1	963	255	67
18	21	5	70	73	11.26	33	84.3	66.4	3 094	4 260	836	3.0	927	119	97
15	43	17	51	55	0.83	116	82.9	54.2	1 902	3 447	188	2.9	376	31	-
81	40	9	57	58	0.45	78	53.1	27.9	2 314	687	66	1.0	419	19	135
3	25	12	56	56	3.97	33	82.8	82.9	2 212	6 471	1 471	3.5	773	63	109
58	48	13	48	50	0.53	104	36.7	21.6	2 668	479	41	1.8	168	9	150
324	35	14	48	50	0.28	108	67.3	52.2	1 631	135	16	3.8	60	8	-
42	37	14	51	52	1.92	87	77.0	59.8	2 239	1 153	284	1.5	323	38	125
125	24	5	66	73	4.88	24	89.4	78.8	2 424	3 131	550	0.5	557	206	105
7	36	17	48	48	0.85	113	64.8	33.5	1 924	408	25	1.6	36	4	-
9	46	17	46	47	0.39	124	43.0	20.8	1 992	535	9	1.0	166	12	153
303	33	7	63	67	1.46	49	80.3	69.8	1 819	751	28	2.8	149	35	142
29	45	17	50	54	1.07	108	80.9	54.1	1 485	153	98	2.0	144	5	151

Country	Capital city	Land area (sq km)	Main languages spoken	Unit of currency	Population (2009)
Congo	Brazzaville	342 000	Kongo, Teke, Lingala, French	CFA franc	3 683 2C
Djibouti	Djibouti	22 000	Somali, Afar, French, Arabic	Djibouti franc	864 2C
Egypt	Cairo	1 001 450	Arabic, French, English, Berber	Egyptian pound	82 999 4C
Equatorial Guinea	Malabo	28 051	Spanish, Fang, Bubi, French	CFA franc	676 3C
Eritrea	Asmara	121 320	Tigrinya, English, Tigre, Afar, Arabic, Saho, Bilen, Kunama, Nara, Hadareb	Nakfa	5 073 3C
Ethiopia	Addis Ababa	1 127 127	Amharic, Tigrinya, Galla, Sidamo, Somali, English, Arabic	Birr	82 824 7C
Gabon	Libreville	267 667	Fang, French, Punu, Sira, Nzebi, Mpongwe	CFA franc	1 474 6C
Gambia	Banjul	11 300	Mandinka, Fulani, Wolof, Jola, Soninke, English	Dalasi	1 705 2C
Ghana	Accra	238 540	Twi, Fanti, Ewe, Ga, Adangbe, Gurma, Dagomba (Dagbani)	Cedi	23 837 3C
Guinea	Conakry	245 857	Pulaar, Malinké, Soussou, French	Guinea franc	10 068 7C
Guinea-Bissau	Bissau	36 120	Portuguese Creole, Balante, Fulani, Malinké, Portuguese	CFA franc	1 610 7C
Ivory Coast	Yamoussoukro	322 460	Akan, French, Krou, Voltaïque	CFA franc	21 075 0C
Kenya	Nairobi	582 650	Kiswahili, English, Kikuyu, Luo, Kalenjin, Kamba	Kenya shilling	39 802 0C
Lesotho	Maseru	30 355	English, Sesotho, isiZulu	Loti	2 066 9▊
Liberia	Monrovia	111 370	Kpelle, Vai, Bassa, Kru, Grebo, Kissi, Gola, Loma, English	Liberian dollar	3 955 0C
Libya	Tripoli	1 759 540	Arabic, Tuareg	Libyan dinar	6 419 9C
Madagascar	Antananarivo	587 040	Malagasy, French	Ariary	19 625 0C
Malawi	Lilongwe	118 480	Chewa, Lomwe, Yao, Ngoni, English	Malawi kwacha	15 263 4C
Mali	Bamako	1 240 000	Bambara, Fulani, Senufo, Soninke, French	CFA franc	13 010 2C
Mauritania	Nouakchott	1 030 700	Hassaniyah Arabic, Wolof, French	Ouguiya	3 290 63
Mauritius	Port Louis	1 860	French Creole, Hindi, Urdu, Tamil, Chinese, English, French	Mauritian rupee	1 288 2C
Morocco	Rabat	446 300	Arabic, Tamazight (Berber), French, Spanish	Moroccan dirham	31 992 6C
Mozambique	Maputo	801 590	Makua, Xitsonga, Sena, Lomwe, Portuguese	New metical	22 894 3C
Namibia	Windhoek	825 418	Ovambo, Kavango, English, Bergdama, German, Afrikaans	Namibian $, S African rand	2 171 1C
Niger	Niamey	1 267 000	Hausa, Djerma, Fulani, Tuareg, Teda, French	CFA franc	15 290 1C
Nigeria	Abuja	923 768	Hausa, English, Yoruba, Ibo	Naira	154 728 89
Rwanda	Kigali	26 338	Kinyarwanda, French, Kiswahili, English	Rwanda franc	9 997 6C
São Tomé & Príncipe	São Tomé	1 001	Portuguese Creole, Portuguese	Dobra	162 8C
Senegal	Dakar	196 190	Wolof, Pulaar, Serer, Diola, Mandinka, Malinké, Soninké, French	CFA franc	12 534 2C
Seychelles	Victoria	455	French Creole, English, French	Seychelles rupee	84 6C
Sierra Leone	Freetown	71 740	Mende, Temne, Krio, English	Leone	5 696 5C
Somalia	Mogadishu	637 657	Somali, Arabic, English, Italian	Somali shilin	9 133 1C
South Africa	Tshwane/Cape Town/Bloemfontein	1 219 912	English, isiZulu, isiXhosa, Afrikaans, Sepedi, Setswana, Sesotho, Xitsonga, siSwati, Tshivenda	Rand	50 109 8C
Sudan	Khartoum	2 505 810	Arabic, Dinka, Nuer, Nubian, Beja, Zande, Bari, Fur, Shilluk, Lotuko	New Sudanese pound/dinar	42 272 4C
Swaziland	Mbabane	17 363	English, siSwati, isiZulu, Xitsonga	Lilangeni	11 849 0C
Tanzania	Dodoma	945 087	Kiswahili, Sukuma, Chagga, Nyamwezi, Hehe, Makonde, Yao, Sandawe, English	Tanzanian shilling	43 739 1C
Togo	Lomé	56 785	Ewe, Kabye, Gurma, French	CFA franc	6 618 6C
Tunisia	Tunis	163 610	Arabic, French	Tunisian dinar	10 271 5C
Uganda	Kampala	236 040	Luganda, Nkole, Chiga, Lango, Acholi, Teso, Lugbara, English	New Uganda shilling	32 709 9C
Western Sahara	Laâyoune	266 000	Arabic, Tamazight (Berber), Spanish	Moroccan dirham	513 2C
Zambia	Lusaka	752 614	Bemba, Tonga, Nyanja, Lozi, Lala-Bisa, Nsenga, English	Zambian kwacha	12 935 4C
Zimbabwe	Harare	390 580	Shona, isiNdebele, English	US $, S African rand*	12 522 8C

EUROPE

Country	Capital city	Land area (sq km)	Main languages spoken	Unit of currency	Population (2009)
Albania	Tirana	28 748	Albanian, Greek	Lek	3 155 3C
Andorra	Andorra la Vella	468	Spanish, Catalan, French, Portuguese	Euro	82 2C
Austria	Vienna	83 858	German, Croatian, Slovenian, Hungarian (Magyar)	Euro	8 363 9C
Belarus	Minsk	207 600	Belarussian, Russian	Belarussian rouble	9 633 5C
Belgium	Brussels	30 510	Dutch, French, German	Euro	10 646 8C
Bosnia & Herzegovina	Sarajevo	51 129	Bosnian, Serbian, Croatian	Marka	3 766 6C
Bulgaria	Sofia	110 910	Bulgarian, Turkish, Romani	Lev	7 544 6C
Croatia	Zagreb	56 542	Croatian	Kuna	4 416 2C

* Zimbabwe dollar suspended in 2009; US dollar and South African rand now legal tenc

POPULATION					HEALTH AND EDUCATION					ECONOMIC DEVELOPMENT			TECHNOLOGICAL DEVELOPMENT		
Population density per sq km (2009)	Birth rate per 1000 population (2005–2010)	Death rate per 1000 population (2005–2010)	Life expectancy at birth (years; 2007)		Medical doctors per 10 000 people (1997–2007)	Infant mortality (deaths per 1000 live births; 2007)	Adult literacy rate (percentage of adults over 15; 2000–2007)		Average calorie intake per person (2005)	GNI per person (US$; 2008)	Annual electricity consumption per person (kWh; 2007)	Annual military expenditure as percentage of GDP (2005–2008)	Mobile telephones per 1000 population (2008)	Internet users per 1000 population (2008)	ICT Dev. Index (IDI), compiled by the ITU (2009)
			Male	Female			Male	Female							
11	35	13	54	56	1.99	79	89.6	78.4	2 351	1 973	112	1.3	500	43	132
37	29	11	53	58	1.77	84	79.9	61.4	2 210	1 130	524	4.1	133	23	-
83	25	6	66	70	24.30	30	74.6	57.8	3 331	1 801	1 354	2.3	506	167	94
24	38	15	52	54	3.02	91	93.4	80.5	-	14 980	47	0.1	525	18	-
43	37	9	61	65	0.50	46	76.2	53.0	1 570	299	49	6.3	22	41	149
75	39	12	55	59	0.27	75	50.0	22.8	1 826	282	39	1.5	24	5	147
6	28	10	57	61	2.82	60	90.2	82.2	2 800	7 243	1 033	1.1	898	62	107
171	37	11	57	61	1.11	81	49.9	35.4	2 131	393	93	0.7	702	69	122
104	33	11	56	58	1.51	73	71.7	58.3	2 759	674	248	0.7	496	43	114
41	40	11	52	56	1.15	93	42.6	18.1	2 559	442	81	1.7	391	9	-
57	41	17	46	51	1.25	118	75.1	54.4	2 052	245	35	4.0	318	24	152
66	35	11	52	57	1.23	89	60.8	38.6	2 542	984	172	1.5	507	32	128
70	39	12	53	56	1.41	80	77.7	70.2	2 079	767	152	1.7	421	87	116
68	29	17	43	47	0.49	68	73.7	90.3	2 440	1 080	287	2.6	284	36	123
41	39	11	54	58	0.29	93	60.2	50.9	2 067	167	93	0.5	193	5	-
4	23	4	70	75	12.40	17	94.5	78.4	3 018	11 590	3 635	1.1	767	51	81
34	36	9	58	61	2.91	70	76.5	65.3	2 049	406	50	1.1	253	17	133
162	41	12	49	51	0.22	71	79.2	64.6	2 143	288	116	1.2	120	21	141
11	43	16	47	50	0.79	117	34.9	18.2	2 579	579	33	2.0	271	16	146
3	34	11	56	61	1.04	75	63.3	48.3	2 808	906	121	3.8	651	19	134
693	14	7	70	76	10.86	15	90.2	84.7	2 869	6 401	1 660	0.2	807	220	62
72	21	6	70	75	5.14	32	68.7	43.2	3 167	2 579	641	3.4	722	330	101
29	40	16	47	48	0.27	115	57.2	33.0	2 085	373	495	0.9	197	16	148
3	28	8	58	61	2.99	47	88.6	87.4	2 315	4 200	1 512	3.1	494	53	112
12	54	15	50	53	0.24	83	42.9	15.1	2 151	329	40	1.3	129	5	154
170	40	17	48	50	2.82	97	80.1	64.1	2 655	1 161	140	0.6	417	159	130
401	41	15	49	51	0.51	109	71.4	59.8	1 956	407	25	1.5	136	31	143
170	32	8	59	63	4.46	64	93.4	82.7	2 615	1 020	90	0.8	306	155	-
65	39	11	57	61	0.58	59	52.3	33.0	2 198	968	113	1.6	441	84	131
313	16	7	68	75	14.97	14	91.4	92.3	2 396	10 292	2 845	1.0	1 115	404	-
80	40	16	39	43	0.31	155	50.0	26.8	1 932	321	13	2.3	181	3	-
15	44	16	50	55	0.30	88	49.7	25.8	1 628	288	30	0.9	70	11	-
41	22	15	52	55	7.71	46	88.9	87.2	2 916	5 819	4 509	1.4	906	84	87
17	32	10	57	58	3.00	70	71.1	51.8	2 300	1 125	91	4.2	290	102	120
69	30	16	47	49	1.55	66	84.0	83.7	2 323	2 522	1 266	2.1	455	69	113
49	42	12	51	52	0.22	73	79.0	65.9	2 019	432	80	0.9	306	12	145
122	33	8	56	61	0.45	65	68.7	38.5	2 033	404	98	2.0	240	54	137
66	16	6	72	76	13.46	18	86.4	69.0	3 264	3 292	1 156	1.3	846	275	83
164	46	13	46	51	0.83	92	91.0	88.5	2 511	417	87	2.2	170	79	140
2	40	11	62	66	-	70	-	-	-	-	-	-	-	-	-
17	43	18	45	47	1.16	103	80.8	60.7	1 895	950	730	1.8	280	56	129
32	30	16	45	44	1.62	59	94.1	88.3	2 063	237	825	3.8	133	114	126
115	15	6	71	74	11.70	13	99.0	98.8	2 855	3 836	1 126	2.0	999	239	85
177	10	6	78	85	34.27	3	99.0	99.0	-	43 975	-	0.0	761	700	-
101	9	9	77	83	36.67	4	99.0	99.0	3 666	46 264	7 547	0.9	1 297	712	20
46	10	15	65	76	47.80	5	99.0	99.0	2 983	5 384	3 181	1.4	840	321	54
324	11	10	77	82	42.40	4	99.0	99.0	3 672	44 326	8 084	1.1	1 116	689	24
74	9	10	73	78	14.20	13	99.0	94.4	2 990	4 506	2 176	1.4	843	347	58
68	10	15	69	76	36.50	10	98.6	97.9	2 815	5 487	4 090	2.2	1 383	349	45
78	10	12	73	79	24.46	5	99.0	98.0	2 983	13 574	3 352	1.8	1 330	506	43

Country	Capital city	Land area (sq km)	Main languages spoken	Unit of currency	Population (2009)
			GENERAL FACTS		
Cyprus	Nicosia	9 250	Greek, Turkish	Euro, New Turkish Lira	871 00●
Czech Republic	Prague	78 866	Czech, Slovak, Hungarian (Magyar)	Czech koruna	10 368 90●
Denmark	Copenhagen	43 094	Danish	Danish krone	5 470 30●
Estonia	Tallinn	45 226	Estonian, Russian	Kroon	1 340 3C●
Finland	Helsinki	337 030	Finnish, Swedish, Sámi	Euro	5 325 6C●
France	Paris	547 030	French, Provençal, German, Breton, Catalan, Basque	Euro	62 342 7C●
Germany	Berlin	357 021	German, Turkish	Euro	82 166 7C●
Greece	Athens	131 940	Greek, Turkish, Macedonian, Albanian	Euro	11 161 33●
Hungary	Budapest	93 030	Hungarian (Magyar)	Forint	9 992 7C●
Iceland	Reykjavík	103 000	Icelandic	Icelandic króna	322 70●
Ireland	Dublin	70 280	English, Irish Gaelic	Euro	4 515 5C●
Italy	Rome	301 230	Italian, German, French, Rhaeto-Romanic, Sardinian	Euro	59 870 1C●
Kosovo	Priština	10 908	Albanian, Serbian, Bosniak, Gorani, Roma, Turkish	Euro	2 100 00●
Latvia	Riga	64 589	Latvian, Russian	Lats	2 249 4C●
Liechtenstein	Vaduz	160	German, Alemannish dialect, Italian	Swiss franc	35 00●
Lithuania	Vilnius	65 200	Lithuanian, Russian	Litas	3 286 5C●
Luxembourg	Luxembourg-Ville	2 586	Luxembourgish, German, French	Euro	486 2C●
Macedonia	Skopje	25 333	Macedonian, Albanian, Turkish, Romani, Serbian	Macedonian denar	2 042 50●
Malta	Valletta	316	Maltese, English	Euro	408 7C●
Moldova	Chisinau	33 843	Moldovan, Ukrainian, Russian	Moldovan leu	3 603 50●
Monaco	Monaco-Ville	1.95	French, Italian, Monégasque, English	Euro	32 00●
Montenegro	Podgorica	13 812	Montenegrin, Serbian, Albanian, Bosniak, Croatian	Euro	624 2C●
Netherlands	Amsterdam/The Hague	41 526	Dutch, Frisian	Euro	16 592 23●
Norway	Oslo	324 220	Norwegian (*Bokmål* "book language" and *Nynorsk* "new Norsk"), Sámi	Norwegian krone	4 812 2C●
Poland	Warsaw	312 685	Polish	Zloty	38 073 7C●
Portugal	Lisbon	92 391	Portuguese	Euro	10 707 1C●
Romania	Bucharest	237 500	Romanian, Hungarian (Magyar), Romani, German	New Romanian leu	21 274 7C●
Russian Federation	Moscow	17 075 200	Russian, Tatar, Ukrainian, Chavash, various other national languages	Russian rouble	140 873 6C●
San Marino	San Marino	61	Italian	Euro	31 4C●
Serbia	Belgrade	77 453	Serbian, Hungarian (Magyar)	Serbian Dinar	7 750 00●
Slovakia	Bratislava	48 845	Slovak, Hungarian (Magyar), Czech	Euro	5 405 7C●
Slovenia	Ljubljana	20 253	Slovenian	Euro	2 020 10●
Spain	Madrid	504 782	Spanish, Catalan, Galician, Basque	Euro	44 903 7C●
Sweden	Stockholm	449 964	Swedish, Finnish, Sámi	Swedish krona	9 249 20●
Switzerland	Bern	41 290	German, Swiss-German, French, Italian, Romansch	Swiss franc	7 567 70●
Ukraine	Kiev	603 700	Ukrainian, Russian, Tatar	Hryvna	45 708 1C●
United Kingdom	London	244 820	English, Welsh, Scottish Gaelic, Irish Gaelic	Pound sterling	61 565 40●
Vatican City	Vatican City	0.44	Italian, Latin	Euro	8C●

ASIA

Country	Capital city	Land area (sq km)	Main languages spoken	Unit of currency	Population (2009)
Afghanistan	Kabul	647 500	Pashtu, Tajik, Dari, Farsi, Uzbek, Turkmen	Afghani	28 149 90●
Armenia	Yerevan	29 800	Armenian, Azeri, Russian	Dram	3 083 00●
Azerbaijan	Baku	86 600	Azeri, Russian	New manat	8 832 20●
Bahrain	Manama	620	Arabic	Bahraini dinar	791 50●
Bangladesh	Dhaka	144 000	Bengali, Urdu, Chakma, Marma (Magh), Garo, Khasi, Santhali, Tripuri, Mro	Taka	162 220 80●
Bhutan	Thimphu	47 000	Dzongkha, Nepali, Assamese	Ngultrum	697 30●
Brunei	Bandar Seri Begawan	5 770	Malay, English, Chinese	Brunei dollar	399 70●
Burma (Myanmar)	Nay Pyi Taw	678 500	Burmese, Shan, Karen, Rakhine, Chin, Yangbye, Kachin, Mon	Kyat	50 019 80●
Cambodia	Phnom Penh	181 040	Khmer, French, Chinese, Vietnamese, Cham	Riel	14 805 40●
China	Beijing	9 596 960	Mandarin, Wu, Cantonese, Hsiang, Min, Hakka, Kan	Renminbi (known as yuan)	1 345 751 00●
East Timor	Dili	14 874	Tetum (Portuguese/Austronesian), Bahasa Indonesia, Portuguese	US dollar	1 133 60●
Georgia	Tbilisi	69 700	Georgian, Russian, Azeri, Armenian, Mingrelian, Ossetian, Abkhazian	Lari	4 260 30●

POPULATION					HEALTH AND EDUCATION					ECONOMIC DEVELOPMENT			TECHNOLOGICAL DEVELOPMENT		
Population density per sq km (2009)	Birth rate per 1000 population (2005–2010)	Death rate per 1000 population (2005–2010)	Life expectancy at birth (years; 2007)		Medical doctors per 10 000 people (1997–2007)	Infant mortality (deaths per 1000 live births; 2007)	Adult literacy rate (percentage of adults over 15; 2000–2007)		Average calorie intake per person (2005)	GNI per person (US$; 2008)	Annual electricity consumption per person (kWh; 2007)	Annual military expenditure as percentage of GDP (2005–2008)	Mobile telephones per 1000 population (2008)	Internet users per 1000 population (2008)	ICT Dev. Index (IDI), compiled by the ITU (2009)
			Male	Female			Male	Female							
94	12	7	78	82	23.10	3	99.0	96.6	3 189	24 940	5 425	2.2	1 179	388	37
131	11	11	74	80	35.88	3	99.0	99.0	3 339	16 605	6 044	1.5	1 335	584	40
129	12	10	76	81	35.70	4	99.0	99.0	3 374	59 129	6 507	1.3	1 257	839	3
30	12	13	67	79	33.95	5	99.0	99.0	3 060	14 270	5 912	2.3	1 882	662	26
17	11	9	76	83	32.70	3	99.0	99.0	3 237	48 125	16 368	1.3	1 288	826	9
113	12	9	77	84	34.10	3	99.0	99.0	3 599	42 250	7 344	2.3	935	682	23
235	8	10	77	82	34.40	4	99.0	99.0	3 510	42 436	6 618	1.3	1 283	753	13
85	10	10	77	82	50.10	4	98.2	96.0	3 698	28 650	5 201	3.5	1 239	435	34
108	10	13	69	78	30.30	6	99.0	98.8	3 435	12 810	3 777	1.2	1 221	587	35
3	15	6	80	83	37.70	2	99.0	99.0	3 283	40 074	37 157	0.0	1 086	906	5
66	16	6	77	82	29.50	3	99.0	99.0	3 675	49 592	5 843	0.6	1 207	625	18
204	9	10	79	84	37.00	3	99.0	98.6	3 685	35 237	5 412	1.8	1 516	419	22
193	16	3	67	71	10.83	11	96.6	87.5	-	1 800	3 294	-	-	-	-
35	10	14	66	76	31.30	9	99.0	99.0	3 146	11 864	2 966	1.9	989	606	36
219	10	7	77	84	13.10	2	99.0	99.0	-	99 160	-	0.0	954	660	-
50	10	13	65	77	39.70	6	99.0	99.0	3 415	11 871	2 827	1.6	1 512	550	33
188	11	8	77	83	27.30	3	99.0	99.0	3 701	84 892	13 587	0.7	1 471	805	7
79	11	9	72	76	25.90	15	98.6	95.4	2 873	4 138	3 679	2.0	1 226	415	65
1 277	9	8	78	82	38.80	5	91.2	93.5	3 553	19 703	4 559	1.5	946	488	30
107	12	13	65	73	26.55	16	99.0	98.9	2 948	1 469	1 040	0.4	667	234	68
16 410	9	13	78	85	66.30	4	99.0	99.0	-	40 421	-	0.0	673	673	-
45	12	10	72	76	18.00	9	-	-	-	6 440	3 294	1.5	1 181	472	-
489	11	8	78	82	37.10	4	99.0	99.0	3 240	50 150	6 720	1.4	1 248	866	4
16	12	9	78	83	38.09	3	99.0	99.0	3 464	87 068	24 352	1.3	1 102	826	6
125	10	10	71	80	19.75	6	99.0	99.0	3 381	11 884	3 359	2.0	1 153	490	39
116	10	10	76	82	34.40	3	96.6	93.3	3 612	20 556	4 602	2.0	1 396	419	31
92	10	12	70	77	19.20	12	98.3	96.9	3 493	7 928	2 300	1.5	1 145	290	46
8	11	15	60	73	43.10	10	99.0	99.0	3 157	9 623	5 922	3.6	1 411	320	50
515	10	9	81	84	25.00	2	99.0	99.0	-	53 910	-	-	770	545	-
100	12	12	71	76	24.17	7	98.9	94.1	2 691	5 705	3 294	2.3	978	335	-
110	10	10	71	78	31.24	6	99.0	99.0	2 860	14 541	4 966	1.6	1 022	661	38
100	10	10	75	81	23.60	3	99.0	99.0	3 351	24 013	6 751	1.6	1 020	559	28
90	11	9	78	84	32.92	4	98.6	97.3	3 326	31 963	6 019	1.2	1 117	567	27
22	12	10	79	83	32.80	2	99.0	99.0	3 137	50 943	14 784	1.3	1 183	878	1
190	10	8	79	84	39.47	4	99.0	99.0	3 387	65 334	7 893	0.8	1 180	770	8
76	10	16	62	73	31.25	14	99.0	99.0	3 182	3 213	3 365	2.7	1 211	106	51
255	12	10	77	82	21.45	5	99.0	99.0	3 401	45 394	5 763	2.5	1 263	762	10
1 818	-	-	79	84	-	-	99.0	99.0	-	-	-	0.0	-	-	-
43	47	20	41	42	2.00	165	43.1	12.6	1 539	429	31	2.1	290	18	-
103	15	9	66	73	37.10	22	99.0	99.0	2 240	3 354	1 592	3.2	1 000	62	72
102	19	7	66	70	36.20	34	99.0	99.0	2 603	3 829	1 845	2.7	750	280	86
1 121	18	3	75	76	27.24	9	90.4	86.4	-	27 248	14 248	3.4	1 858	520	42
1 211	22	7	63	64	3.02	47	58.7	48.0	2 261	516	145	1.1	279	4	138
15	22	7	61	65	0.23	56	65.0	38.7	-	1 896	230	1.0	366	66	115
76	20	3	74	77	11.73	8	96.5	93.1	3 255	37 053	7 811	2.4	959	553	41
76	21	10	53	59	3.55	79	93.9	86.4	2 439	386	85	2.1	7	2	119
84	25	8	58	64	1.51	70	85.8	67.7	2 199	603	87	1.1	291	5	121
144	14	7	72	75	14.30	19	96.5	90.0	2 970	2 940	2 129	2.0	480	223	73
78	40	9	58	64	0.96	77	-	-	2 169	2 464	-	-	92	2	-
61	12	12	68	76	46.80	27	99.0	99.0	2 521	2 472	1 569	8.1	640	238	80

GENERAL FACTS

Country	Capital city	Land area (sq km)	Main languages spoken	Unit of currency	Population (2009)
India	New Delhi	3 287 590	Hindi, English, Urdu, Bengali, Marathi, Telugu, Tamil, Bihari, Gujarati, Kanarese	Indian rupee	1 198 003 300
Indonesia	Jakarta	1 919 440	Javanese, Sundanese, Madurese, Bahasa Indonesia, Dutch	Rupiah	229 964 700
Iran	Tehran	1 648 000	Farsi, Azeri, Luri, Gilaki, Mazanderani, Kurdish, Turkmen, Arabic, Baluchi	Iranian rial	74 195 700
Iraq	Baghdad	437 072	Arabic, Kurdish, Turkic languages, Armenian, Assyrian	New Iraqi dinar	30 747 300
Israel	Jerusalem (disputed)	20 770	Hebrew, Arabic, Yiddish, German, Russian, Polish, Romanian, Persian	Shekel	7 169 600
Japan	Tokyo	377 835	Japanese, Korean, Chinese	Yen	127 156 200
Jordan	Amman	92 300	Arabic	Jordanian dinar	6 316 400
Kazakhstan	Astana	2 717 300	Kazakh, Russian, Ukrainian, German, Uzbek, Tatar, Uighur	Tenge	15 637 000
Kuwait	Kuwait City	17 820	Arabic, English	Kuwaiti dinar	2 985 000
Kyrgyzstan	Bishkek	198 500	Kyrgyz, Russian, Uzbek, Tatar, Ukrainian	Som	5 482 200
Laos	Vientiane	236 800	Lao, Mon-Khmer, Yao, Vietnamese, Chinese, French	New kip	6 320 400
Lebanon	Beirut	10 400	Arabic, French, Armenian, Assyrian	Lebanese pound	4 223 600
Malaysia	Kuala Lumpur/Putrajaya	329 750	Bahasa Malaysia, Malay, Chinese, Tamil, English	Ringgit	27 467 800
Maldives	Male'	300	Dhivehi (Maldivian), Sinhala, Tamil, Arabic	Rufiyaa	309 400
Mongolia	Ulan Bator	1 565 000	Khalkha Mongolian, Kazakh, Chinese, Russian	Tugrik (tögrög)	2 671 000
Nepal	Kathmandu	140 800	Nepali, Maithili, Bhojpuri	Nepalese rupee	29 330 500
North Korea	Pyongyang	120 540	Korean	North Korean won	23 906 100
Oman	Muscat	212 460	Arabic, Baluchi, Farsi, Hindi, Punjabi	Omani rial	2 845 400
Pakistan	Islamabad	803 940	Punjabi, Sindhi, Pashtu, Urdu, Baluchi, Brahui	Pakistani rupee	180 808 100
Philippines	Manila	300 000	Filipino, English, Tagalog, Cebuano, Ilocano, Hiligaynon, many other local languages	Philippine peso	91 983 100
Qatar	Doha	11 437	Arabic	Qatar riyal	1 409 400
Saudi Arabia	Riyadh	1 960 582	Arabic	Saudi riyal	25 720 600
Singapore	Singapore	648	Mandarin, Malay, Tamil, English	Singapore dollar	4 736 870
South Korea	Seoul	98 480	Korean	South Korean won	48 332 800
Sri Lanka	Colombo	65 610	Sinhala, Tamil, Sinhala-Tamil, English	Sri Lanka rupee	20 237 700
Syria	Damascus	184 180	Arabic, French, Kurdish, Armenian, Circassian, Turkic languages, Assyrian, Aramaic	Syrian pound	21 906 150
Taiwan	Taipei	35 980	Amoy Chinese, Mandarin Chinese, Hakka Chinese	Taiwan dollar	22 974 340
Tajikistan	Dushanbe	143 100	Tajik, Uzbek, Russian	Somoni	6 952 200
Thailand	Bangkok	514 000	Thai, Chinese, Malay, Khmer, Mon, Karen, Miao	Baht	67 764 000
Turkey	Ankara	780 580	Turkish, Kurdish, Arabic, Circassian, Armenian, Greek, Georgian, Ladino	New Turkish lira	74 815 700
Turkmenistan	Ashgabat	488 100	Turkmen, Uzbek, Russian, Kazakh, Tatar	New manat	5 109 900
United Arab Emirates	Abu Dhabi	82 880	Arabic, Farsi, Indian and Pakistani languages, English	UAE dirham	4 598 600
Uzbekistan	Tashkent	447 400	Uzbek, Russian, Tajik, Kazakh	Som	27 488 200
Vietnam	Hanoi	329 560	Vietnamese, Chinese, Thai, Khmer, Muong, Nung, Miao, Yao, Jarai	Dông	88 068 900
Yemen	Sana	527 970	Arabic	Yemeni rial	23 580 200

AUSTRALASIA & OCEANIA

Country	Capital city	Land area (sq km)	Main languages spoken	Unit of currency	Population (2009)
Australia	Canberra	7 686 850	English, Italian, Cantonese, Greek, Arabic, Vietnamese, Aboriginal languages	Australian dollar	21 292 900
Fiji	Suva	18 270	Fijian, English, Hindi, Urdu, Tamil, Telugu	Fiji dollar	849 200
Kiribati	Bairiki (Tarawa Atoll)	717	English, Kiribati	Australian dollar	99 000
Marshall Islands	Majuro	181	Marshallese, English, Japanese, German	US dollar	54 100
Micronesia	Palikir (Pohnpei Island)	702	Trukese, Pohnpeian, Kosraean, Yapese, English	US dollar	110 700
Nauru	None	21	Nauruan, Kiribati, Chinese, Tuvaluan, English	Australian dollar	9 800
New Zealand	Wellington	268 680	English, Maori	New Zealand dollar	4 266 500
Palau	Melekeok	458	Palauan, English, Japanese, Angaur, Tobi, Sonsorolese	US dollar	20 400
Papua New Guinea	Port Moresby	462 840	Pidgin English, Papuan, English, Motu, around 800 native languages	Kina	6 732 200
Samoa	Apia	2 860	Samoan, English	Tala	178 800
Solomon Islands	Honiara	28 450	English, Pidgin English, Melanesian Pidgin, around 120 others	Solomon Islands dollar	523 200
Tonga	Nuku'alofa	748	English, Tongan	Pa'anga (Tongan dollar)	104 000
Tuvalu	Fongafale (Funafuti Atoll)	26	Tuvaluan, Kiribati, English	Australian $, Tuvaluan $	11 100
Vanuatu	Port Vila	12 200	Bislama (Melanesian pidgin), English, French, other indigenous languages	Vatu	239 800

POPULATION					HEALTH AND EDUCATION					ECONOMIC DEVELOPMENT			TECHNOLOGICAL DEVELOPMENT		
Population density per sq km (2009)	Birth rate per 1000 population (2005–2010)	Death rate per 1000 population (2005–2010)	Life expectancy at birth (years; 2007)		Medical doctors per 10 000 people (1997–2007)	Infant mortality (deaths per 1000 live births; 2007)	Adult literacy rate (percentage of adults over 15; 2000–2007)		Average calorie intake per person (2005)	GNI per person (US$; 2008)	Annual electricity consumption per person (kWh; 2007)	Annual military expenditure as percentage of GDP (2005–2008)	Mobile telephones per 1000 population (2008)	Internet users per 1000 population (2008)	ICT Dev. Index (IDI), compiled by the ITU (2009)
			Male	Female			Male	Female							
403	23	9	63	65	5.97	54	76.9	54.5	2 348	1 066	500	2.4	294	44	118
128	19	6	67	70	1.34	25	95.2	88.8	2 434	2 007	523	1.0	618	79	108
45	19	6	70	74	8.90	29	87.3	77.2	3 102	4 732	2 160	2.5	586	314	78
70	32	6	58	69	6.60	36	84.1	64.2	2 197	2 815	1 002	2.5	582	10	-
353	20	6	79	82	36.97	4	98.5	95.9	3 622	24 699	6 592	8.1	1 274	496	29
338	8	9	79	86	21.16	3	99.0	99.0	2 739	38 207	7 849	0.9	867	754	12
71	26	4	70	74	24.00	18	95.2	87.0	2 909	3 306	1 733	6.2	866	260	76
6	20	11	59	70	38.90	28	99.0	99.0	3 218	6 140	4 371	1.0	961	110	69
168	18	2	78	79	17.90	9	95.2	93.1	3 099	45 920	14 360	3.9	996	343	57
28	22	7	63	69	23.98	33	99.0	99.0	3 115	741	1 667	2.8	627	157	93
27	28	7	60	62	3.45	56	82.5	63.2	2 340	753	495	0.3	326	85	117
413	16	7	68	73	23.44	26	93.4	86.0	3 180	6 353	2 276	4.5	340	225	64
84	21	5	70	75	7.40	10	94.2	89.6	2 863	6 967	3 788	2.0	1 026	558	52
1 031	19	5	72	75	9.21	26	97.0	97.1	2 657	3 626	518	5.5	1 428	235	71
2	19	7	60	69	25.89	35	96.8	97.7	2 213	1 677	1 045	1.4	668	125	88
214	26	7	62	63	2.09	43	70.3	43.6	2 417	404	80	1.5	146	17	139
199	14	10	64	68	32.86	42	-	-	2 173	555	771	25.0	-	-	-
13	22	3	71	77	16.50	11	89.4	77.5	-	18 988	4 206	11.3	1 156	200	77
235	30	7	63	64	8.00	73	67.7	39.6	2 318	981	439	3.2	497	105	127
308	25	5	67	74	11.50	23	93.1	93.7	2 501	1 886	570	0.8	754	62	91
128	12	2	76	76	26.45	8	93.8	90.4	-	93 204	15 130	4.4	1 314	340	44
12	24	4	69	74	13.76	20	89.1	79.4	3 061	19 345	6 399	8.2	1 429	308	55
7 765	8	5	78	83	14.80	2	97.3	91.6	-	34 762	8 318	4.1	1 382	730	15
490	10	6	76	82	15.73	4	99.0	99.0	3 053	21 525	8 028	2.6	947	765	2
313	18	6	68	75	5.46	17	92.7	89.1	2 350	1 789	377	3.0	552	58	100
119	28	3	70	75	5.30	15	89.7	76.5	3 042	2 094	1 368	3.4	332	168	89
712	9	7	75	82	16.00	5	99.0	95.9		17 273	9 423	3.0	1 103	657	25
49	28	6	66	68	20.10	57	99.0	99.0	2 259	596	2 156	3.9	537	88	106
133	15	9	66	74	3.65	6	95.9	92.6	2 510	2 844	1 896	1.6	920	239	63
97	18	6	71	76	15.64	21	96.2	81.3	3 354	9 345	2 043	2.1	891	344	59
10	22	8	60	67	24.92	45	99.0	99.0	2 767	2 840	2 090	3.4	225	15	104
55	14	2	77	80	18.37	7	89.5	91.5	2 922	54 607	13 745	1.9	2 087	652	32
61	20	7	65	71	26.53	36	98.0	95.8	2 497	906	1 531	2.0	468	91	110
271	17	5	70	75	5.61	13	93.9	86.9	2 698	892	686	2.0	804	239	92
42	37	7	62	66	3.26	55	77.0	40.5	2 001	950	185	4.5	161	16	124
3	13	7	79	84	24.81	5	99.0	99.0	3 077	40 351	10 622	1.9	1 050	720	14
46	21	7	67	72	4.53	16	95.9	92.9	3 001	3 934	939	1.3	711	122	84
139	30	8	61	60	1.44	111	11.1	00.11	2 8.1	1 00%	121	0.0	10	21	-
299	31	4	57	59	5.62	49	-	-	-	3 273	-	0.0	17	36	-
158	26	6	68	70	5.55	33	-	-	-	2 338	-	0.0	308	145	-
467	24	6	59	64	7.81	25	-	-	-	3 433	2 144	0.0	-	-	-
16	14	7	78	83	20.50	5	99.0	99.0	3 282	27 936	9 570	1.1	1 092	720	16
40	11	8	69	76	15.99	9	-	-	-	8 646	-	0.0	599	270	-
15	32	8	61	64	0.57	50	62.1	53.4	2 193	1 009	440	0.4	91	18	144
63	24	5	66	70	2.81	22	98.9	98.4	2 769	2 778	471	0.0	693	50	-
19	31	6	66	68	1.26	53	-	-	2 433	1 180	116	0.0	59	20	-
144	28	6	71	69	2.83	19	99.0	99.0	-	2 561	342	1.5	487	81	-
427	23	7	64	65	8.85	30	-	-	-	3 213	-	0.0	202	430	-
20	30	5	67	70	1.38	28	80.0	76.1	2 752	2 332	184	0.0	154	73	-

GLOSSARY

This glossary defines certain geographical and technical terms used in this Atlas.

Acid rain Rain, sleet, snow or mist that has absorbed waste gases from fossil-fuelled power stations and vehicle exhausts, becoming acidic and poisonous.

Alluvium Material deposited by a river, such as silt, sand and mud.

Archipelago A group, or chain, of islands.

Atoll A circular or horseshoe-shaped coral reef enclosing a shallow area of water (lagoon).

Aquifer A body of rock that can absorb water. It may be a source of water for wells or springs.

Bar, coastal An offshore strip of sand or shingle, either above or below the water.

Biodiversity The quantity of different animal or plant species in a given area.

Birth rate The number of live births per 1000 individuals annually within a population.

Cash crop Agricultural produce grown for sale, often for foreign export, rather than to be consumed within the country or area in which it was grown.

Climate The long-term trends in weather conditions for an area.

Coniferous forest A type of forest containing trees or shrubs, like pines and firs, which have needles instead of leaves. They are found in temperate zones.

Continental plates The huge interlocking plates which make up the Earth's surface. A plate boundary is an area where two plates meet, and is the point at which earthquakes occur most frequently.

Conurbation A large urban area created by the merging of several towns.

Coral reef An underwater barrier created by colonies of coral polyps. The polyps secrete a protective skeleton of calcium carbonate, and reefs develop as live polyps build on the skeletons of dead generations.

Core The layers of liquid rock and solid iron at the centre of the Earth.

Crust The hard, thin outer shell of the Earth. The crust floats on the mantle, which is softer, but more dense.

Deciduous forest A type of broadleaf forest found in temperate regions.

Deforestation Cutting down trees or forest for timber or farmland. It can lead to soil erosion, flooding and landslides.

Delta A low-lying, fan-shaped area at a river mouth, formed by the deposition of successive layers of sediment. Slowing as it enters the sea, a river deposits sediment and may, as a result, split into many smaller channels called distributaries.

Deposition The laying down of material broken down by erosion or weathering and transported by the wind, water or gravity.

Desertification The spread of desert conditions into a region which was not previously a desert.

Drainage basin The land drained by a river and its tributaries.

Drought A long period of continuously low rainfall.

Earthquake A trembling or shaking of the ground caused by the sudden movement of rocks in the Earth's crust – and sometimes deeper than the crust. Earthquakes occur most frequently along continental plate boundaries.

Economy The organization of a country's finances, exports, imports, industry, agriculture and services.

Ecosytem A community of species dependent on each other and on the habitat in which they live.

Equator The 0° line of latitude. Equatorial climates are hot and there is plenty of rain.

Erosion The wearing down of the land surface by running water, waves, moving ice, wind and weather.

Estuary The mouth of a river, where the salt water from the sea meets the fresh water of the river.

Fault A crack or fracture in the Earth along which there has been movement of the rock masses relative to one another.

Fjord A coastal valley that has been was sculpted by glacial action.

Flood plain The broad, flat part of a river valley, next to the river itself, formed by sediment deposited during flooding.

Geyser A fountain of hot water or steam that erupts periodically as a result of underground streams coming into contact with hot rocks.

GDP Gross Domestic Product. The total value of goods and services produced by a country, excluding income from foreign countries.

GIS Geographical Information System. A computerized system for the collection, storage and retrieval of geographical data.

Glacier A huge mass of ice made up of compacted and frozen snow which moves slowly, eroding and depositing rock.

Glaciation The moulding of the land by a glacier or ice sheet.

GNI Gross National Income. The total value of goods and services produced by a country.

Groundwater Water that has seeped into the pores, cavities and cracks of rocks or into soil and water held in an aquifer or permeable rock.

Gully A deep, narrow chasm eroded in the landscape by a fast-flowing stream.

Heavy industry Industry that uses large amounts of energy and raw materials to produce heavy goods, such as machinery, ships or locomotives.

Humidity The moisture content of the air.

Hurricane A Violent tropical storm, also known as a cyclone in the Indian Ocean and a typhoon in the Pacific Ocean.

Hydro-electric power Energy produced by harnessing the rapid movement of water down steep mountain slopes to drive turbines to generate electricity.

Ice Age Periods of time in the past when much of the Earth's surface was covered by massive ice sheets. The most recent Ice Age began two million years ago and ended 10,000 years ago.

Iceberg A floating mass of ice that has broken off from a glacier or ice sheet.

Ice sheet A massive area of ice, thousands of metres thick.

Irrigation The artificial supply of water to dry areas – mainly for agricultural use. Water is carried or pumped to the area through pipes or ditches.

Lagoon A shallow stretch of coastal salt water behind a partial barrier such as a sandbank or coral reef.

Latitude The distance north or south of the Equator, measured in degrees, and shown on a globe as imaginary circles running around the Earth parallel to the Equator.

Lava The molten rock, magma, which erupts onto the Earth's surface through a volcano, or through a fault or crack in the Earth's crust. Lava refers to the rock both in its liquid and its later, solidified form.

Load The material that is carried by a river or stream.

Longitude The distance, measured in degrees, east or west of the Prime Meridian.

Limestone A type of rock, formed by sediment, through which water can pass.

Magma Underground, molten rock, which is very hot and highly charged with gas. It originates in the Earth's lower crust or mantle.

Mantle The layer of the Earth's interior between the crust and the core. It is about 2,900 km thick.

Map projection A mathematical formula that is used to show the curved surface of the Earth on a flat map.

Market gardening The intensive growing of fruit and vegetables close to large local markets.

Meander A loop-like bend in a river. As a river nears the sea, it tends to wind more and more. The bigger the river and the shallower its slope, the more likely it is that meanders will form.

Mediterranean climate A temperate climate of hot, dry summers and warm, damp winters.

Meltwater Water which has melted from glaciers or ice sheets.

Mestizo A person of mixed native American and European origin.

Mineral A chemical compound that occurs naturally in the Earth.

Monsoon Winds that change direction according to the seasons. They are most common in South and East Asia, where they blow from the southwest in summer, bringing heavy rainfall, and the northeast in winter.

Moraine Sand and gravel that have been deposited by a glacier or ice sheet.

Nomads (nomadic) Wandering communities who move around in search of suitable pasture for their herds of animals.

Oasis A fertile area in a desert, usually watered by an underground aquifer.

Pack ice Ice masses more than three metres thick which form on the sea surface and are not attached to a landmass.

Pacific Rim The name given to the economically dynamic countries bordering the Pacific Ocean.

Peat Decomposed vegetation found in bogs. It can be dried and used as fuel.

Per capita A latin term meaning 'for each person'.

Plantation A large farm on which only one crop is usually grown, e.g. bananas or coffee.

Plain A flat, level region of land, often relatively low-lying.

Plateau A large area of high, flat land. When surrounded by steep slopes it is called a tableland.

Peninsula A thin strip of land surrounded on three of its sides by water. Large examples include Italy, Florida and Korea.

Permafrost Permanently frozen ground, in which temperatures have remained below 0°C for more than two years.

Precipitation The fall of moisture from the atmosphere onto the surface of the Earth, as dew, hail, rain, sleet or snow.

Prairie A Spanish-American term for grassy plains, with few or no trees.

Prime Meridian 0° longitude. Also known as the Greenwich Meridian because it runs through Greenwich in England.

Rainforest Dense forests in tropical zones with high rainfall, temperature and humidity.

Rainshadow An area downwind from high terrain which has little or no rainfall because it has fallen upon the high relief.

Remote-sensing A way of obtaining information about the environment by using unmanned equipment, such as a satellite, which relays the information to a point where it is collected.

Ria A flooded V-shaped river valley or estuary flooded by a rise in sea level or sinking land.

Rift valley A long, narrow depression in the Earth's crust, formed by the sinking of rocks between two faults.

Savannah Open grassland, where an annual dry season prevents the growth of most trees. They lie between the tropical rainforest and hot desert regions.

Scale The relationship between distance on a map and on the Earth's surface.

Sediment Grains of rock transported and deposited by rivers, sea, ice or wind.

Semi-arid Areas between deserts and better-watered areas, where there is sufficient moisture to support a little more vegetation than in a true desert.

Service industry An industry that supplies services, such as banking, rather than producing manufactured goods.

Shanty town An area in or around a city where people live in temporary shacks, usually without basic facilities such as running water.

Silt Small particles, finer than sand, often carried by water and deposited on river banks, at river mouths and harbours.

Soil A thin layer of rock particles mixed with the remains of dead plants and animals. Soil occurs naturally on the surface of the Earth and provides a medium for plants to grow.

Soil erosion The wearing away of soil more quickly than it is replaced by natural processes. Over-grazing and the clearing of land for farming speeds up the process.

Sorghum A type of grass found in South America, similar to sugar cane.

Spit A narrow bank of shingle or sand extending out from the sea shore. Spits are made out of material transported along the coast by currents, wind and waves.

Staple crop The main food crop grown in a region, for example rice in Southeast Asia.

Steppe Large areas of dry grassland in the northern hemisphere – particularly found in southeast Europe and central Asia.

Subsistence farming A method of farming where enough food is produced to feed farmers and their families but not providing any extra to generate an income.

Taiga A Russian name given to the belt of coniferous forest found in Russia, which borders tundra in the north and mixed forests and grasslands in the south.

Temperate The mild, variable climate found in areas between the tropics and cold polar regions.

Terrace Steps cut into steep slopes to create flat surfaces for cultivating crops.

Tropics An area between the Equator and the Tropic of Cancer and Tropic of Capricorn that has heavy rainfall and high temperatures, and lacks any clear seasonal variation.

Tundra The land area lying in the very cold northern regions of Europe, Asia and Canada, where winters are long and cold and the ground beneath the surface is permanently frozen.

U-shaped valley A river valley that has been deepened and widened by a glacier. They are flat-bottomed and steep-sided, and usually much deeper than river valleys.

V-shaped valley A typical valley eroded by a river in its upper course.

Volcano An opening or vent in the Earth's crust where magma erupts. Volcanos are caused by the movement of the Earth's plates. When the plates collide or spread apart, magma is forced to the surface, at or near the place where the plates meet.

Watershed The dividing line between one drainage basin and another.

INDEX

● Administrative region ◆ Country ● Country capital ◇ Dependent territory ○ Dependent territory capital ▲ Mountain range ▲ Mountain ▲ Volcano ᴧ River ⊚ Lake ⊡ Reservoir

155

ARDS PENINSULA

Ards Peninsula 89 F2 *peninsula* E Northern Ireland, United Kingdom
Arecibo 51 C Puerto Rico
Arenal, Volcán 55 E6 🌋 NW Costa Rica
Arendal 83 B6 S Norway
Arenig Fawr 93 B5 ▲ NW Wales, United Kingdom
Arenys de Mar 99 G2 NE Spain
Areópoli 107 E6 S Greece
Arequipa 63 C6 SE Peru
Arezzo 103 C4 C Italy
Argenteuil 97 D2 N France
Argentina 65 A6 ◆ *republic* S South America
Argentine Basin 14 *undersea feature* SW Atlantic Ocean
Arghandab, Darya-ye 125 E5 ≈ SE Afghanistan
Argo 75 C1 N Sudan
Argun 129 F1 ≈ China/Russian Federation
Argyle, Lake 137 D2 *salt lake* Western Australia
Århus 83 B7 C Denmark
Arica 65 A2 N Chile
Arizona 44 A2 ◐ *state* SW USA
Arkansas 39 B3 ◐ *state* S USA
Arkansas City 43 D7 Kansas, C USA
Arkansas River 39 B4 ≈ C USA
Arkhangel'sk *see* Archangel
Arklow 89 E5 SE Ireland
Arles 97 E6 SE France
Arlington 44 H3 Texas, SW USA
Arlington 39 H1 Virginia, NE USA
Arlon 84 E9 SE Belgium
Armagh 89 E3 S Northern Ireland, United Kingdom
Armagnac 97 C6 *cultural region* S France
Armenia 63 B2 W Colombia
Armenia 121 H2 ◆ *republic* SW Asia
Armidale 137 H5 New South Wales, SE Australia
Armstrong 35 B4 Ontario, S Canada
Armyans'k 109 F6 S Ukraine
Arnedo 99 E2 N Spain
Arnhem 84 E4 SE Netherlands
Arnhem Land 137 E1 *physical region* Northern Territory, N Australia
Arno 103 C3 ≈ C Italy
Arnold 93 E5 C England, United Kingdom
Arnold 49 C6 California, W USA
Arnold 43 G6 Missouri, C USA
Arorae 141 J1 *atoll* Tungaru, W Kiribati
Arran, Isle of 91 C6 *island* SW Scotland, United Kingdom
Ar Raqqah 123 B2 N Syria
Arras 97 D1 N France
Arriaga 53 G5 SE Mexico
Ar Riyad *see* Riyadh
Arrow, Lough 89 C3 ◎ N Ireland
Ar Rub 'al Khali *see* Empty Quarter
Ar Rustaq 123 F4 N Oman
Árta 107 D5 W Greece
Artashat 121 H3 S Armenia
Artemisa 57 B2 W Cuba
Artesia 44 E3 New Mexico, SW USA
Arthur's Pass 139 C6 *pass* C New Zealand
Artigas 65 C5 N Uruguay
Art'ik 121 H2 W Armenia
Artois 97 D1 *cultural region* N France
Artsyz 109 D6 SW Ukraine
Artvin 121 G2 NE Turkey
Arua 75 C5 NW Uganda
Aruba 57 G7 *Dutch* ◇ S West Indies
Aru, Kepulauan 131 H7 *island group* E Indonesia
Arunachal Pradesh 127 F2 *cultural region* NE India Asia
Arusha 75 D6 N Tanzania
Arviat 33 H5 Nunavut, C Canada
Arvidsjaur 83 D3 N Sweden
Arys' 118 C6 S Kazakhstan
Asadabad 125 G5 E Afghanistan
Asahi-dake 133 G1 ▲ Hokkaidō, N Japan
Asahikawa 133 F1 N Japan
Asamankese 72 D5 SE Ghana
Asansol 127 F4 NE India
Ascension Island 26 *St. Helena* ◇ C Atlantic Ocean
Ascoli Piceno 103 D4 C Italy
'Aseb 75 E3 SE Eritrea
Aşgabat 125 C3 ● C Turkmenistan
Ashbourne 89 F4 E Ireland
Ashburton 139 C6 South Island, New Zealand
Ashburton River 137 B4 ≈ Western Australia
Ashby de la Zouch 93 D5 C England, United Kingdom
Ashdod 123 G6 W Israel
Asheville 39 F3 North Carolina, SE USA
Ashford 95 G4 SE England, United Kingdom
Ashington 93 D2 N England, United Kingdom
Ashland 49 B4 Oregon, NW USA
Ashland 40 B2 Wisconsin, N USA
Ash Sharah 123 H7 ⛰ W Jordan
Ash Shihr 123 D7 SE Yemen
Ashtabula 40 F5 Ohio, N USA
Asia 114 *continent*
Asinara 103 A5 *island* W Italy
Asipovichy 109 D2 C Belarus
Aşkale 121 F3 NE Turkey
Askersund 83 C6 C Sweden
Asmar 125 G5 E Afghanistan
Asmara 75 D2 ● C Eritrea
Asmera *see* Asmara
Aspermont 44 F3 Texas, SW USA
Assad, Lake 121 E5 ◎ N Syria
Assam 127 G3 *cultural region* NE India Asia
Assamakka 72 E2 NW Niger
As Samawah 123 C3 S Iraq
Assen 84 F2 NE Netherlands
Assenede 84 B6 NW Belgium
As Sulaymaniyah 123 C2 NE Iraq
As Sulayyil 123 C5 S Saudi Arabia
Astana 118 C5 ● N Kazakhstan
Asti 103 B2 NW Italy
Astorga 99 C2 N Spain
Astrakhan' 111 B8 SW Russian Federation
Asturias 99 C1 *cultural region* NW Spain
Astypálaia 107 F6 *island* Cyclades, Greece
Asunción 65 C4 ● S Paraguay
Aswan 70 J4 SE Egypt
Asyut 70 I3 C Egypt
Atacama Desert 65 A3 *desert* N Chile
Atamyrat 125 E4 E Turkmenistan
Atâr 72 B2 W Mauritania
Atas Bogd 129 D2 ▲ SW Mongolia
Atascadero 49 B8 California, W USA
Atatürk Baraji 121 F4 ⊡ S Turkey
Atbara 75 C2 NE Sudan
Atbara 75 D2 ≈ Eritrea/Sudan
Atbasar 118 C5 N Kazakhstan
Atchison 43 E6 Kansas, C USA
Ath 84 B7 SW Belgium
Athabasca 33 G6 Alberta, SW Canada
Athabasca 35 E4 ≈ Alberta, SW Canada
Athabasca, Lake 33 G5 ◎ Alberta/Saskatchewan, SW Canada
Athboy 89 E4 E Ireland
Athens 107 E5 ● C Greece
Athens 39 F4 Georgia, SE USA
Athens 40 F7 Ohio, N USA
Athens 44 H3 Texas, SW USA
Atherton 137 G2 Queensland, NE Australia
Athina *see* Athens
Athlone 89 D4 C Ireland
Ati 72 H3 C Chad
Atikokan 35 A4 Ontario, S Canada
Atka 118 H3 E Russian Federation
Atka 50 B2 Atka Island, Alaska, USA
Atlanta 44 I3 Texas, SW USA
Atlanta 39 E4 *state capital* Georgia, SE USA
Atlantic 39 I3 North Carolina, SE USA
Atlantic City 37 D6 New Jersey, NE USA
Atlantic Ocean 14 *ocean*
Atlas Mountains 70 C2 ⛰ NW Africa
Atlasovo 118 I3 E Russian Federation
Atlas, Tell 70 D2 ⛰ N Algeria
Atlin 33 E5 British Columbia, W Canada
At Ta'if 123 B5 W Saudi Arabia
Attawapiskat 35 C3 Ontario, C Canada
Attawapiskat 35 C3 ≈ Ontario, S Canada
Attu Island 50 A1 *island* Aleutian Islands, Alaska, USA
Atyrau 118 B4 W Kazakhstan
Aubagne 97 E7 SE France
Aubange 84 E9 SE Belgium
Auburn 37 D3 New York, NE USA
Auburn 49 B2 Washington, NW USA
Auch 97 C6 S France
Auckland 139 D2 North Island, New Zealand
Audincourt 97 F3 E France
Augathella 137 G4 Queensland, E Australia
Augsburg 101 C7 S Germany
Augusta 137 B6 Western Australia
Augusta 39 F4 Georgia, SE USA
Augusta 37 G3 *state capital* Maine, NE USA
Augustów 105 G2 NE Poland
Auki 141 F3 Malaita, N Solomon Islands
Aunu'u Island 51 *island* W American Samoa
Auob 76 C6 ≈ Namibia/South Africa
Aurangabad 127 D5 C India
Auray 97 B3 NW France
Aurès, Massif de l' 112 D4 ⛰ NE Algeria
Aurillac 97 D5 C France
Aurora 47 F5 Colorado, C USA
Aurora 40 C5 Illinois, N USA
Aurora 43 E7 Missouri, C USA
Aus 76 B6 SW Namibia
Austin 43 E4 Minnesota, N USA
Austin 47 B5 Nevada, W USA
Austin 44 G4 *state capital* Texas, SW USA
Australes, Îles 135 *island group* SW French Polynesia
Australia 137 D3 ◆ *commonwealth republic*
Australian Alps 137 G6 ⛰ SE Australia
Australian Capital Territory 137 G6 ◐ *territory* SE Australia
Austria 101 E8 ◆ *republic* C Europe
Auvergne 97 D5 *cultural region* C France Europe
Auxerre 97 D3 C France
Avarua 135 ○ Rarotonga, S Cook Islands
Aveiro 99 B3 W Portugal
Avellino 103 D6 S Italy
Avesta 83 C5 C Sweden
Aveyron 97 C6 ≈ S France
Avezzano 103 D5 C Italy
Aviemore 91 D4 N Scotland, United Kingdom
Avignon 97 E6 SE France
Ávila 99 D3 C Spain
Avilés 99 C1 NW Spain
Avon 95 D4 ≈ SW England, United Kingdom
Avon 95 E4 ≈ C England, United Kingdom
Avonmouth 95 D4 SW England, United Kingdom
Avranches 97 B2 N France
Awaji-shima 133 E6 *island* SW Japan
Awash 75 E3 NE Ethiopia
Awbari 70 F3 SW Libya
Awe, Loch 91 C5 ◎ W Scotland, United Kingdom
Axe 95 D5 ≈ SW England, United Kingdom
Axel 84 B6 SW Netherlands
Axel Heiberg Island 33 G1 *island* Nunavut, N Canada
Ayacucho 63 C6 S Peru
Ayagoz 118 D6 E Kazakhstan
Ayamonte 99 B5 SW Spain
Aydarko'l Ko'li 125 F3 ◎ C Uzbekistan
Aydın 120 A4 SW Turkey
Ayers Rock *see* Uluru
Aylesbury 95 F3 SE England, United Kingdom
Ayorou 72 D3 W Niger
'Ayoûn el 'Atroûs 72 B3 SE Mauritania
Ayr 91 D6 W Scotland, United Kingdom
Ayr 91 D6 ≈ W Scotland, United Kingdom
Ayre, Point of 93 A3 *headland* N Isle of Man
Ayteke Bi 118 B5 SW Kazakhstan
Aytos 107 F3 E Bulgaria
Ayvalık 120 A3 W Turkey
Azahar, Costa del 99 F4 *coastal region* E Spain
Azaouâd 72 D2 *desert* C Mali
Azerbaijan 121 I2 ◆ *republic* SE Asia
Azoum, Bahr 72 H4 *seasonal river* SE Chad
Azov 118 A4 SW Russian Federation
Azov, Sea of 109 F6 *sea* NE Black Sea
Aztec 44 C1 New Mexico, SW USA
Azuaga 99 C5 W Spain
Azuero, Península de 55 G7 *peninsula* S Panama
Azul 65 C6 E Argentina
Az Zagazig 70 I2 N Egypt
Az Zarqā' 123 A2 NW Jordan
Az Zāwiyah 70 F2 NW Libya

B

Baardheere 75 E5 SW Somalia
Baarle-Hertog 84 D5 N Belgium
Baarn 84 D4 C Netherlands
Babayevo 111 B4 NW Russian Federation
Babeldaob 131 H5 *island* N Palau
Bab el Mandeb 123 B7 *strait* Gulf of Aden/Red Sea
Babruysk 109 D3 E Belarus
Babuyan Channel 131 F3 *channel* N Philippines
Babuyan Island 131 F3 *island* N Philippines
Bacabal 63 G4 E Brazil
Bacău 109 C6 NE Romania
Bacheykava 109 D2 N Belarus
Back 33 G4 ≈ Nunavut, N Canada
Bacton 95 H1 E England, United Kingdom
Badajoz 99 B4 W Spain
Baden-Baden 101 B6 SW Germany
Bad Freienwalde 101 E3 NE Germany
Badgastein 101 D8 NW Austria
Bad Hersfeld 101 C5 C Germany
Bad Homburg vor der Höhe 101 B5 W Germany
Bad Ischl 101 E7 N Austria
Bad Krozingen 101 B7 SW Germany
Badlands 43 A4 *physical region* North Dakota/South Dakota, N USA
Badu Island 137 F1 *island* Queensland, NE Australia
Bad Vöslau 101 F7 NE Austria
Badwater Basin 49 D7 *depression* California, W USA
Bafatá 72 A4 C Guinea-Bissau
Baffin Bay 33 I2 *bay* Canada/Greenland
Baffin Island 33 I3 *island* Nunavut, NE Canada
Bafing 72 B4 ≈ W Africa
Bafoussam 72 F5 W Cameroon
Bafra 121 D2 N Turkey
Bagaces 55 E5 NW Costa Rica
Bagé 63 F9 S Brazil
Baghdad 123 C2 ● C Iraq
Baghlan 125 F4 NE Afghanistan
Baghran 125 E5 S Afghanistan
Bago 131 A3 SW Burma (Myanmar)
Bagoé 72 C4 ≈ Ivory Coast/Mali
Baguio 131 F3 Luzon, N Philippines
Bagzane, Monts 72 F3 ▲ N Niger
Bahamas 57 D2 ◆ *commonwealth republic* N West Indies
Baharly 125 C3 C Turkmenistan
Bahawalpur 127 C2 E Pakistan
Bahia 63 G5 *state* E Brazil
Bahía Blanca 65 B6 E Argentina
Bahir Dar 75 D3 N Ethiopia
Bahraich 127 E3 N India
Bahrain 123 D4 ◆ *monarchy* SW Asia
Bahushewsk 109 D2 NE Belarus
Baia Mare 109 B5 NW Romania
Baïbokoum 72 G5 SW Chad
Baie-Comeau 35 F4 Québec, SE Canada
Baikal, Lake 118 F5 ◎ S Russian Federation
Bailén 99 D5 S Spain
Ba Illi 72 G4 SW Chad
Bainbridge 39 E6 Georgia, SE USA
Bairiki 135 ● Tarawa, NW Kiribati
Bairnsdale 137 G6 Victoria, SE Australia
Baishan 129 H2 NE China
Baiyin 129 E3 N China
Baja 105 E8 S Hungary
Baja, Punta 141 C6 *headland* Easter Island, Chile
Bajram Curri 107 D3 N Albania
Bakala 72 H5 C Central African Republic
Baker 49 C3 Oregon, NW USA
Baker and Howland Islands 135 *US* ◇ W Polynesia
Baker Lake 33 H4 Nunavut, N Canada
Bakersfield 49 C8 California, W USA
Bakhtaran *see* Kermanshah
Baki *see* Baku
Bakony 105 D8 ⛰ W Hungary
Baku 121 J2 ● E Azerbaijan
Bala 93 B5 NW Wales, United Kingdom
Balabac Strait 131 E5 *strait* Malaysia/Philippines
Balaguer 99 G2 NE Spain
Balaïtous 97 B7 ▲ France/Spain
Balakovo 111 C7 W Russian Federation
Bala Morghab 125 E4 NW Afghanistan
Balashov 111 B6 W Russian Federation
Balaton, Lake 105 D8 ◎ W Hungary
Balbina, Represa 63 E3 ⊡ NW Brazil
Balboa 55 H6 C Panama
Balbriggan 89 E4 E Ireland
Balcarce 65 C6 E Argentina
Balclutha 139 B8 South Island, New Zealand
Baldy Mountain 47 D1 ▲ Montana, NW USA
Baldy Peak 44 C3 ▲ Arizona, SW USA
Baleares, Islas *see* Balearic Islands
Balearic Islands 99 G4 *island group* Spain, W Mediterranean Sea
Baleine, Rivière à la 35 E2 ≈ Québec, E Canada
Balen 84 D6 N Belgium
Baleshwar 127 F4 E India
Bali 131 E8 *island* C Indonesia
Balıkesir 120 A3 W Turkey
Balikpapan 131 E7 C Indonesia
Balkanabat 125 B3 W Turkmenistan
Balkan Mountains 107 E3 ⛰ Bulgaria/Serbia
Balkh 125 F4 N Afghanistan
Balkhash 118 C6 SE Kazakhstan
Balkhash, Lake 118 C6 ◎ SE Kazakhstan
Balladonia 137 C5 Western Australia
Ballaghmore 89 D5 C Ireland
Ballantrae 91 C7 W Scotland, United Kingdom
Ballarat 137 F6 Victoria, SE Australia
Ballater 91 E4 NE Scotland, United Kingdom
Ballina 89 C3 W Ireland
Ballinasloe 89 C4 W Ireland
Ballindine 89 C4 NW Ireland
Ballinger 44 G4 Texas, SW USA
Ballinhassig 89 C7 S Ireland
Ballinskelligs 89 A6 SW Ireland
Ballinskelligs Bay 89 A7 *inlet* SW Ireland
Ballinspittle 89 C7 S Ireland
Ballintra 89 D2 NW Ireland
Ballybofey 89 D2 NW Ireland
Ballybunnion 89 B5 SW Ireland
Ballycastle 89 E1 N Northern Ireland, United Kingdom
Ballyclare 89 F2 E Northern Ireland, United Kingdom
Ballyconneely 89 B4 W Ireland
Ballycotton 89 C7 S Ireland
Ballycroy 89 B3 NW Ireland
Ballydehob 89 B7 S Ireland
Ballydonegan 89 A7 S Ireland
Ballyduff 89 B5 SW Ireland
Ballyferriter 89 A6 SW Ireland
Ballyhaunis 89 C3 W Ireland
Ballyhoura Mountains 89 C6 ⛰ S Ireland
Ballymena 89 E2 NE Northern Ireland, United Kingdom
Ballymoe 89 C4 W Ireland
Ballymoney 89 E1 NE Northern Ireland, United Kingdom
Ballynafid 89 D4 C Ireland
Ballyshannon 89 C2 NW Ireland
Ballywalter 89 F2 E Northern Ireland, United Kingdom
Balrath 89 E4 E Ireland
Balsas 63 G4 E Brazil
Balsas, Río 53 E5 ≈ S Mexico
Baltasound 91 B5 NE Scotland, United Kingdom
Bălţi 109 D5 N Moldova
Baltic Sea 83 D7 *sea* N Europe
Baltimore 89 B7 S Ireland
Baltimore 39 H1 Maryland, NE USA
Baltinglass 89 E5 E Ireland
Baluchistan 127 B3 *province* SW Pakistan
Balykchy 125 H2 NE Kyrgyzstan
Bam 123 F3 SE Iran
Bamako 72 C4 ● SW Mali
Bambari 72 H5 C Central African Republic
Bamberg 101 C5 SE Germany
Bamburgh 93 D1 N England, United Kingdom
Bamenda 72 F5 W Cameroon
Banaba 141 H1 *island* W Kiribati
Bananga 127 H6 Nicobar Islands, India
Banbridge 89 E3 SE Northern Ireland, United Kingdom
Banbury 95 E3 S England, United Kingdom
Banchory 91 F4 NE Scotland, United Kingdom
Bandaaceh 131 A5 Sumatra, W Indonesia
Bandama 72 C5 ≈ S Ivory Coast
Bandarbeyla 75 G3 NE Somalia
Bandar-e 'Abbas 123 E4 S Iran
Bandar-e Büshehr 123 D3 S Iran
Bandar-e Kangan 123 D3 S Iran
Bandar Lampung 131 B7 W Indonesia
Bandar Seri Begawan 131 D5 ● N Brunei
Banda Sea 131 G7 *sea* E Indonesia
Bandırma 120 A2 NW Turkey
Bandon 89 B7 ≈ S Ireland
Bandundu 76 B2 W Dem. Rep. Congo
Bandung 131 C8 Java, C Indonesia
Banff 91 E3 NE Scotland, United Kingdom
Bangalore 127 D6 S India
Bangassou 72 I5 SE Central African Republic
Banggai, Kepulauan 131 F6 *island group* C Indonesia
Banghazi *see* Benghazi
Bangka, Pulau 131 C7 *island* W Indonesia
Bangkok 131 B4 ● C Thailand
Bangladesh 127 G3 ◆ *republic* S Asia
Bangor 93 B5 NW Wales, United Kingdom
Bangor 89 F2 E Northern Ireland, United Kingdom
Bangor 37 G2 Maine, NE USA
Bangui 72 H5 ● SW Central African Republic
Bangweulu, Lake 76 D3 ◎ N Zambia
Bani 72 C4 ≈ S Mali
Bani Suwayf 70 I3 N Egypt
Banja Luka 107 C2 Republika Srpska, NW Bosnia and Herzegovina
Banjarmasin 131 E7 C Indonesia
Banjul 72 A3 ● W Gambia
Banks Island 33 F3 *island* Northwest Territories, NW Canada
Banks Islands 141 G4 *island group* N Vanuatu
Banks Lake 49 C2 ⊡ Washington, NW USA
Banks Peninsula 139 C6 *peninsula* South Island, New Zealand
Banks Strait 137 G7 *strait* SW Tasman Sea
Bankura 127 F4 NE India
Banmauk 131 A2 N Burma (Myanmar)
Bann 89 E2 ≈ N Northern Ireland, United Kingdom
Ban Nadou 131 C3 S Laos
Bansha 89 C6 S Ireland
Banská Bystrica 105 E6 C Slovakia
Banteer 89 C6 S Ireland
Bantry 89 B7 SW Ireland
Bantry Bay 89 B7 *bay* SW Ireland
Banyak, Kepulauan 131 A6 *island group* NW Indonesia
Banyo 72 F5 NW Cameroon
Banyoles 99 H2 NE Spain
Baoji 129 E4 C China
Baoro 72 G5 W Central African Republic
Baoshan 129 D5 SW China
Baotou 129 F3 N China
Ba'qubah 123 C2 C Iraq
Baraawe 75 E5 S Somalia
Baranavichy 109 C3 SW Belarus
Barbados 57 K6 ◆ *commonwealth republic* SE West Indies
Barbastro 99 F2 NE Spain
Barbate de Franco 99 C6 S Spain
Barbuda 57 J4 *island* N Antigua and Barbuda
Barcaldine 137 G3 Queensland, E Australia
Barcelona 99 G2 E Spain
Barcelona 63 D1 NE Venezuela
Barcs 105 D9 SW Hungary
Bardaï 72 G2 N Chad
Bardejov 105 F6 E Slovakia
Bareilly 127 E3 N India
Barendrecht 84 C4 SW Netherlands
Barentin 97 C2 N France
Barents Sea 111 C2 *sea* Arctic Ocean
Bar Harbor 37 G2 Mount Desert Island, Maine, NE USA
Bari 103 E6 SE Italy
Barikowt 125 G4 NE Afghanistan
Barillas 55 A2 NW Guatemala
Barinas 63 C2 W Venezuela
Barisal 127 G4 S Bangladesh
Barisan, Pegunungan 131 B7 ⛰ Sumatera, W Indonesia
Barito, Sungai 131 E7 ≈ Borneo, C Indonesia
Barkly Tableland 137 E2 *plateau* Northern Territory/Queensland, N Australia
Bârlad 109 C6 E Romania
Bar-le-Duc 97 E2 NE France
Barlee, Lake 137 B5 ◎ Western Australia
Barlee Range 137 B4 ⛰ Western Australia
Barletta 103 E5 SE Italy
Barlinek 105 C3 NW Poland
Barmouth 93 B5 NW Wales, United Kingdom
Barnard Castle 93 D3 N England, United Kingdom
Barnaul 118 D5 C Russian Federation
Barnsley 93 D4 N England, United Kingdom
Barnstaple 95 B4 SW England, United Kingdom
Barnstaple Bay 95 B4 *bay* SW England, United Kingdom
Baroghil Pass 125 G4 *pass* Afghanistan/Pakistan
Barquisimeto 63 C1 NW Venezuela
Barra 91 A4 *island* NW Scotland, United Kingdom
Barra de Río Grande 55 E4 E Nicaragua
Barranca 63 B5 W Peru
Barrancabermeja 63 B2 N Colombia
Barranquilla 63 B1 N Colombia
Barreiro 99 A4 W Portugal
Barrier Range 137 F5 *hill range* New South Wales, SE Australia
Barrier Reef 55 C1 *reef* E Belize
Barrow 50 E1 Alaska, USA
Barrow 89 D6 ≈ SE Ireland
Barrow-in-Furness 93 C3 NW England, United Kingdom
Barrow Island 137 A3 *island* Western Australia
Barry 93 C7 S Wales, United Kingdom
Barstow 49 D8 California, W USA
Bartang 125 G4 ≈ SE Tajikistan
Bartın 121 C2 NW Turkey
Bartlesville 43 D7 Oklahoma, C USA
Barton-upon-Humber 93 F4 N England, United Kingdom
Bartoszyce 105 E2 NE Poland
Baruun-Urt 129 F2 E Mongolia
Barú, Volcán 55 F6 🌋 W Panama
Barva, Volcán 55 E6 🌋 NW Costa Rica
Barwon River 137 G5 ≈ New South Wales, SE Australia
Barysaw 109 D2 NE Belarus
Basarabeasca 109 D6 SE Moldova
Basel 101 B7 NW Switzerland
Basilan 131 F5 *island* SW Philippines
Basildon 95 G3 E England, United Kingdom
Basingstoke 95 E4 S England, United Kingdom
Basque Country, The 99 E1 *cultural region* N Spain Europe
Basra 123 D3 SE Iraq
Bassano del Grappa 103 C2 NE Italy
Bassenthwaite Lake 93 C2 ◎ NW England, United Kingdom
Basseterre 57 J4 ● C Saint Kitts and Nevis
Basse-Terre 57 J5 ○ SW Guadeloupe
Bassett 43 C4 Nebraska, C USA
Bassikounou 72 C3 SE Mauritania
Bass Strait 137 F7 *strait* SE Australia
Bassum 101 B3 NW Germany
Bastia 97 G5 Corsica, France
Bastogne 84 E8 SE Belgium
Bata 72 F6 NW Equatorial Guinea
Batangas 131 F4 Luzon, N Philippines
Batdambang 131 C4 NW Cambodia
Batéké, Plateaux 76 B2 *plateau* S Congo
Bath 95 D4 SW England, United Kingdom
Bath 37 G3 Maine, NE USA
Bathinda 127 D2 NW India
Bathurst 137 G6 New South Wales, SE Australia
Bathurst 35 F4 New Brunswick, SE Canada
Bathurst Island 137 C1 *island* Northern Territory, N Australia
Bathurst Island 33 G2 *island* Parry Islands, Nunavut, N Canada
Batin, Wadi al 123 C3 *dry watercourse* SW Asia
Batman 121 G4 SE Turkey
Batna 70 E1 NE Algeria
Baton Rouge 39 C6 *state capital* Louisiana, S USA
Batticaloa 127 E8 E Sri Lanka
Battipaglia 103 D6 S Italy
Battle Mountain 47 B5 Nevada, W USA
Bat'umi 121 G2 W Georgia
Batu Pahat 131 C6 W Malaysia
Bauchi 72 F4 NE Nigeria
Bautzen 101 E4 E Germany
Bavaria 101 C7 *cultural region* SE Germany Europe
Bavarian Alps 101 C7 ⛰ Austria/Germany
Bavispe, Río 53 C2 ≈ NW Mexico
Bawiti 70 I3 N Egypt
Bawku 72 D4 N Ghana
Bayamo 57 D3 E Cuba
Bayamón 51 E Puerto Rico
Bayan Har Shan 129 D4 ⛰ C China
Bayanhongor 129 D2 C Mongolia
Bayano, Lago 55 H6 ◎ E Panama
Bayard 44 C3 New Mexico, SW USA
Bay City 40 E4 Michigan, N USA
Bay City 44 H5 Texas, SW USA
Baydhabo 75 E5 SW Somalia
Bayern *see* Bavaria
Bayeux 97 C2 N France
Bay Islands 55 D2 *island group* N Honduras
Baymak 111 D7 W Russian Federation
Bayonne 97 B6 SW France
Baýramaly 125 D4 S Turkmenistan
Bayreuth 101 C5 SE Germany
Baytown 44 I4 Texas, SW USA
Baza 99 E5 S Spain
Beachy Head 95 G5 *headland* SE England, United Kingdom
Beacon 37 E4 New York, NE USA
Beacon Hill 93 C6 *hill* E Wales, United Kingdom
Beagle Channel 65 B9 *channel* Argentina/Chile
Bear Lake 47 D4 ◎ Idaho/Utah, NW USA
Beas de Segura 99 E5 S Spain
Beata, Isla 57 F5 *island* SW Dominican Republic
Beatrice 43 D5 Nebraska, C USA
Beatty 47 B6 Nevada, W USA
Beaufort Sea 50 F1 *sea* Arctic Ocean
Beaufort West 76 C7 SW South Africa
Beauly 91 D3 N Scotland, United Kingdom
Beaumont 44 I4 Texas, SW USA
Beaune 97 E4 C France
Beauvais 97 D2 N France
Beaver Falls 37 A5 Pennsylvania, NE USA
Beaver Island 40 C3 *island* Michigan, N USA
Beaver River 43 B7 ≈ Oklahoma, C USA
Beaverton 49 B3 Oregon, NW USA
Beawar 127 D3 N India
Beccles 95 H2 E England, United Kingdom

156 ◐ Administrative region ◆ Country ● Country capital ◇ Dependent territory ○ Dependent territory capital ⛰ Mountain range ▲ Mountain 🌋 Volcano ≈ River ◎ Lake ⊡ Reservoir

BROOKS RANGE

Béchar *70 D2* W Algeria
Beckley *39 G2* West Virginia, NE USA
Bedford *95 F2* E England, United Kingdom
Bedford *40 D7* Indiana, N USA
Bedford Level *95 F2 physical region* E England, United Kingdom
Bedum *84 F2* NE Netherlands
Bedworth *93 D6* C England, United Kingdom
Be'er Menuha *123 H7* S Israel
Beernem *84 B6* NW Belgium
Be'er Sheva *123 G6* S Israel
Beesel *84 E6* SE Netherlands
Beeston *93 E5* C England, United Kingdom
Beeville *44 G5* Texas, SW USA
Bega *137 G6* New South Wales, SE Australia
Beihai *129 F6* S China
Beijing *129 F3* ● E China
Beilen *84 E3* NE Netherlands
Beinn Dearg *91 D3* ▲ N Scotland, United Kingdom
Beira *76 E5* C Mozambique
Beirut *123 A2* ● W Lebanon
Beja *99 B5* SE Portugal
Béjar *99 C3* N Spain
Békéscsaba *105 F8* SE Hungary
Bekobod *125 F3* E Uzbekistan
Belarus *109 C2* ◆ *republic* E Europe
Bełchatów *105 E4* C Poland
Belcher Islands *35 C2 island group* Nunavut, SE Canada
Beledweyne *75 F4* C Somalia
Belém *63 G3* N Brazil
Belén *55 D5* SW Nicaragua
Belen *44 D2* New Mexico, SW USA
Belep, Îles *141 F6 island group* W New Caledonia
Belfast *89 F2 National region capital,* E Northern Ireland, United Kingdom
Belfield *43 A2* North Dakota, N USA
Belfort *97 F3* E France
Belgaum *127 D6* W India
Belgium *81 B7* ◆ *monarchy* NW Europe
Belgorod *111 A6* W Russian Federation
Belgrade *107 D2* ● N Serbia
Belgrano II *142 B4 Argentinian research station* Antarctica
Belitung, Pulau *131 C7 island* W Indonesia
Belize *55 B2* ◆ *commonwealth republic* Central America
Belize *55 B1* ≈ Belize/Guatemala
Belize City *55 C1* NE Belize
Belkofski *50 C3* Alaska, USA
Bellananagh *89 D3* N Ireland
Bellavary *89 B3* NW Ireland
Belle Île *97 A3 island* NW France
Belle Isle, Strait of *35 G3 strait* Newfoundland and Labrador, E Canada
Belleville *40 B7* Illinois, N USA
Bellevue *43 D5* Nebraska, C USA
Bellevue *49 B2* Washington, NW USA
Bellingham *49 B1* Washington, NW USA
Bellingshausen Sea *142 A4 sea* Antarctica
Bellinzona *101 B8* S Switzerland
Bello *63 B2* W Colombia
Bellona *141 E3 island* S Solomon Islands
Bellville *76 C7* SW South Africa
Belmopan *55 B2* ● C Belize
Belmullet *89 B3* W Ireland
Belo Horizonte *63 G7* SE Brazil
Belomorsk *111 B3* NW Russian Federation
Beloretsk *111 D6* W Russian Federation
Belorussia *see* Belarus
Belozersk *111 B4* NW Russian Federation
Belper *93 D5* C England, United Kingdom
Belton *44 H4* Texas, SW USA
Belturbet *89 D3* N Ireland
Belukha, Gora *118 D5* ▲ Kazakhstan/Russian Federation
Belyy, Ostrov *118 D2 island* N Russian Federation
Bemaraha *76 G5* ⛰ W Madagascar
Bemidji *43 E2* Minnesota, N USA
Bemmel *84 E4* SE Netherlands
Benavente *99 C2* N Spain
Benbecula *91 A3 island* NW Scotland, United Kingdom
Bend *49 B4* Oregon, NW USA
Bendery *see* Tighina
Bendigo *137 F6* Victoria, SE Australia
Benešov *105 B5* W Czech Republic
Benevento *103 D6* S Italy
Bengbu *129 G4* E China
Benghazi *70 G2* NE Libya
Bengkulu *131 B7* Sumatra, W Indonesia
Benguela *76 B4* W Angola
Ben Hope *91 D2* ▲ N Scotland, United Kingdom
Beni *76 D1* NE Dem. Rep. Congo
Benidorm *99 F4* SE Spain
Beni-Mellal *70 C2* C Morocco
Benin *72 D4* ◆ *republic* W Africa
Benin, Bight of *72 E5 gulf* W Africa
Benin City *72 E5* SW Nigeria
Beni, Río *65 A2* ≈ N Bolivia
Ben Klibreck *91 C2* ▲ N Scotland, United Kingdom
Ben Lawers *91 D5* ▲ C Scotland, United Kingdom
Ben Lui *91 C5* ▲ C Scotland, United Kingdom
Ben Macdui *91 E4* ▲ C Scotland, United Kingdom
Ben More *91 B5* ▲ W Scotland, United Kingdom
Ben More *91 D5* ▲ C Scotland, United Kingdom
Ben More Assynt *91 D2* ▲ N Scotland, United Kingdom
Ben Nevis *91 C4* ▲ N Scotland, United Kingdom
Benson *44 C3* Arizona, SW USA
Benton *39 B4* Arkansas, C USA
Benton Harbor *40 D5* Michigan, N USA
Benue *72 F5* ≈ Cameroon/Nigeria
Beograd *see* Belgrade
Berat *107 D4* C Albania
Berau, Teluk *131 H7 bay* Papua, E Indonesia
Berbera *75 F3* NW Somalia
Berbérati *72 G5* SW Central African Republic
Berck-Plage *97 D1* N France
Berdyans'k *109 G6* SE Ukraine
Bereket *125 C3* W Turkmenistan
Berettyó *105 F8* ≈ Hungary/Romania
Berettyóújfalu *105 F7* E Hungary
Berezniki *111 D5* NW Russian Federation
Berga *99 G2* NE Spain
Bergamo *103 B2* N Italy
Bergen *101 D2* NE Germany
Bergen *84 C3* NW Netherlands
Bergen *83 A5* S Norway
Bergerac *97 C5* SW France
Bergeyk *84 D6* S Netherlands
Bergse Maas *84 D5* ≈ S Netherlands
Beringen *84 D6* NE Belgium
Bering Sea *50 B1 sea* N Pacific Ocean
Bering Strait *50 D1 strait* Bering Sea/Chukchi Sea
Berja *99 E6* S Spain
Berkeley *49 B7* California, W USA
Berkhamsted *95 F3* SE England, United Kingdom
Berkner Island *142 B4 island* Antarctica
Berlin *101 D3* ● NE Germany
Berlin *37 F3* New Hampshire, NE USA
Bermejo, Río *65 B3* ≈ N Argentina
Bermeo *99 E1* N Spain
Bermuda *26 UK* ◇ NW Atlantic Ocean
Bern *101 A8* ● W Switzerland
Bernau *101 D3* NE Germany
Bernburg *101 D4* C Germany
Berner Alpen *101 A8* ⛰ SW Switzerland
Berneray *91 A4 island* NW Scotland, United Kingdom
Bernier Island *137 A4 island* Western Australia
Berry *97 D3 cultural region* C France
Berry Islands *57 C1 island group* N Bahamas
Bertoua *72 G5* E Cameroon
Berwick-upon-Tweed *93 D1* N England, United Kingdom
Besançon *97 E4* E France
Bessbrook *89 E3* S Northern Ireland, United Kingdom
Betafo *76 G5* C Madagascar
Betanzos *99 B1* NW Spain
Bethlehem *76 D6* C South Africa
Bethlehem *37 D5* Pennsylvania, NE USA
Bethlehem *123 H6* C West Bank
Béticos, Sistemas *99 D5* ⛰ S Spain
Bétou *76 C1* N Congo
Bette, Picco *70 G4* ▲ S Libya
Betws-y-Coed *93 B5* N Wales, United Kingdom
Beulah *40 D3* Michigan, N USA
Beveren *84 C6* N Belgium
Beverley *93 F4* E England, United Kingdom
Bexhill *95 G4* SE England, United Kingdom
Beyla *72 C4* SE Guinea
Beyrouth *see* Beirut
Beyşehir Gölü *120 B4* ◎ C Turkey
Béziers *97 D6* S France
Bhadravati *127 D6* SW India
Bhagalpur *127 F3* NE India
Bhaktapur *127 F3* C Nepal
Bharuch *127 C4* W India
Bhavnagar *127 C4* W India
Bhopal *127 D4* C India
Bhubaneshwar *127 F4* E India
Bhusawal *127 D4* C India
Bhutan *127 G3* ◆ *monarchy* S Asia
Biak, Pulau *131 H6 island* E Indonesia
Biała Podlaska *105 G3* E Poland
Białogard *105 C2* NW Poland
Białystok *105 G2* NE Poland
Biarritz *97 B6* SW France
Bicester *95 E3* C England, United Kingdom
Biddeford *37 F3* Maine, NE USA
Bideford *95 B4* SW England, United Kingdom
Biel *101 A8* W Switzerland
Bielefeld *101 B4* NW Germany
Bielsko-Biała *105 E5* S Poland
Bielsk Podlaski *105 G3* E Poland
Biên Hoa *131 C4* S Vietnam
Bienville, Lac *35 D3* ◎ Québec, C Canada
Bié Plateau *76 C4 plateau* C Angola
Big Bend National Park *44 E5 national park* Texas, S USA
Bigbury Bay *95 B6 bay* SW England, United Kingdom
Big Cypress Swamp *39 G8 wetland* Florida, SE USA
Biggleswade *95 F2* C England, United Kingdom
Bighorn Mountains *47 E3* ⛰ Wyoming, C USA
Bighorn River *47 E3* ≈ Montana/Wyoming, NW USA
Big Sioux River *43 D4* ≈ Iowa/South Dakota, N USA
Big Smoky Valley *47 B6 valley* Nevada, W USA
Big Spring *44 F3* Texas, SW USA
Bihać *107 B2* NW Bosnia and Herzegovina
Bihar *127 F3 cultural region* N India Asia
Biharamulo *75 C6* NW Tanzania
Bihar Sharif *127 F3* NE India
Bihosava *109 C1* NW Belarus
Bijelo Polje *107 D3* E Montenegro
Bikaner *127 D3* NW India
Bikin *118 H5* SE Russian Federation
Bilaspur *127 E4* C India
Biläsuvar *121 I3* SE Azerbaijan
Bila Tserkva *109 D4* N Ukraine
Bilauktaung Range *131 B4* ⛰ Burma (Myanmar)/Thailand
Bilbao *99 E1* N Spain
Bilecik *120 B3* NW Turkey
Billingham *93 E2* N England, United Kingdom
Billings *47 E2* Montana, NW USA
Bilma, Grand Erg de *72 G2 desert* NE Niger
Biloela *137 H4* Queensland, E Australia
Biloxi *39 C6* Mississippi, S USA
Biltine *72 H3* E Chad
Bilzen *84 D6* NE Belgium
Bimini Islands *57 C1 island group* W Bahamas
Binche *84 C7* S Belgium
Binghamton *37 D4* New York, NE USA
Bingöl *121 F3* E Turkey
Bintulu *131 D6* C Malaysia
Binzhou *129 G3* E China
Bío Bío, Río *65 A6* ≈ C Chile
Bioco, Isla de *72 F6 island* NW Equatorial Guinea
Birak *70 F3* C Libya
Birao *72 I4* NE Central African Republic
Biratnagar *127 F3* SE Nepal
Birdhill *89 C5* S Ireland
Birhar Sharif *127 F3* N India
Birjand *123 F2* E Iran
Birkenfeld *101 A6* SW Germany
Birkenhead *93 C4* NW England, United Kingdom
Birmingham *93 D6* C England, United Kingdom
Birmingham *39 D4* Alabama, S USA
Bîr Mogreïn *72 B1* N Mauritania
Birnin Kebbi *72 E4* NW Nigeria
Birnin Konni *72 E3* SW Niger
Birobidzhan *118 H5* SE Russian Federation
Birr *89 D4* C Ireland
Birsk *111 D6* W Russian Federation
Birżebbuġa *112 B6* SE Malta
Bisbee *44 C4* Arizona, SW USA
Biscay, Bay of *97 B4 bay* France/Spain
Bishah, Wadi *123 B5 dry watercourse* C Saudi Arabia
Bishkek *125 H2* ● N Kyrgyzstan
Bishop *49 C7* California, W USA
Bishop Auckland *93 D2* N England, United Kingdom
Biskra *70 E1* NE Algeria
Biskupiec *105 F2* NE Poland
Bislig *131 G5* S Philippines
Bismarck *43 B2 state capital* North Dakota, N USA
Bismarck Archipelago *141 B1 island group* NE Papua New Guinea
Bismarck Sea *141 B1 sea* W Pacific Ocean
Bissau *72 A4* ● W Guinea-Bissau
Bistrița *109 B6* N Romania
Bitam *76 A1* N Gabon
Bitburg *101 A5* SW Germany
Bitlis *121 G4* SE Turkey
Bitola *107 D4* S Macedonia
Bitonto *103 E6* SE Italy
Bitterfeld *101 D4* E Germany
Bitterroot Range *47 C2* ⛰ Idaho/Montana, NW USA
Biu *72 G4* E Nigeria
Biwa-ko *133 E6* ◎ Honshu, SW Japan
Bizerte *70 F1* N Tunisia
Bjørnøya *143 D5 island* N Norway
Blackall *137 G4* Queensland, E Australia
Blackburn *93 C4* NW England, United Kingdom
Black Drin *107 D3* ≈ Albania/Macedonia
Blackfoot *47 D4* Idaho, NW USA
Black Forest *101 B7* ⛰ SW Germany
Black Hills *43 A4* ⛰ South Dakota/Wyoming, N USA
Black Mountain *47 D5* ▲ Colorado, C USA
Black Mountains *93 C6* ⛰ SE Wales, United Kingdom
Blackpool *93 C4* NW England, United Kingdom
Black Range *44 D3* ⛰ New Mexico, SW USA
Black River *131 B2* ≈ China/Vietnam
Black Rock Desert *47 A4 desert* Nevada, W USA
Black Sea *78 sea* Asia/Europe
Black Sea Lowland *109 E6 depression* SE Europe
Blacksod Bay *89 A3 inlet* W Ireland
Black Volta *72 D4* ≈ W Africa
Blackwater *89 E6* SE Ireland
Blackwater *89 D6* ≈ S Ireland
Blackwater *89 E2* ≈ Ireland/Northern Ireland, United Kingdom
Blaenavon *93 C7* SE Wales, United Kingdom
Blagoevgrad *107 E3* W Bulgaria
Blagoveshchensk *118 H5* SE Russian Federation
Blairgowrie *91 E5* C Scotland, United Kingdom
Blakeney Point *95 G1 headland* E England, United Kingdom
Blanca, Bahía *65 B6 bay* E Argentina
Blanca, Costa *99 F5 physical region* SE Spain
Blanche, Lake *137 F4* ◎ South Australia
Blanc, Mont *97 F5* ▲ France/Italy
Blanco, Cape *49 A4 headland* Oregon, NW USA
Blandford Forum *95 D5* S England, United Kingdom
Blanes *99 H2* NE Spain
Blankenberge *84 B5* NW Belgium
Blankenheim *101 A5* W Germany
Blanquilla, Isla *57 I7 island* N Venezuela
Blantyre *76 E4* S Malawi
Blaricum *84 D4* C Netherlands
Blenheim *139 C5* South Island, New Zealand
Blida *70 D1* N Algeria
Bloemfontein *76 D6* ● C South Africa
Blois *97 C3* C France
Bloody Foreland *89 C1 headland* NW Ireland
Bloomfield *44 C1* New Mexico, SW USA
Bloomington *40 B6* Illinois, N USA
Bloomington *40 D7* Indiana, N USA
Bloomington *43 E3* Minnesota, N USA
Bloomsburg *37 D5* Pennsylvania, NE USA
Bloomsbury *137 G3* Queensland, NE Australia
Bluefield *39 G2* West Virginia, NE USA
Bluefields *55 E4* SE Nicaragua
Blue Mountains *137 G6* ⛰ New South Wales, SE Australia
Blue Mountains *49 C3* ⛰ Oregon/Washington, NW USA
Blue Nile *75 C3* ≈ Ethiopia/Sudan
Bluff *47 D6* Utah, W USA
Blumenau *63 F8* S Brazil
Blyth *93 D2* N England, United Kingdom
Blythe *49 E9* California, W USA
Blytheville *39 C3* Arkansas, C USA
Bo *72 B5* S Sierra Leone
Boaco *55 D4* S Nicaragua
Boa Vista *63 E3* NW Brazil
Bobaomby, Tanjona *76 G4 headland* N Madagascar
Bobo-Dioulasso *72 C4* SW Burkina
Boca Raton *39 G8* Florida, SE USA
Bocay *55 D3* N Nicaragua
Bocholt *101 A4* W Germany
Bochum *101 A4* W Germany
Bodaybo *118 F4* E Russian Federation
Boden *83 D3* N Sweden
Bodmin *95 B5* SW England, United Kingdom
Bodmin Moor *95 B5 moorland* SW England, United Kingdom
Bodø *83 C2* C Norway
Bodrum *120 A4* SW Turkey
Boende *76 C2* C Dem. Rep. Congo
Bofin, Lough *89 D3* ◎ N Ireland
Bogalusa *39 C6* Louisiana, S USA
Bogatynia *105 B4* SW Poland
Boğazlıyan *121 D3* C Turkey
Boggeragh Mountains *89 C6* ⛰ S Ireland
Bogia *141 B1* N Papua New Guinea
Bognor Regis *95 F5* SE England, United Kingdom
Bogor *131 C8* Java, C Indonesia
Bogotá *63 B2* ● C Colombia
Bo Hai *129 G3 gulf* NE China
Bohemia *105 B6 cultural region* W Czech Republic
Bohemian Forest *101 D6* ⛰ C Europe
Bohol Sea *131 F5 sea* S Philippines
Bohoro Shan *129 B2* ⛰ NW China
Boise *47 B3 state capital* Idaho, NW USA
Boise City *43 A7* Oklahoma, C USA
Boizenburg *101 C3* N Germany
Bojnūrd *123 E1* N Iran
Boké *72 A4* W Guinea
Boknafjorden *83 A5 fjord* S Norway
Bol *72 G3* W Chad
Bolesławiec *105 C4* SW Poland
Bolgatanga *72 D4* N Ghana
Bolivia *65 A2* ◆ *republic* W South America
Bollene *97 E6* SE France
Bollnäs *83 C5* C Sweden
Bollon *137 G4* Queensland, C Australia
Bologna *103 C3* N Italy
Bol'shevik, Ostrov *118 F2 island* Severnaya Zemlya, N Russian Federation
Bol'shezemel'skaya Tundra *111 E3 physical region* NW Russian Federation
Bol'shoy Lyakhovskiy, Ostrov *118 G2 island* NE Russian Federation
Bolton *93 C4* NW England, United Kingdom
Bolu *121 C2* NW Turkey
Bolungarvík *83 A1* NW Iceland
Bolus Head *89 A6 headland* SW Ireland
Bolzano *103 C1* N Italy
Boma *76 B3* W Dem. Rep. Congo
Bombay *see* Mumbai
Bomu *76 C1* ≈ Central African Republic/Dem. Rep. Congo
Bonaire *57 H7 island* E Netherlands Antilles
Bonanza *55 E3* NE Nicaragua
Bonaparte Archipelago *137 B2 island group* Western Australia
Bon, Cap *112 E4 headland* N Tunisia
Bondo *76 C1* N Dem. Rep. Congo
Bondoukou *72 D5* E Ivory Coast
Bone, Teluk *131 F7 bay* Celebes, C Indonesia
Bongaigaon *127 G3* NE India
Bongo, Massif des *72 H4* ⛰ NE Central African Republic
Bongor *72 G4* SW Chad
Bonifacio *97 G6* Corsica, France
Bonifacio, Strait of *103 A5 strait* C Mediterranean Sea
Bonin Trench *15 undersea feature* NW Pacific Ocean
Bonn *101 A5* W Germany
Boonville *37 D3* New York, NE USA
Boosaaso *75 F3* N Somalia
Boothia, Gulf of *33 H3 gulf* Nunavut, NE Canada
Boothia Peninsula *33 H3 peninsula* Nunavut, NE Canada
Boppard *101 B5* W Germany
Boquete *55 F6* W Panama
Boquillas *53 D2* NE Mexico
Bor *107 D2* E Serbia
Bor *75 C4* S Sudan
Borah Peak *47 B3* ▲ Idaho, NW USA
Borås *83 C6* S Sweden
Bordeaux *97 B5* SW France
Bordj Omar Driss *70 E3* E Algeria
Bordon *95 F4* S England, United Kingdom
Børgefjelt *83 C3* ⛰ C Norway
Borger *84 F2* NE Netherlands
Borger *44 F2* Texas, SW USA
Borgholm *83 C6* S Sweden
Borisoglebsk *111 B6* W Russian Federation
Borlänge *83 C5* C Sweden
Borne *84 F4* E Netherlands
Borneo *131 D7 island* Brunei/Indonesia/Malaysia
Bornholm *83 C7 island* E Denmark
Borovichi *111 A4* W Russian Federation
Borrisokane *89 C5* S Ireland
Bosanski Novi *107 B1* Republika Srpska, NW Bosnia and Herzegovina
Boskovice *105 C6* SE Czech Republic
Bosna *107 C2* ≈ N Bosnia and Herzegovina
Bosna I Hercegovina, Federacija *107 C2 republic* Bosnia and Herzegovina
Bosnia and Herzegovina *107 C2* ◆ *republic* SE Europe
Boso-hanto *133 G6 peninsula* S Japan
Bosporus *120 B2 strait* NW Turkey
Bossangoa *72 H5* C Central African Republic
Bossembélé *72 H5* C Central African Republic
Bossier City *39 B5* Louisiana, S USA
Bosten Hu *129 C3* ◎ NW China
Boston *93 F5* E England, United Kingdom
Boston *37 F4 state capital* Massachusetts, NE USA
Boston Mountains *39 B3* ⛰ Arkansas, C USA
Botany Bay *137 H6 inlet* New South Wales, SE Australia
Boteti *76 C5* ≈ N Botswana
Bothnia, Gulf of *83 D4 gulf* N Baltic Sea
Botoșani *109 C5* NE Romania
Botrange *84 E7* ▲ E Belgium
Botswana *76 C5* ◆ *republic* S Africa
Bouar *72 G5* W Central African Republic
Bou Craa *70 B3* NW Western Sahara
Bougainville Island *141 D2 island* NE Papua New Guinea
Bougaroun, Cap *112 D4 headland* NE Algeria
Bougouni *72 C4* SW Mali
Boujdour *70 A3* W Western Sahara
Boulder *47 F5* Colorado, C USA
Boulder *47 D2* Montana, NW USA
Boulogne-sur-Mer *97 D1* N France
Boûmdeïd *72 B3* S Mauritania
Boundiali *72 C4* N Ivory Coast
Bountiful *47 D5* Utah, W USA
Bourail *141 G6* C New Caledonia
Bourbonnais *97 D4 cultural region* C France
Bourg-en-Bresse *97 E4* E France
Bourges *97 D4* C France
Bourgogne *see* Burgundy
Bourke *137 G5* New South Wales, SE Australia
Bournemouth *95 E5* S England, United Kingdom
Boutilimit *72 A3* SW Mauritania
Bowen *137 G3* Queensland, NE Australia
Bowland, Forest of *93 C3 forest* N England, United Kingdom
Bowling Green *39 E3* Kentucky, S USA
Bowling Green *40 E5* Ohio, N USA
Bowman *43 A2* North Dakota, N USA
Boxmeer *84 E5* SE Netherlands
Boyle *89 C3* C Ireland
Boyne *89 E4* ≈ E Ireland
Boysun *125 F3* S Uzbekistan
Bozeman *47 D3* Montana, NW USA
Bozüyük *120 B3* NW Turkey
Brač *107 B3 island* S Croatia
Bradford *93 D4* N England, United Kingdom
Bradford *37 B4* Pennsylvania, NE USA
Brady *44 G4* Texas, SW USA
Brae *91 A6* NE Scotland, United Kingdom
Braemar *91 E4* NE Scotland, United Kingdom
Braga *99 B2* NW Portugal
Bragança *99 C2* NE Portugal
Brahmanbaria *127 G3* E Bangladesh
Brahmapur *127 F5* E India
Brahmaputra *127 H3* ≈ S Asia
Brăila *109 D7* E Romania
Braine-le-Comte *84 C7* SW Belgium
Brainerd *43 E2* Minnesota, N USA
Braintree *95 G3* SE England, United Kingdom
Brampton *35 D6* Ontario, S Canada
Brampton *93 C2* NW England, United Kingdom
Brandberg *76 B5* ▲ NW Namibia
Brandenburg *101 D3* NE Germany
Brandon *33 H7* Manitoba, S Canada
Brandon *89 A6* SW Ireland
Brandon Bay *89 A6 bay* SW Ireland
Brandon Mountain *89 A6* ▲ SW Ireland
Braniewo *105 E2* NE Poland
Brasília *63 G6* ● C Brazil
Brașov *109 C6* C Romania
Bratislava *105 D7* ● W Slovakia
Bratsk *118 F5* C Russian Federation
Braunschweig *101 C4* N Germany
Brava, Costa *99 H2 coastal region* NE Spain
Bravo, Río *53 D2* ≈ Mexico/USA North America
Brawley *49 D9* California, W USA
Bray *89 E4* E Ireland
Brazil *63 C4* ◆ *federal republic* South America
Brazil Basin *14 undersea feature* W Atlantic Ocean
Brazilian Highlands *63 G6* ⛰ E Brazil
Brazos River *44 H4* ≈ Texas, SW USA
Brazzaville *76 B2* ● S Congo
Brechin *91 E4* E Scotland, United Kingdom
Brecht *84 C5* N Belgium
Brecon *93 C6* E Wales, United Kingdom
Brecon Beacons *93 B7* ⛰ S Wales, United Kingdom
Breda *84 D5* S Netherlands
Bree *84 D6* NE Belgium
Bregalnica *107 E3* ≈ E Macedonia
Bremen *101 B3* NW Germany
Bremerhaven *101 B3* NW Germany
Bremerton *49 B2* Washington, NW USA
Brenham *44 H4* Texas, SW USA
Brenner Pass *101 C8 pass* Austria/Italy
Brentwood *95 G3* E England, United Kingdom
Brescia *103 C2* N Italy
Bressanone *103 C1* N Italy
Bressay *91 B6 island* NE Scotland, United Kingdom
Brest *109 B3* SW Belarus
Brest *97 A2* NW France
Bretagne *see* Brittany
Brewton *39 D6* Alabama, S USA
Bria *72 H5* C Central African Republic
Briançon *97 F5* SE France
Bride *93 B3* N Isle of Man
Bridgend *93 B7* S Wales, United Kingdom
Bridgeport *49 C6* California, W USA
Bridgeport *37 E5* Connecticut, NE USA
Bridgetown *57 K6* ● SW Barbados
Bridgetown *89 E6* SE Ireland
Bridgwater *95 D4* SW England, United Kingdom
Bridgwater Bay *95 C4 bay* SW England, United Kingdom
Bridlington *93 F3* E England, United Kingdom
Bridlington Bay *93 F3 bay* E England, United Kingdom
Bridport *95 D5* S England, United Kingdom
Brig *101 B8* SW Switzerland
Brigg *93 E4* N England, United Kingdom
Brigham City *47 D4* Utah, W USA
Brighton *95 F5* SE England, United Kingdom
Brighton *47 F5* Colorado, C USA
Brindisi *103 F6* SE Italy
Brisbane *137 H4 state capital* Queensland, E Australia
Bristol *95 D4* SW England, United Kingdom
Bristol *37 E4* Connecticut, NE USA
Bristol *39 F3* Virginia, NE USA North America
Bristol Bay *50 C2 bay* Alaska, USA
Bristol Channel *95 C4 inlet* England/Wales, United Kingdom
British Columbia *33 E5* ◐ *province* SW Canada
British Indian Ocean Territory *27 UK* ◇ C Indian Ocean
British Isles *78 island group* NW Europe
British Virgin Islands *57 I4 UK* ◇ E West Indies
Brittany *97 B2 cultural region* NW France Europe
Brive-la-Gaillarde *97 C5* C France
Brixham *95 C5* SW England, United Kingdom
Brno *105 C6* SE Czech Republic
Broad Bay *91 C2 bay* NW Scotland, United Kingdom
Broadford *91 C4* N Scotland, United Kingdom
Broad Haven *89 B2 inlet* NW Ireland
Broad Law *91 E6* ▲ S Scotland, United Kingdom
Broadstairs *95 H4* SE England, United Kingdom
Broads, The *95 H2 wetland* E England, United Kingdom
Brockton *37 F4* Massachusetts, NE USA
Brodeur Peninsula *33 H3 peninsula* Baffin Island, Nunavut, NE Canada
Brodick *91 C6* W Scotland, United Kingdom
Brodnica *105 E2* C Poland
Broek-in-Waterland *84 D3* C Netherlands
Broken Hill *137 F5* New South Wales, SE Australia
Bromley *95 F4* SE England, United Kingdom
Bromsgrove *93 D6* W England, United Kingdom
Brookhaven *39 C5* Mississippi, S USA
Brookings *43 D3* South Dakota, N USA
Brooks Range *50 E2* ⛰ Alaska, USA

◐ Administrative region ◆ Country ● Country capital ◇ Dependent territory ○ Dependent territory capital ⛰ Mountain range ▲ Mountain △ Volcano ≈ River ◎ Lake ◻ Reservoir

157

D

◆ Administrative region   ◆ Country   ● Country capital   ◇ Dependent territory   ○ Dependent territory capital   ▲ Mountain range   ▲ Mountain   ▲ Volcano   ↗ River   ☒ Lake   ☒ Reservoir

159

◆ Administrative region　◆ Country　● Country capital　◇ Dependent territory　○ Dependent territory capital　▲ Mountain range　▲ Mountain　▲ Volcano　⌁ River　● Lake　⊡ Reservoir

JAMES BAY

Hatch 44 D3 New Mexico, SW USA
Hatfield 95 F3 E England, United Kingdom
Hattem 84 E3 E Netherlands
Hatteras, Cape 39 I3 *headland* North Carolina, SE USA
Hattiesburg 39 C6 Mississippi, S USA
Hat Yai 131 B5 SW Thailand
Haugesund 83 A5 S Norway
Haukeligrend 83 B5 S Norway
Haukivesi 83 F4 ◎ SE Finland
Hauraki Gulf 139 D2 *gulf* North Island, N New Zealand
Hauroko, Lake 139 A8 ◎ SW New Zealand
Hautes Fagnes 84 E7 ▲▲ E Belgium
Hauts Plateaux 70 D2 *plateau* Algeria/Morocco
Hauzenberg 101 E6 SE Germany
Havana 57 B2 ● W Cuba
Havant 95 F5 S England, United Kingdom
Havelock 39 H4 North Carolina, SE USA
Havelock North 139 E4 North Island, New Zealand
Haverfordwest 93 A7 SW Wales, United Kingdom
Haverhill 95 G2 E England, United Kingdom
Havířov 105 D5 E Czech Republic
Havre 47 D1 Montana, NW USA
Havre-St-Pierre 35 F4 Québec, E Canada
Hawi 51 D2 Hawaii, USA
Hawaii 51 C1 ◐ *state* USA, C Pacific Ocean
Hawai'i 51 D3 *island* USA, C Pacific Ocean
Hawea, Lake 139 B7 ◎ South Island, New Zealand
Hawera 139 D4 North Island, New Zealand
Hawes 93 D3 N England, United Kingdom
Hawick 91 E6 SE Scotland, United Kingdom
Hawke Bay 139 E4 *bay* North Island, New Zealand
Hawthorne 47 A6 Nevada, W USA
Hay 137 F6 New South Wales, SE Australia
Hayden 44 B3 Arizona, SW USA
Hayes 35 A2 ~ Manitoba, C Canada
Hay-on-Wye 93 C6 E Wales, United Kingdom
Hay River 33 G5 Northwest Territories, W Canada
Hays 43 C6 Kansas, C USA
Haysyn 109 D5 C Ukraine
Haywards Heath 95 G4 SE England, United Kingdom
Hazar 125 B3 W Turkmenistan
Hearne 44 H4 Texas, SW USA
Hearst 35 C4 Ontario, S Canada
Hebbronville 44 G6 Texas, SW USA
Hebrides, Sea of the 91 B4 *sea* NW Scotland, United Kingdom
Hebron 123 H6 S West Bank
Heemskerk 84 C3 W Netherlands
Heerde 84 E3 E Netherlands
Heerenveen 84 E2 N Netherlands
Heerhugowaard 84 D3 NW Netherlands
Heerlen 84 E6 SE Netherlands
Hefa *see* Haifa
Hefei 129 G4 E China
Hegang 129 H1 NE China
Heide 101 B2 N Germany
Heidelberg 101 B6 SW Germany
Heidenheim an der Brenz 101 C6 S Germany
Heilbronn 101 B6 SW Germany
Heilong Jiang *see* Amur
Heiloo 84 C3 NW Netherlands
Heimdal 83 B4 S Norway
Hekimhan 121 E3 C Turkey
Helena 47 D2 *state capital* Montana, NW USA
Helensburgh 91 D5 W Scotland, United Kingdom
Helensville 139 D2 North Island, New Zealand
Helgoländer Bucht 101 B2 *bay* NW Germany
Hellevoetsluis 84 C5 SW Netherlands
Hellín 99 E4 C Spain
Hells Canyon 49 D3 *valley* Idaho/Oregon, NW USA
Helmand, Darya-ye 125 D6 ~ Afghanistan/Iran
Helmond 84 E5 S Netherlands
Helmsdale 91 E2 N Scotland, United Kingdom
Helmsley 93 D3 N England, United Kingdom
Helsingborg 83 C7 S Sweden
Helsinki 83 E5 ● S Finland
Helston 95 A6 SW England, United Kingdom
Helvellyn 93 C3 ▲ NW England, United Kingdom
Henderson 47 C7 Nevada, W USA
Henderson 44 H3 Texas, SW USA
Hengduan Shan 129 D5 ▲▲ SW China
Hengelo 84 F4 E Netherlands
Hengyang 129 F5 S China
Heniches'k 109 F6 S Ukraine
Henley-on-Thames 95 F3 C England, United Kingdom
Hennebont 97 B3 NW France
Herat 125 D5 W Afghanistan
Heredia 55 E6 C Costa Rica
Hereford 93 C6 W England, United Kingdom
Hereford 44 F2 Texas, SW USA
Herford 101 B4 NW Germany
Herk-de-Stad 84 D6 NE Belgium
Herm 95 G6 *island* Channel Islands
Herma Ness 91 B5 *headland* NE Scotland, United Kingdom
Hermansverk 83 B5 S Norway
Hermiston 49 C3 Oregon, NW USA
Hermit Islands 141 B1 *island group* N Papua New Guinea
Hermon, Mount 123 H5 ▲ S Syria
Hermosillo 53 B2 NW Mexico
Herrera del Duque 99 C4 W Spain
Herselt 84 D6 C Belgium
Herstal 84 E7 E Belgium
Hessen 101 C5 *state* C Germany
Hessle 93 F4 N England, United Kingdom
Hettinger 43 B3 North Dakota, N USA
Hexham 93 D2 N England, United Kingdom
Hidalgo del Parral 53 D3 N Mexico
Hida-sanmyaku 133 E5 ▲▲ Honshū, S Japan
Hienghène 141 G6 C New Caledonia
High Atlas 70 C2 ▲▲ C Morocco
High Point 39 G3 North Carolina, SE USA
High Willhays 95 C5 ▲ SW England, United Kingdom
High Wycombe 95 F3 SE England, United Kingdom
Higüero, Punta 51 *headland* W Puerto Rico
Hiiumaa 83 D6 *island* W Estonia
Hikurangi 139 D2 North Island, New Zealand
Hildesheim 101 C4 N Germany
Hill Bank 55 B1 N Belize
Hillegom 84 C4 W Netherlands
Hillsborough 89 E2 E Northern Ireland, United Kingdom
Hilo 51 D3 Hawaii, USA, C Pacific Ocean
Hilversum 84 D4 C Netherlands
Himalayas 127 E2 ▲▲ S Asia
Himeji 133 E6 SW Japan
Hims 123 B2 C Syria
Hinchinbrook Island 137 G2 *island* Queensland, NE Australia
Hinds 139 C6 SW New Zealand
Hindu Kush 125 F4 ▲▲ Afghanistan/Pakistan
Hinesville 39 G5 Georgia, SE USA
Hinnøya 83 C2 *island* C Norway
Hinthada 131 A3 SW Burma (Myanmar)
Hirfanlı Barajı 121 C3 ⊠ C Turkey
Hirosaki 133 F3 C Japan
Hiroshima 133 D7 SW Japan
Hirson 97 E2 N France
Hisiu 141 B3 SW Papua New Guinea
Hispaniola 57 F4 *island* Dominion Republic/Haiti
Hitachi 133 G5 S Japan
Hitra 83 B4 *island* S Norway
Hjälmaren 83 C6 ◎ C Sweden
Hjørring 83 B6 N Denmark
Hkakabo Razi 131 A1 ▲ Burma (Myanmar)/China
Hlukhiv 109 E3 NE Ukraine
Hlybokaye 109 C2 N Belarus
Hoang Lien Son 131 C2 ▲▲ N Vietnam
Hobart 137 G7 *state capital* Tasmania, SE Australia
Hobbs 44 E3 New Mexico, SW USA
Hobro 83 B6 N Denmark
Ho Chi Minh 131 C4 S Vietnam
Hocking River 40 F7 ~ Ohio, N USA
Hodeida 123 B6 W Yemen
Hódmezővásárhely 105 E8 SE Hungary
Hodna, Chott El 112 D4 *salt lake* N Algeria
Hodonín 105 D6 SE Czech Republic
Hoeryong 133 C3 NE North Korea
Hof 101 D5 SE Germany
Hofu 133 D7 SW Japan
Hohenems 101 C7 W Austria
Hohe Tauern 101 D8 ▲▲ W Austria
Hohhot 129 F3 N China
Hokianga Harbour 139 C2 *inlet* SE Tasman Sea
Hokitika 139 B6 South Island, New Zealand
Hokkaido 133 F1 *island* NE Japan
Holbrook 44 C2 Arizona, SW USA
Holden 47 D5 Utah, W USA
Holguín 57 D3 SE Cuba
Hollabrunn 101 F6 NE Austria
Holland *see* Netherlands
Holly Springs 39 C4 Mississippi, S USA
Hollywood 39 G8 Florida, SE USA
Holman 33 G3 Victoria Island, Northwest Territories, N Canada
Holmsund 83 D4 N Sweden
Holon 123 G6 C Israel
Holstebro 83 B6 W Denmark
Holt 95 H1 E England, United Kingdom
Holycross 89 D5 S Ireland
Holyhead 93 A4 NW Wales, United Kingdom
Holy Island 93 D1 *island* NE England, United Kingdom
Holyoke 37 E4 Massachusetts, NE USA
Hombori 72 D3 S Mali
Homyel' 109 D3 SE Belarus
Hondo 44 G5 Texas, SW USA
Hondo 55 B1 ~ Central America
Honduras 55 C3 ◆ *republic* Central America
Honduras, Gulf of 55 C2 *gulf* W Caribbean Sea
Hønefoss 83 B5 S Norway
Honey Lake 49 B6 ◎ California, W USA
Hong Gai 131 C2 N Vietnam
Hong Kong 129 H6 S China
Honiara 141 E3 ● C Solomon Islands
Honiton 95 C5 SW England, United Kingdom
Honjo 133 F4 C Japan
Honolulu 51 B1 *state capital* O'ahu, Hawaii, USA
Honshu 133 G5 *island* SW Japan
Hoogeveen 84 E3 NE Netherlands
Hoogezand-Sappemeer 84 F2 NE Netherlands
Hoorn 84 D3 NW Netherlands
Hoover Dam 47 C7 *dam* Arizona/Nevada, W USA
Hopa 121 G2 NE Turkey
Hope 33 D4 British Columbia, SW Canada
Hope 50 E3 Alaska, USA
Hopedale 35 F2 Newfoundland and Labrador, NE Canada
Hopkinsville 39 D3 Kentucky, S USA
Horasan 121 G3 NE Turkey
Horki 109 D2 E Belarus
Horley 95 F4 SE England, United Kingdom
Horlivka 109 G5 E Ukraine
Hormuz, Strait of 123 E4 *strait* Iran/Oman
Horn, Cape 65 B9 *cape* S Chile
Horncastle 93 F5 E England, United Kingdom
Hornsea 93 F4 E England, United Kingdom
Horoshiri-dake 133 G2 ▲ Hokkaidō, N Japan
Horseleap 89 D4 C Ireland
Horsham 137 F6 Victoria, SE Australia
Horsham 95 F4 SE England, United Kingdom
Horst 84 E5 SE Netherlands
Horten 83 B5 S Norway
Horyn' 109 C4 ~ NW Ukraine
Hosingen 84 E8 NE Luxembourg
Hotan 129 B3 NW China
Hotazel 76 C6 N South Africa
Hoting 83 C4 C Sweden
Hot Springs 39 B4 Arkansas, C USA
Houayxay 131 B2 N Laos
Houghton 40 C2 Michigan, N USA
Houghton Lake 40 D4 Michigan, N USA
Houilles 97 C6 N France
Houlton 37 G1 Maine, NE USA
Houma 39 C6 Louisiana, S USA
Houston 44 H4 Texas, SW USA
Hovd 129 C2 W Mongolia
Hove 95 F5 SE England, United Kingdom
Hoverla, Hora 109 B5 ▲ W Ukraine
Hövsgöl Nuur 129 D1 ◎ N Mongolia
Howar, Wadi 75 B2 ~ Chad/Sudan
Howth 89 E4 E Ireland
Hoy 91 E1 *island* N Scotland, United Kingdom
Hoyerswerda 101 E4 E Germany
Hradec Králové 105 C5 N Czech Republic
Hranice 105 D6 E Czech Republic
Hrodna 109 B2 W Belarus
Huaihua 129 F5 S China
Huajuapan 53 F5 SE Mexico
Hualapai Peak 44 A2 ▲ Arizona, SW USA
Huambo 76 B4 C Angola
Huancayo 63 B5 C Peru
Huangshi 129 G4 C China
Huánuco 63 B5 C Peru
Huanuni 65 A2 W Bolivia
Huaraz 63 B5 W Peru
Huatabampo 53 C3 NW Mexico
Hubli 127 D6 SW India
Huch'ang 133 B4 N North Korea
Hucknall 93 D5 C England, United Kingdom
Huddersfield 93 D4 N England, United Kingdom
Hudiksvall 83 D4 C Sweden
Hudson Bay 35 B2 *bay* NE Canada
Hudson River 37 E4 ~ New Jersey/New York, NE USA
Hudson Strait 33 J4 *strait* Northwest Territories/Québec, NE Canada
Hue 131 C3 C Vietnam
Huehuetenango 55 A3 W Guatemala
Huelva 99 B5 SW Spain
Huesca 99 F2 NE Spain
Huéscar 99 E5 S Spain
Hughenden 137 G3 Queensland, NE Australia
Hugo 43 D9 Oklahoma, C USA
Huich'on 133 B4 C North Korea
Huíla Plateau 76 B4 *plateau* S Angola
Huixtla 53 H6 SE Mexico
Hulingol 129 G2 N China
Hull 35 D5 Québec, SE Canada
Hull 93 F4 ~ N England, United Kingdom
Hulst 84 C6 SW Netherlands
Hulun Buir 129 G1 NE China
Hulun Nur 129 F2 ◎ NE China
Humacao 51 E Puerto Rico
Humaitá 63 D4 N Brazil
Humber 93 F4 *estuary* E England, United Kingdom
Humboldt River 47 B5 ~ Nevada, W USA
Humphreys Peak 44 A2 ▲ Arizona, SW USA
Humpolec 105 C6 C Czech Republic
Hunedoara 109 B6 SW Romania
Hünfeld 101 C5 C Germany
Hungary 105 D8 ◆ *republic* C Europe
Hunstanton 95 G1 E England, United Kingdom
Hunter Island 137 F7 *island* Tasmania, SE Australia
Huntingdon 95 F2 E England, United Kingdom
Huntington 39 F2 West Virginia, NE USA
Huntington Beach 49 C9 California, W USA
Huntly 139 D3 North Island, New Zealand
Huntly 91 E3 NE Scotland, United Kingdom
Huntsville 39 E4 Alabama, S USA
Huntsville 44 H4 Texas, SW USA
Huon Gulf 141 B2 *gulf* E Papua New Guinea
Hurghada 70 J3 E Egypt
Huron 43 C3 South Dakota, N USA
Huron, Lake 40 E3 ◎ Canada/USA
Hurunui 139 C6 ~ South Island, New Zealand
Húsavík 83 A1 NE Iceland
Husum 101 B2 N Germany
Hutchinson 43 C6 Kansas, C USA
Huy 84 D7 E Belgium
Hvannadalshnúkur 83 B1 ⛰ S Iceland
Hvar 107 B3 *island* S Croatia
Hwange 76 D5 W Zimbabwe
Hyargas Nuur 129 D2 ◎ NW Mongolia
Hyderabad 127 E5 C India
Hyderabad 127 B3 SE Pakistan
Hyères 97 E7 SE France
Hyères, Îles d' 97 E7 *island group* S France
Hyesan 133 B4 NE North Korea
Hythe 95 H4 SE England, United Kingdom
Hyvinkää 83 E5 S Finland

I

Ialomiţa 109 C7 ~ SE Romania
Iaşi 109 C6 NE Romania
Ibadan 72 E5 SW Nigeria
Ibar 107 D2 ~ C Serbia
Ibarra 63 B3 N Ecuador
Iberian Peninsula 78 *physical region* Portugal/Spain
Ibérico, Sistema 99 E2 ▲▲ NE Spain
Ibiza 99 G4 *island* Balearic Islands, Spain
Ica 63 B6 SW Peru
İçel *see* Mersin
Iceland 83 A1 ◆ *republic* N Atlantic Ocean
Iceland Plateau 143 B6 *undersea feature* S Greenland Sea
Idabel 43 E9 Oklahoma, C USA
Idaho 49 D3 ◐ *state* NW USA
Idaho Falls 47 D3 Idaho, NW USA
Idfu 70 J3 SE Egypt
Idini 72 A2 W Mauritania
Idlib 123 B2 NW Syria
Idre 83 C4 C Sweden
Ieper 84 A6 W Belgium
Iferouâne 72 F2 N Niger
Ifôghas, Adrar des 72 E2 ▲▲ NE Mali
Igarka 118 E3 N Russian Federation
Iglesias 103 A6 Sardinia, Italy
Igloolik 33 I3 Nunavut, N Canada
Igoumenitsa 107 D5 W Greece
Iguaçu, Rio 63 F8 ~ Argentina/Brazil
Iguala 53 F5 S Mexico
Iguazu Falls 65 D4 *waterfall* Brazil/Argentina
Iguidi, 'Erg 70 C3 *desert* Algeria/Mauritania
Ihosy 76 G5 S Madagascar
Iisalmi 83 E4 C Finland
IJssel 84 E4 ~ Netherlands
IJsselmeer 84 D3 ◎ N Netherlands
IJsselmuiden 84 E3 E Netherlands
Ijzer 84 A6 ~ W Belgium
Ikaahuk *see* Sachs Harbour
Ikaluktutiak *see* Cambridge Bay
Ikaría 107 F6 *island* Dodecanese, Greece
Ikela 76 C2 C Dem. Rep. Congo
Iki 133 C7 *island* SW Japan
Ilagan 131 F3 Luzon, N Philippines
Iława 105 E2 NE Poland
Ilebo 76 C2 W Dem. Rep. Congo
Île-de-France 97 D3 *region* N France
Ilford 95 G3 SE England, United Kingdom
Ilfracombe 95 B4 SW England, United Kingdom
Ílhavo 99 B3 N Portugal
Iliamna Lake 50 D2 ◎ Alaska, USA
Iligan 131 F5 S Philippines
Ilkeston 93 E5 C England, United Kingdom
Ilkley 93 D4 N England, United Kingdom
Illapel 65 A5 C Chile
Illichivs'k 109 E6 SW Ukraine
Illinois 40 B7 ◐ *state* C USA
Illinois River 40 B6 ~ Illinois, N USA
Iloilo 131 F4 Panay Island, C Philippines
Ilorin 72 E4 W Nigeria
Ilovlya 111 B7 SW Russian Federation
Imatra 83 F4 SE Finland
Imisli 121 I2 C Azerbaijan
Imola 103 C3 N Italy
Imperatriz 63 G4 NE Brazil
Imperia 103 A3 NW Italy
Imphal 127 H3 NE India
Inagh 89 B5 W Ireland
Inarajan 51 SE Guam
Inarijärvi 83 E1 ◎ N Finland
Inawashiro-ko 133 F5 ◎ Honshu, C Japan
İncesu 121 D4 Turkey
Inch'on 133 B5 NW South Korea
Independence 43 E6 Missouri, C USA
Independence Mountains 47 B4 ▲▲ Nevada, W USA
India 127 D4 ◆ *republic* S Asia
Indiana 37 B5 Pennsylvania, NE USA
Indiana 40 C6 ◐ *state* N USA
Indianapolis 40 D7 *state capital* Indiana, N USA
Indian Church 55 B1 N Belize
Indian Ocean 15 *ocean*
Indianola 43 E5 Iowa, C USA
Indigirka 118 G2 ~ NE Russian Federation
Indonesia 131 C7 ◆ *republic* SE Asia
Indore 127 D4 C India
Indus 127 B3 ~ S Asia
Indus, Mouths of the 127 B3 *delta* S Pakistan
İnebolu 121 D2 N Turkey
Infiernillo, Presa del 53 E5 ⊠ S Mexico
Ingleborough 93 C4 ▲ N England, United Kingdom
Ingolstadt 101 C6 S Germany
Inhambane 76 E6 SE Mozambique
Inishannon 89 C7 S Ireland
Inishbofin 89 A4 *island* W Ireland
Inishcrone 89 C3 W Ireland
Inishkea North 89 A3 *island* NW Ireland
Inishkea South 89 A3 *island* NW Ireland
Inishmore 89 B4 *island* W Ireland
Inishshark 89 A4 *island* W Ireland
Inishtrahull 89 D1 *island* NW Ireland
Inishturk 89 A3 *island* W Ireland
Inn 101 D7 ~ C Europe
Inner Hebrides 91 B5 *island group* W Scotland, United Kingdom
Inner Sound 91 C3 *strait* NW Scotland, United Kingdom
Innisfail 137 G2 Queensland, NE Australia
Innsbruck 101 C7 W Austria
Inowrocław 105 D3 C Poland
I-n-Sakane, 'Erg 72 D2 *desert* N Mali
I-n-Salah 70 D3 C Algeria
Inta 111 E3 NW Russian Federation
Interlaken 101 B8 SW Switzerland
International Falls 43 E1 Minnesota, N USA
Inukjuak 35 D2 Québec, NE Canada
Inuvik 33 F4 Northwest Territories, NW Canada
Inver 89 C2 N Ireland
Inveraray 91 C5 W Scotland, United Kingdom
Inverbervie 91 F4 NE Scotland, United Kingdom
Invercargill 139 B8 Sw New Zealand
Invergordon 91 D3 N Scotland, United Kingdom
Inverness 91 D3 N Scotland, United Kingdom
Inverurie 91 F3 NE Scotland, United Kingdom
Investigator Strait 137 E6 *strait* South Australia
Inyangani 76 E5 ▲ NE Zimbabwe
Ioánnina 107 D5 W Greece
Iola 43 E7 Kansas, C USA
Iona 91 B5 *island* W Scotland, United Kingdom
Iónia Nisiá *see* Ionian Islands
Ionian Islands 107 D5 *island group* W Greece
Ionian Sea 112 G3 *sea* C Mediterranean Sea
Íos 107 F6 *island* Cyclades, Greece
Iowa 43 E5 ◐ *state* C USA
Iowa City 43 F5 Iowa, C USA
Iowa Falls 43 E4 Iowa, C USA
Iowa River 40 A5 ~ Iowa, C USA
Ipel' 105 E7 ~ Hungary/Slovakia
Ipoh 131 B5 W Malaysia
Ippy 72 H5 C Central African Republic
Ipswich 137 H5 Queensland, E Australia
Ipswich 95 H2 E England, United Kingdom
Iqaluit 33 J3 *province capital* Baffin Island, Nunavut, NE Canada
Iquique 65 A3 N Chile
Iquitos 63 C4 N Peru
Irákleio 107 F7 Crete, Greece
Iran 123 E2 ◆ *republic* SW Asia
Iranian Plateau 123 E3 *plateau* N Iran
Irapuato 53 E4 C Mexico
Iraq 123 B2 ◆ *republic* SW Asia
Irbid 123 A2 N Jordan
Ireland 89 C4 ◆ *republic* NW Europe
Irian Jaya *see* Papua
Iringa 75 D7 C Tanzania
Iriomote-jima 133 A8 *island* Sakishima-shoto, SW Japan
Iriona 55 D2 NE Honduras
Irish Sea 87 C6 *sea* C British Isles
Irkutsk 118 F5 S Russian Federation
Iroise 97 A2 *sea* NW France
Iron Mountain 40 C3 Michigan, N USA
Ironwood 40 B2 Michigan, N USA
Irrawaddy 131 A2 ~ W Burma (Myanmar)
Irrawaddy, Mouths of the 131 A3 *delta* SW Burma (Myanmar)
Irtysh 118 D4 ~ C Asia
Irún 99 E1 N Spain
Iruña *see* Pamplona
Irvine 91 D6 W Scotland, United Kingdom
Irvinestown 89 D2 W Northern Ireland, United Kingdom
Isabela, Isla 63 A7 *island* Galapagos Islands, Ecuador
Isabella, Cordillera 55 D4 ▲▲ NW Nicaragua
Isachsen 33 G2 Ellef Ringnes Island, Nunavut, N Canada
Ísafjördhur 83 A1 NW Iceland
Isbister 91 A6 NE Scotland, United Kingdom
Ise 133 F6 SW Japan
Isère 97 E5 ~ E France
Isernia 103 D5 C Italy
Ise-wan 133 F6 *bay* S Japan
Isfahan 123 D2 C Iran
Ishigaki-jima 133 A8 *island* Sakishima-shoto, SW Japan
Ishikari-wan 133 F2 *bay* Hokkaidō, NE Japan
Ishim 118 C4 C Russian Federation
Ishim 118 D4 ~ Kazakhstan/Russian Federation
Ishinomaki 133 G4 C Japan
Ishkoshim 125 G4 S Tajikistan
Isiro 76 D1 NE Dem. Rep. Congo
İskenderun 121 E5 S Turkey
Iskur 107 E3 ~ NW Bulgaria
Iskur, Yazovir 107 E3 ⊠ W Bulgaria
Isla Cristina 99 B5 SW Spain
Islamabad 127 D1 ● NE Pakistan
Islay 91 B6 *island* SW Scotland, United Kingdom
Isle 97 C5 ~ W France
Isle of Man 93 B3 UK ◇ NW Europe
Isle of Wight 95 E5 *island* , United Kingdom
Isles of Scilly 95 A3 *island group* SW England, United Kingdom
Ismoili Somoni, Qullai 125 G3 ▲ NE Tajikistan
Isna 70 J3 SE Egypt
Isoka 76 E3 NE Zambia
Isparta 120 B4 SW Turkey
İspir 121 F2 NE Turkey
Israel 123 G6 ◆ *republic* SW Asia
Issoire 97 D5 C France
Issyk-Kul', Ozero 125 H2 ◎ E Kyrgyzstan
Istanbul 120 B2 NW Turkey
Istra 107 A1 *cultural region* NW Croatia
Itabuna 63 H6 E Brazil
Itagüí 63 B2 W Colombia
Itaipú Dam 65 C4 *dam* Brazil/Paraguay
Itaipú, Represa de 63 F7 ⊠ Brazil/Paraguay
Itaituba 63 F4 NE Brazil
Italy 103 C4 ◆ *republic* S Europe
Ithaca 37 D4 New York, NE USA
Itoigawa 133 F5 C Japan
Iturup, Ostrov 118 I5 *island* Kurile Islands, SE Russian Federation
Itzehoe 101 C2 N Germany
Ivalo 83 E2 N Finland
Ivanhoe 137 F5 New South Wales, SE Australia
Ivano-Frankivs'k 109 B5 W Ukraine
Ivanovo 111 B5 W Russian Federation
Ivoire, Côte d' *see* Ivory Coast
Ivory Coast 72 C5 ◆ *republic* W Africa
Ivujivik 35 D1 Québec, NE Canada
Iwaki 133 G5 N Japan
Iwakuni 133 D7 SW Japan
Iwanai 133 F2 NE Japan
Iwate 133 G3 N Japan
Ixtapa 53 E5 S Mexico
Ixtepec 53 G5 SE Mexico
Iyo-nada 131 D7 *sea* S Japan
Izabal, Lago de 55 B3 ◎ E Guatemala
Izad Khvast 123 D3 C Iran
Izegem 84 B6 W Belgium
Izhevsk 111 D6 NW Russian Federation
Izmayil 109 D7 SW Ukraine
İzmir 120 A4 W Turkey
İzmit 120 B2 NW Turkey
İznik Gölü 120 B2 ◎ NW Turkey
Izu-hanto 133 G6 *peninsula* Honshu, S Japan
Izu-shoto 133 G6 *island group* S Japan

J

Jabal ash Shifa 123 A3 *desert* NW Saudi Arabia
Jabalpur 127 E4 C India
Jaca 99 F2 NE Spain
Jacaltenango 55 A3 W Guatemala
Jackman 37 F2 Maine, NE USA
Jackpot 47 C4 Nevada, W USA
Jackson 43 G7 Missouri, C USA
Jackson 39 D3 Tennessee, S USA
Jackson 39 C5 *state capital* Mississippi, S USA
Jacksonville 39 G6 Florida, SE USA
Jacksonville [illegible] Illinois, N USA
Jacksonville 39 H4 North Carolina, SE USA
Jacksonville 44 H3 Texas, SW USA
Jacmel 57 F4 S Haiti
Jacobabad 127 C3 SE Pakistan
Jaén 99 D5 S Spain
Jaffna 127 E7 N Sri Lanka
Jagdalpur 127 E5 C India
Jagdaqi 129 G1 N China
Jaipur 127 D3 N India
Jaisalmer 127 C3 NW India
Jakarta 131 C7 ● Java, C Indonesia
Jakobstad 83 E4 W Finland
Jalalabad 125 G5 E Afghanistan
Jalandhar 127 D2 N India
Jalapa 55 D3 NW Nicaragua
Jalpa 53 E4 C Mexico
Jalu 70 H3 NE Libya
Jamaame 75 E5 S Somalia
Jamaica 57 C5 ◆ *commonwealth republic* W West Indies
Jamaica Channel 57 E4 *channel* Haiti/Jamaica
Jambi 131 C7 Sumatra, W Indonesia
James Bay 35 C3 *bay* Ontario/Québec, E Canada

◐ Administrative region ◆ Country ● Country capital ◇ Dependent territory ○ Dependent territory capital ▲▲ Mountain range ▲ Mountain ⛰ Volcano ~ River ◎ Lake ⊠ Reservoir

K

◆ Administrative region   ◆ Country   ● Country capital   ◇ Dependent territory   ○ Dependent territory capital   ▲ Mountain range   ▲ Mountain   ▣ Volcano   ≈ River   ◎ Lake   ▨ Reservoir

L

▲ Administrative region   ◆ Country   ● Country capital   ◇ Dependent territory   ◎ Dependent territory capital   ▲ Mountain range   ▲ Mountain   ▲ Volcano   ↝ River   ◎ Lake   ▣ Reservoir

165

LIDKÖPING

Lidköping 83 C6 S Sweden
Lidzbark Warmiński 105 E2 N Poland
Liechtenstein 101 C8 ◆ *monarchy* C Europe
Liège 84 D7 E Belgium
Lienz 101 D8 W Austria
Liepāja 83 E6 W Latvia
Liezen 101 E7 C Austria
Liffey 89 E5 ~ E Ireland
Lifford 89 D2 NW Ireland
Lifou 141 G6 *island* Îles Loyauté, E New Caledonia
Ligger Bay 95 A5 *bay* SW England, United Kingdom
Lighthouse Reef 55 C1 *reef* E Belize
Ligure, Appennino 103 B2 ⛰ NW Italy
Ligurian Sea 103 A3 *sea* N Mediterranean Sea
Lihir Group 141 D1 *island group* NE Papua New Guinea
Lihue 51 B1 Kaua'i, Hawaii, USA
Likasi 76 D3 SE Dem. Rep. Congo
Liknes 83 A6 S Norway
Lille 97 D1 N France
Lillehammer 83 B5 S Norway
Lillestrøm 83 B5 S Norway
Lilongwe 76 E4 ● W Malawi
Lima 63 B5 ● W Peru
Limanowa 105 E5 S Poland
Limassol 112 C6 SW Cyprus
Limavady 89 E1 NW Northern Ireland, United Kingdom
Limerick 89 C5 SW Ireland
Límnos 107 F4 *island* E Greece
Limoges 97 C4 C France
Limón 55 F6 E Costa Rica
Limón 55 D2 NE Honduras
Limon 47 F5 Colorado, C USA
Limousin 97 C5 *cultural region* C France Europe
Limoux 97 D7 S France
Limpopo 76 E5 ~ S Africa
Linares 65 A6 C Chile
Linares 53 E3 NE Mexico
Linares 99 D5 S Spain
Lincoln 93 E5 E England, United Kingdom
Lincoln 37 G2 Maine, NE USA
Lincoln 43 D5 *state capital* Nebraska, C USA
Lincoln Edge 93 E4 *ridge* E England, United Kingdom
Lincoln Sea 143 B4 *sea* Arctic Ocean
Linden 63 E2 E Guyana
Lindi 75 E7 SE Tanzania
Líndos 107 G6 Rhodes, Dodecanese, Greece
Line Islands 135 *island group* E Kiribati
Lingen 101 B3 NW Germany
Lingga, Kepulauan 131 C6 *island group* W Indonesia
Linköping 83 C6 S Sweden
Linnhe, Loch 91 C5 *inlet* W Scotland, United Kingdom
Linton 43 C2 North Dakota, N USA
Linz 101 E7 N Austria
Lion, Gulf of 97 D7 *gulf* S France
Lipari 103 D7 *island* Aeolian Islands, Italy
Lipetsk 111 B6 W Russian Federation
Lira 75 C5 N Uganda
Lisala 76 C1 N Dem. Rep. Congo
Lisboa *see* Lisbon
Lisbon 99 A4 ● W Portugal
Lisburn 89 E2 E Northern Ireland, United Kingdom
Lisdoonvarna 89 B5 W Ireland
Lisieux 97 C2 N France
Liski 111 A6 W Russian Federation
Lisnaskea 89 D3 W Northern Ireland, United Kingdom
Lisse 84 C4 W Netherlands
Listowel 89 B5 SW Ireland
Litang 129 D5 C China
Lithgow 137 G6 New South Wales, SE Australia
Lithuania 83 E7 ◆ *republic* NE Europe
Little Alföld 105 D7 *plain* Hungary/Slovakia
Little Andaman 127 H5 *island* Andaman Islands, SE India
Little Barrier Island 139 D2 *island* N New Zealand
Little Cayman 57 C4 *island* E Cayman Islands
Little Colorado River 47 D7 ~ Arizona, SW USA
Little Falls 43 E3 Minnesota, N USA
Littlefield 44 F3 Texas, SW USA
Littlehampton 95 F5 SE England, United Kingdom
Little Inagua 57 E3 *island* S Bahamas
Little Minch, The 91 B3 *strait* NW Scotland, United Kingdom
Little Missouri River 43 A3 ~ NW USA
Little Nicobar 127 H6 *island* Nicobar Islands, SE India
Little Ouse 95 G2 ~ E England, United Kingdom
Little Rock 39 B4 *state capital* Arkansas, C USA
Little Saint Bernard Pass 97 F5 *pass* France/Italy
Little Sandy Desert 137 B4 *desert* Western Australia
Littleton 47 F5 Colorado, C USA
Littleton 37 F3 New Hampshire, NE USA
Liuzhou 129 F5 S China
Liverpool 35 F5 Nova Scotia, SE Canada
Liverpool 93 C4 NW England, United Kingdom
Liverpool Bay 93 E1 *bay* England/Wales, United Kingdom
Livingston 91 E5 C Scotland, United Kingdom
Livingston 47 D3 Montana, NW USA
Livingston 44 H4 Texas, SW USA
Livingstone 76 D4 S Zambia
Livingstone Mountains 139 A7 ⛰ South Island, New Zealand
Livingston, Lake 44 H4 ⊠ Texas, SW USA
Livojoki 83 E3 ~ C Finland
Livonia 40 E5 Michigan, N USA
Livorno 103 B3 C Italy
Lizard Point 95 A6 *headland* SW England, United Kingdom
Ljubljana 101 E8 ● C Slovenia
Ljungby 83 C6 S Sweden
Ljusdal 83 C4 C Sweden
Ljusnan 83 C4 ~ C Sweden
Llandeilo 93 B7 S Wales, United Kingdom
Llandovery 93 B6 S Wales, United Kingdom
Llandrindod Wells 93 C6 E Wales, United Kingdom
Llandudno 93 B4 N Wales, United Kingdom
Llanes 99 D1 N Spain
Llanos 63 C2 *physical region* Colombia/Venezuela
Llanwrtyd Wells 93 B6 C Wales, United Kingdom
Lleida 99 F2 NE Spain
Lleyn Peninsula 93 A5 *peninsula* NW Wales, United Kingdom
Llucmajor 99 H4 Majorca, Spain
Lobatse 76 D6 SE Botswana
Löbau 101 E4 E Germany
Lobito 76 B4 W Angola
Locarno 101 B8 S Switzerland
Lochboisdale 91 A4 NW Scotland, United Kingdom
Lochdon 91 C5 W Scotland, United Kingdom
Lochem 84 E4 E Netherlands
Lochgilphead 91 C5 W Scotland, United Kingdom
Lochinver 91 C2 N Scotland, United Kingdom
Lochmaddy 91 B3 NW Scotland, United Kingdom
Lochnagar 91 E4 ▲ C Scotland, United Kingdom
Lochy, Loch 91 C4 ◎ N Scotland, United Kingdom
Lockerbie 91 E7 S Scotland, United Kingdom
Lockport 37 C3 New York, NE USA
Lodja 76 C2 C Dem. Rep. Congo
Lodwar 75 D5 NW Kenya
Lodz 105 E4 C Poland
Lofoten 83 C2 *island group* C Norway
Logan 47 D4 Utah, W USA
Logan, Mount 33 E5 ▲ Yukon Territory, W Canada
Logansport 40 D6 Indiana, N USA
Logroño 99 E2 N Spain
Loibl Pass 101 E8 *pass* Austria/Slovenia
Loire 97 C3 ~ C France
Loja 63 B4 S Ecuador
Lokitaung 75 D4 NW Kenya
Lokoja 72 E5 C Nigeria
Lola, Mount 49 B6 ▲ California, W USA
Lolland 83 B7 *island* S Denmark
Lom 107 E2 NW Bulgaria
Lomami 76 D2 ~ C Dem. Rep. Congo
Lomas de Zamora 65 C5 E Argentina
Lombardia *see* Lombardy
Lombardy 103 C2 *cultural region* N Italy
Lombok, Pulau 131 E8 *island* Nusa Tenggara, C Indonesia
Lomé 72 D5 ● S Togo
Lomela 76 C2 C Dem. Rep. Congo
Lommel 84 D6 N Belgium
Lomond, Loch 91 D5 ◎ C Scotland, United Kingdom
Lomonosov Ridge 143 C4 *undersea feature* Arctic Ocean
Lompoc 49 C8 California, W USA
Łomża 105 F2 NE Poland
Loncoche 65 A6 C Chile
London 95 G4 ● SE England, United Kingdom
London 35 C6 Ontario, S Canada
London 39 F3 Kentucky, S USA
Londonderry 89 D2 NW Northern Ireland, United Kingdom
Londonderry, Cape 137 C1 *cape* Western Australia
Londrina 63 F7 S Brazil
Lone Pine 49 C7 California, W USA
Long Bay 39 H4 *bay* North Carolina/South Carolina, E USA
Long Beach 49 C9 California, W USA
Long Eaton 93 E5 C England, United Kingdom
Longford 89 D4 C Ireland
Long Island 57 E2 *island* C Bahamas
Long Island 37 E5 *island* New York, NE USA
Long Island Sound 37 F5 *sound* NE USA
Longlac 35 B4 Ontario, S Canada
Longmont 47 F5 Colorado, C USA
Longreach 137 G3 Queensland, E Australia
Long Strait 118 H1 *strait* NE Russian Federation
Longview 44 H3 Texas, SW USA
Longview 49 B3 Washington, NW USA
Longyan 129 G5 SE China
Longyearbyen 143 C5 ○ W Svalbard
Lons-le-Saunier 97 E4 E France
Loop Head 89 A5 *promontory* W Ireland
Lop Nur 129 C3 *seasonal lake* NW China
Loppersum 84 F2 NE Netherlands
Lorca 99 E5 S Spain
Lorengau 141 B1 Manus Island, N Papua New Guinea
Loreto 53 B3 W Mexico
Lorient 97 B3 NW France
Lorn, Firth of 91 B5 *inlet* W Scotland, United Kingdom
Lörrach 101 B7 S Germany
Lorraine 97 F2 *cultural region* NE France Europe
Los Alamos 44 D2 New Mexico, SW USA
Los Amates 55 B3 E Guatemala
Los Ángeles 65 A6 C Chile
Los Angeles 49 C8 California, W USA
Lošinj 107 A2 *island* W Croatia
Los Mochis 53 C3 C Mexico
Los Roques, Islas 57 H7 *island group* N Venezuela
Lossiemouth 91 E3 NE Scotland, United Kingdom
Los Testigos, Islas 57 J7 *island* NE Venezuela
Lot 97 C5 *cultural region* C France Europe
Lot 97 C6 ~ S France
Lotagipi Swamp 75 D4 *wetland* Kenya/Sudan
Louangphabang 131 B3 N Laos
Loudéac 97 B2 NW France
Loudi 129 F5 S China
Louga 72 A3 NW Senegal
Loughborough 93 E5 C England, United Kingdom
Loughrea 89 C4 W Ireland
Louisburgh 89 B3 NW Ireland
Louisiade Archipelago 141 D3 *island group* SE Papua New Guinea
Louisiana 39 A5 ◐ *state* S USA
Louisville 39 E2 Kentucky, S USA
Louisville Ridge 14 *undersea feature* S Pacific Ocean
Loup River 43 C5 ~ Nebraska, C USA
Lourdes 97 C6 S France
Louth 89 E3 NE Ireland
Louth 93 F4 E England, United Kingdom
Loutrá 107 E4 N Greece
Louvain-la Neuve 84 C7 C Belgium
Louviers 97 D2 N France
Loveland 47 F5 Colorado, C USA
Lovelock 47 A5 Nevada, W USA
Lovosice 105 B5 NW Czech Republic
Lóvua 76 C3 NE Angola
Lowell 47 C2 Idaho, NW USA
Lowell 37 F4 Massachusetts, NE USA
Lower California 53 B3 *peninsula* NW Mexico
Lower Hutt 139 D5 North Island, New Zealand
Lower Lough Erne 89 D2 ◎ SW Northern Ireland, United Kingdom
Lower Red Lake 43 E2 ◎ Minnesota, N USA
Lower Tunguska 118 E4 ~ N Russian Federation
Lowestoft 95 H2 E England, United Kingdom
Loyauté, Îles 141 G6 *island group* S New Caledonia
Lualaba 76 D2 ~ SE Dem. Rep. Congo
Luanda 76 B3 ● NW Angola
Luangwa 76 E4 ~ Mozambique/Zambia
Luanshya 76 D4 C Zambia
Luarca 99 C1 N Spain
Lubaczów 105 G5 SE Poland
Lubań 105 B4 SW Poland
Lubango 76 B4 SW Angola
Lubao 76 D2 C Dem. Rep. Congo
Lübben 101 E4 E Germany
Lübbenau 101 E4 E Germany
Lubbock 44 F3 Texas, SW USA
Lübeck 101 C2 N Germany
Lubelska, Wyżyna 105 F4 *plateau* SE Poland
Lubin 105 C4 SW Poland
Lublin 105 F4 E Poland
Lubliniec 105 D5 S Poland
Lubny 109 E4 NE Ukraine
Lubsko 105 B4 W Poland
Lubumbashi 76 D3 SE Dem. Rep. Congo
Lucan 89 E4 E Ireland
Lucano, Appennino 103 E6 ⛰ S Italy
Lucapa 76 C3 NE Angola
Lucca 103 C3 C Italy
Luce Bay 91 C7 *inlet* SW Scotland, United Kingdom
Lucena 131 F4 Luzon, N Philippines
Lucena 99 D5 S Spain
Lučenec 105 E7 C Slovakia
Lucknow 127 E3 N India
Luda Kamchiya 107 F3 ~ E Bulgaria
Lüderitz 76 B6 SW Namibia
Ludhiana 127 D2 N India
Ludington 40 D4 Michigan, N USA
Ludlow 93 C6 W England, United Kingdom
Ludvika 83 C5 C Sweden
Ludwigsburg 101 B6 SW Germany
Ludwigsfelde 101 D4 NE Germany
Ludwigshafen 101 B6 W Germany
Ludwigslust 101 C3 N Germany
Ludza 83 F6 E Latvia
Luena 76 C3 E Angola
Lufira 76 D3 ~ SE Dem. Rep. Congo
Lufkin 44 I4 Texas, SW USA
Luga 111 A4 NW Russian Federation
Lugano 101 B8 S Switzerland
Luganville 141 G4 C Vanuatu
Lugenda, Rio 76 F4 ~ N Mozambique
Lugnaquillia Mountain 89 E5 ▲ E Ireland
Lugo 99 B1 NW Spain
Lugoj 109 A6 W Romania
Luhans'k 109 G5 E Ukraine
Lukenie 76 C2 ~ C Dem. Rep. Congo
Łuków 105 F4 E Poland
Lukuga 76 D3 ~ SE Dem. Rep. Congo
Luleå 83 D3 N Sweden
Luleälven 83 D3 ~ N Sweden
Lulimba 76 D2 E Dem. Rep. Congo
Lulonga 76 C1 ~ NW Dem. Rep. Congo
Luma 51 E American Samoa
Lumberton 39 H4 North Carolina, SE USA
Lumbo 76 F4 NE Mozambique
Lumi 141 A1 NW Papua New Guinea
Lumsden 139 B7 South Island, New Zealand
Lund 83 C7 S Sweden
Lundy 95 B4 *island* SW England, United Kingdom
Lüneburg 101 C3 N Germany
Lungué-Bungo 76 C4 ~ Angola/Zambia
Luninyets 109 C3 SW Belarus
Lunteren 84 D4 C Netherlands
Luoyang 129 F4 C China
Lurgan 89 E2 S Northern Ireland, United Kingdom
Lúrio 76 F4 NE Mozambique
Lúrio, Rio 76 F4 ~ NE Mozambique
Lusaka 76 D4 ● SE Zambia
Lut, Dasht-e 123 F3 *desert* E Iran
Luti 141 E2 NW Solomon Islands
Luton 95 F3 E England, United Kingdom
Lutselk'e 33 G5 Northwest Territories, W Canada
Luts'k 109 C4 NW Ukraine
Lutzow-Holm Bay 142 D3 *bay* Antarctica
Luuq 75 E4 SW Somalia
Luwego 75 D7 ~ S Tanzania
Luxembourg 84 E9 ● S Luxembourg
Luxembourg 84 E8 ◆ *monarchy* NW Europe
Luxor 70 J3 E Egypt
Luza 111 C4 NW Russian Federation
Luzern 101 B8 C Switzerland
Luzon 131 F3 *island* N Philippines
Luzon Strait 131 F3 *strait* Philippines/Taiwan
L'viv 109 B4 W Ukraine
Lycksele 83 D3 N Sweden
Lyepyel' 109 D2 N Belarus
Lyme Bay 95 C5 *bay* S England, United Kingdom
Lyme Regis 95 D5 S England, United Kingdom
Lymington 95 E5 S England, United Kingdom
Lynchburg 39 G2 Virginia, NE USA
Lynn 37 F4 Massachusetts, NE USA
Lynn Lake 33 H6 Manitoba, C Canada
Lynton 95 C4 SW England, United Kingdom
Lyon 97 E5 E France
Lysychans'k 109 G4 E Ukraine
Lytham St Anne's 93 C4 NW England, United Kingdom
Lyttelton 139 C6 South Island, New Zealand

M

Maamturk Mountains 89 B4 ⛰ W Ireland
Maaseik 84 E6 NE Belgium
Maastricht 84 E6 SE Netherlands
Mablethorpe 93 F4 E England, United Kingdom
Macao 129 G6 S China
Macapá 63 F3 N Brazil
Macclesfield 93 D5 C England, United Kingdom
Macdonnell Ranges 137 D3 ⛰ Northern Territory, C Australia
Macduff 91 F3 NE Scotland, United Kingdom
Macedonia 107 D4 ◆ *republic* SE Europe
Maceió 63 I5 E Brazil
Macgillycuddy's Reeks 89 B6 ⛰ SW Ireland
Machala 63 A4 SW Ecuador
Machanga 76 E5 E Mozambique
Machilipatnam 127 E5 E India
Machynlleth 93 B6 C Wales, United Kingdom
Mackay 137 G3 Queensland, NE Australia
Mackay, Lake 137 D3 *salt lake* Northern Territory/Western Australia
Mackenzie 33 F4 ~ Northwest Territories, NW Canada
Mackenzie Bay 142 E4 *bay* Antarctica
Mackenzie Mountains 33 E4 ⛰ Northwest Territories, NW Canada
Macleod, Lake 137 A4 ◎ Western Australia
Macomb 40 B6 Illinois, N USA
Macomer 103 A6 Sardinia, Italy
Mâcon 97 E4 C France
Macon 39 F5 Georgia, SE USA
Macon 43 F6 Missouri, C USA
Macroom 89 B6 SW Ireland
Macuspana 53 H5 SE Mexico
Ma'daba 123 A2 NW Jordan
Madagascar 76 G5 ◆ *republic* W Indian Ocean
Madang 141 B2 N Papua New Guinea
Made 84 C5 S Netherlands
Madeira, Rio 63 E4 ~ Bolivia/Brazil
Madeleine, Îles de la 35 F4 *island group* Québec, E Canada
Madeline 49 C5 California, W USA
Madera 49 C7 California, W USA
Madhya Pradesh 127 E4 *state* C India
Madison 43 D4 South Dakota, N USA
Madison 40 B4 *state capital* Wisconsin, N USA
Madisonville 39 D2 Kentucky, S USA
Madiun 131 D8 C Indonesia
Madras *see* Chennai
Madre de Dios, Río 65 A1 ~ Bolivia/Peru
Madre del Sur, Sierra 53 F5 ⛰ S Mexico
Madre, Laguna 53 F3 *lagoon* NE Mexico
Madre, Laguna 44 H6 *lagoon* Texas, SW USA
Madre Occidental, Sierra 53 C3 ⛰ C Mexico
Madre Oriental, Sierra 53 E4 ⛰ C Mexico
Madrid 99 D3 ● C Spain
Madrid 99 D3 *cultural region* C Spain
Madurai 127 D7 S India
Madura, Pulau 131 E8 *island* C Indonesia
Maebashi 133 G5 S Japan
Mae Nam Nan 131 B3 ~ NW Thailand
Maéwo 141 G4 *island* C Vanuatu
Mafia 75 E7 *island* E Tanzania
Magadan 118 H3 E Russian Federation
Magarida 141 C3 SW Papua New Guinea
Magdalena 65 B1 N Bolivia
Magdalena 53 B2 NW Mexico
Magdalena, Isla 53 B4 *island* W Mexico
Magdalena, Río 63 B3 ~ C Colombia
Magdeburg 101 D4 C Germany
Magee, Island 89 F2 *island* E Northern Ireland, United Kingdom
Magelang 131 C8 C Indonesia
Magellan, Strait of 65 B9 *strait* Argentina/Chile
Magerøya 83 D1 *island* N Norway
Maggiore, Lake 103 B1 ◎ Italy/Switzerland
Maghera 89 E2 C Northern Ireland, United Kingdom
Maglie 103 F6 SE Italy
Magna 47 D5 Utah, W USA
Magnitogorsk 118 C4 C Russian Federation
Magnolia 39 B4 Arkansas, C USA
Magta' Lahjar 72 B3 SW Mauritania
Magtymguly 125 C3 W Turkmenistan
Mahajanga 76 G4 NW Madagascar
Mahakam, Sungai 131 E6 ~ Borneo, C Indonesia
Mahalapye 76 D5 SE Botswana
Mahanadi 127 F4 ~ E India
Maharashtra 127 D5 *state* W India
Mahbubnagar 127 D5 C India
Mahia Peninsula 139 E4 *peninsula* North Island, New Zealand
Mahilyow 109 D2 E Belarus
Mahmud-e Raqi 125 F5 NE Afghanistan
Mahón 99 H3 Minorca, E Spain
Maidenhead 95 F3 S England, United Kingdom
Maidens, The 89 F2 *island group* E Northern Ireland, United Kingdom
Maidstone 95 G4 SE England, United Kingdom
Maiduguri 72 G4 NE Nigeria
Main 101 C5 ~ C Germany
Mai-Ndombe, Lac 76 C2 ◎ W Dem. Rep. Congo
Maine 97 C2 *cultural region* NW France
Maine 37 F2 ◐ *state* NE USA
Maine, Gulf of 37 G3 *gulf* NE USA
Mainland 91 E1 *island* N Scotland, United Kingdom
Mainland 91 A6 *island* NE Scotland, United Kingdom
Mainz 101 B5 SW Germany
Maitri 142 C3 *Indian research station* Antarctica
Maizhokunggar 129 C4 W China
Majorca 99 H4 *island* E Spain
Makarov Basin 143 C4 *undersea feature* Arctic Ocean
Makassar 131 E7 Celebes, C Indonesia
Makassar Straits 131 E7 *strait* C Indonesia
Makay 76 G5 ⛰ SW Madagascar
Makeni 72 B4 C Sierra Leone
Makhachkala 111 B9 SW Russian Federation
Makiyivka 109 G5 E Ukraine
Makkah *see* Mecca
Makkovik 35 G2 Newfoundland and Labrador, NE Canada
Makó 105 F8 SE Hungary
Makoua 76 B2 C Congo
Makran Coast 123 F4 *coastal region* SE Iran
Makrany 109 B3 SW Belarus
Makurdi 72 F5 C Nigeria
Malabo 72 [illegible] ● Isla de Bioco, NW Equatorial Guinea
Malacca, Strait of 131 B6 *strait* Indonesia/Malaysia
Malacky 105 C7 W Slovakia
Maladzyechna 109 C2 C Belarus
Málaga 99 D6 S Spain
Malahide 89 E4 E Ireland
Malaita 141 F3 *island* N Solomon Islands
Malakal 75 C3 S Sudan
Malang 131 D8 Java, C Indonesia
Malanje 76 B3 NW Angola
Mälaren 83 D5 ◎ C Sweden
Malatya 121 E4 SE Turkey
Malawi 76 E4 ◆ *republic* S Africa
Malay Peninsula 131 B5 *peninsula* Malaysia/Thailand
Malaysia 131 C5 ◆ *monarchy* SE Asia
Malbork 105 E2 N Poland
Malchin 101 D2 N Germany
Malden 43 G7 Missouri, C USA
Malden Island 135 *atoll* E Kiribati
Maldives 127 C9 ◆ *republic* N Indian Ocean
Male 127 C8 ● C Maldives
Malekula 141 G5 *island* W Vanuatu
Malheur Lake 49 C4 ◎ Oregon, NW USA
Malheur River 49 C4 ~ Oregon, NW USA
Mali 72 D3 ◆ *republic* W Africa
Mali Kyun 131 A4 *island* Mergui Archipelago, S Burma (Myanmar)
Malin 89 D1 NW Ireland
Malindi 75 E6 SE Kenya
Malin Head 89 D1 *headland* NW Ireland
Mallaig 91 C4 N Scotland, United Kingdom
Mallawi 70 I3 C Egypt
Mallorca *see* Majorca
Mallow 89 C6 SW Ireland
Malmberget 83 D2 N Sweden
Malmédy 84 E7 E Belgium
Malmö 83 C7 S Sweden
Malone 37 E2 New York, NE USA
Małopolska, Wyżyna 105 F5 *plateau* S Poland
Malozemel'skaya Tundra 111 D3 *physical region* NW Russian Federation
Malta 47 E1 Montana, NW USA
Malta 112 A6 ◆ *republic* C Mediterranean Sea
Malta Channel 103 D9 *strait* Italy/Malta
Malton 93 E4 N England, United Kingdom
Maluku *see* Moluccas
Malung 83 C5 C Sweden
Malvern Hills 93 C6 *hill range* W England, United Kingdom
Mamberamo, Sungai 131 I7 ~ Papua, E Indonesia
Mamonovo 83 D7 W Russian Federation
Mamoré, Rio 65 B1 ~ Bolivia/Brazil
Mamou 72 B4 W Guinea
Mamoudzou 76 G4 ○ C Mayotte
Mamuno 76 C5 W Botswana
Manacor 99 H4 Spain
Manado 131 F6 Celebes, C Indonesia
Managua 55 D5 ● W Nicaragua
Managua, Lake 55 D4 ◎ W Nicaragua
Manakara 76 G5 SE Madagascar
Manama 123 D4 ● N Bahrain
Mananjary 76 G5 SE Madagascar
Manapouri, Lake 139 A7 ◎ South Island, New Zealand
Manas, Gora 125 F2 ▲ Kyrgyzstan/Uzbekistan
Manau 141 C2 S Papua New Guinea
Manaus 63 E4 NW Brazil
Manavgat 121 C5 SW Turkey
Manbij 123 B1 N Syria
Manchester 93 D4 NW England, United Kingdom
Manchester 37 F3 New Hampshire, NE USA
Mandalay 131 A2 C Burma (Myanmar)
Mandan 43 B2 North Dakota, N USA
Mand, Rud-e 123 D3 ~ S Iran
Mandurah 137 B5 Western Australia
Manduria 103 F6 SE Italy
Mandya 127 D6 C India
Manfredonia 103 E5 SE Italy
Mangai 76 C2 W Dem. Rep. Congo
Mangalmé 72 H4 SE Chad
Mangalore 127 D6 W India
Mangerton Mountain 89 B6 ▲ SW Ireland
Mangoky 76 F5 ~ W Madagascar
Manhattan 43 D6 Kansas, C USA
Manicouagan, Réservoir 35 E4 ◎ Québec, E Canada
Manihiki 135 *atoll* N Cook Islands
Manila 131 F4 ● N Philippines
Manisa 120 A3 W Turkey
Manistee River 40 D4 ~ Michigan, N USA
Manitoba 33 H6 ◐ *province* S Canada
Manitoba, Lake 33 H6 ◎ Manitoba, S Canada
Manitoulin Island 35 C5 *island* Ontario, S Canada
Manizales 63 B2 W Colombia
Manjimup 137 B6 Western Australia
Mankato 43 E3 Minnesota, N USA
Manlleu 99 G2 NE Spain
Manmad 127 D4 W India
Mannar 127 E7 NW Sri Lanka
Mannar, Gulf of 127 D8 *gulf* India/Sri Lanka
Mannheim 101 B6 SW Germany
Manokwari 131 H6 E Indonesia
Manono 76 D3 SE Dem. Rep. Congo
Manorhamilton 89 C3 NW Ireland
Manosque 97 E6 SE France
Mansa 76 D3 N Zambia
Mansel Island 33 [illegible] *island* Nunavut, NE Canada
Mansfield 93 E5 C England, United Kingdom
Mansfield 40 E6 Ohio, N USA
Mansfield 37 C4 Pennsylvania, NE USA
Mantova 103 C2 NW Italy
Manua Islands 51 *island group* E American Samoa
Manurewa 139 D2 North Island, New Zealand
Manus Island 141 B1 *island* N Papua New Guinea
Manzanares 99 D4 C Spain
Manzanillo 57 D3 E Cuba
Manzanillo 53 D5 SW Mexico
Manzhouli 129 F1 N China
Mao 72 G3 W Chad
Maoke, Pegunungan 131 I7 ⛰ Papua, E Indonesia
Maoming 129 F6 S China
Maputo 76 E6 ● S Mozambique
Maraa 141 A6 W French Polynesia
Marabá 63 G4 NE Brazil
Maracaibo 63 C1 NW Venezuela

◐ Administrative region ◆ Country ● Country capital ◇ Dependent territory ○ Dependent territory capital ⛰ Mountain range ▲ Mountain Volcano ~ River ◎ Lake ⊠ Reservoir

MOROGORO

Maracaibo, Lake *63 B2 inlet* NW Venezuela
Maradah *70 G3* N Libya
Maradi *72 F3* S Niger
Maragheh *123 C1* NW Iran
Marajó, Baía de *63 G3 bay* N Brazil
Marajó, Ilha de *63 F3 island* N Brazil
Maranhão *63 G4 state* E Brazil
Marañón, Río *63 B4* ≈ N Peru
Marathon *35 B4* Ontario, S Canada
Marathon *44 E4* Texas, SW USA
Maraza *121 I2* E Azerbaijan
Marbella *99 D6* S Spain
Marble Bar *137 B3* Western Australia
Marburg an der Lahn *101 B5* W Germany
March *95 G2* E England, United Kingdom
Marche *97 D4 cultural region* C France
Marche-en-Famenne *84 D8* SE Belgium
Mar Chiquita, Laguna *65 B5* ◎ C Argentina
Marcy, Mount *37 E3* ▲ New York, NE USA
Mardan *127 C1* N Pakistan
Mar del Plata *65 C6* E Argentina
Mardin *121 F4* SE Turkey
Maré *141 G6 island* Îles Loyauté, E New Caledonia
Mareeba *137 G2* Queensland, NE Australia
Maree, Loch *91 C3* ◎ N Scotland, United Kingdom
Marfa *44 E4* Texas, SW USA
Margarita, Isla de *63 D1 island* N Venezuela
Margate *95 H4* SE England, United Kingdom
Margherita, Lake *75 D4* ◎ SW Ethiopia
Margow, Dasht-e *125 D6 desert* SW Afghanistan
Mari *141 A3* SW Papua New Guinea
María Cleofas, Isla *53 C5 island* C Mexico
Maria Island *137 G7 island* Tasmania, SE Australia
María Madre, Isla *53 C4 island* C Mexico
María Magdalena, Isla *53 C4 island* C Mexico
Mariana Islands *15 island group* Guam/Northern Mariana Islands
Mariana Trench *15 undersea feature* W Pacific Ocean
Mariánské Lázně *105 A5* W Czech Republic
Maribor *101 F8* NE Slovenia
Maridi *75 B4* SW Sudan
Marie Byrd Land *142 B5 physical region* Antarctica
Marie-Galante *57 K5 island* SE Guadeloupe
Mariental *76 C6* SW Namibia
Mariestad *83 C6* S Sweden
Marietta *39 E4* Georgia, SE USA
Marietta *40 F7* Ohio, N USA
Marília *63 F7* S Brazil
Marín *99 B2* NW Spain
Maringá *63 F7* S Brazil
Marion *40 B8* Illinois, N USA
Marion *43 F4* Iowa, C USA
Marion *40 E6* Ohio, N USA
Mariscal Estigarribia *65 C3* NW Paraguay
Maritsa *107 F3* ≈ SW Europe
Mariupol' *109 G5* SE Ukraine
Marka *75 F5* S Somalia
Market Harborough *93 E6* C England, United Kingdom
Markham, Mount *142 C5* ▲ Antarctica
Markounda *72 H5* NW Central African Republic
Marktredwitz *101 D5* E Germany
Marmande *97 C5* SW France
Marmara, Sea of *120 A2 sea* NW Turkey
Marmaris *120 A5* SW Turkey
Marne *97 E2 cultural region* N France Europe
Marne *97 E3* ≈ N France
Maro *72 H4* S Chad
Maroantsetra *76 G4* NE Madagascar
Maromokotro *76 G4* ▲ N Madagascar
Maroni *63 F2* ≈ French Guiana/Surinam
Maroua *72 G4* N Cameroon
Marquesas Islands *135 island group* N French Polynesia
Marquette *40 C2* Michigan, N USA
Marrakech *70 C2* W Morocco
Marrawah *137 F7* Tasmania, SE Australia
Marree *137 E5* South Australia
Marsa al Burayqah *70 G3* N Libya
Marsabit *75 D5* N Kenya
Marsala *103 C8* Sicily, Italy
Marsberg *101 B4* W Germany
Marseille *97 E7* SE France
Marshall *43 D3* Minnesota, N USA
Marshall *44 I3* Texas, SW USA
Marshall Islands *135* ◆ *republic* W Pacific Ocean
Marsh Harbour *57 D1* Great Abaco, W Bahamas
Martigues *97 E6* SE France
Martin *105 E6* N Slovakia
Martinique *57 K5 French* ◇ E West Indies
Martinique Passage *57 K5 channel* Dominica/Martinique
Marton *139 D4* North Island, New Zealand
Martos *99 D5* S Spain
Mary *125 D4* S Turkmenistan
Maryborough *137 H4* Queensland, E Australia
Maryland *39 I2* ◐ *state* NE USA
Maryville *43 E5* Missouri, C USA
Maryville *39 F3* Tennessee, S USA
Masai Steppe *75 D6 grassland* NW Tanzania
Masaka *75 C5* SW Uganda
Masan *133 C6* S South Korea
Masasi *75 D7* SE Tanzania
Masaya *55 D5* W Nicaragua
Maseru *76 D6* ● W Lesotho
Mashhad *123 F1* NE Iran
Masindi *75 C5* W Uganda
Masira, Gulf of *123 F5 bay* E Oman
Mask, Lough *89 B4* ◎ W Ireland
Mason *44 G4* Texas, SW USA
Mason City *43 E4* Iowa, C USA
Masqat *see* Muscat
Massa *103 B3* C Italy
Massachusetts *37 F4* ◐ *state* NE USA
Massawa *see* Mits'iwa
Massena *37 D2* New York, NE USA
Massenya *72 G4* SW Chad
Massif Central *97 D5 plateau* C France
Masterton *139 D5* North Island, New Zealand
Masuda *133 D7* SW Japan
Masvingo *76 E5* SE Zimbabwe
Matadi *76 B3* W Dem. Rep. Congo
Matagalpa *55 D4* C Nicaragua
Matale *127 E8* C Sri Lanka
Matamata *139 D3* North Island, New Zealand
Matamoros *53 F3* NE Mexico
Matane *35 F4* Québec, SE Canada
Matanzas *57 B2* NW Cuba
Matara *127 E8* S Sri Lanka
Mataram *131 E8* C Indonesia
Mataró *99 G2* E Spain
Matātula, Cape *51 headland* W American Samoa
Mataura *139 B8* South Island, New Zealand
Mataura *139 B7* ≈ South Island, New Zealand
Matautu *141 B5* C Samoa
Matā'utu *141 K4* ○ N Wallis and Futuna
Mataveri *141 C6* Easter Island, Chile
Matera *103 E6* S Italy
Matías Romero *53 G5* SE Mexico
Matlock *93 D5* C England, United Kingdom
Mato Grosso *63 E6 state* W Brazil
Mato Grosso do Sul *63 E7 state* S Brazil
Matosinhos *99 B3* NW Portugal
Matsue *133 D6* SW Japan
Matsumoto *133 F5* S Japan
Matsuyama *133 D7* Shikoku, SW Japan
Matterhorn *101 B9* ▲ Italy/Switzerland
Matthew Town *57 E3* S Bahamas
Maturín *63 D1* NE Venezuela
Mau *127 E3* N India
Maui *51 D2 island* Hawaii, USA
Maun *76 C5* C Botswana
Mauna Loa *51 D3* ⛰ Hawaii, USA
Mauritania *72 A2* ◆ *republic* W Africa
Mauritius *66* ◆ *republic* W Indian Ocean
Mawlamyine *131 B3* S Burma (Myanmar)
Mawson *142 E4 Australian research station* Antarctica
Maya *55 B2* ≈ E Russian Federation
Mayaguana *57 F3 island* SE Bahamas
Mayaguana Passage *57 E3 passage* SE Bahamas
Mayagüez *57 H4* W Puerto Rico
Maybole *91 D6* W Scotland, United Kingdom
Maych'ew *75 D3* N Ethiopia
Maydan Shahr *125 F5* E Afghanistan
Mayfield *139 C6* South Island, New Zealand
May, Isle of *91 F5 island* E Scotland, United Kingdom
Maykop *111 A8* SW Russian Federation
Maymyo *131 A2* C Burma (Myanmar)
Mayor Island *139 D3 island* NE New Zealand
Mayotte *76 G4 French* ◇ E Africa
Mazabuka *76 D4* S Zambia
Mazar-e Sharif *125 F4* N Afghanistan
Mazatlán *53 D4* C Mexico
Mazury *105 F2 physical region* NE Poland
Mazyr *109 D3* SE Belarus
Mbabane *76 E6* ● NW Swaziland
Mbala *76 E3* NE Zambia
Mbale *75 C5* E Uganda
Mbandaka *76 C2* NW Dem. Rep. Congo
M'Banza Congo *76 B3* NW Angola
Mbanza-Ngungu *76 B2* W Dem. Rep. Congo
Mbarara *75 C5* SW Uganda
Mbé *72 G5* N Cameroon
Mbeya *75 C7* SW Tanzania
Mbuji-Mayi *76 C3* S Dem. Rep. Congo
McAlester *43 D8* Oklahoma, C USA
McAllen *44 G6* Texas, SW USA
McCamey *44 F4* Texas, SW USA
McCammon *47 D4* Idaho, NW USA
McClintock Channel *33 G3 channel* Nunavut, N Canada
McComb *39 C6* Mississippi, S USA
McCook *43 B5* Nebraska, C USA
McDermitt *47 B4* Nevada, W USA
McKinley, Mount *50 D2* ▲ Alaska, USA
McKinley Park *50 E2* Alaska, USA
McLaughlin *43 B3* South Dakota, N USA
McMinnville *49 B3* Oregon, NW USA
McMurdo *142 C6 US research station* Antarctica
McNary *44 D4* Texas, SW USA
McPherson *43 D6* Kansas, C USA
Mdantsane *76 D7* SE South Africa
Mead, Lake *47 C7* ⊠ Arizona/Nevada, W USA
Meadville *37 B4* Pennsylvania, NE USA
Mecca *123 B5* W Saudi Arabia
Mechelen *84 C6* C Belgium
Mecklenburger Bucht *101 C2 bay* N Germany
Mecsek *105 D8* ⛰ SW Hungary
Medan *131 B6* E Indonesia
Medellín *63 B2* NW Colombia
Médenine *70 F2* SE Tunisia
Medford *49 B4* Oregon, NW USA
Medias *109 B6* C Romania
Medicine Hat *33 G7* Alberta, SW Canada
Medina *123 B4* W Saudi Arabia
Medinaceli *99 E3* N Spain
Medina del Campo *99 D3* N Spain
Mediterranean Sea *112 D4 sea* Africa/Asia/Europe
Médoc *97 B5 cultural region* SW France
Medvezh'yegorsk *111 B3* NW Russian Federation
Medway *95 G4* ≈ SE England, United Kingdom
Meekatharra *137 B4* Western Australia
Meerssen *84 E6* SE Netherlands
Meerut *127 D2* N India
Mehtar Lām *125 G5* E Afghanistan
Mejillones *65 A3* N Chile
Mek'ele *75 D2* N Ethiopia
Meknès *70 C1* N Morocco
Mekong *131 C4* ≈ SE Asia
Mekong, Mouths of the *131 C5 delta* S Vietnam
Melaka *131 B6* SW Malaysia
Melanesia *141 G3 island group* W Pacific Ocean
Melbourne *39 G7* Florida, SE USA
Melbourne *137 F6 state capital* Victoria, SE Australia
Melekeok *134* ● N Palau
Melghir, Chott *70 E2 salt lake* E Algeria
Melilla *69 D1* S Spain
Melita *33 H7* Manitoba, S Canada
Melitopol' *109 F6* SE Ukraine
Melle *84 B6* NW Belgium
Melleray, Mount *89 D6* ▲ S Ireland
Mellerud *83 C6* S Sweden
Mellieha *112 B6* E Malta
Mellizo Sur, Cerro *65 A8* ▲ S Chile
Melo *65 D5* NE Uruguay
Melsungen *101 C5* C Germany
Melton Mowbray *93 E5* C England, United Kingdom
Melun *97 D3* N France
Melville Island *137 D1 island* Northern Territory, N Australia
Melville Island *33 G2 island* Parry Islands, Northwest Territories, NW Canada
Melville, Lake *35 G3* ◎ Newfoundland and Labrador, E Canada
Melville Peninsula *33 H3 peninsula* Nunavut, NE Canada
Memmingen *101 C7* S Germany
Memphis *39 C3* Tennessee, S USA
Menai Bridge *93 B5* NW Wales, United Kingdom
Ménaka *72 E3* E Mali
Menaldum *84 D2* N Netherlands
Mende *97 D6* S France
Mendeleyev Ridge *143 C3 undersea feature* Arctic Ocean
Mendi *141 B2* W Papua New Guinea
Mendip Hills *95 D4 hill range* S England, United Kingdom
Mendocino, Cape *49 A5 headland* California, W USA
Mendoza *65 A5* W Argentina
Menemen *120 A3* W Turkey
Menengiyn Tal *129 F2 plain* E Mongolia
Menongue *76 B4* C Angola
Menorca *see* Minorca
Mentawai, Kepulauan *131 B7 island group* W Indonesia
Meppel *84 E3* NE Netherlands
Merano *103 C1* N Italy
Mercedes *65 C4* NE Argentina
Mercedes *44 G6* Texas, SW USA
Meredith, Lake *44 E2* ⊠ Texas, SW USA
Mérida *53 H4* SE Mexico
Mérida *99 C4* W Spain
Mérida *63 C2* W Venezuela
Meridian *39 D5* Mississippi, S USA
Mérignac *97 B5* SW France
Merizo *51* SW Guam
Merowe *75 C2 desert* W Sudan
Merredin *137 B5* Western Australia
Merrick *91 D7* ▲ S Scotland, United Kingdom
Merrimack River *37 F4* ≈ Massachusetts/New Hampshire, NE USA
Mersey *93 C4* ≈ NW England, UK
Mersin *121 D5* S Turkey
Merthyr Tydfil *93 C7* S Wales, United Kingdom
Merton *95 F4* SE England, United Kingdom
Meru *75 D5* C Kenya
Merzifon *121 D2* N Turkey
Merzig *101 A6* SW Germany
Mesa *44 B3* Arizona, SW USA
Messalo, Rio *76 F4* ≈ NE Mozambique
Messina *103 D8* Sicily, Italy
Messina *see* Musina
Messina, Strait of *103 E8 strait* SW Italy
Mestia *121 G1* N Georgia
Mestre *103 D2* NE Italy
Metairie *39 C6* Louisiana, S USA
Metán *65 B4* N Argentina
Metapán *55 B3* NW El Salvador
Meta, Río *63 C2* ≈ Colombia/Venezuela
Métsovo *107 D4* C Greece
Metz *97 F2* NE France
Meulaboh *131 A6* Sumatra, W Indonesia
Meuse *97 E2* ≈ W Europe
Mexborough *93 E4* N England, United Kingdom
Mexicali *53 A1* NW Mexico
Mexico *43 F6* Missouri, C USA
Mexico *53 D3* ◆ *federal republic* N Central America
Mexico City *53 E5* ● C Mexico
Mexico, Gulf of *28 G3 gulf* W Atlantic Ocean
Meymaneh *125 E4* NW Afghanistan
Mezen' *111 C3* ≈ NW Russian Federation
Mezőtúr *105 F8* E Hungary
Mġarr *112 A6* N Malta
Miahuatlán *53 G6* SE Mexico
Miami *39 G9* Florida, SE USA
Miami *43 E7* Oklahoma, C USA
Miami Beach *39 G8* Florida, SE USA
Mianyang *129 E4* C China
Miastko *105 C2* N Poland
Michalovce *105 F6* E Slovakia
Michigan *40 D4* ◐ *state* N USA
Michigan, Lake *40 C4* ◎ N USA
Michurinsk *111 B6* W Russian Federation
Micronesia *135* ◆ *federation* W Pacific Ocean
Mid-Atlantic Ridge *14 undersea feature* Atlantic Ocean
Middelburg *84 B5* SW Netherlands
Middelharnis *84 C5* SW Netherlands
Middelkerke *84 A6* W Belgium
Middle Andaman *127 H5 island* SE India
Middle Atlas *70 C2* ⛰ N Morocco
Middlesboro *39 F3* Kentucky, S USA
Middlesbrough *93 E3* N England, United Kingdom
Middletown *37 D6* Delaware, NE USA
Middletown *37 E5* New Jersey, NE USA
Middletown *37 E4* New York, NE USA
Middlewich *93 C5* W England, United Kingdom
Mid-Indian Ridge *15 undersea feature* C Indian Ocean
Midland *35 D5* Ontario, S Canada
Midland *40 E4* Michigan, N USA
Midland *43 B4* South Dakota, N USA
Midland *44 F3* Texas, SW USA
Midleton *89 C6* SW Ireland
Mid-Pacific Mountains *15 undersea feature* NW Pacific Ocean
Midway Islands *27 US* ◇ C Pacific Ocean
Miechów *105 E5* S Poland
Międzyrzec Podlaski *105 G3* E Poland
Międzyrzecz *105 C3* W Poland
Mielec *105 F5* SE Poland
Miercurea-Ciuc *109 C6* C Romania
Mieres del Camino *99 C1* NW Spain
Mī'ēso *75 E3* C Ethiopia
Miguel Asua *53 D3* C Mexico
Mijdrecht *84 D4* C Netherlands
Mikhaylovka *111 B7* SW Russian Federation
Mikun' *111 D4* NW Russian Federation
Mikura-jima *133 G6 island* E Japan
Milan *103 B2* N Italy
Milano *see* Milan
Milas *120 A4* SW Turkey
Mildenhall *95 G2* E England, United Kingdom
Mildura *137 F5* Victoria, SE Australia
Miles *137 G4* Queensland, E Australia
Miles City *47 F2* Montana, NW USA
Milford Haven *93 A7* SW Wales, United Kingdom
Milford Haven *93 A7 inlet* SW Wales, United Kingdom
Milford Sound *139 A7* South Island, New Zealand
Mil'kovo *118 I3* E Russian Federation
Milk River *33 G7* Alberta, SW Canada
Milk River *47 E1* ≈ Montana, NW USA
Milk, Wadi el *75 B2* ≈ C Sudan
Milledgeville *39 F5* Georgia, SE USA
Mille Lacs Lake *43 E2* ◎ Minnesota, N USA
Millennium Island *135 atoll* Line Islands, E Kiribati
Millerovo *111 A7* SW Russian Federation
Millford *89 D1* NW Ireland
Millville *37 D6* New Jersey, NE USA
Mílos *107 F6 island* Cyclades, Greece
Milton *139 B8* South Island, New Zealand
Milton Keynes *95 F3* SE England, United Kingdom
Milwaukee *40 C4* Wisconsin, N USA
Minas Gerais *63 H7 state* E Brazil
Minatitlán *53 G5* E Mexico
[illegible] W Burma (Myanmar)
Minch, The *91 C2 strait* NW Scotland, United Kingdom
Mindanao *131 G5 island* S Philippines
Mindelheim *101 C7* S Germany
Minden *101 B4* NW Germany
Mindoro *131 F4 island* N Philippines
Mindoro Strait *131 E4 strait* W Philippines
Minehead *95 C4* SW England, United Kingdom
Mineral Wells *44 G3* Texas, SW USA
Mingäçevir *121 I2* C Azerbaijan
Mingaora *127 C1* N Pakistan
Mingulay *91 A4 island* NW Scotland, United Kingdom
Minho *99 B2* ≈ Portugal/Spain
Minicoy Island *127 C7 island* SW India
Minna *72 F4* C Nigeria
Minneapolis *43 E3* Minnesota, N USA
Minnesota *43 D3* ◐ *state* N USA
Miño *99 B2* ≈ Portugal/Spain
Minorca *99 H3 island* Balearic Islands, Spain
Minot *43 B1* North Dakota, N USA
Minsk *109 C2* ● C Belarus
Minskaya Wzvyshsha *109 C2* ⛰ C Belarus
Minto, Lac *35 D2* ◎ Québec, C Canada
Miraflores *53 C4* W Mexico
Miranda de Ebro *99 E2* N Spain
Miri *131 D5* E Malaysia
Mirim Lagoon *65 D5 lagoon* Brazil/Uruguay
Mirjaveh *123 F3* SE Iran
Mirny *142 D5 Russian research station* Antarctica
Mirnyy *118 F4* NE Russian Federation
Mirpur Khas *127 C3* SE Pakistan
Mirtoan Sea *107 E6 sea* S Greece
Miskitos, Cayos *55 F3 island group* NE Nicaragua
Miskolc *105 F7* NE Hungary
Misool, Pulau *131 G7 island* Maluku, E Indonesia
Misratah *70 F2* NW Libya
Mission *43 B4* South Dakota, N USA
Mississippi *39 C5* ◐ *state* SE USA
Mississippi Delta *39 C7 delta* Louisiana, S USA
Mississippi River *39 C4* ≈ C USA
Missoula *47 C2* Montana, NW USA
Missouri *43 E6* ◐ *state* C USA
Missouri River *43 C5* ≈ C USA
Mistassini, Lac *35 D4* ◎ Québec, SE Canada
Mistelbach an der Zaya *101 F6* NE Austria
Misti, Volcán *63 C6* 🌋 S Peru
Mitchell *137 G4* Queensland, E Australia
Mitchell *49 C3* Oregon, NW USA
Mitchell *43 C4* South Dakota, N USA
Mitchell, Mount *39 F3* ▲ North Carolina, SE USA
Mitchell River *137 F2* ≈ Queensland, NE Australia
Mito *133 G5* S Japan
Mitrovicë *107 D3* N Kosovo
Mits'iwa *75 D2* E Eritrea
Mitspe Ramon *123 G7* S Israel
Mitú *63 C3* SE Colombia
Mitumba Range *76 D3* ⛰ E Dem. Rep. Congo
Miyako *133 G3* C Japan
Miyako-jima *133 G6 island* SW Japan
Miyakonojo *133 D8* SW Japan
Miyazaki *133 D8* SW Japan
Mizen Head *89 A7 headland* SW Ireland
Mjøsa *83 B5* ◎ S Norway
Mława *105 E3* C Poland
Mljet *107 C3 island* S Croatia
Moab *47 D6* Utah, W USA
Moa Island *137 F1 island* Queensland, NE Australia
Moala *141 J5 island* S Fiji
Moanda *76 B2* SE Gabon
Moate *89 D4* C Ireland
Moba *76 D3* E Dem. Rep. Congo
Mobaye *72 H5* S Central African Republic
Moberly *43 F6* Missouri, C USA
Mobile *39 D6* Alabama, S USA
Mochudi *76 D6* SE Botswana
Mocímboa da Praia *76 F3* N Mozambique
Môco *76 B4* ▲ W Angola
Mocuba *76 F4* NE Mozambique
Modena *103 C3* N Italy
Modesto *49 B7* California, W USA
Modica *103 D8* Sicily, Italy
Modimolle *76 D6* NE South Africa
Moe *137 F6* Victoria, SE Australia
Moffat *91 E6* S Scotland, United Kingdom
Mogadishu *75 F5* ● S Somalia
Mogilno *105 D3* C Poland
Mogollon Rim *44 B2 cliff* Arizona, SW USA
Mohammedia *70 C1* NW Morocco
Mohawk River *37 D4* ≈ New York, NE USA
Mohoro *75 D7* E Tanzania
Moi *83 A6* S Norway
Mo i Rana *83 C3* C Norway
Mõisaküla *83 E6* S Estonia
Moissac *97 C6* S France
Mojácar *99 E5* S Spain
Mojave *49 C8* California, W USA
Mojave Desert *49 D8 plain* California, W USA
Mokp'o *133 B7* SW South Korea
Mol *84 D6* N Belgium
Mold *93 C5* NE Wales, United Kingdom
Moldavia *see* Moldova
Molde *83 B4* S Norway
Moldo-Too, Khrebet *125 H2* ⛰ C Kyrgyzstan
Moldova *109* ◆ *republic* SE Europe
Molfetta *103 E6* SE Italy
Mölndal *83 B6* S Sweden
Molodezhnaya *142 E3 Russian research station* Antarctica
Moloka'i *51 C1 island* Hawaii, USA
Molopo *76 C6 seasonal river* Botswana/South Africa
Moluccas *131 G7 island group* E Indonesia
Molucca Sea *131 F6 sea* E Indonesia
Mombacho, Volcán *55 D5* 🌋 SW Nicaragua
Mombasa *75 E6* SE Kenya
Møn *83 B7 island* SE Denmark
Monach Islands *91 A3 island group* NW Scotland, United Kingdom
Monaco *97 F6* ● S Monaco
Monaco *97 F6* ◆ *monarchy* W Europe
Monadhliath Mountains *91 D4* ⛰ N Scotland, United Kingdom
Monaghan *89 E3* N Ireland
Monahans *44 E4* Texas, SW USA
Mona, Isla *57 H4 island* W Puerto Rico
Mona Passage *57 H4 channel* Dominican Republic/Puerto Rico
Monbetsu *133 G1* NE Japan
Moncalieri *103 A2* NW Italy
Monchegorsk *111 B2* NW Russian Federation
Monclova *53 E3* NE Mexico
Moncton *35 F5* New Brunswick, SE Canada
Mondovì *103 A3* NW Italy
Moneygall *89 D5* C Ireland
Moneymore *89 E2* C Northern Ireland, United Kingdom
Monfalcone *103 D2* NE Italy
Monforte de Lemos *99 B2* NW Spain
Mongo *72 H4* C Chad
Mongolia *129 D2* ◆ *republic* E Asia
Mongu *76 C4* W Zambia
Monkey Bay *76 E4* SE Malawi
Monkey River Town *55 C2* SE Belize
Monmouth *93 C7* SE Wales, United Kingdom
Mono Lake *49 C7* ◎ California, W USA
Monovar *99 F5* E Spain
Monroe *39 B5* Louisiana, S USA
Monrovia *72 B5* ● W Liberia
Mons *84 C7* S Belgium
Monselice *103 C2* NE Italy
Montana *107 E2* NW Bulgaria
Montana *47 D2* ◐ *state* NW USA
Montargis *97 D3* C France
Montauban *97 C6* S France
Montbéliard *97 F3* E France
Mont Cenis, Col du *97 F5 pass* E France
Mont-de-Marsan *97 B6* SW France
Monteagudo *65 B3* S Bolivia
Monte Caseros *65 C5* NE Argentina
Monte Cristi *57 F4* NW Dominican Republic
Montego Bay *57 D4* W Jamaica
Montélimar *97 E6* E France
Montemorelos *53 E3* NE Mexico
Montenegro *107 C3* ◆ *republic* SW Europe
Monte Patria *65 A5* N Chile
Monterey *49 B7* California, W USA
Monterey Bay *49 B7 bay* California, W USA
Montería *63 B2* NW Colombia
Montero *65 B2* C Bolivia
Monterrey *53 E3* NE Mexico
Montes Claros *63 G6* SE Brazil
Montevideo *65 C6* ● S Uruguay
Montevideo *43 D3* Minnesota, N USA
Montgenèvre, Col de *97 F5 pass* France/Italy
Montgomery *93 C6* E Wales, United Kingdom
Montgomery *39 E5 state capital* Alabama, S USA
Monthey *101 A8* SW Switzerland
Monticello *37 D4* New York, NE USA
Monticello *47 E6* Utah, W USA
Montluçon *97 D4* C France
Montoro *99 D5* S Spain
Montpelier *47 D4* Idaho, NW USA
Montpelier *37 E3 state capital* Vermont, NE USA
Montpellier *97 D6* S France
Montréal *35 E5* Québec, SE Canada
Montrose *91 F4* E Scotland, United Kingdom
Montrose *47 E6* Colorado, C USA
Montserrat *57 J5 UK* ◇ E West Indies
Monywa *131 A2* C Burma (Myanmar)
Monza *103 B2* N Italy
Monze *76 D4* S Zambia
Monzón *99 F2* NE Spain
Moonie *137 G4* Queensland, E Australia
Moora *137 B5* Western Australia
Moore *43 D8* Oklahoma, C USA
Moorea *141 A5 island* Îles du Vent, W French Polynesia
Moore, Lake *137 B5* ◎ Western Australia
Moorhead *43 D2* Minnesota, N USA
Moose *47 D3* Wyoming, C USA
Moose *35 C4* ≈ Ontario, S Canada
Moosehead Lake *37 F1* ◎ Maine, NE USA
Moosonee *35 C4* Ontario, SE Canada
Mopti *72 C3* C Mali
Mora *83 C5* C Sweden
Morales *55 B3* E Guatemala
Morar, Loch *91 C4* ◎ N Scotland, United Kingdom
Moratalla *99 E5* SE Spain
Morava *105 D6* ≈ C Europe
Moravia *105 D6 cultural region* E Czech Republic
Moray Firth *91 D3 inlet* N Scotland, United Kingdom
Moreau River *43 B3* ≈ South Dakota, N USA
Morecambe *93 C3* NW England, United Kingdom
Morecambe Bay *93 C3 inlet* NW England, United Kingdom
Moree *137 G5* New South Wales, SE Australia
Morelia *53 E5* S Mexico
Morena, Sierra *99 C5* ⛰ S Spain
Mórfou *see* Güzelyurt
Morgan City *39 B6* Louisiana, S USA
Morghab, Darya-ye *125 E4* ≈ Afghanistan/Turkmenistan
Moriarty *44 D2* New Mexico, SW USA
Morioka *133 G3* C Japan
Morlaix *97 A2* NW France
Morocco *70 B2* ◆ *monarchy* N Africa
Morogoro *75 D6* E Tanzania

◐ Administrative region ◆ Country ● Country capital ◇ Dependent territory ○ Dependent territory capital ⛰ Mountain range ▲ Mountain 🌋 Volcano ≈ River ◎ Lake ⊠ Reservoir

MORO GULF

Moro Gulf *131 F5 gulf* S Philippines
Morón *57 D3* C Cuba
Mörön *129 D1* N Mongolia
Morondava *76 G5* W Madagascar
Moroni *76 F4* ● Grande Comore, NW Comoros
Morotai, Pulau *131 G6 island* Moluccas, E Indonesia
Morpeth *93 D2* N England, United Kingdom
Morrinsville *139 D3* North Island, New Zealand
Morris *43 D3* Minnesota, N USA
Morris Jesup, Kap *143 C4 headland* N Greenland
Morvan *97 E4 physical region* C France
Moscow *111 B5* ● W Russian Federation
Moscow *47 B2* Idaho, NW USA
Mosel *97 F2* ≈ W Europe
Moselle *97 F3* ≈ W Europe
Mosgiel *139 B7* South Island, New Zealand
Moshi *75 D6* NE Tanzania
Mosjøen *83 C3* C Norway
Moskva *125 F4* SW Tajikistan
Moskva *see* Moscow
Mosonmagyaróvár *105 D7* NW Hungary
Mosquito Coast *55 E4 coastal region* E Nicaragua
Mosquito Gulf *55 G6 gulf* N Panama
Moss *83 B5* S Norway
Mosselbaai *76 C7* SW South Africa
Mossendjo *76 B2* SW Congo
Mossoró *63 I4* NE Brazil
Most *105 B5* NW Czech Republic
Mosta *112 B6* C Malta
Mostaganem *70 D1* NW Algeria
Mostar *107 C2* S Bosnia and Herzegovina
Mosul *123 C2* N Iraq
Mota del Cuervo *99 E4* C Spain
Motagua, Río *55 B3* ≈ Guatemala/Honduras
Motherwell *91 D6* C Scotland, United Kingdom
Motril *99 D6* S Spain
Motueka *139 C5* South Island, New Zealand
Motul *53 H4* SE Mexico
Motu Nui *141 C6 island* Easter Island, Chile
Mouila *76 A2* C Gabon
Mould Bay *33 G2* Prince Patrick Island, Northwest Territories, N Canada
Moulins *97 D4* C France
Moundou *72 G4* SW Chad
Mountain Home *39 B3* Arkansas, C USA
Mountain Home *47 B4* Idaho, NW USA
Mountbellew Bridge *89 C4* C Ireland
Mount Desert Island *37 G3 island* Maine, NE USA
Mount Gambier *137 F6* South Australia
Mount Hagen *141 B2* C Papua New Guinea
Mount Isa *137 F3* Queensland, C Australia
Mount Magnet *137 B4* Western Australia
Mount Pleasant *43 F5* Iowa, C USA
Mount Pleasant *40 D4* Michigan, N USA
Mount's Bay *95 A6 inlet* SW England, United Kingdom
Mount Vernon *40 B7* Illinois, N USA
Mount Vernon *49 B1* Washington, NW USA
Mourne Mountains *89 E3* ⛰ SE Northern Ireland, United Kingdom
Mouscron *84 B7* W Belgium
Moussoro *72 G3* W Chad
Moycullen *89 B4* W Ireland
Mo'ynoq *125 D1* NW Uzbekistan
Moyynkum, Peski *125 G1 desert* S Kazakhstan
Mozambique *76 E5* ◆ *republic* S Africa
Mozambique Channel *76 F5 strait* W Indian Ocean
Mpama *76 B2* ≈ C Congo
Mragowo *105 F2* NE Poland
Mtwara *75 E7* SE Tanzania
Muar *131 B6* W Malaysia
Muck *91 B4 island* W Scotland, United Kingdom
Muckle Roe *91 A6 island* NE Scotland, United Kingdom
Mucojo *76 F4* N Mozambique
Mudanjiang *129 H2* NE China
Muddy Gap *47 E4* Wyoming, C USA
Mufulira *76 D4* C Zambia
Muğla *120 A4* SW Turkey
Muine Bheag *89 E5* SE Ireland
Mukacheve *109 B5* W Ukraine
Mula *99 E5* SE Spain
Muleshoe *44 E2* Texas, SW USA
Mulhacén *99 D5* ▲ S Spain
Mulhouse *97 F3* NE France
Mullaghmore *89 C2* N Ireland
Mullan *89 D3* W Northern Ireland, United Kingdom
Mullaranny *89 B3* NW Ireland
Muller, Pegunungan *131 D6* ⛰ Borneo, C Indonesia
Müllheim *101 B7* SW Germany
Mullingar *89 D4* C Ireland
Mull, Isle of *91 B5 island* W Scotland, United Kingdom
Mulongo *76 D3* SE Dem. Rep. Congo
Multan *127 C2* E Pakistan
Multinational Station *142 A3 multinational research station* Antarctica
Mumbai *127 C5* W India
Münchberg *101 D5* E Germany
München *see* Munich
Muncie *40 D6* Indiana, N USA
Munda *141 E2* NW Solomon Islands
Mungbere *76 D1* NE Dem. Rep. Congo
Munich *101 D7* SE Germany
Munster *101 B4* NW Germany
Munster *89 B6 cultural region* S Ireland
Muonio *83 E2* N Finland
Muonionjoki *83 D2* ≈ Finland/Sweden
Muqdisho *see* Mogadishu
Mur *101 F8* ≈ C Europe
Muradiye *121 H3* E Turkey
Murchison River *137 B4* ≈ Western Australia
Murcia *99 F5* SE Spain
Murcia *99 E5 cultural region* SE Spain
Mureş *109 A6* ≈ Hungary/Romania
Murfreesboro *39 E3* Tennessee, S USA
Murgap *125 D4* S Turkmenistan
Murgap *83 D4* ≈ Afghanistan/Turkmenistan
Murghob *125 H3* SE Tajikistan
Murgon *137 H4* Queensland, E Australia
Müritz *101 D3* ◎ NE Germany
Murmansk *111 C2* NW Russian Federation
Murmashi *111 B2* NW Russian Federation
Murom *111 B5* W Russian Federation
Muroran *133 F2* NE Japan
Muros *99 A1* NW Spain
Murray, Lake *141 A2* ◎ SW Papua New Guinea
Murray River *137 F5* ≈ SE Australia
Murrumbidgee River *137 F6* ≈ New South Wales, SE Australia
Murska Sobota *101 F8* NE Slovenia
Murupara *139 E3* North Island, New Zealand
Mururoa *135 atoll* Îles Tuamotu, SE French Polynesia
Murwara *127 E4* N India
Murwillumbah *137 H5* New South Wales, SE Australia
Murzuq, Idhan *70 F4 desert* SW Libya
Mürzzuschlag *101 F7* E Austria
Muş *121 G3* E Turkey
Musa, Jabal *70 I3* ▲ NE Egypt
Musala *107 E3* ▲ W Bulgaria
Muscat *123 F4* ● NE Oman
Muscatine *43 F5* Iowa, C USA
Musgrave Ranges *137 D4* ⛰ South Australia
Musina *76 D5* NE South Africa
Muskegon *40 D4* Michigan, N USA
Muskegon River *40 D4* ≈ Michigan, N USA
Muskogee *43 E8* Oklahoma, C USA
Musoma *75 C5* N Tanzania
Musselshell River *47 E2* ≈ Montana, NW USA
Musters, Lago *65 A7* ◎ S Argentina
Muswellbrook *137 G5* New South Wales, SE Australia
Mut *121 C5* S Turkey
Mutare *76 E5* E Zimbabwe
Muy Muy *55 D4* C Nicaragua
Mwali *76 F4 island* S Comoros
Mwanza *75 C6* NW Tanzania
Mweelrea *89 A4* ▲ W Ireland
Mweka *76 C2* C Dem. Rep. Congo
Mwene-Ditu *76 C3* S Dem. Rep. Congo
Mweru, Lake *76 D3* ◎ Dem. Rep. Congo/Zambia
Myadzyel *109 C2* N Belarus
Myanmar *see* Burma
Myeik *131 B4* S Burma (Myanmar)
Myingyan *131 A2* C Burma (Myanmar)
Myitkyina *131 B1* N Burma (Myanmar)
Mykolayiv *109 E6* S Ukraine
Mykonos *107 F6 island* Cyclades, Greece
Mýrina *107 F4* Limnos, Greece
Myrtle Beach *39 H4* South Carolina, SE USA
Myślibórz *105 B3* NW Poland
Mysore *127 D6* W India
My Tho *131 C4* S Vietnam
Mytilíni *107 F5* Lesbos, Greece
Mzuzu *76 E3* N Malawi

N

Nā'ālehu *51 D3* Hawaii, USA
Naas *89 E4* C Ireland
Naberezhnyye Chelny *111 D6* W Russian Federation
Nacala *76 F1* NE Mozambique
Nacogdoches *44 I3* Texas, SW USA
Nadi *141 J5* Viti Levu, W Fiji
Nadur *112 A6* N Malta
Nadvoitsy *111 B3* NW Russian Federation
Nadym *118 D3* N Russian Federation
Náfpaktos *107 D5* C Greece
Náfplio *107 E6* S Greece
Naga *131 F4* N Philippines
Nagano *133 F5* S Japan
Nagaoka *133 F5* C Japan
Nagasaki *133 C8* SW Japan
Nagato *133 D7* Honshu, SW Japan
Nagercoil *127 D7* SE India
Nagles Mountains *89 C6* ⛰ S Ireland
Nagorno-Karabakh *121 H2 former autonomous region* SW Azerbaijan
Nagoya *133 F6* SW Japan
Nagpur *127 E4* C India
Nagqu *129 C4* W China
Nagykálló *105 F7* E Hungary
Nagykanizsa *105 C8* SW Hungary
Nagykőrös *105 E8* C Hungary
Naha *133 A8* Okinawa, SW Japan
Nahariya *123 H5* N Israel
Nahuel Huapí, Lago *65 A7* ◎ W Argentina
Nain *35 F2* Newfoundland and Labrador, NE Canada
Nairn *91 D3* N Scotland, United Kingdom
Nairobi *75 D5* ● S Kenya
Najin *133 C3* NE North Korea
Najran *123 C6* S Saudi Arabia
Nakamura *133 E7* Shikoku, SW Japan
Nakatsugawa *133 F6* SW Japan
Nakhodka *118 H6* SE Russian Federation
Nakhon Ratchasima *131 B3* E Thailand
Nakhon Sawan *131 B3* W Thailand
Nakhon Si Thammarat *131 B5* SW Thailand
Nakuru *75 D5* SW Kenya
Nal'chik *111 A8* SW Russian Federation
Nalut *70 F2* NW Libya
Namangan *125 G3* E Uzbekistan
Nam Co *129 C4* ◎ W China
Nam Dinh *131 C2* N Vietnam
Namhae-do *133 B7 island* S South Korea
Namib Desert *76 B5 desert* W Namibia
Namibe *76 B4* SW Angola
Namibia *76 B5* ◆ *republic* S Africa
Nam Ou *131 B2* ≈ N Laos
Nampa *47 B3* Idaho, NW USA
Namp'o *133 A5* SW North Korea
Nampula *76 F4* NE Mozambique
Namsan-ni *133 A4* NW North Korea
Namsos *83 C3* C Norway
Namur *84 D7* SE Belgium
Namwon *133 B6* S South Korea
Nanaimo *33 E7* Vancouver Island, British Columbia, SW Canada
Nanchang *129 F5* S China
Nancy *97 F3* NE France
Nandaime *55 D5* SW Nicaragua
Nanded *127 D5* C India
Nandyal *127 E6* E India
Nangnim-sanmaek *133 B4* ⛰ C North Korea
Nanjing *129 G4* E China
Nanning *129 F6* S China
Nanping *129 G5* SE China
Nansen Basin *143 D4 undersea feature* Arctic Ocean
Nansen Cordillera *143 C4 undersea feature* Arctic Ocean
Nanterre *97 D2* N France
Nantes *97 B3* NW France
Nantucket Island *37 G4 island* Massachusetts, NE USA
Nantwich *93 C5* W England, United Kingdom
Nanumaga *141 I2 atoll* NW Tuvalu
Nanumea Atoll *141 I2 atoll* NW Tuvalu
Nanyang *129 F4* C China
Napa *49 B6* California, W USA
Napier *139 E4* North Island, New Zealand
Naples *103 D6* S Italy
Naples *39 G8* Florida, SE USA
Napoli *see* Naples
Napo, Río *63 B3* ≈ Ecuador/Peru
Naracoorte *137 F6* South Australia
Nara Visa *44 E2* New Mexico, SW USA
Narbonne *97 D7* S France
Nares Strait *33 H1 strait* Canada/Greenland
Narew *105 F3* ≈ E Poland
Narowlya *109 D3* SE Belarus
Närpes *83 D4* W Finland
Närpiö *see* Närpes
Narrabri *137 G5* New South Wales, SE Australia
Narrogin *137 B5* Western Australia
Narva *83 F5* NE Estonia
Narvik *83 D2* C Norway
Nar'yan-Mar *111 D3* NW Russian Federation
Naryn *125 H2* C Kyrgyzstan
Nashik *127 D5* W India
Nashua *37 F4* New Hampshire, NE USA
Nashville *39 D3 state capital* Tennessee, S USA
Näsijärvi *83 E4* ◎ SW Finland
Nassau *57 D2* ● New Providence, N Bahamas
Nasser, Lake *70 J4* ◎ Egypt/Sudan
Nata *76 D5* NE Botswana
Natal *63 I4* E Brazil
Natchez *39 B5* Mississippi, S USA
Natchitoches *39 B5* Louisiana, S USA
Natitingou *72 D4* NW Benin
Natuna, Kepulauan *131 C6 island group* W Indonesia
Nauru *141 G1* ◆ *republic* W Pacific Ocean
Navan *89 E4* E Ireland
Navapolatsk *109 D1* N Belarus
Navarra *99 E2 cultural region* N Spain
Navassa Island *57 D4 US* ◇ C West Indies
Navoiy *125 E3* C Uzbekistan
Navojoa *53 C3* NW Mexico
Navolato *53 C3* C Mexico
Nawabshah *127 B3* S Pakistan
Naxcivan *121 H3* SW Azerbaijan
Náxos *107 F6 island* Cyclades, Greece
Nayoro *133 G1* NE Japan
Nay Pyi Taw *130 A3* ● C Burma (Myanmar)
Nazareth *123 H5* N Israel
Nazca Ridge *14 undersea feature* E Pacific Ocean
Naze *133 B7* SW Japan
Nazilli *120 A4* SW Turkey
Nazret *75 D3* C Ethiopia
N'Dalatando *76 B3* NW Angola
Ndélé *72 H4* N Central African Republic
Ndendé *76 A2* S Gabon
Ndindi *76 A2* S Gabon
Ndjamena *72 G4* ● W Chad
Ndola *76 D4* C Zambia
Neagh, Lough *89 E2* ◎ E Northern Ireland, United Kingdom
Neápoli *107 D4* N Greece
Neápoli *107 E6* S Greece
Near Islands *50 A1 island group* Aleutian Islands, Alaska, USA
Neath *93 B7* S Wales, United Kingdom
Nebaj *55 A3* W Guatemala
Neblina, Pico da *63 C3* ▲ NW Brazil
Nebraska *43 B5* ◐ *state* C USA
Nebraska City *43 D5* Nebraska, C USA
Neches River *44 I4* ≈ Texas, SW USA
Neckar *101 B6* ≈ SW Germany
Necochea *65 C6* E Argentina
Neder Rijn *84 D4* ≈ C Netherlands
Nederweert *84 E6* SE Netherlands
Neede *84 F4* E Netherlands
Needles *49 E8* California, W USA
Neerpelt *84 D6* NE Belgium
Neftekamsk *111 D6* W Russian Federation
Negele *75 E4* C Ethiopia
Negev *123 G6 desert* S Israel
Negombo *127 E8* SW Sri Lanka
Negotin *107 D2* E Serbia
Negra, Punta *63 A4 point* NW Peru
Negro, Río *65 B6* ≈ E Argentina
Negro, Río *63 D3* ≈ N South America
Negros *131 F5 island* C Philippines
Neijiang *129 E5* C China
Nellore *127 E6* E India
Nelson *139 C5* South Island, New Zealand
Nelson *33 H6* ≈ Manitoba, C Canada
Néma *72 C3* SE Mauritania
Neman *83 E7* ≈ NE Europe
Nemours *97 D3* N France
Nemuro *133 H1* NE Japan
Nenagh *89 C5* C Ireland
Nendö *141 G3 island* Santa Cruz Islands, E Solomon Islands
Nene *95 G2* ≈ E England, United Kingdom
Nepal *127 E3* ◆ *monarchy* S Asia
Nepean *35 D5* Ontario, SE Canada
Nephin *89 B3* ▲ W Ireland
Neretva *107 C2* ≈ Bosnia and Herzegovina/Croatia
Neris *109 C2* ≈ Belarus/Lithuania
Nerva *99 C5* SW Spain
Neryungri *118 G4* NE Russian Federation
Neskaupstadhur *83 B1* E Iceland
Ness, Loch *91 D4* ◎ N Scotland, United Kingdom
Néstos *107 E4* ≈ Bulgaria/Greece
Netanya *123 G6* C Israel
Netherlands *84 D3* ◆ *monarchy* NW Europe
Netherlands Antilles *57 G7 Dutch* ◇ S Caribbean Sea
Nettilling Lake *33 I3* ◎ Baffin Island, Nunavut, N Canada
Neubrandenburg *101 D3* NE Germany
Neuchâtel *101 A8* W Switzerland
Neuchâtel, Lac de *101 A8* ◎ W Switzerland
Neufchâteau *84 D8* SE Belgium
Neumünster *101 C2* N Germany
Neunkirchen *101 A6* SW Germany
Neuquén *65 A6* SE Argentina
Neuruppin *101 D3* NE Germany
Neusiedler See *101 F7* ◎ Austria/Hungary
Neustadt an der Weinstrasse *101 A6* SW Germany
Neustrelitz *101 D3* NE Germany
Neu-Ulm *101 C7* S Germany
Neuwied *101 B5* W Germany
Nevada *47 B5* ◐ *state* W USA
Nevers *97 D4* C France
Nevinnomyssk *111 A8* SW Russian Federation
Nevşehir *121 D4* C Turkey
Newala *75 D7* SE Tanzania
New Albany *40 D7* Indiana, N USA
New Amsterdam *63 E2* E Guyana
Newark *37 E5* New Jersey, NE USA
Newark-on-Trent *93 E5* C England, United Kingdom
New Bedford *37 F4* Massachusetts, NE USA
New Bern *39 H3* North Carolina, SE USA
New Braunfels *44 G4* Texas, SW USA
Newbridge *89 C4* W Ireland
Newbridge on Wye *93 B6* C Wales, United Kingdom
New Britain *141 C2 island* E Papua New Guinea
New Brunswick *35 F5* ◐ *province* SE Canada
Newbury *95 E4* S England, United Kingdom
New Caledonia *141 D5 French* ◇ SW Pacific Ocean
Newcastle *137 G5* New South Wales, SE Australia
Newcastle *89 F3* SE Northern Ireland, United Kingdom
New Castle *37 B5* Pennsylvania, NE USA
Newcastle *47 F3* Wyoming, C USA
Newcastle-under-Lyme *93 D5* C England, United Kingdom
Newcastle upon Tyne *93 D2* NE England, United Kingdom
Newcastle West *89 B5* SW Ireland
New Delhi *127 D3* ● N India
New England *37 F3* ◐ *cultural region* NE USA
New Forest *95 E5 physical region* S England, United Kingdom
Newfoundland *35 G4 island* Newfoundland and Labrador, SE Canada
Newfoundland and Labrador *35 G3* ◐ *province* E Canada
New Georgia *141 E2 island* New Georgia Islands, NW Solomon Islands
New Georgia Islands *141 D3 island group* NW Solomon Islands
New Glasgow *35 G5* Nova Scotia, SE Canada
New Guinea *141 A2 island* Indonesia/Papua New Guinea
New Hampshire *37 E2* ◐ *state* NE USA
New Hanover *141 C1 island* NE Papua New Guinea
Newhaven *95 G5* SE England, United Kingdom
New Haven *37 E5* Connecticut, NE USA
New Iberia *39 B6* Louisiana, S USA
New Ireland *141 C1 island* NE Papua New Guinea
New Jersey *37 E5* ◐ *state* NE USA
Newman *137 B3* Western Australia
Newmarket *95 G2* E England, United Kingdom
Newmarket on Fergus *89 C5* W Ireland
New Mexico *44 D2* ◐ *state* SW USA
New Orleans *39 C6* Louisiana, S USA
New Plymouth *139 D4* North Island, New Zealand
Newport *95 E5* S England, United Kingdom
Newport *93 C7* SE Wales, United Kingdom
Newport *39 E1* Kentucky, S USA
Newport *37 F4* Rhode Island, NE USA
Newport *37 F2* Vermont, NE USA
Newport News *39 I2* Virginia, NE USA
Newport Pagnell *95 F3* SE England, United Kingdom
New Providence *57 D1 island* N Bahamas
Newquay *95 A5* SW England, United Kingdom
New Ross *89 E6* SE Ireland
Newry *89 E3* SE Northern Ireland, United Kingdom
New Siberian Islands *118 F2 island group* N Russian Federation
New South Wales *137 F5* ◐ *state* SE Australia
Newton *43 E5* Iowa, C USA
Newton *43 D7* Kansas, C USA
Newton Abbot *95 C5* SW England, United Kingdom
Newton Stewart *91 D7* S Scotland, United Kingdom
Newtown *89 C6* S Ireland
Newtownabbey *89 E2* E Northern Ireland, United Kingdom
Newtown St Boswells *91 E6* S Scotland, United Kingdom
Newtownstewart *89 D2* W Northern Ireland, United Kingdom
New Ulm *43 E3* Minnesota, N USA
New York *37 E5* New York, NE USA
New York *37 C4* ◐ *state* NE USA
New Zealand *139 A5* ◆ *commonwealth republic* SW Pacific Ocean
Neyveli *127 E7* SE India
Ngangze Co *129 B4* ◎ W China
Ngaoundéré *72 G5* N Cameroon
Ngazidja *76 G4 island* NW Comoros
N'Giva *76 B4* S Angola
Ngo *76 B2* SE Congo
Ngoko *72 G6* ≈ Cameroon/Congo
Ngourti *72 G3* E Niger
Nguigmi *72 G3* SE Niger
Nguru *72 F4* NE Nigeria
Nha Trang *131 D4* S Vietnam
Nhulunbuy *137 E1* Northern Territory, N Australia
Niagara Falls *35 D6* Ontario, S Canada
Niagara Falls *37 B3* New York, NE USA
Niagara Falls *37 B3 waterfall* Canada/USA
Niamey *72 E3* ● SW Niger
Niangay, Lac *72 D3* ◎ E Mali
Nia-Nia *76 D1* NE Dem. Rep. Congo
Nias, Pulau *131 A6 island* W Indonesia
Nicaragua *55 D4* ◆ *republic* Central America
Nicaragua, Lake *55 E5* ◎ S Nicaragua
Nice *97 F6* SE France
Nicholls Town *57 D1* NW Bahamas
Nicobar Islands *127 H6 island group* SE India
Nicosia *112 C6* ● C Cyprus
Nicoya *55 D6* W Costa Rica
Nicoya, Golfo de *55 E6 gulf* W Costa Rica
Nicoya, Península de *55 D6 peninsula* NW Costa Rica
Nida *83 E7* SW Lithuania
Nidzica *105 E2* NE Poland
Nieuw-Bergen *84 D3* SE Netherlands
Nieuwegein *84 D4* C Netherlands
Nieuw Nickerie *63 E2* NW Surinam
Niğde *121 D4* C Turkey
Niger *72 E3* ◆ *republic* W Africa
Niger *72 E4* ≈ W Africa
Niger Delta *66 delta* S Nigeria
Nigeria *72 E4* ◆ *federal republic* W Africa
Niger, Mouths of the *72 E5 delta* S Nigeria
Niigata *133 F4* C Japan
Niihama *133 E7* Shikoku, SW Japan
Ni'ihau *51 A1 island* Hawaii, USA
Nii-jima *133 G6 island* E Japan
Nijkerk *84 D4* C Netherlands
Nijlen *84 C6* N Belgium
Nijmegen *84 E4* SE Netherlands
Nikel' *111 B2* NW Russian Federation
Nikiniki *131 F8* S Indonesia
Nikopol' *109 F5* SE Ukraine
Nikšić *107 C3* SW Montenegro
Nile *70 I3* ≈ N Africa
Nile Delta *70 I2 delta* N Egypt
Nimes *97 E6* S France
Nine Degree Channel *127 C7 channel* India/Maldives
Ninetyeast Ridge *15 undersea feature* E Indian Ocean
Ningbo *129 G4* SE China
Ninigo Group *141 A1 island group* N Papua New Guinea
Niobrara River *43 C4* ≈ Nebraska/Wyoming, C USA
Nioro *72 B3* W Mali
Niort *97 C4* W France
Nipigon *35 B4* Ontario, S Canada
Nipigon, Lake *35 B4* ◎ Ontario, S Canada
Niš *107 D2* SE Serbia
Nisko *105 F5* SE Poland
Nísyros *107 G6 island* Dodecanese, Greece
Nith *91 D6* ≈ S Scotland, United Kingdom
Nitra *105 D7* SW Slovakia
Nitra *105 D7* ≈ W Slovakia
Niue *135 Self-governing* ◇ S Pacific Ocean
Niulakita *141 J3 atoll* S Tuvalu
Niutao *141 J2 atoll* NW Tuvalu
Nivernais *97 D4 cultural region* C France
Nizamabad *127 D5* C India
Nizhnekamsk *111 C6* W Russian Federation
Nizhnevartovsk *118 D4* C Russian Federation
Nizhniy Novgorod *111 B5* W Russian Federation
Nizhniy Odes *111 D4* NW Russian Federation
Nizhyn *109 E4* NE Ukraine
Njombe *75 D7* S Tanzania
Nkayi *76 B2* S Congo
Nkongsamba *72 F5* W Cameroon
Nmai Hka *131 B1* ≈ N Burma (Myanmar)
Nobeoka *133 D8* SW Japan
Noboribetsu *133 F2* NE Japan
Nogales *53 B2* NW Mexico
Nogales *44 B4* Arizona, SW USA
Nokia *83 E5* W Finland
Nokou *72 G3* W Chad
Nola *72 G5* SW Central African Republic
Nolinsk *111 C5* NW Russian Federation
Nome *143 B1* Alaska, USA
Noord-Beveland *84 B5 island* SW Netherlands
Noordwijk aan Zee *84 C4* W Netherlands
Nora *83 C5* C Sweden
Norak *125 F3* W Tajikistan
Norddeutsches Tiefland *105 A2 plain* N Germany
Norden *101 B3* NW Germany
Norderstedt *101 C3* N Germany
Nordfriesische Inseln *see* North Frisian Islands
Nordhausen *101 C4* C Germany
Nordhorn *101 A3* NW Germany
Nordkapp *see* North Cape
Nore *89 D5* ≈ S Ireland
Norfolk *43 D5* Nebraska, C USA
Norfolk *39 I2* Virginia, NE USA
Norfolk Island *135 Australian* ◇ SW Pacific Ocean
Norias *44 H6* Texas, SW USA
Noril'sk *118 E3* N Russian Federation
Norman *43 D8* Oklahoma, C USA
Normandie *see* Normandy
Normandy *97 C2 cultural region* N France
Normanton *137 F2* Queensland, NE Australia
Norrköping *83 C6* S Sweden
Norrtälje *83 D5* C Sweden
Norseman *137 C5* Western Australia
Norsup *141 G5* Malekula, C Vanuatu
Northallerton *93 D3* N England, United Kingdom
Northam *137 B5* Western Australia
North America *28 continent*
North American Basin *14 undersea feature* W Sargasso Sea
Northampton *95 F2* C England, United Kingdom
North Andaman *127 H4 island* Andaman Islands, SE India
North Bay *35 D5* Ontario, S Canada
North Berwick *91 E5* SE Scotland, United Kingdom
North Canadian River *44 G2* ≈ Oklahoma, C USA
North Cape *139 C1 headland* North Island, New Zealand
North Cape *83 E1 headland* N Norway
North Carolina *39 F3* ◐ *state* SE USA
North Channel *40 E3 lake channel* Canada/USA
North Channel *91 B6 strait* Northern Ireland/Scotland, United Kingdom
North Charleston *39 G5* South Carolina, SE USA
North Dakota *43 B2* ◐ *state* N USA
Northeim *101 C4* C Germany
Northern Cook Islands *135 island group* N Cook Islands
Northern Dvina *111 C4* ≈ NW Russian Federation
Northern Ireland *87 C5* ◐ *national region* United Kingdom
Northern Mariana Islands *135 US* ◇ W Pacific Ocean
Northern Sporades *107 E5 island group* E Greece
Northern Territory *137 D2* ◐ *territory* N Australia
North Esk *91 E4* ≈ E Scotland, United Kingdom
North European Plain *78 plain* N Europe

◐ Administrative region ◆ Country ● Country capital ◇ Dependent territory ○ Dependent territory capital ⛰ Mountain range ▲ Mountain Volcano ≈ River ◎ Lake ⊡ Reservoir

PARTRY MOUNTAINS

Northfield 43 E3 Minnesota, N USA
North Foreland 95 H3 headland SE England, United Kingdom
North Frisian Islands 101 B2 island group N Germany
North Geomagnetic Pole 143 A4 pole Arctic Ocean
North Island 139 B2 island N New Zealand
North Korea 133 C4 ◆ republic E Asia
Northland 139 C1 cultural region North Island, New Zealand
North Las Vegas 47 B7 Nevada, W USA
North Little Rock 39 C4 Arkansas, C USA
North Platte 43 B5 Nebraska, C USA
North Platte River 43 B5 〰 C USA
North Pole 143 C4 pole Arctic Ocean
North Ronaldsay 91 F1 island NE Scotland, United Kingdom
North Saskatchewan 33 G6 〰 Alberta/Saskatchewan, S Canada
North Sea 78 sea NW Europe
North Siberian Lowland 118 E3 lowlands N Russian Federation
North Sound 89 B4 sound W Ireland
North Sound, The 91 E1 sound N Scotland, United Kingdom
North Taranaki Bight 139 C3 gulf North Island, New Zealand
North Tyne 93 D2 〰 N England, United Kingdom
North Uist 91 A3 island NW Scotland, United Kingdom
North West Highlands 91 C3 ⛰ N Scotland, United Kingdom
Northwest Pacific Basin 15 undersea feature NW Pacific Ocean
Northwest Territories 33 F4 ◐ territory NW Canada
Northwich 93 C5 C England, United Kingdom
Northwind Plain 143 B2 undersea feature Arctic Ocean
North York Moors 93 E3 moorland N England, United Kingdom
Norton Sound 50 D1 inlet Alaska, USA
Norway 83 A4 ◆ monarchy N Europe
Norwegian Sea 83 A4 sea NE Atlantic Ocean
Norwich 95 H2 E England, United Kingdom
Noshiro 133 F3 C Japan
Nosop 76 C6 〰 E Namibia
Noteć 105 D3 〰 NW Poland
Nottingham 93 E5 C England, United Kingdom
Nouâdhibou 72 A2 W Mauritania
Nouakchott 72 A2 ● SW Mauritania
Nouméa 141 G6 ○ S New Caledonia
Nova Gorica 101 E8 W Slovenia
Nova Iguaçu 63 G7 SE Brazil
Novara 103 B2 NW Italy
Nova Scotia 37 H2 ◐ province SE Canada
Novaya Sibir', Ostrov 118 G2 island NE Russian Federation
Novaya Zemlya 111 E1 island group N Russian Federation
Novi Sad 107 D1 N Serbia
Novoazovs'k 109 G5 E Ukraine
Novocheboksarsk 111 C6 W Russian Federation
Novocherkassk 111 A7 SW Russian Federation
Novodvinsk 111 C3 NW Russian Federation
Novokuznetsk 118 E5 S Russian Federation
Novolazarevskaya 142 C3 Russian research station Antarctica
Novo mesto 101 E9 SE Slovenia
Novomoskovsk 111 B6 W Russian Federation
Novomoskovs'k 109 F5 E Ukraine
Novorossiysk 111 A8 SW Russian Federation
Novoshakhtinsk 111 A7 SW Russian Federation
Novosibirsk 118 D5 C Russian Federation
Novotroitsk 111 D7 W Russian Federation
Novyy Buh 109 E5 S Ukraine
Nowogard 105 C2 NW Poland
Nowy Dwór Mazowiecki 105 E3 C Poland
Nowy Sącz 105 F6 S Poland
Nowy Tomyśl 105 C3 C Poland
[illegible]
Ntomba, Lac 76 B2 ◎ NW Dem. Rep. Congo
Nubian Desert 75 C1 desert NE Sudan
Nueces River 44 G5 〰 Texas, SW USA
Nueva Gerona 57 B3 NW Cuba
Nueva Guinea 55 E5 SE Nicaragua
Nueva Ocotepeque 55 B3 W Honduras
Nueva Rosita 53 E2 NE Mexico
Nuevitas 57 D3 E Cuba
Nuevo Casas Grandes 53 C2 N Mexico
Nuevo, Golfo 65 B7 gulf S Argentina
Nuevo Laredo 53 E2 NE Mexico
Nui Atoll 141 I2 atoll W Tuvalu
Nuku'alofa 135 ● Tongatapu, S Tonga
Nukufetau Atoll 141 I2 atoll C Tuvalu
Nukulaelae Atoll 141 J3 atoll E Tuvalu
Nukumanu Islands 141 E1 island group NE Papua New Guinea
Nukus 125 D2 W Uzbekistan
Nullarbor Plain 137 D5 plateau South Australia/Western Australia
Nunavut 33 H4 ◐ territory N Canada
Nuneaton 93 D6 C England, United Kingdom
Nunivak Island 50 C2 island Alaska, USA
Nunspeet 84 E4 E Netherlands
Nuoro 103 A6 Sardinia, Italy
Nuremberg 101 C6 S Germany
Nurmes 83 F4 E Finland
Nürnberg see Nuremberg
Nurota 125 E3 C Uzbekistan
Nusaybin 121 G4 SE Turkey
Nyagan' 118 D3 N Russian Federation
Nyainqentanglha Shan 129 C4 ⛰ W China
Nyala 75 B3 W Sudan
Nyamtumbo 75 D7 S Tanzania
Nyandoma 111 B4 NW Russian Federation
Nyantakara 75 C6 NW Tanzania
Nyasa, Lake 76 E4 ◎ Malawi/Mozambique/Tanzania/Zambia
Nyeri 75 D5 C Kenya
Nyíregyháza 105 F7 NE Hungary
Nykobing 83 B7 SE Denmark
Nyköping 83 D6 S Sweden
Nylstroom see Modimolle
Nyngan 137 G5 New South Wales, SE Australia
Nyurba 118 F4 NE Russian Federation
Nzega 75 C6 C Tanzania
Nzérékoré 72 B5 SE Guinea
N'Zeto 76 B3 NW Angola

O

Oahe, Lake 43 C3 ⊡ North Dakota/South Dakota, N USA
Oa'hu 51 B1 island Hawai'ian Islands, Hawaii, USA
Oakham 93 E5 C England, United Kingdom
Oak Harbor 49 B2 Washington, NW USA
Oakland 49 B7 California, W USA
Oakley 43 B6 Kansas, C USA
Oamaru 139 B7 South Island, New Zealand
Oa, Mull of 91 B6 headland W Scotland, United Kingdom
Oaxaca 53 F5 SE Mexico
Ob' 118 D3 〰 C Russian Federation
Oban 91 C5 W Scotland, United Kingdom
Ob', Gulf of 118 D3 gulf N Russian Federation
Obihiro 133 G2 NE Japan
Obo 72 I5 E Central African Republic
Obock 75 E3 E Djibouti
Oborniki 105 C3 W Poland
Ocala 39 F7 Florida, SE USA
Ocaña 99 D3 C Spain
O Carballiño 99 B2 NW Spain
Occidental, Cordillera 65 A2 ⛰ Bolivia/Chile
Ocean Falls 33 E6 British Columbia, SW Canada
Oceanside 49 D9 California, W USA
Och'amch'ire 121 G1 W Georgia
Ochil Hills 91 E5 ⛰ C Scotland, United Kingdom
Ocotal 55 D4 NW Nicaragua
Ocozocuautla 53 G5 SE Mexico
October Revolution Island 118 F2 island N Russian Federation
Ocú 55 G7 S Panama
Odate 133 G3 C Japan
Ödemiş 120 A4 SW Turkey
Odense 83 B7 C Denmark
Oder 101 E3 〰 C Europe
Oderhaff 105 B2 bay Germany/Poland
Odesa 109 E6 SW Ukraine
Odessa 44 F4 Texas, SW USA
Odienné 72 C4 NW Ivory Coast
Odoorn 84 F2 NE Netherlands
Odra see Oder
Of 121 F2 NE Turkey
Ofanto 103 E6 〰 S Italy
Offenbach 101 B5 W Germany
Offenburg 101 B7 SW Germany
Ofu 51 island E American Samoa
Ogaden 75 F4 plateau Ethiopia/Somalia
Ogaki 133 F6 SW Japan
Ogallala 43 B5 Nebraska, C USA
Ogbomosho 72 E5 W Nigeria
Ogden 47 D5 Utah, W USA
Ogdensburg 37 D2 New York, NE USA
Ohio 40 E6 ◐ state N USA
Ohio River 40 F7 〰 N USA
Ohrid, Lake 107 D4 ◎ Albania/Macedonia
Ohura 139 D3 North Island, New Zealand
Oil City [illegible] Pennsylvania, NE USA
Oirschot 84 D5 S Netherlands
Oise 97 D2 〰 N France
Oita 133 D7 Kyushu, SW Japan
Ojinaga 53 D2 N Mexico
Ojos del Salado, Cerro 65 A4 ▲ W Argentina
Okaihau 139 C1 North Island, New Zealand
Okanogan River 49 C1 〰 Washington, NW USA
Okara 127 D2 E Pakistan
Okavango 76 C5 〰 S Africa
Okavango Delta 76 C5 wetland N Botswana
Okayama 133 E6 SW Japan
Okazaki 133 F6 C Japan
Okeechobee, Lake 39 F8 ◎ Florida, SE USA
Okefenokee Swamp 39 F6 wetland Georgia, SE USA
Okehampton 95 C5 SW England, United Kingdom
Okhotsk 118 H3 E Russian Federation
Okhotsk, Sea of 118 H4 sea NW Pacific Ocean
Okhtyrka 109 F4 NE Ukraine
Okinawa 133 A8 SW Japan
Okinawa-shoto 133 A8 island group SW Japan
Oki-shoto 133 D6 island group SW Japan
Oklahoma 43 C8 ◐ state C USA
Oklahoma City 43 D8 state capital Oklahoma, C USA
Okmulgee 43 D8 Oklahoma, C USA
Oko, Wadi 75 D1 〰 NE Sudan
Oktyabr'skiy 111 D6 SW Russian Federation
Okushiri-to 133 F2 island NE Japan
Öland 83 D7 island S Sweden
Olavarría 65 C6 E Argentina
Oława 105 D4 SW Poland
Olbia 103 B5 Sardinia, Italy
Oldebroek 84 E3 E Netherlands
Oldenburg 101 B3 NW Germany
Oldenburg 101 C2 N Germany
Oldenzaal 84 F4 E Netherlands
Oldham 93 D4 NW England, United Kingdom
Old Head of Kinsale 89 C7 headland SW Ireland
Olëkma 118 G4 〰 C Russian Federation
Olëkminsk 118 G4 NE Russian Federation
Oleksandriya 109 E5 C Ukraine
Olenegorsk 111 B2 NW Russian Federation
Olenek 118 F3 NE Russian Federation
Olenëk 118 F3 〰 NE Russian Federation
Oléron, Île d' 97 B4 island W France
Olevs'k 109 C4 N Ukraine
Ölgiy 129 C1 W Mongolia
Olhão 99 B5 S Portugal
Olifa 76 B4 NW Namibia
Oliva 99 F4 E Spain
Olivet 97 D3 C France
Olmaliq 125 F3 E Uzbekistan
Olomouc 105 D6 E Czech Republic
Olonets 111 B4 NW Russian Federation
Olosega 51 island E American Samoa
Olovyannaya 118 G5 S Russian Federation
Olpe 101 B5 W Germany
Olsztyn 105 E2 N Poland
Olt 109 B7 〰 S Romania
Olvera 99 C6 SW Spain
Olympia 49 B2 state capital Washington, NW USA
Olympic Mountains 49 A2 ⛰ Washington, NW USA
Olympus, Mount 107 D4 ▲ N Greece
Omagh 89 D2 W Northern Ireland, United Kingdom
Omaha 43 D5 Nebraska, C USA
Oman 123 E6 ◆ monarchy SW Asia
Oman, Gulf of 123 F4 gulf N Arabian Sea
Omboué 76 A2 W Gabon
Omdurman 75 C2 C Sudan
Ometepe, Isla de 55 D5 island S Nicaragua
Ommen 84 E3 E Netherlands
Omsk 118 D5 C Russian Federation
Omuta 133 D7 SW Japan
Onda 99 F3 E Spain
Öndörhaan 129 F2 E Mongolia
Onega 111 B3 NW Russian Federation
Onega 111 B4 〰 NW Russian Federation
Onega, Lake 111 B4 ◎ NW Russian Federation
Oneida Lake 37 D3 ◎ New York, NE USA
O'Neill 43 C4 Nebraska, C USA
Oneonta 37 D4 New York, NE USA
Onex 101 A8 SW Switzerland
Ongjin 133 A5 SW North Korea
Ongole 127 E6 E India
Onitsha 72 F5 S Nigeria
Onon Gol 129 F2 〰 N Mongolia
Onslow 137 A3 Western Australia
Onslow Bay 39 H4 bay North Carolina, E USA
Ontario 35 B4 ◐ province S Canada
Ontario, Lake 37 C3 ◎ Canada/USA
Ontinyent 99 F4 E Spain
Ontong Java Atoll 141 E2 atoll N Solomon Islands
Oostakker 84 B6 NW Belgium
Oostburg 84 B5 SW Netherlands
Oostende see Ostend
Oosterbeek 84 E4 SE Netherlands
Oosterhout 84 D5 S Netherlands
Opava 105 D5 E Czech Republic
Opelika [illegible] Alabama, S USA
Opelousas 39 B6 Louisiana, S USA
Opmeer 84 D3 NW Netherlands
Opochka 111 A4 W Russian Federation
Opole 105 D5 S Poland
Oporto 99 B3 NW Portugal
Opotiki 139 E3 North Island, New Zealand
Oqtosh 125 E3 C Uzbekistan
Oradea 109 B6 NW Romania
Oran 70 D1 NW Algeria
Orange 137 G5 New South Wales, SE Australia
Orange 97 E6 SE France
Orangeburg 39 G4 South Carolina, SE USA
Orange River 76 C6 〰 S Africa
Orange Walk 55 C1 N Belize
Oranienburg 101 D3 NE Germany
Oranjemund 76 B6 SW Namibia
Oranjestad 57 G7 ○ W Aruba
Oranmore 89 C4 W Ireland
Orbetello 103 C4 C Italy
Orcadas 142 A2 Argentinian research station South Orkney Islands, Antarctica
Orchard Homes 47 C2 Montana, NW USA
Ord River 137 D2 〰 N Australia Oceania
Ordu 121 E2 N Turkey
Örebro 83 C5 C Sweden
Oregon 49 B4 ◐ state NW USA
Oregon City 49 B3 Oregon, NW USA
Orël 111 A6 W Russian Federation
Orem 47 D5 Utah, W USA
Ore Mountains 101 D5 ⛰ Czech Republic/Germany
Orenburg 111 D7 W Russian Federation
Orense see Ourense
Orford Ness 95 H2 cape E England, United Kingdom
Organ Peak 44 D3 ▲ New Mexico, SW USA
Oriental, Cordillera 65 B3 ⛰ Bolivia/Peru
Orihuela 99 F5 E Spain
Orikhiv 109 F5 SE Ukraine
Orin 47 F4 Wyoming, C USA
Orinoco, Río 63 D2 〰 Colombia/Venezuela
Oriomo 141 A3 SW Papua New Guinea
Orissa 127 F5 state NE India
Oristano 103 A6 Sardinia, Italy
Orkney Islands 91 D1 island group N Scotland, United Kingdom
Orlando 39 G7 Florida, SE USA
Orléanais 97 D3 cultural region C France
Orléans 97 D3 C France
Orleans 37 G4 Massachusetts, NE USA
Ormskirk 93 C4 NW England, United Kingdom
Örnsköldsvik 83 D4 C Sweden
Orohena, Mont 141 B6 🌋 Tahiti, W French Polynesia
Oromocto 35 F5 New Brunswick, SE Canada
Orsha 109 D2 NE Belarus
Orsk 111 D7 W Russian Federation
Orthez 97 B6 SW France
Ortona 103 D5 C Italy
Oruro 65 A2 W Bolivia
Orwell 95 H2 〰 E England, United Kingdom
Osaka 133 E6 SW Japan
Osa, Península de 55 E7 peninsula S Costa Rica
Osborne 43 C6 Kansas, C USA
Osh 125 G3 SW Kyrgyzstan
Oshakati 76 B5 N Namibia
Oshawa 35 D6 Ontario, SE Canada
Oshikango 76 B4 N Namibia
O-shima 133 G6 island S Japan
Oshkosh 40 C4 Wisconsin, N USA
Osijek 107 C1 E Croatia
Oskaloosa 43 F5 Iowa, C USA
Oskarshamn 83 C6 S Sweden
Oslo 83 B5 ● S Norway
Osmaniye 121 E5 S Turkey
Osnabrück 101 B4 NW Germany
Osorno 65 A7 C Chile
Oss 84 D5 S Netherlands
Ossa, Serra d' 99 B4 ⛰ SE Portugal
Ossora 118 I3 E Russian Federation
Ostend 84 A6 NW Belgium
Östersund 83 C4 C Sweden
Ostfriesische Inseln see East Frisian Islands
Ostiglia 103 C2 N Italy
Ostrava 105 D5 E Czech Republic
Ostróda 105 E2 NE Poland
Ostrołęka 105 F3 C Poland
Ostrov 111 A4 W Russian Federation
Ostrowiec Świętokrzyski 105 F4 C Poland
Ostrów Mazowiecka 105 F3 NE Poland
Ostrów Wielkopolski 105 D4 C Poland
Osumi-shoto 133 A7 island group SW Japan
Osumit, Lumi i 107 D4 〰 SE Albania
Osuna 99 C5 SW Spain
Oswego 37 D3 New York, NE USA
Oswestry 93 C5 W England, United Kingdom
Otago Peninsula 139 B7 peninsula South Island, New Zealand
Otaki 139 D5 North Island, New Zealand
Otaru 133 F2 NE Japan
Otavi 76 B5 N Namibia
Otira 139 C6 South Island, New Zealand
Otjiwarongo 76 B5 N Namibia
Otley 93 D4 N England, United Kingdom
Otorohanga 139 D3 North Island, New Zealand
Otranto 112 G5 SE Italy
Otranto, Strait of 103 F7 strait Albania/Italy
Otrokovice 105 D6 E Czech Republic
Ōtsu 133 E6 Honshu, SW Japan
Ottawa 35 D5 ● Ontario, SE Canada
Ottawa 40 B5 Illinois, N USA
Ottawa 43 E6 Kansas, C USA
Ottawa Islands 35 C2 island group Nunavut, C Canada
Otterburn 93 D2 N England, United Kingdom
Ottignies 84 C7 C Belgium
Ottumwa 43 F5 Iowa, C USA
Ouachita Mountains 39 A3 ⛰ Arkansas/Oklahoma, C USA
Ouachita River 39 B5 〰 Arkansas/Louisiana, C USA
Ouagadougou 72 D4 ● C Burkina
Ouahigouya 72 D3 NW Burkina
Oualâta 72 C3 SE Mauritania
Ouanda Djallé 72 I4 NE Central African Republic
Ouarâne 72 B2 desert C Mauritania
Ouargla 70 E2 NE Algeria
Ouarzazate 70 C2 S Morocco
Oubangui 72 H5 〰 C Africa
Ouessant, Île d' 97 A2 island NW France
Ouésso 76 B1 NW Congo
Oughterard 89 B4 W Ireland
Oujda 70 D1 NE Morocco
Oujeft 72 B2 C Mauritania
Oulu 83 E3 C Finland
Oulujärvi 83 E3 ◎ C Finland
Oulujoki 83 E3 〰 C Finland
Ounasjoki 83 E2 〰 N Finland
Ounianga Kébir 72 H2 N Chad
Oupeye 84 D7 E Belgium
Our 84 E8 〰 NW Europe
Ourense 99 B2 NW Spain
Ourique 99 B5 S Portugal
Ourthe 84 E8 〰 E Belgium
Ou-sanmyaku 133 G3 ⛰ Honshū, C Japan
Ouse 93 E4 〰 N England, United Kingdom
Outer Hebrides 91 A3 island group NW Scotland, United Kingdom
Outes 99 B1 NW Spain
Out Skerries 91 B6 island group NE Scotland, United Kingdom
Ouvéa 141 G6 island Îles Loyauté, NE New Caledonia
Ouyen 137 F6 Victoria, SE Australia
Ovalle 65 A5 N Chile
Ovar 99 B3 N Portugal
Overflakkee 84 B5 island SW Netherlands
Overijse 84 C7 C Belgium
Oviedo 99 C1 NW Spain
Owando 76 B2 C Congo
Owase 133 F6 SW Japan
Owatonna 43 E4 Minnesota, N USA
Owen, Mount 139 C5 ▲ South Island, New Zealand
Owensboro 39 D2 Kentucky, S USA
Owens Lake 49 D7 salt flat California, W USA
Owen Stanley Range 141 B3 ⛰ S Papua New Guinea
Owerri 72 F5 S Nigeria
Owyhee River 49 D4 〰 Idaho/Oregon, NW USA
Oxford 139 C6 South Island, New Zealand
Oxford 95 E3 S England, United Kingdom
Oxford Canal 95 E2 canal S England, United Kingdom
Oxkutzcab 53 H4 SE Mexico
Oxnard 49 C8 California, W USA
Oyama 133 G5 Honshu, S Japan
Oyem 76 A1 N Gabon
Oykel 91 D3 〰 N Scotland, United Kingdom
Oyo 76 B2 C Congo
Oyo 72 E5 W Nigeria
Ozark 39 E6 Alabama, S USA
Ozark Plateau 43 E7 plain Arkansas/Missouri, C USA
Ozarks, Lake of the 43 F6 ⊡ Missouri, C USA
Ózd 105 E7 NE Hungary
Ozieri 103 A5 Sardinia, Italy

P

Pabbay 91 A3 island NW Scotland, United Kingdom
Pabna 127 G3 W Bangladesh
Pachuca 53 F5 C Mexico
Pacific Ocean 14 ocean
Padang 131 B6 Sumatra, W Indonesia
Paderborn 101 B4 NW Germany
Padova see Padua
Padre Island 44 H6 island Texas, SW USA
Padua 103 C2 NE Italy
Paducah 39 D2 Kentucky, S USA
Paektu-san 133 B3 ▲ China/North Korea
Paengnyong-do 133 A5 island NW South Korea
Paeroa 139 D3 North Island, New Zealand
Páfos 112 C6 W Cyprus
Pag 107 B2 island C Croatia
Page 44 B1 Arizona, SW USA
Pago Pago 135 ○ W American Samoa
Pāhala 51 D3 Hawaii, USA
Pahiatua 139 D4 North Island, New Zealand
[illegible] Hawaii, USA
Paignton 95 C5 SW England, United Kingdom
Paihia 139 D1 North Island, New Zealand
Päijänne 83 E4 ◎ S Finland
Pailolo Channel 51 C2 channel Hawaii, USA
Paine, Cerro 65 A9 ▲ S Chile
Painted Desert 47 D7 desert Arizona, SW USA
Paisley 91 D6 W Scotland, United Kingdom
País Valenciano 99 F3 cultural region NE Spain
País Vasco see Basque Country, The
Pakistan 127 B2 ◆ republic S Asia
Pakokku 131 A2 C Burma (Myanmar)
Pakruojis 83 E7 N Lithuania
Paks 105 E8 S Hungary
Pakwach 75 C5 NW Uganda
Pakxe 131 C3 S Laos
Palafrugell 99 H2 NE Spain
Palagruža 107 B3 island SW Croatia
Palamós 99 H2 NE Spain
Palanpur 127 C4 W India
Palapye 76 D5 SE Botswana
Palatka 39 G6 Florida, SE USA
Palau 131 H6 ◆ republic W Pacific Ocean
Palawan 131 E5 island W Philippines
Palawan Passage 131 E4 passage W Philippines
Palembang 131 C7 W Indonesia
Palencia 99 D2 NW Spain
Palermo 103 C7 Sicily, Italy
Palestine 44 H3 Texas, SW USA
Pali 127 C3 N India
Palikir 135 ● Pohnpei, E Micronesia
Palk Strait 127 E7 strait India/Sri Lanka
Palliser, Cape 139 D5 headland North Island, New Zealand
Palma 99 H4 Balearic Islands, E Spain
Palma del Río 99 C5 S Spain
Palmar Sur 55 F6 SE Costa Rica
Palma Soriano 57 E4 E Cuba
Palmer 37 F4 Massachusetts, NE USA
Palmer 142 A4 US research station Antarctica
Palmer Land 142 B4 physical region Antarctica
Palmerston North 139 D4 North Island, New Zealand
Palmi 103 E8 SW Italy
Palm Springs 49 D9 California, W USA
Palmyra Atoll 135 US ◇ C Pacific Ocean
Palo Alto 49 B7 California, W USA
Palu 131 E6 Celebes, C Indonesia
Pamiers 97 C7 S France
Pamir 125 G4 〰 Afghanistan/Tajikistan
Pamirs 125 G4 ⛰ C Asia
Pamlico Sound 39 I3 sound North Carolina, SE USA
Pampa 44 F2 Texas, SW USA
Pampas 65 B6 plain C Argentina
Pamplona 99 E2 N Spain
Panaji 127 C6 W India
Panama 55 G7 ◆ republic Central America
Panama Canal 55 G6 shipping canal E Panama
Panama City 55 H6 ● C Panama
Panama City 39 E6 Florida, SE USA
Panama, Gulf of 55 H7 gulf S Panama
Panama, Isthmus of 55 H6 isthmus E Panama
Panay Island 131 E4 island C Philippines
Pančevo 107 D2 N Serbia
Panevėžys 83 E7 C Lithuania
Pangkalpinang 131 C7 W Indonesia
Panguitch 47 C6 Utah, W USA
Pantanal 63 E6 swamp SW Brazil
Pantelleria 103 B8 Sicily, Italy
Pantelleria, Isola di 112 F4 island SW Italy
Pánuco 53 F4 E Mexico
Paola 112 B6 E Malta
Papagayo, Golfo de 55 D5 gulf NW Costa Rica
Papakura 139 D2 North Island, New Zealand
Papantla 53 F4 E Mexico
Papa Stour 91 A6 island NE Scotland, United Kingdom
Papa Westray 91 E1 island NE Scotland, United Kingdom
Papeete 141 A5 ○ W French Polynesia
Papillion 43 D5 Nebraska, C USA
Papua 131 I7 province E Indonesia
Papua, Gulf of 141 B3 gulf S Papua New Guinea
Papua New Guinea 141 B2 ◆ commonwealth republic NW Melanesia
Papuk 107 C1 ⛰ NE Croatia
Pará 63 F4 state NE Brazil
Paracel Islands 131 C3 Disputed ◇ SE Asia
Paraguay 65 B3 ◆ republic C South America
Paraguay 65 C3 〰 C South America
Paraíba 63 I5 state E Brazil
Parakou 72 E4 C Benin
Paramaribo 63 F2 ● N Surinam
Paramushir, Ostrov 118 I4 island SE Russian Federation
Paraná 65 C5 E Argentina
Paraná 63 F8 state S Brazil
Paraná 65 C5 〰 C South America
Paraparaumu 139 D5 North Island, New Zealand
Parchim 101 D3 N Germany
Parczew 105 G4 E Poland
Pardubice 105 C5 C Czech Republic
Parecis, Chapada dos 65 D1 ⛰ W Brazil
Parepare 131 E7 Celebes, C Indonesia
Paria, Gulf of 57 J7 gulf Trinidad and Tobago/Venezuela
Paris 97 D2 ● N France
Paris 44 H2 Texas, SW USA
Parkersburg 39 F1 West Virginia, NE USA
Parkes 137 G5 New South Wales, SE Australia
Parma 103 C3 N Italy
Parnaíba 63 H4 E Brazil
Pärnu 83 E6 SW Estonia
Páros 107 F6 island SE Greece
Parral 65 A6 C Chile
Parramatta 137 G6 New South Wales, SE Australia
Parras 53 E3 NE Mexico
Parrett 95 D4 〰 SW England, United Kingdom
Parsons 43 E7 Kansas, C USA
Partney 93 F5 E England, United Kingdom
Partry 89 B3 NW Ireland
Partry Mountains 89 B4 ⛰ W Ireland

◐ Administrative region ◆ Country ● Country capital ◇ Dependent territory ○ Dependent territory capital ⛰ Mountain range ▲ Mountain 🌋 Volcano 〰 River ◎ Lake ⊡ Reservoir

PASADENA

Pasadena 49 C8 California, W USA
Pasadena 44 H4 Texas, SW USA
Pasco 49 C3 Washington, NW USA
Pasewalk 101 E3 NE Germany
Pasinler 121 G3 NE Turkey
Pasłęk 105 E2 NE Poland
Pasni 127 A3 SW Pakistan
Paso de Indios 65 A7 S Argentina
Passau 101 D6 SE Germany
Passo Fundo 63 F8 S Brazil
Pasto 63 B3 SW Colombia
Patagonia 65 B7 semi arid region Argentina/Chile
Patea 139 D4 North Island, New Zealand
Paterson 37 E5 New Jersey, NE USA
Pathein 131 A3 SW Burma (Myanmar)
Pátmos 107 F6 island Dodecanese, Greece
Patna 127 F3 N India
Patnos 121 G3 E Turkey
Patos, Lagoa dos 63 F9 lagoon S Brazil
Pátra 107 D5 S Greece
Patrickswell 89 C5 SW Ireland
Patuca, Río 55 E3 ≈ E Honduras
Pau 97 B6 SW France
Paulatuk 33 F3 Northwest Territories, NW Canada
Pavia 103 B2 N Italy
Pavlodar 118 D5 NE Kazakhstan
Pavlohrad 109 F5 E Ukraine
Pawn 131 B3 ≈ C Burma (Myanmar)
Paxoí 107 D5 island Ionian Islands, Greece
Paysandú 65 C5 W Uruguay
Pazar 121 F2 NE Turkey
Pazardzhik 107 E3 C Bulgaria
Peach Springs 44 A2 Arizona, SW USA
Peak District 93 D5 physical region C England, United Kingdom
Pearl City 51 B1 O'ahu, Hawaii, USA
Pearl Harbor 51 B2 inlet O'ahu, Hawaii, USA, C Pacific Ocean
Pearl Islands 55 H6 island group SE Panama
Pearl Lagoon 55 F4 lagoon E Nicaragua
Pearl River 39 C6 ≈ Louisiana/Mississippi, S USA
Pearsall 44 G5 Texas, SW USA
Peawanuk 35 C3 Ontario, C Canada
Pechora 111 D4 NW Russian Federation
Pechora 111 D3 ≈ NW Russian Federation
Pechora Sea 111 D2 sea NW Russian Federation
Pecos 44 E4 Texas, SW USA
Pecos River 44 F4 ≈ New Mexico/Texas, SW USA
Pécs 105 D9 SW Hungary
Pedro Juan Caballero 65 C3 E Paraguay
Peebles 91 E6 SE Scotland, United Kingdom
Peel 93 A3 W Isle of Man
Peer 84 D6 NE Belgium
Pegasus Bay 139 C6 bay South Island, New Zealand
Pehuajó 65 B6 E Argentina
Peine 101 C4 C Germany
Peipus, Lake 83 E5 ◎ Estonia/Russian Federation
Peiraías see Piraeus
Pejë 107 D3 W Kosovo
Pekalongan 131 D7 Java, C Indonesia
Pekanbaru 131 B6 Sumatra, W Indonesia
Pekin 40 B6 Illinois, N USA
Peking see Beijing
Pelagie 103 C9 island group SW Italy
Pelly Bay see Kugaaruk
Peloponnese 107 D6 peninsula S Greece
Pematangsiantar 131 A6 Sumatra, W Indonesia
Pemba 76 F4 NE Mozambique
Pemba 75 E6 island E Tanzania
Pembroke 35 D5 Ontario, SE Canada
Pembroke 93 A7 SW Wales, United Kingdom
Pembroke Dock 93 A7 SW Wales, United Kingdom
Penas, Golfo de 65 A8 gulf S Chile
Pendleton 49 C3 Oregon, NW USA
Pend Oreille, Lake 47 B1 ◎ Idaho, NW USA
Peniche 99 A4 W Portugal
Penn Hills 37 B5 Pennsylvania, NE USA
Pennine Alps 101 B8 ⛰ Italy/Switzerland
Pennines 93 D3 ⛰ N England, United Kingdom
Pennsylvania 37 C5 ◐ state NE USA
Penobscot River 37 G2 ≈ Maine, NE USA
Penong 137 E5 South Australia
Penonomé 55 G6 C Panama
Penrhyn 135 atoll N Cook Islands
Penrith 93 C2 NW England, United Kingdom
Pensacola 39 D6 Florida, SE USA
Pentecost 141 H4 island C Vanuatu
Pentland Firth 91 E1 strait N Scotland, United Kingdom
Pentland Hills 91 E6 hill range S Scotland, United Kingdom
Pen y Fan 93 B7 ▲ SE Wales, United Kingdom
Pen-y-ghent 93 D3 ▲ N England, United Kingdom
Penza 111 B6 W Russian Federation
Penzance 95 A6 SW England, United Kingdom
Peoria 40 B6 Illinois, N USA
Perchtoldsdorf 101 F7 NE Austria
Percival Lakes 137 C3 lakes Western Australia
Perdido, Monte 99 F2 ▲ NE Spain
Pergamino 65 C5 E Argentina
Périgueux 97 C5 SW France
Perito Moreno 65 A8 S Argentina
Perleberg 101 D3 N Germany
Perm' 111 D5 NW Russian Federation
Pernambuco 63 H5 state E Brazil
Pernik 107 E3 W Bulgaria
Perote 53 F5 E Mexico
Perpignan 97 D7 S France
Perryton 44 F1 Texas, SW USA
Perryville 43 G7 Missouri, C USA
Persian Gulf 123 D3 gulf SW Asia
Perth 91 E5 C Scotland, United Kingdom
Perth 137 B5 state capital Western Australia
Peru 65 A2 ◆ republic W South America
Peru Basin 14 undersea feature E Pacific Ocean
Peru-Chile Trench 14 undersea feature E Pacific Ocean
Perugia 103 C4 C Italy
Péruwelz 84 B7 SW Belgium
Pervomays'k 109 E5 S Ukraine
Pervyy Kuril'skiy Proliv 118 I4 strait E Russian Federation
Pesaro 103 D3 C Italy
Pescara 103 D5 C Italy
Peshawar 127 C1 N Pakistan
Pessac 97 B5 SW France
Petah Tikva 123 H6 C Israel
Pétange 84 E9 SW Luxembourg
Petén Itzá, Lago 55 B2 ◎ N Guatemala
Peterborough 137 E5 South Australia
Peterborough 35 D6 Ontario, SE Canada
Peterborough 95 F2 E England, United Kingdom
Peterhead 91 F3 NE Scotland, United Kingdom
Peter I Island 142 A4 Norwegian ◇ Antarctica
Peterlee 93 E3 N England, United Kingdom
Petersburg 39 H2 Virginia, NE USA
Petersfield 95 F4 S England, United Kingdom
Peto 53 H4 SE Mexico
Petrich 107 E4 SW Bulgaria
Petrodvorets 111 A4 NW Russian Federation
Petropavlovsk 118 C4 N Kazakhstan
Petropavlovsk-Kamchatskiy 118 I3 E Russian Federation
Petrozavodsk 111 B4 NW Russian Federation
Pevek 118 H2 NE Russian Federation
Pezinok 105 D7 W Slovakia
Pforzheim 101 B6 SW Germany
Pfungstadt 101 B6 W Germany
Phangan, Ko 131 B4 island SW Thailand
Phenix City 39 E5 Alabama, S USA
Phetchaburi 131 B4 SW Thailand
Philadelphia 37 D5 Pennsylvania, NE USA
Philippines 131 D4 ◆ republic SE Asia
Philippine Sea 131 F3 sea W Pacific Ocean
Philippine Trench 15 undersea feature W Philippine Sea
Phitsanulok 131 B3 C Thailand
Phnom Penh 131 C4 ● S Cambodia
Phoenix 44 B3 state capital Arizona, SW USA
Phoenix Islands 135 island group C Kiribati
Phra Thong, Ko 131 A5 island SW Thailand
Phuket 131 B5 SW Thailand
Phuket, Ko 131 A5 island SW Thailand
Piacenza 103 B2 N Italy
Piatra-Neamţ 109 C6 NE Romania
Piauí 63 G5 state E Brazil
Picardie see Picardy
Picardy 97 D2 cultural region N France Europe
Pichilemu 65 A5 C Chile
Pickering 93 E3 N England, United Kingdom
Picos 63 H4 E Brazil
Picton 139 D5 South Island, New Zealand
Piedmont 103 A2 cultural region NW Italy
Piedmont 39 G3 escarpment E USA
Piedras Negras 53 E2 NE Mexico
Pielavesi 83 E4 C Finland
Pielinen 83 F4 ◎ E Finland
Piemonte see Piedmont
Pierre 43 C3 state capital South Dakota, N USA
Pieštany 105 D6 W Slovakia
Pietarsaari see Jakobstad
Pietermaritzburg 76 D6 E South Africa
Pietersburg see Polokwane
Pigs, Bay of 57 C3 bay SE Cuba
Pijijiapán 53 H6 SE Mexico
Pikes Peak 47 E6 ▲ Colorado, C USA
Pikeville 39 F2 Kentucky, S USA
Piła 105 C3 C Poland
Pilar 65 C4 S Paraguay
Pilcomayo, Rio 65 C3 ≈ C South America
Pillsbury Sound 51 strait C Virgin Islands (USA) North America Caribbean Sea Atlantic Ocean
Pinar del Rio 57 B2 W Cuba
Pindus Mountains 107 D5 ⛰ C Greece
Pine Bluff 39 B4 Arkansas, C USA
Pine Creek 137 D1 Northern Territory, N Australia
Pinega 111 C4 ≈ NW Russian Federation
Pineiós 107 E4 ≈ C Greece
Pineland 44 I4 Texas, SW USA
Pingdingshan 129 F4 C China
Ping, Mae Nam 131 B3 ≈ W Thailand
Pinotepa Nacional 53 F6 SE Mexico
Pins, Île des 141 G6 island E New Caledonia
Pinsk 109 C3 SW Belarus
Piombino 103 B4 C Italy
Piotrków Trybunalski 105 E4 C Poland
Piraeus 107 E5 C Greece
Pirata, Monte 51 ▲ E Puerto Rico
Piripiri 63 H4 E Brazil
Pirna 101 E5 E Germany
Pisa 103 B3 C Italy
Pisco 63 B6 SW Peru
Písek 105 B6 S Czech Republic
Pishan 129 B3 NW China
Pistoia 103 C3 C Italy
Pisz 105 F2 NE Poland
Pita 72 B4 NW Guinea
Pitcairn Islands 135 UK ◇ C Pacific Ocean
Piteå 83 D3 N Sweden
Piteşti 109 B7 S Romania
Pitlochry 91 D4 C Scotland, United Kingdom
Pit River 49 B5 ≈ California, W USA
Pittsburg 43 E7 Kansas, C USA
Pittsburgh 37 B5 Pennsylvania, NE USA
Pittsfield 37 E4 Massachusetts, NE USA
Piura 63 A4 NW Peru
Pivdennyy Buh 109 E5 ≈ S Ukraine
Placetas 57 C3 C Cuba
Plainview 44 F2 Texas, SW USA
Plano 44 H3 Texas, SW USA
Plasencia 99 C3 W Spain
Plate, River 65 C5 estuary Argentina/Uruguay
Platinum 50 D2 Alaska, USA
Platte River 43 D5 ≈ Nebraska, C USA
Plattsburgh 37 E2 New York, NE USA
Plauen 101 D5 E Germany
Play Cu 131 C4 C Vietnam
Plenty, Bay of 139 E3 bay North Island, New Zealand
Plérin 97 B2 NW France
Plesetsk 111 C4 NW Russian Federation
Pleszew 105 D4 C Poland
Pleven 107 E2 N Bulgaria
Płock 105 E3 C Poland
Plöcken Pass 101 D8 pass SW Austria
Ploieşti 109 C7 SE Romania
Płońsk 105 E3 C Poland
Plovdiv 107 F3 C Bulgaria
Plymouth 57 J5 Trinidad and Tobago
Plymouth 95 B5 SW England, United Kingdom
Plynlimon 93 B6 ▲ C Wales, United Kingdom
Plzeň 105 A5 W Czech Republic
Po 103 C3 ≈ N Italy
Pobedy, Pik 129 B2 ▲ China/Kyrgyzstan
Pocahontas 39 C3 Arkansas, C USA
Pocatello 47 C4 Idaho, NW USA
Pochinok 111 A5 W Russian Federation
Pocking 101 D7 SE Germany
Pocklington Reef 141 E3 reef SE Papua New Guinea
Poděbrady 105 B5 C Czech Republic
Podgorica 107 C3 ● S Montenegro
Podil's'ka Vysochyna 109 C5 ⛰ SW Ukraine
Podol'sk 111 A5 W Russian Federation
P'ohang 133 C6 E South Korea
Poinsett, Cape 142 E5 cape Antarctica
Pointe-à-Pitre 57 J5 C Guadeloupe
Pointe-Noire 76 A2 S Congo
Point Lay 50 E1 Alaska, USA
Poitiers 97 C4 W France
Poitou 97 B4 cultural region W France
Pokhara 127 F3 C Nepal
Pola de Lena 99 C1 N Spain
Poland 105 D4 ◆ republic C Europe
Polatlı 121 C3 C Turkey
Polatsk 109 D1 N Belarus
Pol-e Khomri 125 F4 NE Afghanistan
Pólis 112 C6 W Cyprus
Pollença 99 H3 Majorca, Spain
Polokwane 76 D6 NE South Africa
Poltava 109 F4 NE Ukraine
Polyarnyy 111 C2 NW Russian Federation
Polynesia 135 island group C Pacific Ocean
Pomerania 105 C2 cultural region Germany/Poland
Pomeranian Bay 101 E2 bay Germany/Poland
Pomio 141 C2 E Papua New Guinea
Pomorskiy Proliv 111 D3 strait NW Russian Federation
Pompano Beach 39 G8 Florida, SE USA
Ponca City 43 D7 Oklahoma, C USA
Ponce 57 H4 C Puerto Rico
Pondicherry 127 E6 SE India
Pond Inlet 143 A4 Baffin Island, Nunavut, NE Canada
Ponferrada 99 C2 NW Spain
Poniatowa 105 F4 E Poland
Ponta Grossa 63 F8 S Brazil
Pontarlier 97 F4 E France
Ponteareas 99 B2 NW Spain
Ponte da Barca 99 B2 N Portugal
Pontevedra 99 B2 NW Spain
Pontiac 40 E5 Michigan, N USA
Pontianak 131 D6 C Indonesia
Pontivy 97 B3 NW France
Pontoise 97 D2 N France
Pontypool 93 C7 SE Wales, United Kingdom
Pontypridd 93 C7 S Wales, United Kingdom
Ponziane Island 103 C6 island C Italy
Poole 95 E5 S England, United Kingdom
Poole Bay 95 E5 bay S England, United Kingdom
Popayán 63 B3 SW Colombia
Poperinge 84 A6 W Belgium
Poplar Bluff 43 G7 Missouri, C USA
Popocatépetl 53 F5 🌋 S Mexico
Popondetta 141 C3 S Papua New Guinea
Poprad 105 E6 E Slovakia
Poprád 105 E6 ≈ Poland/Slovakia
Porbandar 127 C4 W India
Pordenone 103 D2 NE Italy
Pori 83 E5 SW Finland
Porirua 139 D5 C New Zealand
Porkhov 111 A4 W Russian Federation
Póros 107 D5 Kefallonía, Greece
Porsangenfjorden 83 E1 fjord N Norway
Porsgrunn 83 B5 S Norway
Portadown 89 E2 S Northern Ireland, United Kingdom
Portaferry 89 F3 E Northern Ireland, United Kingdom
Portalegre 99 B4 E Portugal
Port Alexander 50 F4 Baranof Island, Alaska, USA
Port Alfred 76 D7 S South Africa
Port Angeles 49 B2 Washington, NW USA
Port Arthur 44 I4 Texas, SW USA
Port Askaig 91 B6 W Scotland, United Kingdom
Port Augusta 137 E5 South Australia
Port-au-Prince 57 ● C Haiti
Port Blair 127 H5 Andaman Islands, SE India
Port Charlotte 39 F8 Florida, SE USA
Port Douglas 137 G2 Queensland, NE Australia
Port Elizabeth 76 D7 S South Africa
Port Ellen 91 B6 W Scotland, United Kingdom
Port Erin 93 A4 SW Isle of Man
Porterville 49 C8 California, W USA
Port-Gentil 76 A2 W Gabon
Port Harcourt 72 E5 S Nigeria
Port Hardy 33 E7 Vancouver Island, British Columbia, SW Canada
Port Harrison see Inukjuak
Port Hedland 137 B3 Western Australia
Port Huron 40 E4 Michigan, N USA
Portimão 99 B5 S Portugal
Port Isaac Bay 95 A5 bay SW England, United Kingdom
Portishead 95 D4 SW England, United Kingdom
Portland 137 F6 Victoria, SE Australia
Portland 37 F3 Maine, NE USA
Portland 49 B3 Oregon, NW USA
Portland 44 H5 Texas, SW USA
Portland Bill 95 D5 headland S England, United Kingdom
Portland, Isle of 95 D5 island SW England, United Kingdom
Port Laoise 89 D5 C Ireland
Port Lavaca 44 H5 Texas, SW USA
Port Lincoln 137 E6 South Australia
Port Louis 67 ● NW Mauritius
Port Macquarie 137 H5 New South Wales, SE Australia
Port Moresby 141 B3 ● New Guinea, SW Papua New Guinea
Porto see Oporto
Porto Alegre 63 F8 S Brazil
Portobelo 55 H6 N Panama
Port O'Connor 44 H5 Texas, SW USA
Portoferraio 103 B4 C Italy
Port of Ness 91 B2 NW Scotland, United Kingdom
Port-of-Spain 57 K7 ● C Trinidad and Tobago
Portogruaro 103 D2 NE Italy
Porto-Novo 72 E5 ● S Benin
Porto Torres 103 A5 Sardinia, Italy
Porto Velho 63 D5 W Brazil
Portoviejo 63 A4 W Ecuador
Port Pirie 137 E5 South Australia
Portree 91 B3 N Scotland, United Kingdom
Portrush 89 E1 N Northern Ireland, United Kingdom
Port Said 70 I2 N Egypt
Portskerra 91 D2 N Scotland, United Kingdom
Portsmouth 95 F5 S England, United Kingdom
Portsmouth 37 F3 New Hampshire, NE USA
Portsmouth 40 E7 Ohio, N USA
Portsmouth 39 I2 Virginia, NE USA
Port Šudan 75 D1 NE Sudan
Portugal 99 A3 ◆ republic SW Europe
Port-Vila 141 H5 ● Éfaté, C Vanuatu
Porvenir 65 A1 NW Bolivia
Porvenir 65 B9 S Chile
Porvoo 83 E5 S Finland
Posadas 65 C4 NE Argentina
Post 44 F3 Texas, SW USA
Posterholt 84 E6 SE Netherlands
Postojna 101 E9 SW Slovenia
Potenza 103 E6 S Italy
P'ot'i 121 G1 W Georgia
Potiskum 72 F4 NE Nigeria
Potomac River 39 H1 ≈ NE USA
Potosí 65 B3 S Bolivia
Potsdam 101 D3 NE Germany
Potsdam 37 D2 New York, NE USA
Pottsville 37 D5 Pennsylvania, NE USA
Pouébo 141 G6 C New Caledonia
Poulton-le-Fylde 93 C4 NW England, United Kingdom
Po Valley 103 C3 valley N Italy
Považská Bystrica 105 D6 W Slovakia
Poverty Bay 139 E4 inlet North Island, New Zealand
Póvoa de Varzim 99 B2 NW Portugal
Powder River 47 F3 ≈ Montana/Wyoming, NW USA
Powell 47 E3 Wyoming, C USA
Powell, Lake 47 D6 ◎ Utah, W USA
Poza Rica 53 F4 E Mexico
Poznań 105 C3 C Poland
Pozoblanco 99 D5 S Spain
Pozzallo 103 D9 Sicily, Italy
Prachatice 105 B6 S Czech Republic
Prague 105 ● NW Czech Republic
Praha see Prague
Praia 69 ● Santiago, S Cape Verde
Prairie du Chien 40 B4 Wisconsin, N USA
Prato 103 C3 C Italy
Pratt 43 C7 Kansas, C USA
Prattville 39 E5 Alabama, S USA
Pravia 99 C1 N Spain
Prenzlau 101 D3 NE Germany
Přerov 105 D6 E Czech Republic
Prescott 44 B2 Arizona, SW USA
Preseli, Mynydd 93 A6 ⛰ SW Wales, United Kingdom
Presidio 44 E5 Texas, SW USA
Prešov 105 F6 E Slovakia
Prespa, Lake 107 D4 ◎ SE Europe
Presque Isle 37 G1 Maine, NE USA
Prestatyn 93 C4 N Wales, United Kingdom
Preston 93 C4 NW England, United Kingdom
Prestwick 91 D6 W Scotland, United Kingdom
Pretoria 76 D6 ● NE South Africa (see also Tshwane)
Préveza 107 D5 W Greece
Pribilof Islands 50 B2 island group Alaska, USA
Price 47 D5 Utah, W USA
Prichard 39 D6 Alabama, S USA
Prilep 107 D4 S Macedonia
Prince Albert 33 G6 Saskatchewan, S Canada
Prince Edward Island 35 G5 ◐ province SE Canada
Prince George 33 F6 British Columbia, SW Canada
Prince of Wales Island 137 F1 island Queensland, E Australia
Prince of Wales Island 33 H3 island Queen Elizabeth Islands, Nunavut, NW Canada
Prince Patrick Island 33 F2 island Parry Islands, Northwest Territories, NW Canada
Prince Rupert 33 E6 British Columbia, SW Canada
Princess Charlotte Bay 137 G1 bay Queensland, NE Australia
Princess Elizabeth Land 142 D4 physical region Antarctica
Príncipe 72 E6 island N Sao Tome and Principe
Prinzapolka 55 E4 NE Nicaragua
Pripet 109 C3 ≈ Belarus/Ukraine
Pripet Marshes 109 C3 forested and swampy region Belarus/Ukraine
Prishtinë see Pristina
Pristina 107 D3 ● C Kosovo
Privas 97 E5 E France
Prizren 107 D3 S Kosovo
Probolinggo 131 D8 C Indonesia
Progreso 53 H4 SE Mexico
Prokhladnyy 111 B8 SW Russian Federation
Promyshlennyy 111 E3 NW Russian Federation
Prostějov 105 D6 E Czech Republic
Provence 97 E6 cultural region SE France
Providence 37 F4 state capital Rhode Island, NE USA
Provideniya 143 C1 NE Russian Federation
Provo 47 D5 Utah, W USA
Prudhoe Bay 50 F1 Alaska, USA
Pruszków 105 E3 C Poland
Prut 109 D6 ≈ E Europe
Prydz Bay 142 E4 bay Antarctica
Pryluky 109 E4 NE Ukraine
Przemyśl 105 G5 C Poland
Psará 107 F5 island E Greece
Psël 109 F4 ≈ Russian Federation/Ukraine
Pskov 111 A4 W Russian Federation
Ptsich 109 D3 ≈ SE Belarus
Ptuj 101 F8 NE Slovenia
Pucallpa 63 B5 C Peru
Puck 105 D1 N Poland
Pudasjärvi 83 E3 C Finland
Puebla 53 F5 S Mexico
Pueblo 47 F6 Colorado, C USA
Puerto Acosta 65 A2 W Bolivia
Puerto Aisén 65 A7 S Chile
Puerto Ángel 53 G6 SE Mexico
Puerto Ayacucho 63 D2 SW Venezuela
Puerto Baquerizo Moreno 63 B7 Galapagos Islands, Ecuador
Puerto Barrios 55 C2 E Guatemala
Puerto Cabezas 55 E3 NE Nicaragua
Puerto Cortés 55 C2 NW Honduras
Puerto Deseado 65 B8 SE Argentina
Puerto Escondido 53 F6 SE Mexico
Puerto Lempira 55 E3 E Honduras
Puertollano 99 D4 C Spain
Puerto Maldonado 63 C5 E Peru
Puerto Montt 65 A7 C Chile
Puerto Natales 65 A9 S Chile
Puerto Obaldía 55 I6 NE Panama
Puerto Plata 57 G4 N Dominican Republic
Puerto Princesa 131 E4 Palawan, W Philippines
Puerto Rico 51 US ◇ C West Indies
Puerto San Julián 65 B8 SE Argentina
Puerto Suárez 65 C2 E Bolivia
Puerto Vallarta 53 D5 SW Mexico
Puerto Varas 65 A7 C Chile
Puerto Viejo 55 E5 NE Costa Rica
Puget Sound 49 B2 sound Washington, NW USA
Pukaki, Lake 139 B6 ◎ SW New Zealand
Pukatikei, Maunga 141 D6 🌋 Easter Island, Chile
Pukch'ong 133 B4 E North Korea
Pukekohe 139 D3 North Island, New Zealand
Pula 107 A2 NW Croatia
Pulaski 39 G2 Virginia, NE USA
Puławy 105 F4 E Poland
Pullman 49 D2 Washington, NW USA
Pułtusk 105 E3 C Poland
Pune 127 C5 W India
Punjab 127 D2 cultural region India/Pakistan
Puno 63 C6 SE Peru
Punta Alta 65 B6 E Argentina
Punta Arenas 65 A9 S Chile
Punta, Cerro de 51 ▲ C Puerto Rico
Punta Gorda 55 B2 SE Belize
Punta Gorda 55 E5 SE Nicaragua
Puntarenas 55 E6 W Costa Rica
Puntland 75 F3 cultural region NE Somalia
Pupuya, Nevado 65 A2 ▲ W Bolivia
Puri 127 F5 E India
Purmerend 84 D3 C Netherlands
Purus, Rio 63 D4 ≈ Brazil/Peru
Pusan 133 C6 SE South Korea
Püspökladány 105 F7 E Hungary
Putney 37 E3 Vermont, NE USA
Putorana Mountains 118 E3 ⛰ N Russian Federation
Putrajaya 131 B6 ● Peninsular Malaysia
Puttalam 127 E7 W Sri Lanka
Puttgarden 101 C2 N Germany
Putumayo, Río 63 C4 ≈ NW South America
Pu'u 'Ula'ula 51 C2 ▲ Maui, Hawaii, USA
Pu'uwai 51 A1 Ni'ihau, Hawaii, USA
Pwllheli 93 B5 NW Wales, United Kingdom
Pyatigorsk 111 A8 SW Russian Federation
Pyay 131 A3 C Burma (Myanmar)
Pyongyang 133 A5 ● SW North Korea
Pyramid Lake 47 A5 ◎ Nevada, W USA
Pyrenees 99 F2 ⛰ SW Europe
Pyrgos 107 D6 S Greece
Pyrzyce 105 B3 NW Poland

Q

Qaidam Pendi 129 D3 basin C China
Qal'aikhum 125 G3 S Tajikistan
Qalat 125 F6 S Afghanistan
Qal'eh-ye Now 125 E4 NW Afghanistan
Qamdo 129 D4 China
Qarokul 125 G3 E Tajikistan
Qarshi 125 E3 S Uzbekistan
Qasr al Farafirah 70 I3 W Egypt
Qatar 123 D4 ◆ monarchy SW Asia
Qattara Depression 70 I3 desert NW Egypt
Qausuittuq see Resolute
Qazimämmäd 121 J2 SE Azerbaijan
Qazvin 123 D2 N Iran
Qilian Shan 129 D3 ⛰ N China
Qina 70 J3 E Egypt
Qingdao 129 G3 E China
Qinghai Hu 129 D3 ◎ C China
Qinhuangdao 129 G3 E China
Qinzhou 129 F6 S China
Qiqihar 129 G2 NE China
Qira 129 B3 NW China
Qitai 129 C2 NW China
Qizilrabot 125 H4 SE Tajikistan
Qom 123 D2 N Iran
Qo'ng'irot 125 D2 NW Uzbekistan
Qo'qon 125 G3 E Uzbekistan
Quang Ngai 131 D3 C Vietnam
Quanzhou 129 G5 SE China
Quanzhou 129 F5 S China
Qu'Appelle 33 H7 ≈ Saskatchewan, S Canada
Quarles, Pegunungan 131 E7 ⛰ Sulawesi, C Indonesia
Quartu Sant' Elena 103 A6 Sardegna, Italy
Quba 121 I2 N Azerbaijan
Québec 35 D3 province capital Québec, SE Canada
Québec 35 E5 ◐ province SE Canada
Queen Charlotte Islands 33 D6 island group British Columbia, SW Canada
Queen Charlotte Sound 33 D6 sea area British Columbia, W Canada
Queen Elizabeth Islands 33 G2 island group Nunavut, N Canada
Queensland 137 F3 ◐ state N Australia
Queenstown 139 B7 South Island, New Zealand
Queenstown 76 D7 S South Africa
Quelimane 76 E5 NE Mozambique
Quemado 44 C2 New Mexico, SW USA
Quepos 55 E6 S Costa Rica
Querétaro 53 E4 C Mexico
Quesada 55 E6 N Costa Rica
Quetta 127 B2 SW Pakistan
Quezaltenango 55 A3 W Guatemala
Quilon 127 D7 SW India (see also Kollam)
Quilty 89 B5 W Ireland
Quimper 97 A2 NW France
Quimperlé 97 A3 NW France

◐ Administrative region ◆ Country ● Country capital ◇ Dependent territory ○ Dependent territory capital ⛰ Mountain range ▲ Mountain 🌋 Volcano ≈ River ◎ Lake ⊠ Reservoir

SALINA

Quinault *49 B2* Washington, NW USA
Quincy *40 A6* Illinois, N USA
Quito *63 B3* ● N Ecuador
Qurghonteppa *125 F4* SW Tajikistan
Quy Nhon *131 D4* C Vietnam

R

Raahe *83 E3* W Finland
Raalte *84 E3* E Netherlands
Raamsdonksveer *84 D5* S Netherlands
Raasay *91 B3 island* NW Scotland, United Kingdom
Rába *105 C8* ≈ Austria/Hungary
Rabat *70 C1* ● NW Morocco
Rabat *112 A5* W Malta
Rabaul *141 D1* E Papua New Guinea
Rabinal *55 B3* C Guatemala
Rabka *105 E6* S Poland
Rabyanah Ramlat *70 G4 desert* SE Libya
Race, Cape *35 H4 cape* Newfoundland, E Canada
Rach Gia *131 C4* S Vietnam
Racine *40 C5* Wisconsin, N USA
Radom *105 F4* C Poland
Radomsko *105 E4* C Poland
Radzyń Podlaski *105 F4* E Poland
Raetihi *139 D4* North Island, New Zealand
Rafaela *65 B5* E Argentina
Raga *75 B4* SW Sudan
Ragged Island Range *57 D3 island group* S Bahamas
Ragusa *103 D8* Sicily, Italy
Rahimyar Khan *127 C3* SE Pakistan
Raichur *127 D5* C India
Rainier, Mount *49 B2* ✱ Washington, NW USA
Rainy Lake *43 E1* ◎ Canada/USA
Raipur *127 E4* C India
Rajahmundry *127 E5* E India
Rajang, Batang *131 D6* ≈ East Malaysia
Rajapalaiyam *127 D7* SE India
Rajasthan *127 C3 state* NW India
Rajkot *127 C4* W India
Rajshahi *127 G3* W Bangladesh
Rakaia *139 C6* ≈ South Island, New Zealand
Raleigh *39 H3 state capital* North Carolina, SE USA
Râmnicu Vâlcea *109 B7* C Romania
Ramree Island *131 A3 island* W Burma (Myanmar)
Ramsey *93 B3* NE Isle of Man
Ramsgate *95 H4* SE England, United Kingdom
Rancagua *65 A5* C Chile
Ranchi *127 F4* N India
Randers *83 B6* C Denmark
Rangiora *139 C6* South Island, New Zealand
Rangitikei *139 D4* ≈ North Island, New Zealand
Rangoon *131 A3* S Burma (Myanmar)
Rangpur *127 G3* N Bangladesh
Rankin Inlet *33 H4* Nunavut, C Canada
Rannoch Moor *91 D4 heathland* C Scotland, United Kingdom
Rapid City *43 A3* South Dakota, N USA
Rāpina *83 F6* SE Estonia
Rarotonga *135 island* S Cook Islands
Rasht *123 D1* NW Iran
Ratān *83 C4* C Sweden
Rathfriland *89 E3* SE Northern Ireland, United Kingdom
Rathkeale *89 C5* SW Ireland
Rathlin Island *89 E1 island* N Northern Ireland, United Kingdom
Ráth Luirc *89 C6* S Ireland
Rathmelton *89 D1* N Ireland
Rathmore *89 B6* SW Ireland
Rathmullan *89 D1* N Ireland
Rathnew *89 E5* E Ireland
Rat Islands *50 A1 island group* Aleutian Islands, Alaska, USA
Ratlam *127 D4* C India
Ratnapura *127 E8* S Sri Lanka
Raton *44 E1* New Mexico, SW USA
Rättvik *83 C5* C Sweden
Raufarhöfn *83 B1* NE Iceland
Raukumara Range *139 E3* ▲▲ North Island, New Zealand
Raurkela *127 F4* E India
Rauma *83 D5* SW Finland
Ravenglass *93 B3* NW England, United Kingdom
Ravenna *103 C3* N Italy
Ravi *127 C2* ≈ India/Pakistan
Rawalpindi *127 D1* NE Pakistan
Rawa Mazowiecka *105 E4* C Poland
Rawicz *105 C4* C Poland
Rawlinna *137 C5* Western Australia
Rawlins *47 E4* Wyoming, C USA
Rawson *65 B7* SE Argentina
Rayong *131 B4* S Thailand
Razazah, Buhayrat ar *123 B2* ◎ C Iraq
Razgrad *107 F2* N Bulgaria
Razim, Lacul *109 D7 lagoon* NW Black Sea
Reading *95 F4* S England, United Kingdom
Reading *37 D5* Pennsylvania, NE USA
Real, Cordillera *58 B4* ▲▲ C Ecuador
Realicó *65 B5* C Argentina
Rebecca, Lake *137 C5* ◎ Western Australia
Rebun-to *133 F1 island* NE Japan
Recife *63 I5* E Brazil
Recklinghausen *101 A4* W Germany
Recogne *84 D8* SE Belgium
Reconquista *65 C4* C Argentina
Red Bluff *49 B5* California, W USA
Redcar *93 E2* N England, United Kingdom
Red Deer *33 G7* Alberta, SW Canada
Redding *49 B5* California, W USA
Redditch *93 D6* W England, United Kingdom
Redhill *95 F4* SE England, United Kingdom
Redon *97 B3* NW France
Red River *43 D1* ≈ Canada/USA
Red River *131 B2* ≈ China/Vietnam
Red River *44 G2* ≈ S USA
Red River *39 B6* ≈ Louisiana, S USA
Redruth *95 A6* SW England, United Kingdom
Red Sea *123 A4 sea* Africa/Asia
Red Wing *43 F3* Minnesota, N USA
Reefton *139 C5* South Island, New Zealand
Ree, Lough *89 D4* ◎ C Ireland
Reese River *47 B5* ≈ Nevada, W USA
Refahiye *121 F3* C Turkey
Regensburg *101 D6* SE Germany
Regenstauf *101 D6* SE Germany
Reggane *70 D3* C Algeria
Reggio di Calabria *103 E8* SW Italy
Reggio nell'Emilia *103 C3* N Italy
Regina *33 H7 province capital* Saskatchewan, S Canada
Rehoboth *76 B5* C Namibia
Rehovot *123 G6* C Israel
Reid *137 D5* Western Australia
Ré, Île de *97 B4 island* W France
Reims *97 E2* N France
Reindeer Lake *33 H5* ◎ Manitoba/Saskatchewan, C Canada
Reinga, Cape *139 C1 headland* North Island, New Zealand
Reinosa *99 D1* N Spain
Reliance *33 G5* Northwest Territories, C Canada
Rendsburg *101 C2* N Germany
Rengat *131 B6* Sumatra, W Indonesia
Rennell *141 E3 island* S Solomon Islands
Rennes *97 B3* NW France
Reno *47 A5* Nevada, W USA
Republican River *47 G5* ≈ Kansas/Nebraska, C USA
Repulse Bay *33 I3* Northwest Territories, N Canada
Resistencia *65 C4* NE Argentina
Reşiţa *109 A7* W Romania
Resolute *33 H2* Cornwallis Island, Nunavut, N Canada
Resolution Island *35 E1 island* Nunavut, NE Canada
Réthymno *107 F7* SE Greece
Réunion *76 H6 French* ◇ W Indian Ocean
Reus *99 G3* E Spain
Reutlingen *101 B7* S Germany
Reuver *84 E6* SE Netherlands
Revillagigedo, Islas *53 B5 island group* W Mexico
Rexburg *47 D3* Idaho, NW USA
Reyes *65 A2* NW Bolivia
Rey, Isla del *55 H6 island* Archipiélago de las Perlas, SE Panama
Reykjavík *83 A1* ● W Iceland
Reynosa *53 F3* C Mexico
Rezé *97 B3* NW France
Rhein *see* Rhine
Rheine *101 B4* NW Germany
Rheinisches Schiefergebirge *101 A5* ▲▲ W Germany
Rhine *84 E4* ≈ W Europe
Rhinelander *40 B3* Wisconsin, N USA
Rho *103 B2* N Italy
Rhode Island *37 F5* ◐ *state* NE USA
Rhodes *107 G6 island* Dodecanese, Greece
Rhodope Mountains *107 E3* ▲▲ Bulgaria/Greece
Rhône *97 E6* ≈ France/Switzerland
Rhossili *93 B7* S Wales, United Kingdom
Rhum *91 B4 island* W Scotland, United Kingdom
Ribble *93 C4* ≈ NW England, United Kingdom
Ribeira *99 A2* NW Spain
Ribeirão Preto *63 G7* S Brazil
Riberalta *65 B1* N Bolivia
Rice Lake *40 A3* Wisconsin, N USA
Richard Toll *72 A3* N Senegal
Richfield *47 D6* Utah, W USA
Richland *49 C3* Washington, NW USA
Richmond *139 C5* South Island, New Zealand
Richmond *93 D3* N England, United Kingdom
Richmond *39 E2* Kentucky, S USA
Richmond *39 H2 state capital* Virginia, NE USA
Richmond Range *139 C5* ▲▲ South Island, New Zealand
Ricobayo, Embalse de *99 B2* ⊡ NW Spain
Ridgecrest *49 D8* California, W USA
Ridsdale *93 D2* N England, United Kingdom
Ried im Innkreis *101 D7* NW Austria
Riemst *84 D7* NE Belgium
Riesa *101 D4* E Germany
Riga *83 E6* ● C Latvia
Riga, Gulf of *83 E6 gulf* Estonia/Latvia
Rigestan *125 E6 desert region* S Afghanistan
Riggins *47 B3* Idaho, NW USA
Riihimäki *83 E5* S Finland
Rijeka *107 B1* NW Croatia
Rijn *see* Rhine
Rijssen *84 E4* E Netherlands
Rimah, Wadi ar *123 C4 dry watercourse* C Saudi Arabia
Rimini *103 D3* N Italy
Rimouski *35 E4* Québec, SE Canada
Ringebu *83 B4* S Norway
Ringkøbing Fjord *83 A7 fjord* W Denmark
Ringvassøya *83 C1 island* N Norway
Ringwood *95 E5* S England, United Kingdom
Rio Branco *63 D5* W Brazil
Río Bravo *53 F3* C Mexico
Río Cuarto *65 B5* C Argentina
Rio de Janeiro *63 H7* SE Brazil
Río Gallegos *65 B9* S Argentina
Rio Grande *65 B9* S Argentina
Rio Grande *63 F9* S Brazil
Río Grande *53 D4* C Mexico
Rio Grande *47 F7* ≈ Texas, SW USA
Rio Grande do Norte *63 I4 state* E Brazil
Rio Grande do Sul *63 F8 state* S Brazil
Riohacha *63 C1* N Colombia
Río Lagartos *53 I4* SE Mexico
Riom *97 D5* C France
Rio Verde *53 E4* C Mexico
Ripoll *99 G2* NE Spain
Ripon *93 D3* N England, United Kingdom
Rishiri-to *133 F1 island* NE Japan
Ritidian Point *51 headland* N Guam
Rivas *55 D5* SW Nicaragua
Rivera *65 C5* NE Uruguay
River Falls *40 A3* Wisconsin, N USA
Riverside *49 D9* California, W USA
Riverstown *89 C6* S Ireland
Riverton *139 A8* South Island, New Zealand
Riverton *47 E4* Wyoming, C USA
Riviera *44 G6* Texas, SW USA
Rivière-du-Loup *35 E5* Québec, SE Canada
Rivne *109 C4* NW Ukraine
Rivoli *103 A2* NW Italy
Riyadh *123 C4* ● C Saudi Arabia
Rize *121 F2* NE Turkey
Rkiz *72 A3* W Mauritania
Road Town *57 I4* ○ C British Virgin Islands
Roag, Loch *91 A2 inlet* NW Scotland, United Kingdom
Roanne *97 E4* E France
Roanoke *39 G2* Virginia, NE USA
Roanoke River *39 H3* ≈ North Carolina/Virginia, SE USA
Roatán *55 D2* N Honduras
Robin Hood's Bay *93 E3* N England, United Kingdom
Robson, Mount *33 F6* ▲ British Columbia, SW Canada
Robstown *44 H5* Texas, SW USA
Roca Partida, Isla *53 B5 island* W Mexico
Rocas, Atol das *63 I4 island* E Brazil
Rochdale *93 D4* NW England, United Kingdom
Rochefort *84 D8* SE Belgium
Rochefort *97 B4* W France
Rochester *43 F4* Minnesota, N USA
Rochester *37 F3* New Hampshire, NE USA
Rochester *37 C3* New York, NE USA
Rockford *40 B5* Illinois, N USA
Rockhampton *137 H4* Queensland, E Australia
Rock Hill *39 G4* South Carolina, SE USA
Rock Island *40 B5* Illinois, N USA
Rock Sound *57 E2* Eleuthera Island, C Bahamas
Rock Springs *47 E4* Wyoming, C USA
Rocky Mount *39 H3* North Carolina, SE USA
Rocky Mountains *28* ▲▲ Canada/USA
Roden *84 E2* NE Netherlands
Rodez *97 D6* S France
Rodos *see* Rhodes
Roermond *84 E6* SE Netherlands
Roeselare *84 B6* W Belgium
Rogers *39 B3* Arkansas, C USA
Roi Et *131 C3* E Thailand
Rokiškis *83 F7* NE Lithuania
Rokycany *105 B5* W Czech Republic
Rolla *43 F6* Missouri, C USA
Roma *137 G4* Queensland, E Australia
Roma *see* Rome
Roman *109 C6* NE Romania
Romania *109 B6* ◆ *republic* SE Europe
Rome *103 C5* ● C Italy
Rome *39 E4* Georgia, SE USA
Romford *95 G3* SE England, United Kingdom
Romney Marsh [illegible] *physical region* SE England, United Kingdom
Romny *109 E4* NE Ukraine
Rømø *83 A7 island* SW Denmark
Romsey *95 E4* S England, United Kingdom
Ronda *99 C6* S Spain
Rondônia *63 D5 state* W Brazil
Rondonópolis *63 F6* W Brazil
Rønne *83 C7* E Denmark
Ronne Ice Shelf *142 B4 ice shelf* Antarctica
Roosendaal *84 C5* S Netherlands
Roosevelt Island *142 C6 island* Antarctica
Roraima *63 D3 state* N Brazil
Roraima, Mount *63 D2* ▲ N South America
Røros *83 B4* S Norway
Rosa, Lake *57 E3* ◎ S Bahamas
Rosalia, Punta *141 C5 headland* Easter Island, Chile
Rosario *65 C5* C Argentina
Rosario *65 C3* C Paraguay
Rosarito *53 A1* NW Mexico
Roscommon *89 C4* C Ireland
Roscommon *40 D4* Michigan, N USA
Roscrea *89 D5* C Ireland
Roseau *57 K5* ● SW Dominica
Roseburg *49 B4* Oregon, NW USA
Rosenberg *44 H4* Texas, SW USA
Rosengarten *101 C3* N Germany
Rosenheim *101 D7* S Germany
Roslavl' *111 A5* W Russian Federation
Rosmalen *84 D5* S Netherlands
Ross *139 B6* SW New Zealand
Rossano *103 E7* SW Italy
Ross Carbery *89 B7* S Ireland
Ross Ice Shelf *142 C5 ice shelf* Antarctica
Rosslare *89 E6* SE Ireland
Rosslare Harbour *89 E6* SE Ireland
Rosso *72 A3* SW Mauritania
Ross-on-Wye *93 C6* W England, United Kingdom
Rossosh' *111 A7* W Russian Federation
Ross Sea *142 C6 sea* Antarctica
Rostock *101 D2* NE Germany
Rostov-na-Donu *111 A7* SW Russian Federation
Roswell *44 E3* New Mexico, SW USA
Rother *95 F4* ≈ S England, United Kingdom
Rothera *142 A4 UK research station* Antarctica
Rotherham *93 E4* N England, United Kingdom
Rothesay *91 C6* W Scotland, United Kingdom
Rotorua *139 D3* North Island, New Zealand
Rotorua, Lake *139 D3* ◎ NE New Zealand
Rotterdam *84 C4* SW Netherlands
Rottweil *101 B7* S Germany
Rotuma *141 I4 island* NW Fiji
Roubaix *97 D1* N France
Rouen *97 D2* N France
Round Rock *44 G4* Texas, SW USA
Roundstone *89 B4* W Ireland
Roundwood *89 E5* E Ireland
Rousay *91 E1 island* N Scotland, United Kingdom
Roussillon *97 D7 cultural region* S France
Rouyn-Noranda *35 D5* Québec, SE Canada
Rovaniemi *83 E3* N Finland
Rovigo *103 C3* NE Italy
Rovuma, Rio *76 F4* ≈ Mozambique/Tanzania
Roxas City *131 F4* C Philippines
Royale, Isle *40 C1 island* Michigan, N USA
Royal Leamington Spa *93 D6* C England, United Kingdom
Royal Tunbridge Wells *95 G4* SE England, United Kingdom
Royan *97 B4* W France
Royston *95 G3* E England, United Kingdom
Rožňava *105 E6* E Slovakia
Ruapehu, Mount *139 D4* ✱ North Island, New Zealand
Ruapuke Island *139 B8 island* SW New Zealand
Ruatoria *139 E3* North Island, New Zealand
Ruawai *139 D2* North Island, New Zealand
Rubizhne *109 G4* E Ukraine
Ruby Mountains *47 B5* ▲▲ Nevada, W USA
Rudnyy *118 C4* N Kazakhstan
Rufiji *75 D7* ≈ E Tanzania
Rufino *65 B5* C Argentina
Rugby *93 E6* C England, United Kingdom
Rugeley *93 D5* C England, United Kingdom
Rügen *101 D2 cape* NE Germany
Ruhr Valley *101 A4 industrial region* W Germany
Rukwa, Lake *75 C7* ◎ SE Tanzania
Rumbek *75 B4* S Sudan
Rum Cay *57 E2 island* C Bahamas
Rumia *105 D1* N Poland
Runanga *139 C5* South Island, New Zealand
Runcorn *93 C4* C England, United Kingdom
Rundu *76 C5* NE Namibia
Ruoqiang *129 C3* NW China
Rupel *84 C6* ≈ N Belgium
Rupert, Rivière de *35 D4* ≈ Québec, C Canada
Ruse *107 F2* N Bulgaria
Rushden [illegible] England, United Kingdom
Rushmore, Mount *43 A4* ▲ South Dakota, N USA
Russellville *39 B3* Arkansas, C USA
Russian Federation *118 D4* ◆ *republic* Asia/Europe
Rust'avi *121 H2* SE Georgia
Ruston *39 B5* Louisiana, S USA
Rutland *37 E3* Vermont, NE USA
Rutland Water *93 E5* ◎ C England, United Kingdom
Rutog *129 A4* W China
Ruvuma *75 D7* ≈ Mozambique/Tanzania
Ruwenzori *75 B5* ▲▲ Dem. Rep. Congo/Uganda
Ružomberok *105 E6* N Slovakia
Rwanda *75 B6* ◆ *republic* C Africa
Ryazan' *111 B6* W Russian Federation
Rybinsk *111 B5* W Russian Federation
Rybnik *105 D5* S Poland
Rye *95 G4* SE England, United Kingdom
Rye *93 E3* ≈ N England, United Kingdom
Ryki *105 F4* E Poland
Rypin *105 E3* C Poland
Rysy *105 E6* ▲ S Poland
Ryukyu Islands *133 A7 island group* SW Japan
Rzeszów *105 F5* SE Poland
Rzhev *111 A5* W Russian Federation

S

Saale *101 D4* ≈ C Germany
Saalfeld *101 C5* C Germany
Saarbrücken *101 A6* SW Germany
Saaremaa *83 D6 island* W Estonia
Saariselkä *83 E2* N Finland
Šabac *107 D2* W Serbia
Sabadell *99 G2* E Spain
Sabah *131 E5 cultural region* Borneo, E Malaysia Asia
Sab'atayn, Ramlat as *123 C7 desert* C Yemen
Sabaya *65 A3* S Bolivia
Saberi, Hamun-e *123 F3* ◎ Afghanistan/Iran
Sabha *70 F3* C Libya
Sabinas *53 E2* NE Mexico
Sabinas Hidalgo *53 E3* NE Mexico
Sabine Lake *39 A6* ◎ Louisiana/Texas, S USA
Sabine River *44 I4* ≈ Louisiana/Texas, SW USA
Sable, Cape *39 G9 headland* Florida, SE USA
Sable, Île de *141 E5 island* NW New Caledonia
Sable Island *35 G5 island* Nova Scotia, SE Canada
Sabzevar *123 E1* NE Iran
Sachsen *see* Saxony
Sachs Harbour *33 F3* Banks Island, Northwest Territories, N Canada
Sacramento *49 B6 state capital* California, W USA
Sacramento Mountains *44 D3* ▲▲ New Mexico, SW USA
Sacramento River *49 B6* ≈ California, W USA
Sacramento Valley *49 B6 valley* California, W USA
Sa'dah *123 C6* NW Yemen
Sado *133 F4 island* C Japan
Säffle *83 C5* C Sweden
Safford *44 C3* Arizona, SW USA
Saffron Walden *95 G3* SE England, United Kingdom
Safi *70 B2* W Morocco
Safid Kuh, Selseleh-ye *125 D5* ▲▲ W Afghanistan
Saga *133 D7* Kyūshū, SW Japan
Sagaing *131 A2* C Burma (Myanmar)
Sagami-nada *133 G6 inlet* SW Japan
Saganaga Lake *43 F1* ◎ Minnesota, N USA
Sagar *127 E4* C India
Saginaw *40 E4* Michigan, N USA
Saginaw Bay *40 E4 lake bay* Michigan, N USA
Sagua la Grande *57 C2* C Cuba
Sagunt *see* Sagunto
Sagunto *99 F4* E Spain
Sahara *72 D2 desert* Libya/Algeria
Saharan Atlas *70 D2* ▲▲ Algeria/Morocco
Sahel *72 E3 physical region* C Africa
Sahiwal *127 D2* E Pakistan
Saidpur *127 F3* NW Bangladesh
Saimaa *83 F4* ◎ SE Finland
St Albans *95 F3* E England, United Kingdom
Saint Albans *39 F2* West Virginia, NE USA
St Aldhelm's Head *95 E5 headland* S England, United Kingdom
St Andrews *91 E5* E Scotland, United Kingdom
St Anne *95 H5* Alderney, Channel Islands
St. Anthony *35 G3* Newfoundland, SE Canada
Saint Augustine *39 G6* Florida, SE USA
St Austell *95 B5* SW England, United Kingdom
St Austell Bay *95 B6 bay* SW England, United Kingdom
St-Barthélemy *57 J4 island* N Guadeloupe
St Bees Head *93 B3 headland* NW England, United Kingdom
St-Brieuc *97 B2* NW France
St. Catharines *35 D6* Ontario, S Canada
St Catherine's Point *95 E5 headland* S England, United Kingdom
St-Chamond *97 E5* E France
Saint Clair, Lake *37 A4* ◎ Canada/USA
St-Claude *97 E4* E France
Saint Cloud *43 E3* Minnesota, N USA
St. Croix *51 island* S Virgin Islands (USA)
Saint Croix River *40 A3* ≈ Minnesota/Wisconsin, N USA
St David's *93 A7* SW Wales, United Kingdom
St-Dié *97 F3* NE France
St-Egrève *97 E5* E France
Saintes *97 B4* W France
St-Étienne *97 E5* E France
St-Flour *97 D5* C France
St-Gaudens *97 C6* S France
Saint George *137 G4* Queensland, E Australia
Saint George *47 C6* Utah, W USA
St. George's *57 K7* ● SW Grenada
St-Georges *35 E5* Québec, SE Canada
St George's Channel *89 F6 channel* Ireland/Wales, United Kingdom
Saint Helena *26 UK* ◇ C Atlantic Ocean
St. Helena Bay *76 B7 bay* SW South Africa
St Helens *93 C4* NW England, United Kingdom
Saint Helens, Mount *49 B2* ✱ Washington, NW USA
St Helier *95 H6* ○ S Jersey, Channel Islands
Saint Ignace *40 D3* Michigan, N USA
St Ives *95 A6* E England, United Kingdom
St Ives *95 B3* SW England, United Kingdom
St-Jean, Lac *35 E4* ◎ Québec, SE Canada
St. John *35 F5* New Brunswick, SE Canada
St John *95 H6* N Jersey
St. John *51 island* Virgin Islands (USA)
Saint John River *37 G1* ≈ Canada/USA
St John's *57 J4* ● Antigua, Antigua and Barbuda
St. John's *35 H4* Newfoundland, E Canada
Saint Johns *44 C2* Arizona, SW USA
St John's Point *89 C2 headland* N Ireland
Saint Joseph *43 E6* Missouri, C USA
St Julian's *112 B6* N Malta
Saint Kitts and Nevis *57 I5* ◆ *commonwealth republic* E West Indies
St. Lawrence, Gulf of *35 F4 gulf* NW Atlantic Ocean
Saint Lawrence Island *50 C1 island* Alaska, USA
Saint Lawrence River *37 D2* ≈ Canada/USA
St. Lawrence Seaway *35 F4 seaway* Canada/USA North America Gulf of St.Lawrence N Atlantic Ocean
St-Lô *97 C2* N France
St-Louis *97 F3* NE France
Saint Louis *72 A3* NW Senegal
Saint Louis *43 G6* Missouri, C USA
St Lucia *57 J6* ◆ *commonwealth republic* SE West Indies
St. Lucia Channel *57 K6 channel* Martinique/Saint Lucia North America Atlantic Ocean
St Magnus Bay *91 A6 bay* N Scotland, United Kingdom
St-Malo *97 B2* NW France
St-Malo, Golfe de *97 B2 gulf* NW France
St Margaret's Hope *91 E1* NE Scotland, United Kingdom
St-Martin *57 J4 island* N Guadeloupe
St Mary *95 H6* Jersey, Channel Islands
St. Matthias Group *141 C1 island group* NE Papua New Guinea
St. Moritz *101 C8* SE Switzerland
St-Nazaire *97 B3* NW France
St Neots *95 F2* E England, United Kingdom
St-Omer *97 D1* N France
Saint Paul *43 E3 state capital* Minnesota, N USA
St Peter Port *95 G6* ○ C Guernsey, Channel Islands
Saint Petersburg *111 A4* NW Russian Federation
Saint Petersburg *39 F7* Florida, SE USA
St-Pierre and Miquelon *35 G4 French* ◇ NE North America
St-Quentin *97 D2* N France
St. Thomas *51 island* Virgin Islands (USA)
Saint Vincent *57 J6 island* N Saint Vincent and the Grenadines
Saint Vincent and the Grenadines *57 I6* ◆ *commonwealth republic* SE West Indies
Saint Vincent Passage *57 K6 passage* Saint Lucia/Saint Vincent and the Grenadines
Sajama, Nevado *65 A2* ▲ W Bolivia
Sajószentpéter *105 F7* NE Hungary
Sakakawea, Lake *43 B2* ⊡ North Dakota, N USA
Sakata *133 F4* C Japan
Sakhalin *118 I4 island* SE Russian Federation
Saki *121 I2* NW Azerbaijan
Sakishima-shoto *133 A8 island group* SW Japan
Sala *83 C5* C Sweden
Sala Consilina *103 E6* S Italy
Salado, Río *65 B4* ≈ E Argentina
Salado, Río *65 B5* ≈ C Argentina
Salalah *123 E6* SW Oman
Salamá *55 B3* C Guatemala
Salamanca *65 A5* C Chile
Salamanca *99 C3* NW Spain
Salang Tunnel *125 F4 tunnel* C Afghanistan Asia
Salantai *83 E7* NW Lithuania
Salavat *111 D6* W Russian Federation
Šalčininkai *83 F7* SE Lithuania
Salcombe *95 C6* SW England, United Kingdom
Sale *137 G6* Victoria, SE Australia
Salé *70 C1* NW Morocco
Salekhard *118 D3* N Russian Federation
Salelologa *141 A5* C Samoa
Salem *127 D7* SE India
Salem *49 B3 state capital* Oregon, NW USA
Salerno *103 D6* S Italy
Salerno, Gulf of *103 D6 gulf* S Italy
Salford *93 D4* NW England, United Kingdom
Salihorsk *109 C3* S Belarus
Salina *43 D6* Kansas, C USA

◐ Administrative region ◆ Country ● Country capital ◇ Dependent territory ○ Dependent territory capital ▲▲ Mountain range ▲ Mountain ✱ Volcano ≈ River ◎ Lake ⊡ Reservoir

SALINA

Salina 47 D6 Utah, W USA
Salina Cruz 53 G6 SE Mexico
Salinas 49 B7 California, W USA
Salisbury 95 E4 S England, United Kingdom
Salisbury Plain 95 E4 plain S England, United Kingdom
Salmon 47 C3 Idaho, NW USA
Salmon River 47 B3 ≈ Idaho, NW USA
Salmon River Mountains 47 B3 ▲▲ Idaho, NW USA
Salo 83 E5 SW Finland
Salon-de-Provence 97 E6 SE France
Salonica 107 E4 N Greece
Sal'sk 111 A8 SW Russian Federation
Salta 65 B4 NW Argentina
Saltash 95 B5 SW England, United Kingdom
Saltillo 53 E3 NE Mexico
Salt Lake City 47 D5 state capital Utah, W USA
Salto 65 C5 N Uruguay
Salton Sea 49 D9 ◎ California, W USA
Salvador 63 H6 E Brazil
Salween 131 B2 ≈ SE Asia
Salyan 127 E3 W Nepal
Salzburg 101 D7 N Austria
Salzgitter 101 C4 C Germany
Salzwedel 101 C3 N Germany
Samalayuca 53 C2 N Mexico
Samar 131 F4 island C Philippines
Samara 111 C6 W Russian Federation
Samarinda 131 E6 C Indonesia
Samarqand 125 F3 C Uzbekistan
Sambalpur 127 F4 E India
Sambava 76 H4 NE Madagascar
Sambir 109 B4 NW Ukraine
Sambre 97 E1 ≈ Belgium/France
Samfya 76 D3 N Zambia
Samoa 141 B4 ◆ monarchy W Polynesia
Sámos 107 F5 island Dodecanese, SE Greece
Samothraki 107 F4 island NE Greece
Sampit 131 D7 C Indonesia
Sam Rayburn Reservoir 44 I4 ⊠ Texas, SW USA
Samsun 121 E2 N Turkey
Samtredia 121 G1 W Georgia
Samui, Ko 131 B5 island SW Thailand
San 72 C3 C Mali
San 105 G5 ≈ SE Poland
Sana 123 C6 ● W Yemen
Sana 107 B2 ≈ NW Bosnia and Herzegovina
San'a' see Sana
Sanae 142 B3 South African research station Antarctica
Sanaga 72 G5 ≈ C Cameroon
Sanandaj 123 C2 W Iran
San Andrés, Isla de 55 F4 island NW Colombia
San Andrés Tuxtla 53 G5 E Mexico
San Angelo 44 F4 Texas, SW USA
San Antonio 55 B2 S Belize
San Antonio 65 A5 C Chile
San Antonio 44 G5 Texas, SW USA
San Antonio Oeste 65 B7 E Argentina
Sanaw 123 D6 NE Yemen
San Benedicto, Isla 53 B5 island W Mexico
San Benito 55 B2 N Guatemala
San Bernardino 49 D8 California, W USA
San Blas 53 C3 C Mexico
San Blas, Cape 39 D7 headland Florida, SE USA
San Blas, Cordillera de 55 H6 ▲▲ NE Panama
San Carlos 55 E5 S Nicaragua
San Carlos 44 C3 Arizona, SW USA
San Carlos de Bariloche 65 A7 SW Argentina
San Clemente Island 49 C9 island Channel Islands, California, W USA
San Cristóbal 63 C2 W Venezuela
San Cristobal 141 F3 island SE Solomon Islands
San Cristóbal de Las Casas 53 H5 SE Mexico
San Cristóbal, Isla 63 B7 island Galapagos Islands, Ecuador
Sancti Spíritus 57 C3 C Cuba
Sancy, Puy de 97 D5 ▲ C France
Sandakan 131 E5 E Malaysia
Sandanski 107 E3 SW Bulgaria
Sanday 91 E1 island NE Scotland, United Kingdom
Sandbach 93 D5 W England, United Kingdom
Sanders 44 C2 Arizona, SW USA
Sand Hills 43 B4 ▲▲ Nebraska, C USA
San Diego 49 D9 California, W USA
Sandnes 83 A5 S Norway
Sandomierz 105 F5 C Poland
Sandown 95 E5 S England, United Kingdom
Sandpoint 47 B1 Idaho, NW USA
Sandray 91 A4 island NW Scotland, United Kingdom
Sand Springs 43 D7 Oklahoma, C USA
Sandusky 40 E5 Ohio, N USA
Sandvika 83 B5 S Norway
Sandviken 83 D5 C Sweden
Sandy City 47 D5 Utah, W USA
Sandy Lake 35 A3 ◎ Ontario, C Canada
San Esteban 55 D3 C Honduras
San Fernando 99 C6 S Spain
San Fernando 57 K7 Trinidad, Trinidad and Tobago
San Fernando del Valle de Catamarca 65 B4 NW Argentina
San Francisco 49 B7 California, W USA
San Francisco del Oro 53 D3 N Mexico
San Francisco de Macorís 57 G4 C Dominican Republic
Sangan, Kuh-e 125 E5 ▲ C Afghanistan
Sangir, Kepulauan 131 F6 island group N Indonesia
Sangli 127 D5 W India
Sangmélima 72 G6 S Cameroon
Sangre de Cristo Mountains 44 E1 ▲▲ Colorado/New Mexico, C USA
San Ignacio 55 B2 W Belize
San Ignacio 65 B2 N Bolivia
San Ignacio 53 B3 W Mexico
San Joaquin Valley 49 C7 valley California, W USA
San Jorge, Gulf of 65 B8 gulf S Argentina
San José 55 E6 ● C Costa Rica
San José 65 C2 E Bolivia
San José 55 A4 S Guatemala
San Jose 49 B7 California, W USA
San José del Guaviare 63 C3 S Colombia
San Juan 65 A5 W Argentina
San Juan 51 ○ NE Puerto Rico
San Juan Bautista 65 C4 S Paraguay
San Juan de Alicante 99 F5 E Spain
San Juan del Norte 55 E5 SE Nicaragua
San Juanito, Isla 53 C4 island C Mexico
San Juan Mountains 47 E6 ▲▲ Colorado, C USA
San Juan, Río 55 E5 ≈ Costa Rica/Nicaragua
San Juan River 47 E6 ≈ Colorado/Utah, W USA
Sankt Gallen 101 B7 NE Switzerland
Sankt-Peterburg see Saint Petersburg
Sankt Pölten 101 E7 N Austria
Sankuru 76 C2 ≈ C Dem. Rep. Congo
Şanlıurfa 121 F4 S Turkey
San Lorenzo 65 B3 S Bolivia
Sanlúcar de Barrameda 99 C6 S Spain
San Lucas Cape 53 C4 headland W Mexico
San Luis 65 B5 C Argentina
San Luis 55 B2 NE Guatemala
San Luis 53 A1 NW Mexico
San Luis Obispo 49 B8 California, W USA
San Luis Potosí 53 E4 C Mexico
San Marcos 55 A3 W Guatemala
San Marcos 44 G4 Texas, SW USA
San Marino 103 D3 ● C San Marino
San Marino 103 D3 ◆ republic S Europe
San Martín 142 A4 C Argentina
San Matías 65 C2 E Bolivia
San Matías, Gulf of 65 B7 gulf E Argentina
Sanmenxia 129 F4 C China
San Miguel 55 B4 SE El Salvador
San Miguel 53 D2 N Mexico
San Miguel de Tucumán 65 B4 N Argentina
San Miguelito 55 E5 S Nicaragua
San Miguelito 55 H6 C Panama
San Miguel, Río 65 B2 ≈ E Bolivia
Sanok 105 F6 SE Poland
San Pablo 65 B3 S Bolivia
San Pedro 55 C1 NE Belize
San-Pédro 72 C5 S Ivory Coast
San Pedro 53 D3 NE Mexico
San Pedro de la Cueva 53 C2 NW Mexico
San Pedro Mártir, Sierra 53 A2 ▲▲ NW Mexico
San Pedro Sula 55 C3 NW Honduras
San Rafael 65 A5 W Argentina
San Rafael Mountains 49 C8 ▲▲ California, W USA
San Ramón de la Nueva Orán 65 B3 N Argentina
San Remo 103 A3 NW Italy
San Salvador 55 B4 ● SW El Salvador
San Salvador 57 E2 island E Bahamas
San Salvador de Jujuy 65 B3 N Argentina
Sansanné-Mango 72 D4 N Togo
Sansepolcro 103 C4 C Italy
San Severo 103 E5 SE Italy
Santa Ana 65 B2 N Bolivia
Santa Ana 55 B4 NW El Salvador
Santa Ana 49 D9 California, W USA
Santa Barbara 53 D3 N Mexico
Santa Barbara 49 C8 California, W USA
Santa Catalina 55 G6 W Panama
Santa Catalina Island 49 C9 island Channel Islands, California, W USA
Santa Catarina 63 F8 state S Brazil
Santa Clara 57 C3 C Cuba
Santa Comba 99 B1 NW Spain
Santa Cruz 65 B2 C Bolivia
Santa Cruz 49 B7 California, W USA
Santa Cruz del Quiché 55 A3 W Guatemala
Santa Cruz, Isla 63 B7 island Galapagos Islands, Ecuador
Santa Cruz Islands 141 G3 island group E Solomon Islands
Santa Cruz, Río 65 A8 ≈ S Argentina
Santa Elena 55 B2 W Belize
Santa Fe 65 C5 C Argentina
Santa Fe 44 D2 state capital New Mexico, SW USA
Santa Genoveva 53 B4 ▲ W Mexico
Santa Isabel 141 E2 island N Solomon Islands
Santa Lucia Range 49 B8 ▲▲ California, W USA
Santa Margarita, Isla 53 B4 island W Mexico
Santa Maria 63 F8 S Brazil
Santa Maria 49 C8 California, W USA
Santa Maria 141 G4 island N Vanuatu
Santa María, Isla 63 A7 island Galapagos Islands, Ecuador
Santa Marta 63 B1 N Colombia
Santander 99 D1 N Spain
Santarém 63 F4 N Brazil
Santarém 99 A4 W Portugal
Santa Rosa 65 B6 C Argentina
Santa Rosa 49 B6 California, W USA
Santa Rosa 44 E2 New Mexico, SW USA
Santa Rosa de Copán 55 B3 W Honduras
Santa Rosa Island 49 B9 island California, W USA
Sant Carles de la Ràpita 99 F3 NE Spain
Santiago 65 A5 ● C Chile
Santiago 57 G4 N Dominican Republic
Santiago 55 G7 S Panama
Santiago 99 B1 NW Spain
Santiago de Cuba 57 E4 E Cuba
Santiago del Estero 65 B4 C Argentina
Santo Domingo 57 G4 ● SE Dominican Republic
Santorini 107 F6 island Cyclades, SE Greece
Santos 63 G7 S Brazil
Santo Tomé 65 C4 NE Argentina
San Valentín, Cerro 65 A8 ▲ S Chile
San Vicente 55 C4 C El Salvador
São Francisco, Rio 63 G6 ≈ E Brazil
Sao Hill 75 D7 S Tanzania
São João da Madeira 99 B3 N Portugal
São Luís 63 G4 NE Brazil
São Manuel, Rio 63 E5 ≈ C Brazil
Saona, Isla 57 G4 island SE Dominican Republic
Saône 97 E5 ≈ E France
São Paulo 63 G7 S Brazil
São Paulo 63 F7 state S Brazil
São Roque, Cabo de 63 I4 headland E Brazil
São Tomé 72 E6 ● S Sao Tome and Principe
São Tomé 72 F6 island S Sao Tome and Principe
Sao Tome and Principe 72 E6 ◆ republic E Atlantic Ocean
São Vicente, Cabo de 99 A5 cape S Portugal
Sapele 72 E5 S Nigeria
Sa Pobla 99 H4 Majorca, Spain
Sappir 123 H7 S Israel
Sapporo 133 F2 NE Japan
Sapri 103 E6 S Italy
Sapulpa 43 D8 Oklahoma, C USA
Saqqez 123 C2 NW Iran
Sarahs 125 D4 S Turkmenistan
Sarajevo 107 C2 ● SE Bosnia and Herzegovina
Saraktash 111 D7 W Russian Federation
Saran' 118 C5 C Kazakhstan
Sarandë 107 D4 S Albania
Saransk 111 B6 W Russian Federation
Sarasota 39 F8 Florida, SE USA
Saratoga Springs 37 E3 New York, NE USA
Saratov 111 B7 W Russian Federation
Sarawak 131 D6 cultural region Borneo, S Malaysia
Sardegna see Sardinia
Sardinia 103 B6 island W Italy
Sargodha 127 C2 NE Pakistan
Sarh 72 H4 S Chad
Sari 123 D1 N Iran
Saría 107 G7 island SE Greece
Sarıkamış 121 G3 NE Turkey
Sarikol Range 125 H3 ▲▲ China/Tajikistan
Sariwon 133 A5 SW North Korea
Sark 95 H6 island SE Guernsey
Şarkışla 121 E3 C Turkey
Sarmiento 65 B7 S Argentina
Sarnia 35 C6 Ontario, S Canada
Sarny 109 C4 NW Ukraine
Sarpsborg 83 B5 S Norway
Sartène 97 G6 Corsica, France
Sarthe 97 C3 cultural region N France Europe
Sárti 107 E4 N Greece
Sarygamyş Köli 125 C2 salt lake Kazakhstan/Uzbekistan
Sary-Tash 125 G3 SW Kyrgyzstan
Sasalaguan, Mount 51 ▲ S Guam
Sasebo 133 C7 SW Japan
Saskatchewan 33 G5 ◐ province SW Canada
Saskatchewan 33 H6 ≈ Manitoba/Saskatchewan, C Canada
Saskatoon 33 G7 Saskatchewan, S Canada
Sasovo 111 B6 W Russian Federation
Sassandra 72 C5 S Ivory Coast
Sassandra 72 C5 ≈ S Ivory Coast
Sassari 103 A5 Sardinia, Italy
Sassenheim [illegible] W Netherlands
Sassnitz 101 D2 NE Germany
Sátoraljaújhely 105 F7 NE Hungary
Satpura Range 127 D4 ▲▲ C India
Satsunan-shoto 133 A7 island group SW Japan
Sattanen 83 E2 NE Finland
Satu Mare 109 B5 NW Romania
Saudi Arabia 123 C5 ◆ monarchy SW Asia
Saulkrasti 83 E6 C Latvia
Sault Sainte Marie 40 D2 Michigan, N USA
Sault Ste. Marie 35 C5 Ontario, S Canada
Saumur 97 C3 NW France
Saurimo 76 C3 NE Angola
Savá 55 D2 N Honduras
Savai'i 141 A4 island NW Samoa
Savannah 39 G5 Georgia, SE USA
Savannah River 39 G5 ≈ Georgia/South Carolina, SE USA
Save 107 D2 ≈ SE Europe
Save, Rio 76 E5 ≈ Mozambique/Zimbabwe
Saverne 97 F3 NE France
Savigliano 103 A2 NW Italy
Savinskiy 111 C4 NW Russian Federation
Savissivik 143 A4 N Greenland
Savoie 97 E5 cultural region E France Europe
Savona 103 B3 NW Italy
Savu Sea 131 F8 sea S Indonesia
Sawel Mountain 89 E2 ▲ C Northern Ireland, United Kingdom
Sawhaj 70 I3 C Egypt
Sawqirah 123 E6 S Oman
Saxony 101 D4 cultural region E Germany
Saýat 125 E3 E Turkmenistan
Sayaxché 55 B2 N Guatemala
Sayhut 123 D6 E Yemen
Saynshand 129 F2 SE Mongolia
Sayre 37 D4 Pennsylvania, NE USA
Say'un 123 D6 C Yemen
Scafell Pike 93 C3 ▲ NW England, United Kingdom
Scandinavia 78 geophysical region NW Europe
Scapa Flow 91 E1 sea basin N Scotland, United Kingdom
Scarborough 57 K7 N Trinidad and Tobago
Scarborough 93 F3 N England, United Kingdom
Scarp 91 A2 island NW Scotland, United Kingdom
Schaerbeek 84 C6 C Belgium
Schaffhausen 101 B7 N Switzerland
Schagen 84 C3 NW Netherlands
Scheessel 101 C3 NW Germany
Schefferville 35 E3 Québec, E Canada
Scheldt 84 C6 ≈ W Europe
Schell Creek Range 47 C5 ▲▲ Nevada, W USA
Schenectady 37 E4 New York, NE USA
Schertz 44 G5 Texas, SW USA
Schiermonnikoog 84 E1 island Waddeneilanden, N Netherlands
Schijndel 84 D5 S Netherlands
Schiltigheim 97 F3 NE France
Schleswig 101 C2 N Germany
Schleswig-Holstein 101 C2 state N Germany
Schönebeck 101 D4 C Germany
Schoten 84 C6 N Belgium
Schouwen 84 B5 island SW Netherlands
Schwäbische Alb 101 B7 ▲▲ S Germany
Schwandorf 101 D6 SE Germany
Schwarzwald see Black Forest
Schwaz 101 D7 W Austria
Schweinfurt 101 C5 SE Germany
Schwerin 101 C3 N Germany
Schwyz 101 B8 C Switzerland
Scioto River 40 E7 ≈ Ohio, N USA
Scotch Corner 93 D3 N England, United Kingdom
Scotia Sea 142 A2 sea SW Atlantic Ocean
Scotland 91 C4 ◐ national region , United Kingdom
Scott Base 142 C6 NZ research station Antarctica
Scottsbluff 43 A5 Nebraska, C USA
Scottsboro 39 E4 Alabama, S USA
Scottsdale 44 B3 Arizona, SW USA
Scousburgh 91 A7 NE Scotland, United Kingdom
Scranton 37 D4 Pennsylvania, NE USA
Scunthorpe 93 E4 E England, United Kingdom
Scutari, Lake 107 C3 ◎ Albania/Montenegro
Seaford 95 G5 SE England, United Kingdom
Searcy 39 B3 Arkansas, C USA
Seascale 93 B3 NW England, United Kingdom
Seattle 49 B2 Washington, NW USA
Sébaco 55 D4 W Nicaragua
Sebastián Vizcaíno, Bahía 53 A2 bay NW Mexico
Secunderabad 127 E5 C India
Sedan 97 E2 N France
Seddon 139 D5 C New Zealand
Seddonville 139 C5 South Island, New Zealand
Sédhiou 72 A4 SW Senegal
Sedona 44 B2 Arizona, SW USA
Seesen 101 C4 C Germany
Segezha 111 B3 NW Russian Federation
Ségou 72 C3 C Mali
Segovia 99 D3 C Spain
Séguédine 72 G2 NE Niger
Seguin 44 G5 Texas, SW USA
Segura 99 E5 ≈ S Spain
Seinäjoki 83 E4 W Finland
Seine 97 D2 ≈ N France
Seine, Baie de la 97 C2 bay N France
Sekondi-Takoradi 72 D5 S Ghana
Selby 93 E4 N England, United Kingdom
Selenga 129 E2 ≈ Mongolia/Russian Federation
Sélestat 97 F3 NE France
Selfoss 83 A1 SW Iceland
Sélibabi 72 B3 S Mauritania
Selkirk 91 E6 SE Scotland, United Kingdom
Selma 49 C7 California, W USA
Semarang 131 D8 Java, C Indonesia
Sembé 76 B1 NW Congo
Seminole 44 E3 Texas, SW USA
Seminole, Lake 39 E6 ⊠ Florida/Georgia, SE USA
Semipalatinsk 118 D5 E Kazakhstan
Semnān 123 E2 N Iran
Semois 84 D8 ≈ SE Belgium
Senachwine Lake 40 B6 ◎ Illinois, N USA
Sendai 133 D8 SW Japan
Sendai 133 G4 C Japan
Sendai-wan 133 G4 bay E Japan
Senec 105 D7 W Slovakia
Senegal 72 A3 ◆ republic W Africa
Senegal 72 A3 ≈ W Africa
Seney Marsh 40 D2 wetland Michigan, N USA
Senftenberg 101 E4 E Germany
Sênggê Zangbo 129 B4 ≈ W China
Senica 105 D6 W Slovakia
Senja 83 C1 island N Norway
Senkaku-shoto 133 A8 island group SW Japan
Senlis 97 D2 N France
Sennar 75 C3 C Sudan
Sens 97 D3 C France
Seoul 133 B6 ● NW South Korea
Sepik 141 A2 ≈ Indonesia/Papua New Guinea
Sept-Îles 35 F4 Québec, SE Canada
Serahs 125 D4 S Turkmenistan
Seraing 84 D7 E Belgium
Seram, Pulau 131 G7 island Maluku, E Indonesia
Serang 131 C7 Java, C Indonesia
Serasan, Selat 131 D6 strait Indonesia/Malaysia
Serbia 107 C3 ◆ federal republic SE Europe
Serdar 125 C3 W Turkmenistan
Seremban 131 B6 SW Malaysia
Serengeti Plain 75 C6 plain N Tanzania
Serenje 76 D4 E Zambia
Serhetabat 125 D4 S Turkmenistan
Sérifos 107 E6 island Cyclades, Greece
Serov 118 C4 C Russian Federation
Serowe 76 D5 SE Botswana
Serpukhov 111 A5 W Russian Federation
Sesto San Giovanni 103 B2 N Italy
Sète 97 D6 S France
Setesdal 83 B5 valley S Norway
Sétif 70 E1 N Algeria
Setté Cama 76 A2 SW Gabon
Settle 93 D3 N England, United Kingdom
Setúbal 99 A4 W Portugal
Setúbal, Baía de 99 A5 bay W Portugal
Seul, Lac 35 A4 ◎ Ontario, S Canada
Sevan 121 H2 C Armenia
Sevan, Lake 121 H2 ◎ E Armenia
Sevastopol' 109 F7 S Ukraine
Sevenoaks 95 G4 SE England, United Kingdom
Severn 35 B3 ≈ Ontario, S Canada
Severn 93 C5 ≈ England/Wales, United Kingdom
Severnaya Zemlya 118 E2 island group N Russian Federation
Severnyy 111 E3 NW Russian Federation
Severodvinsk 111 C3 NW Russian Federation
Severomorsk 111 C2 NW Russian Federation
Sevier Lake 47 C6 ◎ Utah, W USA
Sevilla see Seville
Seville 99 B5 SW Spain
Seychelles 66 ◆ republic W Indian Ocean
Seydhisfjördhur 83 B1 E Iceland
Seýdi 125 E3 E Turkmenistan
Seymour 44 G3 Texas, SW USA
Sfântu Gheorghe 109 C6 C Romania
Sfax 70 F2 E Tunisia
's-Gravenhage see Hague, the
's-Gravenzande 84 C4 W Netherlands
Sgurr Na Lapaich 91 C3 ▲ NW Scotland, United Kingdom
Shache 129 A3 NW China
Shackleton Ice Shelf 142 E5 ice shelf Antarctica
Shaftesbury 95 D4 S England, United Kingdom
Shahany, Ozero 109 D6 ◎ SW Ukraine
Shahrak 125 E5 C Afghanistan
Shahr-e Kord 123 D2 C Iran
Shahrud 123 E1 N Iran
Shalkar 118 B5 W Kazakhstan
Shamrock 44 F2 Texas, SW USA
Shanghai 129 G4 E China
Shangrao 129 G5 S China
Shannon 89 C5 W Ireland
Shannon 89 B5 ≈ W Ireland
Shannon Erne Waterway 89 D3 canal N Ireland
Shannon, Mouth of the 89 A5 estuary W Ireland
Shan Plateau 131 B2 plateau E Burma (Myanmar)
Shantou 129 G5 S China
Shaoguan 129 F5 S China
Shapinsay 91 E1 island NE Scotland, United Kingdom
Shar 118 D5 E Kazakhstan
Sharjah 123 E4 NE United Arab Emirates
Shark Bay 137 A4 bay Western Australia
Sharon 37 B4 Pennsylvania, NE USA
Shashe 76 D5 ≈ Botswana/Zimbabwe
Shasta Lake 49 B5 ⊠ California, W USA
Shawnee 43 D8 Oklahoma, C USA
Shchëkino 111 A6 W Russian Federation
Shchors 109 E3 N Ukraine
Shchuchinsk 118 C5 N Kazakhstan
Shchuchyn 109 B2 W Belarus
Shebekino 111 A6 W Russian Federation
Shebeli 75 E4 ≈ Ethiopia/Somalia
Sheberghan 125 E4 N Afghanistan
Sheboygan 40 C4 Wisconsin, N USA
Shebshi Mountains 72 F4 ▲▲ E Nigeria
Sheelin, Lough 89 D3 ◎ C Ireland
Sheerness 95 G4 SE England, United Kingdom
Sheffield 93 D4 N England, United Kingdom
Shelby 47 D1 Montana, NW USA
Sheldon 43 D4 Iowa, C USA
Shelekhov Gulf 118 H3 gulf E Russian Federation
Shendi 75 C2 NE Sudan
Shenyang 129 G2 NE China
Shepherd Islands 141 H5 island group C Vanuatu
Shepparton 137 F6 Victoria, SE Australia
Shepton Mallet 95 D4 SW England, United Kingdom
Sherbrooke 35 E5 Québec, SE Canada
Shereik 75 C1 N Sudan
Sheridan 47 E3 Wyoming, C USA
Sherman 44 H3 Texas, SW USA
's-Hertogenbosch 84 D5 S Netherlands
Shetland Islands 91 A7 island group NE Scotland, United Kingdom
Shevchenko see Aktau
Shiant Islands 91 B3 island group NW Scotland, United Kingdom
Shibetsu 133 G1 NE Japan
Shibushi-wan 133 D8 bay SW Japan
Shihezi 129 C2 NW China
Shijiazhuang 129 F3 E China
Shikarpur 127 C3 S Pakistan
Shikoku 133 E7 island SW Japan
Shilabo 75 F4 E Ethiopia
Shildon 93 D2 N England, United Kingdom
Shiliguri 127 G3 NE India
Shilka 118 G5 ≈ S Russian Federation
Shillelagh 89 E5 E Ireland
Shillong 127 G3 NE India
Shimbiris 75 F3 ▲ N Somalia
Shimoga 127 D6 W India
Shimonoseki 133 D7 Honshu, SW Japan
Shinano-gawa 133 F5 ≈ Honshū, C Japan
Shindand 125 D5 W Afghanistan
Shingū 133 F7 Honshu, SW Japan
Shinjō 133 G4 Honshu, C Japan
Shin, Loch 91 D2 ◎ N Scotland, United Kingdom
Shinyanga 75 C6 NW Tanzania
Shiprock 44 C1 New Mexico, SW USA
Shiraz 123 D3 S Iran
Shivpuri 127 D3 C India
Shizugawa 133 G4 NE Japan
Shizuoka 133 F6 Honshu, S Japan
Shkodër 107 D3 NW Albania
Shoreham-by-Sea 95 F5 SE England, United Kingdom
Shoshoni 47 E4 Wyoming, C USA
Shostka 109 E3 NE Ukraine
Show Low 44 C2 Arizona, SW USA
Shreveport 39 A5 Louisiana, S USA
Shrewsbury 93 C5 W England, United Kingdom
Shu 118 C6 SE Kazakhstan
Shumagin Islands 50 C3 island group Alaska, USA
Shumen 107 F2 NE Bulgaria
Shuqrah 123 C7 SW Yemen
Shymkent 118 B6 S Kazakhstan
Sialum 141 B2 C Papua New Guinea
Šiauliai 83 E7 N Lithuania
Sibay 111 D7 W Russian Federation
Siberia 118 E4 physical region NE Russian Federation
Siberut, Pulau 131 A6 island Kepulauan Mentawai, W Indonesia
Sibi 127 B2 SW Pakistan
Sibiti 76 B2 S Congo
Sibiu 109 B6 C Romania
Sibolga 131 B6 Sumatra, W Indonesia
Sibu 131 D6 E Malaysia
Sibut 72 H5 S Central African Republic
Sibuyan Sea 131 F4 sea W Pacific Ocean
Sichon 131 B5 SW Thailand
Sichuan Pendi 129 E4 basin C China
Sicilia see Sicily
Sicily 103 C8 island S Italy
Sicily, Strait of 103 B8 strait C Mediterranean Sea
Siderno 103 E8 SW Italy
Sidi Barrâni 70 H2 NW Egypt
Sidi Bel Abbès 70 D1 NW Algeria
Sidlaw Hills 91 E5 ▲▲ E Scotland, United Kingdom
Sidley, Mount 142 B5 ▲ Antarctica
Sidmouth 95 C5 SW England, United Kingdom
Sidney 47 F2 Montana, NW USA
Sidney 43 A5 Nebraska, C USA
Sidney 40 E6 Ohio, N USA
Siedlce 105 F3 C Poland
Siegen 101 B5 W Germany
Siemiatycze 105 G3 NE Poland
Siena 103 C4 C Italy
Sieradz 105 D4 C Poland
Sierpc 105 E3 C Poland
Sierra Leone 72 A5 ◆ republic W Africa
Sierra Madre 55 A3 ▲▲ Guatemala/Mexico
Sierra Morena 112 B4 ▲▲ SW Spain Europe
Sierra Nevada 99 D6 ▲▲ S Spain
Sierra Nevada 49 B6 ▲▲ W USA
Sierra Vieja 44 E4 ▲▲ Texas, SW USA
Sierra Vista 44 C4 Arizona, SW USA
Sífnos 107 E6 island Cyclades, Greece
Sigli 131 A5 Sumatra, W Indonesia
Siglufjördhur 83 A1 N Iceland
Signal Peak 44 A3 ▲ Arizona, SW USA
Signy 142 A3 UK research station South Orkney Islands, Antarctica
Siguatepeque 55 C3 W Honduras
Siguiri 72 B4 NE Guinea
Siilinjärvi 83 F4 C Finland
Siirt 121 G4 SE Turkey
Sikasso 72 C4 S Mali
Sikeston 43 G7 Missouri, C USA
Siklós 105 D9 SW Hungary
Silchar 127 H3 NE India
Silesia 105 D4 physical region SW Poland
Silicon Valley 49 B7 ◐ industrial region California, SW USA North America

◐ Administrative region ◆ Country ● Country capital ◇ Dependent territory ○ Dependent territory capital ▲▲ Mountain range ▲ Mountain ▲ Volcano ≈ River ◎ Lake ⊠ Reservoir

◆ Administrative region   ◆ Country   ● Country capital   ◇ Dependent territory   ○ Dependent territory capital   ▲ Mountain range   ▲ Mountain   ▲ Volcano   ⊿ River   ⊚ Lake   ⊡ Reservoir

173

◆ Administrative region   ◆ Country   ● Country capital   ◇ Dependent territory   ○ Dependent territory capital   ▲ Mountain range   ▲ Mountain   ▼ Volcano   ➤ River   ● Lake   ☒ Reservoir

U

V

W

● Administrative region ◆ Country ● Country capital ◇ Dependent territory ○ Dependent territory capital ▲ Mountain range ▲ Mountain ⛰ Volcano ≈ River ⊚ Lake ⊡ Reservoir